Speaking for Ourselves

Speaking for Ourselves
American Ethnic Writing   Second Edition

Lillian Faderman
California State University, Fresno

Barbara Bradshaw

Scott, Foresman and Company • Glenview, Illinois
Dallas, Tex. • Oakland, N.J. • Palo Alto, Cal. • Tucker, Ga.
Brighton, England

To my mother, MARY LIFTON GORDIN,
who came to America from Latvia

—L.F.

In memory of my grandfathers,
RENIER J. STRAETEN *and* JACK BRADSHAW,
who came to America from Holland and England

—B.B.

Library of Congress Catalog Card Number: 74-82641
ISBN: 0-673-07925-2

Acknowledgments

"Perla Is a Pig" by Oscar Zeta Acosta from *Con Safos*, 2(2). Reprinted by permission of Mr. Arturo Flores, Editor-in-Chief, *Con Safos Magazine*. ". . . in Chihuahua, Villa was shooting traitors" and "in december's air" by Leonard Adamé. Reprinted by permission of the author. "Must Be the Season of the Witch" and "We've Played Cowboys" by Alurista from *Floricanto*. Copyright © 1971. Reprinted by permission of the author. "Glyph," from *The American Rhythm*, translated by Mary Austin. Reprinted by permission of the publisher, Houghton Mifflin Company. From *Go Tell It on the Mountain* by James Baldwin. Reprinted from *Go Tell It on the Mountain* by James Baldwin. Copyright © 1953, 1952 by James Baldwin and used by permission of the publisher, The Dial Press, Inc., and Michael Joseph Limited. From *After Pentecost* by Richard Bankowsky. Copyright © 1961 by Richard Bankowsky. Reprinted by permission of Random House, Inc. From *The Adventures of Augie March* by Saul Bellow. Copyright 1953 by Saul Bellow. Reprinted by permission of The Viking Press, Inc., and Weidenfeld & Nicolson Ltd. "The Chance" by Harold Bond. Reprinted with permission of the author from *The Northern Wall* (Northeastern University Press, 1969), copyright © 1969 by Harold Bond, appearing originally in *Ararat* magazine, 9, no. 3 (Summer 1968). "Letter to an Aunt" by Harold Bond. Reprinted with permission of the author from *The Armenian Review*, 19, no. 1 (Spring 1966), copyright © 1966 by the Hairenik Assn. "a light and diplomatic bird" by Gwendolyn Brooks. From *Annie Allen* by Gwendolyn Brooks. Copyright 1949 by Gwendolyn Brooks Blakely. Reprinted by permission of Harper & Row, Publishers. "Langston Hughes," "sick man looks at flowers," and "weaponed woman" by Gwendolyn Brooks. From *Selected Poems* by Gwendolyn Brooks. Copyright © 1963 by Gwendolyn Brooks Blakely. Reprinted by permission of Harper & Row, Publishers. "History of a Moment" by Carlos Bulosan. Reprinted from *Voices*, 1938. "On Seeing My Great Aunt in a Funeral Parlor" by Diana Chang. Reprinted from *The American Scholar*, 38, no. 1 (Winter 1958–59). Copyright © 1958 by the United Chapters of Phi Beta Kappa. By permission of the publishers and the author. "Four Views in Praise of Reality" by Diana Chang. Reprinted from *The American Scholar*, 35, no. 1 (Winter 1955–56). Copyright © 1955 by the United Chapters of Phi Beta Kappa. By permission of the publishers and author. "Garden of My Childhood" by Kuangchi C. Chang. Reprinted from *The American Scholar*, 26 (Winter 1956–57). Copyright © 1956 by the United Chapters of Phi Beta Kappa. By permission of the publishers and the author. "Confessions of a Number One Son" by Frank Chin. Copyright © 1973 by Noah's Ark, Inc., *Ramparts Magazine*. Reprinted by permission of the editors. "Elegy" by John Ciardi. From *As If* by John Ciardi. Copyright © 1955 by the Trustees of Rutgers College in New Jersey. Reprinted by permission of the author. "Letter to Mother" by John Ciardi from *Homeward to America*. Copyright 1940 by Holt, Rinehart & Winston, Inc., copyright © 1968 by John Ciardi. Reprinted by permission of the author. "Birthplace Revisited" and "Uccello" by Gregory Corso. From *Gasoline* by Gregory Corso. Copyright © 1958 by Gregory Corso. Reprinted by permission of City Lights Books. "Energy" and "today is a day of great joy" from *Snaps*, by Victor Hernandez Cruz. Copyright © 1969 by Victor Hernandez Cruz. Reprinted by permission of Random House, Inc. "The Man Who Came to the Last Floor" from *Mainland*, by Victor Hernandez Cruz. Copyright © 1973 by Victor Hernandez Cruz. Reprinted by permission of Random House, Inc. "Yet Do I Marvel" and "Incident" from *On These I Stand* by Countee Cullen. Copyright 1925 by Harper & Row, Publishers; renewed © 1953 by Ida M. Cullen. Reprinted by permission of Harper & Row, Publishers. *Purlie Victorious* by Ossie Davis. Copyright © 1961 by Ossie Davis. Reprinted by permission of the author. "The Cheyenne Experience" by Vine Deloria, Jr. Copyright © 1972 by The American Museum of Natural History. Reprinted with permission from *Natural History* magazine, November 1972. "Conquistador" by Prudencio de Pereda. From *Commentary*, February 1952. Reprinted by permission of the author. "Damián Sánchez, G.I." by Emilio Díaz Valcárel. From *San Juan Review*, September 1965. Reprinted by permission of the author. "Christ in Concrete" by Pietro di Donato. Reprinted by permission of the author and the author's agents, Scott Meredith Literary Agency, Inc., 580 Fifth Avenue, New York, N.Y. 10036. "Jonathan's Song" and "Sorrow Is the Only Faithful One" by Owen Dodson. Reprinted with the permission of Farrar, Straus & Giroux, Inc., from *Powerful Long Ladder* by Owen Dodson. Copyright 1946 by Owen Dodson. "At Candle-Lightin' Time" and "We Wear the Mask" by Paul Laurence Dunbar. Reprinted by permission of Dodd, Mead & Company, Inc., from *The Complete Poems of Paul Laurence Dunbar*. From *From the Deep Woods to Civilization* by Charles A. Eastman. Reprinted from *From the Deep Woods to Civilization* (Little, Brown and Company, 1916), copyright 1916 by Charles A. Eastman. Reprinted by permission of Mrs. Ernest E. Mensel. From *The Soul of the Indian* by Charles A. Eastman. Reprinted from *The Soul of the Indian* (Houghton Mifflin, 1911). "Did You Ever Dream Lucky?" by Ralph Ellison. Copyright © 1954 by Ralph Ellison. Reprinted by permission of William Morris Agency, Inc., on behalf of the author. "Status Symbol" and "Vive Noir!" by Mari Evans from *I Am a Black Woman*. Published 1970 by William Morrow and Company. Reprinted by permission of the author. "The Oratory Contest" reprinted from *The Short Stories of James T. Farrell* by permission of the publisher, the Vanguard Press, Inc. Copyright 1935, 1937 by Vanguard Press, Inc. Copyright renewed 1963, 1965 by James T. Farrell. "Saul Bellow" by Leslie A. Fiedler. Copyright © 1957 by the University of Nebraska Press. Reprinted by permission of the author and *Prairie Schooner*. "Inviting a Tiger" and "Be Beautiful, Noble, Like the Antique Ant" from *Selected Poems and New* by José Garcia Villa. Copyright © 1958 by José Garcia Villa. Reprinted by permission of the author. From *Kaddish* by Allen Ginsberg. Copyright © 1961 by Allen Ginsberg. Reprinted by permission of City Lights Books. "Nikki-Rosa," "Seduction," and "Adulthood" by Nikki Giovanni. From *Black Feeling, Black Talk*, copyright © 1970 by Nikki Giovanni. Reprinted by permission of Broadside Press. "Frederick Douglass" and "Middle Passage" by Robert Hayden from *Selected Poems*. Copyright © 1966 by Robert Hayden. Reprinted by permission of October House, Inc. "Genealogy" and "Awakening" by Sharon Hucklenbroich. Reprinted by permission. "Let America Be America Again" by Langston Hughes. From *A New Song* by Langston Hughes. Reprinted by permission of Harold Ober Associates, Inc. Copyright © 1938 by Langston Hughes. Renewed. "Madam and Her Madam" and "Madam's Past History" by Langston Hughes. Copyright 1948 by Alfred A. Knopf, Inc. Reprinted from *Selected Poems*, by Langston Hughes, by permission of the publisher. "My People" by Langston Hughes. Copyright 1926 by Alfred A. Knopf, Inc., and renewed 1954 by Langston Hughes. Reprinted from *Selected Poems*, by Langston Hughes, by permission of the publisher. "Asian Brother, Asian Sister" by Lawson Fusao Inada from *Roots: An Asian American Reader*. Published 1971 by the University of California at Los Angeles Asian American Studies Center. Reprinted by permission of the author. "O Black and Unknown Bards" by James Weldon Johnson. From *St. Peter Relates an Incident* by James Weldon Johnson. Copyright 1917, 1921, 1935 by James Weldon Johnson. Copyright © 1963 by Grace Nail Johnson. Reprinted by permission of the Viking Press, Inc. "Black Bourgeoisie" by LeRoi Jones. From *Rights and Reviews*. Copyright © New York CORE. Reprinted by permission of New York CORE and Ronald Hobbs Literary Agency. "Hard Rock Returns to Prison" and "The Warden Said to Me the Other Day" by Etheridge Knight. From *Poems from Prison*, copyright © 1968 by Etheridge Knight. Reprinted by permission of Broadside Press. "Pauline" by Pam Koo. Copyright © 1975 by Pam Koo. Printed by permission. "10/9 Afternoon" and "In the Hardware Store" by Pam Koo from *Backwash*, 1972–73. Reprinted by permission of the author. From "Behold the Sea" by Aaron Kurtz. Reprinted from *Jewish Currents*, January 1957, by permission of the publisher. "Vision of a Past Warrior" from the record *As Long As the Grass Shall Grow* by Peter La Farge. Copyright © 1963 United International Copyright Representatives Ltd. Used by permission. All Rights Reserved. From *Sweet Promised Land* by Robert Laxalt. Copyright © 1957 by Robert Laxalt. Reprinted by permission of Harper & Row, Publishers, and Curtis Brown, Ltd. "Gwendolyn Brooks," "black music/a beginning," and "But He Was Cool" by Don L. Lee. From *Don't Cry, Scream*, copyright © 1969 by Don L. Lee. Reprinted by permission of Broadside Press. "Illustrious Ancestors" by Denise Levertov from *The Jacob's Ladder*. Copyright © 1958 by Denise Levertov Goodman. Reprinted by permission of New Directions Publishing Corporation and Jonathan Cape Ltd. "Somebody Trying" and "A Hunger" by Denise Levertov from *Relearning the Alphabet*. Copyright © 1968, 1970 by Denise Levertov Goodman. Reprinted by permission of New Directions Publishing Corporation and Jonathan Cape

Ltd. "Jíbaro" by Luis Lloréns Torres. From *Poet in the Fortress* by Thomas Aitken, Jr. Copyright © 1964 by Thomas Aitken, Jr. Reprinted by permission of The New American Library, Inc., New York. "Untitled," "Direction," "I Am Crying from Thirst," and "I Go Forth to Move About the Earth" by Alonzo Lopez from *The Whispering Wind*, edited by Terry Allen. Copyright © 1972 by The Institute of American Indian Arts. Reprinted by permission of Doubleday & Company, Inc. "Message to a Dope Fiend" and "The Library" by Felipe Luciano from *The Puerto Rican Poets* published by Bantam Books, Inc. Reprinted by permission of the author. "The First Seven Years" by Bernard Malamud. Reprinted with the permission of Farrar, Straus & Giroux, Inc., and Eyre & Spottiswoode (Publishers) Ltd., London, from *The Magic Barrel* by Bernard Malamud. Copyright © 1950, 1958 by Bernard Malamud. "The Art of the Chicano Movement and the Movement of Chicano Art" by Manuel J. Martinez from *Aztlan: An Anthology of Mexican-American Literature*, edited by Valdez and Steiner. Copyright © 1972 by Alfred A. Knopf, Inc. Reprinted by permission of Harold Matson Company, Inc., and A. D. Peters and Company. "If We Must Die" and "The White House" by Claude McKay from *Selected Poems of Claude McKay*. Copyright © 1953 and reprinted by permission of Twayne Publishers, Inc. "Summer Water and Shirley" by Durango Mendoza. Reprinted from *Prairie Schooner*, Fall 1966, by permission of the University of Nebraska Press. Copyright © 1966 by the University of Nebraska Press. "The Four Directions" by Emerson Blackhorse Mitchell from *The Whispering Wind*, edited by Terry Allen. Copyright © 1972 by The Institute of American Indian Arts. Reprinted by permission of Doubleday & Company, Inc. "A Vision Beyond Time and Place" by N. Scott Momaday, *Life*, copyright © 1971 Time Inc. Reprinted with permission. "The Eggs of the World" and "The Seventh Street Philosopher" by Toshio Mori. Reprinted from *Yokahama, California* by Toshio Mori by permission of the publisher, The Caxton Printers, Ltd. "O Hana San," "Speak Not Again, Voice," and "Ah Thou, World of This Day" by Yone Noguchi. Reprinted from *The Selected Poems of Yone Noguchi*. Permission granted by Branden Press.

"White Ethnic" by Michael Novak from *The Rise of the Unmeltable Ethnics*. Copyright © 1971, 1972 by Michael Novak. Originally published in *Harper's Magazine*. Reprinted by permission of the Macmillan Publishing Co., Inc., and Curtis Brown, Ltd. "Relocation" and "Missing That Indian Name of Roy or Ray" by Simon J. Ortiz from *Navaho Rough Rock News*. Reprinted by permission of the author. "The Long-Distance Runner" by Grace Paley, reprinted with permission of Farrar, Straus & Giroux, Inc., and Elaine Greene Ltd. from *Enormous Changes at the Last Minute* by Grace Paley. Copyright © 1960, 1962, 1965, 1967, 1968, 1971, 1972, 1974 by Grace Paley. British edition to be published by André Deutsch Ltd. in 1975. "Italian to the Moon Over New York" by Joe Papaleo. Reprinted from *Common Ground*, 10 (Autumn 1949) by permission of the American Council for Nationalities Service. "The Legend of Gregorio Cortez" by Americo Paredes. From *With His Pistol in His Hand* by Americo Paredes (Austin: University of Texas Press,

1958), pp. 33–54. Reprinted by permission of the publisher. "The Wooing of Ariadne" by Harry Mark Petrakis from *Pericles on 31st Street*. Copyright © 1965. By permission of Toni Strassman, Agent. "Miserere" by William Pillin. From *Pavanne for a Fading Memory* by William Pillin (Denver: Alan Swallow, 1963). Reprinted by permission of the author. "Chee's Daughter" by Juanita Platero and Siyowin Miller. Reprinted from *Common Ground*, 8 (Winter 1948), by permission of the American Council for Nationalities Service. "Argumentum ad Hominem" and "On the Photograph of a Man I Never Saw" by Hyam Plutzik. From *Aspects of Proteus* by Hyam Plutzik. Copyright 1949 by Hyam Plutzik. Reprinted by permission of Harper & Row, Publishers. "Memorial Wreath" by Dudley Randall. Reprinted from *New Negro Poets*, ed. Langston Hughes, by permission of the publisher, Indiana University Press. "Booker T. and W. E. B." by Dudley Randall. From *Poem Counterpoem*, copyright © 1966 by Dudley Randall. Reprinted by permission of Broadside Press. Excerpts from Introduction to *19 Necromancers from Now*, edited by Ishmael Reed. Copyright © 1970 by Ishmael Reed. Reprinted by permission of Doubleday & Company, Inc., and Ishmael Reed. "Prayer" and "Smoke" by Josef Rodriguez. Used by permission of the author. "Grebes at Sunset," "Hopi Roadrunner, Dancing, Dancing," and "West Side of the Valley" by Wendy Rose. Used by permission of the author. "Eli, the Fanatic" by Philip Roth. From *Goodbye, Columbus* by Philip Roth. Copyright © 1959 by Philip Roth. Reprinted by permission of the publisher, Houghton Mifflin Company, and André Deutsch Limited. Publishers. "Beast in View" by Muriel Rukeyser. From *Beast in View* by Muriel Rukeyser. Reprinted by permission of Monica McCall, Inc. Copyright © 1944 by Muriel Rukeyser. From "Letter to the Front" by Muriel Rukeyser. From *Beast in View* by Muriel Rukeyser. Reprinted by permission of Monica McCall, Inc. Copyright © 1944 and 1962 by Muriel Rukeyser. "This Day of Quixotic Expectation" and from "Aztec Angel" by Luis Omar Salinas. Used by permission of the author. "The Day the Dancers Came" by Bienvenido Santos. Used by permission of the author. "Abraham" by Delmore Schwartz. Copyright © 1959 by Delmore Schwartz. From *Summer Knowledge* by Delmore Schwartz. Reprinted by permission of Doubleday & Company, Inc. "The Self Unsatisfied Runs Everywhere" by Delmore Schwartz. From *Vaudeville for a Princess* by Delmore Schwartz. Copyright 1950 by New Directions. Reprinted by permission of New Directions Publishing Corporation. "Dark Moon" and "Grand-Mama" by Rhoda Schwartz. Copyright © 1975 by Rhoda Schwartz. Printed by permission of the author. "Old Photographs" by Rhoda Schwartz from *Jewish-American Literature: An Anthology*. Published by New American Library. Copyright © 1974 by Rhoda Schwartz. Reprinted by permission of Rhoda Schwartz. "The 151st Psalm" by Karl Shapiro. Copyright © 1957 by Karl Shapiro. Reprinted from *Poems of a Jew*, by Karl Shapiro, by permission of Random House, Inc. "University" by Karl Shapiro. Copyright 1940 and renewed 1968 by Karl Shapiro. Reprinted from *Selected Poems*, by Karl Shapiro, by permission of Random House, Inc. "The Little Shoemakers" by Isaac Bashevis Singer, translated by Isaac Rosenfeld. From *A Treasurey of Yiddish Stories* edited by Irving Howe and Eliezer Greenberg. Copyright 1954 by The Viking Press, Inc. Reprinted by permission of The Viking Press, Inc., and André Deutsch Limited, Publishers. "I Was My Father" by Jacob Sloan. Reprinted from *Commentary*, by permission. Copyright 1950 by the American Jewish Committee. "The Parade," "Once Again," and "The Indian Market" by Liz Sohappy from *The Whispering Wind*, edited by Terry Allen. Copyright © 1972 by The Institute of American Indian Arts. Reprinted by permission of Doubleday & Company, Inc. "Jumping Mouse" from *Seven Arrows* (pp. 66–85) by Hyemeyohsts Storm. Copyright © 1972 by Hyemeyohsts Storm. Reprinted by permission of Harper & Row, Publishers. "Gift of Quince" and "Retrospect" by Toyo Suyemoto. From *The Yale Review*, 35, no. 2 (December 1945). Copyright 1945 by Yale University Press. Reprinted by permission of the publisher. "Daffodils," "The Magnolia," and "Things in Common" by May Swenson. "The Magnolia" and "Daffodils" (Copyright © 1966 by May Swenson), which appeared first in *The New Yorker*, and "Things in Common" are reprinted with the permission of Charles Scribner's Sons from *Half Sun, Half Sleep* by May Swenson. Copyright © 1967 by May Swenson. "Nisei, Nisei!" by Ferris (Mary) Takahashi (M. H. Constable). Reprinted from *Common Ground*, 6 (Spring 1946) by permission of the American Council for Nationalities Service. "The Widower" by Ferris Takahashi from *The Pacific Citizen*, December 21, 1956. Reprinted by permission of Mrs. Ferris Takahashi. "Photograph of Five Ancestors" by Virginia Tatarian. Reprinted by permission of the author. "Alien Turf" by Piri Thomas. From *Down These Mean Streets* by Piri Thomas. Copyright © 1967 by Piri Thomas. Reprinted by permission of Alfred A. Knopf, Inc., and Ashley Famous Agency, Inc. "Poem" and "To Ripen" by Lloyd Tsugawa. Used by permission of the author. "Five Haiku" by Shisei Tsuneishi. Used by permission of the author. "Las Dos Caras del Patroncito" by Luis Valdez from *Actos: El Teatro Campesino*. Copyright © 1971 by Cucaracha Publication/El Centro Campesino Cultural. Reprinted by permission. "The Man Who Saw the Flood" by Richard Wright. Copyright 1937 by Weekly Masses Co., Inc. Reprinted by permission of Paul R. Reynolds, Inc., 599 Fifth Avenue, New York, N.Y. 10017. "Hokkus" by Richard Wright. Copyright © by Richard Wright. Reprinted by permission of Paul R. Reynolds, Inc., 599 Fifth Avenue, New York, N.Y. 10017 "The Legend of Miss Sasagawara" by Hisaye Yamamoto. Originally published in the Winter 1950 *Kenyon Review*. Copyright © 1960 by Kenyon College. Reprinted by permission of the publisher. "Arrival at Boston" from *The Silent Traveller in Boston* by Chiang Yee. Copyright © 1959 by W. W. Norton & Company, Inc. Reprinted by permission of W. W. Norton & Company, Inc., and Methuen & Co. From "A Dance for Militant Dilettantes" from *Dancing: Poems* by Al Young. Copyright © 1969 by Al Young. Reprinted by permission of Corinth Books. From *Chinatown Family* by Lin Yutang. Reprinted from *Chinatown Family* by Lin Yutang (New York: The John Day Co., 1948) by permission of the author.

Preface

The Second Edition of *Speaking for Ourselves* updates the 1969 edition and continues our original purpose of bringing together in one literary anthology writers of different ethnic backgrounds, some who have received considerable critical recognition and others who have been known only to their own ethnic groups.

We are concerned in the Second Edition, as we were in the First, with the two-thirds of the American population that is *not* white Anglo-Saxon Protestant native-born of native parentage. The writers included here represent groups that have had distinct problems of adjustment to American life: many members of these groups have lived in ghettos, experienced the discomforts of poverty, had their identities diminished by others to a pejorative term, and most of them have suffered from the alienation that takes place between the generations within ethnic groups.

The concerns of the writers are reflected in the questions following the selections. In each case—poem, story, play, or essay—the "Suggestions for Discussion" are designed to aid students of varying levels in careful analytical reading. The "Suggestions for Writing and Comparison" are typically more difficult and generally suggest dealing with the work as an entity and relating it to other works of literature, philosophy, or sociology. The student majoring in English who uses this anthology as a basic text will therefore find the "Discussion" questions helpful in understanding the literature; but both the non-English major and the more advanced student will want to consult the "Writing and Comparison" questions as suggestions for further study.

In the six years since the First Edition was published, much has changed with regard to ethnic writing in America. There have even been changes in the terms with which almost all the ethnic groups considered in this book identify themselves. Most Black writers have rejected the term Negro; Mexican Americans often prefer to be called Chicanos; the group that was called Indian has now stated a preference for Native American as an identifying term; Asian Americans often reject the term Oriental; and many Americans of Polish, Irish, Italian, Greek, German, and other European backgrounds think of themselves as White Ethnics.

The last few years have also seen a renaissance of ethnic writing in America. While previous to 1969 there were a few fine writers in most of the ethnic groups considered here, since that time there has been a great flourish of creative activity in almost all of these ethnic groups, and many more excellent ethnic writers have recently been published. The proliferation of ethnic periodicals and anthologies mentioned in the chapter introductions is further proof of this burst of activity.

As ethnic consciousness has grown over the past several years, ethnic writers have turned increasingly to the essay to examine the relationship of their groups to the larger American society and, more particularly, to explore the dual allegiance of ethnic writers to their people and to their art. For this reason, seven essays have been introduced into this edition of *Speaking for Ourselves.*

In preparing the First Edition of *Speaking for Ourselves,* our major problem was hunting down, often with great difficulty, good writing by members of American minority groups. In preparing the Second Edition, our major problem has been reading through the tremendous mass of fine new material that we found everywhere in order to select the very best and most representative examples of American minority-group writing. We are confident that we have done just that.

Lillian Faderman
Barbara Bradshaw

Contents

2
BLACK AMERICAN WRITERS

3

ASIAN AMERICAN WRITERS

4

HISPANIC AMERICAN WRITERS

Chapter 1
Native American Writers

Introduction

Alcatraz and Wounded Knee seem to have provided us with a turning point in history—or at least in the mythology surrounding white and Native American relations. The white conception of the Indian has varied between that of the noble savage and the bloodthirsty savage—but savage he was because the history books told us that his culture was "primitive" and that Custer was massacred at the Little Big Horn. Today the public knows about the common burial ground at Wounded Knee and what happened to the Sioux after they defeated Custer. The recent popularity of *Custer Died for Your Sins* (1969), by Vine Deloria, Jr., *Bury My Heart at Wounded Knee* (1970), by Dee Brown, and *Black Elk Speaks* (1932 and 1961), by John Neihardt, has helped Wounded Knee and Alcatraz replace the Little Big Horn in the American consciousness.

All three books deal with the problem of Custer and the defeat of the Native Americans by descendants of Europeans. Vine Deloria and Black Elk, Native Americans, also deal with life since 1890 and with the problem of the future. In his last vision Black Elk, the holy man, prayed, "O make my people live." However, Dee Brown (a white man) ends his sympathetic book with the song,

> The old men
> say
> the earth
> only
> endures.
> You spoke
> truly.
> You are right.

It remains to be seen whether the Native American will live or whether the enduring earth will serve as his grave, but for now Black Elk's vision prevails.

In a nation of over 200 million people, however, Native Americans number only about one million. It is estimated that before 1492 there were more than two thousand independent tribes, of which only slightly more than three hundred survive today. Of the tribes that have survived, almost all have been moved in forced migrations, and a few have lately prospered and increased. The figure of one million may be inaccurate, as census taking is difficult on remote reservations, and Spanish surnames (as, for instance, that of Simon Ortiz) may lead census takers to count Native Americans with another group.

The view of the Indian from a European perspective has been inaccurate from the first—as is evident in the name "Indian." Although "Native American" may prove too cumbersome a term, it is at least an attempt at accuracy. Some history books still state that "Columbus discovered America," suggesting that the people who were already here, the non-Europeans, counted for nothing. And it is not only history books, but our literature as well, which has provided a false mythology of the "Indian."

For instance, most high-school graduates have read Cooper's *The Last of the Mohicans;* they have heard of *Hiawatha* and some can even quote the first few lines. But the *Walam Olum* and the "Rite of the Condoling Council," original Delaware (or Lenape) and Iroquois chronicles, are generally unknown. Longfellow's inaccurate but romanticized portrayal of the Indian is a part of the myth. James Fenimore Cooper's Leatherstocking tales, most of which were published in the 1820's, also contributed to the myth. Many of Cooper's Indians, such as Chingachgook and Uncas, are sympathetic characters in that they are noble savages. Natty Bumppo's friends are the Delaware and the Pawnee. Yet even among his Indian friends, Bumppo seems ambivalent. On the one hand he says, "I am not a prejudiced man," but in the same sentence he adds, "though the worst enemy I have on earth . . . daren't deny that I am genuine white," and he surveys "with secret satisfaction the faded color of his bony and sinewy hand." Bumppo, the white man, obviously sees himself as a superior being and the Indian as a savage.

Charles A. Eastman (Ohiyesa) added a new dimension to the question when he appeared in print in the first decade of the twentieth century. Himself a Sioux driven by troopers into Canada as a result of Sitting Bull's victory at the Little Big Horn, Eastman had become a Christian, graduated from Dartmouth, and received an M. D. degree from Boston University. A story of his youth, *Indian Boyhood* (1902 and reissued 1968), was followed by *The Soul of the Indian* (1911 and reissued 1970), an introduction to Indian religion, and by *From the Deep Woods to Civilization* (1916), an autobiography. Eastman's account of massacres which occurred at the time when the Ghost Dance religion flourished (see p. 50) reveals that the hope of the Ghost Dance was peace with the white man. Eastman points out that there were massacres—but of Indians by troopers—when Indian agents outlawed the performance of dances and members of the religion refused to comply. In summary of the incident Eastman wrote:

> I have tried to make it clear that there was no "Indian outbreak" in 1890–91, and that such trouble as we had may justly be charged to the dishonest politicians, who through unfit appointees first robbed the Indians, then bullied them, and finally in a panic called for troops to suppress them.
> —*From the Deep Woods to Civilization*

That Eastman felt it necessary for an Indian to speak for himself is evident in *The Soul of the Indian.* In the foreword he explains:

I have attempted to paint the religious life of the typical American Indian as it was before he knew the white man. I have long wished to do this, because I cannot find that it has ever been seriously, adequately, and sincerely done. The religion of the Indian is the last thing about him that the man of another race will ever understand. First, the Indian does not speak of these deep matters so long as he believes in them, and when he has ceased to believe he speaks inaccurately and slightingly. Second, even if he can be induced to speak, the racial and religious prejudice of the other stands in the way of his sympathetic comprehension. Third, practically all existing studies on this subject have been made during the transition period, when the original beliefs and philosophy of the native American were already undergoing rapid disintegration.

It is indeed true that Native Americans needed a spokesman. At the turn of the century they were fewer in number than before or since. Resistance had been crushed: Captain Jack of the Modocs was hanged in 1873, Sitting Bull shot in 1890, and Chief Joseph of the Nez Percé died quietly in Indian Territory in 1904. Most Native Americans had been "resettled" and were faced with reservation life. Helen Hunt Jackson, a well-intentioned friend of the Native American, had written *A Century of Dishonor* (1881) in which she discussed "the fashion of making treaties with tribes and then breaking them." Unfortunately, and paradoxically, her book resulted in a reform—the General Allotment Act of 1887—which worsened the situation. Each Native American was allotted 140 to 160 acres, which was supposed to encourage individual initiative; but within two years 20 percent of the land was lost through misunderstanding, bribery, or trickery. In spite of Eastman's efforts in Washington, Native Americans continued losing their lands until, in 1933, 90 million of the Allotment Act's 138 million acres were gone.

Another Dakota Sioux writer, who lived at about the same time as Eastman, was Gertrude Bonnin (Zitkala-Sa). Her *Old Indian Legends* (1901), a children's book, was written with the intention of promoting understanding between "white" and "red" youngsters. She did not become a Christian convert as did Eastman, and her essay about her beliefs, "Why I Am a Pagan," was published in *The Atlantic Monthly*. A collection of her writing, *American Indian Stories* (1921), contains a variety of depictions of Indian life, and includes legends, reminiscences, stories, and polemics. But her books, unlike Charles Eastman's, have not been reissued, despite the fact that many of the social situations she describes still prevail.

Anthropologists sought out the Native American on his reservation during the years following his "resettlement," and it is from them we have gained a "scientific outlook" and some translations of Native American literature. Most anthropologists and linguists were interested in recording sacred songs and ceremonies, perhaps fearing their disappearance in the process of acculturation. Occasionally Native Americans were truly interested in sharing their literature and music. Francis La Flésche, an Omaha, worked with Alice Fletcher on *The Omaha Tribe* (1911) and later, on his own, published *The Osage Tribe: The Rite of the Vigil* (1925) and *The War Ceremony and Peace Ceremony of the Osage Indians* (1939). Ella Deloria, a Teton who had worked with Franz Boas, published *Dakota Texts* in 1932.

After Charles A. Eastman's *From the Deep Woods to Civilization* (1916) many other Indian autobiographies appeared, although they were usually told to or edited by an anthropologist. *The Autobiography of a Fox Woman,* edited by Truman Michelson, was published in 1919, and was followed by, among others, *Crashing Thunder: The Autobiography of an American Indian* (1926), edited by Paul Radin; the previously mentioned *Black Elk Speaks: The Life of an Oglala Sioux* (1932 and 1961), as told to John Neihardt; *Autobiography of a Papago Woman* (1936), edited by Ruth Underhill; *Son of Old Man Hat: A Navaho Autobiography* (1938), recorded by Walter Dyk; *Smoke from Their Fires* (1940) by the Kwakiutl C. J. Nowell, and edited by Chellan S. Ford; and Don C. Talayesva's *Sun Chief: Autobiography of a Hopi* (1942), edited by Leo W. Simmons.

One of the few earlier autobiographies completely written and edited by a Native American was *The Land of the Spotted Eagle* (1933) by Chief Standing Bear of the Lakota. Although Eastman was a Sioux and Chief Standing Bear a Lakota, their attitudes toward life and literary statement are similar. The works of both men do more than relate facts; they explain customs and values. For example, their observations on silence reveal the same basic perspective:

> Training began with children who were taught to sit still and enjoy it. They were taught to use their organs of smell, to look when there was apparently nothing to see, and to listen intently when all seemingly was quiet . . .
> A pause giving time for thought was the truly courteous way of beginning and conducting a conversation . . . In the midst of sorrow, sickness, and death, or misfortune of any kind, and in the presence of the notable and great, silence was the mark of respect.
>
> —Chief Standing Bear, *The Land of the Spotted Eagle*

> [The Indian] believes profoundly in silence—the sign of a perfect equilibrium. Silence is the absolute poise or balance of body, mind, and spirit. The man who preserves his selfhood is ever calm and unshaken by the storms of existence—not a leaf, as it were, astir on the tree; not a ripple upon the surface of the pool.
>
> —Charles A. Eastman, *The Soul of the Indian*

Silence and keeping still in both cases suggest an ordering of the self and an awareness of one's surroundings—not just the absence of physical activity.

Many of the autobiographies contain descriptions and explanations of the traditional way of life, and include myths and legends that reveal symbolic significance. The coyote, the raven, and the crow, for instance, appear in a number of songs, and their significance has been discussed in *Crashing Thunder.* The raven and the crow are sacred birds, messengers of the gods, with parallels to many Biblical birds and to the dove of peace. The coyote is a figure who shares many traits with other animals—for example, the cunning and guile of Reynard the Fox or Brer Rabbit. In addition, the Navajo credit the coyote rather than Prometheus with stealing fire from the gods and giving it to man.

After Cooper and Longfellow, very few major American mainstream writers of the nineteenth century mentioned the Native American. When they did, they were ignored. For instance, Henry David Thoreau spent his last twelve years filling notebooks with information on customs, legends, and chants from interviews with well over a hundred Native Americans. He died before editing these notebooks and they have never been published. Another nineteenth-century rebel, Walt Whitman, studied Native American poetry and oratory, and he concluded that we would never have a truly "American" literature until the work of the original American poets was recognized. His advice to the American literary world has gone largely unheeded.

More recently, Willa Cather and William Faulkner included a few Native Americans in their canvases crowded with European immigrants, blacks, and Hispanos. Cather's story "The Enchanted Bluff" (1909) concerns the vanished civilization of the New Mexican mesa, symbolic of the "American heritage" of the Indian that contrasted with the immigrant's old "European heritage." In a similar way, Faulkner pictures an elderly Sam Fathers teaching a young white about "Indian ways" in the novella *The Bear*.

Two westerners, Oliver La Farge and Frank Waters, wrote novels of the Native American in his ghetto, the reservation, during the 1920's, '30's, and '40's. Oliver La Farge's *Laughing Boy* takes place on the Navajo's Arizona reservation, where La Farge lived for a number of years. Frank Waters' *The Man Who Killed the Deer* takes place in the New Mexican Taos Pueblo and in the surrounding mountains. Frank Waters has also written studies of Navajo and Hopi religious ceremonies in *Masked Gods* (1950) and *Book of the Hopi* (1963). In 1970 the sacred Blue Lake mentioned in Waters' novel was restored to the Taos Pueblo after years of petition and protest.

■ We have come to a time, in the 1970's, when Native American writers are speaking for themselves without anthropologists or historians to translate. We now have three major Native American writers of stature—N. Scott Momaday, Hyemeyohsts Storm, and Vine Deloria, Jr., several books making major statements, and a number of younger writers appearing in the wake of these events.

N. Scott Momaday's *House Made of Dawn* won the 1969 Pulitzer Prize for fiction, a sign that the literary establishment is changing and that there may be a new willingness to listen to minority group writers. In *House Made of Dawn* Momaday is particularly involved with the problem of adapting to two cultures. The hunt becomes a ritual in which man attempts to share the animal's "at homeness" in nature. Through this ritual the hunter also attains manhood. But Momaday's character, who hunts alone, must also live in the larger American society and deal with conflicting cultures, as represented by the army and the reservation. Simon Ortiz, a younger poet also concerned with the problem of adaptation (see pp. 58–61), uses a bus ride to express disorientation and transition from the reservation to the big city.

The new aim of the B.I.A. (Bureau of Indian Affairs) to "relocate" Native Americans from reservations to the megalopolis is seen by Deloria and other writers as an attempt at "deculturing the Indian" and placing him on the lowest rung of the American social and economic ladder. In *Custer Died for Your Sins* (1969) and *We Talk, You Listen* (1970), Deloria documents the struggle of the American Indian Movement (A.I.M.) to regain civil rights and land and water rights. These two books of essays are concerned with political history, past and present.

Deloria's newest book, *God Is Red* (1973), is also a book of essays, but in it he turns to a new subject, Native American religion and the future of this country. In this new theme, Deloria joins Momaday in *The Way to Rainy Mountain* and Hyemeyohsts Storm in *Seven Arrows*. Although each author approaches the subject differently, all three deal with mysticism, philosophy, ecology, and psychology.

Momaday, in *The Way to Rainy Mountain,* writes of the Kiowa genesis, of Spider Grandmother, and of Tai-Me, the sacred Sun Dance Stone. Sacred myth, Kiowa history, and personal reflection are combined, and there emerges an acceptance of the integration of an ethnic awareness, a tribal awareness, within the twentieth-century "persona."

Deloria's *God Is Red* explores the use of religion beyond the personal. As a lawyer and political activist, Deloria is interested in the future of this country. He explores the relation of religion to history and science, noting that modern Christian thinkers may be wrong in believing the parting of the Red Sea to be mere fantasy. He investigates the possibility of a worldwide flood and other widely recorded catastrophes which indicate that so-called myths may indeed be historic fact. Ancient religious legends, as well as providing historical insights, may also provide ways for us to save the land, Deloria believes, and he notes that modern science has been unable to prevent the present crises in energy and ecology. Deloria says,

> Religion . . . is a force in itself and it calls for the integration of lands and people in harmonious unity. . . . Who will find peace with the lands? The future of mankind lies waiting for those who will come to understand their lives and take up their responsibilities to all living things. Who will listen to the trees, the animals and birds, the voices of the places of the lands?

Hyemeyohsts Storm's *Seven Arrows* (1972) is a new kind of book. As Vine Deloria suggests (see p. 9), *Seven Arrows* may be a novel, but it is not a novel written in the western European tradition. The book presents a different view, a Cheyenne view of the universe. Storm's use of Cheyenne legends is comparable to the Christian use of the parable and the Buddhist jataka tales. In *Seven Arrows* the American buffalo, hawk, mouse, and bear replace the Near Eastern camel and the Asian monkey. Learning is a medicine, and the medicine wheel and the sacred hoop are Cheyenne mandalas.

In Storm's *Seven Arrows,* Deloria's *God Is Red,* and Momaday's *The Way to Rainy Mountain,* we have a kind of trilogy of Native American philosophy, all three containing new literary and conceptual approaches. They seem a fulfillment of Alonzo Lopez's prediction about the Native American creative spirit:

> Let those among us
> who have left us to die
> Know that we only slept,
> And now,
> We live again.

Vine Deloria, Jr.

Vine Deloria, Jr., a Sioux, was born on the Pine Ridge Reservation in South Dakota. He attended Iowa State University, Lutheran School of Theology in Illinois, and the University of Colorado Law School. Deloria is a political activist and a practicing lawyer. He has taught at the College of Ethnic Studies, Western Washington State College. For three years he was executive director of the National Congress of American Indians. His books include *Custer Died for Your Sins* (1969), *We Talk, You Listen* (1970), and *God Is Red* (1973).

"The Cheyenne Experience" appeared as a review of *Seven Arrows* in *Natural History* magazine in November 1972. It deals with Native American literature, publishing history, and the public response to books by and about Native Americans.

The Cheyenne Experience

For decades one had little choice when looking for books on the American Indian. Most books followed a standard format so dull and traditional that the subject appeared unimportant. A friendly white with an interest in Indians would contact a publisher and make arrangements for a book on the history of some tribe. He would devour the dozen or so books already written on the tribe, draft a good summary of the material, being careful not to be too obvious in using other people's words, and hand in his manuscript. Little new material was incorporated into the book, the viewpoint stayed the same, and only the book jacket changed.

Outside of a number of smaller paperbacks of limited distribution by Ruth Bronson Muskrat, Ella Deloria, and D'Arcy McNickle, few Indians had written books since the early decades of this century, when Charles Eastman, a Sioux physician, produced a series of books on his recollections of Indian culture. Other than these works, none of which became known to the general reading public, no books on American Indians by American Indians had ever been written.

In the early 1960's the first breakthrough occurred when Emerson Blackhorse Mitchell published *Miracle Hill,* a recounting of his experiences as a young Navaho trying to understand the white man's culture. Mitchell was just entering his teen years when the book was released and perhaps the novelty of a teen-ager writing a book overshadowed the fact that the book was an excellent presentation of a unique and difficult story.

The real breakthrough in American Indian literature came in 1968 when Stan Steiner published *The New Indians* with Harper and Row. The book was a chronicle of the rising Indian movement, particularly as it has been experienced by postcollege Indians of the National Indian Youth Council and the National Congress of American Indians. *The New Indians* sold well in non-Indian circles and virtually exploded in Indian circles. It spoke to the countless frustrated Indian college students who were increasingly concerned that the social movements of the 1960's had passed Indians by. Alcatraz followed, and the movement was under way.

Almost immediately, publishers began beating the bushes for Indian authors, and Indians thought that the time had actually come for a presentation of their concerns to the reading public. Alas, the desire for income weighed heavier than the thirst for literature and despite N. Scott Momaday's *House Made of Dawn,* which won the Pulitzer Prize in 1969, the trend swept from books *by* American Indians to books *on* American Indians.

As the movement grew, the reading public latched on to Dee Brown's *Bury My Heart at Wounded Knee* and made it a phenomenal bestseller. McGraw-Hill, erasing the barriers between fiction and nonfiction, presented the thrilling *Memoirs of Chief Red Fox,* the story of an alleged Sioux chief whose supposed tribe had never heard of him and whose chief claim to Indian ancestry was his pitch as a sausage seller during the 1950's. Those publishers who had been caught short at the cash register promptly came forth with some hurried anthologies of great Indian speeches; and a maudlin collection of sentimental trivia followed, highlighted by T. C. McLuhan's *Touch the Earth,* with sepia pictures and Chief Joseph's surrender speech reprinted for the hundredth time.

Two books by Indians on current political problems, *The Tortured Americans* and *Custer Died for Your Sins*, only spurred readers to flee to the past glory and romance of Indians, rather than to consider their responsibility for the current depredations against Indians by their favorite senators, congressmen, and governors. Momaday's second book, *The Way to Rainy Mountain*, was fairly well received since it did not deal with contemporary problems but made a poetic presentation of past Kiowa history.

The problem in judging literature on American Indians, then, has been establishing the categories of what exactly constitutes a book on Indians. At the start we can discard the anthologies since they show a remarkable similarity, as if only a certain number of documents were ever available to the compilers. With the exception of *The Way*, by Stan Steiner and Shirley Hill Witt, the anthologies are merely the reshuffling of speeches taken out of obscure journals and reprinted periodically as Indians wax and wane in favor with the reading public. *The Way* is a collection of writings and sayings of young Indians as yet unpublished and displaying, in some cases, considerable talent.

Another category in Indian literature must surely consist of the standard tribal histories and traditional stories of the American Indian, generalized histories that follow the interpretive scheme of western conquest, ending, of course, in 1890. If one is only interested in what the people were doing in 1876 these books are all right. If one cares to examine the present state or location of the people, these books are dangerously misleading since they appear to arrive at the unanimous conclusion that the particular tribes vanished in 1891.

The final category must be books by American Indians covering some particular concern of the Indian community. A good number are political tracts involving contemporary problems. These are important books but lack the support of a unified Indian political force to give them impact. It was not, remember, until the Civil Rights movement heated up that James Baldwin became a philosopher in the eyes of white America.

Seven Arrows, it seems to me, begins a new and very important development in Indian literature. It is first a book that makes a statement without any reference to external buttressing evidence. That is to say, one need not have the foggiest idea of what Indians are like in order to understand the book. Consequently, the usual concepts by which books are judged are not available for analysis of *Seven Arrows*. It appears to be a novel in that it traces the Cheyennes over a period of years and often incorporates their friends, the Sioux, and neighbors, the Crow, into the story with such smooth transitions that one does not question where they came from and why they are present.

But to classify *Seven Arrows* solely as a novel would lead readers astray, for it lacks the rigid structure that defines the novel in Western European traditions. It has no definite starting and finishing points, and thus time, so important to Western man, appears in the Indian context as a relative, an extremely relative, determining force. One day we are in the past, the next day we are on the reservation in the early days, the following day we are apparently talking about modern times. Time, as such, is useful only to keep the non-Indian readers from losing their orientation with respect to the major themes of the book. The format, if we look at the sequence of the story, is solidly and traditionally Indian.

Within the general theme of the people's experiences we find a willingness—through the questions and storytelling answers of the leading characters of the Brotherhood of the Shield—to articulate the major archetypal themes of Indian communal existence. Thus, at the beginning of the book, when we are in the prereservation period, members of the camp bring their questions to the elders and receive the medicine stories concerning the meaning and origin of things. With the text rapidly shifting between happenings and explanations of the religious beliefs and doctrines, the reader comes to understand the importance of expanding religious conceptions of life as a growth phenomenon of a community.

Numerous characters dot the pages of the book but not as extraneous figures in a colossal, historical sense. Rather, each character illustrates the gradual shifting of sensitivity and outlook as it has been experienced by the community as a whole. Incidents of the story become departure points for bringing the events of daily life into a cosmic focus. We are told at the beginning that the Medicine Wheel and the Sun Dance teaching present a mirror in which everything is reflected. Characters thus merge and emerge as the reflections of the universe change through continued growth.

What we have in *Seven Arrows*, therefore, is a statement about the universe and an intense effort to illustrate how that statement validates itself in the continual reintegration of experiences of a community of people. The importance of this concept for theology and related social sciences is tremendous. Religion is conceived of and presented by Storm as a continuing presence of powers and the ways that these powers identify with and involve the people. When we consider that most other religious statements are concerned with proving historical facts, such as the Resurrection, the location of the Garden of Eden, or the reality of divinity in concrete terms of salvation or escape on an individual basis, the startling statements of *Seven Arrows* take on a deep meaning. For a world that is utterly convinced that divinity exists at its pleasure, the revelations of the book may draw skepticism and derision. But then all fundamentally different religious conceptions are initially rejected for their doctrinal impossibility, only to be later accepted because they are meaningful in the collapse of doctrinal certainty.

One is tempted to compare *Seven Arrows* with the two books on Don Juan, which have proved so popular with young whites seeking the real substance behind Indian religious and communal ideas. *Seven Arrows* is solidly and triumphantly an Indian book. By comparison, *The Teachings of Don Juan* and *A Separate Reality* are peripherally Indian; that is, they have references to the Yaqui in them. But *Seven Arrows* is concerned with land and the centering of the universe, rivers, mountains, and other hard facts of Indian existence that are determining factors in the vast majority of Indian tribal religions.

One might conclude by mentioning the outstanding paintings and sepia pictures that dominate one's recollections of the book's impact. They are skillfully chosen so that when one is reading about the buffalo people he has a picture of the buffalo to see. Many times a picture often only previews the possibility that what is shown will somehow be confronted at some point in the text. If Marshall McLuhan is skillful in combining text and visual presentations, Hyemeyohsts Storm is equally adept at merging visual and textual presentations for maximum impact.

Scattered throughout the book are stark paintings of shields portraying the stories of the book. Some people have remarked that these pictures are hardly the rigid figures to be found on traditional paintings of religious themes by American Indians. It is this objection that indicates a misunderstanding of the book in a dreadful and total sense. *Seven Arrows* is not, like Peter Powell's *Sweet Medicine* (a book covering the same Cheyenne religion), an explanation of what the religion was or how it is practiced today. *Seven Arrows* is a religious statement, not a statement about religion, if the difference can be understood.

When one considers the nature of the Indian movement, the importance of this book appearing at this time is evident. Almost every Indian activist event has involved establishment of a particular Indian community at a particular place to do a particular job. The seizing of Alcatraz was an effort to establish a religious study center and ecological laboratory. Fort Lawton, in Seattle, was invaded by Indians seeking a cultural center for training Indians to be Indians. The activists have expressed in political deeds what Storm is saying in poetic-novel-teaching form.

Seven Arrows is thus totally political if politics can be severed from man's total experience and made a discipline or career. It is totally sociological if sociology can also be severed and made a cold and abstract subject matter. The presentation of this sense of totality without apologies to recorded data on Indian religions or to the critiques of purists, the simple statements of understanding — these attributes make *Seven Arrows* important and qualitatively distinct from everything else written on or by Indians with the exception of Neihardt's Black Elk material to which *Seven Arrows* has great and consistent affinity.

Hyemeyohsts Storm and Douglas Latimer of the Harper and Row Indian series are to be applauded for the publication of *Seven Arrows*. The book forces the field of Indian literature beyond simple explanations of gathered facts or recitation of cherished stereotypes, no matter how sympathetic. It presents a statement of integrity about the nature of man's existence in an Indian communal sense. Indian literature must take this statement seriously and pass beyond trivia to the issues of our existence.

Suggestions for Discussion

1. State Deloria's reasons for liking or disliking the books mentioned in the first few pages of the essay. Are they convincing?
2. How would you interpret Deloria's saying that *Seven Arrows* "is a statement about the universe"? How does this differentiate *Seven Arrows* from most other novels?
3. Compare Deloria's essay with the introduction to this chapter. Do you find any areas of disagreement? Discuss.

Suggestions for Writing and Comparison

1. Read Hyemeyohsts Storm's "Jumping Mouse," p. 35. Show how that story is "concerned with land and the centering of the universe, rivers, mountains, and other hard facts of Indian existence."
2. Read Bruce Iwasaki's essay on Asian American literature in *Roots: An Asian American Reader* (1972). Compare the publishing history of Native American writers with that of Asian American writers.

N. Scott Momaday

N. Scott Momaday, of Kiowa and Cherokee descent, received his Ph.D. at Stanford University and is presently an associate professor of English at the University of California, Berkeley. He is the author of *The Owl in the Cedar Tree* (1965), *House Made of Dawn* (1968), and *The Way to Rainy Mountain* (1969). *House Made of Dawn* is about a Native American who returns from the Army during World War II and finds that he can neither recover his tribal identity nor escape the cultural context in which he grew up. He is torn between two worlds and cannot become the whole man in either one. The novel concerns his struggle to survive in contemporary American society. *House Made of Dawn* won the 1969 Pulitzer Prize for fiction.

The following essay, "A Vision Beyond Time and Place," appeared in *Life* magazine in 1971, after Momaday won the Pulitzer Prize.

A Vision Beyond Time and Place

When my father was a boy, an old man used to come to [my grandfather] Mammedaty's house and pay his respects. He was a lean old man in braids and was impressive in his age and bearing. His name was Cheney, and he was an arrowmaker. Every morning, my father tells me, Cheney would paint his wrinkled face, go out, and pray aloud to the rising sun. In my mind I can see that man as if he were there now. I like to watch him as he makes his prayer. I know where he stands and where his voice goes on the rolling grasses and where the sun comes up on the land. There, at dawn, you can feel the silence. It is cold and clear and deep like water. It takes hold of you and will not let you go. (From *The Way to Rainy Mountain*. The University of New Mexico Press.)

I often think of old man Cheney, and of his daily devotion to the sun. He died before I was born, and I never knew where he came from or what of good and bad entered into his life. But I think I know who he was, essentially, and what his view of the world meant to him and to me. He was a man who saw very deeply into the distance, I believe, one whose vision extended far beyond the physical boundaries of his time and place. He perceived the wonder and meaning of Creation itself. In his mind's eye he could integrate all the realities and illusions of the earth and sky; they became for him profoundly intelligible and whole.

Once, in the first light, I stood where Cheney has stood, next to the house which my grandfather Mammedaty had built on a rise of land near Rainy Mountain Creek, and watched all the sun come out of the black horizon of the world. It was an irresistible and awesome emergence, as waters gather to the flood, of weather and of light. I could not have been more sensitive to the cold, nor to the heat which came upon it. And I could not have foreseen the break of day. The shadows on the rolling plains became large and luminous in a moment, impalpable, then faceted, dark and distinct again as they were run through with splinters of light. And the sun itself, when it appeared, was pale and immense, original in the deepest sense of the word. It is no wonder, I thought, that an old man should pray to it. It is no wonder . . . and yet, of course, wonder is the principal part of such a vision. Cheney's prayer was an affirmation of his wonder and regard, a testament to the realization of a quest for vision.

This native vision, this gift of seeing truly, with wonder and delight, into the natural world, is informed by a certain attitude of reverence and self-respect. It is a matter of extrasensory as well as sensory perception, I believe. In addition to the eye, it involves the intelligence, the instinct, and the imagination. It is the perception not only of objects and forms but also of essences and ideals, as in this Chippewa song:

> as my eyes
> search
> the prairie
> I feel the summer
> in the spring.

Even as the singer sees into the immediate landscape, he perceives a now and future dimension that is altogether remote, yet nonetheless real and inherent within it, a quality of evanescence and evolution, a state at once of being and of becoming. He beholds what is there; nothing of the scene is lost upon him. In the integrity of his vision he is wholly in possession of himself and of the world around him; he is quintessentially alive.

Most Indian people are able to see in these terms. Their view of the world is peculiarly native and distinct, and it determines who and what they are to a great extent. It is indeed the basis upon which they identify themselves as individuals and as a race. There is something of genetic significance in such a thing, perhaps, an element of being which resides in the blood and which is, after all, the very nucleus of the self. When old man Cheney looked into the sunrise he saw as far into himself, I suspect, as he saw into the distance. He knew certainly of his existence and of his place in the scheme of things.

In contrast, most of us in this society are afflicted with a kind of cultural nearsightedness. Our eyes, it may be, have been trained too long upon the superficial, and artificial, aspects of our environment; we do not see beyond the buildings and billboards that seem at times to be the monuments of our civilization, and consequently we fail to see into the nature and meaning of our own humanity. Now, more than ever, we might do well to enter upon a vision quest of our own, that is a quest after vision itself. And in this the Indian stands to lead by his example. For with respect to such things as a sense of heritage, of a vital continuity in terms of origin and of destiny, a profound investment of the mind and spirit in the oral traditions of literature, philosophy, and religion—those things, in short, which constitute his vision of the world—the Indian is perhaps the most culturally secure of all Americans.

As I see him, that old man, he walks very slowly to the place where he will make his prayer, and it is always the same place, a small mound where the grass is sparse and the hard red earth shows through. He limps a little, with age, but when he plants his feet he is tall and straight and hard. The bones are fine and prominent in his face and hands. And his face is painted. There are red and yellow bars under his eyes, neither bright nor sharply defined on the dark, furrowed skin, but soft and organic, the colors of sandstone and of pollen. His long braids are wrapped with blood-red cloth. His eyes are deep and open to the wide world. At sunrise, precisely, they catch fire and close, having seen. The low light descends upon him. And when he lifts his voice, it enters upon the silence and carries there, like the call of a bird.

Suggestions for Discussion

1. Discuss Momaday's vision of old man Cheney. The essay begins and ends with a descriptive portrait. Which details are repeated? Why are colors emphasized in the final paragraph?
2. What does Momaday mean by the phrases "quest for vision" and "vision of the world"? What does he suggest that the Native American can contribute to American culture and society?
3. Reread the final sentence of the essay. What does it suggest about man's relationship to animals, to nature, to the universe?

Suggestion for Writing and Comparison

1. Read *God Is Red* by Vine Deloria, Jr., and compare his view of the Native American's vision of this continent with N. Scott Momaday's view.

Juanita Platero and Siyowin Miller

Juanita Platero and Siyowin Miller met in California in 1929 through Standing Bear, chief of the Lakota Indians and a writer himself. Juanita Platero and her husband Luciano, who were both Navajo Indians, lived on a Navajo reservation in New Mexico; Siyowin Miller was a resident of California. In 1940 Mrs. Miller and Mrs. Platero began working on a novel, *The Winds Erase Your Footprints*, which was concerned with an Indian couple's search for a middle path between the divergent Anglo and Navajo cultures. Their work on this book led to short stories dealing with the same background and characters. "Chee's Daughter," along with several other stories by these two writers, was published in the periodical *Common Ground* during the 1940's.

Chee's Daughter

The hat told the story, the big, black, drooping Stetson. It was not at the proper angle, the proper rakish angle for so young a Navaho. There was no song, and that was not in keeping either. There should have been at least a humming, a faint, all-to-himself "he he he heya," for it was a good horse he was riding, a slender-legged, high-stepping buckskin that would race the wind with light knee-urging. This was a day for singing, a warm winter day, when the touch of the sun upon the back belied the snow high on distant mountains.

Wind warmed by the sun touched his high-boned cheeks like flicker feathers, and still he rode on silently, deeper into Little Canyon, until the red rock walls rose straight upward from the stream bed and only a narrow piece of blue sky hung above. Abruptly the sky widened where the canyon walls were pushed back to make a wide place, as though in ancient times an angry stream had tried to go all ways at once.

This was home — this wide place in the canyon — levels of jagged rock and levels of rich red earth. This was home to Chee, the rider of the buckskin, as it had been to many generations before him.

He stopped his horse at the stream and sat looking across the narrow ribbon of water to the bare-branched peach trees. He was seeing them each springtime with their age-gnarled limbs transfigured beneath veils of blossom pink; he was seeing them in autumn laden with their yellow fruit, small and sweet. Then his eyes searched out the indistinct furrows of the fields beside the stream, where each year the corn and beans and squash drank thirstily of the overflow from summer rains. Chee was trying to outweigh today's bitter betrayal of hope by gathering to himself these reminders of the integrity of the land. Land did not cheat! His mind lingered deliberately on all the days spent here in the sun caring for the young plants, his songs to the earth and to the life springing from it— ". . . In the middle of the wide field . . . Yellow Corn Boy . . . He has started both ways . . . ," then the harvest and repayment in full measure. Here was the old feeling of wholeness and of oneness with the sun and earth and growing things.

Chee urged the buckskin toward the family compound where, secure in a recess of overhanging rock, was his mother's dome-shaped hogan, red rock and red adobe like the ground on which it nestled. Not far from the hogan was the half-circle of brush like a dark shadow against the canyon wall — corral for sheep and goats. Farther from the hogan, in full circle, stood the horse corral made of heavy cedar branches sternly interlocked. Chee's long thin lips curved into a smile as he passed his daughter's tiny hogan squatted like a round Pueblo oven beside the corral. He remembered the summer day when together they sat back on their heels and plastered wet adobe all about the circling wall of rock and the woven dome of piñon twigs. How his family laughed when the Little One herded the bewildered chickens into her tiny hogan as the first snow fell.

Then the smile faded from Chee's lips and his eyes darkened as he tied his horse to a corral post and turned to the strangely empty compound. "Someone has told them," he thought, "and they are inside weeping." He passed his mother's deserted loom on the south side of the hogan and pulled the rude wooden door toward him, bowing his head, hunching his shoulders to get inside.

His mother sat sideways by the center fire, her feet drawn up under her full skirts. Her hands were busy kneading dough in the chipped white basin. With her head down, her voice was muffled when she said, "The meal will soon be ready, son."

Chee passed his father sitting against the wall, hat over his eyes as though asleep. He passed his older sister who sat turning mutton ribs on a crude wire grill over the coals, noticed tears dropping on her hands. "She cared more for my wife than I realized," he thought.

Then because something must be said sometime, he tossed the black Stetson upon a bulging sack of wool and said, "You have heard, then." He could not shut from his mind how confidently he had set the handsome new hat on his head that very morning, slanting the wide brim over one eye: he was going to see his wife and today he would ask the doctors about bringing her home; last week she had looked so much better.

His sister nodded but did not speak. His mother sniffled and passed her velveteen sleeve beneath her nose. Chee sat down, leaning against the wall. "I suppose I was a fool for hoping all the time. I should have expected this. Few of our people get well from the coughing sickness. But *she* seemed to be getting better."

His mother was crying aloud now and blowing her nose noisily on her skirt. His father sat up, speaking gently to her.

Chee shifted his position and started a cigarette. His mind turned back to the Little One. At least she was too small to understand what had happened, the Little One who had been born three years before in the sanitarium where his wife was being treated for the coughing sickness, the Little One he had brought home to his mother's hogan to be nursed by his sister whose baby was a few months older. As she grew fat-cheeked and sturdy-legged, she followed him about like a shadow; somehow her baby mind had grasped that of all those at the hogan who cared for her and played with her, he – Chee – belonged most to her. She sat cross-legged at his elbow when he worked silver at the forge; she rode before him in the saddle when he drove the horses to water; often she lay wakeful on her sheep-pelts until he stretched out for the night in the darkened hogan and she could snuggle warm against him.

Chee blew smoke slowly and some of the sadness left his dark eyes as he said, "It is not as bad as it might be. It is not as though we are left with nothing."

Chee's sister arose, sobs catching in her throat, and rushed past him out the doorway. Chee sat upright, a terrible fear possessing him. For a moment his mouth could make no sound. Then: "The Little One! Mother, where is she?"

His mother turned her stricken face to him. "Your wife's people came after her this morning. They heard yesterday of their daughter's death through the trader at Red Sands."

Chee started to protest but his mother shook her head slowly. "I didn't expect they would want the Little One either. But there is nothing you can do. She is a girl child and belongs to her mother's people; it is custom."

Frowning, Chee got to his feet, grinding his cigarette into the dirt floor. "Custom! When did my wife's parents begin thinking about custom? Why, the hogan where they live doesn't even face the East!" He started toward the door. "Perhaps I can overtake them. Perhaps they don't realize how much we want her here with us. I'll ask them to give my daughter back to me. Surely, they won't refuse."

His mother stopped him gently with her outstretched hand. "You couldn't overtake them now. They were in the trader's car. Eat and rest, and think more about this."

"Have you forgotten how things have always been between you and your wife's people?" his father said.

That night, Chee's thoughts were troubled—half-forgotten incidents became disturbingly vivid—but early the next morning he saddled the buckskin and set out for the settlement of Red Sands. Even though his father-in-law, Old Man Fat, might laugh, Chee knew that he must talk to him. There were some things to which Old Man Fat might listen.

Chee rode the first part of the fifteen miles to Red Sands expectantly. The sight of sandstone buttes near Cottonwood Spring reddening in the morning sun brought a song almost to his lips. He twirled his reins in salute to the small boy herding sheep toward many-colored Butterfly Mountain, watched with pleasure the feathers of smoke rising against tree-darkened western mesas from the hogans sheltered there. But as he approached the familiar settlement sprawled in mushroom growth along the highway, he began to feel as though a scene from a bad dream was becoming real.

Several cars were parked around the trading store which was built like two log hogans side by side, with red gas pumps in front and a sign across the tar-paper roofs: *Red Sands Trading Post—Groceries Gasoline Cold Drinks Sandwiches Indian Curios*. Back of the trading post an unpainted frame house and outbuildings squatted on the drab, treeless land. Chee and the Little One's mother had lived there when they stayed with his wife's people. That was according to custom—living with one's wife's people—but Chee had never been convinced that it was custom alone which prompted Old Man Fat and his wife to insist that their daughter bring her husband to live at the trading post.

Beside the Post was a large hogan of logs, with brightly painted pseudo-Navaho designs on the roof—a hogan with smoke-smudged windows and a garish blue door which faced north to the highway. Old Man Fat had offered Chee a hogan like this one. The trader would build it if he and his wife would live there and Chee would work at his forge making silver jewelry where tourists could watch him. But Chee had asked instead for a piece of land for a cornfield and help in building a hogan far back from the highway and a corral for the sheep he had brought to this marriage.

A cold wind blowing down from the mountains began to whistle about Chee's ears. It flapped the gaudy Navaho rugs which were hung in one long bright line to attract tourists. It swayed the sign *Navaho Weaver at Work* beside the loom where Old Man Fat's wife sat hunched in her striped blanket, patting the colored thread of a design into place with a wooden comb. Tourists stood watching the weaver. More tourists stood in a knot before the hogan where the sign said: *See Inside a Real Navaho Home 25c*.

Then the knot seemed to unravel as a few people returned to their cars; some had cameras; and there against the blue door Chee saw the Little One standing uncertainly. The wind was plucking at her new purple blouse and wide green skirt; it freed truant strands of soft dark hair from the meager queue into which it had been tied with white yarn.

"Isn't she cunning!" one of the women tourists was saying as she turned away.

Chee's lips tightened as he began to look around for Old Man Fat. Finally he saw him passing among the tourists collecting coins.

Then the Little One saw Chee. The uncertainty left her face and she darted through the crowd as her father swung down from his horse. Chee lifted her in his arms, hugging her tight. While he listened to her breathless chatter, he watched Old Man Fat bearing down on them, scowling.

As his father-in-law walked heavily across the gravelled lot, Chee was reminded of a statement his mother sometimes made: "When you see a fat Navaho, you see one who hasn't worked for what he has."

Old Man Fat was fattest in the middle. There was indolence in his walk even though he seemed to hurry, indolence in his cheeks so plump they made his eyes squint, eyes now smoldering with anger.

Some of the tourists were getting into their cars and driving away. The old man said belligerently to Chee, "Why do you come here? To spoil our business? To drive people away?"

"I came to talk with you," Chee answered, trying to keep his voice steady as he faced the old man.

"We have nothing to talk about," Old Man Fat blustered and did not offer to touch Chee's extended hand.

"It's about the Little One." Chee settled his daughter more comfortably against his hip as he weighed carefully all the words he had planned to say. "We are going to miss her very much. It wouldn't be so bad if we knew that *part* of each year she could be with us. That might help you too. You and your wife are no longer young people and you have no young ones here to depend upon." Chee chose his next words remembering the thriftlessness of his wife's parents, and their greed. "Perhaps we could share the care of this little one. Things are good with us. So much snow this year will make lots of grass for the sheep. We have good land for corn and melons."

Chee's words did not have the expected effect. Old Man Fat was enraged. "Farmers, all of you! Long-haired farmers! Do you think everyone must bend his back over the short-handled hoe in order to have food to eat?" His tone changed as he began to brag a little. "We not only have all the things from cans at the trader's, but when the Pueblos come past here on their way to town we buy their salty jerked mutton, young corn for roasting, dried sweet peaches."

Chee's dark eyes surveyed the land along the highway as the old man continued to brag about being "progressive." *He* no longer was tied to the land. He and his wife made money easily and could *buy* all the things they wanted. Chee realized too late that he had stumbled into the old argument between himself and his wife's parents. They had never understood his feeling about the land—that a man took care of his land and it in turn took care of him. Old Man Fat and his wife scoffed at him, called him a Pueblo farmer, all during that summer when he planted and weeded and harvested. Yet they ate the green corn in their mutton stews, and the chili paste from the fresh ripe chilis, and the tortillas from the cornmeal his wife ground. None of this working and sweating in the sun for Old Man Fat, who talked proudly of his easy way of living—collecting money from the trader who rented this strip of land beside the highway, collecting money from the tourists.

Yet Chee had once won that argument. His wife had shared his belief in the integrity of the earth, that jobs and people might fail one but the earth never would. After that first year she had turned from her own people and gone with Chee to Little Canyon.

Old Man Fat was reaching for the Little One. "Don't be coming here with plans for my daughter's daughter," he warned. "If you try to make trouble, I'll take the case to the government man in town."

The impulse was strong in Chee to turn and ride off while he still had the Little One in his arms. But he knew his time of victory would be short. His own family would uphold the old custom of children, especially girl children, belonging to the mother's people. He would have to give his daughter up if the case were brought before the Headman of Little Canyon, and certainly he would have no better chance before a strange white man in town.

He handed the bewildered Little One to her grandfather who stood watching every movement suspiciously. Chee asked, "If I brought you a few things for the Little One, would that be making trouble? Some velvet for a blouse, or some of the jerky she likes so well . . . this summer's melon?"

Old Man Fat backed away from him. "Well," he hesitated, as some of the anger disappeared from his face and beads of greed shone in his eyes. "Well," he repeated. Then as the Little One began to squirm in his arms and cry, he said, "No! No! Stay away from here, you and all your family."

The sense of his failure deepened as Chee rode back to Little Canyon. But it was not until he sat with his family that evening in the hogan, while the familiar bustle of meal preparing went on about him, that he began to doubt the wisdom of the things he'd always believed. He smelled the coffee boiling and the oily fragrance of chili powder dusted into the bubbling pot of stew; he watched his mother turning round crusty fried bread in the small black skillet. All around him was plenty—a half of mutton hanging near the door, bright strings of chili drying, corn hanging by the braided husks, cloth bags of dried peaches. Yet in his heart was nothing.

He heard the familiar sounds of the sheep outside the hogan, the splash of water as his father filled the long drinking trough from the water barrel. When his father came in, Chee could not bring himself to tell a second time of the day's happenings. He watched his wiry, soft-spoken father while his mother told the story, saw his father's queue of graying hair quiver as he nodded his head with sympathetic exclamations.

Chee's doubting, acrid thoughts kept forming: Was it wisdom his father had passed on to him or was his inheritance only the stubbornness of a long-haired Navaho resisting change? Take care of the land and it will take care of you. True, the land had always given him food, but now food was not enough. Perhaps if he had gone to school he would have learned a different kind of wisdom, something to help him now. A schoolboy might even be able to speak convincingly to this government man whom Old Man Fat threatened to call, instead of sitting here like a clod of earth itself—Pueblo farmer indeed. What had the land to give that would restore his daughter?

In the days that followed, Chee herded sheep. He got up in the half-light, drank the hot coffee his mother had ready, then started the flock moving. It was necessary to drive the sheep a long way from the hogan to find good winter forage. Sometimes Chee met friends or relatives who were on their way to town or to the road camp where they hoped to get work; then there was friendly banter and an exchange of news. But most of the days seemed endless; he could not walk far enough or fast enough from his memories of the Little One or from his bitter thoughts. Sometimes it seemed his daughter trudged beside him, so real he could almost hear her footsteps—the muffled pad-pad of little feet clad in deerhide. In the glare of a snow bank he would see her vivid face, brown eyes sparkling. Mingling with the tinkle of sheep bells he heard her laughter.

When, weary of following the small sharp hoof marks that crossed and recrossed in the snow, he sat down in the shelter of a rock, it was only to be reminded that in his thoughts he had forsaken his brotherhood with the earth and sun and growing things. If he remembered times when he had flung himself against the earth to rest, to lie there in the sun until he could no longer feel where he left off and the earth began, it was to remember also that now he sat like an alien against the same earth; the belonging-together was gone. The earth was one thing and he was another.

It was during the days when he herded sheep that Chee decided he must leave Little Canyon. Perhaps he would take a job silversmithing for one of the traders in town. Perhaps, even though he spoke little English, he could get a job at the road camp with his cousins; he would ask them about it.

■ Springtime transformed the mesas. The peach trees in the canyon were shedding fragrance and pink blossoms on the gentled wind. The sheep no longer foraged for the yellow seeds of chamiso but ranged near the hogan with the long-legged new lambs, eating tender young grass.

Chee was near the hogan on the day his cousins rode up with the message for which he waited. He had been watching with mixed emotions while his father and his sister's husband cleared the fields beside the stream.

"The boss at the camp says he needs an extra hand, but he wants to know if you'll be willing to go with the camp when they move it to the other side of the town?" The tall cousin shifted his weight in the saddle.

The other cousin took up the explanation. "The work near here will last only until the new cut-off beyond Red Sands is finished. After that, the work will be too far away for you to get back here often."

That was what Chee had wanted—to get away from Little Canyon—yet he found himself not so interested in the job beyond town as in this new cut-off which was almost finished. He pulled a blade of grass, split it thoughtfully down the center as he asked questions of his cousins. Finally he said: "I need to think more about this. If I decide on this job I'll ride over."

Before his cousins were out of sight down the canyon Chee was walking toward the fields, a bold plan shaping in his mind. As the plan began to flourish, wild and hardy as young tumbleweed, Chee added his own voice softly to the song his father was singing: ". . . In the middle of the wide field . . . Yellow Corn Boy . . . I wish to put in."

Chee walked slowly around the field, the rich red earth yielding to his footsteps. His plan depended upon this land and upon the things he remembered most about his wife's people.

Through planting time Chee worked zealously and tirelessly. He spoke little of the large new field he was planting because he felt so strongly that just now this was something between himself and the land. The first days he was ever stooping, piercing the ground with the pointed stick, placing the corn kernels there, walking around the field and through it, singing, ". . . His track leads into the ground . . . Yellow Corn Boy . . . his track leads into the ground." After that, each day Chee walked through his field watching for the tips of green to break through; first a few spikes in the center and then more and more until the corn in all parts of the field was above ground. Surely, Chee thought, if he sang the proper songs, if he cared for this land faithfully, it would not forsake him now, even though through the lonely days of winter he had betrayed the goodness of the earth in his thoughts.

Through the summer Chee worked long days, the sun hot upon his back, pulling weeds from around young corn plants; he planted squash and pumpkin; he terraced a small piece of land near his mother's hogan and planted carrots and onions and the moisture-loving chili. He was increasingly restless. Finally he told his family what he hoped the harvest from this land would bring him. Then the whole family waited with him, watching the corn: the slender graceful plants that waved green arms and bent to embrace each other as young winds wandered through the field, the maturing plants flaunting their pollen-laden tassels in the sun, the tall and sturdy parent corn with new-formed ears and a froth of purple, red and yellow corn-beards against the dusty emerald of broad leaves.

Summer was almost over when Chee slung the bulging packs across two pack ponies. His mother helped him tie the heavy rolled pack behind the saddle of the buckskin. Chee knotted the new yellow kerchief about his neck a little tighter, gave the broad black hat brim an extra tug, but these were only gestures of assurance and he knew it. The land had not failed him. That part was done. But this he was riding into? Who could tell?

When Chee arrived at Red Sands, it was as he had expected to find it—no cars on the highway. His cousins had told him that even the Pueblo farmers were using the new cut-off to town. The barren gravel around the Red Sands Trading Post was deserted. A sign banged against the dismantled gas pumps *Closed until further notice.*

Old Man Fat came from the crude summer shelter built beside the log hogan from a few branches of scrub cedar and the sides of wooden crates. He seemed almost friendly when he saw Chee.

"Get down, my son," he said, eyeing the bulging packs. There was no bluster in his voice today and his face sagged, looking somewhat saddened; perhaps because his cheeks were no longer quite full enough to push his eyes upward at the corners. "You are going on a journey?"

Chee shook his head. "Our fields gave us so much this year, I thought to sell or trade this to the trader. I didn't know he was no longer here."

Old Man Fat sighed, his voice dropping to an injured tone. "He says he and his wife are going to rest this winter; then after that he'll build a place up on the new highway."

Chee moved as though to be traveling on, then jerked his head toward the pack ponies. "Anything you need?"

"I'll ask my wife," Old Man Fat said as he led the way to the shelter. "Maybe she has a little money. Things have not been too good with us since the trader closed. Only a few tourists come this way." He shrugged his shoulders. "And with the trader gone — no credit."

Chee was not deceived by his father-in-law's unexpected confidences. He recognized them as a hopeful bid for sympathy and, if possible, something for nothing. Chee made no answer. He was thinking that so far he had been right about his wife's parents: their thriftlessness had left them with no resources to last until Old Man Fat found another easy way of making a living.

Old Man Fat's Wife was in the shelter working at her loom. She turned rather wearily when her husband asked with noticeable deference if she would give him money to buy supplies. Chee surmised that the only income here was from his mother-in-law's weaving.

She peered around the corner of the shelter at the laden ponies, and then she looked at Chee. "What do you have there, my son?"

Chee smiled to himself as he turned to pull the pack from one of the ponies, dragged it to the shelter where he untied the ropes. Pumpkins and hardshelled squash tumbled out, and the ears of corn — pale yellow husks fitting firmly over plump ripe kernels, blue corn, red corn, yellow corn, many-colored corn, ears and ears of it — tumbled into every corner of the shelter.

"Yooooh," Old Man Fat's Wife exclaimed as she took some of the ears in her hands. Then she glanced up at her son-in-law. "But we have no money for all this. We have sold almost everything we own — even the brass bed that stood in the hogan."

Old Man Fat's brass bed. Chee concealed his amusement as he started back for another pack. That must have been a hard parting. Then he stopped, for, coming from the cool darkness of the hogan was the Little One, rubbing her eyes as though she had been asleep. She stood for a moment in the doorway and Chee saw that she was dirty, barefoot, her hair uncombed, her little blouse shorn of all its silver buttons. Then she ran toward Chee, her arms outstretched. Heedless of Old Man Fat and his wife, her father caught her in his arms, her hair falling in a dark cloud across his face, the sweetness of her laughter warm against his shoulder.

It was the haste within him to get this slow waiting game played through to the finish that made Chee speak unwisely. It was the desire to swing her before him in the saddle and ride fast to Little Canyon that prompted his words. "The money doesn't matter. You still have something. . . ."

Chee knew immediately that he had overspoken. The old woman looked from him to the corn spread before her. Unfriendliness began to harden in his father-in-law's face. All the old arguments between himself and his wife's people came pushing and crowding in between them now.

Old Man Fat began kicking the ears of corn back onto the canvas as he eyed Chee angrily. "And you rode all the way over here thinking that for a little food we would give up our daughter's daughter?"

Chee did not wait for the old man to reach for the Little One. He walked dazedly to the shelter, rubbing his cheek against her soft dark hair and put her gently into her grandmother's lap. Then he turned back to the horses. He had failed. By his own haste he had failed. He swung into the saddle, his hand touching the roll behind it. Should he ride on into town?

Then he dismounted, scarcely glancing at Old Man Fat, who stood uncertainly at the corner of the shelter, listening to his wife. "Give me a hand with this other pack of corn, Grandfather," Chee said, carefully keeping the small bit of hope from his voice.

Puzzled, but willing, Old Man Fat helped carry the other pack to the shelter, opening it to find more corn as well as carrots and round pale yellow onions. Chee went back for the roll behind the buckskin's saddle and carried it to the entrance of the shelter where he cut the ropes and gave the canvas a nudge with his toe. Tins of coffee rolled out, small plump cloth bags; jerked meat from several butcherings spilled from a flour sack, and bright red chilis splashed like flames against the dust.

"I will leave all this anyhow," Chee told them. "I would not want my daughter nor even you old people to go hungry."

Old Man Fat picked up a shiny tin of coffee, then put it down. With trembling hands he began to untie one of the cloth bags — dried sweet peaches.

The Little One had wriggled from her grandmother's lap, unheeded, and was on her knees, digging her hands into the jerked meat.

"There is almost enough food here to last all winter," Old Man Fat's Wife sought the eyes of her husband.

Chee said, "I meant it to be enough. But that was when I thought you might send the Little One back with me." He looked down at his daughter noisily sucking jerky. Her mouth, both fists were full of it. "I am sorry that you feel you cannot bear to part with her."

Old Man Fat's Wife brushed a straggly wisp of gray hair from her forehead as she turned to look at the Little One. Old Man Fat was looking too. And it was not a thing to see. For in that moment the Little One ceased to be their daughter's daughter and became just another mouth to feed.

"And why not?" the old woman asked wearily.

■ Chee was settled in the saddle, the barefooted Little One before him. He urged the buckskin faster, and his daughter clutched his shirtfront. The purpling mesas flung back the echo: ". . . My corn embrace each other. In the middle of the wide field . . . Yellow Corn Boy embrace each other."

Suggestions for Discussion

    1. Are the opening paragraphs effective in their characterization of Chee? Which descriptive details suggest the Navajo way of life? Are they intrusive as "information" or integral to the story?

    2. In what way does the death of Chee's wife serve as an introduction to the story proper? What caused her death? Was it expected?

    3. Discuss the description of the Red Sands Trading Post. How would the description change if it were rendered from the point of view of one of the tourists instead of Chee?

4. How does Chee regard the earth and corn? What does he feel are his responsibilities to them? What is the significance of ending the story with Chee's singing about Yellow Corn Boy?
5. What is the major theme of the story? How is it related to Old Man Fat and his wife?

Suggestions for Writing and Comparison

1. Compare and contrast the character of Chee with Old Man Fat. What, aside from their different adjustments to "the way of the white man," differentiates the two men?
2. Read Pearl Buck's *The Good Earth* and one of the following autobiographies: *Son of Old Man Hat* recorded by Walter Dyk, *Sun Chief: Autobiography of a Hopi* by Don Talayesva, or *Kaibah* by Kay Bennett. Compare the Chinese and Native American attitudes toward the land.

Durango Mendoza

Durango Mendoza was born in 1946 in Oklahoma, where he grew up. He is half Native American (Creek) and half Mexican. While attending the University of Missouri, Mendoza wrote the following story, "Summer Water and Shirley," which won the annual Mahan Fiction Contest. His work has been published in various university magazines, among them *Prairie Schooner*.

"Summer Water and Shirley," which is concerned with twentieth-century Native Americans, combines elements of the traditional folk tale with realistic contemporary characters and setting. The particular ethnic interest of the story is subordinate to its universal romantic theme: that love (specifically the love of a brother for his sister) can overcome even death.

Summer Water and Shirley

It was in the summer that had burned every stalk of corn and every blade of grass and dried up the creek until it only flowed in trickles across the ford below the house where in the pools the boy could scoop up fish in a dishpan.

The boy lived with his mother and his sister, Shirley, and the three smaller children eleven miles from Weleetka, and near Lthwathlee Indian church where it was Eighth Sunday meeting and everyone was there. The boy and his family stayed at the camp house of his dead father's people.

Shirley and her brother, who was two years older and twelve, had just escaped the deacon and were lying on the brown, sun-scorched grass behind the last camp house. They were out of breath and giggled as they peeped above the slope and saw the figure of the deacon, Hardy Eagle, walking toward the church house.

"Boy, we sure out-fooled him, huh?" Shirley laughed lightly and jabbed her elbow in her brother's shaking side. "Whew!" She ran her slim hand over her eyes and squinted at the sky. They both lay back and watched the cloudless sky until the heat in their blood went down and their breath slowed to normal. They lay there on the hot grass until the sun became too much for them.

"Hey, let's go down to the branch and find a pool to wade in, okay?" She had rolled over suddenly and spoke directly into the boy's ear.

"I don't think we better. Mama said to stay around the church grounds."

"Aw, you're just afraid."

"No, it's just that—"

"'Mama said to stay around the church grounds!' Fraidy-cat, I'll go by myself then." She sat up and looked at him. He didn't move and she sighed. Then she nudged him. "Hey." She nudged him again and assumed a stage whisper. "Looky there! See that old man coming out of the woods?"

The boy looked and saw the old man shuffling slowly through the high johnson grass between the woods and the clearing for the church grounds. He was very old and still wore his hair in the old way.

"Who is he?" Shirley whispered. "Who is he?"

"I can't tell yet. The heat makes everything blurry." The boy was looking intently at the old man who was moving slowly in the weltering heat through the swaying grass that moved with the sound of light tinsel in the dry wind.

"Let's go sneak through the grass and scare him," Shirley suggested. "I bet that'd make him even run." She moved her arms as if she were galloping and broke down into giggles. "Come on," she said, getting to one knee.

"Wait!" He pulled her back.

"What do you mean, 'wait'? He'll be out of the grass pretty soon and we won't—" She broke off. "What's the matter? What're you doing?"

The boy had started to crawl away on his hands and knees and was motioning for her to follow. "Come on, Shirley," he whispered. "That's old Ansul Middlecreek!"

"Who's *he?*"

"Don't you remember? Mama said he's the one that killed Haskell Day —with witchcraft. He's a *stiginnee!*"

"A *stiginnee?* Aw, you don't believe that, do you? Mama says you can tell them by the way they never have to go to the toilet, and that's where he's been. Look down there." She pointed to the little unpainted house that stood among the trees.

"I don't care *where* he's been! Come on, Shirley! Look! Oh my gosh! He saw you pointing!"

"I'm coming," she said and followed him quickly around the corner of the camp house.

They sat on the porch. Almost everyone was in for the afternoon service and they felt alone. The wind was hot and it blew from the southwest. It blew past them across the dry fields of yellow weeds that spread before them up to the low hills that wavered in the heat and distance. They could smell the dry harshness of the grass and they felt the porch boards hot underneath them. Shirley bent over and wiped her face with the skirt of her dress.

"Come on," she said. "Let's go down to the creek branch before that deacon comes back." She pulled at his sleeve and they stood up.

"Okay," he said and they skirted the outer camp houses and followed the dusty road to the bridge, stepping from tuft to tuft of scorched grass.

■ Toward evening and suppertime they climbed out of the dry bed of the branch, over the huge boulders to the road and started for the camp grounds. The sun was in their eyes as they trudged up the steep road from the bridge. They had found no water in the branch so they had gone on down to the creek. For the most part it too was dry.

Suddenly they saw a shadow move into the dust before them. They looked up and saw old Ansul Middlecreek shuffling toward them. His cracked shoes raised little clouds of dust that rose around his ankles and made whispering sounds as he moved along.

"Don't look when you go by," the boy whispered intently, and he pushed her behind him. But as they passed by Shirley looked up.

"Hey, Ansul Middlecreek," she said cheerfully. "*Henkschay!*" Then with a swish of her skirt she grabbed her brother and they ran. The old man stopped and the puffs of dust around his feet moved ahead as he grumbled, his face still in shadow because he did not turn around. The two didn't stop until they had reached the first gate. Then they slowed down and the boy scolded his sister all the way to their camp. And all through supper he looked at the dark opening of the door and then at Shirley who sat beside him, helping herself with childish appetite to the heavy, greasy food that was set before her.

"You better eat some," she told her brother. "Next meetin's not 'til next month."

Soon after they had left the table she began to complain that her head hurt and their mother got them ready to go home. They took the two little girls and the baby boy from where they were playing under the arbor and cleaned them up before they started out. Their uncle, George Hulegy, would go with them and carry the biggest girl. The mother carried the other one while the boy struggled in the rear with the baby. Shirley followed morosely behind them all as they started down the road that lay white and pale under the rising moon.

She began to fall further behind and shuffled her bare feet into the warm underlayer of dust. The boy gave to his uncle the sleeping child he carried and took Shirley by the hand, surprised that it was so hot and limp.

"Come on, Shirley, come on. Mama, Shirley's got a fever. Don't walk so fast — we can't keep up. Come on, Shirley," he coaxed. "Hurry."

They turned into their lane and followed it until they were on the little hill above the last stretch of road and started down its rocky slope to the sandy road below. Ahead, the house sat wanly under the stars, and Rey, the dog, came out to greet them, sniffing and wriggling his black body and tail.

George Hulegy and the mother were already on the porch as the boy led his sister into the yard. As they reached the porch they saw the lamp begin to glow orange in the window. Then Shirley took hold of the boy's arm and pointed weakly toward the back yard and the form of the storehouse.

"Look, Sonny! Over there, by the storehouse." The boy froze with fear but he saw nothing. "They were three little men," she said vaguely and then she collapsed.

"Mama!" But as he screamed he saw a great yellow dog with large brown spots jump off the other end of the porch with a click of its heavy nails and disappear into the shadows that led to the creek. The boy could hear the brush rustle and a few pebbles scatter as it went. Rey only whined uneasily and did not even look to where the creature had gone.

"What is it? What's wrong?" The two older persons had come quickly onto the porch and the mother bent immediately to help her daughter.

"Oh, Shirley! George! Help me. Oh gosh! She's burning up. Sonny, put back the covers of the big bed. Quick now!"

They were inside now and the boy spoke.

"She saw dwarfs," he said solemnly and the mother looked at George Hulegy. "And there was a big yellow dog that Rey didn't even see."

"Oh, no, no," the mother wailed and leaned over Shirley who had begun to writhe and moan. "Hush, baby, hush. Mama's here. Hush, baby, your Mama's here." She began to sing softly a very old song while George Hulegy took a lantern from behind the stove.

"I'm going to the creek and get some pebbles where the water still runs," he said. "I have to hurry." He closed the screen quietly behind him and the boy watched him as he disappeared with the swinging lantern through the brush and trees, down into the darkness to the ford. Behind him the mother still sang softly as Shirley's voice began to rise, high and thin like a very small child's. The boy shivered in the heat and sat down in the corner to wait helplessly as he tried not to look at the dark space of the window. He grew stiff and tired trying to control his trembling muscles as they began to jump.

Then George Hulegy came in with some pebbles that still were dripping and they left little wet spots of dark on the floor as he placed them above all the doors and windows throughout the house. Finally he placed three round ones at the foot of the bed where Shirley lay twisting and crying with pain and fever.

The mother had managed to start a small fire in the kitchen stove and told the boy to go out and bring in a few pieces of cook wood from the woodpile. He looked at her and couldn't move. He stood stiff and alert and heard George Hulegy, who was bending close over Shirley, muttering some words that he could not understand. He looked at the door but the sagging screen only reflected the yellow lamplight so that he couldn't see through into the darkness; he froze even tighter.

"Hurry, son!"

He looked at Shirley lying on the bed and moving from side to side.

"Sonny, I have to make Shirley some medicine!" His body shook from a spasm. The mother saw and turned to the door. "I'll get them," she said.

"Mama!"

She stopped and he barged through the door and found the darkness envelop him. As he fixed his wide-open gaze on the woodpile that faintly reflected the starlight and that of the moon which had risen above the trees, he couldn't look to either side nor could he run. When he reached for the first piece of wood, the hysteria that was building inside him hardened into an aching bitter core. He squeezed the rough cool wood to his chest and felt the fibers press into his bare arms as he staggered toward the house and the two rectangles of light. The closer he came the higher the tension inside him stretched until he could scarcely breathe. Then he was inside again and he sat limply in the corner, light and drained of any support. He could feel nothing except that Shirley was lying in the big feather bed across the room, wailing with hurt and a scalding fever.

His mother was hurrying from the kitchen with a tin cup of grass tea when Shirley began to scream, louder and louder until the boy thought that he would never hear another sound as he stood straight and hard, not leaning at all.

She stopped.

In the silence he saw his mother standing above and behind the lamp, casting a shadow on the ceiling, stopped with fear as they heard the other sound. The little girls had come into the room from their bedroom and were standing whimpering in their nightgowns by the door. The mother signaled and they became still and quiet, their mouths slightly open and their eyes wide. They heard nothing.

Then like a great, beating heart the sound rose steadily until they could smell the heat of a monstrous flesh, raw and hot. Steadily it grew to a gagging, stifling crescendo—then stopped. They heard the click of dog's nails on the porch's wooden planks, and afterwards, nothing. In the complete silence the air became cold for an instant and Shirley was quiet.

■ It was three days now since Shirley had begun to die and everyone knew how and had given up any hope. Even the white doctor could find nothing wrong and all the old Indians nodded their solemn heads when he went away saying that Shirley would be up in a few days, for now, to them, her manner of death was confirmed. He said to send for him if there was any "real" change. No need to move her—there was nothing wrong—nothing physically wrong, he had said. He could not even feel her raging fever. To him Shirley was only sleeping.

Everyone had accepted that Shirley was going to die and they were all afraid to go near her. "There is evil around her," they said. They even convinced the mother to put her in the back room and close off all light and only open it after three days. She would not die until the third day's night, nor would she live to see the fourth day's dawn. This they could know. A very old woman spoke these words to the mother and she could not disbelieve.

On this third day the boy sat and watched the flies as they crawled over the dirty floor, over the specks and splotches, the dust and crumbs. They buzzed and droned about some drops of water, rubbing their legs against themselves, nibbling, strutting, until the drops dried into meaningless little rings while the hot wind blew softly through the open window, stirring particles of dust from the torn screen. A droplet of sweat broke away from above his eyebrow and ran a crooked rivulet down his temple until he wiped it away. In his emptiness the boy did not want his sister to die.

"Mama?"

"What is it, son?"

"Is Shirley going to die?"

"Yes, son."

He watched her as she stood with her back to him. She moved the heavy skillet away from the direct heat and turned the damper so that the flames would begin to die. She moved automatically, as if faster movement would cause her to breathe in too much of the stifling heat. And as she moved the floor groaned under the shift in weight and her feet made whispering sounds against the sagging boards. The flies still flitted about, mindless and nasty, as the boy looked away from them to his mother.

"Does she have to, Mama?"

"Shirley is dying, son."

Again he saw how the flies went about, unaware of the heat, himself, his mother across the room or that Shirley lay in her silence in the back room. He splashed some more water from his glass and they knew he was there but immediately forgot and settled back to their patternless walking about. And even though the table was clean they walked jerkily among the dishes and inspected his tableware. The boy had lived all his life among these creatures but now he could not stand their nature.

"Darn flies!"

"Well, we won't have to worry when cold weather gets here," she said. "Now go call the kids and eat. I want to get some sewing done this afternoon."

He said nothing and watched her as she went into the other room. He went to the door and leaned out to call the small children. Then he slipped quietly into the back room and closed the door behind him, fastening the latch in the dark. The heat was almost choking and he blinked away the saltiness that stung his eyes. He stood by the door until he could see a little better. High above his head a crack in the shingles filtered down a star of daylight and he stepped to the bed that stood low against the rough planks of the wall. There were no flies in this room and there was no sound.

The boy sat down on a crate and watched the face of his sister emerge from the gloom where she lay. Straining his eyes he finally saw the rough army blanket rise and fall, but so slight was the movement that when his eyes lost their focus he could not see it and he quickly put out his hand but stopped. Air caught in his throat and he stifled a cough, still letting his hand hover over the motionless face. Then he touched the smooth forehead and jerked his hand away as if he had been burned.

He sat and watched his sister's well-formed profile and saw how the skin of the nose and forehead had become taut and dry and now gleamed pale and smooth like old ivory in the semi-darkness. A smell like that of hot wood filled the room but underneath it the boy could smell the odor of something raw, something evil—something that was making Shirley die.

The boy sat on the empty crate in the darkness through the late afternoon and did not answer when his mother called him. He knew that she would not even try the door to this room. He waited patiently for his thoughts to come together, not moving in the lifeless heat, and let the sweat flow from his body. He smelled the raw smell and when it became too strong he touched the smooth, round pebbles that had come from the creek where it still flowed, and the smell receded.

For many hours he sat, and then he got up and took down the heavy blanket that had covered the single window and let the moonlight fall across the face of his sister through the opening. He began to force his thoughts to remember, to relive every living moment of his life and every part that Shirley had lived in it with him. And then he spoke softly, saying what they had done, and how they would do again what they had done because he had not given up, for he was alive, and she was alive, and they had lived and would *still* live. And so he prayed to his will and forced his will out through his thoughts and spoke softly his words and was not afraid to look out through the window into the darkness through which came the coolness of the summer night. He smelled its scents and let them touch his flesh and come to rest around the "only sleeping" face of his sister. He stood, watching, listening, living.

Then they came, silently, dark-bellied clouds drifting up from the south, and the wind, increasing, swept in the heavy scent of the approaching storm. Lightning flashed over the low, distant hills and the clouds closed quietly around the moon as the thunder rumbled and the heavy drops began to fall, slowly at first, then irregularly, then increasing to a rhythmic rush of noise as the gusts of wind forced the rain in vertical waves across the shingled roof.

Much later, when the rain had moved ahead and the room became chilly when the water began to drip from the roof and the countless leaves, the boy slipped out of his worn denim pants and took off his shirt and lay down beside his sister. She felt him and woke up.

"You just now gettin' to bed?" she asked. "It's pretty late for that, ain't it?"

"No, Shirley," he said. "Go on back to sleep. It'll be morning pretty soon and when it gets light again we'll go see how high the water's risen in the creek."

He pulled the cover over him and drew his bare arms beneath the blanket and pulled it over their shoulders as he turned onto his side. Lying thus he could see in the darkness the even darker shapes of the trees and the storehouse his father had built.

Suggestions for Discussion

1. How is Shirley characterized in the first few pages of the story? Is the relationship of Shirley to her brother, particularly in the beginning of the story, a typical one?

2. Why has the author chosen to include in the same paragraph two episodes as dissimilar as Shirley's calling out "Hey, Ansul Middlecreek" and her eating of the "heavy, greasy food" for supper?

3. What is the significance of the brother's seeing the "great yellow dog with brown spots"? What kind of an atmosphere does the author create in the paragraph beginning "Then like a great, beating heart . . ."? How has the reader's perception of "the truth" changed with the sentence "*They* heard the click of the dog's nails on the porch's wooden planks, and afterwards, nothing"?

4. What aspect of nature in relation to man is made evident as the boy watches the flies? Why then can touching pebbles from the creek make "the smell" recede? Are these incidents contradictory statements about nature or the revelation of two different aspects of nature?

5. What is the implied reason for the boy's ability to "cure" his sister? Is his "curing" foreshadowed in previous incidents?

6. What is the significance of the thunderstorm? What is the meaning of the title of the story?

Suggestion for Writing and Comparison

1. Read Paul Radin's *The Coyote Myth* or *Hero Cycles of the Winnebago*. Does "Summer Water and Shirley" contain elements of the folk tale as discussed by Radin?

Hyemeyohsts Storm

Hyemeyohsts Storm, a Cheyenne, was born on the Lame Deer Agency in Montana. *Seven Arrows* is his first book. The title refers to the seven teaching arrows; they include the six directions—north, the direction of wisdom; south, trust; west, introspection; east, illumination; the earth below; the sky above; and the seventh arrow, which is the Spirit "spoken of as Universal Harmony." Although *Seven Arrows* has been called a novel, it is not written within the European tradition. It contains many old stories from the oral tradition of the Cheyenne. In commenting on stories such as "Jumping Mouse," the author has said,

> The stories are about animals and people. You will find stories about Mice, Wolves, Raccoons, and Buffalo. These stories are almost entirely allegorical in form, and everything in them should be read symbolically. Every story can be symbolically unfolded for you through your own . . . Reflections and Seekings.

Storm also describes the "Mouse Person," who is the subject of the following selection, in this way:

> A Mouse Person would be one who saw everything close up, and whose vision would be limited to the immediate world around him. He would be a gatherer of things. He might gather facts, information, material objects, or even ideas. But because he could not see far enough to connect his world with that of the great prairie of the world around him, he would never be able to use or understand all he saw and gathered.

Jumping Mouse

Day Woman and Prairie Rose entered Flying Cloud's lodge and hugged Dancing Water. Both girls peeked at the newborn baby before sitting down next to Dancing Water. Two Sioux women were working on buckskins, their eyes so full of tears that they could hardly work. Day Woman saw the tears in Dancing Water's eyes and looked down at her hands.

"You must know quickly," said Dancing Water through her tears. "Grey Owl, Painted Elk, Four Bears, and many more are all dead." Day Woman was crying hard herself now, but still she could not help but see the brightly colored material that Dancing Water dried her eyes with.

Early the next morning the men returned. Day Woman was awakened by the barking of the camp dogs. She slipped on her dress and stepped from the lodge just as Lame Bear dismounted.

"I will put your horse in hobbles for you," she said, walking to Lame Bear's horse.

"No," Lame Bear answered, his voice tired. "Picket him in front of the lodge and leave the weapons tied."

As Day Woman busied herself making her uncle's meal, she noticed his haggard face but said nothing, waiting for him to talk.

"We will have to move soon," he finally said as he began to eat. "The people who murdered your brothers and uncles were not whitemen, Day Woman." His voice was full of emotion. "We have known, we all have known, for a very long time. The Brotherhood is dead. The men of the Shield are no more. The Way of the Medicine Wheel that bound us together in the Brotherhood is truly dead."

"The Way is not dead!" the Medicine Chief said as he entered the lodge. He was a big man, over six feet tall, with broad shoulders and muscular arms, a man of about forty winters. Hawk followed the man into the lodge and sat with him across from Lame Bear. Reaching for more bowls, Day Woman set them before the men. Lame Bear was silent, not looking at his guests.

"Wars," continued the Peace Chief, "have been with man for so long that man has forgotten when they began. I am amazed to hear you speak this way, Lame Bear. The very Power that has made our Way possible has been in those of the People who have held fast to the Ways of the Shield."

"What," Lame Bear exploded, "has the Great Spirit been so horribly blind and deaf then? Or has our Way been only the foolish Way of children? By the Power, man! Look around you! Look what the Power has given to the whiteman! The gifts to these men overwhelm the mind! And they are a People of war! They despise peace! Yet still the Power given them by the Universe is a far greater Medicine than ours! Their gifts of wealth and power are a living proof!"

"Is the love of the universe reflected only in material gifts?" the Chief answered quickly. "Lame Bear, I do not claim to understand these men, but if their Way is one of war and death, then they cannot be a full people. And remember, my brother, their gifts are ours too. And one day we will find peace and live together. And we will grow."

"Grow!" Lame Bear barked, holding his head with both hands. "Did you hear him, Day Woman? He said grow!" Lame Bear laughed almost hysterically. "Will Grey Owl grow? Or the others who have died? Will there be anyone left alive to grow, other than the whitemen? I have dreamed, Man of the Shield, and in my dreams it has all been made clear to me. I asked to understand. And do you know what has been told to me? The whitemen are determined to destroy all People whose Ways do not reflect their own. They have set the People one against the other and will kill whichever is left when the wars have ended. And know this! The universe has given them even the Power to have talking leaves. Go away, Man of the Shield. I am weary. I want to sleep. Even the power of talking leaves," he mumbled as he lay down.

Deep sorrow etched the eyes of the Peace Chief as he rose to leave. Day Woman and Hawk followed him from the lodge. He sat down under the shade of the lodge arbor and rubbed his forehead hard, as if trying to erase some thought.

"Is it true?" asked Day Woman timidly, addressing the Chief. "Do they really have leaves that talk?"

The Peace Chief raised his head and stared quietly at the distant mountains. They stood out sharply above the green landscape. "Yes," he said gently, turning to Day Woman, "they do."

"Great Father," said Hawk, looking straight into the eyes of the chief, "if they have these wonderful gifts, then why do they kill?"

"That, my son, is one of the riddles of men," answered the Chief. "Would you listen to a Story concerning men?"

"A Story?" asked Day Woman excitedly, "Great Shield, please let me run for my sister, Prairie Rose, so that she too may hear it."

"Bring as many of my children who will listen as you can!" smiled the Chief as Day Woman flew to find her friend.

Soon half a dozen children were clustered around the Story-Teller. He lit his Pipe and began:

Once there was a Mouse.

Squinting his eyes, he touched his nose to the nose of a little girl near him.

He was a Busy Mouse, Searching Everywhere, Touching his Whiskers to the Grass, and Looking. He was Busy as all Mice are, Busy with Mice things. But Once in a while he would Hear an odd Sound. He would Lift his Head, Squinting hard to See, his Whiskers Wiggling in the Air, and he would Wonder. One Day he Scurried up to a fellow Mouse and asked him, "Do you Hear a Roaring in your Ears, my Brother?"

"No, no," answered the Other Mouse, not Lifting his Busy Nose from the Ground. "I Hear Nothing. I am Busy now. Talk to me Later."

He asked Another Mouse the same Question and the Mouse Looked at him Strangely. "Are you Foolish in your Head? What Sound?" he asked and Slipped into a Hole in a Fallen Cottonwood Tree.

The little Mouse shrugged his Whiskers and Busied himself again, Determined to Forget the Whole Matter. But there was that Roaring again. It was faint, very faint, but it was there! One Day, he Decided to investigate the Sound just a little. Leaving the Other Busy Mice, he Scurried a little Way away and Listened again. There It was! He was Listening hard when suddenly, Someone said Hello.

"Hello, little Brother," the Voice said, and Mouse almost Jumped right Out of his Skin. He Arched his Back and Tail and was about to Run.

"Hello," again said the Voice. "It is I, Brother Raccoon." And sure enough, It was! "What are you Doing Here all by yourself, little Brother?" asked the Raccoon. The Mouse blushed, and put his Nose almost to the Ground. "I Hear a Roaring in my Ears and I am Investigating it," he answered timidly.

"A Roaring in your Ears?" replied the Raccoon as he Sat Down with him. "What you Hear, little Brother, is the River."

"The River?" Mouse asked curiously. "What is a River?"

"Walk with me and I will Show you the River," Raccoon said.

Little Mouse was terribly Afraid, but he was Determined to Find Out Once and for All about the Roaring. "I can Return to my Work," he thought, "after this thing is Settled, and possibly this thing may Aid me in All my Busy Examining and Collecting. And my Brothers All said it was Nothing. I will

Show them. I will Ask Raccoon to Return with me and I will have Proof."

"All right Raccoon, my Brother," said Mouse. "Lead on to the River. I will *Walk with you."*

"Get me another brand from the fire, my son," the Chief said to Hawk. "And we will talk more about this Mouse."

Hawk ran for the brand and brought it to the Chief. Lighting his Pipe, the Chief looked up at the little girl nearest him. "And what will happen to little Mouse?" he asked, grabbing the end of her nose. She blushed and looked down at her hands.

"He will fall into the river," she answered in a voice almost too small to be heard.

"Aai ya hey!" the Chief said, gripping his Pipe. "Did Seven Arrows visit you and whisper the Story in your ear?"

"No," she giggled. "Grandfather told me the beginning."

"That is exactly what will happen," the Chief smiled. "But let us talk about it before we continue."

Hawk squirmed in his impatience. What did this have to do with the Power and the riddle he had asked? He looked at a group of boys who were playing the hoop game nearby, and he wished he could join them. "If nothing more interesting happens soon," he thought, "I will go play with them."

Just then Bull Looks Back's wife stuck her head out of her lodge and called. Two of the children sitting in the group got up and ran to their lodge.

"As you already know," began the Chief, "we were discussing the riddle of men. Men are like little Mouse. They are so busy with the things of this world that they are unable to perceive things at any distance. They scrutinize some things very carefully, and only brush others over lightly with their whiskers. But all of these things must be close to them. The roaring that they hear in their ears is life, the river. This great sound in their ears is the sound of the Spirit. The lesson is timely, Hawk, because the cries of mankind now are everywhere, but men are too busy with their little Mouse lives to hear. Some deny the presence of these sounds, other do not hear them at all, and still others, my son, hear them so clearly that it is a screaming in their hearts. Little Mouse heard the sounds and went a short distance from the world of Mice to investigate them."

"And met Raccoon," Hawk added. "Is the Raccoon the Great Spirit?"

"In a manner of speaking he is, little brother, but he is also the things that man will discover, if he seeks them, that will lead him to the Great River. The Raccoon can also be a man, or men."

"Men?" said Day Woman. "What kind of men?"

"Men," continued the Chief, "who know of the Medicine River. Men who have experienced and are familiar with life. The Raccoon washes his food in this Medicine. These types of men are unique, my children."

"Now, let us continue the Story," the Chief began again, glancing quickly at Hawk. "That is, if you wish."

Hawk looked fleetingly towards the hoop game and turned his eyes back to the Teacher. "Yes, please continue," he said, settling himself in place.

The man turned his smiling face to the mountains, clapped his hands together, and began.

Little Mouse Walked with Raccoon. His little Heart was Pounding in his

Breast. The Raccoon was Taking him upon Strange Paths and little Mouse Smelled the Scent of many things that had Gone by this Way. Many times he became so Frightened he almost Turned Back. Finally, they Came to the River! It was Huge and Breathtaking, Deep and Clear in Places, and Murky in Others. Little Mouse was unable to See Across it because it was so Great. It Roared, Sang, Cried, and Thundered on its Course. Little Mouse Saw Great and Little Pieces of the World Carried Along on its Surface.

"It is Powerful!" little Mouse said, Fumbling for Words.

"It is a Great thing," answered the Raccoon, "but here, let me Introduce you to a Friend."

In a Smoother, Shallower Place was a Lily Pad, Bright and Green. Sitting upon it was a Frog, almost as Green as the Pad it sat on. The Frog's White Belly stood out Clearly.

"Hello, little Brother," said the Frog. "Welcome to the River."

"I must Leave you Now," cut in Raccoon, "but do not Fear, little Brother, for Frog will Care for you Now." And Raccoon Left, Looking along the River Bank for Food that he might Wash and Eat.

Little Mouse Approached the Water and Looked into it. He saw a Frightened Mouse Reflected there.

"Who are you?" little Mouse asked the Reflection. "Are you not Afraid being that Far out into the Great River?"

"No," answered the Frog, "I am not Afraid. I have been Given the Gift from Birth to Live both Above and Within the River. When Winter Man Comes and Freezes this Medicine, I cannot be Seen. But all the while Thunderbird Flies, I am here. To Visit me, One must Come when the World is Green. I, my Brother, am the Keeper of the Water."

"Amazing!" little Mouse said at last, again Fumbling for Words.

"Would you like to have some Medicine Power?" Frog asked.

"Medicine Power? Me?" asked little Mouse. "Yes, yes! If it is Possible."

"Then Crouch as Low as you Can, and then Jump as High as you are Able! You will have your Medicine!" Frog said.

Little Mouse did as he was Instructed. He Crouched as Low as he Could and Jumped. And when he did, his Eyes Saw the Sacred Mountains.

"Like those over there," the Chief said, pointing to the distant mountains. Then he went on.

Little Mouse could hardly Believe his Eyes. But there They were! But then he Fell back to Earth, and he Landed in the River!

The Chief laughed and looked at the little girl.

Little Mouse became Frightened and Scrambled back to the Bank. He was Wet and Frightened nearly to Death.

"You have Tricked me," little Mouse Screamed at the Frog!

"Wait," said the Frog. "You are not Harmed. Do not let your Fear and Anger Blind you. What did you See?"

"I," Mouse stammered, "I, I Saw the Sacred Mountains!"

"And you have a New Name!" Frog said. "It is Jumping Mouse."

"Thank you. Thank you," Jumping Mouse said, and Thanked him again. "I want to Return to my People and Tell them of this thing that has Happened to me."

"Go. Go then," Frog said. "Return to your People. It is Easy to Find them. *Keep the Sound of the Medicine River to the Back of your Head. Go Opposite to the Sound and you will Find your Brother Mice."*

Jumping Mouse Returned to the World of the Mice. But he Found Disappointment. No One would Listen to him. And because he was Wet, and had no Way of explaining it because there had been no Rain, many of the other Mice were Afraid of him. They believed he had been Spat from the Mouth of Another Animal that had Tried to Eat him. And they all Knew that if he had not been Food for the One who Wanted him, then he must also be Poison for them.

Jumping Mouse Lived again among his People, but he could not Forget his Vision of the Sacred Mountains.

The Medicine Chief reached again for his Pipe, and Hawk ran for a new brand from the fire to light it for him.

"Is this Story about the Green of the South?" asked Hawk as he sat down. "I remember you talked before about the Man of the South and his Sister. Is this Man the Frog?"

"Yes," the Chief answered. He blew a long puff in the air. "The South is the place of innocence. Men who walk there must walk with a heart of trust."

"Your own Shield is bordered with lodges of green," Day Woman said, pointing to a Shield that hung a few lodges away.

"Those marks are Signs of the Mirroring, just as when Jumping Mouse looked into the river and saw his Reflection," said the Chief.

"But," Hawk added quickly, "that Sign you have upon your Shield is the Medicine Wheel, the Sun Dance. How is it then also the Mirroring?"

"The Medicine Wheel, my children," said the Chief, "is the Mirroring of the Great Spirit, the Universe, among men. We are all the Medicine River. And the Universe is the Medicine River that man is Mirrored upon, my children. And we in our turn see the Medicines of men Mirrored in the Universe."

"Then who is the Frog?" Hawk asked. "I am confused. I do not understand."

"Nor I," Day Woman chimed in.

"Do not make this matter complicated for yourselves," the Chief said. "Little Mouse heard the roaring in his ears and sought to solve its mystery. He met Raccoon and was taken to see the Medicine River, which represents Life. He saw himself Mirrored there in Life.

"All of us are so Mirrored, my children, but many men have not visited the Great River and have not witnessed it. Some have followed Raccoon to the River, seen their Reflection, but become frightened and retreated among the mice again. But the lesson is always there for those who seek it. It is in the place of the South. The place of trust."

"Will you explain more to us about the Raccoon?" asked Day Woman.

"No, little Day Woman, because it is for you to visit this place yourself. The Raccoon and the Frog will then become clear to you."

The Chief immediately began the Story again.

The Memory Burned in the Mind and Heart of Jumping Mouse, and One Day he Went to the Edge of the River Place . . .

"Come with me, children," the Peace Chief said, getting to his feet. They walked through the camp, and past it to the river. Even though it was a warm, almost a hot day, many of the People were still busy about the camp.

A group of young men were riding into the camp laughing and teasing with one another. When they rode past Hawk and Day Woman they turned their teasing to the boy and girl. As they rode by, one of the young men slipped from his horse and walked up to the Medicine Chief.

"Good Father," he said, not looking at the Chief, "You are invited to the lodge of my parents for the evening meal. Medicine Crow, my grandfather, has been made well from sickness. The Medicine Power has healed him. My father told me to tell you these things, and also that he will sponsor a dance and Give-Away to the People in thanksgiving tonight."

"A dance!" squeaked Day Woman and Prairie Rose, almost together. "We must prepare," the girls explained to the Chief, and then they were off, running hand in hand to their lodge.

"Well, it appears that now only we three are left," said the Chief.

As they began to walk again, a girl the same age as Singing Flower ran up and grabbed her hand, said something, and left to play. Singing Flower hesitated for a moment and then ran off to join her.

"This," explained the Chief after he and Hawk had reached the brush and trees along the river, "is where Jumping Mouse began. Do you see those lodges of our People? Those, my son, we will pretend are the Sacred Mountains. Lie down here upon your stomach and see how a Mouse would perceive the Prairie."

Hawk lay on his stomach and looked. The expanse of Prairie appeared to him as a measureless sea of grass. The Chief helped Hawk back to his feet and found them a cool place to sit. There he began the Story again.

Jumping Mouse went to the Edge of the Place of Mice and Looked out onto the Prairie. He Looked up for Eagles. The Sky was Full of many Spots, each One an Eagle. But he was Determined to Go to the Sacred Mountains. He Gathered All of his Courage and Ran just as Fast as he Could onto the Prairie. His little Heart Pounded with Excitement and Fear.

He Ran until he Came to a Stand of Sage. He was Resting and trying to Catch his Breath when he Saw an Old Mouse. The Patch of Sage Old Mouse Lived in was a Haven for Mice. Seeds were Plentiful and there was Nesting Material and many things to be Busy with.

"Hello," said Old Mouse. "Welcome."

Jumping Mouse was Amazed. Such a Place and such a Mouse. "You are Truly a great Mouse," Jumping Mouse said with all the Respect he could Find. "This is Truly a Wonderful Place. And the Eagles cannot See you here, either," Jumping Mouse said.

"Yes," said Old Mouse, "and One can See All the Beings of the Prairie here: the Buffalo, Antelope, Rabbit, and Coyote. One can See them All from here and Know their Names."

"That is Marvelous," Jumping Mouse said. "Can you also See the River and the Great Mountains?"

"Yes and No," Old Mouse Said with Conviction. "I Know there is the Great River. But I am Afraid that the Great Mountains are only a Myth. Forget your Passion to See Them and Stay here with me. There is Everything you Want here, and it is a Good Place to Be."

"How can he Say such a thing?" Thought Jumping Mouse. "The Medicine

of the Sacred Mountains is Nothing One can Forget."

"Thank you very much for the Meal you have Shared with me, Old Mouse, and also for sharing your Great Home," Jumping Mouse said. "But I must Seek the Mountains."

"You are a Foolish Mouse to Leave here. There is Danger on the Prairie! Just Look up there!" Old Mouse said, with even more Conviction. "See all those Spots! They are Eagles, and they will Catch you!"

It was hard for Jumping Mouse to Leave, but he Gathered his Determination and Ran hard Again. The Ground was Rough. But he Arched his Tail and Ran with All his Might. He could Feel the Shadows of the Spots upon his Back as he Ran. All those Spots! Finally he Ran into a Stand of Chokecherries. Jumping Mouse could hardly Believe his Eyes. It was Cool there and very Spacious. There was Water, Cherries and Seeds to Eat, Grasses to Gather for Nests, Holes to be Explored and many, many Other Busy Things to do. And there were a great many things to Gather.

He was Investigating his New Domain when he Heard very Heavy Breathing. He Quickly Investigated the Sound and Discovered its Source. It was a Great Mound of Hair with Black Horns. It was a Great Buffalo. Jumping Mouse could hardly Believe the Greatness of the Being he Saw Lying there before him. He was so large that Jumping Mouse could have Crawled into One of his Great Horns. "Such a Magnificent Being," Thought Jumping Mouse, and he Crept Closer.

"Hello, my Brother," said the Buffalo. "Thank you for Visiting me."

"Hello, Great Being," said Jumping Mouse. "Why are you Lying here?"

"I am Sick and I am Dying," the Buffalo said, "And my Medicine has Told me that only the Eye of a Mouse can Heal me. But little Brother, there is no such Thing as a Mouse."

Jumping Mouse was Shocked. "One of my Eyes!" he Thought, "One of my Tiny Eyes." He Scurried back into the Stand of Chokecherries. But the Breathing came Harder and Slower.

"He will Die," Thought Jumping Mouse, "If I do not Give him my Eye. He is too Great a Being to Let Die."

He Went Back to where the Buffalo Lay and Spoke. "I am a Mouse," he said with a Shaky Voice. "And you, my Brother, are a Great Being, I cannot Let you Die. I have Two Eyes, so you may have One of them."

The minute he had Said it, Jumping Mouse's Eye Flew Out of his Head and the Buffalo was Made Whole. The Buffalo Jumped to his Feet, Shaking Jumping Mouse's Whole World.

"Thank you, my little Brother," said the Buffalo. "I Know of your Quest for the Sacred Mountains and of your Visit to the River. You have Given me Life so that I may Give-Away to the People. I will be your Brother Forever. Run under my Belly and I will Take you right to the Foot of the Sacred Mountains, and you need not Fear the Spots. The Eagles cannot See you while you Run under Me. All they will See will be the Back of a Buffalo. I am of the Prairie and I will Fall on you if I Try to Go up the Mountains."

Little Mouse Ran under the Buffalo, Secure and Hidden from the Spots, but with only One Eye it was Frightening. The Buffalo's Great Hooves Shook the Whole World each time he took a Step. Finally they Came to a Place and Buffalo Stopped.

"This is Where I must Leave you, little Brother," said the Buffalo.

"Thank you very much," said Jumping Mouse. "But you Know, it was very Frightening Running under you with only One Eye. I was Constantly in Fear of your Great Earth-Shaking Hooves."

"Your Fear was for Nothing," said Buffalo. "For my Way of Walking is the Sun Dance Way, and I Always Know where my Hooves will Fall. I now must Return to the Prairie, my Brother. You can Always Find me there."

"Come with me, Hawk," the Chief said. "Let us walk to those pines on that hill."

"Tell me," said Hawk, "What is the meaning within this Teaching?"

The Chief walked in silence until he was almost to the top of the hill. A coyote jumped from behind a small rock and ran over the top of the hill, but not before stopping once and looking back at the two men.

The smell of the campfires and cooking food drifted up from the camp below. The voices of children laughing at their play blended with the sounds of the wind in the pines and the songbirds of the prairie.

"When you experience this seeking," the Chief began, "You will meet the Old Mice of the world. They can name for you the beings of the Prairie, but they have neither touched nor known them. These people have received a great Gift, but they spend their lives hidden within the sage. They have not yet run out on to the Prairie, the everyday world. Like Jumping Mouse, they fear the spots the most.

"But remember, my son, that Mice see clearly only that which is very near to them. To those people who perceive in this way, the sky will always be full of spots because of their nearsightedness. And of course in their fear they will always perceive them as Eagles," the Chief chuckled.

"But Jumping Mouse does not stay, he runs. As you already know, the Buffalo is the great Spirit's greatest Gift to the People. He is the Spirit of Giving. Jumping Mouse Gives-Away one of his own eyes, one of his Mouse's ways of perceiving, and heals the Buffalo."

"Why must he Give-Away an eye to heal the Buffalo?" Hawk asked.

"Because this kind of person, this Mouse, must give up one of his Mouse ways of seeing things in order that he may grow. People never are forced to do these things, Hawk. The Buffalo did not even know Jumping Mouse was a Mouse. He could have just stayed hidden like the Old Mouse."

"What would have happened if he had let the Buffalo die?" asked Hawk.

"He would have had to live with the stink of the rotting flesh, my son. Or he would have had to retreat to the place of Old Mouse. And if he had decided to live there instead of moving and growing, then he would have experienced thirst. The chokecherries he would have eaten would have made him thirst mightily for water.

"Believe me, Hawk, many men have reached these places. Some choose to live with the stink, and others, refusing to leave the Old Mouse's place, thirst constantly. Still others run endlessly under the great Buffalo. These are probably the most powerful of men, but no doubt the worst. They have the Power, but they speak always from fear. Fear of the great hooves of the Spirit, and of course the fear of the spots, the high Eagles, the unknown."

"Is there yet more, Shield Man?" Hawk asked.

"Yes, there is," answered the Teacher. "But do you wish to eat first?"

"No," said Hawk quickly, "I can eat later. Please finish the Story."

The Man of the Shield smiled and let his eyes rest on the camp below him.

Jumping Mouse Immediately Began to Investigate his New Surroundings. There were even more things here than in the Other Places, Busier things, and an Abundance of Seeds and Other things Mice Like. In his Investigation of these things, Suddenly he Ran upon a Gray Wolf who was Sitting there doing absolutely Nothing.

"Hello, Brother Wolf," Jumping Mouse said.

The Wolf's Ears Came Alert and his Eyes Shone. "Wolf! Wolf! Yes, that is what I am, I am a Wolf!" But then his mind Dimmed again and it was not long before he Sat Quietly again, completely without Memory as to who he was. Each time Jumping Mouse Reminded him who he was, he became Excited with the News, but soon would Forget again.

"Such a Great Being," thought Jumping Mouse, "but he has no Memory."

Jumping Mouse Went to the Center of this New Place and was Quiet. He Listened for a very long time to the Beating of his Heart. Then Suddenly he Made up his Mind. He Scurried back to where the Wolf Sat and he Spoke.

"Brother Wolf," Jumping Mouse said. . . .

"Wolf! Wolf," said the Wolf. . . .

"Please, Brother Wolf," said Jumping Mouse, "Please Listen to me. I Know what will Heal you. It is One of my Eyes. And I Want to Give it to you. You are a Greater Being than I. I am only a Mouse. Please Take it."

When Jumping Mouse Stopped Speaking his Eye Flew out of his Head and the Wolf was made Whole.

Tears Fell down the Cheeks of Wolf, but his little Brother could not See them, for Now he was Blind.

"You are a Great Brother," said the Wolf, "for Now I have my Memory. But Now you are Blind. I am the Guide into the Sacred Mountains. I will Take you there. There is a Great Medicine Lake there. The most Beautiful Lake in the World. All the World is Reflected there. The People, the Lodges of the People, and All the Beings of the Prairies and Skies."

"Please Take me there," Jumping Mouse said.

The Wolf Guided him through the Pines to the Medicine Lake. Jumping Mouse Drank the Water from the Lake. The Wolf Described the Beauty to him.

"I must Leave you here," said Wolf, "for I must Return so that I may Guide Others, but I will Remain with you as long as you Like."

"Thank you, my Brother," said Jumping Mouse. "But although I am Frightened to be Alone, I Know you must Go so that you may Show Others the Way to this Place." Jumping Mouse Sat there Trembling in Fear. It was no use Running, for he was Blind, but he Knew an Eagle would Find him Here. He Felt a Shadow on his Back and Heard the Sound that Eagles Make. He Braced himself for the Shock. And the Eagle Hit! Jumping Mouse went to Sleep.

Then he Woke Up. The surprise of being Alive was Great, but Now he could See! Everything was Blurry, but the Colors were Beautiful.

"I can See! I can See!" said Jumping Mouse over again and again.

A Blurry Shape Came toward Jumping Mouse. Jumping Mouse Squinted hard but the Shape Remained a Blur.

"Hello, Brother," a Voice said. "Do you Want some Medicine?"

"Some Medicine for me?" asked Jumping Mouse. "Yes! Yes!"

"Then Crouch down as Low as you Can," the Voice said, "and Jump as High as you Can."

Jumping Mouse did as he was Instructed. He Crouched as Low as he Could and Jumped! The Wind Caught him and Carried him Higher.

"Do not be Afraid," the Voice called to him. "Hang on to the Wind and Trust!"

Jumping Mouse did. He Closed his Eyes and Hung on to the Wind and it Carried him Higher and Higher. Jumping Mouse Opened his Eyes and they were Clear, and the Higher he Went the Clearer they Became. Jumping Mouse Saw his Old Friend upon a Lily Pad on the Beautiful Medicine Lake. It was the Frog.

"You have a New Name," Called the Frog. "You are Eagle!"

Suggestions for Discussion

1. What is the emotional setting for the story of "Jumping Mouse"? Who tells the story and to what purpose?
2. On p. 36 the powers of the white men are discussed. What seems to be meant by the "power of talking leaves"? You might discuss the relationship between power, wisdom (or medicine here), and knowledge. For instance, has the free public school meant an increase in knowledge, in wisdom?
3. The story of the mouse is interrupted by discussion and questioning. Is this method of writing effective? Would you prefer the story without interpretation? Does this method clarify the symbolism of Raccoon, Frog, and Buffalo, for example, or does it overexplain?
4. Do you find this story of renunciation appropriate for or relevant to the 1970's? On p. 43 the narrator speaks of men who "have the Power, but . . . speak always from fear." Do the wealthy and politically powerful in American society seem to speak from fear?

Suggestion for Writing and Comparison

1. Read Arthur Waley's *Monkey* or any other translation of the Buddhist jataka tales. Compare Storm's use of animal stories with that of the Buddhists as a way of teaching philosophy. Are there any similarities between the Asian and Native American attitudes towards animals?

History and the American Dream

Peter La Farge

Peter La Farge, of part Native American ancestry, was born in
Colorado in 1931. He has earned a national reputation as a folk
singer and a composer of folk songs. Much of La Farge's work is
concerned specifically with Indian themes, although he has also
recorded albums such as *Peter La Farge Sings of the Cowboys*
(1965). The poem "Vision of a Past Warrior" which follows was
written by La Farge and included in his album *As Long As the
Grass Shall Grow* (1963). (Buffy Sainte-Marie, another folk
singer of Native American descent, has composed and recorded
"Now That the Buffalo's Gone" as a further commentary on
"Vision of a Past Warrior." Buffy Saint-Marie's song is dedicated to La Farge: see Buffy Sainte-Marie's *It's My Way*.)

"Vision of a Past Warrior" was composed to be sung. However, the poem is not written in the traditional ballad form
—pentameter is used instead of tetrameter and trimeter and
there is no use of repetition or refrain. The dream or vision of
the future in the poem is one seen by an Indian warrior of the
past, as indicated by the title; the Indian's version of the American dream is made explicit; and the tone of the poem is at
once nostalgic and bitter, far more bitter than that of Langston
Hughes' "Let America Be America Again" (p. 108) or even Aaron
Kurtz's "Behold the Sea" (p. 503).

Vision of a Past Warrior

I have within me such a dream of pain
That all my silver horseman hopes rust still—
Beyond quick silver mountains, on the plain,
The buffalo are gone, none left to kill.

5 I see the plains grow blackened with that dawn,
No robes for winter warmth, no meat to eat—
The ghost white buffalos' medicine gone,
No hope for Indians then; I see defeat.

Then there will be changes to another way,
10 We will fight battles that are legends long.
But of all our glory none will stay—
Who will remember that I sang this song?

Suggestions for Discussion

1. What are "silver horseman hopes"? Why do they "rust"? Is "rust" an appropriate verb here? Can "still" be read in more than one way?
2. Who is the speaker and from what vantage point does he speak? In which stanza is the "present time" of the poem made explicit?
3. How is color used in the poem? In "the plains grow blackened with that dawn," why is the normal order of things reversed?
4. Discuss meter and rhyme scheme in the poem. Is there internal evidence that this poem was written to be sung? Does the poem work alone, without music?

Suggestions for Writing and Comparison

1. Compare "O Black and Unknown Bards" by James Weldon Johnson (p. 114) to "Vision of a Past Warrior." How do La Farge and Johnson celebrate the past?
2. Discuss Buffy Sainte-Marie's "Now That the Buffalo's Gone" in contrast to Peter La Farge's "Vision of a Past Warrior." Which is the better poem, song, or statement of social protest?

Wendy Rose
(Chiron Khanshendel)

Wendy Rose, whose pen name is Chiron Khanshendel, was born in Oakland, California. She is half Hopi; her Indian name is Schiacalega, "Child of the Horse."

Wendy Rose attended a Catholic elementary school and a public high school. She dropped out of high school "from sheer boredom" in the eleventh grade and waited until she was eighteen so that she could go to a junior college. She then attended Contra Costa College and Cabrillo College in California.

Ms. Rose's poetry has been published in many journals and in two anthologies, *From the Belly of the Shark* and *Carriers of the Dream Wheel*. She is the author of two books of poetry, *Inside a God's Eye* and *Hopi Roadrunner Dancing*. Her poetry is generally concerned with man's relationship to the land and nature and the Indian's relationship to twentieth-century American society.

(See p. 66 for two other poems by Wendy Rose, "Grebes at Sunset" and "Hopi Roadrunner, Dancing, Dancing.")

West Side of the Valley

To the Apache Guardians

The rocks are unstable
     and they give way beneath
  the chestnut's unshod hooves;
I am thankful for the sun——
5   it dries the land to let the
        dust swirl, forming
patterns in the red loam; the air
  hangs humid, the steam rising from
the irrigation canals
10   converging upon
       the city; they grow cabbages here.
Above the city I can breathe
  clean, dry air, for the
      mountains of the Lost Dutchman
15   purify all things that come asking for
purification—such as I.

     No questions—I will leave the gold to
those who guard it. I mind my business and that of my horse.
  The Superstitions mind their business and those who
20   are part of them watch me but do not hide. We have

never met but we are friends. But for them on the ridge,
                    I am alone with my horse and the wild ones.

I can climb the Superstition Mountains
and look down upon the steaming valley
25 where herefords and cabbages grow.

Suggestions for Discussion

1. Who is the speaker in the poem? What is the connection between this *persona* and the "Apache Guardians" of the dedication?
2. What is meant by "The Superstitions mind their business and those who/are part of them watch me but do not hide"? Who are "those who"? Are they necessarily people?
3. What images in the previous stanzas are in opposition to herefords, cabbages, and "the steaming valley"? What is the theme of the poem?

Suggestion for Writing and Comparison

1. Discuss the use of understatement in the poem. How does the poet imply a comparison of the white man's way of life with the Indians'? Is the poem an effective statement?

Ghost Dance Songs

The influence of Christianity on Indian religion is evident in the Ghost Dance. In northern California, about 1870, an Indian prophet started a new religious cult. His son, a Paiute medicine man named Wovoka, had a vision in which God told him to tell his people "they must be good and love one another, have no quarreling and live in peace with the whites . . . If they faithfully obeyed his instructions they would at last be reunited with their friends in the other world, where there would be no more death or sickness or old age." If the people performed this dance "at intervals, for five successive days each time, they would secure this happiness to themselves and hasten the event."

The teachings of Wovoka spread east to the Plains Indians, among them the Cheyennes and the Sioux or Dakotas, from whom the following songs come. The Ghost Dance itself and the use of peyote induced trancelike states in the participants; individuals were encouraged to sing of their visions. The following songs indicate the hope for the return of the buffalo and the dead "nation." Dream messages are brought by birds—here by the sacred eagle, the crow, and the raven.

The Whole World Is Coming

The whole world is coming.
A nation is coming, a nation is coming,
The Eagle has brought the message to the tribe.
The father says so, the father says so.
5 Over the whole earth they are coming.
The buffalo are coming, the buffalo are coming,
The Crow has brought the message to the tribe,
The father says so, the father says so.

—*Sioux*

The Raven Says

Our father above, I have seen.
The raven says, "There is going to be another judgment day."

—*Cheyenne*

Suggestions for Discussion

1. What are the "nation" and the "tribe" that are referred to in the first poem?
2. Were the buffalo important to the Plains Indians only for their food? What do the buffalo symbolize?
3. What is the effect of the use of parallelism and repetition in "The Whole World Is Coming"? How does the prophecy in "The Raven Says" relate to the vision of "The Whole World Is Coming"?
4. What parallels are there in Christianity for the crow, eagle, and raven? Who is "the father" and "our father"? How might the use of these terms indicate the influence of Christianity?

Suggestion for Writing and Comparison

1. Compare "The Whole World Is Coming" with the poem by Peter La Farge on p. 47. Were the tragic implications of "The Whole World Is Coming" realized by its writer? How do the two poems differ in their visionary quality?

Emerson Blackhorse Mitchell

Emerson Blackhorse Mitchell, a Navajo, was born in 1945 near "Four Corners," where New Mexico, Arizona, Utah, and Colorado meet. He learned English as a second language when he attended school in Ignacio, Colorado.

As a student at the Institute of American Indian Arts, Mitchell wrote an autobiographical novel, *Miracle Hill,* which was published in 1967. Mitchell's poetry has appeared in several Native American and multi-ethnic anthologies.

"The Four Directions" should be compared with the poems of other young Native American writers such as Liz Sohappy (pp. 55–57, 70) and Alonzo Lopez (pp. 53, 68) in its view of the Native American future.

The Four Directions

A century and eight more years,
    Since Kit Carson rode from four directions,
Deep into the heart of nomadic Navajos,
    Burning, ravishing the Land of Enchantment.

5 Prairie grasses are once more
    Growing as high as the horse's belly.
Cradles of wrapped babies in colors
    Of the rainbow again span the land.

I know my people will stand and rise again.
10   Now it is time.
Pollen of yellow grain,
    Scatter in the four directions.

Suggestions for Discussion

1. See the traditional Navajo song "May I Walk" (p. 64), and discuss Mitchell's use of pollen.
2. Aside from the mention of corn pollen, how does Mitchell use Navajo traditions in this poem?

Suggestion for Writing and Comparison

1. Compare Mitchell's "The Four Directions" with Alonzo Lopez's "Untitled" (p. 53). On what does each base the conviction that it is time for the Native American to rise again?

Alonzo Lopez

Alonzo Lopez, a Papago, was born in 1947, in Pima County, Arizona. He attended high school at the Institute of American Indian Arts and graduated in 1967. Since then he has attended Yale and done graduate work at Wesleyan in the field of American Indian Studies. One of his projects was recording and translating his native Papago language. Lopez has also taught classes in Native American poetry. His poems have appeared in the anthologies *The Whispering Wind* (1972) and *American Indian Authors* (1972).

The poetry of Alonzo Lopez is consciously traditional in both form and content. The poems "Direction," "I Am Crying from Thirst," and "I Go Forth to Move About the Earth" (p. 68) are chants or prayers using rhythmic parallel phrasing without rhyme. "Untitled" is at once a statement of poetic intent for the author and a plan for future Native American poets. In it Lopez envisions the poet's job to be that of awakening his people, finding "all that has been lost," and making the public aware that "We only slept,/And now,/We live again." This kind of vitality among the younger generation of writers has led to a rebirth of Native American poetic traditions within the English language.

Untitled

Go, my child,
   to the lands of your people.
Awaken them.
They have slept too long.
5 Many years have passed.
Traditions have been carried away
   by the wind.
Old tales have fled into the night.
The way of the Ancient Ones is dying.
10 Wash away the evil and harm
   that have befallen them.
Lead them in traditional song.
Lead them in ceremonial dance.
Send them forth to the far edges
15   of the earth
To find all that has been lost.
Let those among us
   who have left us to die
Know that we only slept,
20 And now,
We live again.

Suggestions for Discussion

1. Who are the Ancient Ones mentioned in line 9?
2. Does this poem seem more a vain hope or a statement of reality? Explain your answer in relation to recent historical events.

Suggestion for Writing and Comparison

1. Compare Lopez's view of the Native American's future with Peter La Farge's "Vision of a Past Warrior." Are there any historical reasons that might account for their differences in outlook?

Liz Sohappy

Liz Sohappy, a Palouse, was born in 1948 and lives in Topper-
ish, Washington. She attended the Institute of American Indian
Arts for two years and has studied art in Portland, Oregon. Like
Alonzo Lopez, Liz Sohappy is interested in both anthropology
and the arts. Her poetry has appeared in the Institute of American Indian Arts anthology, *The Whispering Wind* (1972).

"The Indian Market" (see p. 70) contains an implied comparison of the city's mechanized supermarket with nature's trees
and rivers, the Indian's market. The return to Indian ways is a
return home.

The poem "Once Again" presents an even more direct argument for the return to Native American history and values. Sohappy suggests the building of "a small fire, a huge angry fire"
to combat darkness and death. This angry fire which the poet
builds lets her re-create from memories her heritage so that it
lives again.

The Parade

The light glows bright
as the parade begins.
Not everyone has come,
only the old ones.
5 The Eastern tribes came far,
dressed in cloth, wearing silver.
From the southeast trailed teared travelers
of the Five Civilized Tribes.
From the plains came buffalo hunters
10 dressed in beaded, fringed buckskin.
The light glows brighter
as each tribe passes.

It was such a long time ago
when he was first sighted,
15 running through the forest
like a frightened, swift lean deer.
When he danced in bird feathers,
dancing frenzied around blue ashes.
In the twilight of dawn, again he dances.
20 Drums thunder over creeks
to the swishing grasses on the plains.
Chants echo across the land of yellow maize,
along the paths of the sacred buffalo.

The years flow like running water.
25 Grasses grow yellow, rocks crumble to crust
as old ones come, they pass.

Once Again

Let go of the present and death.
Go to the place nearest the stars,
gather twigs, logs;
build a small fire,
5 a huge angry fire.

Gather nature's skin,
wet it, stretch it,
make a hard drum,
fill it with water
10 to muffle the sound.

Gather dry leaves, herbs,
feed into the fire.
Let the smoke rise
up to the dark sky,
15 to the roundness of the sun.

Moisten your lips,
loosen your tongue,
let the chant echo
from desert, to valley, to peak —
20 wherever your home may be.

Remember the smoke,
the chants, the drums,
the stick grandfather held
as he spoke in the dark
25 of the power of his fathers?

Gather your memories
into a basket, into a pot,
into your cornhusk bag, and
grandfather is alive
30 for us to see once again.

Suggestions for Discussion

1. What does the title "The Parade" refer to? What kind of parade?
2. Discuss the last three lines of "The Parade." What mood do they convey?
3. Who does the poet seem to be addressing throughout "Once Again"? Do the commands seem to include you or do they alienate you? Explain.
4. If the author is discussing the poet's task in "Once Again," what does she seem to say it consists of? Do you agree?

Suggestion for Writing and Comparison

1. Read Michael Novak's essay "White Ethnic" (p. 543). Compare Novak's view of the importance of rediscovering our family and ethnic history with that of Liz Sohappy.

Simon Ortiz

Simon Ortiz was raised at the Acoma Pueblo in New Mexico. He is the editor of the *Navajo Rough Rock News* and now lives in Albuquerque, New Mexico. His books of poems include *Naked in the Wind* and *Going for the Rain.*

Ortiz has experimented with the use of tapes to record extemporaneous narratives of his experiences and his people, which have become the source of some of his poems. "Missing That Indian Name of Roy or Ray" shows Ortiz's concern with the spoken word; the poem's form derives from the way people tell a story. Conversation, backtracking, recollections of violence, a sudden recognition of the obscenity of oil wells all occur in "Missing That Indian Name of Roy or Ray." "Relocation," which is less conversational, is an interior monologue on the pain of loss.

Relocation

don't talk to me no words
don't frighten me
for i am in the blinding city
the lights
5 the cars
the deadened glares
   tear my heart
   & close my mind

who questions my pain
10 the tight knot of anger
in my breast
i swallow hard and often
and taste my spit
and it does not taste good
15 who questions my mind

i came here because i was tired
the BIA taught me to cleanse myself
daily to keep a careful account of my time
efficiency was learned in catechism
20 the sisters spelled me god in white
and i came here to feed myself
corn & potatoes and chili and mutton
did not nourish me it was said

so i agreed to move
25 i see me walking in sleep

down streets down streets grey with cement
and glaring glass and oily wind
armed with a pint of wine
i cheated my children to buy
30 i am ashamed
i am tired
i am hungry
i speak words
i am lonely for hills
35 i am lonely for myself

Missing That Indian Name of Roy or Ray

1.

can't even remember his name
maybe it was Roy, or Ray,
tell Leslie that,
drinking on Des Moines to K. C. bus,
5 throbbing with dull nerves,
going home; coming home,
talk to nobody until K. C. depot.
   Meet Roy,
he's wobbling down from Chicago bus
10 first I see him.
Ya-ta-heh, where you from?
Sanders.
I know where Sanders is.
West of Gallup right off 66.

15 Two Indians going for a drink.
Wink at a barmaid. Two whiskies
two beers settle down warm
but in a hurry. Look for danger.
In the early morning, when it's getting light,
20 we're outside of Tulsa, and you see those oil wells,
pumping the juice, the nodding bastards.
Up and down, up and down, all day, getting rich.
On the outskirts, we see a sign:
   Tulsa Screw Products, Co., and laugh and laugh.

2.

25 He gets lost in Amarillo.
Went to get a couple of hamburgers
and then didn't show back up.

"Where's that Indian that was back there?"
the bus driver asked.
30 "Went to get some hamburgers," I told him.
And then ran around the block,
but couldn't find him.
At least he took his expensive transistor
with him.
35 Me and the black guy and the hippie girl
keep looking out the back window
when we pull out of Amarillo.

3.

The black guy gets off in Tucumcari.
Roy, Navajo, coming from places,
40 new levis, new shirt, everything new,
right in style man, don't talk English
too good, but fuck it, and expensive transistor
we listen to. That's okay, brother,
I like cowboy music, sentimental bullshit,
45 go to dances at Milan's in Gallup,
saw somebody getting laid out in back once,
saw somebody get knifed there too,
red blood black and shiny in neon light,
quick footsteps running away,
50 me and my buddy careful to approach him,
don't touch him, and then make a phone call.

Later on in the bus he sings me Navajo songs.
Squaw dance singing, you sing when there's
a crowd, girls, some wine, and fires
55 that smell good. "Give me two dollars.
"And I will like you."
A black guy and a hippie-looking girl
come and join us in the back.
"No more dollar.
60 "No more dollar."
And I wonder that it's a strange place
for a black man to get off at.
Tucumcari.

4.

When I get off in Albuquerque
65 the girl stays on. "See you
in Portland," she says.
And I walk up the street
missing that Indian we left
behind in Amarillo.

Suggestions for Discussion

1. In "Relocation," what statement about religious missionaries does the line "efficiency was learned in catechism" make?
2. Why is the narrator ashamed? Do you think the author feels that he should be more ashamed or more angry?
3. What statement about relocation does the final line, "i am lonely for myself," make? Is this an effective way to end the poem? Why?
4. "Ya-ta-heh," in "Missing That Indian Name of Roy or Ray," is a Navajo greeting. Discuss phrases you may not understand at first. If you were to hear them in the middle of a conversation, would they make more sense? Why has the poet used this language?
5. What happened to the Indian? Why did he get off the bus? What was the relationship between the narrator, the Navajo, "the black guy," and "the hippie girl"?

Suggestion for Writing and Comparison

1. Which other selections in this text talk about similarities or coalitions between groups that have been deprived or feel themselves to be oppressed? (See, for example, "Jonathan's Song," "Behold the Sea," etc.) Compare Ortiz's treatment of such a situation in "Missing That Indian" with that of one or two other authors.

POEMS

The Old Truths

Traditional Native American Songs (I)

Child's Night Song

Very much, very much
I of the owl am afraid,
Sitting alone in the wigwam.

—Chippewa

Song of Failure

A wolf
I considered myself,
But the owls are hooting
And the night
5 I fear.

—Teton Sioux

Suggestions for Discussion

1. Frances Densmore, who collected Chippewa songs, was told that "Child's Night Song" was composed by a child of the tribe to drive away his dread of the owl's hooting. The people heard him singing and the song became popular in the village. Is there evidence in the poem to suggest an unsophisticated composer, or does the poem indicate, rather, that it was created by a skilled poet?
2. In the "Song of Failure" why does the speaker equate himself with the wolf? What are the connotations of the word "wolf"?
3. Which of the two poems best conveys the experiences of fear? Is either of the poems necessarily naive? Is the appeal of the poems limited — that is, parochial or tribal — or is it universal?

Suggestions for Writing and Comparison

1. Compare the form of "Child's Night Song" to Japanese haiku. Does the imagery serve to evoke emotion in the same way in both cases?
2. Read Wallace Stevens' "Thirteen Ways of Looking at a Blackbird," verse XI: "He rode over Connecticut/In a glass coach." In the "Song of Failure," does the man's opening statement "A wolf I considered myself" function in a similar way to Stevens' description of the character riding over Connecticut in a glass coach? How is it suggested each man deals with fear? What do the images of the blackbird and the owl have in common?

Traditional Native American Songs (II)

Spring Song

As my eyes search the prairie
I feel the summer in the spring.

—Chippewa

Glyph

Truly buzzards
Around my sky are circling!

For my soul festers,
And an odor of corruption
5 Betrays me to disaster.

Meanness, betrayal and spite
Come flockwise,
To make me aware
Of sickness and death within me.
10 My sky is full of the dreadful sound
Of the wings of unsuccesses.

—Washoe-Paiute

May I Walk

On the trail marked with pollen may I walk,
With grasshoppers about my feet may I walk,
With dew about my feet may I walk,
With beauty may I walk,
5 With beauty before me, may I walk,
With beauty behind me, may I walk,
With beauty above me, may I walk,
With beauty under me, may I walk,
With beauty all around me, may I walk,
10 In old age wandering on a trail of beauty, lively, may I walk,
In old age wandering on a trail of beauty, living again, may I walk,
It is finished in beauty.

—Navajo

Suggestions for Discussion

1. What is the mood of "Spring Song"? Why is it *suggested* in the poem rather than stated?
2. What is the central metaphor in the poem "Glyph"? What aspect of the buzzard is explored in each stanza? How is this image appropriate to the tone of the poem?
3. What is the effect of the repetition of "may I walk" in every line but the last? What qualities of a prayer does this poem contain? Does "May I Walk" give the impression from internal evidence that it is to be said, sung, or chanted? Would it be performed by an individual or a group?
4. What is the relationship between "the trail marked with pollen" in the first line of "May I Walk" and "a trail of beauty" mentioned twice in the conclusion?

Suggestions for Writing and Comparison

1. Compare the Chippewa "Spring Song" with Emily Dickinson's "To Make a Prairie." Do the Chippewa word "feel" and Miss Dickinson's word "reverie" suggest the same human response?
2. See Oliver La Farge's novel *Laughing Boy* for other Navajo songs which mention the "trail of beauty" (see particularly Chapter XXI). Discuss the use and value of such songs outside their ceremonies.

Wendy Rose

(See p. 48 for Rose's poem "West Side of the Valley" and a biographical sketch of the author.)

Grebes at Sunset

The grebes' mad wings
    sucking air
thru the long
    flight-feathers all evening
5 long bidding the sun
    farewell . . .

the sheltered
    Eucalyptus trees hide
where the tides cannot
10   reach, above on a
crumbling cliff
    away from the
water that will soon
    be their purgatory . . .

15 The ocean showered with
    twilight pigments
is the new moon's
    special child.

Hopi Roadrunner, Dancing, Dancing

There's a bay twig cross
on the crest of the Saguaro hill
  where twine of many colors
  winds around—an Eye of God in the presence
5   of a desert mandala—the flower of an ocotillo—
watchers in the mesquite branches are
      beings with big eyes that stare—no blinking—no trembling—
the cold of the still night cuts,
but through the deepness of the slash comes
10   warmth and light—

blueness, brightness, Hopi roadrunner, dancing, dancing,
      blood upon the beavertail spines—

Suggestions for Discussion

1. What kind of birds are grebes? What makes their wings seem to suck air?
2. What image is explored in each stanza of "Grebes at Sunset"? Are the three stanzas related to each other explicitly or implicitly?
3. If you are unfamiliar with plants and animals of the Southwest, consult a dictionary for a description of saguaro, ocotillo, mesquite, and roadrunner as they occur in the second poem. From what languages are the four words derived? What colors are the flowers of the ocotillo and saguaro?
4. Who are the "watchers in the mesquite branches" in the second poem? What is an "Eye of God"? Why is the flower of an ocotillo described as "a desert mandala"? How are the watchers, the Eye, and the mandala related? Do they each have a symbolic significance?
5. Is the tone of the title, "Hopi Roadrunner, Dancing, Dancing," fulfilled in the poem proper? How does the imagery relate to the tone?

Suggestion for Writing and Comparison

1. Discuss the meaning of the images of the desert plants as well as the Eye of God and the mandala. Do they have significance for a twentieth-century urban dweller? (See also Carl Jung's *Man and His Symbols* or Maud Bodkin's *Archetypal Patterns in Poetry*.)

Alonzo Lopez

(See p. 53 for Lopez's "Untitled" and for a biographical sketch of the author.)

Direction

I was directed by my grandfather
To the East,
  so I might have the power of the bear;
To the South,
5   so I might have the courage of the eagle;
To the West,
  so I might have the wisdom of the owl;
To the North,
  so I might have the craftiness of the fox;
10 To the Earth,
  so I might receive her fruit;
To the Sky,
  so I might lead a life of innocence.

I Am Crying from Thirst

I am crying from thirst.
I am singing for rain.
I am dancing for rain.
The sky begins to weep,
5   for it sees me
  singing and dancing
  on the dry, cracked
  earth.

I Go Forth to Move About the Earth

I go forth to move about the earth.
I go forth as the owl, wise and knowing.
I go forth as the eagle, powerful and bold.
I go forth as the dove, peaceful and gentle.
5 I go forth to move about the earth
  in wisdom, courage, and peace.

Suggestions for Discussion

1. Reread the introduction to "Jumping Mouse" by Hyemeyohsts Storm (see p. 35). Do the meanings of the six directions explained there vary from the meanings in Lopez's "Direction"? For example, what is the relation of the wisdom of the north to the "craftiness of the fox"?
2. Why is the poem entitled "Direction"? What relation does it have to a "direction in life"? Compare the idea with that in Frost's "The Road Not Taken."
3. Discuss the traditional elements in "I Am Crying from Thirst" and "I Go Forth to Move About the Earth." Does either one require a belief in a religion?

Suggestion for Writing and Comparison

1. Compare Lopez's work to the traditional anonymous Native American songs in this text such as "May I Walk." Which elements has Lopez borrowed from traditional Native American poetry?

Liz Sohappy

(See pp. 55–56 for Sohappy's "The Parade" and "Once Again" and for a biographical sketch of the author.)

The Indian Market

Come! What shall it be?
Bitterroot noodles,
sweetroot carrots,
and baby potatoes
5 for our supper tonight?

Quick! Look about! No one is near.
That tree, that leafy branch,
it blackens my hair, makes it grow.
That other tree, with red buds hanging,
10 we will drink it for our sweating bodies.

Look! Up there, it is yellow.
Grasp it gently, now pull it slow,
here, into my beaded pouch—
Rouge for our faces,
15 war paint for our men.

Come! There is work to be done.
There are salmon to be cleaned,
venison to be dried,
eels to be roasted,
20 and berries to be picked.

Come! Our moccasin prints lead us home.
We will return tomorrow.

Suggestions for Discussion

1. Where is the Indian market located? How is this contrasted with the city's supermarket?
2. What do the last two lines in the poem mean? Can they be read on both a figurative and a literal level? Explain.

Suggestion for Writing and Comparison

1. Compare "The Indian Market" with Alonzo Lopez's "Untitled." What views do these authors hold concerning traditions and the future of the Native American?

Chapter 2
Black American Writers

Introduction

Black American writing began in the colonial period before there was a United States and has developed through various stages as this country has developed. In the eighteenth century Black poets wrote almost exclusively in heroic couplets—as was the style in England at the time. In the nineteenth century, with the growth of the abolitionist movement, Black writers turned to the documentary style to record their escapes from slavery and to provide the source for abolitionist oratory. With the end of legal slavery, writers could turn to less political subjects and forms, so that by the turn of the century Black poets were reemerging and Black novelists appeared for the first time. Generally, however, if they were to be published, Black writers had to fulfill white expectations. What was most frequently published was written in dialect and contained characters that white readers expected to find. We do not know, of course, what was written that violated publishers' taboos—and so was never published. When Harlem came to be known throughout the country as a Black haven, independent writing that ignored stereotypes began to emerge, and in the 1920's a Black artists' movement called the Harlem Renaissance was born. This movement marked the beginning of the conscious development of a Black aesthetic.

Traditional Black forms—the sermon and spiritual of the church and the secular music of jazz—were the beginnings of a distinctively Black art. However, with few exceptions, such as the experiments of Langston Hughes, the conscious creation of new literary forms had to wait until the 1960's and 1970's. The 1960's brought an upsurge of ethnic awareness and the assertion of the right to a variety of life-styles, the right to differ politically, the right to differ in language and culture. Ethnic pluralism meant to Black Americans a belief in the "rightness" of a pride in Black language, Black music, and the ability to produce Black art. The acceptance of the word "Black" not as a pejorative term but as a source of pride is a case in point, and inventive speech became not bad grammar but Black English, with its own previously unacknowledged grammatical rules. Use of this language flowered in such novels as *His Own Where,* by June Jordan, and *Yellow Back Radio Broke-Down,* by Ishmael Reed.

The sonnet, eloquently refashioned by Claude McKay in "If We Must Die" during the 1919 riots, reappeared in the Attica prison riots of the 1970's. However, the younger poets have largely been rejecting forms from the British literary tradition such as the sonnet, and they have been creating new forms using Black English.

This awareness of the right to be one's own person, to speak from a different perspective, and to illuminate various facets of the Black American experience is implied in Gwendolyn Brooks' definition of Black writing:

> The juice from tomatoes is not called merely juice. It is always called tomato juice. If you go into a restaurant desiring tomato juice you do not order the waiter to bring you "juice"; you request, distinctly, TOMATO juice. The juice from cranberries is called cranberry juice. The juice from oranges is called orange juice. The [writing] from Black [writers] is called Black [writing].

■ Phyllis Wheatley and Jupiter Hammon, both New England slaves, were the earliest Black American writers to be published. But after their work few Black writers emerged for some time, perhaps as a result of the passage of laws against reading, writing, and assembling by slaves in the South — statutes conceived in reaction to slave revolts. In the North the literary efforts of Blacks during this period were largely dedicated to the cause of slavery's abolition. However, the reprisals against literacy in the South which worked to increase the activities of the "underground railroad" did lead indirectly to the creation of a whole new genre: the narrative of the ex-slave and his experiences in escaping from slavery.

The most famous author of such a narrative was Frederick Douglass, who escaped from slavery in Maryland in 1841. He became an orator and journalist, and also wrote short stories for William Lloyd Garrison's abolitionist newspaper, *The Liberator*. His autobiography, less famous but perhaps more realistic and of better literary quality than *Uncle Tom's Cabin,* is entitled *Narrative of the Life of Frederick Douglass, an American Slave,* and is a classic of the genre.

Later authors, once the war was over, were able to turn their talents to less didactic writings. The ability of Paul Laurence Dunbar (1872–1906) was recognized by the influential editor William Dean Howells, who published his poems in the *Atlantic Monthly.* But Dunbar often fulfilled white expectations by writing rhythmic dialect poems such as "At Candle-Lightin' Time" and "When de Co'n Pone's Hot." Dunbar's formal English lyrics generally met with much less popular acclaim. Charles W. Chesnutt, whose early stereotyped stories were also published by the *Atlantic Monthly,* was similarly less well received when he dealt realistically with the subjects of race riots and miscegenation. His novel *The Marrow of Tradition* (1901) is still a moving account of the 1898 race riots in North Carolina.

The movement that was to be called the "Renaissance of the New Negro" was gaining impetus as early as 1912, but several events had to occur to make possible its culmination in the 1920's. Many Blacks moved North during World War I, often as a result of recruiting by factories. This was the first of the large-scale migrations which led eventually to the movement from the rural South to the urban North and West of approximately half of Black

America. Migration was to make a great impact on Black artistic and intellectual achievement. For, unlike white American writers such as William Faulkner and Carson McCullers, who lived all their lives in the South, Black American writers were, in the main, either to be born outside the South, as were authors such as Paul Laurence Dunbar and Gwendolyn Brooks, or they were to move away from the South by their twenties, as did Richard Wright. Then too, the migration of other Blacks to the North meant both a larger reading audience and the experience of an urban way of life — as that in Harlem — which was to be reflected in subject matter and theme.

The "New Negro" took a new stance, at once more cosmopolitan and more independent. Yet as the new music of blues and jazz had grown from the spirituals, so the new writing grew from a previous tradition. But the newness was in attitude, a refusal to be apologetic; or as Langston Hughes, fresh from Europe and Africa, put it:

> We younger Negro artists who create now intend to express our individual dark-skinned selves without fear or shame. If white people are pleased, we are glad. If they are not, it doesn't matter. We know we are beautiful. And ugly, too. If colored people are pleased, we are glad. If they are not, their displeasure doesn't matter either. *We build our temples for tomorrow, strong as we know how, and we stand on top of the mountain, free within ourselves.*

> — *"The Negro Artist and the Racial Mountain"*

Among the many talented writers of that time, James Weldon Johnson, Countee Cullen, Claude McKay, and Langston Hughes are represented in this anthology. James Weldon Johnson often made use of the cadence and rhetoric of the Black sermon. In "O Black and Unknown Bards" (p. 114) he pays tribute to his ancestors in art, the unknown composers of spirituals such as "Go Down, Moses" and "Steal Away to Jesus." Countee Cullen (pp. 117–18) wrote in the older European literary forms of sonnets and lyrics in regular rhymed stanzas, but in those traditional forms he expresses a definite social consciousness. His sonnet "From the Dark Tower" is representative:

> We shall not always plant while others reap
> The golden increment of bursting fruit,
> Not always countenance, abject and mute,
> That lesser men should hold their brothers cheap . . .
> We were not made eternally to weep.

Langston Hughes (pp. 107–10, 121–23), one of the most versatile writers, often invented poetic forms based on blues and jazz, although occasionally he worked in the literary form of a declarative free verse made famous by Walt Whitman and Carl Sandburg. Both Hughes and Claude McKay brought to Black literature an atmosphere and a social consciousness that attracted white readers' attention. More importantly, they presented for Black readers a lifestyle that their audience could have known firsthand and articulated an intellectual stance which was theirs and which had rarely been expressed in American literature before.

In 1940 a novel by an unknown writer appeared which forced critics to take note. Richard Wright's *Native Son,* which came out of the Depression, was a powerful statement of social protest. Wright, like Hughes, is an author who still serves as a touchstone. Yet, unlike Hughes, he has been in recent years the center of a controversy. The critic Irving Howe has suggested that James Baldwin and Ralph Ellison would do better to write books more nearly like *Native Son,* a scathing criticism of white hypocrisy and stupidity, and an effective warning that the product of such hypocrisy and stupidity will be violence. Early in his career, Baldwin rejected the notion that Black writers must protest the Black condition rather than be primarily concerned with artistic craftsmanship and universal themes (see Baldwin's essays "Everybody's Protest Novel" in *Partisan Review,* 1949, and "Alas Poor Richard" in *Nobody Knows My Name,* 1961). He did, however, pay some homage to Wright in the title of his essay collection *Notes of a Native Son;* and in his latest works, such as *Tell Me How Long the Train's Been Gone* (1968) and *No Name in the Streets* (1974), he seems to be assuming Wright's position as his own.

Ralph Ellison, author of *Invisible Man,* continues to be the most eloquent spokesman for the school of Black writers that Irving Howe opposed to Richard Wright. Ellison distinguishes between his intention and purpose and those of Wright in his essay "The World and the Jug":

> Wright believed in the much-abused idea that novels are weapons. . . . But I believe that true novels, even when most pessimistic and bitter, arise out of an impulse to celebrate human life and are therefore ritualistic and ceremonial at their core. Thus they would preserve as they destroy, affirm as they reject.

This controversy became a central concern of Black writers of the 1960's and 1970's. Many young Black writers, led in the beginning by Imamu Amira Baraka (LeRoi Jones), often absorbed and then totally rejected the traditional forms and techniques of white writers. In contrast to the writers of the Harlem Renaissance such as Cullen and McKay, who wrote almost exclusively in traditional forms, these young writers often extended Langston Hughes' experiments in form far beyond the point where he left off. They turned increasingly to street idiom and Black English. They challenged traditional conceptions of "good English" and "proper form" with four-letter words, abbreviated words, words combined with slashes, slashes in place of usual punctuation, omission of capitals, and omissions of helping verbs and word endings.

Prior to the 1960's Black writers often attacked American hypocrisy and injustice — but they did so using formal phrases such as "the murderous cowardly pack" (McKay, "If We Must Die"). Many of the younger writers of today have adopted the idiom that Baraka popularized in poems such as "Black People!" The popularity among whites of Baraka's violent language and militant attitude has been satirized by Al Young:

> Dont nobody want no nice nigger no more . . .
> they dont want no bourgeois woogie
> they want them a militant nigger.

It must also be emphasized that although much of the new Black writing has shown an increasing hostility toward whites, it shows too an increasingly healthy self-love and even humanism. Don Lee points out in his preface to *We Walk the Way of the New World* (1970):

We need innovators and producers of positive change. The older generation's resistance to change is natural; so how do we change without alienating them? How can we reduce if not completely eliminate all the negativism, pettiness, and cliquishness that exist and are so damaging? . . . How can we create a common consciousness, based on a proven humanism—as we stop trying to prove our humanism to those who are inhuman?

Perhaps the attempt to create this common consciousness is best characterized by the constant insistence of these writers on an awareness of Blackness suggested even in the titles they select for their writing. Lee calls one of his books *Think Black*. Nikki Giovanni's first volume of poetry was *Black Judgment* (1968). This was followed by *Black Feeling, Black Talk* (1970). And both these poets insist that there is no neutral Black art, that Black writing must be political. In taking this view they agree with Richard Wright that literature is a political weapon and disagree with Langston Hughes who felt the reaction of a contemporary audience—black or white—did not matter, and that his audience was posterity.

This controversy still rages in the 1970's among active Black writers. The artist's independence from a particular audience and his reliance on the criteria of literary merit are upheld in the 1970's by Robert Hayden, one of the most accomplished living Black poets who is of the same generation as Ralph Ellison, Owen Dodson, and Gwendolyn Brooks. In a critical essay from his anthology *Afro-American Literature,* Hayden states, "The work of the best Afro-American authors transcends insularity and achieves a social vision and significant literary form." Hayden attacks critics who evaluate the work of Black authors in racial or sociological or political terms, and he calls on the Harlem Renaissance poet Countee Cullen as an ally, repeating Cullen's statement that poetry must be judged as poetry, not as something considered racial utterance. Black writing, both Cullen and Hayden insist, must be judged by the same criteria applied to the work of other American poets.

Thus it is clear that there is no one agreed-upon concept among Black authors today or at any time in the past as to what Black writing is or should be. We turn again to Gwendolyn Brooks for the only unarguable definition of Black writing—Black writing is writing from Black authors.

Ishmael Reed

Ishmael Reed was born in Chattanooga, Tennessee, in 1938. His first novel, *Freelance Pallbearers* (1968), was followed by *Yellow Back Radio Broke-Down* (1969), and the anthology *19 Necromancers from Now* (1970). His poetry has been widely published in periodicals and anthologies. Reed is also one of the founders of *The East Village Other.*

In the following essay, an excerpt from the introduction to *19 Necromancers from Now,* Reed takes to task both white and Black critics who want to circumscribe what Black literature is and should be.

from
19 Necromancers from Now

> *According to ancient legend the white race results from a nuclear
> explosion in what is now the Gobi desert some 30,000 years ago.
> The civilization and techniques which made the explosion possible
> were wiped out. The only survivors were slaves marginal to the
> area who had no knowledge of its science or techniques. They be-
> came albinos as a result of radiation and scattered in different
> directions. Some of them went into Persia, northern India, Greece
> and Turkey. Others moved westward and settled in the caves of
> Europe. The descendants of the cave dwelling albinos are the pres-
> ent inhabitants of America and Western Europe.*

The above is an excerpt from a "story" which appeared in the *Village Voice*
on September 12, 1968. It goes on to recount the atrocities committed by
the "cave dwelling albinos" and to describe them as "a hideous threat to
life on this planet." The story was no narrative of the myth of Yacub, nor was
it written by an author who ducked the pigfire in Watts of 1964.

The author of *Astronauts Return* is none other than William Burroughs, a
White writer whose grandfather invented the adding machine. This demon-
strates the difficulty you encounter when talking of "Black writing," the
"Black Aesthetic," or the "Black Experience."

The matter is further complicated when a young "militant" Black poet
names a color in a story after a White impressionist painter (Soutine), or another Black writer congratulates a "militant" colleague's outstanding oratory
as "Churchillian splendor."

The fact remains that the history of literature is replete with examples of
writers not being what their writing represents them to be. In the Western
nineteenth-century literature women used male pseudonyms because at the
time a female who wrote was considered just a step above the common
whore. The category of print is not a racial or sexual category — and when one
is reading print; decoding someone else's experience or non-experience, fairy
tales, science fiction, fantasy, etc., the author may be a thousand miles away
or dead.

■ In 1967 I went to Berkeley, California, for the purpose of writing a Western. A counselor at Merritt College heard that I was in town and invited me
to teach a course in Afro-American literature, but when I told him I could not
in good conscience twist the works of Ralph Ellison and Richard Wright to
accommodate a viewpoint he at the time believed irresistible, the bureaucrat
told me that the job was unavailable.

This counselor, like many people, views Afro-American culture as something to be exploited for the pursuit of certain political ends. Students who
would never think of turning a seminar on Melville into a political rally would
not hesitate to dictate to a Black instructor what emphasis should be made, or
what works should be covered, in his course. Their unconscious racism is
sometimes just as rigid as that of their elders. After all, in this country art is
what White people do. All other people are "propagandists." One can see this
in the methodology used by certain White and Black critics in investigating

Black literature. Form, Technique, Symbology, Imagery are rarely investigated with the same care as Argument, and even here, the Argument must be one that appeals to the critics' prejudices. Novels that don't have the right "message" are cast aside as "pretentious," for it is assumed that the native who goes the way of art is "uppity." He loses his seat in Congress, or is dethroned as Heavyweight Champion of the World.

After my experience with the counselor at Merritt College, I was invited to do a course at the University of California at Berkeley.

Originally, the position of the English Department was that there was no need for a course in Afro-American literature, since no literature had appeared until after World War II—a statement that could be rendered foolish even upon cursory examination. This view, I must say, was not shared by the Department Chairman, James D. Hart, compiler and editor of *The Oxford Companion to American Literature,* who, although Afro-American literature was not his field, solicited materials on the subject, and is now able to hold his own in a discussion with any student of the field. But there were those on the faculty who held this opinion. They confused a fanatical defense of Western religion with "education," just as their counterparts in the critical field confuse this defense with "reviews."

■ I was to learn that White authors, as well as Afro-American authors, are neglected by the American university. Before I arrived at Berkeley, there was no room in the curriculum for detective novels or Western fiction, even though some of the best contributions to American literature occur in these genres. At another major university, the library did not carry books by William Burroughs, who at least manages to get it up beyond the common, simple, routine narrative that critics become so thrilled about.

I found that some of the students who didn't understand the language of Chester Himes or Charles Wright were equally at a loss when it came to Horace McCoy or Damon Runyon. I had them translate these works with the same enthusiasm encouraged by the English faculty for explicating a later poem of Yeats. I suspect that the inability of some students to "understand" works written by Afro-American authors is traceable to an inability to understand the American experience as rooted in slang, dialect, vernacular, argot, and all of the other putdown terms the faculty uses for those who have the gall to deviate from the true and proper way of English.

"Slang and colloquial speech have rarely been so creative. It is as if the common man (or his anonymous spokesman) would in his speech assert his humanity against the powers that be, as if the rejection and revolt subdued in the political sphere would burst out in a vocabulary that calls things by their names: 'head-shrinker' and 'egghead', 'boob tube', 'think tank' and 'beat it', 'dig it' and 'gone man gone'," Herbert Marcuse wrote in *The One-Dimensional Man.*

And it may turn out that the great restive underground language rising from the American slums and fringe communities is the real American poetry and prose, that can tell you the way things are happening now. If this is not the case, then it is mighty strange that a whole new generation exploits this language, in what White racist critics call "folk rock lyrics."

Composers of rock lyrics have exploited "Black Talk," and the contemporary "Neo-Slave Narrative" confessional may have revolutionized the essay form. An English writer recently complained that he and his colleagues desired the same freedom as a leading Black exponent of this autobiographical genre, which dates back as early as *A Narrative of the Uncommon Sufferings and Surprising Deliverance of Britan Hammon, A Negro Man,* published in 1760. Admittedly, there is a frenzy for this kind of writing in publishing circles, and its authors are celebrities on the lecture circuit. At times it seems that the stampede for these books is so great that Afro-American authors who go the route of Art are trampled. Al Young wrote in his book of poems, *Dancing:*

> Dont nobody want no nice nigger no more
> these honkies man that put out
> these books & things
> they want an angry splib
> a furious nigrah
> they dont want no bourgeois woogie
> they want them a militant nigger
> in a fiji haircut
> fresh out of some secret boot camp
> with a bad book in one hand
> & a molotov cocktail in the other
> subject to turn up at one of their conferences
> or soirees
> & shake the shit out of them

But even among the "Neo-Slave Narrative" writers, who somehow confuse their experience with that of thirty million other people, one has to search for the kind of bad writing that typifies the current American "bestseller" scene—a scene that so woefully neglects its own younger White writers: John Harriman, Donald Phelps, Willard Bain—just to mention a few.

■ What distinguishes the present crop of Afro-American and Black writers from their predecessors is a marked independence from Western form. This holds true even for the authors of the "Neo-Slave Narrative."

The history of Afro-American literature is abundant with examples of writers using other people's literary machinery and mythology in their work. W. E. B. DuBois, in some of his writing, is almost embarrassing in his use of White classical references. And what does one do with a modern writer who terms Egyptians "villains," or equates Babylon with America?

Black writers have in the past written sonnets, iambic pentameter, ballads, every possible Western gentleman's form. They have been neo-classicists, Marxists, existentialists, and infected by every Western disease available. I have a joke I tell friends about a young Black poet who relies upon other people's systems, and does not use his head. He wears sideburns and has seen every French film in New York. While dining at Schrafft's he chokes to death on nut-covered ice cream and dies. He approaches the river Styx and pleads with Charon to ferry him across: "I don't care how often you've used me as a mythological allusion," Charon says. "You're still a nigger—swim!"

One has to return to what some writers would call "dark heathenism" to find original tall tales, and yarns with the kind of originality that some modern writers use as found poetry—the enigmatic street rhymes of some of Ellison's minor characters, or the dozens. I call this neo-hoodooism; a spur to originality, which prompted Julia Jackson, a New Orleans soothsayer, when asked the origin of the amulets, talismans, charms, and potions in her workshop, to say: "I make all my own stuff. It saves me money and it's as good. People who has to buy their stuff ain't using their heads."

■ Sometimes I feel that the condition of the Afro-American writer in this country is so strange that one has to go to the supernatural for an analogy. Manipulation of the word has always been related in the mind to manipulation of nature. One utters a few words and stones roll aside, the dead are raised and the river beds emptied of their content.

The Afro-American artist is similar to the Necromancer (a word whose etymology is revealing in itself!). He is a conjuror who works JuJu upon his oppressors; a witch doctor who frees his fellow victims from the psychic attack launched by demons of the outer and inner world.

For *The Man* there has always been something spooky about the slave who begins to handle clay or word music, or talks to his fellow victims in what for him are undecipherable codes. One must remember that we live in a country where at one time *literacy for Blacks was a crime.*

Alex Gross, a young White painter, wrote in the *East Village Other:* "The artist is the new preacher, the prophet of the modernist religion. But as soon as a black man appears using the cult words of the religion, the devout begin to feel ill at ease. Why is this? It is because the assumption that art is only white man's work is built into the very culture itself. Art which pays homage to the idea of reaching all of society and influencing it, becomes embarrassed when it is actually expected to do so. . . . The phrases and opinions which seemed like revealed truth when uttered by the white artist have tended to cause doubt and embarrassment when spoken by a black one."

This racism even affects the so-called counter culture—whose scholars write of the Indian and Zen influence, but leave out the Black influence upon those who are seeking to transform the wicked old. Yet the Black influence is pervasive. There were more people doing the boogaloo at Woodstock than chanting, *"Hare krishna hare hare."*

Nevertheless, in certain radical bookstores on the Lower East Side, Berkeley, and other focal points of what is called the "counter culture or the alternative culture," Claude McKay and Robert Hayden are consigned to the Black section, whereas Ezra Pound and Hermann Hesse are in the poetry and fiction sections. And a volume which was audaciously called *The New American Poetry 1945–1960,* edited by Donald Allen and influenced by Allen Ginsberg, carried the work of only one Black poet.

And if you think that things have changed since 1956, I would direct your attention to *The Young American Poets,* edited by Paul Carroll, and *31 New American Poets,* edited by Ron Schreiber, where the absence of adequate Black representation (they printed three!) was so conspicuous that even a reviewer for the *Village Voice* was called upon to comment.

The exclusionary policy of the traditional American anthology is a mysterious phenomenon. It can't be based upon "inferior quality"—that well-worn private dick the White art world dials when threatened by an invasion of creative gangsters—because many of those Afro-Americans who have chosen to emulate Western form and content excel at their adopted literary devices. Some Afro-American poets can write about flowers, girlfriends and being miserable along with the best of them.

Perhaps those White writers who think American writing is like hunting Big Game (firing from a helicopter while sipping a martini), or going a couple of rounds with a champion boxer have a point.

Perhaps at the roots of American art is a rivalry between the oppressor and the oppressed, with a secret understanding that the oppressor shall always prevail and make off with the prizes, no matter how inferior his art to that of his victims. Art in America may even be related to sexual competition. In the beginning was The Word and The Word is the domain of the White patriarchy. Beware. Women and natives are not to tamper with The Word.

If in Mayan or ancient Egyptian culture writing was considered a royal profession, and the writer a necromancer, soothsayer, priest, prophet; a man who opened doors to the divine, here in America writing is related to bullfighting, or to sports in which men disfigure other men or animals—or sometimes it is compared to wreaking sexual vengeance upon a woman:

"The novel is the great bitch," Norman Mailer said, in *Cannibals and Christians*. "We've all had a piece of her," and he gave a long list of writers who had presumably balled the bitch. Only one Black writer was invited to join the orgy—James Baldwin.

If writing has these *extra-literary* connotations, then it is no surprise when Afro-American writers are treated in the same manner as Afro-American boxers—whatever the arena, they end up giving each other lumps in the semi-finals. . . .

■ Afro-American or Black literature is food for a deep, lifetime study, not something to be squeezed into a quarter or semester as a concession to student demands, nor a literature to be approached one-dimensionally, as do critics Robert Bone, Edward Margolies, and David Littlejohn. In Bone's case, for example, the categories he uses—Amalgamation, Open Revolt, Separatism, or Back-to-Africa—are not literary categories, but essentially political ones. This is to deprive the student of Black literature of the broad universe the most creative Black authors have painstakingly structured in their work. Black writing requires the same multi-dimensional critical approach that has been traditionally applied to Western literature, and critics Addison Gayle, Adam David Miller, Ron Welburn, Sarah Fabio, Nick Aaron Ford, Darwin Turner, Wilmer Lucas, Elizabeth Postell and Toni Cade are educating serious students of Afro-American or Black literature on these matters.

Marshall McLuhan surveyed—in predictably White scholarly fashion—a Western body of literature up to James Joyce, and his conclusions led many students of communications to assume that print had just about run its course. "Words are 'oxcarts' and may disappear sooner than we think," William Burroughs wrote.

If Marshall McLuhan and Burroughs had opened their reading to include the new Afro-American, Indian-American, and Chinese-American writers, they would have found that print and words are not dead at all. To the contrary, they are very much alive and kicking.

Suggestions for Discussion

1. What point does Reed wish to demonstrate with his examples of Burroughs' writing on "cave dwelling albinos," a Black writer congratulating a militant colleague's outstanding oratory as "Churchillian splendor," and nineteenth-century women writers using male pseudonyms?
2. What is Reed's view towards the use of literature for sociopolitical purposes? How does the poem he quotes by Al Young illustrate his argument? What is "Black literature" according to Reed?
3. What criticism does Reed make of the approach taken by white critics such as Robert Bone, Edward Margolies, and David Littlejohn toward Black literature?

Suggestion for Writing and Comparison

1. Note the various ways in which Reed compares the plight of the woman writer with that of the Black writer, e.g., "In the beginning was The Word and The Word is the domain of white patriarchy. Beware. Women and natives are not to tamper with The Word." Then read Shirley Chisholm's essay "Racism and Anti-Feminism" (in *Black Scholar,* January–February 1970). Write an essay in which you discuss the problems of white patriarchal oppression which Blacks and women have shared.

STORIES

Richard Wright

Richard Wright was born on a plantation near Natchez, Mississippi, in 1908. His early education was often interrupted by the
family's moves and his mother's illness. At the age of fifteen he
left home to work in Memphis where he spent most of his nights
reading and making up for his lack of formal education.

During the Depression he moved to Chicago where he was
employed by the WPA Federal Writer's Project. In 1939 he was
the recipient of a Guggenheim Fellowship. The publication of
his naturalistic novel *Native Son* (1940) brought him international recognition.

Several years later Wright relocated in Paris where he continued to write until his death in 1960. *Native Son* remains his best-
known work. But during his prolific career he produced numerous books, among them his autobiography, *Black Boy* (1945), a
novel, *The Outsider* (1953), several collections of essays, and
two collections of short stories, *Uncle Tom's Children* (1938)
and *Eight Men* (1961). Richard Wright was the first major Black
American novelist.

The story which follows, "The Man Who Saw the Flood," was
included in *Eight Men*. It is characteristic of Wright's fiction in
its feeling of hopelessness and in its tone of despair. Wright's
deterministic philosophy, which is apparent in this story as in
most of his work, is reminiscent of other American naturalist
writers such as Theodore Dreiser and Stephen Crane.

(See p. 153 for Richard Wright's "Hokku Poems.")

The Man Who Saw the Flood

When the flood waters recede,
the poor folk along the river
start from scratch.

At last the flood waters had receded. A black father, a black mother, and a black child tramped through muddy fields, leading a tired cow by a thin bit of rope. They stopped on a hilltop and shifted the bundles on their shoulders. As far as they could see the ground was covered with flood silt. The little girl lifted a skinny finger and pointed to a mud-caked cabin.

"Look, Pa! Ain tha our home?"

The man, round-shouldered, clad in blue, ragged overalls, looked with bewildered eyes. Without moving a muscle, scarcely moving his lips, he said: "Yeah."

For five minutes they did not speak or move. The flood waters had been more than eight feet high here. Every tree, blade of grass, and stray stick had its flood mark; caky, yellow mud. It clung to the ground, cracking thinly here and there in spider web fashion. Over the stark fields came a gusty spring wind. The sky was high, blue, full of white clouds and sunshine. Over all hung a first-day strangeness.

"The henhouse is gone," sighed the woman.

"N the pigpen," sighed the man.

They spoke without bitterness.

"Ah reckon them chickens is all done drowned."

"Yeah."

"Miz Flora's house is gone, too," said the little girl.

They looked at a clump of trees where their neighbor's house had stood.

"Lawd!"

"Yuh reckon anybody knows where they is?"

"Hard t tell."

The man walked down the slope and stood uncertainly.

"There wuz a road erlong here somewheres," he said.

But there was no road now. Just a wide sweep of yellow, scalloped silt.

"Look, Tom!" called the woman. "Here's a piece of our gate!"

The gatepost was half buried in the ground. A rusty hinge stood stiff, like a lonely finger. Tom pried it loose and caught it firmly in his hand. There was nothing particular he wanted to do with it; he just stood holding it firmly. Finally he dropped it, looked up, and said:

"C mon. Les go down n see whut we kin do."

Because it sat in a slight depression, the ground about the cabin was soft and slimy.

"Gimme tha bag o lime, May," he said.

With his shoes sucking in mud, he went slowly around the cabin, spreading the white lime with thick fingers. When he reached the front again he had a little left; he shook the bag out on the porch. The fine grains of floating lime flickered in the sunlight.

"Tha oughta hep some," he said.

"Now, yuh be careful, Sal!" said May. "Don yuh go n fall down in all this mud, yuh hear?"

"Yessum."

The steps were gone. Tom lifted May and Sally to the porch. They stood a moment looking at the half-opened door. He had shut it when he left, but somehow it seemed natural that he should find it open. The planks in the porch floor were swollen and warped. The cabin had two colors; near the bottom it was a solid yellow; at the top it was the familiar gray. It looked weird, as though its ghost were standing beside it.

The cow lowed.

"Tie Pat t the pos on the en of the porch, May."

May tied the rope slowly, listlessly. When they attempted to open the front door, it would not budge. It was not until Tom placed his shoulder against it and gave it a stout shove that it scraped back jerkily. The front room was dark and silent. The damp smell of flood silt came fresh and sharp to their nostrils. Only one-half of the upper window was clear, and through it fell a rectangle of dingy light. The floors swam in ooze. Like a mute warning, a wavering flood mark went high around the walls of the room. A dresser sat cater-cornered, its drawers and sides bulging like a bloated corpse. The bed, with the mattress still on it, was like a giant casket forged of mud. Two smashed chairs lay in a corner, as though huddled together for protection.

"Les see the kitchen," said Tom.

The stovepipe was gone. But the stove stood in the same place.

"The stove's still good. We kin clean it."

"Yeah."

"But where's the table?"

"Lawd knows."

"It must've washed erway wid the rest of the stuff, Ah reckon."

They opened the back door and looked out. They missed the barn, the henhouse, and the pigpen.

"Tom, yuh bettah try tha ol pump n see ef eny watah's there."

The pump was stiff. Tom threw his weight on the handle and carried it up and down. No water came. He pumped on. There was a dry, hollow cough. Then yellow water trickled. He caught his breath and kept pumping. The water flowed white.

"Thank Gawd! We's got some watah. Yuh bettah boil it fo yuh use it," he said.

"Yeah. Ah know."

"Look, Pa! Here's yo ax," called Sally.

Tom took the ax from her. "Yeah. Ah'll need this."

"N here's somethin else," called Sally, digging spoons out of the mud.

"Waal, Ahma git a bucket n start cleanin," said May. "Ain no use in waitin, cause we's gotta sleep on them floors tonight."

When she was filling the bucket from the pump, Tom called from around the cabin. "May, look! Ah done foun mah plow!" Proudly he dragged the silt-caked plow to the pump. "Ah'll wash it n it'll be awright."

"Ahm hongry," said Sally.

"Now, yuh jus wait! Yuh et this mawnin," said May. She turned to Tom. "Now, whutcha gonna do, Tom?"

He stood looking at the mud-filled fields.

"Yuh goin back t Burgess?"

"Ah reckon Ah have to."

"Whut else kin yuh do?"

"Nothin," he said. "Lawd, but Ah sho hate t start all over wid tha white man. Ah'd leave here ef Ah could. Ah owes im nigh eight hundred dollahs. N we needs a hoss, grub, seed, n a lot mo other things. Ef we keeps on like this tha white man'll own us body n soul."

"But, Tom, there ain nothin else t do," she said.

"Ef we try t run erway they'll put us in jail."

"It coulda been worse," she said.

Sally came running from the kitchen. "Pa!"

"Hunh?"

"There's a shelf in the kitchen the flood didn git!"

"Where?"

"Right up over the stove."

"But, chile, ain nothin up there," said May.

"But there's somethin on it," said Sally.

"C mon. Les see."

High and dry, untouched by the flood-water, was a box of matches. And beside it a half-full sack of Bull Durham tobacco. He took a match from the box and scratched it on his overalls. It burned to his fingers before he dropped it.

"May!"

"Hunh?"

"Look! Here's ma bacco n some matches!"

She stared unbelievingly. "Lawd!" she breathed.

Tom rolled a cigarette clumsily.

May washed the stove, gathered some sticks, and after some difficulty, made a fire. The kitchen stove smoked, and their eyes smarted. May put water on to heat and went into the front room. It was getting dark. From the bundles they took a kerosene lamp and lit it. Outside Pat lowed longingly into the thickening gloam and tinkled her cowbell.

"Tha old cow's hongry," said May.

"Ah reckon Ah'll have t be gittin erlong t Burgess."

They stood on the front porch.

"Yuh bettah git on, Tom, fo it gits too dark."

"Yeah."

The wind had stopped blowing. In the east a cluster of stars hung.

"Yuh goin, Tom?"

"Ah reckon Ah have t."

"Ma, Ah'm hongry," said Sally.

"Wait erwhile, honey. Ma knows yuh's hongry."

Tom threw his cigarette away and sighed.

"Look! Here comes somebody!"

"Thas Mistah Burgess now!"

A mud-caked buggy rolled up. The shaggy horse was splattered all over. Burgess leaned his white face out of the buggy and spat.

"Well, I see you're back."

"Yessuh."

"How things look?"

"They don look so good, Mistah."

"What seems to be the trouble?"

"Waal. Ah ain got no hoss, no grub, nothin. The only thing Ah got is tha ol cow there . . ."

"You owe eight hundred dollahs down at the store, Tom."

"Yessuh, Ah know. But, Mistah Burgess, can't yuh knock somethin off of tha, seein as how Ahm down n out now?"

"You ate that grub, and I got to pay for it, Tom."

"Yessuh, Ah know."

"It's going to be a little tough, Tom. But you got to go through with it. Two of the boys tried to run away this morning and dodge their debts, and I had to have the sheriff pick em up. I wasn't looking for no trouble out of you, Tom . . . The rest of the families are going back."

Leaning out of the buggy, Burgess waited. In the surrounding stillness the cowbell tinkled again. Tom stood with his back against a post.

"Yuh got t go on, Tom. We ain't got nothin here," said May.

Tom looked at Burgess.

"Mistah Burgess, Ah don wanna make no trouble. But this is jus *too* hard. Ahm worse off now than befo. Ah got to start from scratch."

"Get in the buggy and come with me. I'll stake you with grub. We can talk over how you can pay it back." Tom said nothing. He rested his back against the post and looked at the mud-filled fields.

"Well," asked Burgess. "You coming?" Tom said nothing. He got slowly to the ground and pulled himself into the buggy. May watched them drive off.

"Hurry back, Tom!"

"Awright."

"Ma, tell Pa t bring me some 'lasses," begged Sally.

"Oh, Tom!"

Tom's head came out of the side of the buggy.

"Hunh?"

"Bring some 'lasses!"

"Hunh?"

"Bring some 'lasses for Sal!"

"Awright!"

She watched the buggy disappear over the crest of the muddy hill. Then she sighed, caught Sally's hand, and turned back into the cabin.

Suggestions for Discussion

1. How does Wright create the impression of despair through the use of setting, characters, and action in the first few paragraphs?
2. How does the author appeal to the reader's senses in order to arouse his emotions?

3. What effect does the sharecropping system have on the relationship of Tom to Burgess? What impression does Wright give of Burgess through dialogue? What words are used which suggest tone and attitude?
4. Why does Wright twice state that Tom had "his back against a post" while talking to Burgess? How does this image relate to the theme of the story?
5. How does the author want the conclusion to affect the reader? Is he successful? What is the dominant tone of the story?

Suggestions for Writing and Comparison

1. Discuss fear, choice, and absurdity as related aspects of Wright's story.
2. Read Theodore Dreiser's *An American Tragedy* and Richard Wright's *Native Son*. Compare the two novels as examples of naturalism.

James Baldwin

James Baldwin was born in Harlem in 1924, the oldest of nine children. His father was a fundamentalist preacher, and as a boy Baldwin also preached until the world of literature drew his attention.

Baldwin has been awarded a number of literary fellowships —Rosenwald, Guggenheim, and Partisan Review—as well as other literary honors. His stories and essays have appeared in leading magazines such as *Harper's, The Reporter, Atlantic Monthly*, and *Esquire*. In addition, he has published four novels, *Go Tell It On The Mountain* (1952), *Giovanni's Room* (1956), *Another Country* (1963), *Tell Me How Long the Train's Been Gone* (1968), a book of short stories, *Going to Meet the Man* (1965), several volumes of essays, *Notes of a Native Son* (1955), *Nobody Knows My Name* (1961), *The Fire Next Time* (1963), and *No Name in the Streets* (1974), and two plays, *The Amen Corner* (1953) and *Blues for Mister Charlie* (1964). Baldwin's literary reputation is international. He is considered one of the best contemporary American essayists.

His first novel, *Go Tell It On the Mountain*, as well as several of his short stories, are somewhat autobiographical, depicting the struggle to attain manhood in Harlem. His later books, set in the American South, Greenwich Village, and Europe, show an increasing bitterness at the contrast between Americans' and Europeans' regard for Black Americans.

Baldwin's familarity with the prose of sermons and the Bible is especially apparent in the following excerpt from his novel *Go Tell It On the Mountain*. Baldwin is concerned in this story with a double exodus: that of the slave from legal bondage and that of the Black from the bondage of custom.

from

Go Tell It On the Mountain

She had always seemed to Florence the oldest woman in the world, for she often spoke of Florence and Gabriel as the children of her old age, and she had been born, innumerable years ago, during slavery, on a plantation in another state. On this plantation she had grown up as one of the field workers, for she was very tall and strong; and by and by she had married and raised children, all of whom had been taken from her, one by sickness and two by auction; and one, whom she had not been allowed to call her own, had been raised in the master's house. When she was a woman grown, well past thirty as she reckoned it, with one husband buried—but the master had given her another—armies, plundering and burning, had come from the North to set them free. This was in answer to the prayers of the faithful, who had never ceased, both day and night, to cry out for deliverance.

For it had been the will of God that they should hear, and pass thereafter, one to another, the story of the Hebrew children who had been held in bondage in the land of Egypt; and how the Lord had heard their groaning, and how His heart was moved; and how He bid them wait but a little season till He should send deliverance. Florence's mother had known this story, so it seemed, from the day that she was born. And while life she lived—rising in the morning before the sun came up, standing and bending in the fields when the sun was high, crossing the fields homeward while the sun went down at the gates of Heaven far away, hearing the whistle of the foreman and his eerie cry across the fields; in the whiteness of winter when hogs and turkeys and geese were slaughtered, and lights burned bright in the big house, and Bathsheba, the cook, sent over in a napkin bits of ham and chicken and cakes left over by the white folks—in all that befell: in her joys, her pipe in the evening, her man at night, the children she suckled, and guided on their first short steps; and in her tribulations, death, and parting, and the lash, she did not forget that deliverance was promised, and would surely come. She had only to endure and trust in God. She knew that the big house, the house of pride where the white folks lived, would come down: it was written in the Word of God. They, who walked so proudly now, had not fashioned for themselves or their children so sure a foundation as was hers. They walked on the edge of a steep place and their eyes were sightless—God would cause them to rush down, as the herd of swine had once rushed down, into the sea. For all that they were so beautiful, and took their ease, she knew them, and she pitied them, who would have no covering in the great day of His wrath.

Yet, she told her children, God was just, and He struck no people without first giving many warnings. God gave men time, but all the times were in His hand, and one day the time to forsake evil and do good would all be finished: then only the whirlwind, death riding on the whirlwind, awaited those people who had forgotten God. In all the days that she was growing up, signs failed not, but none heeded. "Slaves done ris," was whispered in the cabin and at the master's gate: slaves in another county had fired the masters' houses and fields and dashed their children to death against the stones. "Another slave in Hell," Bathsheba might say one morning, shooing the pickaninnies away from the great porch: a slave had killed his master, or his overseer, and had gone down to Hell to pay for it. "I ain't got long to stay here," someone crooned beside her in the fields, someone who would be gone by morning on his journey north. All these signs, like the plagues with which the Lord had afflicted Egypt, only hardened the hearts of these people against the Lord. They thought the lash would save them, and they used the lash; or the knife, or the gallows, or the auction block; they thought that kindness would save them, and the master and mistress came down, smiling, to the cabins, making much of the pickaninnies and bearing gifts. These were great days, and they all, black and white, seemed happy together. But when the Word has gone forth from the mouth of God nothing can turn it back.

The word was fulfilled one morning, before she was awake. Many of the stories her mother told meant nothing to Florence; she knew them for what they were, tales told by an old black woman in a cabin in the evening to distract her children from their cold and hunger. But the story of this day she was never to forget; it was a day for which she lived. There was a great running and shouting, said her mother, everywhere outside, and, as she opened her eyes to the light of that day, so bright, she said, and cold, she was certain that the judgment trumpet had sounded. While she still sat, amazed, and wondering what, on the judgment day, would be the best behavior, in rushed Bathsheba, and behind her many tumbling children and field hands and house niggers, all together, and Bathsheba shouted, "Rise up, rise up, Sister Rachel, and see the Lord's deliverance! He done brought us out of Egypt, just like He promised, and we's free at last!" Bathsheba grabbed her, tears running down her face; she, dressed in the clothes in which she had slept, walked to the door to look out on the new day God had given them.

On that day she saw the proud house humbled; green silk and velvet blowing out of windows, and the garden trampled by many horsemen, and the big gate open. The master and mistress, and their kin, and one child she had borne were in that house — which she did not enter. Soon it occurred to her that there was no longer any reason to tarry here. She tied her things in a cloth that she put on her head, and walked out through the big gate, never to see that country any more.

And this became Florence's deep ambition: to walk out one morning through the cabin door, never to return. . . .

In nineteen hundred, when she was twenty-six, Florence walked out through the cabin door. She had thought to wait until her mother, who was so ill now that she no longer stirred out of bed, should be buried — but suddenly she knew that she would wait no longer, the time had come. She had been working as cook and serving-girl for a large white family in town, and it was on the day her master proposed that she become his concubine that she knew her life among these wretched had come to its destined end. She left her employment that same day (leaving behind her a most vehement conjugal bitterness), and with part of the money that with cunning, cruelty, and sacrifice she had saved over a period of years, bought a railroad ticket to New York. When she bought it, in a kind of scarlet rage, she held like a talisman at the back of her mind the thought: "I can give it back, I can sell it. This don't mean I got to go." But she knew that nothing could stop her.

And it was this leave-taking that came to stand, in Florence's latter days, and with many another witness, at her bedside. Gray clouds obscured the sun that day, and outside the cabin window she saw that mist still covered the ground. Her mother lay in bed, awake; she was pleading with Gabriel, who had been out drinking the night before, and who was not really sober now, to mend his ways and come to the Lord. And Gabriel, full of the confusion, and pain, and guilt that were his whenever he thought of how he made his mother suffer, but that became nearly insupportable when she taxed him with it, stood before the mirror, head bowed, buttoning his shirt. Florence knew that he could not unlock his lips to speak; he could not say yes to his mother, and to the Lord; and he could not say no.

"Honey," their mother was saying, "don't you *let* your old mother die without you look her in the eye and tell her she going to see you in glory. You hear me, boy?"

In a moment, Florence thought with scorn, tears would fill his eyes, and he would promise to "do better." He had been promising to "do better" since the day he had been baptized.

She put down her bag in the center of the hateful room.

"Ma," she said, "I'm going. I'm a-going this morning."

Now that she had said it, she was angry with herself for not having said it the night before, so that they would have had time to be finished with their weeping and their arguments. She had not trusted herself to withstand the night before; but now there was almost no time left. The center of her mind was filled with the image of the great, white clock at the railway station, on which the hands did not cease to move.

"You going where?" her mother asked sharply. But she knew that her mother had understood, had indeed long before this moment known that this time would come. The astonishment with which she stared at Florence's bag was not altogether astonishment, but a startled, wary attention. A danger imagined had become present and real, and her mother was already searching for a way to break Florence's will. All this Florence knew in a moment, and it made her stronger. She watched her mother, waiting.

But at the tone of his mother's voice Gabriel, who had scarcely heard Florence's announcement, so grateful had he been that something had occurred to distract from him his mother's attention, dropped his eyes and saw Florence's traveling-bag. And he repeated his mother's question in a stunned, angry voice, understanding it only as the words hit the air:

"Yes, girl. Where you think you going?"

"I'm going," she said, "to New York. I got my ticket."

And her mother watched her. For a moment no one said a word. Then, Gabriel, in a changed and frightened voice, asked:

"And when you done decide that?"

She did not look at him, nor answer his question. She continued to watch her mother. "I got my ticket," she repeated. "I'm going on the morning train."

"Girl," asked her mother, quietly, "is you sure you know what you's doing?"

She stiffened, seeing in her mother's eyes a mocking pity. "I'm a woman grown," she said, "I know what I'm doing."

"And you going," cried Gabriel, "this morning—just like that? And you going to walk off and leave your mother—just like that?"

"You hush," she said, turning to him for the first time, "she got you, ain't she?"

This was indeed, she realized as he dropped his eyes, the bitter, troubling point. He could not endure the thought of being left alone with his mother, with nothing whatever to put between himself and his guilty love. With Florence gone, time would have swallowed up all his mother's children, except himself; and *he*, then, must make amends for all the pain that she had borne, and sweeten her last moments with all his proofs of love. And his mother required of him one proof only, that he tarry no longer in sin. With Florence gone, his stammering time, his playing time, contracted with a bound to the sparest interrogative second, when he must stiffen himself, and answer to his mother, and all the host of heaven, yes, or no.

Florence smiled inwardly a small, malicious smile, watching his slow bafflement, and panic, and rage; and she looked at her mother again. "She got you," she repeated. "She don't need me."

"You going north," her mother said, then. "And when you reckon on coming back?"

"I don't reckon on coming back," she said.

"You come crying back soon enough," said Gabriel, with malevolence, "soon as they whip your butt up there four or five times."

She looked at him again. "Just don't you try to hold your breath till then, you hear?"

"Girl," said her mother, "you mean to tell me the Devil's done made your heart so hard you can just leave your mother on her dying bed, and you don't care if you don't never see her in this world no more? Honey, you can't tell me you done got so evil as all that?"

She felt Gabriel watching her to see how she would take this question—the question that, for all her determination, she had dreaded most to hear. She looked away from her mother, and straightened, catching her breath, looking outward through the small, cracked window. There, outside, beyond the slowly rising mist, and farther off than her eyes could see, her life awaited her. The woman on the bed was old, her life was fading as the mist rose. She thought of her mother as already in the grave; and she would not let herself be strangled by the hands of the dead.

"I'm going, Ma," she said. "I got to go."

Her mother leaned back, face upward to the light, and began to cry. Gabriel moved to Florence's side and grabbed her arm. She looked up into his face and saw that his eyes were full of tears.

"You can't go," he said. "You can't go. You can't go and leave your mother thisaway. She need a woman, Florence, to help look after her. What she going to do here, all alone with me?"

She pushed him from her and moved to stand over her mother's bed.

"Ma," she said, "don't be like that. Ain't a blessed thing for you to cry about so. Ain't a thing can happen to me up North can't happen to me here. God's everywhere, Ma. Ain't no need to worry."

She knew that she was mouthing words; and she realized suddenly that her mother scorned to dignify these words with her attention. She had granted Florence the victory—with a promptness which had the effect of making Florence, however dimly and unwillingly, wonder if her victory was real. She was not weeping for her daughter's future, she was weeping for the past, and weeping in an anguish in which Florence had no part. And all of this filled Florence with a terrible fear, which was immediately transformed into anger. "Gabriel can take care of you," she said, her voice shaking with malice. "Gabriel ain't never going to leave you. Is you, boy?" and she looked at him. He stood, stupid with bewilderment and grief, a few inches from the bed. "But me," she said, "I got to go." She walked to the center of the room again, and picked up her bag.

"Girl," Gabriel whispered, "ain't you got no feelings at *all?*"

"*Lord!*" her mother cried; and at the sound her heart turned over; she and Gabriel, arrested, stared at the bed. "Lord, Lord, Lord! Lord, have mercy on my sinful daughter! Stretch out your hand and hold her back from the lake that burns forever! Oh, my Lord, my Lord!" and her voice dropped, and broke, and tears ran down her face. "Lord, I done my best with all the children what you give me. Lord, have mercy on my children, and my children's children."

"Florence," said Gabriel, "please don't go. Please don't go. You ain't really fixing to go and leave her like this?"

Tears stood suddenly in her own eyes, though she could not have said what she was crying for. "Leave me be," she said to Gabriel, and picked up her bag again. She opened the door; the cold, morning air came in. "Good-by," she said. And then to Gabriel: "Tell her I said good-by." She walked through the cabin door and down the short steps into the frosty yard. Gabriel watched her, standing frozen between the door and the weeping bed. Then, as her hand was on the gate, he ran before her, and slammed the gate shut.

"Girl, where you going? What you doing? You reckon on finding some men up North to dress you in pearls and diamonds?"

Violently, she opened the gate and moved out into the road. He watched her with his jaw hanging, and his lips loose and wet. "If you ever see me again," she said, "I won't be wearing rags like yours."

Suggestions for Discussion

1. What does the author mean to imply by leaving the mother unnamed at the beginning? When is she first called by name? How is her situation reminiscent of that of her Biblical namesake, Rachel?

2. In what various ways has Baldwin used the Bible? For instance, who are the American "Hebrew people"? Who or what is "Egypt"? In what way do the "signs" in the story resemble the Biblical plagues?

3. What part does faith in God's justice play in the lives of the slaves?

4. How is Florence's life parallel to her mother's? What is the basis of conflict between mother and daughter? What justification does Florence have for desiring freedom, for wanting to leave? What does she hope to find in "the promised land"?

5. What evidence is there of the influence of Baldwin's early experiences, both as the son of a preacher and as a preacher himself, on his prose style? What elements of his noted expository writing are contained in the story?

Suggestion for Writing and Comparison

1. Read Claude Brown's *Manchild in the Promised Land* (1965). To what extent has Brown's generation realized Florence's hope of "the promised land"?

Ralph Ellison

Ralph Ellison, one of the foremost contemporary American writers, was born in Oklahoma City, Oklahoma, in 1914. He trained as a musician at Tuskegee Institute from the age of nineteen to the age of twenty-two. But after a visit to New York where Ellison met Richard Wright, he decided to try his hand at writing fiction. Since 1939 his works have appeared in numerous national magazines and anthologies. He is best known for his novel *Invisible Man* (1952), which won him both the National Book Award and the Russwurm Award. In a poll of two hundred authors, critics, and editors in 1965, *Invisible Man* was voted the novel "most memorable and likely to endure of the past twenty years." His second full-length book, *Shadow and Act* (1964), is a collection of essays.

Ellison has been appointed a fellow to the American Academy in Rome and to the American Institute of Arts and Letters. He has taught at the University of Chicago, Rutgers University, and several other distinguished colleges and universities.

The following short story, "Did You Ever Dream Lucky?," was written after publication of *Invisible Man* and contains the character Mary Rambo from that novel. She becomes here a superb storyteller who slowly spins a tragicomic yarn of the older generation in Harlem.

Did You Ever Dream Lucky?

After the hurried good-bys the door had closed and they sat at the table with the tragic wreck of the Thanksgiving turkey before them, their heads turned regretfully toward the young folks' laughter in the hall. Then they could hear the elevator open and shut and the gay voices sinking swiftly beneath the floor and they were left facing one another in a room suddenly quiet with disappointment. Each of them, Mary, Mrs. Garfield, and Portwood, missed the young roomers, but in his disappointment Portwood had said something about young folks being green and now Mary was challenging him.

"Green," she said, "shucks, you don't know nothing about green!"

"Just wait a minute now," Portwood said, pushing back from the table, "Who don't? Who you talking about?"

"I'm talking about you," Mary said. "Them chillun is gone off to the dance, so *I must* be talking 'bout you. And like I *shoulda* said, you don't even know green when you see it."

"Let me get on out of here," Portwood said, getting up. "Mrs. Garfield, she's just tuning up to lie. I can't understand why we live here with an ole lying woman like her anyway. And contentious with it too. Talking 'bout *I* don't know nothing 'bout green. Why, I been meeting green folks right at the dam' station for over twenty-five years. . . ."

"Sit down, man. Just sit on back down," said Mary, placing her hand upon the heavy cut-glass decanter. "You got nowhere in this whole wide world to go — probably cause you make so much noise with your mouth . . ."

Mrs. Garfield smiled with gentle amusement. She'd been through it all before. A retired cook whose husband was dead, she had roomed with Mary almost as long as Portwood and knew that just as this was his way of provoking Mary into telling a story, it was Mary's way of introducing the story she would tell. She watched Mary cut her eyes from Portwood's frowning face to look through the window to where, far beyond the roofs of Harlem, mist-shrouded buildings pierced the sky. It was raining.

"It's gon' be cold out there on the streets this winter," Mary said. "I guess you know all about that."

"Don't be signifying at me," Portwood said. "You must aim to *lie* me into the streets. Well, I ain't even thinking about moving."

"You'll move," Mary said. "You'll be glad to move. And you still won't know nothing 'bout green."

"Then you tell us, Miss Mary," Mrs. Garfield said. "Don't pay Portwood any mind."

Portwood sat down, shaking his head hopelessly. "Now she's bound to lie. Mrs. Garfield, you done *guaranteed* she go' lie. And just look at her," he said, his voice rising indignantly, "sitting there looking like a lady preacher or something!"

"Portwood, I done tole you 'bout your way of talking," Mary began, but suddenly the stern façade of her face collapsed and they were all laughing.

"Hush, y'all," Mary said, her eyes gleaming. "Hush!"

"Don't try to laugh out of it," Portwood said, "I maintain these youngsters nowadays is green. They black and trying to git to heaven in a Cadillac. They think their education proves that we old southern folks is fools who don't know nothing 'bout life or loving or nothing 'bout living in the world. They green, I tell you! How we done come this far and lived this long if we didn't learn nothing 'bout life? Answer me that!"

"Now, Portwood," Mrs. Garfield said gently, "They're not that bad, the world just looks different to their eyes."

"Don't tell me, I see 'em when they get off the trains. Long as I been a Red Cap I've seen thousands of 'em, and dam' nigh everyone of 'em is green. And just cause these here is rooming with you, Moms, don't make 'em no different. Here you done fixed this fine Thanksgiving dinner and they caint hardly finish it for rushing off somewhere. Too green to be polite. Don't even know there ain't no other ole fool woman like you renting rooms in Harlem who'll treat 'em like kinfolks. Don't tell me 'bout . . ."

"Shh," Mrs. Garfield said, as the sound of voices leaving the elevator came to them, "they might be coming back."

They listened. The voices grew gaily up the hall, then, blending with a remote peal of chimes, faded beyond a further wall. Mrs. Garfield sighed as they looked at one another guiltily.

"Shucks," Portwood said, "by now they just about beating the door down, trying to get into that dance. Like I was telling y'all . . ."

"Hush, Portwood!" Mary said. "What *green?*" She said, singing full-throatedly now, her voice suddenly folk-toned and deep with echoes of sermons and blue trombones, "Lawd, *I* was green. That's what I'm trying to tell you. Y'all hear me? *I, Me, Mary Raaaam-bo*, was green."

"You telling me?" Portwood laughed. "Is you telling *me?*" Nevertheless he leaned forward with Mrs. Garfield now, surrendering once more to Mary's once-upon-a-time antiphonal spell, waiting to respond to her stated theme: green.

"Here y'all," she said, beckoning for their glasses with one hand and lifting the decanter with the other. "Git some wine in y'all's stomachs so's it can warm y'all's old-time blood."

They drank ceremoniously with lowered eyes, waiting for Mary's old contralto to resume its flight, its tragic-comic ascendence.

"Sho, I was green," she continued. "Green as anybody what ever left the farm and come to town. Shucks, here you criticizing those youngsters for rushing to the dance 'cause they hope to win that auto—that ain't nothing, not to what I done. Cause like them chillun and everybody else, I was after money. And I was full grown, too. Times was hard. My husband had done died and I couldn't get nothing but part-time work and didn't nobody have enough to eat. My daughter Lucy and me couldn't even afford a ten cents movies so we could go forget about it. So Lawd, this evening we're sitting in the window watching the doings down in the streets. Y'all know how it gits round here in the summertime, after it has been hot all day and has cooled off a bit: Folks out strolling or hanging on the stoops and hollering out the windows, chillun yelling and ripping and romping and begging for pennies to buy that there shaved ice with the red sirup poured over it. Dogs barking—y'all know how it is round here in the summertime. All that talk and noise and Negroes laughing loud and juke boxes blaring and like-a-that. Well, it's 'bout that time on one of them kinda days, and one of them store-front churches is just beginning to jump. You can hear them clapping their hands and shouting and the tambourines is a-shaking and a-beating, and that ole levee camp trombone they has is going *Wah-wah, Wah-wah, Wah-wah-wah!* Y'all know, just like it really has something to do with the good Lawd's business—when all of a sudden two autos decides to see which is the toughest."

"A wreck?" Portwood said. "What the newspapers call a *collision?*"

"That's it," Mary said, sipping her wine, "one of the biggest smashups you ever seen. Here we is up in the window on the fourth floor and it's happening right down below us. Why, it's like two big bulls has done charged and run head-on. I tell you, Mrs. Garfield, it was something! Here they is," she said, shifting two knives upon the cloth, "one's coming thisa way, and the other's coming thata way, and when they gits right here, WHAM! They done come together and something flies out of there like a cannon ball. Then for a second it gets real quiet. It's like everybody done stopped to take a breath at the same time—all except those clapping hands and tambourines and that ole nasty-mouthed trombone (that fool was sounding like he done took over and started preaching the gospel by now). Then, Lawd," she said, rocking forward for emphasis, "*glass* is falling, *dust* is rising, *women* is screaming—Oh, such a commotion. Then all of a sudden all you can hear is Negroes' feet slapping the sidewalks . . ."

"Never mind them feet," Portwood said, "what was it that flew out of there?"

"I'm fixing to tell you now, fool. When the cars come together me and Lucy sees that thing bust outa there like a comet and fly off to one side somewhere. Lucy said, 'Mama, did you see what I seen?' 'Come on, chile,' I says, 'Let's us get ourselfs on down there!' And good people, that's when we started to move! Lawd, we flew down them stairs. I didn't even take time to pull off my apron or my house shoes. Just come a-jumping. Oh, it was a sight, I tell you. Everybody and his brother standing round trying to see if anybody was killed and measuring the skid marks and waiting for the ambulance to come — the man coulda died before that ambulance got there ——"

"Well, how about it, Moms, was anybody hurt?"

"Yes, they was, but I ain't your mama, an ole rusty Negro like you! Sho' they was hurt. One man was all cut up and bleeding and the other knocked cold as a big deep freeze. They thought he was dead.

"But me and Lucy don't waste no time with none of that. We gets busy looking for what we seen shoot out of them cars. I whispers, 'Chile, where did it hit?' And she points over near the curb. And sho 'nough, when I starts slow-dragging my leg along the gutter my foot hits against something heavy, and when I hears it clink together my heart almost flies out of my mouth . . ."

"My Lord, Miss Mary! What was it?" Mrs. Garfield said, her eyes intense. "You don't mean to tell me it was ——"

Mary gave her a flat look. "I'm goin' to tell you," she said, taking a taste of wine. "I give y'all my word I'm gon' tell you — I calls to Lucy, 'Gal, come over here a minute,' justa looking 'round to see if anybody'd seen me. And she come and I whispers to her, 'Now don't let on we found anything, just get on the other side of me and make like you trying to kick me on the foot. Go on, gal,' I says, 'Don't argue with me — And watch out for my bunion!' And Lawd, she kicks that bag and this time I'm sho, 'cause I hear that sweet metal-like sound. 'What you think it is?' I says and she leans close to me, eyes done got round as silver dollars, says, 'Mother' (always called me *mother* steada 'mama,' when she was excited or trying to be proper or something) says, 'Mother, that's money!' 'Shhh, fool,' I tole her, 'you don't have to tell *eve'y*body.'

" 'But, Mother, what are we going to do?'

" 'Just stand still a secon',' I says. 'Just quiet down. Don't move. Take it easy! Make out like you watching what they doing over yonder with those cars. Gimme time to figure this thing out . . .' "

She laughed. "Lawd, I was sweating by the gallon. Here I am standing in the street with my foot on a bag full of somebody's money! I don't know what to do. By now the police is all around us and I don't know when whichever one of them men who was hurt is gonna rise up and start yelling for it. I tell you, I musta lost five pounds in five minutes, trying to figure out the deal."

"Miss Mary, I wish I could have seen you," Mrs. Garfield said.

"Well, I'm glad you didn't; I was having trouble enough. Oh it was agonizing. Everytime somebody walks toward us I almost faint. And Lucy, she's turning this-away and that-away, real fast, like she's trying to invent a new dance. 'Do something, Mother,' she says. 'Please hurry up and do something!' Till finally I caint stand it and just flops down on the curbstone and kicks the bag kinda up under my skirts. Lawd, today!" she sang, then halted to inspect Portwood, who, with his head on his arms, laughed in silent glee. "What's the matter with you, fool?"

"Go on, tell the lie," Portwood said. "Don't mind poor me. You really had larceny in your heart that day."

"Well," Mary grinned, " 'bout this time old Miz Brazelton, a meddlesome ole lady who lived across the hall from me, she comes up talking 'bout, 'Why, Miss Mary, don't you know a woman of your standing in the community oughtn't to be sitting on the curb like some ole common nobody?' Like all Mary Rambo's got to do is worry 'bout what somebody might think about her—I looks and I knows the only way to git rid of the fool is to bawl her out. 'Look here, Miz Brazelton,' I says, 'this here's my own ole rusty tub I'm sitting on and long as I can haul it 'round without your help I guess I can put it down wherever I please . . .' "

"You a rough woman, Moms," Portwood said with deep resonance, his face a judicial frown. "Rough!"

"I done tole you 'bout calling me Moms!" Mary warned.

"Just tell the lie," Portwood said. "Then what happen?"

"I know that type," Mrs. Garfield said. "With them you do sometimes have to be radical."

"You know it too?" Mary said. "Radical sho is the word. You shoulda seen her face. I really didn't want to hurt that ole woman's feelings, but right then I had to git shed of the fool.

"Well, she leaves and I'm still sitting there fighting with myself over what I oughta do. Should I report what we'd found, or just take it on upstairs? Not that I meant to be dishonest, you know, but like everybody else in New York if something-for-nothing comes along, I wanted to be the one to git it. Besides, anybody fool enough to have that much money riding around with him in a car *deserves* to lose it."

"He sho dam' do," Portwood said. "He *dam*' sho do!"

"Well, all at once Lucy shakes me and here comes the ambulance, justa screaming.

" 'Mother, we better go,' Lucy says. And me I don't know *what* to do. By now the cops is pushing folks around and I knows soon as they see me they bound to find out what kinda egg this is I'm nesting on. Then all of a sudden it comes over me that I'm still wearing my apron! Lawd, I reaches down and touches that bag and my heart starts to going ninety miles a minute. It feels like a heapa money! And when I touches that thick cloth bag you can hear it clinking together. 'Lucy, chile,' I whispers, 'stand right in front of me while the ole lady rolls this heavy stuff up in her apron . . .' "

"Oh, Miss Mary," Mrs. Garfield said, shaking her head, "You'd given in to the devil."

"I'm in his arms, girl, in his hairy arms! And Lucy in on the deal. She's hurrying me up and I picks up that bag and no sooner'n I do, here comes a cop!"

"Oh my Jesus, Miss Mary!" cried Mrs. Garfield.

"Woman," said Mary, "you don't know; you have no *idea*. He's one of these tough-looking young cops, too. One of them that thinks he has to beat you up just to prove he's in command of things. Here he comes, swinging up to Lucy like a red sledge hammer, telling folks to move along—Ain't seen *me*, cause I'm still sitting down. And when he comes up to Lucy I starts to moaning like I'm sick: 'Please, mister officer,' I says, kinda hiding my face, 'we just fixin' to leave.' Well, suh, his head shoots round Lucy like a turkey gobbler's and he sees me. Says, 'What's the matter, madam, wuz you in this wreck?' —and in a real nice voice too. Then Lucy—Lawd, that Lucy was smart; up to that time I didn't know my chile could lie. But Lucy looks the cop dead in the eye and says, 'Officer, we be going in a minute. My mother here is kinda nauchus from looking at all that blood.' "

"Oh, Miss Mary, she didn't say that!"

"She sho did, and it worked! Why the cop bends down and tries to help me to my feet and I says, 'Thank you, officer, just let me rest here a second and I be all right.' Well, suh, he leaves us and goes on off. But by now I got the bag in my apron and gets up moaning and groaning and starts out across the street, kinda bent over like, you know, with Lucy helping me along. Lawd, that bag feels like a thousand pounds. And everytime I takes a step it gets heavier. And on top of that, looks like we never going to cross the street, cause everybody in the block is stopping us to ask what's wrong: 'You sick Miss Mary?'; 'Lucy, what done happen to your mother?'; 'Do she want a doctor?'; 'Po' thing, she done got herself over-excited'—and all likea that. Shucks! I'm overexcited, all right, that bag's 'bout to give me a nervous breakdown!

"When we finally make it up to the apartment, I'm so beat that I just flops into a chair and sits there panting. Don't even take the bag outa my apron, and Lucy, she's having a fit. 'Open it up, Mother, let's see what's in it,' she says. But I figures we better wait, cause after all, they might miss the money and come searching for it. You see, after I done worked so hard gitting it up there, I had decided to keep it sho 'nough . . ."

"You had given in to the devil," Mrs. Garfield said.

"Who?" said Mary, reaching for the wine, "I'm way, *way* past the giving-in stage."

"This world is surely a trial," Mrs. Garfield mused. "It truly is."

"And you can say that again," said Mary, "cause it's the agonizing truth."

"What did you do then, Miss Mary?"

"Pass me your glass, Portwood," Mary said, reaching for the decanter.

"Never mind the wine," said Portwood, covering his glass with his hand. "Get back to what *happened!*"

"Well, we goes to the bathroom—wait, don't say it!" she warned, giving Portwood a frown. "We goes to the bathroom and I gits up on a chair and drops that bag dead into the flush box."

"Now Miss Mary, really!"

"Girl, yes! I knowed wouldn't nobody think to look for it up there. It coulda been hid up in heaven somewhere. Sho! I dropped it in there, then I sent Lucy on back downstairs to see if anybody'd missed it. She musta hung 'round there for over an hour. Police and the newspaper people come and made pictures and asked a heapa questions and everything, but nothing 'bout the bag. Even after the wreckers come and dragged that pile of brand new junk away—still nothing 'bout the bag."

"Everything going in y'all's favor," Portwood said.

"Uhhuh, everything going our way."

"Y'all had it made, Moms," Portwood said, "Why you never tole this lie before?"

"The devil is truly powerful," Mrs. Garfield said, "Almost as powerful as the Lord. Even so, it's strange nobody missed that much money!"

"Now that's what me and Lucy thought . . ."

Portwood struck the table, "What I want to know is how much money was in the bag?"

"I'm coming to that in a second," Mary said.

"Yeah, but why you taking so long?"

"Who's telling this lie, Portwood, me or you?" said Mary.

"You was 'til you got off the track."

"Don't forget your manners, Portwood," Mrs. Garfield said.

"I'm not, but looks like to me y'all think money ought to be as hard to get in a lie somebody's telling as it is to get carrying folks' bags."

"Or as 'tis to git you to hush your mouth," said Mary. "Anyway, we didn't count it right then. We was scaird. I knowed I was doing wrong, holding on to something wasn't really mine. But that wasn't stopping me."

"Y'all was playing a little finders-keepers," Portwood said, resting back.

"Yeah, and concentrating on the keeping part."

"But why didn't you just *look* at the money, Miss Mary?"

"Cause we mighta been tempted to spend some of it, girl."

"Yeah, and y'all mighta give yourself away," Portwood said.

"Ain't it the truth! And that bag was powerful enough as it was. It was really working on us. Me and Lucy just sitting 'round like two ole hens on a nest, trying to guess how much is in it. Then we tries to figure whether it was dollars or fifty-centies. Finally we decides that it caint be less'n five or ten dollar gold pieces to weigh so much."

"But how on earth could you resist looking at it?" Mrs. Garfield said.

"Scaird, chile; scaird. We was like a couple kids who somebody's done give a present and tole 'em it would disappear if they opened it before Christmas. And know something else, neither one of us ever had to go to the bathroom so much as when us had that bag up there in that flush box. I got to flushing it just to hear it give out that fine clinking sound."

Portwood groaned. "I knew you was gon' lie," he said. "I *knowed* it."

"Hush, man, hush!" Mary laughed. "I know our neighbors musta got sick and tired of hearing us flush that thing. But I tell you, everytime I pulled the chain it was like ringing up money in the cash register! I tell you, it was disintegrating! Whew! I'd go in there and stay a while and come out. Next thing I know there'd be Lucy going in. Then we got shamed and started slipping past one another. She'd try to keep hid from me, and me from her. I tell you, that stuff was working on us like a dose of salts! Why, after a few days I got so I couldn't work, just sat 'round thinking 'bout that doggone bag. And naturally, I done most of my thinking up there on the throne."

"Didn't I tell you she was tuning up to lie," Portwood laughed. "If she don't stop I'm dead gon' call the police."

"This here's the agonizing truth I'm telling y'all," said Mary.

"I wouldn't have been able to stand it, Miss Mary. I would have had to get it over with."

"They shoulda been looking for it by now," Portwood said, "all that money."

"That's what us thought," said Mary. "And we got to figuring why they didn't. First we figgers maybe it was because the man who was hurt so bad had died. But then we seen in the papers that he got well . . ."

"Maybe they was gangsters," Portwood said.

"Yeah, we thought of that too; gangsters or bootleggers."

"Yeah, yeah, either one of them coulda been carrying all that money—or gamblers even."

"Sho they could. Me and Lucy figgered that maybe they thought the cops had took the money or that they was trying to find it theyselves on the q.t., y'know."

"Miss Mary, you were either very brave or very reckless."

"Neither one, girl," Mary said, "just broke and hongry. And don't talk about brave, shucks, we was scaird to answer the doorbell at night. Let me tell you, we was doing some tall figuring. Finally I got so I couldn't eat and Lucy couldn't sleep. We was evil as a coupla lady bears at cubbing time."

"You just couldn't stand all that prosperity, huh, Moms?"

"It was a burden, all right. And everytime we pulled the chain it got a few dollars more so."

Mrs. Garfield smiled. "Mr. Garfield often said that the possession of great wealth brought with it the slings and arrows of outrageous responsibility."

"Mrs. Garfield," Mary mused, "you know you had you a right smart man in him? You really did. And looks like when you got stuff saved up like that you got the responsibility of keeping some of it circulating. Even without looking at it we got to figuring how to spend it. Lucy, she wants to go into business. Why she *almost* persuaded me to see about buying a building and opening a restaurant! And as if *that* wasn't enough trouble to git into, she decides she's goin' take the third floor and open her a beauty shop. Oh, we had it all planned!" She shook her head.

"And y'all still ain't looked at it," Portwood said.

"Still ain't seen a thing."

"Dam!"

"You had marvelous self-control," Mrs. Garfield said.

"Yeah, I did," Mary said, "until that day Lucy went to the dentist. Seems I just couldn't hold out no longer. Seems like I got to thinking 'bout that bag and couldn't stop. I looked at the newspaper and all those ads. Reminded me of things I wanted to buy; looked out the window and saw autos; I tried to read the Bible and as luck would have it I opened it to where it says something 'bout 'Store ye up riches in heaven,' or 'Cast your bread upon the waters.' It really had me on a merry-go-round. I just had to take a peep! So I went and pulled down all the shades and started the water running in the tub like I was taking me a bath—turned on every faucet in the house—then I climbed up there with a pair of scissors and reached in and raised that bag up and just looked at it awhile.

"It had done got *cooold*! It come up *cooold*, with the water dripping off it like some old bucket been deep down in a well. Done turned green with canker, y'all!! I just couldn't resist it no longer. I really couldn't, I took them scissors and snipped me a piece outa that bag and took me a good, *looong* look. And let me tell you, dear people, after I looked I was so excited I had to get down from there and put myself to bed. My nerves just couldn't take it . . ."

"It surely must have been an experience, Miss Mary."

"Woman, you don't know. You really don't know. You hear me? *I had to go to bed!*"

"Heck, with that much money you could afford to go to bed," said Portwood.

"Wait, le'me tell you. I'm laying up there moaning and groaning when here come Lucy and she's in one of her talking moods. Soon as I seen her I knowed pretty soon she was going to want to talk 'bout that bag and I truly dreaded telling her that I'd done looked into it without her. I says, 'Baby, I don't feel so good. You talk to me later' . . . But y'all think that stopped her? Shucks, all she does is to go get me a bottle of cold beer she done brought me and start to running her mouth again. And, just like I knowed she was gon' do, she finally got round to talking 'bout that bag. What ought we to buy *first,* she wants to know. Lawd, that pore chile, whenever she got her mind set on a thing! Well suh, I took me a big swoller of beer and just lay there like I was thinking awhile."

"You were really good companions," Mrs. Garfield said. "There is nothing like young people to make life rich and promising. Especially if they're your own children. If only Mr. Garfield and I . . ."

"Mrs. Garfield, let her finish this lie," Portwood said, "*then* we can talk about you and Mr. Garfield."

"Oh, of course," Mrs. Garfield said, "I'm sorry, Miss Mary, you know I didn't really mean to interrupt."

"Pay that pore fool no min'," Mary said. "I wish I had Lucy with me right this minit!"

"Is this lie about money or chillun?" Portwood said. "Y'all here'bout to go serious. I want to know what you tole Lucy *then.* What did y'all start out to buy?"

"If you hadn't started monkeying with Mrs. Garfield you'da learned by now," Mary said. "Well, after I lay there and thought awhile I tole her, 'Well, baby, if you want to know the truth 'bout what I think, *I* think we oughta buy us an auto.'

"Well suh, you coulda knocked her over with a feather. 'A car!' she says, 'why Mother, I didn't know you was interested in a car. We don't want to be like these ole ignorant Negroes who buy cars and don't have anything to go with it and no place to keep it,' she says. Says, 'I'm certainly surprised at you, Mother. I never would've dreamed you wanted a *car,* not the very first thing.'

"Oh, she was running off a mile a minute. And looking at me like she done caught me kissing the preacher or the iceman or somebody! 'We want to be practical,' she says. 'We don't want to throw our money away . . .'

"Well, it almost killed me. 'Lucy, honey,' I says, 'that's just what your mama's trying to do, be practical. That's why I say let's git us an auto.'

" 'But, Mama,' she says, 'a car isn't practical at all.'

" 'Oh yes it is,' I says, 'Cause how else is we gon' use two sets of auto chains?'———

"And do y'all know," said Mary, sitting up suddenly and balancing the tips of her fingers on her knees, her face a mask of incredulity, "I had to hop outa bed and catch that chile before she swayed dead away in a faint!"

"Yeah," Portwood laughed, falling back in his chair, "and you better hop up from there and catch me."

Mrs. Garfield's voice rose up girlishly, "Oh Miss Mary," she laughed, "you're just fooling."

Mary's bosom heaved, "I wish I was, girl," she said, "I sho wish I was."

"How 'bout that? Tire chains," Portwood said. "All that larceny for some dam' tire chain!"

"Fool," said Mary, "didn't I tell you you didn't know nothing 'bout green? There *I* was thinking I done found me a bird nest on the ground. C'mon now," she said chuckling at the gullibility of all mankind, "let's us finish the wine."

Portwood winked at Mrs. Garfield. "Hey, Moms, tell us something . . ."

"I ain't go' tell you again that I ain't yo' mama," said Mary.

"I just want you to tell us one last thing . . ."

Mary looked at him warily, "What is it? I got no more time for your foolishness now, I got to git up from here and fix for them chillun."

"Never mind them youngsters," said Portwood, "just tell us if you ever dreamed lucky?"

Mary grinned, "Ain't I just done tole you?" she said. "Sho I did, but I woke up cold in hand. Just the same though," she added thoughtfully, "I still hope them youngsters win that there auto."

"Yes," Mrs. Garfield said. "And wouldn't it be a comfort, Miss Mary? Just to know that they *can* win one, I mean . . . ?"

Mary said that it certainly would be.

Suggestions for Discussion

1. What mood does the aftermath of a Thanksgiving dinner evoke? How is the setting appropriate to the story?
2. How are the tensions of expectation aroused in the first few pages? What part does each of the three characters play in the telling of the story? What is Ellison suggesting by the use of terms such as "antiphonal," "contralto," and "tragic-comic"?
3. Mary's stated theme of "green" operates on a number of levels. What are they? What variations on "green" are acknowledged by Portwood and Mrs. Garfield?
4. How does Mary's manner of storytelling indicate that she is a master of the art?
5. How do the characters' religious attitudes and their use of Biblical quotations provide an ironic commentary on their actions and thought?
6. What is the answer to the question in the title of the story? Is Ellison a pessimist, a realist, a moralist, or a humorist?

Suggestions for Writing and Comparison

1. Discuss the conflicts between reality and appearance, and the material and spiritual, as treated in "Did You Ever Dream Lucky?" Are these conflicts related somehow to the American dream?
2. In a brief essay show how "green" and "larceny" are related to the main theme in Ellison's story.

Langston Hughes

Langston Hughes was born in Joplin, Missouri, in 1902. His grandmother, Mary Samson Langston, with whom he lived for several years, had been the last surviving widow of John Brown's raid at Harper's Ferry: her first husband was one of the five Blacks to die in that raid.

After high-school graduation Hughes lived in Mexico for a year and then traveled throughout Africa and Europe. In 1925 he received the poetry award from *Opportunity* magazine. Returning to America, he attended Lincoln University in Pennsylvania, graduating in 1929. Hughes won a Witter Bynner poetry contest in 1926, a Harmon Gold Award in 1931, and later received Guggenheim and Rosenwald fellowships.

In the mid-1920's a literary renaissance occurred in Harlem, which brought such poets as James Weldon Johnson (pp. 114–16), Claude McKay (pp. 119–20), and Countee Cullen (pp. 117–18) to national attention. Langston Hughes became the foremost writer of this Harlem Renaissance, often celebrating the urban working-class Black as in his "Alberta K." series of poems (pp. 121–23). He retained his literary fame over a period of more than forty years, until his death in 1967. He is the author of several volumes of poetry such as *The Weary Blues* (1926), *Fields of Wonder* (1947), *Montage of a Dream Deferred* (1951), and *The Panther and the Lash* (1967); an autobiography, *The Big Sea* (1940); a number of story collections such as *The Ways of White Folks* (1934); and the famous series of "Simple" sketches.

Langston Hughes, who outlived his contemporary, Countee Cullen, wrote more distinctly original poems and more memorable lines than he. Whereas Cullen was a skilled sonneteer in the style of Keats, Hughes was especially interested in experimental forms. His poems frequently indicate his attention to jazz rhythms and the distinctive qualities of Black speech.

The following poem, "Let America Be America Again," written in a free-verse style somewhat reminiscent of that of Carl Sandburg, is less typical in form than "My People" (p. 121) and the "Alberta K." poems; but it is representative of Langston Hughes' work in content, revealing his sympathy with those who felt "America never was America to me" as well as his attempt to be for future generations as Gwendolyn Brooks described him, "helmsman, hatchet, headlight" (see p. 157).

Let America Be America Again

Let America be America again.
Let it be the dream it used to be.
Let it be the pioneer on the plain
Seeking a home where he himself is free.

5 (America never was America to me.)

Let America be the dream the dreamers dreamed—
Let it be that great strong land of love
Where never kings connive nor tyrants scheme
That any man be crushed by one above.

10 (It never was America to me.)

O, let my land be a land where Liberty
Is crowned with no false patriotic wreath,
But opportunity is real, and life is free,
Equality is in the air we breathe.

15 (There's never been equality for me,
Nor freedom in this "homeland of the free.")

Say who are you that mumbles in the dark?
And who are you that draws your veil across the stars?

I am the poor white, fooled and pushed apart,
20 I am the red man driven from the land.
I am the refugee clutching the hope I seek—
But finding only the same old stupid plan
Of dog eat dog, of mighty crush the weak.
I am the Negro, "problem" to you all.
25 I am the people, humble, hungry, mean—
Hungry yet today despite the dream.
Beaten yet today—O, Pioneers!
I am the man who never got ahead,
The poorest worker bartered through the years.

30 Yet I'm the one who dreamt our basic dream
In that Old World while still a serf of kings,
Who dreamt a dream so strong, so brave, so true,
That even yet its mighty daring sings
In every brick and stone, in every furrow turned
35 That's made America the land it has become.
O, I'm the man who sailed those early seas
In search of what I meant to be my home—
For I'm the one who left dark Ireland's shore,
And Poland's plain, and England's grassy lea,
40 And torn from Black Africa's strand I came
To build a "homeland of the free."

The free?
Who said the free? Not me?
Surely not me? The millions on relief today?
45 The millions who have nothing for our pay
For all the dreams we've dreamed
And all the songs we've sung
And all the hopes we've held
And all the flags we've hung,
50 The millions who have nothing for our pay—
Except the dream we keep alive today.

O, let America be America again—
The land that never has been yet—
And yet must be—the land where *every* man is free.
55 The land that's mine—the poor man's, Indian's, Negro's, ME—
Who made America,
Whose sweat and blood, whose faith and pain,
Whose hand at the foundry, whose plow in the rain,
Must bring back our mighty dream again.

60   O, yes,
        I say it plain,
        America never was America to me,
        And yet I swear this oath—
        America will be!

Suggestions for Discussion

1. What qualities of this poem can best be appreciated from hearing it read aloud? What is the cumulative effect of repetitions such as "Let America be . . ." and "I am the one . . ."?

2. What internal evidence confirms the 1930's as the date of composition of this poem? How can historical situations influence writers?

3. Examine the stanza which begins "Yet I'm the one who dreamt our basic dream" for content and form. Show how the following stanza "answers" in ideas and form. Who is the speaker in each stanza?
4. Discuss Hughes' interpretation of the American dream. Does he emphasize one set of rights over another? How does his interpretation relate to the choice of the phrase "life, liberty, and *the pursuit of happiness*" over the phrase "life, liberty, and *property*" by the framers of the Constitution?

Suggestions for Writing and Comparison

1. Read Carl Sandburg's "The People, Yes," especially section 51, and Walt Whitman's "Song of Myself." Compare and contrast Hughes', Sandburg's, and Whitman's visions of America.
2. Compose a free-verse list based on your conception of the American dream. What have you added that Hughes omitted?

Paul Laurence Dunbar

Paul Laurence Dunbar, the first nationally known Black poet, born in 1872 in Dayton, Ohio, was the son of former slaves. His father had escaped to the North by way of the "underground railroad." Unable to attend college, Dunbar worked as an elevator operator, but he continued writing poetry as he had been doing since grammar school. His first book, *Oak and Ivy* (1893), was privately printed. His second volume, *Majors and Minors* (1895), attracted the attention of William Dean Howells of the *Atlantic Monthly*, under whose sponsorship *Lyrics of Lowly Life* (1896) was published. This volume of dialect poems won a national reputation for Dunbar. In spite of failing health, he produced many volumes in quick succession: *Lyrics of the Hearthside* (1899), *Lyrics of Love and Laughter* (1903), *Lyrics of Sunshine and Shadow* (1905), four collections of short stories, and four novels. He died at the age of thirty-four, having turned from the writing of dialect verse in poems such as "At Candle-Lightin' Time" to formal English lyrics.

Dunbar's great misfortune is that he was lionized for sentimental dialect poems which strengthened the prevailing turn-of-the-century stereotypes of Blacks as childlike, ignorant, and basic. His formal poems, which were generally more honest and often directly destructive of the stereotype, were neglected. "We Wear the Mask" is representative of the latter, and provides its own ironic comment on "At Candle-Lightin' Time."

At Candle-Lightin' Time

When I come in f'om de co'n-fiel' aftah wo'kin' ha'd all day,
It's amazin' nice to fin' my suppah all erpon de way;
An' it's nice to smell de coffee bubblin' ovah in de pot,
An' it's fine to see de meat a-sizzlin' teasin'-lak an' hot.

5 But when suppah-time is ovah, an' de t'ings is cleahed away;
Den de happy hours dat foller are de sweetes' of de day.
When my co'ncob pipe is sta'ted, an' de smoke is drawin' prime,
My ole 'ooman says, "I reckon, Ike, it's candle-lightin' time."

Den de chillun snuggle up to me, an' all commence to call,
10 "Oh, say, daddy, now it's time to mek de shadders on de wall."
So I puts my han's togethah — evah daddy knows de way, —
An' de chillun snuggle closer roun' ez I begin to say: —

"Fus' thing, hyeah come Mistah Rabbit; don' you see him wo'k his eahs?
Huh, uh! dis mus' be a donkey, — look, how innercent he 'pears!
15 Dah's de ole black swan a'swimmin' — ain't she got a' awful neck?
Who's dis feller dat's a-còmin'? Why, dat's ole dog Tray, I 'spec'!"

Dat's de way I run on, tryin' fu' to please 'em all I can;
Den I hollahs, "Now be keerful—dis hyeah las's de buga-man!"
An' dey runs an' hides dey faces; dey ain't skeered—dey's lettin' on:
20 But de play ain't raaly ovah twell dat buga-man is gone.

So I jes' teks up my banjo, an' I plays a little chune,
An' you see dem haids come peepin' out to listen mighty soon.
Den my wife says, "Sich a pappy fu' to give you sich a fright!
Jes' you go to baid, an' leave him: say yo' prayers an' say good-night."

We Wear the Mask

We wear the mask that grins and lies,
It hides our cheeks and shades our eyes,—
This debt we pay to human guile;
With torn and bleeding hearts we smile,
5 And mouth with myriad subtleties.

Why should the world be over-wise,
In counting all our tears and sighs?
Nay, let them only see us, while
      We wear the mask.

10 We smile, but, O great Christ, our cries
To thee from tortured souls arise.
We sing, but oh the clay is vile
Beneath our feet, and long the mile;
But let the world dream otherwise,
15   We wear the mask.

Suggestions for Discussion

1. In "We Wear the Mask" for whom does the poet speak when he uses the collective "we"? What is the nature of "the mask"?

2. Who is the speaker in "At Candle-Lightin' Time"? For what kind of audience did Dunbar write this poem? What are the turn-of-the-century stereotypes that this poem reinforces? Does Dunbar appear to strive for verisimilitude in his language?

3. In what way could the picture presented in "At Candle-Lightin' Time" be said to be a "wearing of the mask"? What kind of mask did the literary world seem to be asking Dunbar—as a Black poet in 1900—to wear?

Suggestions for Writing and Comparison

1. Compare the rationale for "wearing the mask" as Dunbar sees it with the grandfather's last words to the protagonist in Ellison's novel *Invisible Man*. Do "yes 'em to death" and "let the world dream otherwise" exhibit similar attitudes towards the Black man's "pose" for white society?
2. See the poems of Edgar Guest, James Whitcomb Riley, or Eugene Field. What qualities does "At Candle-Lightin' Time" share with the work of any of these poets?

James Weldon Johnson

James Weldon Johnson, who at the time of his death in 1938 was regarded as one of the most important Black American writers of his generation, was born in Jacksonville, Florida, in 1871. He had a varied career as a school teacher, principal, lawyer, diplomat, Broadway lyricist, executive secretary of the NAACP, Professor of Creative Literature at Fisk University, and noted poet. He wrote the lyrics for the song "Lift Every Voice and Sing," which has been called the Black national anthem. Johnson also translated into English the libretto of *Goyescas,* a Spanish grand opera which was performed by the Metropolitan Opera Company in 1915. He produced several volumes of poetry, including *"Fifty Years" and Other Poems* (1917), *God's Trombones* (1927), and *St. Peter Relates an Incident* (1930). His autobiography, *Along This Way,* was published in 1933, five years before his death. In 1912 he wrote the fictional *Autobiography of an Ex-Colored Man,* which was concerned particularly with race relations in the early decades of the twentieth century.

A contemporary of Paul Laurence Dunbar (pp. 111–12), James Weldon Johnson outlived him by more than thirty years. While Dunbar used Black dialect to depict "plantation scenes," Johnson frequently used the form of the Black sermon in poems such as those in *St. Peter Relates an Incident,* as well as in the more famous "The Creation." Johnson objected to the tradition of "blackface dialect" as untrue caricature and as "limited to two stops—pathos and humor." The following poem, "O Black and Unknown Bards," is a formal ode which deals with racial subject matter. Johnson's appreciation of the spirituals that were first composed by talented slaves is evident in such lines as "How like a mighty trumpet-call they stir the blood."

O Black and Unknown Bards

O black and unknown bards of long ago,
How came your lips to touch the sacred fire?
How, in your darkness, did you come to know
The power and beauty of the minstrel's lyre?

5 Who first from midst his bonds lifted his eyes?
  Who first from out the still watch, lone and long,
  Feeling the ancient faith of prophets rise
  Within his dark-kept soul, burst into song?

  Heart of what slave poured out such melody
10 As "Steal Away to Jesus"? On its strains
  His spirit must have nightly floated free,
  Though still about his hands he felt his chains.
  Who heard great "Jordan roll"? Whose starward eye
  Saw chariot "swing low"? And who was he
15 That breathed that comforting, melodic sigh,
  "Nobody Knows De Trouble I See"?

  What merely living clod, what captive thing,
  Could up toward God through all its darkness grope,
  And find within its deadened heart to sing
20 These songs of sorrow, love, and faith, and hope?
  How did it catch that subtle undertone,
  That note in music heard not with the ears?
  How sound the elusive reed so seldom blown,
  Which stirs the soul or melts the heart to tears?

25 Not that great German master in his dream
  Of harmonies that thundered amongst the stars
  At the creation, ever heard a theme
  Nobler than "Go Down, Moses." Mark its bars,
  How like a mighty trumpet-call they stir
30 The blood. Such are the notes that men have sung
  Going to valorous deeds; such tones there were
  That helped make history when Time was young.

  There is a wide, wide wonder in it all,
  That from degraded rest and servile toil
35 The fiery spirit of the seer should call
  These simple children of the sun and soil.
  O black slave singers, gone, forgot, unfamed,
  You—you alone, of all the long, long line
  Of those who've sung untaught, unknown, unnamed,
40 Have stretched out upward, seeking the divine.

  You sang not deeds of heroes or of kings;
  No chant of bloody war, no exulting paean
  Of arms-won triumphs; but your humble strings
  You touched in chord with music empyrean.
45 You sang far better than you knew; the songs
  That for your listeners' hungry hearts sufficed
  Still live—but more than this to you belongs:
  You sang a race from wood and stone to Christ.

Suggestions for Discussion

1. What is the significance of "the sacred fire" (see line 2)? What is the origin of the word "minstrel"? How is a minstrel with a lyre different from the American minstrel of the nineteenth century?
2. To what is the poet referring when he says "that subtle undertone/That note in music heard not with the ears" (see stanza three)? Is he able to capture that quality in this poem?
3. What lines in particular from "Go Down, Moses" sound "a mighty trumpet-call" (see stanza four)? What "valorous deeds" does the song call for? Why was Harriet Tubman called "the Moses of her people"?
4. In the final stanza Johnson says of the black and unknown bards, "You sang far better than you knew." What two reasons does he give for this statement? Is the spiritual a unique contribution to music and literature?
5. What elements of the ode does "O Black and Unknown Bards" contain? How do the rhyme scheme and meter contribute to the poem as a whole?

Suggestions for Writing and Comparison

1. Discuss the concepts of form and content in art in relation to Black American spirituals. Does their utilitarian value of sustaining people during suffering add or detract from their intrinsic worth? Do the spirituals fulfill Horace's requisite that art must be both *dulce et utile*, sweet (or beautiful) and useful?
2. Describe an artistic contribution made by someone untaught who "sang far better than he knew" (for instance, the French painter Rousseau, the poet Robert Burns, or the builder of the Watts towers, Simon Rodia, all of whom had little education).

Countee Cullen

Countee Cullen, born in 1903, was educated in the public schools of New York City. He received recognition for his poetry while still in high school. As an undergraduate at New York University he won the Witter Bynner Poetry Award for American students. In 1925, when he was twenty-two years old, he published his first volume of poetry, *Color*, which was very well received by the critics and won him the Harmon Gold Award for literature. Two years later two more of his books were published, *Copper Sun* and *The Ballad of the Brown Girl*. Between the publication of his first book and his second and third books he also received a master's degree from Harvard University. In 1929 he went to France on a Guggenheim Fellowship and there he wrote a fourth book, *The Black Christ*. This was followed by a novel, *One Way to Heaven* (1932), an anthology of Black American poetry, *Caroling Dusk* (1927), a play, and several other volumes of verse, including *The Medea and Other Poems* (1938). He was a prolific writer until his death in 1946.

With few exceptions, Cullen limited himself to the English sonnet and traditional ballad forms. His contribution to the Harlem Renaissance was in the romantic attitude he took to a distant Africa of the past:

> One three centuries removed
> From the scenes his fathers loved,
> Spicy grove, cinnamon tree,
> What is Africa to me?
>
> *—from "Heritage"*

"Yet Do I Marvel" shows Cullen's ease in handling the sonnet, and like "Heritage," and many other of his poems, it also demonstrates his particular concern with Blackness. "Incident," despite its surface simplicity, is perhaps the most potent statement in American poetry on the cruelty of prejudice.

Yet Do I Marvel

I doubt not God is good, well-meaning, kind,
And did He stoop to quibble could tell why
The little buried mole continues blind,
Why flesh that mirrors Him must some day die,
5 Make plain the reason tortured Tantalus
Is baited by the fickle fruit, declare
If merely brute caprice dooms Sisyphus
To struggle up a never-ending stair.
Inscrutable His ways are, and immune

10 To catechism by a mind too strewn
   With petty cares to slightly understand
   What awful brain compels His awful hand.
   Yet do I marvel at this curious thing:
   To make a poet black, and bid him sing!

Incident

Once riding in old Baltimore
Heart-filled, head-filled with glee,
I saw a Baltimorean
Keep looking straight at me.

5 Now I was eight and very small,
And he was no whit bigger,
And so I smiled, but he poked out
His tongue, and called me, "Nigger."

I saw the whole of Baltimore
10 From May until December;
Of all the things that happened there
That's all that I remember.

Suggestions for Discussion

1. Is "Yet Do I Marvel" a Petrarchan or a Shakespearean sonnet? Note the thought pattern as well as the rhyme scheme.
2. What attributes of God are listed in this poem? How does the reference to the poet's situation relate to God?
3. What is the tone of the conclusion of the poem? Is the reader prepared for the conclusion by suggestions earlier in the poem or does it have a shock effect?
4. What effect do the form and language of "Incident" have on the message of the poem?
5. What is the meaning of the title "Incident"? At what point in the poem do we understand its meaning?

Suggestions for Writing and Comparison

1. Read William Blake's poems "The Tiger" and "The Lamb." Compare Blake's treatment of paradox, such as the coexistence of ferocity and gentleness, with Cullen's in "Yet Do I Marvel."
2. Write a brief essay in which you describe an incident which you experienced as a child. Use simple language, and match the form with the content.

Claude McKay

Claude McKay was born in 1891 in Jamaica and emigrated to the United States in 1912. He attended Tuskegee Institute and Kansas State University. Collections of his poetry include *Songs of Jamaica* (1912), *Harlem Shadows* (1922), and *Selected Poems* (1953). *A Long Way from Home* (1937) is his autobiography. McKay's most important novels are *Home to Harlem* (1928), *Banjo* (1929), and *Banana Bottom* (1935).

Claude McKay was a major figure in the Harlem Renaissance. *Home to Harlem* was exceptionally popular as it presented Harlem's "exotic" side—cabarets, the streets, and jazz—which most interested white readers.

Ironically, the passage of time has not dealt well with Claude McKay. Originally his poems were very popular. "If We Must Die" was written after the race riots of 1919. It was still well known in the 1940's, and was quoted during World War II by Winston Churchill to encourage Englishmen standing up to the Nazis. However, by 1973 it must have been forgotten by many, as, following the Attica prison uprising, *Time* magazine quoted it as a poem written by an unnamed Attica inmate. The error was corrected later by a letter to the editor from Gwendolyn Brooks, but the lesson for literary history remains.

If We Must Die

If we must die, let it not be like hogs
Hunted and penned in an inglorious spot,
While round us bark the mad and hungry dogs,
Making their mock at our accursed lot.
5 If we must die, O let us nobly die,
So that our precious blood may not be shed
In vain; then even the monsters we defy
Shall be constrained to honor us though dead!
O kinsmen! we must meet the common foe!
10 Though far outnumbered let us show us brave,
And for their thousand blows deal one deathblow!
What though before us lies the open grave?
Like men we'll face the murderous, cowardly pack,
Pressed to the wall, dying, but fighting back!

The White House

Your door is shut against my tightened face,
And I am sharp as steel with discontent;
But I possess the courage and the grace

To bear my anger proudly and unbent.
5 The pavement slabs burn loose beneath my feet,
A chafing savage, down the decent street;
And passion rends my vitals as I pass,
Where boldly shines your shuttered door of glass,
Oh, I must search for wisdom every hour,
10 Deep in my wrathful bosom sore and raw,
And find in it the superhuman power
To hold me to the letter of your law!
Oh, I must keep my heart inviolate
Against the potent poison of your hate.

Suggestions for Discussion

1. Discuss the effectiveness of the traditional Shakespearean sonnet form, used in "If We Must Die," as a vehicle for social protest. (See also William Wordsworth's sonnet "To Toussaint L'Ouverture.") Does the rhymed couplet increase the effectiveness of the argument in the final lines?
2. Examine the use of animal imagery in "If We Must Die." To what purpose does McKay employ such imagery?
3. McKay uses a phrase such as "decent street" in "The White House" to convey a tone of bitter irony. What other phrases in the poem contribute to that tone?
4. What does the title of the poem mean? Is the title purposefully ambiguous?

Suggestion for Writing and Comparison

1. Read Claude McKay's *Selected Poems* (1953). Compare the militancy in McKay's poems of the 1920's and 1930's with that of contemporary Black militant poetry of the 1970's. See, for example, Don Lee's *Don't Cry, Scream* (1969).

Langston Hughes

(See pp. 107–8 for Hughes' "Let America Be America Again"
and a biographical sketch of the author.)

My People

The night is beautiful,
So the faces of my people.

The stars are beautiful,
So the eyes of my people.

5 Beautiful, also, is the sun.
Beautiful, also, are the souls of my people.

Madam's Past History

My name is Johnson—
Madam Alberta K.
The Madam stands for business.
I'm smart that way.

5 I had a
HAIR-DRESSING PARLOR
Before
The depression put
The prices lower.

10 Then I had a
BARBECUE STAND
Till I got mixed up
With a no-good man.

Cause I had a insurance
15 The WPA
Said, We can't use you
Wealthy that way.

I said,
DON'T WORRY 'BOUT ME!
20 Just like the song,
Take care of yourself—
And I'll get along.

I do cooking,
Day's work, too!
25 Alberta K. Johnson
Madam to you.

Madam and Her Madam

I worked for a woman,
She wasn't mean—
But she had a twelve-room
House to clean.

5 Had to get breakfast,
Dinner, and supper, too—
Then take care of her children
When I got through.

Wash, iron, and scrub,
10 Walk the dog around—
It was too much,
Nearly broke me down.

I said, Madam,
Can it be
15 You trying to make a
Pack-horse out of me?

She opened her mouth.
She cried, Oh, no!
You know, Alberta,
20 I love you so!

I said, Madam,
That may be true—
But I'll be dogged
If I love you!

Suggestions for Discussion

1. Is the imagery in "My People" more nearly in the form of metaphor or simile? What qualities do these "comparisons" have in common with the following poem by Ezra Pound?

> In a Station of the Metro
> The apparition of these faces in the crowd;
> Petals on a wet, black bough.

2. What is the relationship between the images of night, stars, and sun in "My People"? What do the images suggest about the people who share their qualities? How is this brief poem more than "the sum of its parts"?

3. How does the poet avoid the merely picturesque or caricature in "My People"? In what way are his images romantic?

4. What is Alberta K.'s stance or attitude toward the world in "Madam's Past History" and "Madam and Her Madam"? How

has she been treated by individuals and social forces, and what has her response been?

5. How does Hughes reveal the character of the two women in the last two stanzas of "Madam and Her Madam"? How would you characterize their respective personalities?

6. What is the tone of both Alberta K. poems? Describe the beat, meter, and diction. Are there any elements in the poems which suggest particularly ethnic qualities?

Suggestions for Writing and Comparison

1. Compare Langston Hughes' portrait poems about Alberta K. with any sociological portrait of people "on welfare" (see, for example, *The Negro American,* edited by Talcott Parsons and Kenneth B. Clark, or *Minorities in a Changing World,* edited by Milton L. Barrow). What insights does Hughes present that are often garbled or overlooked by scientific surveys? In what sense can Madam's outspoken statements be said to be subtle or sophisticated comments?

2. Read some of Langston Hughes' "Simple" sketches for prose portraits and comments on Harlem (see *Simple's Uncle Sam* and *The Best of Simple* for the most recent collections).

Imamu Amira Baraka (LeRoi Jones)

LeRoi Jones was born in Newark, New Jersey, in 1934 and attended Howard University, from which he graduated at the age of nineteen, and Columbia University. After service in the Air Force, Jones was an editor of the avant-garde magazine *Yungen*, a jazz critic for *Downbeat*, *Metronome*, and *Jazz Review*, and a teacher of creative writing at the New School for Social Research in New York. He has published a variety of works, including the novel *The System of Dante's Hell* (1963), the collection of poems *The Dead Lecturer* (1964), the collection of essays *Home* (1966), and two volumes of plays. *Dutchman* (1964), which received the off-Broadway theatrical Obie Award, has met with a good deal of critical acclaim, and has been called the most important imaginative literary document of the American race war since *Native Son*.

In the late 1960's Jones changed his name to Imamu Amira Baraka, with the conviction that "LeRoi Jones" and other names that Black Americans hold are slave names and serve only to obscure the Black man's true roots. While his later works are increasingly militant, "Black Bourgeoise" reflects a concern which he continues to hold: the middle-class Black's alienation from his true self.

Black Bourgeoisie

has a gold tooth, sits long hours
on a stool, thinking about money.
sees white skin in a secret room
rummages his sense for sense
5 dreams about Lincoln(s)
conks his daughter's hair
sends his coon to school
works very hard
grins politely in restaurants
10 has a good word to say
never says it
does not hate ofays
hates, instead, him self
him black self.

Suggestions for Discussion

1. What is the poet's attitude towards the character described in "Black Bourgeoisie"? What does the poet suggest about traits that are generally considered admirable or pleasant, such as "works very hard," "grins politely," "has a good word to say," and "does not hate ofays"?
2. What are the various offenses of the "black bourgeoisie"? How many of these offenses are suggested through *double entendre* — for example, "dreams about Lincoln(s)"?
3. What is the function of the ungrammatical last line of "Black Bourgeoisie" — "him black self"?

Suggestion for Writing and Comparison

1. Read Baraka's one act play, *Dutchman*. How does his characterization of Clay in that play help to explain the tone of "Black Bourgeoisie"?

Owen Dodson

Owen Dodson, born in Brooklyn, New York, in 1914, received a B.A. degree from Bates College and an M.F.A. degree from Yale University. Dodson has written not only plays such as *Divine Comedy* (1938) and *Garden of Time* (1940), but also poems, short stories, and a novel, *Boy at the Window* (1951). With his theatrical group, the Howard Players, he has toured Norway, Denmark, Sweden, and Germany under the auspices of the U.S. State Department and the Government of Norway. He is the recipient of Guggenheim, Rosenwald, and General Education Board fellowships. A number of his poems and plays have won various prizes and awards, such as the Maxwell Anderson verse play contest and the *Paris Review* prize for the short story. His poems have been collected in *Powerful Long Ladder* and *Cages*.

In "Jonathan's Song" Dodson compares the historical persecution of the Jew with that of the Black and concludes that he too is a Jew, for "Jew" no longer designates a particular group, but rather a condition.

Jonathan's Song

A Negro Saw the Jewish Pageant, "We Will Never Die"

(For Sol Gordon)

I am a part of this:
Four million starving
And six million dead:
I am flesh and bone of this.

5 I have starved
In the secret alleys of my heart
And died in my soul
Like Ahab at the white whale's mouth.

The twisted cross desire
10 For final annihilation
Of my race of sufferers:
I am Abel, too.

Because my flesh is whole
Do not think that it signifies life.
15 I am the husk, believe me.
The rest is dead, remember.

I am a part of this
Memorial to suffering,
Militant strength:
20 I am a Jew.

Jew is not a race
Any longer—but a condition.
All the desert flowers have thorns;
I am bleeding in the sand.

25 Take me for your own David:
My father was not cruel,
I will sing your psalms,
I have learned them by heart.

I have loved you as a child,
30 We pledged in blood together.
The union is not strange,
My brother and my lover.

There was a great scent of death
In the garden when I was born.
35 Now it is certain:
Love me while you can.

The wedding is powerful as battle,
Singular, dread, passionate, loud,
Ahab screaming and the screaming whale
40 And the destination among thorns.

Love is a triple desire:
Flesh, freedom, hope:
No wanton thing is allowed.
I will sing thy psalms, all thy psalms,
45 Take me while you can.

Suggestions for Discussion

1. What are the various comparisons that Dodson makes between the Black and the Jew? What does he mean when he asserts, "I am a Jew"?
2. Explain the reference to the six million dead. Who are Ahab, Abel, and David? How are they used in the context of this poem? Explain the wedding and love imagery of the poem.

Suggestion for Writing and Comparison

1. See Aaron Kurtz's excerpt from *Behold the Sea* on p. 503 of the Jewish American chapter. Compare the similarities that Kurtz draws between the Jewish and the Black experience with those that Dodson draws.

Robert Hayden

Robert Hayden was born in Detroit, Michigan, in 1913. He attended graduate school at the University of Michigan, which later, in 1938 and 1942, granted him the Hopwood Award for Poetry. Hayden has been a professor of English at Fisk University and the University of Michigan. He is one of the best established contemporary Black poets of the older generation. His first book of poems, *Heartshape in the Dust,* appeared in 1940. This was followed by *The Lion and the Archer* (1948), *Figure of Time* (1955), *A Ballad of Remembrance* (1962), and *Selected Poems* (1966). Hayden. is also the editor of *Kaleidoscope: Poems by American Negro Poets* (1967) and *Afro-American Literature: An Introduction* (1971).

Hayden's poetry is often public in tone and intent. "Middle Passage" takes as its subject matter the slave trade between Africa and America which was still flourishing in the nineteenth century. The "middle passage" of the title refers specifically to the horrifying sea voyage between the two continents which took thousands of slaves' lives, making it indeed a "voyage through death." The *Amistad* revolt which is referred to in Part III of this poem was an early slave revolt; its leader, Cinquez, is comparable to Nat Turner, who was brought to popular attention by William Styron's novel *The Confessions of Nat Turner.* Hayden's poem "Frederick Douglass" extolls a different kind of hero—a man of love and logic, who was heroic by virtue of his vision.

While Hayden's themes are generally Black, he rejects what he calls the "sociological fallacy" of critics who evaluate the work of Black authors in strictly racial terms, and who allow the impact of social statement to supersede considerations of literary quality.

Middle Passage

I

Jesús, Estrella, Esperanza, Mercy:

> Sails flashing to the wind like weapons,
> sharks following the moans the fever and the dying;
> horror the corposant and compass rose.

5 Middle Passage:
> voyage through death
>> to life upon these shores.

> "10 April 1800—
> Blacks rebellious. Crew uneasy. Our linguist says
10 their moaning is a prayer for death,
ours and their own. Some try to starve themselves.

Lost three this morning leaped with crazy laughter
to the waiting sharks, sang as they went under."

Desire, Adventure, Tartar, Ann:

15   Standing to,America, bringing home
       black gold, black ivory, black seed.

          Deep in the festering hold thy father lies,
          of his bones New England pews are made,
          those are altar lights that were his eyes.

20 Jesus Saviour Pilot Me
    Over Life's Tempestuous Sea

    We pray that Thou wilt grant, O Lord,
    safe passage to our vessels bringing
    heathen souls unto Thy chastening.

25 Jesus Saviour

       "8 bells. I cannot sleep, for I am sick
       with fear, but writing eases fear a little
       since still my eyes can see these words take shape
       upon the page & so I write, as one
30   would turn to exorcism. 4 days scudding,
       but now the sea is calm again. Misfortune
       follows in our wake like sharks (our grinning
       tutelary gods). Which one of us
       has killed an albatross? A plague among
35   our blacks — Ophthalmia: blindness — & we
       have jettisoned the blind to no avail.
       It spreads, the terrifying sickness spreads.
       Its claws have scratched sight from the Capt.'s eyes
       & there is blindness in the fo'c'sle
40   & we must sail 3 weeks before we come
       to port."

       What port awaits us, Davy Jones'
       or home? I've heard of slavers drifting, drifting,
       playthings of wind and storm and chance, their crews
45   *gone blind, the jungle hatred*
       crawling up on deck.

    Thou Who Walked On Galilee

       "Deponent further sayeth *The Bella J*
       left the Guinea Coast
50   with cargo of five hundred blacks and odd
       for the barracoons of Florida:

       "That there was hardly room 'tween-decks for half
       the sweltering cattle stowed spoon-fashion there;

that some went mad of thirst and tore their flesh
55   and sucked the blood:

"That Crew and Captain lusted with the comeliest
of the savage girls kept naked in the cabins;
that there was one they called The Guinea Rose
and they cast lots and fought to lie with her:

60   "That when the Bo's'n piped all hands, the flames
spreading from starboard already were beyond
control, the negroes howling and their chains
entangled with the flames:

"That the burning blacks could not be reached,
65   that the Crew abandoned ship,
leaving their shrieking negresses behind,
that the Captain perished drunken with the wenches:

"Further Deponent sayeth not."

Pilot Oh Pilot Me

II

70 Aye, lad, and I have seen those factories,
Gambia, Rio Pongo, Calabar;
have watched the artful mongos baiting traps
of war wherein the victor and the vanquished

Were caught as prizes for our barracoons.
75 Have seen the nigger kings whose vanity
and greed turned wild black hides of Fellatah,
Mandingo, Ibo, Kru to gold for us.

And there was one — King Anthracite we named him —
fetish face beneath French parasols
80 of brass and orange velvet, impudent mouth
whose cups were carven skulls of enemies:

He'd honor us with drum and feast and conjo
and palm-oil-glistening wenches deft in love,
and for tin crowns that shone with paste,
85 red calico and German-silver trinkets

Would have the drums talk war and send
his warriors to burn the sleeping villages
and kill the sick and old and lead the young
in coffles to our factories.

90 Twenty years a trader, twenty years,
for there was wealth aplenty to be harvested
from those black fields, and I'd be trading still
but for the fevers melting down my bones.

III

Shuttles in the rocking loom of history,
95 the dark ships move, the dark ships move,
their bright ironical names
like jests of kindness on a murderer's mouth;
plough through thrashing glister toward
fata morgana's lucent melting shore,
100 weave toward New World littorals that are
mirage and myth and actual shore.

Voyage through death,
            voyage whose chartings are unlove.

A charnel stench, effluvium of living death
105 spreads outward from the hold,
where the living and the dead, the horribly dying,
lie interlocked, lie foul with blood and excrement.

>   *Deep in the festering hold thy father lies,*
>   *the corpse of mercy rots with him,*
110 *rats eat love's rotten gelid eyes.*

>   *But, oh, the living look at you*
>   *with human eyes whose suffering accuses you,*
>   *whose hatred reaches through the swill of dark*
>   *to strike you like a leper's claw.*

115 *You cannot stare that hatred down*
>   *or chain the fear that stalks the watches*
>   *and breathes on you its fetid scorching breath;*
>   *cannot kill the deep immortal human wish,*
>   *the timeless will.*

120 "But for the storm that flung up barriers
of wind and wave, *The Amistad*, señores,
would have reached the port of Príncipe in two,
three days at most; but for the storm we should
have been prepared for what befell.
125 Swift as the puma's leap it came. There was
that interval of moonless calm filled only
with the water's and the rigging's usual sounds,
then sudden movement, blows and snarling cries
and they had fallen on us with machete
130 and marlinspike. It was as though the very
air, the night itself were striking us.
Exhausted by the rigors of the storm,
we were no match for them. Our men went down
before the murderous Africans. Our loyal
135 Celestino ran from below with gun
and lantern and I saw, before the cane-
knife's wounding flash, Cinquez,

that surly brute who calls himself a prince,
directing, urging on the ghastly work.
140 He hacked the poor mulatto down, and then
he turned on me. The decks were slippery
when daylight finally came. It sickens me
to think of what I saw, of how these apes
threw overboard the butchered bodies of
145 our men, true Christians all, like so much jetsam.
Enough, enough. The rest is quickly told:
Cinquez was forced to spare the two of us
you see to steer the ship to Africa,
and we like phantoms doomed to rove the sea
150 voyaged east by day and west by night,
deceiving them, hoping for rescue,
prisoners on our own vessel, till
at length we drifted to the shores of this
your land, America, where we were freed
155 from our unspeakable misery. Now we
demand, good sirs, the extradition of
Cinquez and his accomplices to La
Havana. And it distresses us to know
there are so many here who seem inclined
160 to justify the mutiny of these blacks.
We find it paradoxical indeed
that you whose wealth, whose tree of liberty
are rooted in the labor of your slaves
should suffer the august John Quincy Adams
165 to speak with so much passion of the right
of chattel slaves to kill their lawful masters
and with his Roman rhetoric weave a hero's
garland for Cinquez. I tell you that
we are determined to return to Cuba
170 with our slaves and there see justice done. Cinquez—
or let us say 'the Prince'—Cinquez shall die."

The deep immortal human wish,
the timeless will:

Cinquez its deathless primaveral image,
175 life that transfigures many lives.

Voyage through death
to life upon these shores.

Frederick Douglass

When it is finally ours, this freedom, this liberty, this beautiful
and terrible thing, needful to man as air,

usable as earth; when it belongs at last to all,
when it is truly instinct, brain matter, diastole, systole,
5 reflex action; when it is finally won; when it is more
than the gaudy mumbo jumbo of politicians:
this man, this Douglass, this former slave, this Negro
beaten to his knees, exiled, visioning a world
where none is lonely, none hunted, alien,
10 this man, superb in love and logic, this man
shall be remembered. O, not with statues' rhetoric,
not with legends and poems and wreaths of bronze alone,
but with the lives grown out of his life, the lives
fleshing his dream of the beautiful, needful thing.

Suggestions for Discussion

Part I of "Middle Passage"

1. How are the names of the ships, such as *Jesús, Esperanza, Mercy,* and *Desire,* an ironic comment? Is the prayer for "safe passage" ironic in any way?

2. One of the many allusions in the poem is to Ariel's song from Shakespeare's *The Tempest*:

> Full fathom five thy father lies;
>   Of his bones are coral made;
> Those are pearls that were his eyes:
>   Nothing of him that doth fade
> But doth suffer a sea-change
> Into something rich and strange.
> Sea nymphs hourly ring his knell.
>   Ding-dong.
> Hark! Now I hear them,—ding-dong, bell.

Note the changes Hayden has made, particularly with regard to the "sea-change." How do Hayden's alterations affect the tone of his poem?

3. To what poem does the killing of an albatross refer? What connection has the albatross to the "plague" of blindness?

4. What is suggested by the line "and they cast lots and fought to lie with her"? How is this reference related to the Christian symbolism of the poem?

Part II

1. Who is the narrator of this section of the poem? How is Part II different from Part I? In what way might Part II be said to be counterpoint to Parts I and III?

2. What is the narrator's purpose in relating this tale? Why does this narrator not refer to "bringing heathen souls into Thy chastening"? (Compare Parts I and III.)

Part III

1. Discuss how the author has expanded the previous themes suggested by a) the names of the slave ships, b) the albatross, c) the song from *The Tempest,* and d) quotations from written affidavits concerning actual voyages.
2. How is Cinquez a deathless image of "the deep immortal human wish, the timeless will"? How does Hayden's symbolic use of Cinquez relate to the historical fact that he was one of the leaders of slave revolts?
3. Compare and contrast the themes of "Middle Passage" with those of "Let America Be America Again" (p. 108). How are the tones of bitterness, hope, and despair revealed in each poem?

"Frederick Douglass"

1. Which characteristics of the traditional sonnet form does Hayden retain? How has he fit his argument into the sonnet structure? What variation has he made on the structure of the Petrarchan sonnet?

Suggestions for Writing and Comparison

1. Read an account of the passage from Europe to America by anyone who came "steerage" class (see, for example, Abraham Cahan's *The Rise of David Levinsky* or George and Helen Papashvily's *Anything Can Happen*). Compare and contrast the mental and physical discomforts in each case. What were the special horrors of the "middle passage"?
2. Compare the slave revolts of Rome with those in the New World (for example, see Howard Fast's *Spartacus* for a fictionalized account of an ancient uprising).
3. Read Frederick Douglass' autobiography, *Narrative of the Life of Frederick Douglass, An American Slave*. Which aspects of his life make him merit Hayden's praise?

Dudley Randall

Dudley Randall, born in 1914 in Washington, D.C., graduated from Wayne University in Detroit and received a Master's degree in library science from the University of Michigan. His poems have appeared in numberous anthologies. Randall is the coauthor of *Poem Counterpoem* (1966) and *For Malcolm* (1967), and the author of *Cities Burning* (1968) and *Love You* (1970).

"Memorial Wreath" commemorates the death of the Black soldiers who fought on the Union side during the American Civil War. The facts of the Black man's role in the War have been well-documented in James M. McPherson's study *The Negro's Civil War* (1965). "Booker T. and W. E. B." captures the philosophical differences between two Black historical figures and, by implication, comments on militancy and "Uncle Tom-ism" today.

Memorial Wreath

(For the more than 200,000 Negroes who served in the Union Army during the Civil War)

In this green month when resurrected flowers,
Like laughing children ignorant of death,
Brighten the couch of those who wake no more,
Love and remembrance blossom in our hearts
5 For you who bore the extreme sharp pang for us,
And bought our freedom with your lives.

                              And now,
Honoring your memory, with love we bring
These fiery roses, white-hot cotton flowers
10 And violets bluer than cool northern skies
You dreamed of in the burning prison fields
When liberty was only a faint north star,
Not a bright flower planted by your hands
Reaching up hardy nourished with your blood.

15 Fit gravefellows you are for Lincoln, Brown
And Douglass and Toussaint . . . all whose rapt eyes
Fashioned a new world in this wilderness.

American earth is richer for your bones;
Our hearts beat prouder for the blood we inherit.

Booker T. and W. E. B.

(Booker T. Washington and W. E. B. Du Bois)

"It seems to me," said Booker T.,
"It shows a mighty lot of cheek
To study chemistry and Greek
When Mister Charlie needs a hand
5 To hoe the cotton on his land,
And when Miss Ann looks for a cook,
Why stick your nose inside a book?"

"I don't agree," said W. E. B.
"If I should have the drive to seek
10 Knowledge of chemistry or Greek,
I'll do it. Charles and Miss can look
Another place for hand or cook.
Some men rejoice in skill of hand,
And some in cultivating land,
15 But there are others who maintain
The right to cultivate the brain."

"It seems to me," said Booker T.,
"That all you folks have missed the boat
Who shout about the right to vote,
20 And spend vain days and sleepless nights
In uproar over civil rights.
Just keep your mouths shut, do not grouse,
But work, and save, and buy a house."

"I don't agree," said W. E. B.,
25 "For what can property avail
If dignity and justice fail?
Unless you help to make the laws,
They'll steal your house with trumped-up clause.
A rope's as tight, a fire as hot,
30 No matter how much cash you've got.
Speak soft, and try your little plan,
But as for me, I'll be a man."

"It seems to me," said Booker T. —

"I don't agree,"
35 Said W. E. B.

Suggestions for Discussion

    1. Discuss the symbolism of the colors of the flowers in "Memorial Wreath." What is the controlling image in the poem? How does the image relate to the dead men?

2. What is the significance of the change from "faint north star" to "bright flower"? In what way did Lincoln, Brown, Douglass, and Toussaint share in "planting" and "fashioning"?
3. What is the tone of "Booker T. and W. E. B."? How does the author convey the tone to the reader?
4. Which figure does the author seem to sympathize with? Does Randall present the arguments of both figures with equal seriousness?

Suggestions for Writing and Comparison

1. Read James M. McPherson's *The Negro's Civil War* (1965), particularly Chapters X through XV which deal with Blacks' contributions to the Union war effort.
2. Read Booker T. Washington's *Up from Slavery* and W. E. B. Du Bois' *The Souls of Black Folk*. Compare their attitudes toward whites, education for Blacks, and civil rights.

Mari Evans

Mari Evans was born in Toledo, Ohio. She is presently an assistant professor and writer-in-residence at Indiana University, Bloomington. Her poems have been collected in various anthologies, such as Langston Hughes' *New Negro Poets: U.S.A.* and Walter Lowenfels' *Poets of Today.* Mari Evans' first poem included here, "Status Symbol," is characteristic of her style in its ironic tone, its short line length, and its verse techniques which indicate the influence of twentieth-century American writers such as Langston Hughes. "Vive Noir!", a later poem in a bold, declamatory style, extends the commentary on the American dream in relation to the Black American. The speaker in "Status Symbol" has been asked by American society to view possession of the key of the white restroom, or "tokenism," as a great mark of progress; but the speaker in "Vive Noir!" refuses to be satisfied with tokenism, and demands a complete reversal of the positions which had hitherto defined the races.

Status Symbol

i
Have Arrived

i
am the
5 New Negro

i
am the result of
President Lincoln
World War I
10 and Paris
the
Red Ball Express
white drinking fountains
sitdowns and
15 sit-ins
Federal Troops
Marches on Washington
and
prayer meetings . . .

20 today
They hired me
it

is a status
job . . .
25 along
with my papers
They
gave me my
Status Symbol
30 the
key
to the
White . . . Locked . . .
John

Vive Noir!

i
am going to rise
en masse
from Inner City
5   sick
                           of newyork ghettos
                           chicago tenements
                           l a's slums
weary
10   of exhausted lands
         sagging privies
         saying yessuh yessah
         yesSIR
         in an assortment
15   of geographical dialects i
have seen my last
broken down plantation
even from a
distance
20   i
will load all my goods
in '50 Chevy pickups '53
Fords fly United and '66
caddys i
25   have packed in
         the old man and the old lady and
         wiped the children's noses
                 I'm tired
                     of hand me downs
30   shut me ups
                         pin me ins
                             keep me outs

<pre>
                                        messing me over have
                                    just had it
    35   baby
                                    from
                                    you . . .
                i'm
                gonna spread out
    40   over America
                        intrude
                my proud blackness
                all
                        over the place
    45   i have wrested wheat fields
                                from the forests

                                turned rivers
                                from their courses

                                leveled mountains
    50   at a word
                                festooned the land with
                                bridges
                                            gemlike
                                        on filaments of steel
    55   moved
                                glistening towersofBabel in place

                                sweated a whole
                                civilization

                                    now
    60   i'm
                                gonna breathe fire
                                through flaming nostrils BURN
                                    a place for

                                    me

    65   in the skyscrapers and the
                                schoolrooms on the green
                                lawns and the white
                                beaches
                                            i'm
    70   gonna wear the robes and
                                sit on the benches
                                make the rules and make
                                the arrests say
                                who can and who
    75   can't
                                        baby you don't stand
                                        a
                                        chance
</pre>

i'm
80 gonna put black angels
    in all the books and a black
    Christchild in Mary's arms i'm
    gonna make black bunnies black
    fairies black santas black
85 nursery rhymes and
                        black

    ice cream
                    i'm
    gonna make it a
90 crime
        to be anything BUT   black
        pass the coppertone

    gonna make white
    a twentyfourhour
95 lifetime
    J.O.B.
            an' when all the coppertone's gone . . . . ?

Suggestions for Discussion

1. How has the poet employed capitalization and the lack of it in "Status Symbol" as a literary device?
2. How does the "New Negro" of "Status Symbol" relate to the "New Negro" of the Harlem Renaissance of the 1920's? When did the March on Washington of Mari Evans' generation take place? In what sense was the March on Washington during the Depression different from this one? Is there a comment on the "progress" of the 1960's and 1970's implied in this poem?
3. In what ways is the last stanza of "Status Symbol" an answer to the one preceding it? How complex is the tone of the poem?
4. Who is the "i" in "Vive Noir!" that rises from "newyork ghettos/ chicago tenements/ l a's slums" and leaves by way of "'50 Chevy pickups '53/ Fords fly United and '66/ caddys"?
5. Whom does the "i" of "Vive Noir!" address in the lines "just had it/ baby/ from/ you"? What action does the "i" promise? Why does he feel "baby you don't stand/a/chance"?
6. In the lines "gonna make white/ a twentyfourhour/ lifetime/ J.O.B." in "Vive Noir!", what are the various meanings of "J.O.B."? What does the ellipsis suggest in the final line "an' when all the coppertone's gone . . . . ?"
7. What is the tone of "Vive Noir!"? How does it relate to the tone of "Status Symbol"?

Suggestions for Writing and Comparison

1. Compare the techniques employed by Mari Evans with those of William Carlos Williams and E. E. Cummings (see particularly Williams' "The Jungle" and Cummings' "as freedom is a breakfast food").
2. Discuss "Status Symbol" as a comment on the American Dream. Compare this poem with either Langston Hughes' "Let America Be America Again" (p. 108) or Dudley Randall's "Memorial Wreath" (p. 135).
3. Trace the "progress" of the American Dream as found in the poems of this section.

Nikki Giovanni

Nikki Giovanni, born in 1943 in Knoxville, Tennessee, graduated from Fisk University in 1967. She has taught creative writing at Rutgers University. Hers was a new voice to emerge in the late 60's and the 70's. She has lectured extensively on college campuses, and her poems have appeared in *Ebony,* and *The Journal of Black Poetry*, and the anthology *New Black Voices*. Her first books of poems, entitled *Black Feeling, Black Talk* and *Black Judgment,* were followed by *Gemini, Re-Creation,* and *Night Comes Softly.*

Nikki Giovanni has committed herself and her writing to the Black revolution. Her poetry, though it may be personal in details, is political in purpose, and she writes with the conscious objective of reaching a Black audience. Her first poem here, "Nikki-Rosa," is an autobiographical statement which takes issue with the notion that to be Black and poor is of necessity to be deprived. In "Seduction" the poet teases the revolutionary whose rhetoric interferes with life. Finally, "Adulthood" is more than an autobiographical statement; it is a political commitment to being a "for real Black person."

Nikki-Rosa

childhood remembrances are always a drag
if you're Black
you always remember things like living in Woodlawn
with no inside toilet
5 and if you become famous or something
they never talk about how happy you were to have your mother
all to yourself and
how good the water felt when you got your bath from one of
those big tubs that folk in chicago barbecue in
10 and somehow when you talk about home
it never gets across how much you
understood their feelings
as the whole family attended meetings about Hollydale
and even though you remember
15 your biographers never understand
your father's pain as he sells his stock
and another dream goes
and though you're poor it isn't poverty that
concerns you
20 and though they fought a lot
it isn't your father's drinking that makes any difference
but only that everybody is together and you
and your sister have happy birthdays and very good christmasses

and I really hope no white person ever has cause to write
25 about me because they never understand Black love is Black
wealth and they'll probably talk about my hard childhood
and never understand that all the while I was quite happy

Seduction

one day
you gonna walk in this house
and i'm gonna have on a long African
gown
5 you'll sit down and say "The Black . . ."
and i'm gonna take one arm out
then you—not noticing me at all—will say "What about
this brother . . ."
and i'm going to be slipping it over my head
10 and you'll rap on about "The revolution . . ."
while i rest your hand against my stomach
you'll go on—as you always do—saying
"I just can't dig . . ."
while i'm moving your hand up and down
15 and i'll be taking your dashiki off
then you'll say "What we really need . . ."
and i'll be licking your arm
and "The way I see it we ought to . . ."
and unbuckling your pants
20 "And what about the situation . . ."
and taking your shorts off
then you'll notice
your state of undress
and knowing you you'll just say
25 "Nikki,
isn't this counterrevolutionary . . . ?"

Adulthood

(for claudia)

i usta wonder who i'd be

when i was a little girl in indianapolis
sitting on doctors porches with post-dawn pre-debs
(wondering would my aunt drag me to church sunday)
5 i was meaningless
and i wondered if life
would give me a chance to mean

i found a new life in the withdrawal from all things
not like my image

10 when i was a teen-ager i usta sit
on front steps conversing
the gym teachers son with embryonic eyes
about the essential essence of the universe
(and other bullshit stuff)
15 recognizing the basic powerlessness of me

but then i went to college where i learned
that just because everything i was was unreal
i could be real and not just real through withdrawal
into emotional crosshairs or colored bourgeoisie intellectual pretensions
20 but from involvement with things approaching reality
i could possibly have a life

so catatonic emotions and time wasting sex games
were replaced with functioning commitments to logic and
necessity and the gray area was slowly darkened into
25 a black thing
for a while progress was being made along with a certain degree
of happiness cause i wrote a book and found a love
and organized a theatre and even gave some lectures on
Black history
30 and began to believe all good people could get
together and win without bloodshed
then
hammarskjold was killed
and lumumba was killed
35 and diem was killed
and kennedy was killed
and malcolm was killed
and evers was killed
and schwerner, chaney and goodman were killed
40 and liuzzo was killed
and stokely fled the country
and le roi was arrested
and rap was arrested
and pollard, thompson and cooper were killed
45 and king was killed
and kennedy was killed
and i sometimes wonder why i didn't become a debutante
sitting on porches, going to church all the time, wondering
is my eye make-up on straight
50 or a withdrawn discoursing on the stars and moon
instead of a for real Black person who must now feel
and inflict
pain

Suggestions for Discussion

1. Discuss the stereotypes about a Black childhood which are prevalent. Which details in "Nikki-Rosa" challenge those stereotypes?
2. How do we know "Seduction" is a fantasy? Does the tone of the poem suggest it is more a "put-on" or a "put-down"?
3. What are the three stages in development of the poet's awareness in "Adulthood"?
4. What is the effect on the reader of the list of people who were killed or arrested? What statement about contemporary history does the list make?
5. What is the tone of the line "and i sometimes wonder why . . ." at the end of the list? Does the final stanza of the poem suggest puzzlement or commitment?

Suggestion for Writing and Comparison

1. Read Grier and Cobbs' *Black Rage* (1968). Compare and contrast the Black psychiatrists' and the Black poet's views of mental health.

Etheridge Knight

Etheridge Knight was born in 1933 in Corinth, Mississippi. He has said of himself, "I died in Korea from a shrapnel wound and narcotics resurrected me. I died in 1960 from a prison sentence and poetry brought me back to life."

Knight has had stories and poems published in *Negro Digest, Journal of Black Poetry,* and the anthology *Dices or Black Bones.* His first book of poems, *Poems from Prison,* was printed by Broadside Press in 1968. Etheridge Knight, like Malcolm X and Eldridge Cleaver, found his voice in prison. However he may have forged his own identity, his poetry is less self-concerned than that of Nikki Giovanni and more concerned with the observable and often tragic facts of human nature.

Hard Rock Returns to Prison From the Hospital for the Criminal Insane

Hard Rock was "known not to take no shit
From nobody," and he had the scars to prove it:
Split purple lips, lumped ears, welts above
His yellow eyes, and one long scar that cut
5   Across his temple and plowed through a thick
Canopy of kinky hair.

The WORD was that Hard Rock wasn't a mean nigger
Anymore, that the doctors had bored a hole in his head,
Cut out part of his brain, and shot electricity
10 Through the rest. When they brought Hard Rock back,
Handcuffed and chained, he was turned loose,
Like a freshly gelded stallion, to try his new status.
And we all waited and watched, like indians at a corral,
To see if the WORD was true.

15 As we waited we wrapped ourselves in the cloak
Of his exploits: "Man, the last time, it took eight
Screws to put him in the Hole." "Yeah, remember when he
Smacked the captain with his dinner tray?" "He set
The record for time in the Hole—67 straight days!"
20 "Ol Hard Rock! man, that's one crazy nigger."
And then the jewel of a myth that Hard Rock had once bit
A screw on the thumb and poisoned him with syphilitic spit.

The testing came, to see if Hard Rock was really tame.
A hillbilly called him a black son of a bitch
25 And didn't lose his teeth, a screw who knew Hard Rock
From before shook him down and barked in his face.
And Hard Rock did *nothing.* Just grinned and looked silly,
His eyes empty like knot holes in a fence.

And even after we discovered that it took Hard Rock
30 Exactly 3 minutes to tell you his first name,
We told ourselves that he had just wised up,
Was being cool; but we could not fool ourselves for long,
And we turned away, our eyes on the ground. Crushed.
He had been our Destroyer, the doer of things
35 We dreamed of doing but could not bring ourselves to do,
The fears of years, like a biting whip,
Had cut grooves too deeply across our backs.

The Warden Said to Me the Other Day

The warden said to me the other day
(innocently, I think), "Say, etheridge,
why come the black boys don't run off
like the white boys do?"
5 I lowered my jaw and scratched my head
and said (innocently, i think), "Well, suh,
I ain't for sure, but I reckon it's cause
we ain't got no wheres to run to."

Suggestions for Discussion

1. Explain the symbolism in the similes in stanza two of "Hard
   Rock." How is Hard Rock "like a freshly gelded stallion" and
   how are the inmates "like indians at a corral"?
2. "Cool," "nigger," "shit," and "screw" are all words used in
   "Hard Rock." Has the poet been effective in transforming ex-
   pletives and prison argot into poetry, or are these words used
   merely for shock value? Notice also the difference in tone between "frontal lobotomy" and "the doctors had bored a hole in
   his head." Why does the poet's phrase have more immediacy
   than the technical term?
3. Why does the inmate in "The Warden Said" scratch his head?
   What kind of a game is being enacted in the poem?
4. Discuss the irony and the levels of meaning in "we ain't got no
   wheres to run to."

Suggestion for Writing and Comparison

1. Read Ken Kesey's *One Flew Over the Cuckoo's Nest* in either
   the play or novel form. Compare Kesey's and Knight's attitudes
   toward the use of shock treatment and lobotomy in restraining
   the "troublemaker" rather than curing mental disease.

Don L. Lee

Don L. Lee was born in Detroit, Michigan, in 1942 and attended college in Chicago. He has been Black Poet in Residence at Cornell and has taught at Harvard University. Collections of his verse include *Think Black* (1967), *Black Pride* (1968), *Don't Cry, Scream* (1969), *We Walk the Way of the New World* (1970), and *Directionscore: Selected and New Poems* (1971).

The three poems included here are from *Don't Cry, Scream.* And they do that. "Blackmusic/a beginning" records the theft of black music and style by whites. "But He Was Cool" takes us through the changes in Black identity of the 60's—from cool dashikis and naturals and speaking Swahili to "after detroit" when "to be black/is/to be/very-hot." The poem-portrait of Gwendolyn Brooks contains a list of kinds of Blackness and juxtaposes the label "the lady 'negro poet.'" By the end of the poem we know Gwendolyn Brooks is not a lady negro poet but a Black poet whose "makeup is total-real!"

Perhaps more than any other writer, Don L. Lee has reinvented the word Black for our times.

Gwendolyn Brooks

she doesn't wear
costume jewelry
& she knew that walt disney
was/is making a fortune off
5 false-eyelashes and that time magazine is the
authority on the knee/grow.
her makeup is total-real.

a negro english instructor called her:
    "a fine negro poet."
10 a whi-te critic said:
    "she's a credit to the negro race."
somebody else called her:
    "a pure negro writer."
johnnie mae, who's a senior in high school said:
15   "she & langston are the only negro poets we've
    read in school and i understand her."
pee wee used to carry one of her poems around in his
  back pocket;
    the one about being cool. that was befo pee wee
20   was cooled by a cop's warning shot.

into the sixties
a word was born . . . . BLACK
& with black came poets
& from the poet's ball points came:

25 black doubleblack purpleblack blueblack beenblack was
   black daybeforeyesterday blackerthan ultrablack super
   black blackblack yellowblack niggerblack blackwhi-te-
      man
   blackerthanyoueverbes ¼ black unblack coldblack clear
30 black my momma's blackerthanyourmomma pimpleblack
      fall
   black so black we can't even see you black on black in
   black by black technically black mantanblack winter
   black coolblack 360degreesblack coalblack midnight
35 black black when it's convenient rustyblack moonblack
   black starblack summerblack electronblack spaceman
   black shoeshineblack jimshoeblack underwearblack ugly
   black auntjimammablack, uncleben'srice black
      williebest
40 black blackisbeautifulblack i justdiscoveredblack negro
   black unsubstanceblack.

   and everywhere the
   lady "negro poet"
   appeared the poets were there.
45 they listened & questioned
   & went home feeling uncomfortable/unsound & so-
      untogether
   they read/re-read/wrote & re-wrote
   & came back the next time to tell the
50 lady "negro poet"
   how beautiful she was/is & how she had helped them
   & she came back with:
      how necessary they were and how they've helped her.
   the poets walked & as space filled the vacuum between
55   them & the
   lady "negro poet"
   u could hear one of the blackpoets say:
      "bro, they been callin that sister by the wrong name."

blackmusic/a beginning

   pharaoh sanders
   had
   finished
   playing
5 &
   the whi-
   te boy was to
   go on next.

   him didn't

10 him sd
    that
    his horn
    was
    broke.

15 they sat
    there
    dressed in
    african garb
    & dark sun glasses
20 listening to the brothers
    play.   (taking notes)
    we
    didn't realize
    who they
25 were un
    til their
    next recording
    had been
    released: the beach boys play soulmusic.

30 real sorry about
    the supremes
    being dead,
    heard some whi
    te girls
35 the other day —
    all wigged-down
    with a mean tan —
    soundin just like them,
    singin
40 rodgers & hart
    & some country & western.

But He Was Cool
    or: he even stopped for green lights

    super-cool
    ultrablack
    a tan/purple
    had a beautiful shade.

 5 he had a double-natural
    that wd put the sisters to shame.
    his dashikis were tailor made
    & his beads were imported sea shells
        (from some blk/country i never heard of)
10 he was triple-hip.

his tikis were hand carved
out of ivory
& came express from the motherland.
he would greet u in swahili
15 & say good-by in yoruba.
woooooooooooo-jim he bes so cool & ill tel li gent
        cool-cool is so cool he was un-cooled by
            other niggers' cool
        cool-cool ultracool was bop-cool/ice box
20   cool so cool cold cool
        his wine didn't have to be cooled, him was
            air conditioned cool
        cool-cool/real cool made me cool — now
            ain't that cool
25   cool-cool so cool him nick-named refrig-
            erator.

cool-cool so cool
he didn't know,

after detroit, newark, chicago &c.,
30 we had to hip
        cool-cool/super-cool/real cool
   that
to be black
is
35 to be
very-hot.

Suggestions for Discussion

1. Notice the progression in the comments about Gwendolyn
   Brooks in the first poem. Which ones does the poet lead us to
   believe are nearest the truth?
2. Try various ways of reading the third stanza aloud. Three or
   four students might prepare a choral reading.
3. With reference to "blackmusic/a beginning," what popular white
   groups are imitating black music styles today?
4. Discuss the difference between the Beatles' use of black music
   and that of the Beach Boys.
5. Discuss "being cool" as a survival mechanism. What kind of a
   political situation allows for being "very-hot"?

Suggestion for Writing and Comparison

1. Read Don Lee's and Gwendolyn Brooks' poem-portraits of
   their contemporaries. How do the poets vary the form of the
   poems to express the personalities of the subjects?

POEMS
The Old Truths

Richard Wright

(See p. 85 for Wright's story "The Man Who Saw the Flood" and a biographical sketch of the author.)

Hokku Poems

1

In the falling snow
A laughing boy holds out his palms
Until they are white

2

Keep straight down this block
Then turn right where you will find
A peach tree blooming

3

With a twitching nose
A dog reads a telegram
On a wet tree trunk

4

The spring lingers on
In the scent of a damp log
Rotting in the sun

5

Whose town did you leave
O wild and drowning spring rain
And where do you go?

6

The crow flew so fast
That he left his lonely caw
Behind in the fields

Suggestions for Discussion

1. The "hokku"' or "haiku" verse form originated as an abbreviation of the "tanka" verse form in sixteenth-century Japan. It is made up of seventeen syllables divided into three lines: five syllables, seven syllables, five syllables. Severely limited in length, the poem contains suggestive images rather than rhetorically expressed ideas. Ezra Pound, Amy Lowell, Wallace Stevens, and many imagist poets were influenced by the haiku form. (For haiku by Japanese Americans, see the Asian American chapter of this book.) The haiku traditionally includes references both to the world of nature and to the seasons of the year. List the words Wright uses to indicate changes in the physical surroundings.
2. Is the evocative sensory imagery of the haiku more nearly like the simile or the metaphor? How is it different from both?
3. Compare the tone of these poems with the tone of Wright's short story "The Man Who Saw the Flood" (p. 85). Do the story and the poems indicate the same attitude toward life? If there is a difference, can you account for it?

Suggestions for Writing and Comparison

1. Read Wallace Stevens' poem "Thirteen Ways of Looking at a Blackbird." How has he changed or expanded the form of the haiku? Compare Wright's poems to any of the thirteen sections of Stevens' poem.
2. Discuss the haiku as an experience in the tangible, necessary in order to offset our emphasis on the abstract.

Owen Dodson

(See p. 126 for Dodson's "Jonathan's Song" and a biographical sketch of the author.)

Sorrow Is the Only Faithful One

Sorrow is the only faithful one:
The lone companion clinging like a season
To its original skin no matter what the variations.

If all the mountains paraded
5 Eating the valleys as they went
And the sun were a cliffure on the highest peak,

Sorrow would be there between
The sparkling and the giant laughter
Of the enemy when the clouds come down to swim.

10 But I am less, unmagic, black,
Sorrow clings to me more than to doomsday mountains
Or erosion scars on a palisade.

Sorrow has a song like a leech
Crying because the sand's blood is dry
15 And the stars reflected in the lake

Are water for all their twinkling
And bloodless for all their charm.
I have blood, and a song.
SORROW IS THE ONLY FAITHFUL ONE.

Suggestions for Discussion

1. Rhymed tercets were popular with medieval Provençal and Italian poets. English, however, has far fewer rhymes than French or Italian. How does Dodson accommodate his rhyme to modern English?
2. The structure of the rondel (of which this poem is an example) dictates the use of the same lines for the opening and closing of the poem. How many "investigations" of sorrow are there that expand our understanding of "Sorrow is the only faithful one"? Is the ending redundant or is it an effective closure?
3. The following lines present a clear image:

   And the stars reflected in the lake
   Are water for all their twinkling
   And bloodless for all their charm.

Compare and contrast Dodson's use of imagery with the imagery in a haiku by Richard Wright (p. 153) or Shisei Tsuneishi (pp. 302–3).

4. What is the emotional center of the poem? How does the poet suggest climbing and being pulled back? Is the rondel an appropriate form for the "emotional progress" of the poem?

Suggestions for Writing and Comparison

1. Discuss Dodson's use of symbolism. How are mountains, lakes, and stars related to human sorrow?
2. Compare "Sorrow Is the Only Faithful One" with Countee Cullen's "Yet Do I Marvel" (p. 117). How is the theme of Blackness treated in each poem?

Gwendolyn Brooks

Gwendolyn Brooks was born in Topeka, Kansas, in 1917, but she has lived most of her life in Chicago. Before the publication of her first book of poetry, *A Street in Bronzeville* (1945), she received four awards for her work from the Midwestern Writers Conference. She also received several grants and fellowships, and in 1950, following publication of her second volume of poetry, *Annie Allen* (1950), she was the recipient of the Pulitzer Prize. Since then she has written a novel, *Maud Martha* (1953), and several volumes of poems, including *The Bean Eaters* (1960), *Selected Poems* (1963), *In the Mecca* (1968), and *Riot* (1969).

Gwendolyn Brooks, one of the most accomplished modern poets in this anthology, is an admirer of another woman poet familiar to students of American literature, Emily Dickinson. In manner and skill she has also been compared to T. S. Eliot by critics such as David Littlejohn (see *Black on White: A Critical Survey of Writing by American Negroes*). Her sure hand at phrasing and idiosyncratic diction are evident in the personal complex lyric "a light and diplomatic bird," as well as in "weaponed woman" and "sick man looks at flowers." In the poem "Langston Hughes" she adopts that writer's rhythm and vocabulary in making a perceptive sketch of both the man and the poet.

Langston Hughes

      is merry glory.
Is saltatory.
Yet grips his right of twisting free.

Has a long reach,
5 Strong speech,
Remedial fears.
Muscular tears.

Holds horticulture
In the eye of the vulture
10 Infirm profession.
In the Compression —
In mud and blood and sudden death —
In the breath
Of the holocaust he
15 Is helmsman, hatchet, headlight.
See
One restless in the exotic time! and ever,
Till the air is cured of its fever.

weaponed woman

Well, life has been a baffled vehicle
And baffling. But she fights, and
Has fought, according to her lights and
The lenience of her whirling-place.

5 She fights with semi-folded arms,
Her strong bag, and the stiff
Frost of her face (that challenges "When" and "If.")
And altogether she does Rather Well.

sick man looks at flowers

You are sick and old, and there is a closing in —
The eyes gone dead to all that would beguile.
Echoes are dull and the body accepts no touch
Except its pain. Mind is a little isle.
5 But now invades this impudence of red!
This ripe rebuke, this burgeoning affluence
Mocks me and mocks the desert of my bed.

a light and diplomatic bird

A light and diplomatic bird
Is lenient in my window tree.
A quick dilemma of the leaves
Discloses twist and tact to me.

5 Who strangles his extremest need
For pity of my imminence
On utmost ache and lacquered cold
Is prosperous in proper sense:

He can abash his barmecides;
10 The fantoccini of his range
Pass over. Vast and secular
And apt and admirably strange.

Augmented by incorrigible
Conviction of his symmetry,
15 He can afford his sine die.
He can afford to pity me

Whose hours at best are wheats or beiges
Lashed with riot-red and black.
Tabasco at the lapping wave.
20 Search-light in the secret crack.

Oh open, apostolic height!
And tell my humbug how to start
Bird balance, bleach: make miniature
Valhalla of my heart.

Suggestions for Discussion

1. In "Langston Hughes," define "saltatory." How is salt salutary? What relation is there of "merry glory" to "salatory," and "remedial fears" to "muscular tears"?
2. When is horticulture an "infirm profession," as in "Langston Hughes"? Might "horticulture" refer to cultivating one's own garden, as in *Candide?*
3. Do Langston Hughes' poems or short stories or essays (see particularly the latest collection of his poems, *The Panther and the Lash*) give the impression he was "helmsman, hatchet, headlight"? What do you imagine was Hughes' purpose in writing "Let America Be America Again" (p. 108)?
4. Notice the effective use of internal rhyme—alliteration, assonance, and slant rhyme—in connection with strong caesural pauses in "weaponed woman." How do these techniques, as well as the meter and end-rhyme, relate to the title of the poem?
5. What is the effect of the final line of "weaponed woman" being set off, a sentence unto itself, and the capitalizing of the last two words "Rather Well"? Is the poem a sympathetic portrait?
6. How clear is the picture of sickness in "sick man looks at flowers"? What is meant by the phrase "mind is a little isle"? How does the sick man come to see his bed as a desert?
7. The two poems "weaponed woman" and "sick man looks at flowers" were originally published in a section of poems entitled "a catch of shy fish." What is the significance of that title in relation to "weaponed woman" and "sick man looks at flowers"? What qualities do these lyric portraits share?
8. In what sense does the author of "a light and diplomatic bird" mean the bird is "lenient" (see lines 1 and 2)? Consult an unabridged dictionary. Many words in this poem are used in their original sense rather than the sense we give them in ordinary speech. For example, a "dilemma" was orginally the offering of two arguments. In the poem, a "dilemma of the leaves/Discloses twist and tact." What is there in the origins of "twist" that suggests the actions of a tree? How do the origins of "tact" lead us back to the diplomatic bird?
9. How are colors used in the fifth quatrain? *Synesthesia* is a literary term for the substitution of the qualitites of one sense, such as taste, for those of another, such as sight. In what way is "Tabasco at the lapping wave" an ironic used of synesthesia?

10. In what way has the bird been an apostle to the poet (see the final stanza)? What specifically does the poet mean when she says "make miniature/Valhalla of my heart"? How does the closing stanza enlarge the meaning of the opening line, "A light and diplomatic bird"?

Suggestions for Writing and Comparison

1. Compare Gwendolyn Brooks' poems with those of Elizabeth Bishop or Marianne Moore, with particular reference to the use of internal rhyme and "irregular" rhythms.
2. Examine the structure of "Langston Hughes" in comparison to Brooks' "weaponed woman" and "sick man looks at flowers." Show how she has modified her style to fit the subject.
3. Compare Gerard Manley Hopkins' "The Windhover" with "a light and diplomatic bird." How do both poets convey the movement and color of birds through rhythm and diction?
4. Discuss the use of imagery and argument in the poems in this section. Show how Wright (p. 153) uses one or the other, whereas Dodson (p. 155) and Brooks use both in combination. Compare the effectiveness of these approaches in creating memorable lyric poems.

Ossie Davis

Ossie Davis was born in 1917, in Georgia, which is the setting for his play *Purlie Victorious* (1961). He attended Howard University before beginning his career in the theatre as an actor, producer, and playwright.

Davis made his acting debut in 1941 in the play *Joy Exceeding Glory*. Since then he has appeared in several Broadway plays, including *Green Pastures*, *Raisin in the Sun*, and his own *Purlie Victorious*. He has also played a number of television and motion picture roles.

Although *Purlie Victorious* (1961) preceded the popular trend of "sick" humor of the middle and late 1960's, it is written with the same attitude toward convention and institutions. However, *Purlie Victorious* is sane rather than sick comedy. The character of Purlie is that of a man bursting with ideas and rhetoric— often exuberant and exaggerating, but clearly sane—and he establishes for the reader a new perspective from which to view the racial situation.

Purlie Victorious

Act I / Scene 1

> **Scene:** *The setting is the plain and simple interior of an antiquated, run-down farmhouse such as Negro sharecroppers still live in, in South Georgia. Threadbare but warm-hearted, shabby but clean. In the Center is a large, rough-hewn table with three homemade chairs and a small bench. This table is the center of all family activities. The main entrance is a door in the Upstage Right corner, which leads in from a rickety porch which we cannot see. There is a small archway in the opposite corner, with some long strips of gunny-sacking hanging down to serve as a door, which leads off to the kitchen. In the center of the Right wall is a window that is wooden, which opens outward on hinges. Downstage Right is a small door leading off to a bedroom, and opposite, Downstage Left, another door leads out into the backyard, and on into the cotton fields beyond. There is also a smaller table and a cupboard against the wall. An old dresser stands against the Right wall, between the window and the Downstage door. There is a shelf on the Left wall with a pail of drinking water, and a large tin dipper. Various cooking utensils, and items like salt and pepper are scattered about in appropriate places.*

> **At Rise:** *The CURTAIN rises on a stage in semi-darkness. After a moment, when the LIGHTS have come up, the door in the Up Right corner bursts open: Enter* PURLIE JUDSON. PURLIE JUD-SON *is tall, restless, and commanding. In his middle or late thir-ties, he wears a wide-brim, ministerial black hat, a string tie, and a claw hammer coat, which, though far from new, does not fit him too badly. His arms are loaded with large boxes and parcels, which must have come fresh from a department store.* PURLIE *is a man consumed with that divine impatience, without which nothing truly good, or truly bad, or even truly ridiculous, is ever accomplished in this world—with rhetoric and flourish to match.*

PURLIE. (*Calling out loudly.*) Missy! (*No answer.*) Gitlow!—It's me—Purlie Victorious! (*Still no answer.* PURLIE *empties his overloaded arms, with obvious relief, on top of the big Center table. He stands, mops his brow, and blows.*) Nobody home it seems. (*This last he says to someone he as-sumes has come in with him. When there is no answer he hurries to the door through which he entered.*) Come on—come on in!

(Enter LUTIBELLE JENKINS, *slowly, as if bemused. Young, eager, well-built: though we cannot tell it at the moment. Clearly a girl from the backwoods, she carries a suitcase tied up with a rope in one hand, and a greasy shoebox with what's left of her lunch, together with an out-moded, out-sized handbag, in the other. Obviously she has traveled a great distance, but she still manages to look fresh and healthy. Her hat is a horror with feathers, but she wears it like a banner. Her shoes are flat-heeled and plain white, such as a good servant girl in the white folks' kitchen who knows her place is absolutely bound to wear. Her fall coat is dowdy, but well-intentioned with a stingy strip of rabbit fur around the neck.* LUTIEBELLE *is like thousands of Negro girls you might know. Eager, desirous—even anxious, keenly in search for life and for love, trembling on the brink of self-confident and vigorous young womanhood—but afraid to take the final leap: because no one has ever told her it is no longer necessary to be white in order to be virtuous, charming, or beautiful.)*

LUTIEBELLE. *(Looking around as if at a museum of great importance.)* Nobody home it seems.

PURLIE. *(Annoyed to find himself so exactly echoed, looks at her sharply. He takes his watch from his vest pocket, where he wears it on a chain.)* Cotton-picking time in Georgia it's against the law to be home. Come in— unload yourself. *(Crosses and looks out into the kitchen.* LUTIEBELLE *is so enthralled, she still stands with all her bags and parcels in her arm.)* Set your suitcase down.

LUTIEBELLE. What?

PURLIE. It's making you lopsided.

LUTIEBELLE. *(Snapping out of it.)* It is? I didn't even notice. *(Sets suitcase, lunch box, and parcels down.)*

PURLIE. *(Studies her for a moment; goes and gently takes off her hat.)* Tired?

LUTIEBELLE. Not stepping high as I am!

PURLIE. *(Takes the rest of her things and sets them on the table.)* Hungry?

LUTIEBELLE. No, sir. But there's still some of my lunch left if you—

PURLIE. *(Quickly.)* No, thank you. Two ham-hock sandwiches in one day is my limit. *(Sits down and fans himself with his hat.)* Sorry I had to walk you so far so fast.

LUTIEBELLE. *(Dreamily.)* Oh, I didn't mind, sir. Walking's good for you, Miz Emmylou sez—

PURLIE. Miz Emmylou can afford to say that: Miz Emmylou got a car. While all the transportation we got in the world is tied up in second-hand shoe leather. But never mind, my sister, never-you-mind! *(Rises, almost as if to dance, exaltation glowing in his eyes.)* And toll the bell, Big Bethel—toll that big, black, fat and sassy liberty bell! Tell Freedom the bridegroom cometh; the day of her deliverance is now at hand! *(*PURLIE *catches sight of* MISSY *through door Down Left.)* Oh, there she is. *(Crosses to door and calls out.)* Missy!—Oh, Missy!

MISSY. *(From a distance.)* Yes-s-s-s-!

PURLIE. It's me!—Purlie!

MISSY. Purlie Victorious?

PURLIE. Yes. Put that battling stick down and come on in here!

MISSY. All right!

PURLIE. (*Crosses hurriedly back to above table at Center.*) That's Missy, my sister-in-law I was telling you about. (*Clears the table of everything but one of the large cartons, which he proceeds to open.*)

LUTIEBELLE. (*Not hearing him. Still awe-struck to be in the very house, in perhaps the very same room that* PURLIE *might have been born in.*) So this is the house where you was born and bred at.

PURLIE. Yep! Better'n being born outdoors.

LUTIEBELLE. What a lovely background for your homelife.

PURLIE. I wouldn't give it to my dog to raise fleas in!

LUTIEBELLE. So clean—and nice—and warm-hearted!

PURLIE. The first chance I get I'ma burn the damn thing down!

LUTIEBELLE. But—Reb'n Purlie!—It's yours, and that's what counts. Like Miz Emmylou sez—

PURLIE. Come here! (*Pulls her across to the window, flings it open.*) You see that big white house, perched on top of that hill with them two windows looking right down at us like two eyeballs: that's where Ol' Cap'n lives.

LUTIEBELLE. Ol' Cap'n?

PURLIE. Stonewall Jackson Cotchipee. He owns this dump, not me.

LUTIEBELLE. Oh—

PURLIE. And that ain't all: hill and dale, field and farm, truck and tractor, horse and mule, bird and bee and bush and tree—and cotton!—cotton by bole and by bale—every bit o' cotton you see in this county!—Everything and everybody he owns!

LUTIEBELLE. Everybody? You mean he owns people?

PURLIE. (*Bridling his impatience.*) Well—look!—ain't a man, woman or child working in this valley that ain't in debt to that ol' bastard!—(*Catches himself.*) bustard!—(*This still won't do.*) buzzard!—And that includes Gitlow and Missy—everybody—except me.—

LUTIEBELLE. But folks can't own people no more, Reb'n Purlie. Miz Emmylou sez that—

PURLIE. (*Verging on explosion.*) You ain't working for Miz Emmylou no more, you're working for me—Purlie Victorious. Freedom is my business, and I say that ol' man runs this plantation on debt: the longer you work for Ol' Cap'n Cotchipee, the more you owe at the commissary; and if you don't pay up, you can't leave. And I don't give a damn what Miz Emmylou nor nobody else sez—that's slavery!

LUTIEBELLE. I'm sorry, Reb'n Purlie—

PURLIE. Don't apologize, wait!—Just wait!—til I get my church;—wait til I buy Big Bethel back—(*Crosses to window and looks out.*) Wait til I stand once again in the pulpit of Grandpaw Kinkaid, and call upon my people—and talk to my people—About Ol' Cap'n, that miserable son-of-a—

LUTIEBELLE. (*Just in time to save him.*) Wait—!

PURLIE. Wait, I say! And we'll see who's gonna dominize this valley!—him or me! (*Turns and sees* MISSY *through door Down Left.*) Missy—!

(*Enter* MISSY, *ageless, benign, and smiling. She wears a ragged old straw hat, a big house apron over her faded gingham, and low-cut, dragged-out tennis shoes on her feet. She is strong and of good cheer—of a certain shrewdness, yet full of the desire to believe. Her eyes light on* LUTIE-BELLE, *and her arms go up and outward automatically.*)

MISSY. Purlie!

PURLIE. (*Thinks she is reaching for him.*) Missy!

MISSY. (*Ignoring him, clutching* LUTIEBELLE, *laughing and crying.*) Well—well—well!

PURLIE. (*Breaking the stranglehold.*) For God's sake, Missy, don't choke her to death!

MISSY. All my life—all my life I been praying for me a daughter just like you. My prayers is been answered at last. Welcome to our home, whoever you is!

LUTIEBELLE. (*Deeply moved.*) Thank you, ma'am.

MISSY. "M'am—m'am." Listen to the child, Purlie. Everybody down here calls me Aunt Missy, and I'd be much obliged if you would, too.

LUTIEBELLE. It would make me very glad to do so—Aunt Missy.

MISSY. Uhmmmmmm! Pretty as a pan of buttermilk biscuits. Where on earth did you find her, Purlie? (PURLIE *starts to answer.*) Let me take your things—now, you just make yourself at home—Are you hungry?

LUTIEBELLE. No, m'am, but cheap as water is, I sure ain't got no business being this thirsty!

MISSY. (*Starts forward.*) I'll get some for you—

PURLIE. (*Intercepts her; directs* LUTIEBELLE.) There's the dipper. And right out yonder by the fence just this side of that great big live oak tree you'll find the well—sweetest water in Cotchipee county.

LUTIEBELLE. Thank you, Reb'n Purlie. I'm very much obliged. (*Takes dipper from water pail and exits Down Left.*)

MISSY. Reb'n who?

PURLIE. (*Looking off after* LUTIEBELLE.) Perfection—absolute Ethiopian perfect. Hah, Missy?

MISSY. (*Looking off after* LUTIEBELLE.) Oh, I don't know about that.

PURLIE. What you mean you don't know? This girl looks more like Cousin Bee than Cousin Bee ever did.

MISSY. No resemblance to me.

PURLIE. Don't be ridiculous; she's the spitting image—

MISSY. No resemblance whatsoever!

PURLIE. I ought to know how my own cousin looked—

MISSY. But I was the last one to see her alive—

PURLIE. Twins, if not closer!

MISSY. Are you crazy? Bee was more lean, loose, and leggy—

PURLIE. Maybe so, but this girl makes it up in—

MISSY. With no chin to speak of—her eyes: sort of fickle one to another—

PURLIE. I know, but even so—

MISSY. (*Pointing off in* LUTIEBELLE'S *direction.*) Look at her head—it ain't nearly as built like a rutabaga as Bee's own was!

PURLIE. (*Exasperated.*) What's the difference! White folks can't tell one of us from another by the head!

MISSY. Twenty years ago it was, Purlie, Ol' Cap'n laid bull whip to your natural behind—

PURLIE. Twenty years ago I swore I'd see his soul in hell!

MISSY. And I don't think you come full back to your senses yet—That ol' man ain't no fool!

PURLIE. That makes it one "no fool" against another.

MISSY. He's dangerous, Purlie. We could get killed if that old man was to find out what we was trying to do to get that church back.

PURLIE. How can he find out? Missy, how many times must I tell you, if it's one thing I am foolproof in it's white folks' psychology.

MISSY. That's exactly what I'm afraid of.

PURLIE. Freedom, Missy, that's what Big Bethel means. For you, me and Gitlow. And we can buy it for five hundred dollars, Missy. Freedom!— You want it, or don't you?

MISSY. Of course I want it, but—After all, Purlie, that rich ol' lady didn't exactly leave that $500 to us.

PURLIE. She left it to Aunt Henrietta—

MISSY. Aunt Henrietta is dead—

PURLIE. Exactly—

MISSY. And Henrietta's daughter Cousin Bee is dead, too.

PURLIE. Which makes us next in line to inherit the money by law!

MISSY. All right, then, why don't we just go on up that hill man-to-man and tell Ol' Cap'n we want our money?

PURLIE. Missy! You have been black as long as I have—

MISSY. (*Not above having her own little joke.*) Hell, boy, we could make him give it to us.

PURLIE. Make him—how? He's a white man, Missy. What you plan to do, sue him?

MISSY. (*Drops her teasing; thinks seriously for a moment.*) After all, it is our money. And it was our church.

PURLIE. And can you think of a better way to get it back than that girl out there?

MISSY. But you think it'll work, Purlie? You really think she can fool Ol' Cap'n?

PURLIE. He'll never know what hit him.

MISSY. Maybe—but there's still the question of Gitlow.

PURLIE. What about Gitlow?

MISSY. Gitlow has changed his mind.

PURLIE. Then you'll have to change it back.

GITLOW. (*Offstage.*) Help, Missy; help, Missy; help, Missy; help, Missy! (GITLOW *runs on.*)

MISSY. What the devil's the matter this time?

GITLOW. There I was, Missy, picking in the high cotton, twice as fast as the human eye could see. All of a sudden I missed a bole and it fell—it fell on the ground, Missy! I stooped as fast as I could to pick it up and—(*He stoops to illustrate. There is a loud tearing of cloth.*) ripped the seat of my britches. There I was, Missy, exposed from stem to stern.

MISSY. What's so awful about that? It's only cotton.

GITLOW. But cotton is white, Missy. We must maintain respect. Bring me my Sunday School britches.

MISSY. What!

GITLOW. Ol' Cap'n is coming down into the cotton patch today, and I know you want your Gitlow to look his level best. (MISSY *starts to answer.*) Hurry, Missy, hurry! (GITLOW *hurries her off.*)

PURLIE. Gitlow—have I got the girl!

GITLOW. Is that so—what girl?

PURLIE. (*Taking him to the door.*) See? There she is! Well?

GITLOW. Well what?

PURLIE. What do you think?

GITLOW. Nope; she'll never do.

PURLIE. What you mean, she'll never do?

GITLOW. My advice to you is to take that girl back to Florida as fast as you can!

PURLIE. I can't take her back to Florida.

GITLOW. Why can't you take her back to Florida?

PURLIE. 'Cause she comes from Alabama. Gitlow, look at her: she's just the size—just the type—just the style.

GITLOW. And just the girl to get us all in jail. The answer is no! (*Crosses to kitchen door.*) MISSY! (*Back to* PURLIE.) Girl or no girl, I ain't getting mixed up in no more of your nightmares—I got my own. Dammit, Missy, I said let's go!

MISSY. (*Entering with trousers.*) You want me to take my bat to you again?

GITLOW. No, Missy, control yourself. It's just that every second Gitlow's off the firing line-up, seven pounds of Ol' Cap'n's cotton don't git gotten. (*Snatches pants from* MISSY, *but is in too much of a hurry to put them on—starts off.*)

PURLIE. Wait a minute, Gitlow. . . . Wait! (GITLOW *is off in a flash.*) Missy! Stop him!

MISSY. He ain't as easy to stop as he used to be. Especially now Ol' Cap'n's made him Deputy-For-The-Colored.

PURLIE. Deputy-For-The-Colored? What the devil is that?

MISSY. Who knows? All I know is Gitlow's changed his mind.

PURLIE. But Gitlow can't change his mind!

MISSY. Oh, it's easy enough when you ain't got much to start with. I warned you. You don't know how shifty ol' Git can git. He's the hardest man to convince and keep convinced I ever seen in my life.

PURLIE. Missy, you've got to make him go up that hill, he's got to identify this girl—Ol' Cap'n won't believe nobody else.

MISSY. I know—

PURLIE. He's got to swear before Ol' Cap'n that this girl is the real Cousin Bee—

MISSY. I know.

PURLIE. Missy, you're the only person in this world ol' Git'll really listen to.

MISSY. I know.

PURLIE. And what if you do have to hit him a time or two—it's for his own good!

MISSY. I know.

PURLIE. He'll recover from it, Missy. He always does—

MISSY. I know.

PURLIE. Freedom, Missy—Big Bethel; for you; me; and Gitlow—!

MISSY. Freedom—and a little something left over—that's all I ever wanted all my life. (*Looks out into the yard.*) She do look a little somewhat like Cousin Bee—about the feet!

PURLIE. Of course she does—

MISSY. I won't guarantee nothing, Purlie—but I'll try.

PURLIE. (*Grabbing her and dancing her around.*) Everytime I see you, Missy, you get prettier by the pound!

(LUTIEBELLE *enters.* MISSY *sees her.*)

MISSY. Stop it, Purlie, stop it! Stop it. Quit cutting the fool in front of company!

PURLIE. (*Sees* LUTIEBELLE, *crosses to her, grabs her about the waist and swings her around too.*)
How wondrous are the daughters of my people,
Yet knoweth not the glories of themselves!
(*Spins her around for* MISSY'S *inspection. She does look better with her coat off, in her immaculate blue and white maid's uniform.*)
Where do you suppose I found her, Missy—
This Ibo prize—this Zulu Pearl—
This long lost lily of the black Mandingo—
Kikuyu maid, beneath whose brown embrace
Hot suns of Africa are burning still: where—where?
A drudge; a serving wench; a feudal fetch-pot:
A common scullion in the white man's kitchen.
Drowned is her youth in thankless Southern dishpans;
Her beauty spilt for Dixiecratic pigs!
This brown-skinned grape! this wine of Negro vintage—

MISSY. (*Interrupting.*) I know all that, Purlie, but what's her name?

(PURLIE *looks at* LUTIEBELLE *and turns abruptly away.*)

LUTIEBELLE. I don't think he likes my name so much; it's Lutiebelle, ma'am —Lutiebelle Gussiemae Jenkins!

MISSY. (*Gushing with motherly reassurance.*) Lutiebelle Gussiemae Jenkins! My, that's nice.

PURLIE. Nice! It's an insult to the Negro people!

MISSY. Purlie, behave yourself!

PURLIE. A previous condition of servitude, a badge of inferiority, and I refuse to have it in my organization—change it!

MISSY. You want me to box your mouth for you!

PURLIE. Lutiebelle Gussiemae Jenkins! What does it mean in Swahili? Cheap labor!

LUTIEBELLE. Swahili?

PURLIE. One of the thirteen silver tongues of Africa: Swahili, Bushengo, Ashanti, Baganda, Herero, Yoruba, Bambora, Mpongwe, Swahili: a language of moons, of velvet drums; hot days of rivers, red-splashed, and bird-song bright!, black fingers in rice white at sunset red!—ten thousand Queens of Sheba—

MISSY. (*Having to interrupt.*) Just where did Purlie find you, honey?

LUTIEBELLE. It was in Dothan, Alabama, last Sunday, Aunt Missy, right in the junior choir!

MISSY. The junior choir—my, my, my!

PURLIE. (*Still carried away.*)

Behold! I said, this dark and holy vessel,
In whom should burn that golden nut-brown joy
Which Negro womanhood was meant to be.
Ten thousand queens, ten thousand Queens of Sheba:

(*Pointing at* LUTIEBELLE.)

Ethiopia herself—in all her beauteous wonder,
Come to restore the ancient thrones of Cush!

MISSY. Great Gawdamighty, Purlie, I can't hear myself think—!

LUTIEBELLE. That's just what I said last Sunday, Aunt Missy, when Reb'n Purlie started preaching that thing in the pulpit.

MISSY. Preaching it!?

LUTIEBELLE. Lord, Aunt Missy, I shouted clear down to the Mourners' Bench.

MISSY. (*To* PURLIE.) But last time you was a professor of Negro Philosophy.

PURLIE. I told you, Missy: my intention is to buy Big Bethel back; to reclaim the ancient pulpit of Grandpaw Kincaid, and preach freedom in the cotton patch—I told you!

MISSY. Maybe you did, Purlie, maybe you did. You got yourself a license?

PURLIE. Naw!—but—

MISSY. (*Looking him over.*) Purlie Victorious Judson: Self-made minister of the gospel-claw-hammer coattail, shoe-string tie and all.

PURLIE. (*Quietly but firmly holding his ground.*) How else can you lead the Negro people?

MISSY. Is that what you got in your mind: leading the Negro people?

PURLIE. Who else is they got?

MISSY. God help the race.

LUTIEBELLE. It was a sermon, I mean, Aunt Missy, the likes of which has never been heard before.

MISSY. Oh, I bet that. Tell me about it, son. What did you preach?

PURLIE. I preached the New Baptism of Freedom for all mankind, according to the Declaration of Independence, taking as my text the Constitution of the United States of America, Amendments First through Fifteenth, which readeth as follow: "Congress shall make no law—"

MISSY. Enough—that's enough, son—I'm converted. But it is confusing, all the changes you keep going through. (*To* LUTIEBELLE.) Honey, every time I see Purlie he's somebody else.

PURLIE. Not any more, Missy; and if I'm lying may the good Lord put me down in the book of bad names: Purlie is put forever!

MISSY. Yes. But will he stay put forever?

PURLIE. There is in every man a finger of iron that points him what he must and must not do—

MISSY. And your finger points up the hill to that five hundred dollars with which you'll buy Big Bethel back, preach freedom in the cotton patch, and live happily ever after!

PURLIE. The soul-consuming passion of my life! (*Draws out watch.*) It's 2:15, Missy, and Gitlow's waiting. Missy, I suggest you get a move on.

MISSY. I already got a move on. Had it since four o'clock this morning!

PURLIE. Time, Missy—exactly what the colored man in this country ain't got, and you're wasting it!

MISSY. (*Looks at* PURLIE, *and decides not to strike him dead.*) Purlie, would you mind stepping out into the cotton patch and telling your brother Gitlow I'd like a few words with him? (PURLIE, *overjoyed, leaps at* MISSY *as if to hug and dance her around again, but she is too fast.*) Do like I tell you now—go on! (PURLIE *exits singing.* MISSY *turns to* LUTIEBELLE *to begin the important task of sizing her up.*) Besides, it wouldn't be hospitable not to set and visit a spell with our distinguished guest over from Dothan, Alabama.

LUTIEBELLE. (*This is the first time she has been called anything of importance by anybody.*) Thank you, ma'am.

MISSY. Now. Let's you and me just set back and enjoy a piece of my potato pie. You like potato pie, don't you?

LUTIEBELLE. Oh, yes, ma'am, I like it very much.

MISSY. And get real acquainted. (*Offers her a saucer with a slice of pie on it.*)

LUTIEBELLE. I'm ever so much obliged. My, this looks nice! Uhm, uhn, uhn!

MISSY. (*Takes a slice for herself and sits down.*) You know—ever since that ol' man—(*Indicates up the hill.*) took after Purlie so unmerciful with that bull whip twenty years ago—he fidgets! Always on the go; rattling around from place to place all over the country: one step ahead of the white folks—something about Purlie always did irritate the white folks.

LUTIEBELLE. Is that the truth!

MISSY. Oh, my yes. Finally wound up being locked up a time or two for safe-keeping—(LUTIEBELLE *parts with a loud, sympathetic grunt. Changing her tack a bit.*) Always kept up his schooling, though. In fact that boy's got one of the best second-hand educations in this country.

LUTIEBELLE. (*Brightening considerably.*) Is that a fact!

MISSY. Used to read everything he could get his hands on.

LUTIEBELLE. He did? Ain't that wonderful!

MISSY. Till one day he finally got tired, and throwed all his books to the hogs—not enough "Negro" in them, he said. After that he puttered around with first one thing then another. Remember that big bus boycott they had in Montgomery? Well, we don't travel by bus in the cotton patch, so Purlie boycotted mules!

LUTIEBELLE. You don't say so?

MISSY. Another time he invented a secret language, that Negroes could understand but white folks couldn't.

LUTIEBELLE. Oh, my goodness gracious!

MISSY. He sent it C.O.D. to the NAACP but they never answered his letter.

LUTIEBELLE. Oh, they will, Aunt Missy; you can just bet your life they will.

MISSY. I don't mind it so much. Great leaders are bound to pop up from time to time 'mongst our people—in fact we sort of look forward to it. But Purlie's in such a hurry I'm afraid he'll lose his mind.

LUTIEBELLE. Lose his mind—no! Oh, no!

MISSY. That is unless you and me can do something about it.

LUTIEBELLE. You and me? Do what, Aunt Missy? You tell me—I'll do any-thing!

MISSY. (*Having found all she needs to know.*) Well, now; ain't nothing ever all that peculiar about a man a good wife—and a family—and some steady home cooking won't cure. Don't you think so?

LUTIEBELLE. (*Immensely relieved.*) Oh, yes, Aunt Missy, yes. (*But still not getting* MISSY's *intent.*) You'd be surprised how many tall, good-looking, great big, ol' handsome looking mens—just like Reb'n Purlie—walking around, starving theyselves to death! Oh, I just wish I had one to aim my pot at!

MISSY. Well, Purlie Judson is the uncrowned appetite of the age.

LUTIEBELLE. He is! What's his favorite?

MISSY. Anything! Anything a fine-looking, strong and healthy—girl like you could put on the table.

LUTIEBELLE. Like me? Like ME! Oh, Aunt Missy—!

MISSY. (PURLIE's *future is settled.*) Honey, I mind once at the Sunday School picnic Purlie et a whole sack o' pullets!

LUTIEBELLE. Oh, I just knowed there was something—something—just reeks about that man. He puts me in the mind of all the good things I ever had in my life. Picnics, fish-fries, corn-shuckings, and love-feasts, and gospel-singings—picking huckleberries, roasting groundpeas, quilting-bee parties and barbecues; that certain kind of—welcome—you can't get nowhere else in all this world. Aunt Missy, life is so good to us—sometimes!

MISSY. Oh, child, being colored can be a lotta fun when ain't nobody look-ing.

LUTIEBELLE. Ain't it the truth! I always said I'd never pass for white, no matter how much they offered me, unless the things I love could pass, too.

MISSY. Ain't it the beautiful truth!

(PURLIE *enters again*; *agitated.*)

PURLIE. Missy—Gitlow says if you want him come and get him!

MISSY. (*Rises, crosses to door Down Left*; *looks out.*) Lawd, that man do take his cotton picking seriously. (*Comes back to* LUTIEBELLE *and takes her saucer.*) Did you get enough to eat, honey?

LUTIEBELLE. Indeed I did. And Aunt Missy, I haven't had potato pie like that since the senior choir give—

MISSY. (*Still ignoring him.*) That's where I met Gitlow, you know. On the senior choir.

LUTIEBELLE. Aunt Missy! I didn't know you could sing!

MISSY. Like a brown-skin nightingale. Well, it was a Sunday afternoon—Big Bethel had just been—

PURLIE. Dammit, Missy! The white man is five hundred years ahead of us in this country, and we ain't gonna ever gonna catch up with him sitting around on our non-Caucasian rumps talking about the senior choir!

MISSY. (*Starts to bridle at this sudden display of passion, but changes her mind.*) Right this way, honey. (*Heads for door Down Right.*) Where Cousin Bee used to sleep at.

LUTIEBELLE. Yes, ma'am. (*Starts to follow* MISSY.)

PURLIE. (*Stopping her.*) Wait a minute—don't forget your clothes! (*Gives her a large carton.*)

MISSY. It ain't much, the roof leaks, and you can get as much September inside as you can outside any time; but I try to keep it clean.

PURLIE. Cousin Bee was known for her clothes!

MISSY. Stop nagging, Purlie— (*To* LUTIEBELLE.) There's plenty to eat in the kitchen.

LUTIEBELLE. Thank you, Aunt Missy. (*Exits Down Right.*)

PURLIE. (*Following after her.*) And hurry! We want to leave as soon as Missy gets Gitlow in from the cotton patch!

MISSY. (*Blocking his path.*) Mr. Preacher—(*She pulls him out of earshot.*) If we do pull this thing off—(*Studying him a moment.*) what do you plan to do with her after that—send her back where she came from?

PURLIE. Dothan, Alabama? Never! Missy, there a million things I can do with a girl like that, right here in Big Bethel!

MISSY. Yeah! Just make sure they're all legitimate. Anyway, marriage is still cheap, and we can always use another cook in the family! (PURLIE *hasn't the slightest idea what* MISSY *is talking about.*)

LUTIEBELLE. (*From Offstage.*) Aunt Missy.

MISSY. Yes, honey.

LUTIEBELLE. (*Offstage.*) Whose picture is this on the dresser?

MISSY. Why, that's Cousin Bee.

LUTIEBELLE. (*A moment's silence. Then she enters hastily, carrying a large photograph in her hand.*) Cousin Bee!

MISSY. Yes, poor thing. She's the one the whole thing is all about.

LUTIEBELLE. (*The edge of panic.*) Cousin Bee—Oh, my!—Oh, my goodness! My goodness gracious!

MISSY. What's the matter?

LUTIEBELLE. But she's pretty—she's so pretty!

MISSY. (*Takes photograph; looks at it tenderly.*) Yes—she was pretty. I guess they took this shortly before she died.

LUTIEBELLE. And you mean—you want me to look like her?

PURLIE. That's the idea. Now go and get into your clothes. (*Starts to push her off.*)

MISSY. They sent it down to us from the college. Don't she look smart? I'll bet she was a good student when she was living.

LUTIEBELLE. (*Evading* PURLIE.) Good student!

MISSY. Yes. One more year and she'd have finished.

LUTIEBELLE. Oh, my gracious Lord have mercy upon my poor soul!

PURLIE. (*Not appreciating her distress or its causes.*) Awake, awake! Put on thy strength, O, Zion—put on thy beautiful garments. (*Hurries her Offstage.*) And hurry! (*Turning to* MISSY.) Missy, Big Bethel and Gitlow is waiting. Grandpaw Kincaid gave his life. (*Gently places the bat into her hand.*) It is a far greater thing you do now, than you've ever done before —and Gitlow ain't never got his head knocked off in a better cause. (MISSY *nods her head in sad agreement, and accepts the bat.* PURLIE *helps her to the door Down Left, where she exits, a most reluctant executioner.* PURLIE *stands and watches her off from the depth of his satisfaction. The door Down Right eases open, and* LUTIEBELLE, *her suitcase, handbag, fall coat and lunch box firmly in hand, tries to sneak out the front door.* PURLIE *hears her, and turns just in time.*) Where do you think you're going?

LUTIEBELLE. Did you see that, Reb'n Purlie? (*Indicating bedroom from which she just came.*) Did you see all them beautiful clothes—slips, hats, shoes, stockings? I mean nylon stockings like Miz Emmylou wears—and a dress, like even Miz Emmylou don't wear. Did you look at what was in that big box?

PURLIE. Of course I looked at what was in that big box—I bought it—all of it—for you.

LUTIEBELLE. For me!

PURLIE. Of course! I told you! And as soon as we finish you can have it!

LUTIEBELLE. Reb'n Purlie, I'm a good girl. I ain't never done nothing in all this world, white, colored or otherwise, to hurt nobody!

PURLIE. I know that.

LUTIEBELLE. I work hard; I mop, I scrub, I iron; I'm clean and polite, and I know how to get along with white folks' children better'n they do. I pay my church dues every second and fourth Sunday the Lord sends; and I can cook catfish—and hushpuppies—You like hushpuppies, don't you, Reb'n Purlie?

PURLIE. I love hushpuppies!

LUTIEBELLE. Hushpuppies—and corn dodgers; I can cook you a corn dodger would give you the swimming in the head!

PURLIE. I'm sure you can, but—

LUTIEBELLE. But I ain't never been in a mess like this in all my life!

PURLIE. Mess—what mess?

LUTIEBELLE. You mean go up that hill, in all them pretty clothes, and pretend—in front of white folks—that—that I'm your Cousin Bee—somebody I ain't never seen or heard of before in my whole life!

PURLIE. Why not? Some of the best pretending in the world is done in front of white folks.

LUTIEBELLE. But Reb'n Purlie, I didn't know your Cousin Bee was a student at the college; I thought she worked there!

PURLIE. But I told you on the train—

LUTIEBELLE. Don't do no good to tell ME nothing, Reb'n Purlie! I never listen. Ask Miz Emmylou and 'em, they'll tell you I never listen. I didn't know it was a college lady you wanted me to make like. I thought it was for a sleep-in like me. I thought all that stuff you bought in them boxes was stuff for maids and cooks and—Why, I ain't never even been near a college!

PURLIE. So what? College ain't so much where you been as how you talk when you get back. Anybody can do it; look at me.

LUTIEBELLE. Nawsir, I think you better look at me like Miz Emmylou sez—

PURLIE. (*Taking her by the shoulders, tenderly.*) Calm down—just take it easy, and calm down. (*She subsides a little, her chills banished by the warmth of him.*) Now—don't tell me, after all that big talking you done on the train about white folks, you're scared.

LUTIEBELLE. Talking big is easy—from the proper distance.

PURLIE. Why—don't you believe in yourself?

LUTIEBELLE. Some.

PURLIE. Don't you believe in your own race of people?

LUTIEBELLE. Oh, yessir—a little.

PURLIE. Don't you believe the black man is coming to power some day?

LUTIEBELLE. Almost.

PURLIE. Ten thousand Queens of Sheba! What kind of a Negro are you! Where's your race pride?

LUTIEBELLE. Oh, I'm a great one for race pride, sir, believe me—it's just that I don't need it much in my line of work! Miz Emmylou sez—

PURLIE. Damn Miz Emmylou! Does her blond hair and blue eyes make her any more of a woman in the sight of her men folks than your black hair and brown eyes in mine?

LUTIEBELLE. No, sir!

PURLIE. Is her lily-white skin any more money-under-the-mattress than your fine fair brown? And if so, why does she spend half her life at the beach trying to get a sun tan?

LUTIEBELLE. I never thought of that!

PURLIE. There's a whole lotta things about the Negro question you ain't thought of! The South is split like a fat man's underwear; and somebody beside the Supreme Court has got to make a stand for the everlasting glory of our people!

LUTIEBELLE. Yessir.

PURLIE. Snatch Freedom from the jaws of force and filibuster!

LUTIEBELLE. Amen to that!

PURLIE. Put thunder in the Senate—!

LUTIEBELLE. Yes, Lord!

PURLIE. And righteous indignation back in the halls of Congress!

LUTIEBELLE. Ain't it the truth!

PURLIE. Make Civil Rights from Civil Wrongs; and bring that ol' Civil War to a fair and a just conclusion!

LUTIEBELLE. Help him, Lord!

PURLIE. Remind this white and wicked world there ain't been more'n a dime's worth of difference twixt one man and another'n, irregardless of race, gender, creed, or color—since God Himself Almighty set the first batch out to dry before the chimneys of Zion got hot! The eyes and ears of the world is on Big Bethel!

LUTIEBELLE. Amen and hallelujah!

PURLIE. And whose side are you fighting on this evening, sister?

LUTIEBELLE. Great Gawdamighty, Reb'n Purlie, on the Lord's side! But Miss Emmylou sez—

PURLIE. (Blowing up.). This is outrageous—this is a catastrophe! You're a disgrace to the Negro profession!

LUTIEBELLE. That's just what she said all right—her exactly words.

PURLIE. Who's responsible for this? Where's your Maw and Paw at?

LUTIEBELLE. I reckon I ain't rightly got no Maw and Paw, wherever they at.

PURLIE. What!

LUTIEBELLE. And nobody else that I knows of. You see, sir—I been on the go from one white folks' kitchen to another since before I can remember. How I got there in the first place—whatever became of my Maw and Paw, and my kinfolks—even what my real name is—nobody is ever rightly said.

PURLIE. (*Genuinely touched.*) Oh. A motherless child—

LUTIEBELLE. That's what Miz Emmylou always sez—

PURLIE. But—who cared for you—like a mother? Who brung you up—who raised you?

LUTIEBELLE. Nobody in particular—just whoever happened to be in charge of the kitchen that day.

PURLIE. That explains the whole thing—no wonder; you've missed the most important part of being somebody.

LUTIEBELLE. I have? What part is that?

PURLIE. Love—being appreciated, and sought out, and looked after; being fought to the bitter end over even.

LUTIEBELLE. Oh, I have missed that, Reb'n Purlie, I really have. Take mens—all my life they never looked at me the way other girls get looked at!

PURLIE. That's not so. The very first time I saw you—right up there in the junior choir—I give you that look!

LUTIEBELLE. (*Turning to him in absolute ecstasy.*) You did! Oh, I thought so!—I prayed so. All through your sermon I thought I would faint from hoping so hard so. Oh, Reb'n Purlie—I think that's the finest look a person could ever give a person—Oh, Reb'n Purlie! (*She closes her eyes and points her lips at him.*)

PURLIE. (*Starts to kiss her, but draws back shyly.*) Lutiebelle—

LUTIEBELLE. (*Dreamily, her eyes still closed.*) Yes, Reb'n Purlie—

PURLIE. There's something I want to ask you—something I never—in all my life—thought I'd be asking a woman—Would you—I don't know exactly how to say it—would you—

LUTIEBELLE. Yes, Reb'n Purlie?

PURLIE. Would you be my disciple?

LUTIEBELLE. (*Rushing into his arms.*) Oh, yes, Reb'n Purlie, yes!

(*They start to kiss, but are interrupted by a NOISE coming from Offstage.*)

GITLOW. (*Offstage; in the extremity of death.*) No, Missy. No—no!—NO!— (*This last plea is choked off by the sound of some solid object brought smartly into contact with sudden flesh. "CLUNK!"* PURLIE *and* LUTIE-BELLE *stand looking off Left, frozen for the moment.*)

LUTIEBELLE. (*Finally daring to speak.*) Oh, my lord, Reb'n Purlie, what happened?

PURLIE. Gitlow has changed his mind. (*Grabs her and swings her around bodily.*) Toll the bell, Big Bethel!—toll that big, fat, black and sassy liberty bell. Tell Freedom—(LUTIEBELLE *suddenly leaps from the floor into his arms and plants her lips squarely on his. When finally he can come up for air.*) Tell Freedom—tell Freedom—WOW!

Curtain

Act 1 / Scene 2

Time: *It is a little later the same afternoon.*

Scene: *We are now in the little business office off from the commissary, where all the inhabitants of Cotchipee Valley buy food, clothing, and supplies. In the back a traveler has been drawn with just enough of an opening left to serve as the door to the main part of the store. On Stage Left and on Stage Right are simulated shelves where various items of reserve stock are kept: A wash tub, an axe, sacks of peas, and flour; bolts of gingham and calico, etc. Downstage Right is a small desk, on which an ancient typewriter, and an adding machine, with various papers and necessary books and records of commerce are placed. There is a small chair at this desk. Downstage Left is a table, with a large cash register, that has a functioning drawer. Below this is an entrance from the street.*

At Rise: *As the CURTAIN rises, a young white* MAN *of 25 or 30, but still gawky, awkward, and adolescent in outlook and behavior, is sitting on a high stool Downstage Right Center. His face is held in the hands of* IDELLA, *a Negro cook and woman of all work, who has been in the family since time immemorial. She is the only mother* CHARLIE, *who is very much oversized even for his age, has ever known.* IDELLA *is as little as she is old and as tough as she is tiny, and is busily applying medication to* CHARLIE'S *black eye.*

CHARLIE. Ow, Idella, ow! — Ow!

IDELLA. Hold still, boy.

CHARLIE. But it hurts, Idella.

IDELLA. I know it hurts. Whoever done this to you musta meant to knock your natural brains out.

CHARLIE. I already told you who done it — OW!

IDELLA. Charlie Cotchipee, if you don't hold still and let me put this hot poultice on your eye, you better! (CHARLIE *subsides and meekly accepts her ministrations.*) First the milking, then the breakfast, then the dishes, then the washing, then the scrubbing, then the lunch time, next the dishes, then the ironing — and now; just where the picking and plucking for supper ought to be — you!

CHARLIE. You didn't tell Paw?

IDELLA. Of course I didn't — but the sheriff did.

CHARLIE. (*Leaping up.*) The sheriff!

IDELLA. (*Pushing him back down.*) Him and the deputy come to the house less than a hour ago.

CHARLIE. (*Leaping up again.*) Are they coming over here?

IDELLA. Of course they're coming over here — sooner or later.

CHARLIE. But what will I do, Idella, what will I say?

IDELLA. (*Pushing him down.* CHARLIE *subsides.*) "He that keepeth his mouth keepeth his life — "

CHARLIE. Did they ask for me?

IDELLA. Of course they asked for you.

CHARLIE. What did they say?

IDELLA. I couldn't hear too well; your father took them into the study and locked the door behind them.

CHARLIE. Maybe it was about something else.

IDELLA. It was about YOU: that much I could hear! Charlie – you want to get us both killed!

CHARLIE. I'm sorry, Idella, but –

IDELLA. (Overriding; finishing proverb she had begun.) "But he that openeth wide his lips shall have destruction!"

CHARLIE. But it was you who said it was the law of the land –

IDELLA. I know I did –

CHARLIE. It was you who said it's got to be obeyed –

IDELLA. I know it was me, but –

CHARLIE. It was you who said everybody had to stand up and take a stand against –

IDELLA. I know it was me, dammit! But I didn't say take a stand in no barroom!

CHARLIE. Ben started it, not me. And you always said never to take low from the likes of him!

IDELLA. Not so loud; they may be out there in the commissary! (Goes quickly to door Up Center and peers out; satisfied no one has overheard them she crosses back down to CHARLIE.) Look, boy, everybody down here don't feel as friendly towards the Supreme Court as you and me do – you big enough to know that! And don't you ever go outta here and pull a fool trick like you done last night again and not let me know about it in advance. You hear me!

CHARLIE. I'm sorry.

IDELLA. When you didn't come to breakfast this morning, and I went upstairs looking for you, and you just setting there, looking at me with your big eyes, and I seen that they had done hurt you – my, my, my! Whatever happens to you happens to me – you big enough to know that!

CHARLIE. I didn't mean to make trouble, Idella.

IDELLA. I know that, son, I know it. (Makes final adjustments to the poultice.) Now. No matter what happens when they do come I'll be right behind you. Keep your nerves calm and your mouth shut. Understand?

CHARLIE. Yes.

IDELLA. And as soon as you get a free minute come over to the house and let me put another hot poultice on that eye.

CHARLIE. Thank you, I'm very much obliged to you. Idella –

IDELLA. What is it, son?

CHARLIE. Sometimes I think I ought to run away from home.

IDELLA. I know, but you already tried that, honey.

CHARLIE. Sometimes I think I ought to run away from home – again!

(OL' CAP'N has entered from the Commissary just in time to hear this last remark.)

OL' CAP'N. Why don't you, boy – why don't you? (OL' CAP'N COTCHIPEE is aged and withered a bit, but by no means infirm. Dressed in traditional southern linen, the wide hat, the shoestring tie, the long coat, the twirling *moustache of the Ol' Southern Colonel. In his left hand he carries a cane, and in his right a coiled bull whip: his last line of defense. He stops long enough to establish the fact that he means business, threatens them both with a mean cantankerous eye, then hangs his whip — the definitive answer to all who might foolishly question his Confederate power and glory — upon a peg.* CHARLIE *freezes at the sound of his voice.* IDELLA *tenses but keeps working on* CHARLIE'S *eye.* OL' CAP'N *crosses down, rudely pushes her hand aside, lifts up* CHARLIE'S *chin so that he may examine the damage, shakes his head in disgust.*) You don't know, boy, what a strong stomach it takes to stomach you. Just look at you, sitting there — all slopped over like something the horses dropped; steam, stink and all!

IDELLA. Don't you dare talk like that to this child!

OL' CAP'N. (*This stops him — momentarily.*) When I think of his grandpaw, God rest his Confederate soul, hero of the battle of Chicamauga — (*It's too much.*) Get outta my sight! (CHARLIE *gets up to leave.*) Not you — you! (*Indicates* IDELLA. *She gathers up her things in silence and starts to leave.*) Wait a minute — (IDELLA *stops.*) You been closer to this boy than I have, even before his ma died — ain't a thought ever entered his head you didn't know 'bout it first. You got anything to do with what my boy's been thinking lately?

IDELLA. I didn't know he had been thinking lately.

OL' CAP'N. Don't play with me, Idella — and you know what I mean! Who's been putting these integrationary ideas in my boy's head? Was it you — I'm asking you a question, dammit! Was it you?

IDELLA. Why don't you ask him?

OL' CAP'N. (*Snorts.*) Ask him! ASK HIM! He ain't gonna say a word unless you tell him to, and you know it. I'm asking you again, Idella Landy, have you been talking integration to my boy!?

IDELLA. I can't rightly answer you any more on that than he did.

OL' CAP'N. By God, you will answer me. I'll make you stand right there — right there! — all day and all night long, till you do answer me!

IDELLA. That's just fine.

OL' CAP'N. What's that! What's that you say?

IDELLA. I mean I ain't got nothing else to do — supper's on the stove; rice is ready, okra's fried, turnip's simmered, biscuits' baked, and stew is stewed. In fact them lemon pies you wanted special for supper are in the oven right now, just getting ready to burn —

OL' CAP'N. Get outta here!

IDELLA. Oh — no hurry, Ol' Cap'n —

OL' CAP'N. Get the hell out of here! (IDELLA *deliberately takes all the time in the world to pick up her things. Following her around trying to make his point.*) I'm warning both of you; that little lick over the eye is a small skimption compared to what I'm gonna do. (IDELLA *pretends not to listen.*) I won't stop till I get to the bottom of this! (IDELLA *still ignores him.*) Get outta here, Idella Landy, before I take my cane and — (*He raises his cane but* IDELLA *insists on moving at her own pace to exit Down Left.*) And save me some buttermilk to go with them lemon pies, you hear me! (*Turns to* CHARLIE; *not knowing how to approach him.*) The sheriff was here this morning.

CHARLIE. Yessir.

OL' CAP'N. Is that all you got to say to me: "Yessir"?

CHARLIE. Yessir.

OL' CAP'N. You are a disgrace to the southland!

CHARLIE. Yessir.

OL' CAP'N. Shut up! I could kill you, boy, you understand that? Kill you with my own two hands!

CHARLIE. Yessir.

OL' CAP'N. Shut up! I could beat you to death with that bull whip — put my pistol to your good-for-nothing head — my own flesh and blood — and blow your blasted brains all over this valley! (*Fighting to retain his control.*) If — if you wasn't the last living drop of Cotchipee blood in Cotchipee County, I'd — I'd —

CHARLIE. Yessir. (*This is too much.* OL' CAP'N *snatches* CHARLIE *to his feet. But* CHARLIE *does not resist.*)

OL' CAP'N. You trying to get non-violent with me, boy? (CHARLIE *does not answer, just dangles there.*)

CHARLIE. (*Finally.*) I'm ready with the books, sir — that is — whenever you're ready.

OL' CAP'N. (*Flinging* CHARLIE *into a chair.*) Thank you — thank you! What with your Yankee propaganda, your barroom brawls, and all your other non-Confederate activities, I didn't think you had the time.

CHARLIE. (*Picks up account book; reads.*) "Cotton report. Fifteen bales picked yesterday and sent to the cotton gin; bringing our total to 357 bales to date."

OL' CAP'N. (*Impressed.*) 357 — boy, that's some picking. Who's ahead?

CHARLIE. Gitlow Judson, with seventeen bales up to now.

OL' CAP'N. Gitlow Judson; well I'll be damned; did you ever see a cotton-pickinger darky in your whole life?!

CHARLIE. Commissary report —

OL' CAP'N. Did you ever look down into the valley and watch ol' Git a-picking his way through that cotton patch? Holy Saint Mother's Day! I'll bet you —

CHARLIE. Commissary report!

OL' CAP'N. All right! — commissary report.

CHARLIE. Yessir — well, first, sir, there's been some complaints: the flour is spoiled, the beans are rotten, and the meat is tainted.

OL' CAP'N. Cut the price on it.

CHARLIE. But it's also a little wormy —

OL' CAP'N. Then sell it to the Negras — Is something wrong?

CHARLIE. No, sir — I mean, sir . . . , we can't go on doing that, sir.

OL' CAP'N. Why not? It's traditional.

CHARLIE. Yessir, but times are changing — all this debt — (*Indicates book.*) According to this book every family in this valley owes money they'll never be able to pay back.

OL' CAP'N. Of course — it's the only way to keep 'em working. Didn't they teach you nothin' at school?

CHARLIE. We're cheating them — and they know we're cheating them. How long do you expect them to stand for it?

OL' CAP'N. As long as they're Negras—

CHARLIE. How long before they start a-rearing up on their hind legs, and saying: "Enough, white folks—now that's enough! Either you start treating me like I'm somebody in this world, or I'll blow your brains out"?

OL' CAP'N. (*Shaken to the core.*) Stop it—stop it! You're tampering with the economic foundation of the southland! Are you trying to ruin me? One more word like that and I'll kill—I'll shoot— (CHARLIE *attempts to answer.*) Shut up! One more word and I'll—I'll fling myself on your Maw's grave and die of apoplexy. I'll—! I'll—! Shut up, do you hear me? Shut up! (*Enter* GITLOW, *hat in hand, grin on face, more obsequious today than ever.*) Now what the hell *you* want?

GITLOW. (*Taken aback.*) Nothing, sir, nothing!—That is—Missy, my ol' 'oman—well, suh, to git to the truth of the matter, I got a little business—

OL' CAP'N. Negras ain't got no business. And if you don't get the hell back into that cotton patch you better. Git, I said! (GITLOW *starts to beat a hasty retreat.*) Oh, no—don't go. Uncle Gitlow—good ol' faithful ol' Gitlow. Don't go—don't go.

GITLOW. (*Not quite sure.*) Well—you're the boss, boss.

OL' CAP'N. (*Shoving a cigar into* GITLOW's *mouth.*) Just the other day, I was talking to the Senator about you— What's that great big knot on your head?

GITLOW. Missy—I mean, a mosquito!

OL' CAP'N. (*In all seriousness, examining the bump.*) Uh! Musta been wearin' brass knuck—And he was telling me, the Senator was, how hard it was —impossible, he said, to find the old-fashioned, solid, hard-earned, Uncle Tom type Negra nowadays. I laughed in his face.

GITLOW. Yassuh. By the grace of God, there's still a few of us left.

OL' CAP'N. I told him how you and me growed up together. Had the same mammy—my mammy was your mother.

GITLOW. Yessir! Bosom buddies!

OL' CAP'N. And how you used to sing that favorite ol' spiritual of mine: (*Sings.*) "I'm a-coming . . . I'm a-coming, For my head is bending low," (GITLOW *joins in on harmony.*) "I hear the gentle voices calling, Ol' Black Joe. . . ." (*This proves too much for* CHARLIE; *he starts out.*) Where you going?

CHARLIE. Maybe they need me in the front of the store.

OL' CAP'N. Come back here! (CHARLIE *returns.*) Turn around—show Gitlow that eye. (CHARLIE *reluctantly exposes black eye to view.*)

GITLOW. Gret Gawdamighty, somebody done cold cocked this child! Who hit Mr. Charlie, tell Uncle Gitlow who hit you? (CHARLIE *does not answer.*)

OL' CAP'N. Would you believe it? All of a sudden he can't say a word. And just last night, the boys was telling me, this son of mine made hisself a full-fledged speech.

GITLOW. You don't say.

OL' CAP'N. All about Negras—NeGROES he called 'em—four years of college, and he still can't say the word right—seems he's quite a specialist on the subject.

GITLOW. Well, shut my hard-luck mouth!

OL' CAP'N. Yessireebob. Told the boys over at Ben's bar in town, that he was all for mixing the races together.

GITLOW. You go on 'way from hyeah!

OL' CAP'N. Said white children and darky children ought to go the same schoolhouse together!

GITLOW. Tell me the truth, Ol' Cap'n!

OL' CAP'N. Got hisself so worked up some of 'em had to cool him down with a co-cola bottle!

GITLOW. Tell me the truth—again!

CHARLIE. That wasn't what I said!

OL' CAP'N. You calling me a liar, boy!

CHARLIE. No, sir, but I just said, that since it was the law of the land—

OL' CAP'N. It is not the law of the land no sucha thing!

CHARLIE. I didn't think it would do any harm if they went to school together —that's all.

OL' CAP'N. That's all—that's enough!

CHARLIE. They do it up North—

OL' CAP'N. This is down South. Down here they'll go to school together over me and Gitlow's dead body. Right, Git?!

GITLOW. Er, you the boss, boss!

CHARLIE. But this is the law of the—

OL' CAP'N. Never mind the law! Boy—look! You like Gitlow, you trust him, you always did—didn't you?

CHARLIE. Yessir.

OL' CAP'N. And Gitlow here, would cut off his right arm for you if you was to ask him. Wouldn't you, Git?

GITLOW. (*Gulping.*) You the boss, boss.

OL' CAP'N. Now Gitlow ain't nothing if he ain't a Negra!—Ain't you, Git?

GITLOW. Oh—two-three hundred percent, I calculate.

OL' CAP'N. Now, if you really want to know what the Negra thinks about this here integration and all lacka-that, don't ask the Supreme Court—ask Gitlow. Go ahead—ask him!

CHARLIE. I don't need to ask him.

OL' CAP'N. Then I'll ask him. Raise your right hand, Git. You solemnly swear to tell the truth, whole truth, nothing else but, so help you God?

GITLOW. (*Raising hand.*) I do.

OL' CAP'N. Gitlow Judson, as God is your judge and maker, do you believe in your heart that God intended white folks and Negra children to go to school together?

GITLOW. Nawsuh, I do not!

OL' CAP'N. Do you, so help you God, think that white folks and black should mix and 'sociate in street cars, buses, and railroad stations, in any way, shape, form, or fashion?

GITLOW. Absolutely not!

OL' CAP'N. And is it not your considered opinion, God strike you dead if you lie, that all my Negras are happy with things in the southland just the way they are?

GITLOW. Indeed I do!

OL' CAP'N. Do you think ary single darky on my place would ever think of changing a single thing about the South, and to hell with the Supreme Court as God is your judge and maker?

GITLOW. As God is my judge and maker and you are my boss, I do not!

OL' CAP'N. (*Turning in triumph to* CHARLIE.) The voice of the Negra himself! What more proof do you want!

CHARLIE. I don't care whose voice it is—it's still the law of the land, and I intend to obey it!

OL' CAP'N. (*Losing control.*) Get outta my face, boy—get outta my face, before I kill you! Before I—

(CHARLIE *escapes into the commissary.* OL' CAP'N *collapses.*)

GITLOW. Easy, Ol' Cap'n, easy, suh, easy! (OL' CAP'N *gives out a groan.* GITLOW *goes to shelf and comes back with a small bottle and a small box.*) Some aspirins, suh . . . , some asaphoetida? (PURLIE *and* LUTIEBELLE *appear at door Left.*) Not now—later—later! (*Holds bottle to* OL' CAP'N'S *nose.*)

OL' CAP'N. Gitlow—Gitlow!

GITLOW. Yassuh, Ol' Cap'n—Gitlow is here, suh; right here!

OL' CAP'N. Quick, ol' friend—my heart. It's—quick! A few passels, if you please—of that ol' speritual.

GITLOW. (*Sings most tenderly.*) "Gone are the days, when my heart was young and gay . . ."

OL' CAP'N. I can't tell you, Gitlow—how much it eases the pain— (GITLOW *and* OL' CAP'N *sing a phrase together.*) Why can't he see what they're doing to the southland, Gitlow? Why can't he see it, like you and me? If there's one responsibility you got, boy, above all others, I said to him, it's these Negras—your Negras, boy. Good, honest, hard-working cotton choppers. If you keep after 'em.

GITLOW. Yes, Lawd. (*Continues to sing.*)

OL' CAP'N. Something between you and them no Supreme Court in the world can understand—and wasn't for me they'd starve to death. What's gonna become of 'em, boy, after I'm gone—?

GITLOW. Dass a good question, Lawd—you answer him. (*Continues to sing.*)

OL' CAP'N. They belong to you, boy—to you, evah one of 'em! My ol' Confederate father told me on his deathbed: feed the Negras first—after the horses and cattle—and I've done it evah time! (*By now* OL' CAP'N *is sheltered in* GITLOW's *arms. The LIGHTS begin slowly to fade away.* GITLOW *sings a little more.*) Ah, Gitlow ol' friend—something, absolutely sacred 'bout that speritual—I live for the day you'll sing that thing over my grave.

GITLOW. Me, too, Ol' Cap'n, me, too! (GITLOW's *voice rises to a slow, gentle, yet triumphant crescendo, as our LIGHTS fade away.*)

Blackout

Curtain

Act II / Scene 1

Time: *A short while later.*

Scene: *The scene is the same: the little commissary office.*

At Rise: *The Stage is empty. After a moment* GITLOW *hurries in from the commissary proper, crosses down to the little back door and opens it.*

PURLIE. (*Entering hurriedly.*) What took you so long?

GITLOW. S-sh! Not so loud! He's right out there in the commissary! (PURLIE *crosses over and looks out into the commissary, then crosses back to the little back door and holds out his hands.* LUTIEBELLE *enters. She is dressed in what would be collegiate style. She is still full of awe and wonder, and—this time—of fear, which she is struggling to keep under cover.*) Ain't she gonna carry no school books?

PURLIE. What are they doing out there?

GITLOW. The watermelon books don't balance.

PURLIE. What!

GITLOW. One of our melons is in shortage!

PURLIE. You tell him about Lutiebelle—I mean, about Cousin Bee?

GITLOW. I didn't have time. Besides, I wanted you to have one more chance to get out of here alive!

PURLIE. What's the matter with you!? Don't five hundred dollars of your own lawful money mean nothing to you? Ain't you got no head for business?

GITLOW. No! The head I got is for safekeeping, and—besides—(PURLIE *lifts* OL' CAP'N'S *bull whip down from its peg.*) don't touch that thing, Purlie! (GITLOW *races over, snatches it from him, replaces it, and pats it soothingly into place, while at the same time looking to see if* OL' CAP'N *is coming—and all in one continuous move.*)

PURLIE. Why not? It touched me!

GITLOW. (*Aghast.*) Man, ain't nothing sacred to you!?

OL' CAP'N. (*Calling from Off in the commissary.*) Gitlow, come in here!

GITLOW. (*Racing off.*) Coming, Ol' Cap'n, coming!

OL' CAP'N. (*Offstage.*) Now! We are going to cross-examine these water-melons one more time—one watermelon—

GITLOW. (*Offstage.*) One watermelon!

CHARLIE. (*Offstage.*) One watermelon!

OL' CAP'N. Two watermelons—

GITLOW. Two watermelons—

CHARLIE. Two watermelons—

(*The sound of the watermelon count-down continues in the background.* PUR-LIE, *finding he's got a moment, comes over to reassure* LUTIEBELLE.)

PURLIE. Whatever you do, don't panic!

LUTIEBELLE. (*Repeating after him: almost in hypnotic rote.*) Whatever you do, don't panic!

PURLIE. Just walk like I taught you to walk, and talk like I taught you to talk—

LUTIEBELLE. Taught like I walked you to—

PURLIE. (*Shaking her shoulders.*) Lutiebelle!

LUTIEBELLE. Yes, Reb'n Purlie!

PURLIE. Wake up!

LUTIEBELLE. Oh my goodness, Reb'n Purlie—was I sleep?

PURLIE. Alert!

LUTIEBELLE. Alert!—

PURLIE. Wide awake!—

LUTIEBELLE. Wide awake!—

PURLIE. Up on your toes!

LUTIEBELLE. (*Starting to rise on toes.*) Up on your—

PURLIE. No. No, that's just a figure of speech. Now! You remember what I told you—?

LUTIEBELLE. No, sir. Can't say I do, sir.

PURLIE. Well—first: chit-chat—small-talk!

LUTIEBELLE. Yessir—how small?

PURLIE. Pass the time of day—you remember? The first thing I taught you on the train?

LUTIEBELLE. On the train— Oh! "Delighted to remake your acquaintance, I am sure."

PURLIE. That's it—that's it exactly! Now. Suppose he was to say to you: (PURLIE *imitates* OL' CAP'N.) "I bet you don't remember when you wasn't kneehigh to a grasshopper and Ol' Cap'n took you by the hand, and led you down on your first trip to the cotton patch?"

LUTIEBELLE. Just like you told me on the train?

PURLIE. Yes!

LUTIEBELLE. "I must confess—that much of my past life is vague and hazy."

PURLIE. (*Imitating.*) Doggone my hide—you're the cutest li'l ol' piece of brown skin sugar I ever did see!

LUTIEBELLE. Oh, thank you, Reb'n Purlie!

PURLIE. I ain't exactly me, saying that—it's Ol' Cap'n. (*Continues imitation.*) And this is my land, and my cotton patch, and my commissary, and my bull whip—still here, just like you left us. And what might be your name, li'l gal?

LUTIEBELLE. (*Warming to the game.*) Beatrice Judson, sir.

PURLIE. And what is your daddy's name, li'l gal?

LUTIEBELLE. Horace Judson, sir.

PURLIE. And what did they teach you up in that college, li'l gal?

LUTIEBELLE. It was my major education, Ol' Cap'n—

PURLIE. You mean you majored in education. (*Resumes imitation.*) Well —nothing wrong with Negras getting an education, I always say— But then again, ain't nothing right with it, either. Cousin Bee—heh, heh, heh—you don't mind if I call you Cousin Bee, do you, honey?

LUTIEBELLE. Oh, sir, I'd be delighted!

PURLIE. Don't! Don't be delighted until he puts the money in your hands. (*Resumes imitation.*) And where did you say your Maw worked at?

LUTIEBELLE. In North Carolina.

PURLIE. Where is your maw at now?

LUTIEBELLE. She's at the cemetery: she died.

PURLIE. And how much is the inheritance?

LUTIEBELLE. Five hundred dollars for the next of kin.

PURLIE. (*Delighted at her progress.*) Wonderful, just—just—wonderful! (*Enjoying his own imitation now.*) (OL' CAP'N *enters from the commissary, followed by* GITLOW. LUTIEBELLE *sees* OL' CAP'N, *but* PURLIE *is so wrapped up in his own performance he does not.*) Say, maybe you could teach a old dog like me some new tricks. (*He tries to get a rise out of* LU-TIEBELLE *but she is frozen in terror.* OL' CAP'N *becomes aware of* PURLIE'S *presence, and approaches.*) By swickety—a gal like you could doggone well change a joker's luck if she had a mind to—see what I mean? (PURLIE *hunches what he expects to be an invisible* GITLOW *in the ribs. His blow lands upon* OL' CAP'N *with such force, he falls onto a pile of sacks of chicken feed.*)

OL' CAP'N. (*Sputtering.*) What! What in the name of— (GITLOW *and* PURLIE *scramble to help him to his feet.*)

PURLIE. My compliments, sir—are only exceeded by my humblest apologies. And allow me, if you please, to present my Aunt Henrietta's daughter, whom you remember so well; Beatrice Judson—or as we call her—Cousin Bee.

OL' CAP'N. (*He is so taken by what he sees he forgets his anger.*) Well I'll be switched!

PURLIE. Come, Cousin Bee. Say "howdo" to the man.

LUTIEBELLE. How do to the man. I mean— (*Takes time to correct herself, then.*) Delighted to remake your acquaintance, I'm sure.

OL' CAP'N. What's that? What's that she's saying?

PURLIE. College, sir.

OL' CAP'N. College?

PURLIE. That's all she ever talks.

OL' CAP'N. You mean Henrietta's little ol' button-eyed pickaninny was in college? Well bust my eyes wide open! Just LOOK at that! (*Gets closer, but she edges away.*) You remember me, honey. I'm still the Ol' Cap'n round here.

LUTIEBELLE. Oh, sir, it would not be the same without you being the Ol' Cap'n around here.

OL' CAP'N. You don't say! Say, I'll bet you don't remember a long time ago when—

LUTIEBELLE. When I wasn't but knee high to a hoppergrass, and you took me by the hand, and led me on my very first trip to the cotton patch.

OL' CAP'N. (*Ecstatic.*) You mean you remember that!

LUTIEBELLE. Alert, wide awake, and up on my toes—if you please, sir! (*Rises up on her toes.*)

OL' CAP'N. (*Moving in.*) Doggone my hide. You're the cutest li'l ol' piece of brown sugar I ever did see—

LUTIEBELLE. (*Escaping.*) And this is your land, and your cotton patch, and your commissary, and your bull whip—

OL' CAP'N. What's that?

LUTIEBELLE. Just a figure of speech or two—

OL' CAP'N. Well, Beatrice—you wouldn't mind if Ol' Cap'n was to call you Cousin Bee?

LUTIEBELLE. Oh, positively not, not!—since my mother's name was Henrietta Judson; my father's name was Horace Judson—

OL' CAP'N. But most of all, I remember that little ol' dog of yours—"Spicey," wasn't it?

LUTIEBELLE. Oh, we wasn't much for eating dogs, sir—

OL' CAP'N. No, no! Spicey was the name—wasn't it?

(LUTIEBELLE *looking to* PURLIE *for help, but* PURLIE *cannot help. He looks to* GITLOW, *who also cannot remember.*)

LUTIEBELLE. You, er, really think we really called him "Spicey"?

OL' CAP'N. Not him—her!

PURLIE. HER!

LUTIEBELLE. Oh, her! Her! I am most happy to recollect that I do.

OL' CAP'N. You do! You don't say you do!

LUTIEBELLE. I did, as I recall it, have a fond remembrance of you and "Spicey," since you-all went so well together—and at the same time!

OL' CAP'N. You do? Well hush my mouth, eh, Git?

GITLOW. Hush your mouth indeed, sir.

LUTIEBELLE. Cose soon it is my sworn and true confession that I disremembers so many things out of my early pastime that mostly you are haze and vaguey!

OL' CAP'N. Oh, am I now!

LUTIEBELLE. Oh, yes, and sir—indeedy.

OL' CAP'N. Doggone my hide, eh, Git?

GITLOW. Doggone your hide indeed, suh.

LUTIEBELLE. You see of coursely I have spount—

PURLIE. Spent—

LUTIEBELLE. Spunt so much of my time among the college that hardly all of my ancient maidenhead—

PURLIE. Hood.

LUTIEBELLE. Is a thing of the past!

OL' CAP'N. You don't say!

LUTIEBELLE. But yes, and most precisely.

OL' CAP'N. Tell me, Li'l Bee—what did they teach you up at that college?

LUTIEBELLE. Well, mostly they taught me an education, but in between I learned a lot, too.

OL CAP'N. Is that a fact?

LUTIEBELLE. Reading, writing, 'rithmetic—oh, my Lord—just sitting out on the rectangular every evening after four o' clock home work and you have your regular headache—

OL' CAP'N. You know something, I been after these Negras down here for years: Go to school, I'd say, first chance you get—take a coupla courses in advanced cotton picking. But you think they'd listen to me? No sireebob. By swickety! A gal like you could doggone well change a joker's luck if she was a mind to. (*Gives* GITLOW *a broad wink and digs him in his ribs.* GITLOW *almost falls.*) See what I mean?

LUTIEBELLE. Oh, most indo I deed.

OL' CAP'N. Look—anything! Ask me anything! Whatever you want—name it and it's yours!

LUTIEBELLE. You mean—really, really, really?

OL' CAP'N. Ain't a man in Cotchipee County can beat my time when I see something I want—name it! (*Indicates with a sweep the contents of the commissary.*) Some roasted peanuts; a bottle of soda water; a piece of pepmint candy?

LUTIEBELLE. Thank you, sir, but if it's all the same to you I'd rather have my money.

OL' CAP'N. (*As if shot.*) Your WHAT!

LUTIEBELLE. (*Frightened but determined to forge ahead under her own steam.*) Now I'm gonna tell you like it was, Your Honor: You see, Reb'n Purlie and Uncle Gitlow has one aunty between them, name of Harrietta—

PURLIE. Henrietta!

LUTIEBELLE. Henrietta—who used to cook for this rich ol' white lady up in North Carolina years ago; and last year this ol' lady died—brain tumor—

PURLIE. Bright's disease!

LUTIEBELLE. Bright's disease—leaving five hundred dollars to every servant who had ever worked on her place, including Henrietta. But Henrietta had already died, herself: largely from smallpox—

PURLIE. No!

LUTIEBELLE. Smally from large pox?

PURLIE. Influenza!

LUTIEBELLE. Influenza—and since Henrietta's husband Harris—

PURLIE. Horace!

LUTIEBELLE. Horace—was already dead from heart trouble—

PURLIE. Gunshot wounds!—

LUTIEBELLE. (*Exploding.*) His heart stopped beating, didn't it?!

PURLIE. Yes, but—

LUTIEBELLE. Precisely, Reb'n Purlie, precisely! (*Turning back to* OL' CAP'N.) Since, therefore and where-in-as Cousin Bee, her daughter, was first-in-line-for-next-of-kinfolks, the five hundred dollars left in your care and keep by Aunt Henrietta, and which you have been saving just for me all these lonesome years—

OL' CAP'N. I ain't been saving no damn sucha thing!

PURLIE. (*Stepping swiftly into the breach.*) Oh, come out from behind your modesty, sir!

OL' CAP'N. What!

PURLIE. Your kindness, sir; your thoughtfulness, sir; your unflagging consideration for the welfare of your darkies, sir: have rung like the clean clear call of the clarion from Maine to Mexico. Your constant love for them is both hallmark and high water of the true gentility of the dear old South.

OL' CAP'N. Gitlow, Gitlow—go get Charlie. I want him to hear this. (GITLOW *exits Upstage Center.*) Go on, boy, go on!

PURLIE. And as for your faithful ol' darkies themselves, sir—why, down in the quarters, sir, your name stands second only to God Himself Almighty.

OL' CAP'N. You don't mean to tell me!

PURLIE. Therefore, as a humble token of their high esteem and their deep and abiding affection, especially for saving that five hundred dollar inheritance for Cousin Bee, they have asked me to present to you . . . this plaque! (PURLIE *unveils a "sheepskin scroll" from his inside coat pocket.* OL' CAP'N *reaches for it, but* PURLIE *draws it away.* CHARLIE *appears in the doorway Upstage Center followed by* GITLOW.) Which bears the following citation to wit, and I quote: "Whereas Ol' Cap'n has kindly allowed us to remain on his land, and pick his cotton, and tend his cattle, and drive his mules, and whereas Ol' Cap'n still lets us have our hominy grits and fat back on credit and whereas Ol' Cap'n never resorts to bull whip except as a blessing and a benediction, therefore be it resolved, that Ol' Cap'n Cotchipee be cited as the best friend the Negro has ever had, and officially proclaimed Great White Father of the Year!"

OL' CAP'N. (*Stunned.*) I can't believe it—I can't believe it! (*Sees* CHARLIE.) Charlie, boy—did you hear it? Did you hear it, Charlie, my boy—GREAT WHITE FATHER OF THE YEAR!

PURLIE. (*Like a professional undertaker.*) Let me be the first to congratulate you, sir. (*They shake hands solemnly.*)

OL' CAP'N. Thank you, Purlie.

LUTIEBELLE. And me. (*They shake hands solemnly.*)

OL' CAP'N. Thank you, Cousin Bee.

GITLOW. And me, too, Ol' Cap'n.

OL' CAP'N. (*On the verge of tears, as they shake hands.*) Gitlow—Gitlow. I know this is some of your doings—my old friend. (*He turns expectantly to* CHARLIE.) Well, boy—(CHARLIE *is trapped.*) ain't you gonna congratulate your father?

CHARLIE. Yessir. (*Shakes his hand.*)

OL' CAP'N. This—is the happiest day of my life. My darkies—my Negras—my own— (*Chokes up; unable to continue.*)

PURLIE. Hear, hear!

GITLOW AND LUTIEBELLE. Hear, hear!

(CHARLIE *tries to sneak off again, but* OL' CAP'N *sees him.*)

OL' CAP'N. I am just too overcome to talk. Come back here, boy. (CHARLIE *comes back and stands in intense discomfort.*) Silent—speechless—dumb, my friends. Never in all the glorious hoary and ancient annals of all Dixie —never before— (*Chokes up with tears; blows nose with big red handkerchief, and pulls himself together.*) My friends, in the holy scripture —and I could cite you chapter and verse if I was a mind to— "In the beginning God created white folks and He created black folks," and in the name of all that's white and holy, let's keep it that way. And to hell with Abraham Lincoln and Martin Luther King!

PURLIE. I am moved, Ol' Cap'n—

GITLOW AND LUTIEBELLE. Uhn!

PURLIE. Moved beyond my jurisdiction; as for example, I have upon my person a certificate of legal tender duly affixed and so notarized to said itemized effect— (*Hands over an official-looking document.*) a writ of Habeas Corpus.

OL' CAP'N. (*Taking the document.*) Habeas who?

PURLIE. Habeas Corpus. It means I can have the body.

OL' CAP'N. Body—what body?

PURLIE. The body of the cash—the five hundred dollars—that they sent you to hold in trust for Cousin Bee.

OL' CAP'N. (*Pauses to study the eager faces in the room; then*) Charlie—

CHARLIE. Yessir.

OL' CAP'N. Bring me—five hundred dollars—will you? (CHARLIE *starts for safe.*) No, no, no—not that old stuff. Fresh money, clean money out of my private stock out back. Nothin's too good for my Negras.

CHARLIE. Yessir—yessir! (*Starts out, stops.*) And Paw?

OL' CAP'N. Yes, son?

CHARLIE. All I got to say is "Yessir!" (*Crosses to cash register.*)

OL' CAP'N. Just wait—wait till I tell the Senator: "Great White Father of the Year."

CHARLIE. (*Returns with roll of bills which he hands to his father.*) Here you are, Paw.

OL' CAP'N. Thank you, boy.

(*Enter* IDELLA, *followed by the* SHERIFF *and the* DEPUTY.)

IDELLA. Here everybody is, back in the office.

OL' CAP'N. (*Overjoyed to see them.*) Just in time, Sheriff, for the greatest day of my life. Gentlemen—something has happened here today, between me and my Negras, makes me proud to call myself a Confederate: I have just been named Great White Father of the Year. (*To* PURLIE.) Right?

PURLIE. Right. And now if you'll just—

SHERIFF AND DEPUTY. Great White Father of the Year! Congratulations! (*They shake his hands warmly.*)

OL' CAP'N. True, there are places in this world where the darky is rebellious, running hog wild, rising up and sitting down where he ain't wanted, acting sassy in jail, getting plumb out of hand, totally forgetting his place and his manners—but not in Cotchipee County! (*To* PURLIE.) Right?

PURLIE. Right! And now perhaps we could get back to the business at hand.

OL' CAP'N. (*Finishing his count.*) All right—five hundred dollars. (PURLIE *impulsively reaches for the money, but* OL' CAP'N *snatches it back.*) Just a moment. There's still one small formality: a receipt.

PURLIE. A receipt? All right, I'll—

OL' CAP'N. Not you— You! (*Thrusts a printed form toward* LUTIEBELLE.) . . . just for the record. (*Offers her a fountain pen.*) Sign here. Your full and legal name—right here on the dotted line.

PURLIE. (*Reaching for the pen.*) I'll do it—I have her power of attorney.

LUTIEBELLE. (*Beating* PURLIE *to the pen.*) It's all right, Reb'n Purlie, I can write. (*Takes pen and signs paper with a flourish.*)

OL' CAP'N. (*Takes up paper and reads the signature.*) Sheriff, I want this woman arrested!

PURLIE. Arrested?! For what?

OL' CAP'N. She came into my presence, together with him—(*Indicates* PURLIE.) and with him— (*Indicates* GITLOW.) And they all swore to me that she is Beatrice Judson.

PURLIE. She IS Beatrice Judson!

OL' CAP'N. (*Pouncing.*) Then how come she to sign her name: Lutiebelle Gussiemae Jenkins!

PURLIE. Uhn-uhn!

GITLOW. Uhn-uhn!

LUTIEBELLE. Uhn-uhn!

GITLOW. (*Starting off suddenly.*) Is somebody calling my name out there—

OL' CAP'N. Come back here, Gitlow— (GITLOW *halts in his tracks.*) You'll go out of that door when the Sheriff takes you out. And that goes for all of you. (*The* SHERIFF *starts forward.*) Just a minute, Sheriff. Before you take 'em away there's something I've got to do. (*Crosses to where the whip is hung.*)

GITLOW. (*Horrified at the thought of the whip.*) I'll make it up to you in cotton, Ol' Cap'n—

OL' CAP'N. Shut up, Gitlow. (*Takes whip down, and starts to uncoil it.*) Something I started twenty years ago with this bull whip— (*Fastening his eyes on* PURLIE.) Something I intend to finish.

GITLOW. (*Drops to his knees and begins to sing.*) "Gone are the days—"

OL' CAP'N. (*Turning to* GITLOW.) Dammit! I told you to shut up! (*Then back to* PURLIE.) I'm gonna teach you to try to make a damn fool outta white folks; all right, boy, drop them britches.

PURLIE. The hell you preach!

OL' CAP'N. What's that you said?

LUTIEBELLE. He said, "The hell you preach!"

CHARLIE. Paw, wait, listen—!

OL' CAP'N. I thought I told you to shut up! (*Back to* PURLIE.) Boy, I'm gonna teach you to mind what I say!

(PURLIE *doesn't move.* OL' CAP'N *takes a vicious cut at him with the bull whip, and* PURLIE, *leaping back to get out of the way, falls into the arms of the* SHERIFF.)

SHERIFF. I distinctly heard that gentleman order you to drop your britches. (*Spins* PURLIE *around, sets him up, and swings with all his might.* PURLIE *easily ducks and dances away.*)

DEPUTY. Save a little taste for me, Sheriff!

(*The* SHERIFF *swings again; and, again,* PURLIE *dances away. He swings still again, but to no avail.*)

SHERIFF. (*Aggravated.*) Hold still, dammit! (*Swings again, and once more* PURLIE *ducks away.*) Confound it, boy! You trying to make me hurt myself?

DEPUTY. What's the matter, Sheriff—can't you find him?! (*Laughs.*)

SHERIFF. (*Desperate.*) Now, you listen to me, boy! Either you stand up like a man, so I can knock you down, or—

LUTIEBELLE (*Stepping between the* SHERIFF *and* PURLIE.) Don't you dare!

SHERIFF. What!

LUTIEBELLE. Insultin' Reb'n Purlie, and him a man of the cloth! (*Grabs his gun arm and bites it.*)

SHERIFF. Owwww! (*She kicks him in the shin.*) Owwwwwww!

(*The* DEPUTY *charges in to the rescue. He attempts to grab* LUTIEBELLE, *but she eludes him and steps down hard on his corns.*)

DEPUTY. Owwwwwwwwww!
PURLIE. (*Going for the* DEPUTY.) Keep your hands off her, you hypothetical baboon, keep your hands OFF her! (*Grabs the* DEPUTY, *spins him around and knocks him across the room, starts to follow, but the* SHERIFF *grabs him and pins his arms behind him.*)
CHARLIE. (*Breaks loose from* IDELLA, *snatching at the* SHERIFF.) You let him go, dammit, let him go! (*With one arm the* SHERIFF *pushes* CHARLIE *away.*)
SHERIFF. (*Still holding* PURLIE'S *arms pinned back.*) All right, Dep, he's all yours. Throw him your fast ball—high, tight and inside!
DEPUTY. Glad to oblige you, Sheriff! (*He draws back like a big league baseball pitcher.*)
CHARLIE. (*Rushing into the breach.*) Stop! Stop—stop in the name of the— (*The* DEPUTY *swings from the floor,* PURLIE *ducks and rolls his head sharply to one side.* CHARLIE *runs full into the force of the blow. Collapsing heavily.*) Idella—aaaaaaa!
OL' CAP'N. (*Rushing to him.*) Charlie—!
IDELLA. Charlie—!

(PURLIE, *taking advantage of the confusion, snatches* LUTIEBELLE *by the arms and dashes with her out the back door.*)

OL' CAP'N. After them, you idiots, after them!
SHERIFF. (*To the* DEPUTY.) After them, you idiot! (*They both run off after* PURLIE *and* LUTIEBELLE.)

(OL' CAP'N *and* IDELLA *are kneeling beside the prostrate* CHARLIE. GITLOW, *after a moment, comes into the picture.*)

OL' CAP'N. His eyes, Idella, his eyes! Where are his eyes?
IDELLA. Gitlow, fetch me the asaphoetida, Ol' Cap'n, you rub his hands.
GITLOW. Yes'm.
IDELLA. (*Slapping his face.*) Charlie, honey, wake up—wake up! It's me, Idella.

(OL' CAP'N *is too disorganized to be of any assistance.* GITLOW *has returned with a bottle which he hands to* IDELLA. *He then kneels and starts rubbing* CHARLIE'S *hands.*)

GITLOW. Mr. Charlie, wake up—

(*With* GITLOW *and* IDELLA'S *help,* CHARLIE *slowly rises to his feet. Still unsteady, his eyes glazed and vacant.*)

OL' CAP'N. (*Snapping his fingers in front of his eyes.*) It's me, Charlie, me—
It's your daddy, boy! Speak to me—talk to me—say something to me!

CHARLIE. (*Snaps suddenly into speech—but still out on his feet.*) Fourscore
and seven years ago, our fathers brought forth—

OL' CAP'N. Shut up!

Curtain

Act II / Scene 2

> **Time:** *Two days later.*
>
> **Scene:** *Back at the shack, outside in the yard area.*
>
> **At Rise:** MISSY *is discovered, busy working on some potted plants.
> She is preoccupied, but we feel some restlessness, some antici-
> pation in the manner in which she works.* PURLIE *enters.*

PURLIE. (*The great prophet intones his sorrows.*) Toll the bell—Big Bethel;
toll the big, black, ex-liberty bell; tell Freedom there's death in the family.

MISSY. Purlie—

PURLIE. All these wings and they still won't let me fly!

MISSY. Where you been these last two days, Purlie? We been lookin' for you.
All this plotting and planning—risking your dad-blasted neck like a crazy
man! And for what—FOR WHAT! (IDELLA *enters.*) Oh, come in, Miz
Idella.

IDELLA. Is anybody here seen Charlie Cotchipee this morning?

MISSY. No, we haven't.

PURLIE. Is something wrong, Miz Idella?

IDELLA. He left home this morning right after breakfast—here it is after
lunch and I ain't seen him since. I can't find Charlie—first time in forty-
five years I been working up there in that house I ever misplaced anything! You don't suppose he'd run away from home and not take me—?

MISSY. Oh, no, Miz Idella! Not li'l Charlie Cotchipee.

IDELLA. Well, I guess I'd better be getting back. If you should see him—

MISSY. Miz Idella, we all want to thank you for keeping Purlie out of jail so
kindly. (*Hands her flowers.*)

IDELLA. Oh, that was nothing; I just told that ol' man if he didn't stop all that
foolishness about chain gangs and stuff, I would resign from his kitchen
and take Charlie right along with me! But now I've lost Charlie. First time
in forty-five years I ever misplaced anything! (*She exits.*)

MISSY. (*Turns to* PURLIE.) Don't you know there's something more important
in this world than having that broken down ol' ex-church of a barn to
preach in?

PURLIE. Yeah—like what?

MISSY. Like asking Lutiebelle to marry you.

PURLIE. Asking Lutiebelle to marry me?

MISSY. She worships the ground you walk on. Talks about you all the time. You two could get married, settle down, like you ought to, and raise the cutest little ol' family you ever did see. And she's a cookin', po' child—she left you some of her special fritters.

PURLIE. Freedom, Missy, not fritters. The crying need of this Negro day and age is not grits, but greatness; not cornbread but courage; not fat-back, but fight-back; Big Bethel is my Bethel; it belongs to me and to my people; and I intend to have it back if I have to pay for it in blood!

MISSY. All right—come on in and I'll fix you some dinner.

GITLOW. (*Enters front door, singing.*) "I'm comin', I'm comin'—"

MISSY. (*Entering house.*) Not so loud, Gitlow. You want to wake up the mule?

GITLOW. Not on his day off. "For my head is bendin' low—" (GITLOW *sits, unfolds comic section and reads.*)

MISSY. Where's Lutiebelle, Gitlow?

GITLOW. "The history of the War Between the States will be continued next week." That sure is a good story—I wonder how that's gonna come out?

MISSY. Grown man, deacon in the church, reading the funny-paper. And your shirt. You sneaked outta here this morning in your clean white shirt, after I told you time and time again I was saving it!

GITLOW. Saving it for what?

MISSY. It's the only decent thing you got to get buried in! (*Exits side door.*)

GITLOW. Don't you know that arrangements for my funeral has been taken over by the white folks? (*To* PURLIE.) Besides, I got the money!

PURLIE. What kinda money?

GITLOW. The five hundred dollar kinda money.

PURLIE. Five hundred dollars! You mean Ol' Cap'n give the money to you?

GITLOW. "Gitlow," he said. "Ain't another man in this valley, black, white, or otherwise, I would trust to defend and protect me from the N double ACP but you."

PURLIE. Is that a fact?

GITLOW. Well, now. Whatever become of you? All them gretgawdamighty plans your mouth runneth over—all that white folks' psychology?

PURLIE. Gitlow! Er, Deacon Gitlow— Big Bethel is waiting!

GITLOW. So you're the good-for-nothing, raggedy ass high falute 'round here that goes for who-tied-the-bear!

PURLIE. Naw, Git, man—ain't nothing to me.

GITLOW. Always so high and mighty—can't nobody on earth handle white folks but you—don't pay no 'tention to Gitlow; naw—he's a Tom. Tease him—low-rate him—laugh at ol' Gitlow; he ain't nothing but a fool!

PURLIE. Aw, Git, man, you got me wrong. I didn't mean nothing like that!

GITLOW. Who's the fool now, my boy—who's the fool now?

PURLIE. Er—I'm the fool, Gitlow.

GITLOW. Aw, man, you can talk plainer than that.

PURLIE. I'm the fool, Gitlow.

GITLOW. Uh-huh! Now go over to that window, open it wide as it will go and say it so everybody in this whole damn valley can hear you! Go on! Go on, man—I ain't got all day!

PURLIE. (*Goes to window.*) I'm the fool, Gitlow!

GITLOW. Nice. Now beg me!

PURLIE. What!

GITLOW. I said if you want to see the money, beg me! Do it like you do white folks.

PURLIE. I'd rather die and go to hell in a pair gasoline drawers— (GITLOW *starts to put money away.*) No, wait. Holy mackerel, dere, Massa Gitlow—hee, hee, hee. Hey! Boss, could I possible have a look at that there five hundred dollars dere, suh? Hyuh, hyuh, hyuh!

GITLOW. Man, you sure got style! You know together you and me could make the big time! (PURLIE *reaches for money.*) Come in and see me during office hours! As Deputy-For-The-Colored, I guess I'll just sort of step outside for a minute and let that low September sun shine down on a joker as rich as he is black!

PURLIE. Gitlow—Gitlow! (GITLOW *starts for side door.*) If slavery ever comes back I want to be your agent!

GITLOW. Now that was a snaggy-toothed, poverty-struck remark if I ever heard one.

MISSY. (*Enters side door.*) Youall wash your hands and git ready—Gitlow! Where's Lutiebelle?

GITLOW. (*Evasive.*) She didn't get back yet.

MISSY. We know she didn't get back yet.

PURLIE. Where is Lutiebelle, Gitlow?

GITLOW. What I mean is—on our way home from church, we stopped by Ol' Cap'n's awhile, and he asked me to leave her there to help with the Sunday dinner.

PURLIE. And you left her!

MISSY. With that frisky ol' man?

GITLOW. For goodness' sakes, she's only waiting on table.

PURLIE. The woman I love don't wait on table for nobody, especially Ol' Cap'n; I know that scoun'. I'm going and get her!

GITLOW. Wait a minute—you can't get her right now!

PURLIE. (*Studying him.*) What you mean, I can't get her right now?

GITLOW. Not right this minute—that'll spoil everything. Ol' Cap'n wouldn't like it.

MISSY. How low can you git, Gitlow!

GITLOW. I mean she's got to stay and bring us the $500.00.

MISSY. What 500 dollars?

PURLIE. I thought you already had the money?

GITLOW. Well, not exactly. But he promised me faithful to send it down by Lutiebelle.

PURLIE. I'm going and get Lutiebelle—

GITLOW. Wait a minute, wait a minute; you want to buy Big Bethel back or don't you?

PURLIE. (*A glimmering of truth.*) I hope I misunderstand you!

GITLOW. You said it yourself: It is meet that the daughters of Zion should sacrifice themselves for the cause.

PURLIE. (*Grabbing up* MISSY's *bat.*) Gitlow, I'll kill you—!

GITLOW. Wait a minute, wait a minute, wait a MINUTE!

(*The door opens suddenly, and there stands* LUTIEBELLE. *She, too, has on her Sunday best, but it is disheveled. She has a work apron over her dress, with her hat completely askew, the once proud feather now hanging over her face. In her hands she still clutches a rolling pin.*)

MISSY. Lutiebelle—Lutiebelle, honey!

LUTIEBELLE. I think I am going to faint. (*She starts to collapse, and they rush toward her to help; but suddenly she straightens up and waves them off.*) No, I ain't, either—I'm too mad! (*She shudders in recollection.*) I was never so insulted in all my dad-blamed life!

PURLIE. Lutiebelle!

LUTIEBELLE. Oh, excuse me, Reb'n Purlie—I know I look a mess, but—

MISSY. What happened up there?

LUTIEBELLE. (*Boiling again.*) I'm a maid first class, Aunt Missy, and I'm proud of it!

MISSY. Of course you are.

LUTIEBELLE. I ain't had no complaints to speak of since first I stepped into the white folks' kitchen. I'm clean; I'm honest, and I work hard—but one thing: I don't stand for no stuff from them white folks.

PURLIE. Of course you don't. You don't have to—

LUTIEBELLE. I mean, I KNOW my job, and I DO my job—and the next ol' sweaty, ol' grimey, ol' drunkeny man puts his hands on me—so much as touch like he got no business doing—God grant me strength to kill him! Excuse me, Reb'n Purlie.

GITLOW. Well, Ol' Cap'n do get playful at times—did he send the money?

LUTIEBELLE. Money! What money? There ain't none!

GITLOW. What! Naw, naw! He wouldn't do that to me—not to good ol', faithful ol' Gitlow, nawsir!

LUTIEBELLE. The whole thing was a trick—to get you out of the house—

GITLOW. Not to ME he didn't!

LUTIEBELLE. So he could—sneak up behind me in the pantry!

MISSY. What I tell you!—what I tell you!

LUTIEBELLE. I knowed the minute I—Come grabbing on me, Reb'n Purlie; come grabbing his dirty ol' hands on me!

PURLIE. He did!

LUTIEBELLE. And twisting me around, and—and pinching me, Reb'n Purlie!

PURLIE. Pinching you—where? Where?

LUTIEBELLE. Must I, Reb'n Purlie—?

PURLIE. I demand to know—where did he pinch you!

(LUTIEBELLE *diffidently locates a spot on her left cheek. They all examine it anxiously.*)

MISSY. That's him all right!

GITLOW. Aw, Missy—

MISSY. I'd know them fingerprints anywhere!

LUTIEBELLE. Right in the pantry—and then he, he—Oh, Reb'n Purlie, I'm so ashamed!

PURLIE. What did he do? Tell me, woman, tell me: what did he do? WHAT DID HE DO?

LUTIEBELLE. He kissed me!

PURLIE AND MISSY. No!

LUTIEBELLE. He kissed me — right here.

MISSY. (*Squinting, it is a very small spot indeed.*) Right where? (LUTIEBELLE *is so broken up, she can only point to her other cheek.*)

GITLOW. Aw, for Pete's sakes.

PURLIE. (*Almost out of control.*) He kissed my woman, Gitlow — he kissed the woman I love!

GITLOW. So what!

PURLIE. So what do you mean, "So what"? No man kisses the woman I love and lives! (GITLOW *laughs.*) Go ahead, laugh! Laugh. Let's have one last look at your teeth before I knock 'em down your throat!

GITLOW. Aw, man, git off my nerves.

PURLIE. I'm going up that hill, and I'm gonna call that buzzardly ol' bastard out, and I wouldn't be surprised if I didn't beat him until he died.

LUTIEBELLE. (*Suddenly not so sure.*) Reb'n Purlie —

GITLOW. (*Also wondering about* PURLIE.) Now looka here, Purlie — don't you be no fool, boy — you still in Georgia. If you just got to defend the honor of the woman you love, do it somewhere else.

PURLIE. Kissing my woman — kissing my woman! (*Runs to window, flings it open and shouts out.*) Man, I'll break your neck off!

LUTIEBELLE. (*Helping* GITLOW *and* MISSY *to wrestle* PURLIE *away from the window.*) Please, Reb'n Purlie!

PURLIE. (*Breaks away and goes to window and shouts again.*) I'll stomp your eyeballs in!

LUTIEBELLE. (*They snatch him from the window again.*) Don't, Reb'n Purlie — oh my goodness! —

PURLIE. (*Breaks away still again and shouts from window.*) I'll snatch your right arm outta the socket, and beat the rest of you to death!

LUTIEBELLE. (*This time they get him away, and close the window.*) Don't talk like that, Rebn' Purlie!

MISSY. (*Standing at the window, arms widespread to block him.*) Have you gone crazy?

GITLOW. (*Still struggling with* PURLIE.) You go up that hill tonight, boy, and they'll kill you!

PURLIE. Let 'em kill me, it won't be the first time.

LUTIEBELLE. Aunt Missy, stop him —

GITLOW. Listen, boy! This is your Deputy-For-The-Colored telling you you ain't gonna leave this house, and that's an order!

PURLIE. You try and stop me!

GITLOW. Good gracious a life, what's the matter with you? The man only kissed your woman.

PURLIE. Yeah! And what you suppose he'd a done to me if I'd a kissed his? (*The one question too obvious to answer.*) And that's exactly what I'm gonna do to him!

LUTIEBELLE. Please, Reb'n Purlie. I beg you on bended knees. (*She throws her arms around him.*)

PURLIE. (*Holds her close.*) For the glory and honor of the Negro National Anthem; for the glory and honor of brown-skin Negro womanhood; for the glory and honor of— (LUTIEBELLE *suddenly kisses him big and hard.*) —for LUTIEBELLE! (*His emotions explode him out of the door which slams shut behind him.*)

GITLOW.(*Singing.*) "I hear them gentle bloodhounds callin'—Old Black Joe." . . .

(LUTIEBELLE *finds the deepest spot in* MISSY'S *shoulder to bury her head and cry, as:*)

Curtain

Act III / Scene 1

> **Scene:** *The shack.*
>
> **Time:** *Later that same night.*
>
> **At Rise:** *There is light only from a KEROSENE LAMP turned down low. The air of Sunday is gone from the room. The table-cloth has been changed, and things are as they were before.* LUTIEBELLE *enters Down Right.*

LUTIEBELLE. Is it him, Aunt Missy, is it him?

MISSY. No, honey, not yet.

LUTIEBELLE. Oh, I could have sworn I thought it was him. What time is it?

MISSY. About four in the morning from the sound of the birds. Now, why ain't you sleep after all that hot toddy I give you?

LUTIEBELLE. I can't sleep. The strangest thing. I keep hearing bells—

MISSY. Bells?

LUTIEBELLE. Wedding bells. Ain't that funny? Oh, Lord, please don't let him be hurt bad, please! Where can he be, Aunt Missy?

MISSY. Now don't you worry 'bout Purlie. My! You put on your pretty pink dress!

LUTIEBELLE. Yes, ma'am. It's the only thing I got fitting to propose in.

MISSY. Oh?

LUTIEBELLE. I thought, to sort of show my gratitude, I'd offer him my hand in matrimony—it's all I've got.

MISSY. It's a nice hand, and a nice dress—just right for matrimony.

LUTIEBELLE. You really think so, Aunt Missy: really, really, really?

MISSY. I know so, and wherever Reb'n Purlie is this morning, you can bet your bottom dollar he knows it, too.

LUTIEBELLE. Ten thousand Queens of Sheba! Aunt Missy—

MISSY. Yes—

LUTIEBELLE. (*Letting it out in a gush.*) I wanted him to get mad; I wanted him to tear out up that hill; I wanted him to punch that sweaty ol' buzzard in his gizzard— You think I was wrong?

MISSY. I should say not!

LUTIEBELLE. Course I coulda punched him myself, I reckon.

MISSY. Why should you? Why shouldn't our men folks defend our honor with the white folks once in a while? They ain't got nothing else to do.

LUTIEBELLE. You really, really, really think so?

MISSY. (*Shrugs.*) Ten thousand Queens of Sheba—

LUTIEBELLE. Oh, my goodness, when he walks through that door, I'm just gonna—

(*Door Down Left suddenly swings open to reveal* GITLOW.)

GITLOW. (*Entering.*) Well, well, Lutiebelle.

LUTIEBELLE. Did you find him, Uncle Git?

MISSY. Don't depend on Gitlow for nothing, honey—(*Exits to kitchen.*)

LUTIEBELLE. Where can he be, Uncle Gitlow, where can he be?

GITLOW. Oh—good wind like this on his tail oughta put him somewhere above Macon long 'bout now, if his shoes hold out!

LUTIEBELLE. You mean—running!

GITLOW. What's wrong with running? It emancipated more people than Abe Lincoln ever did.

LUTIEBELLE. How dare you! The finest, bravest man—

GITLOW. The finer they come, the braver they be, the deader these white folks gonna kill 'em when they catch 'em!

MISSY. (*Entering from the kitchen.*) Gitlow, I'll skin you!

GITLOW. All that talk about calling that man out, and whipping him—

MISSY. The man is duty-bound to defend the honor of the woman he loves, and any woman worth her salt will tell you so.

LUTIEBELLE. Love can make you do things you really can't do—can't it, Aunt Missy?

GITLOW. Look. That man's got the president, the governor, the courthouse, and both houses of the congress—on his side!

MISSY. Purlie Judson is a man the Negro woman can depend on!

LUTIEBELLE. An honor to his race, and a credit to his people!

GITLOW. (*Not to be sidetracked.*) The army, the navy, the marines; the sheriff, the judge, the jury, the police, the F.B.I.—all on his side. Not to mention a pair of brass knucks and the hungriest dogs this side of hell! Surely youall don't expect that po' boy to go up against all that caucasiatic power empty-handed!

MISSY. O, ye of little faith!

LUTIEBELLE. Didn't my Lord deliver Daniel?

GITLOW. Of course he did—but lions is one thing and white folks is another!

MISSY. Where there's a will there's a woman—

LUTIEBELLE. And where there's a woman there's a way!

GITLOW. (*Exasperated.*) Great Gawdamighty! All right—go ahead and have it your way. But I'll lay you six bits 'gainst half my seat on the heavenly choir, Purlie ain't been up that hill. And the minute he walks in that door—if he ever shows up again around here—I'm gonna prove it! Oh, damn—I can make better time out there talkin' to that mule.

MISSY. Why not—it's one jackass to another.

(GITLOW *exits to the kitchen.* MISSY *and* LUTIEBELLE *look at each other, both determined not to give way to the very real fright they feel. There is a long, uncomfortable pause.*)

LUTIEBELLE. It sure is a lovely year—for this time of morning, I mean. (*There is a pause.*) I can't tell you how much all this fresh air, wine-smoke, and apple-bite reminds me of Alabama.

MISSY. Oh, yes—Ol' Georgia can sure smile pretty when she's of a mind to—

PURLIE. (*Bursts in.*) "Arise and shine for thy light has come."

MISSY. Purlie—Purlie Victorious! (*They embrace.*)

LUTIEBELLE. Oh, you Reb'n Purlie you!

PURLIE. "Truth and Mercy are met together, Righteousness and Peace have kissed each other!" (*They embrace.*)

MISSY. Let me look at you—behold the man!—knee-deep in shining glory. Great day the righteous marching! What happened to you?

PURLIE. Mine enemy hath been destroyed!

MISSY. What!

PURLIE. I told that ol' man twenty years ago, Missy, that over his dead body, Big Bethel would rise again!

MISSY. Purlie—! You mean you done—

PURLIE. "Have I any pleasure that the wicked should die, saith the Lord, and not turn from his ways and live?" Lutiebelle, put on your hat and coat, and hurry!

LUTIEBELLE. Yessir!

PURLIE. Missy, throw us some breakfast into a paper sack, and quick!

MISSY. Yessir!

PURLIE. Gitlow, I'm calling on you and your fellow mule to write a new page in the annals of Negro History Week.

GITLOW. (*Entering.*) Well, if it ain't ol' little black riding hood, dere! How was the mean ol' peckerwolf tonight, dere, kingfish?

MISSY. Tell him, Purlie boy, what you told us: how you sashayed up that hill with force and fistfight!

GITLOW. Hallelujah!

MISSY. How you fit Ol' Cap'n to a halt and a stand-still!

GITLOW. Talk that talk!

MISSY. And left him laying in a pool of his own Confederate blood!

GITLOW. For Pete sakes, Missy—quit lying!

MISSY. Don't you dare call Purlie Judson a liar!

LUTIEBELLE. No man calls Reb'n Purlie a liar and lives!

GITLOW. What's the matter with you people? Purlie ain't been up that hill; Purlie ain't seen Ol' Cap'n; Purlie ain't done doodley squat! And all that gabble about leaving somebody in a pool of his own Confederate blood ain't what the bull left in the barnyard!

PURLIE. Five hundred dollars says it is! (*Draws roll of bills from his pocket, for all to see.*)

ALL. Five hundred dollars!

PURLIE. In cool September cash!

GITLOW. Money! (*Lunges forward, but* PURLIE *slaps his hand.*)

PURLIE. And that ain't all I got— (*Opens bag he has brought. They look in.*)
GITLOW. (*Almost choking in awe.*) Oh, my goodness, Missy—great day in the morning time—Missy—Missy!
MISSY. (*Also impressed.*) Gitlow, that's *it!*
GITLOW. That's *it*, Missy—that's *it!*
MISSY. Of course that's *it!*—ain't nothing in the world but *it!* (PURLIE *slowly pulls out* OL' CAP'N'S *bull whip.*)
GITLOW. Ain't but one way—one way in all this world—for nobody to get that bull whip off'n Ol' Cap'n!
MISSY. And that's off'n his dead body!
GITLOW. And that's the everlovin' truth, so help me.
PURLIE. Here, take it—and burn it in a public place. Lutiebelle—
LUTIEBELLE. Yes, Reb'n Purlie.
PURLIE. This money belongs to the Negro people—
GITLOW. Reb'n Purlie, my boy, I apologize from the bottom of my knees. (*Kneels and starts to sing.*) "Gone are the days—"
MISSY. (*Snatching him to his feet.*) Get up and shut up!
PURLIE. (*Deliberately continuing to* LUTIEBELLE.) Take it, and wear it next to your heart.
LUTIEBELLE. (*Very conscious of the great charge laid upon her, turns her back to* GITLOW *and hides the money in her bosom.*) Until death us do part.
MISSY. (*To* GITLOW.) If I ever catch you with that song in your mouth again I'll choke you with it!
PURLIE. And go wake up the mule. We due in Waycross to buy Big Bethel.
GITLOW. I'm going, I'm going. (*Starts, but can't tear himself away.*) Cash— five hundred dollars in cash. And a bull whip, from Ol' Cap'n Cotchipee himself— Man, I'd give a pretty piece of puddin' to know how you did it!
MISSY. You go and wake up that mule! (*Turning back to* PURLIE.) Me, too! How did you do it, Purlie?
LUTIEBELLE. What happened when you first got there?
PURLIE. (*Almost laughing.*) Now wait a minute—don't rush me!
MISSY. That's what I say: don't rush him—let the man talk!
PURLIE. Talk! Missy, I told you. I haven't got time—
GITLOW. That's all right, Purlie, we'll listen in a hurry.
LUTIEBELLE. What happened when you called him out and whipped him?
PURLIE. I didn't call him out and whip him!
GITLOW. What!
MISSY. You didn't!
LUTIEBELLE. Reb'n Purlie—?
PURLIE. I mean, I did call him out—!
LUTIEBELLE. (*In ecstatic relief.*) Oh— You did call him out!
PURLIE. Yeah—but he didn't come.
ALL. What!
PURLIE. So—er—I went in to get him!
ALL. You did! Sure enough! What happened then?
PURLIE. (*Still seeking escape.*) Well, like I told you—
LUTIEBELLE. Tell us, Reb'n Purlie—please!
PURLIE. (*No escape.*) Well—here was me; and there was him—twisted and bent like a pretzel! Face twitchified like a pan of worms; eyes bugging out;

sweat dreening down like rain; tongue plumb clove to the roof of his mouth! (*He looks to his audience, and is impelled to go on.*) Well—this thief! This murderer; this adulterer—this oppressor of all my people, just a sitting there: Stonewall Jackson Cotchipee, just a sitting there. (*Begins to respond to his own fantasy.*) "Go to, rich man, weep and howl, for your sorrows shall come upon you." And-a "Wherefore abhor yourself, and repent Ye in sackcloth and ashes!" cause ol' Purlie is done come to get you!

LUTIEBELLE. (*Swept away.*) Oh, my Lord!

MISSY. What he do, Purlie—what he do!?

PURLIE. Fell down on bended knees and cried like a baby!

MISSY. Ol' Cap'n Cotchipee on his knees!?

GITLOW. Great day in the morning time!

PURLIE. (*Warming to the task.*) Don't beg me, white folks, it's too late. "Mercy?" What do you know about mercy?! Did you have mercy on Ol' Uncle Tubb when he asked you not to cheat him out of his money so hard, and you knocked him deaf in his left ear?—Did you have mercy on Lolly's boy when he sassed you back, and you took and dipped his head in a bucket of syrup! And twenty years ago when little Purlie, black and manly as he could be, stood naked before you and your bull whip and pleaded with tears in his li'l ol' eyes, did you have mercy!?

GITLOW. Naw!

PURLIE. —And I'll not have mercy now!

ALL. Amen! Help him, Lawd! Preach it, boy, preach it! (*Etc.*)

PURLIE. Vengeance is mine saith the Lord! (*Hallelujah!*) Ye serpents; ye vipers; ye low-down sons of—! (*Amen!*) How can ye escape the damnation of hell!

MISSY. Throw it at him, boy!

PURLIE. And then, bless my soul, I looked up—up from the blazing depths of my righteous indignation! And I saw tears spill over from his eyeballs; and I heard the heart be-clutching anguish of his outcry! His hands was both a-tremble; and slobber a-dribblin' down his lips!

GITLOW. Oh, my Lawd!

PURLIE. And he whined and whimpered like a ol' hound dog don't want you to kick him no more!

LUTIEBELLE. Great goodness a mighty!

PURLIE. And I commenced to ponder the meaning of this evil thing that groveled beneath my footstool—this no-good lump of nobody!—not fit to dwell on this earth beside the children of the blessed—an abomination to the Almighty and stench in the nostrils of his people! And yet— (*Pause for effect.*) And yet—a man! A weak man; a scared man; a pitiful man; like the whole southland bogged down in sin and segregation crawling on his knees before my judgment seat—but still a MAN!

GITLOW. A man, Lawd!

PURLIE. He, too, like all the South, was one of God's creatures—

MISSY. Yes, Lawd!

PURLIE. He, too, like all the South, could never be beyond the reach of love, hope, and redemption.

LUTIEBELLE. Amen!

PURLIE. Somewhere for him—even for him, some father's heart was broken, some mother's tears undried.

GITLOW. Dry 'em, Lawd!

PURLIE. I am my brother's keeper!

ALL. Yes, Lawd.

PURLIE. And thinking on these things, I found myself to pause, and stumble in my great resolve—and sorrow squeezed all fury from my heart—and pity plucked all hatred from my soul—and the racing feet of an avenging anger slowed down to a halt and a standstill—and the big, black, and burly fist of my strong correction—raised on high like a stroke of God's own lightning—fell useless by my side. The book say, "Love one another."

MISSY. Love one another!

PURLIE. The book say, "Comfort ye one another."

LUTIEBELLE. Comfort ye one another.

PURLIE. The book say, "Forgive ye one another."

GITLOW. Forgive Ol' Cap'n, Lord.

PURLIE. Slowly I turned away—to leave this lump of human mess and misery to the infinite darkness of a hell for white folks only, when suddenly—

MISSY. Suddenly, Lord.

PURLIE. Suddenly I put on my brakes—Purlie Victorious Judson stopped dead in his tracks—and stood stark still, and planted his feet, and rared back, asked himself and all the powers—that—be some mighty important questions.

LUTIEBELLE. Yes, he did, Lawd.

MISSY. And that is the truth!

PURLIE. How come—I asked myself, it's always the colored folks got to do all the forgiving?

GITLOW. Man, you mighty right!

PURLIE. How come the only cheek gits turned in this country is the Negro cheek!

MISSY. Preach to me, boy!

PURLIE. What was this, this—man—Ol' Cap'n Cotchipee—that in spite of all his sins and evils, he still had dominion over me?

LUTIEBELLE. Ain't that the truth!

PURLIE. God made us all equal—God made us all brothers—

ALL. Amen, amen.

PURLIE. "And hath made of one blood all nations of men for to dwell on the face of the earth."—Who changed all that!?

GITLOW. (*Furious.*) Who changed it, he said.

PURLIE. Who took it and twisted it around!

MISSY. (*Furious.*) Who was it, he said!

LUTIEBELLE. (*Furious.*) And where's that scoun' hiding?!

PURLIE. So that the Declarator of Independence himself might seem to be a liar?

GITLOW. Who, that's what I want to know, who?

PURLIE. That a man the color of his face—(*Pointing up Cotchipee Hill.*) could live by the sweat of a man the color of mine!

LUTIEBELLE. Work with him, Lawd, work with him!

PURLIE. —Could live away up there in his fine, white mansion, and us down here in a shack not fitting to house the fleas upon his dogs!

GITLOW. Nothing but fleas!

PURLIE. —Could wax hisself fat on the fat of the land; steaks, rice, chicken, roastineers, sweet potato pies, hot buttered biscuits and cane syrup anytime he felt like it and never hit a lick at a snake! And us got to every day git-up-and-git-with-it, sunup-to-sundown, on fatback and cornmeal hoecakes—and don't wind up owning enough ground to get buried standing up in!

MISSY. Do, Lord!

PURLIE. —And horses and cadillacs, bull whips and bourbon, and two for 'leven dollar seegars—and our fine young men to serve at his table; and our fine young women to serve in his bed!

LUTIEBELLE. Help him, Lawd.

PURLIE. Who made it like this—who put the white man on top?

GITLOW. That's what I wants to know!

PURLIE. Surely not the Lord God of Israel who is a just God!

MISSY. Hah, Lord!

PURLIE. And no respecter of persons! Who proved in the American Revolution that all men are created equal!

GITLOW. Man, I was there when he proved it!

PURLIE. Endowed with Civil Rights and First Class Citizenship, Ku Klux Klan, White Citizens Council notwithstanding!

MISSY. Oh, yes, he did!

PURLIE. And when my mind commenced to commemorate and to reconsider all these things—

GITLOW. Watch him, Lawd!

PURLIE. And I thought of the black mother in bondage—(Yes.) and I thought of the black father in prison—(Ha, Lawd!) And of Momma herself—Missy can tell how pretty she was—

MISSY. Indeed I can!

PURLIE. How she died outdoors on a dirty sheet cause the hospital doors said—"For white folks only." And of Papa, God rest his soul—who brought her tender loving body back home—and laid her to sleep in the graveyard—and cried himself to death among his children!

MISSY. (Crying.) Purlie, Purlie—

PURLIE. (Really carried away.) Then did the wrath of a righteous God possess me; and the strength of the host and of ten thousand swept into my good right arm—and I arose and I smote Ol' Cap'n a mighty blow! And the wind from my fist ripped the curtains from the eastern walls—and I felt the weight of his ol' bull whip nestling in my hands—and the fury of a good Gawd-almighty was within me; and I beat him—I whipped him—and I flogged him—and I cut him—I destroyed him!

(IDELLA enters.)

GITLOW. Great day and the righteous marching—Whoeeeee! Man, I ain't been stirred that deep since the tree caught fire on a possum hunt and the dogs pushed Papa in the pot.

MISSY. Idella, you shoulda heard him!

IDELLA. I did hear him—all the way across the valley. I thought he was calling hogs. Well, anyway: all hell is broke loose at the big house. Purlie, you better get outta here. Ol' Cap'n is on the phone to the sheriff.

MISSY. Ol' Cap'n Cotchipee is dead.

IDELLA. The hell you preach.

ALL. What!

IDELLA. Ol' Cap'n ain't no more dead than I am.

LUTIEBELLE. That's a mighty tacky thing to say about your ex-fellow man.

MISSY. Mighty tacky.

LUTIEBELLE. Reb'n Purlie just got through preaching 'bout it. How he marched up Cotchipee hill—

GITLOW. (*Showing the bull whip.*) And took Ol' Cap'n by the bull whip—

MISSY. And beat that ol' buzzard to death!

IDELLA. That is the biggest lie since the devil learned to talk!

LUTIEBELLE. I am not leaving this room till somebody apologizes to Reb'n Purlie V. Judson, the gentleman of my intended.

IDELLA. Purlie Judson! Are you gonna stand there sitting on your behind, and preach these people into believing you spent the night up at the big house whipping Ol' Cap'n to death when all the time you was breaking into the commissary!

MISSY. Breaking into the commissary!

GITLOW. Something is rotten in the cotton!

PURLIE. It's all right, Miz Idella—I'll take it from there—

MISSY. It is not all right—!

PURLIE. While it is true that, maybe, I did not go up that hill just word for word, and call that ol' man out, and beat him to death so much on the dotted line—!

MISSY. (*Snatching up the paper bag.*) I'm goin' to take back my lunch!

PURLIE. Missy! Wait a minute!

LUTIEBELLE. You know what, Aunt Missy?

MISSY. Yes, honey?

LUTIEBELLE. Sometimes I just wish I could drop dead for a while!

PURLIE. Wait, Lutiebelle, give me a chance to—

LUTIEBELLE. Here's your money!—(*Puts roll into* PURLIE'S *hand.*) And that goes for every other great big ol' handsome man in the whole world!

PURLIE. What you want me to do? Go up that hill by myself and get my brains knocked out?

MISSY. It's little enough for the woman you love!

LUTIEBELLE. Why'd you have to preach all them wonderful things that wasn't so?

GITLOW. And why'd you have to go and change your mind?

PURLIE. I didn't mean for them not to be so: it was a—a parable! A prophecy! Believe me! I ain't never in all my life told a lie I didn't mean to make come true, some day! Lutiebelle—!

IDELLA. Purlie: unless you want to give heartbreak a headache, you better run!

PURLIE. Run—run for what!

MISSY. You want Ol' Cap'n to catch you here!?

PURLIE. Confound Ol' Cap'n! Dad-blast Ol' Cap'n! Damn, damn, damn, and double-damn Ol' Cap'n!

(The front door swings open and in walks OL' CAP'N *steaming with anger.)*

OL' CAP'N. *(Controlling himself with great difficulty.)* Somebody—I say somebody—is calling my name!

GITLOW. Ol' Cap'n, you just in time to settle a argument: is Rudolph Valentino still dead?

OL' CAP'N. Shut up!

GITLOW. *(To* MISSY.*)* See—I told you.

OL' CAP'N. One thing I have not allowed in my cotton patch since am-I-born-to-die! And that's stealin'! Somebody broke into my commissary tonight —took two cans of sardines, a box of soda crackers, my bull whip!—*(Picks up whip from table.)* And five hundred dollars in cash. And, boy—*(Walking over to* PURLIE.*)* I want it back!

LUTIEBELLE. Stealing ain't all that black and white.

MISSY. And we certainly wasn't the ones that started it!

GITLOW. Who stole me from Africa in the first place?

LUTIEBELLE. Who kept me in slavery from 1619 to 1863, working me to the bone without no social security?

PURLIE. And tonight—just because I went up that hill, and disembezzled my own inheritance that you stole from me—!

OL' CAP'N. *(Livid.)* I have had a belly full of your black African sass—!

(The door bursts open again; this time it is the SHERIFF *who comes in with pistol drawn.)*

SHERIFF. All right, everybody, drop that gun!

PURLIE. Drop what gun?

OL' CAP'N. So there you are, you idiot—what kept you so long?

SHERIFF. Like you told us to do on the phone, suh, we was taking a good, long, slow snoop 'round and 'bout the commissary looking for clues! And dog-gone if one didn't, just a short while ago, stumble smack into our hands!

OL' CAP'N. What!

SHERIFF. We caught the culprit red-handed—bring in the prisoner, Dep!

DEPUTY. Glad to oblige you, Sheriff.

(Enter DEPUTY, *dragging* CHARLIE, *who has his hands cuffed behind him; wears heavy leg shackles and has a large white gag stuck into his mouth.)*

SHERIFF. Southern justice strikes again!

OL' CAP'N. Charlie!—oh, no!

IDELLA. Charlie, my baby!

OL' CAP'N. Release him, you idiots! Release him at once! (EVERYBODY *pitches in to set* CHARLIE *free.)* What have they done to you, my boy?

IDELLA. What have they done to you!

CHARLIE. *(Free from the gag.)* Hello, Paw—Idella—Purlie—

OL' CAP'N. I'll have your thick, stupid necks for this!

SHERIFF. It was you give the orders, suh!

OL' CAP'N. Not my son, you idiot!

DEPUTY. It was him broke into the commissary.

OL' CAP'N. What!

SHERIFF. It was him stole the five hundred dollars—he confessed!

OL' CAP'N. Steal? A Cotchipee? Suh, that is biologically impossible! (*To* CHARLIE.) Charlie, my boy. Tell them the truth—tell them who stole the money. It was Purlie, wasn't it, boy?

CHARLIE. Well, as a matter of fact, Paw—it was mostly me that broke in and took the money, I'd say. In fact it WAS me!

OL' CAP'N. No!

CHARLIE. It was the only thing I could do to save your life, Paw.

OL' CAP'N. Save my life! Idella, he's delirious—!

CHARLIE. When Purlie come up that hill after you last night, I seen him, and lucky for you I did. The look he had on his face against you was not a Christian thing to behold! It was terrible! I had to get into that commissary, right then and there, open that safe, and pay him his inheritance—even then I had to beg him to spare your life!

OL' CAP'N. (*To* PURLIE.) You spare my life, boy? How dare you? (*To* CHARLIE.) Charlie, my son, I know you never recovered from the shock of losing your mother—almost before you were born. But don't worry—it was Purlie who stole that money and I'm going to prove it. (*Starts to take out gun.* GITLOW *grabs gun.*) Gitlow, my old friend, arrest this boy, Gitlow! As Deputy-For-The-Colored—I order you to arrest this boy for stealing!

GITLOW. (*With a brand new meaning.*) "Gone are the days—" (*Still twirls pistol safely out of* OL' CAP'N'S *reach.*)

PURLIE. "Stealin," is it? Well, I'm gonna really give you something to arrest me for. (*Snatches bull whip.*)

OL' CAP'N. Have a care, boy: I'm still a white man.

PURLIE. Congratulations! Twenty years ago, I told you this bull whip was gonna change hands one of these days!

MISSY. Purlie, wait—!

PURLIE. Stay out of my struggle for power!

MISSY. You can't do wrong just because it's right!

GITLOW. Never kick a man when he's down except in self-defense!

LUTIEBELLE. And no matter what you are, and always will be—the hero of Cotchipee Hill.

PURLIE. Am I?

LUTIEBELLE. Ten thousand queens!

PURLIE. I bow to the will of the Negro people. (*Throws whip away. Back to* OL' CAP'N.) But one thing, Ol' Cap'n, I am released of you—the entire Negro people is released of you! No more shouting hallelujah! every time you sneeze, nor jumping jackass every time you whistle "Dixie"! We gonna love you if you let us and laugh as we leave if you don't. We want our cut of the Constitution, and we want it now: and not with no teaspoon, white folks—throw it at us with a shovel!

OL' CAP'N. Charlie, my boy—my own, lily white, Anglo-Saxon, semi-confederate son. I know you never recovered from the shock of losing your mother almost before you were born. But don't worry: there is still time to take these insolent, messy cotton-picking ingrates down a peg—and prove by word and deed that God is still a white man. Tell 'em! Boy, tell 'em!

CHARLIE. Tell 'em what, Paw?

OL' CAP'N. Tell 'em what you and me have done together. Nobody here would believe me. Tell 'em how you went to Waycross, Saturday night, in my name —

CHARLIE. Yes, sir — I did.

OL' CAP'N. Tell 'em how you spoke to Ol' Man Pelham in my name —

CHARLIE. Yes, sir — I spoke to him.

OL' CAP'N. And paid him cash for that ol' barn they used to call Big Bethel!

CHARLIE. Yes, sir; that's what I did, all right.

OL' CAP'N. And to register the deed in the courthouse in my name —

CHARLIE. Yes, sir, that's exactly what you told me to do —

OL' CAP'N. Then — ain't but one thing left to do with that ramshackle dung-soaked monstrosity — that's burn the damn thing down. (*Laughs aloud in his triumph.*)

CHARLIE. But, Paw —

OL' CAP'N. First thing, though — let me see the deed: I wouldn't want to destroy nothing that didn't — legally — belong to me. (*Snatches deed from* CHARLIE'S *hand. Begins to mumble as he reads it.*)

IDELLA. Twenty years of being more than a mother to you!

CHARLIE. Wait, Idella, wait. I did go to Waycross, like Paw said; I did buy the barn — excuse me Purlie: the church — like he said; and I registered the deed at the courthouse like he told me — but not in Paw's name —

OL' CAP'N. (*Startled by something he sees on the deed.*) What's this?

CHARLIE. (*To* IDELLA.) I registered the deed in the name of —

OL' CAP'N. (*Reading, incredulous.*) "Purlie Victorious Judson —" No!

IDELLA. PURLIE VICTORIOUS Judson?

OL' CAP'N. (*Choking on the words.*) Purlie Victorious Judsssss — aaaarrrrgggghhhhh! (*The horror of it strikes him absolutely still.*)

CHARLIE. (*Taking the deed from* OL' CAP'N'S *limp hand.*) It was the only thing I could do to save your life. (*Offering deed to* PURLIE.) Well, Purlie, here it is.

PURLIE. (*Counting out the five hundred dollars.*) You did a good job, Charlie — I'm much obliged!

CHARLIE. (*Refuses money; still holds out deeds to* PURLIE.) Thank you, Purlie, but —

PURLIE. Big Bethel is my Bethel, Charlie: it's my responsibility. Go on, take it.

CHARLIE. No, no! I couldn't take your money, Purlie —

IDELLA. Don't be a fool, boy — business is business. (*She takes the deed from* CHARLIE *and gives it to* PURLIE, *while at the same time taking the money from* PURLIE.)

CHARLIE. Idella — I can't do that!

IDELLA. I can! I'll keep it for you.

CHARLIE. Well — all right. But only, if — if —

IDELLA. Only if what?

CHARLIE. (*To* PURLIE.) Would you let me be a member of your church?

MISSY. You?

GITLOW. Li'l Charlie Cotchipee!

LUTIEBELLE. A member of Big Bethel?

CHARLIE. May I? That is—that is, if you don't mind—as soon as you get it started?

PURLIE. Man, we're already started: the doors of Big Bethel, Church of the New Freedom for all Mankind, are hereby declared "Open for business!"

GITLOW. Brother Pastor, I move we accept Brother Charlie Cotchipee as our first candidate for membership to Big Bethel on a integrated basis—

MISSY. I second that motion!

PURLIE. You have heard the motion. Are you ready for the question?

ALL. (*Except* OL' CAP'N.) Question!

PURLIE. Those in favor will signify by saying "Aye." (EVERYBODY, *except* OL' CAP'N, *crowds around* CHARLIE, *saying "Aye" over and over, in such a crescendo of welcome that* PURLIE *has to ride over the noise.*) Those opposed? (*Looks at* OL' CAP'N, *who is still standing, as if frozen, as we last saw him. He does not answer.*) Those opposed will signify by saying—

(*He stops . . . all eyes focus on* OL' CAP'N *now, still standing in quiet, frozen-like immobility. There is a moment of silence, an unspoken suspicion in everybody's face. Finally,* GITLOW *goes over and touches* OL' CAP'N, *still standing rigid. Still he does not move.* GITLOW *feels his pulse, listens to his heart, and lifts up his eyelids. Nothing.*)

GITLOW. The first man I ever seen in all this world to drop dead standing up!

Blackout

Act III / Epilogue

Time: *Immediately following.*

Scene: *We are at Big Bethel at funeral services for* OL' CAP'N.

At Rise: *We cannot see the coffin. We hear the ringing of the CHURCH BELL as we come out of the blackout.* PURLIE *is in the pulpit.*

PURLIE. And toll the bell, Big Bethel, toll the bell! Dearly beloved, recently bereaved, and friends, we welcome you to Big Bethel, Church of the New Freedom: part Baptist; part Methodist; part Catholic—with the merriness of Christmas and the happiness of Hanukkah; and to the first integrated funeral in the sovereign, segregated state of Georgia. Let there be no merriments in these buryments! Though you are dead, Ol' Cap'n, and in hell, I suspect—as post-mortal guest of honor, at our expense: it is not too late to repent. We still need togetherness; we still need each otherness—with faith in the futureness of our cause. Let us, therefore, stifle the rifle of conflict, shatter the scatter of discord, smuggle the struggle, tickle the pickle, and grapple the apple of peace!

GITLOW. This funeral has been brought to you as a public service.

PURLIE. Take up his bones. For he who was my skin's enemy, was brave enough to die standing for what he believed. . . . And it is the wish of his family—and his friends—that he be buried likewise— (*The* PALLBEARERS *enter, carrying* OL' CAP'N's *ornate coffin just as he would have wished: standing up! It is draped in a Confederate flag; and his hat, his bull whip, and his pistol, have been fastened to the lid in appropriate places.*) Gently, gently. Put kindness in your fingers. He was a man—despite his own example. Take up his bones. (*The* PALLBEARERS *slowly carry the upright coffin across the stage.*) Tonight, my friends—I find, in being black, a thing of beauty: a joy; a strength; a secret cup of gladness; a native land in neither time nor place—a native land in every Negro face! Be loyal to yourselves: your skin; your hair; your lips, your southern speech, your laughing kindness—are Negro kingdoms, vast as any other! Accept in full the sweetness of your blackness—not wishing to be red, nor white, nor yellow: nor any other race, or face, but this. Farewell, my deep and Africanic brothers, be brave, keep freedom in the family, do what you can for the white folks, and write me in care of the post office. Now, may the Constitution of the United States go with you; the Declaration of Independence stand by you; the Bill of Rights protect you; and the State Commission Against Discrimination keep the eyes of the law upon you, henceforth, now and forever. Amen.

Curtain

Suggestions for Discussion

1. As well as being the name of the play's main character, what is the meaning of the title *Purlie Victorious*? The movie version of the play was called *Gone Are the Days*. What is the significance of that phrase as found within the play? Which seems the most appropriate title?

2. Purlie Judson is described as "consumed with . . . divine impatience." What evidence is there from his behavior in Act I that this statement is true?

3. What are the various implications in Purlie's statement, "Lutiebelle Gussiemae Jenkins! What does it mean in Swahili? Cheap labor!"? Why does Purlie repeat the phrase "ten thousand Queens of Sheba"?

4. What does Charlie personify? What is the significance of his name? What is Charlie's relationship to Idella? What does the characterization of Charlie suggest about the playwright's attitude towards this type?

5. Discuss the significance of the names of the characters, particularly Gitlow, Ol' Cap'n, Purlie, and Idella.

6. What are the various Southern institutions and stereotypes that are satirized in *Purlie Victorious*?

7. What does the church mean to Purlie, to the other Blacks in the play, and to Ol' Cap'n? What is the meaning of its names — Big Bethel and The Church of the New Freedom? Note particularly Purlie's final speech concerning the church. Why is it important both that Charlie asks to be a member and that he is voted in?
8. In the context of the entire play, why is it necessary that Ol' Cap'n die? What do the titles of the play (*Purlie Victorious* and *Gone Are the Days*) suggest in this respect?
9. Who is Ossie Davis' audience? That is, to whom do you think this play is addressed? What is the purpose of the play? In your opinion, is its purpose achieved?

Suggestions for Writing and Comparison

1. Read Ben Jonson's *Volpone*. Compare and contrast the functions of satire in *Volpone* and *Purlie Victorious*. Compare Ol' Cap'n Cotchipee and Volpone as symbolic characters. Are the characters in satire usually rounded (fully developed) or are they symbolic of abstractions such as virtue and vice? In *Volpone* and *Purlie Victorious* specifically, how does characterization function in relation to satire?
2. Read James Baldwin's play *Blues for Mr. Charlie*. Compare Baldwin's and Davis' plays as social comment. Which is most effective? How are the various representations of the white liberal, the bigot, the Uncle Tom, and the Black militant treated in each play? Does the use of humor in *Purlie Victorious* make its overall effect different from that of Baldwin's play?

Chapter 3
Asian American Writers

Carlos Bulosan
Diana Chang
Kuangchi C. Chang
Frank Chin
José Garcia Villa
Lawson Fusao Inada

Pam Koo
Toshio Mori
Bienvenido Santos
Toyo Suyemoto
Ferris Takahashi
Lloyd Tsugawa

Shisei Tsuneishi
Hisaye Yamamoto
Chiang Yee
Lin Yutang

Introduction

American writers have long acknowledged their debt to Asian art and philosophy. The imagist movement in poetry, which dominated the early decades of twentieth-century American literature, was influenced by the conciseness of the Japanese haiku and tanka poems. The stylized form of the Noh play has been adapted to the Western Expressionistic drama, and American playwrights such as Thornton Wilder have used the bare-stage technique of Noh. More recently, poets such as Allen Ginsberg and Gary Snyder have spent years in Asia acquiring firsthand knowledge of non-Western culture.

Ironically, however, Asian American writers have long been neglected in America both by the general reading public and by much of the Asian American reading public. In part this neglect has been due to racist attitudes that were manifested in the Chinese Exclusion Act and the relocation camps of World War II. In part it has been due to a self-fulfilling prophecy: if publishers had little interest in Asian American writing, then few Asian Americans would write for publication. This neglect was also due to the public's belief that it "understood the Oriental," and that he had nothing to write except what would fulfill the stereotype.

■ The three groups that are represented in this section—Chinese, Japanese, and Filipino—were first permitted to enter this country when there were labor shortages on the West Coast. Of the three groups, the Chinese have the oldest history of immigration to the United States, many of them having been brought to America as workers to help lay the tracks for the Central Pacific Railroad. With the completion of this job in 1869, they were thrown into the labor market and aroused hostility because they were offered lower wages and therefore became threateningly competitive to the non-Asian workers. The derogatory expression "coolie wages" is derived from this nineteenth-century situation.

The depression of 1873 caused a panic among unemployed workers who felt that their conditions were aggravated by having to compete for the few available jobs with "cheap" Chinese labor. A series of anti-Chinese riots soon followed. The anti-Chinese feeling, particularly on the West Coast, was so strong that California politicians succeeded in pressuring the federal government to pass the Chinese Exclusion Act in 1882. This piece of legislation denied entry to Chinese laborers for ten years. In 1892 the Chinese Exclusion Act was renewed, and in 1902 Chinese immigration was suspended indefinitely. American citizenship was denied to native-born Chinese until World War II, when China became an American ally.

■ In the nineteenth century, Japanese immigration was less than one percent of the total annual immigration into America. The 1870 census showed that there were only fifty Japanese Americans. But in 1885 the Imperial government legalized emigration of laborers, and by 1900 the number of Japanese Americans had risen to 12,628. The Japanese experienced the same initial hostility afforded to all immigrant groups who had to compete with native Americans for jobs. Because of this hostility Japan made a "gentleman's agreement" with America to stop further emigration. The agreement was largely ineffective: by 1920 Japanese Americans numbered 111,010. The Exclusion Act of 1924 resulted in a sharp decline in Japanese immigration, although business and professional people continued to come to this country in fair numbers.

By 1941 there were 71,000 Nisei and Sansei (the first and second generations of Japanese born in the United States, and therefore American citizens) and 41,000 Issei (the Japanese immigrants to America who were barred from citizenship); most of these people lived on the West Coast. Four months after America entered the war with Japan, all Japanese living on the West Coast, whether Issei, Nisei, or Sansei, alien or citizen, were evacuated to relocation centers. This evacuation came in the wake of the hysteria that was led by the Hearst newspapers. The immediate reasons given for the order were that evacuation would protect the Japanese Americans from mob violence and would guard against the possibility of spies living near the Pacific. While the first reason had roots in reality, it has been conclusively proven that the second did not.

■ In the first decade of the twentieth century many Filipinos migrated to Hawaii for jobs as a result of the economic situation at home. At the end of the First World War the movement shifted to the mainland; the peak of this migration occurred between 1920 and 1930. With the Depression and the job shortage which followed, however, the Filipinos suffered the same experience as several of the newer immigrant groups: certain states passed discriminatory laws against them, and their immigration into America was restricted to a small annual quota which was finally abolished in 1965. The Filipino population in the United States is now approximately 200,000.

■ A few native Asians, who immigrated to the United States during the period when their immigration was severely restricted, were artists and scholars. But most often Asian immigrants followed the pattern of other ethnic groups in the United States: the first generation concerned itself with the stern business of settling in a new land, and it was not until the second or even the third generation that the young were free to get an education and enter the professions and the arts.

The early Asian American writers who were most acceptable were those who best fulfilled the reading public's expectations. Yone Noguchi, the first Asian poet to be published in America, came to this country from Japan at the age of eighteen. His first collection of poems, *Seen and Unseen,* published in 1897, was followed by a half-dozen other volumes of poetry and criticism. Noguchi combines Asian and American influences, often in an obvious or disturbingly superficial way. He begins "O Hana San" with the lines:

> It was many and many a year ago
> In a garden of the cherry-blossom
> On a far off isle you may know
> By the fairy name of Nippon . . .

In more serious poems he frequently demonstrates the influence of Whitman:

> Ah thou, world of this day, sigh not of the poets who have deserted
> thee—aye, I hail myself as I do Homer!
> Behold, a baby flower hymns the creation of the universe in the
> breeze, charming my soul as the lover-moon!

Noguchi's haiku poems also reflect what was an expected combination of Asian and American influences. He retains the seventeen-syllable form, but his mood often suggests nineteenth-century Western Romanticism; and his imagery is less realistic, more allegorical than that of traditional haiku poems:

> Speak not again, Voice!
> The silence washes off sins:
> Come not again, Light!

In later decades, too, the Asian American writers who were most successful were those who best confirmed expectations and accepted images of the Asian American. For example, Chin Y. Lee's *Flower Drum Song* (1957), a light story of San Francisco's Chinatown, became a Rodgers and Hammerstein Broadway hit and a Hollywood film. Jade Snow Wong's autobiographical *Fifth Chinese Daughter* (1945), a view of growing up between two cultures —replete with old-fashioned parents, Americanizing schools, and generally admirable adjustments—was perhaps the most widely read of all Asian American writing. Lin Yutang's philosophical works such as *The Importance of Living* (1937) presented the reading public with an acceptable and enigmatic mandarin wisdom. Even more successful were works that did not permit Asian Americans to speak for themselves, but did it for them, such as the famous Charlie Chan novels, which later became a popular series of motion pictures.

Serious Asian American writing, literature that was less concerned with the light touch and made no contribution to the stereotypes, first began to emerge in the 1940's. *Yokohama, California,* Toshio Mori's collection of short stories which viewed life in a Japanese American ghetto not as the general public conceived it but as the writer lived it, was ready for publication in 1941, before war was declared on Japan. With the outbreak of war publication of the book was postponed, and Mori, along with all the other Japanese Americans on the West Coast, was sent to a relocation camp. *Yokohama, California* was finally published in 1949, but the experience which preceded its publication was enough to silence the author for the future. However, the relocation camp experience did serve to foster a new Japanese American literature. Camp newspapers were a proving ground for the young artist Miné Okubo, who collected her drawings and reminiscences of internment in *Citizen 13660*. This book, published in 1946 and now out of print, was the first to reveal the day-to-day reality of imprisonment. Monica Itoi Sone's autobiographical *Nisei Daughter* (1953) contains scenes involving life in a relocation camp ironically called "Camp Harmony." A third woman writer, Hisaye Yamamoto, used the relocation camp as a background to explore perceptions of reality: Is Miss Sasagawara insane or are those who accept the life of the camp insane? (See p. 235 for "The Legend of Miss Sasagawara.")

One of the most impressive literary efforts to come out of the Japanese American experience of World War II was John Okada's *No-No Boy* (1957), a strangely neglected novel about a Japanese American who refuses to be inducted into the American army during the Second World War and finds himself without any roots after the war, having said "no" to both his American and Japanese backgrounds.

The popular success of works such as Chin Y. Lee's *Flower Drum Song*, Jade Snow Wong's *Fifth Chinese Daughter*, Pardee Lowe's *Father and Glorious Descendant*, and Chiang Yee's *Silent Traveller* series (a collection of poems, prose, and drawings which trace an Asian's travels around the world) indicates that readers had some interest in the writings of Asian Americans, but only in such works as did not probe very far beneath a surface. The neglect of Hisaye Yamamoto, of Okada's *No-No Boy*, and of Louis Chu's disturbingly unromantic novel of Chinatown, *Eat a Bowl of Tea* (1961), suggests that a new reading public had to develop, a public of American readers – and particularly but not exclusively Asian American readers – who truly wanted Asian American writers to speak for themselves, from their own observations and sensibilities. Perhaps it is true that before writers can speak for themselves, they must have some hope of being heard; and an expectation of an audience, the ready receptivity of an audience, go a long way toward fostering talent which might have lain dormant.

Such an audience emerged in the late 1960's, in the wake of the movement for Black awareness. While there has long been an active Asian American press that has produced periodicals, little was done to encourage Asian American belletristic writing. (The publication of stories and poems in periodicals such as *Pacific Citizen* was generally limited to the holiday issues.) With the publication of a spate of Asian American and multi-ethnic periodicals and readers in recent years (e.g., *Third World Women, Roots: An Asian American Reader, Yellow Pearl, Gidra*), Asian American poetry and prose is experiencing a renaissance.

Much of this literary renaissance is concerned with defining the Asian American and Asian American writing. Is the Asian American one who combines the cultures of Asia and America into a unified whole, or is he one who must reject both cultures and find a new and separate definition for himself?

Is he one who identifies himself primarily as Chinese or Japanese or Filipino American rather than Asian American, or does he identify himself, through being an Asian, with Blacks, Chicanos, and Native Americans? Is the Asian American of the 1970's another ingredient in the so-called melting pot of American culture who is free to intermarry and have children who more than symbolically combine the meeting of two continents (see Jon Shirota's novel, *Pineapple White*, 1972), or should he adopt a separatist position in order to survive as a cultural entity? Is the Asian American writer any Asian, regardless of the place of his birth, who is living and writing in America—as Lin Yutang, Diana Chang, and Bienvenido Santos would maintain? Or is the Asian American writer one who is born in the United States of Asian parents and grandparents and who has a sensibility that is neither Asian nor American nor a combination of the two—as Frank Chin, Jeffery Chan, Lawson Inada, and Shawn Hsu Wong would maintain? Does Asian American writing ideally reflect the influence of Asian writing forms (e.g., haiku, tanka, Noh drama), or does it ideally evolve new forms which express Asian American culture in the ways that contemporary Black American writing has been able to express Black American culture? These are the questions with which students of Asian American literature must deal.

Frank Chin

Frank Chin, born in San Francisco, California, is a playwright, critic, and fiction writer. His plays have been produced off-Broadway and on the West Coast. Chin has received various awards for his fiction, including the Joseph Honey Jackson and James T. Phelan awards. He is presently completing an anthology of Asian American writing and a novel under contract with Harper and Row.

Chin is recognized as one of the strongest voices among young Asian American writers. His work is frequently concerned with the alienation and deculturization of the Asian American, as the following essay will illustrate.

Confessions of a Number One Son

I was born and last seen being carried off by alleycats into a dark neighborhood. William Bendix found me in the rubble of a village during a Japanese air raid at my dead momma's withered tit wailing hoarsely. The movie was *China*. I was the symbol of helpless, struggling China in the arms of William Bendix. He named me "Donald Duck."

The wail went from movie to movie. The Japs have tortured me into giving up the secret position and are driving the little life of me left in my little battered body in a truck full of Jap soldiers out to get the jump on John Wayne and my missionary teacher from Indiana and all my friends. I grabbed the wheel of the truck and pulled that truck right off the world and sent it down the darkness. My body rolled out of the burning truck to the feet of John Wayne and all my surprised friends working their stealthy way through the jungle. America saw my face by the flamelight of the burning truck full of Japs. They saw me trying not to cry out in pain while tears streamed down my cheeks.

"Don't try to talk," John Wayne said softly. And John Wayne and the missionary teacher who'd failed to teach me how to properly spell A-M-E-R-I-C-A instead of A-M-E-L-L-I-C-A exchanged looks and sadly shook their heads. And all the soldiers and all my friends were getting down on their knees around me. "I failed," I said. "I guess I'll never be promoted to sergeant now," and my eyes began to roll back into my skull and my breath, a quiet shriek from my lungs, was the sound of metal scraped with a long file. Now and then I coughed and blood rosebudded out of my mouth. John Wayne took the colonel's bird off his collar and pinned it on me.

By the light of burning Japs sputtering and sizzling in the background, women in the shopper's matinees with their paper sacks and red meat tokens saw tears in John Wayne's eyes. "You didn't fail," he said to me and had to gulp something back before he could say, "He-yeck! You got that promotion! I got orders from the President himself to promote you all the way to colonel." And the women in the shopper's matinee sighed at the vision of my face filling the darkness. My eyes opened up big and buzzed with an orchestra playing the *Battle Hymn of the Republic*. And the missionary teacher from Indiana put her ear to my mouth as I agonized out my last words, "Ayeeee! Emmmm!" My eyes came open, shining gleaming silver like something crazy. She wiped the blood from my lips, from my eyes, and arranged my hair a bit at a time. "Eee," I continued. "Easy, champ," John Wayne said. He shrugged violently, suddenly, and looked into the flames of the burning truckful of Japs. "Ell! Ell!" I screamed. "Eye! See! Ayy! AMELLICA!" I cried struggling up to my elbows suddenly. The missionary teacher screamed. John Wayne said, "At ease, colonel," and I fell back into a shot of John Wayne with his mouth open and was dead in his arms.

One summer vacation from college I was Frank Sinatra's gunbearer in the jungle south of the Chinese border in World War II. The Japs ambushed us, wiped out the field hospital and Frank Sinatra stuck his gun out to me while continuing to glare off after the direction of the runoff Japs.

And his arm stayed out there awhile until he got the idea something was wrong. I hadn't taken the gun from him. He turned around to see I wasn't there. I was on the ground awhile back, been blinking sweat out of my eyes a long time now, on my back with a twenty-two pound Browning Automatic Rifle and bipod, a six pound M-1 Garand rifle, a Thompson machine gun with a drum magazine and sack of hand grenades, spare parts and extra Zippo lighters. "I have failed you," I said. "Don't talk now," Frank Sinatra said. Then they were all around my cot. The doctor and Sinatra exchanged looks and shook their heads no at each other. I'm shuddering, trying not to cry. In this movie I'm as tall as Frank Sinatra. Breath comes whinneying from my lungs. Frank Sinatra draws his Colt forty-five and chambers a round. He tells everyone to leave the tent. "You can't do it!" someone says. "It's murder!"

"It's either this way, quick, or letting him scream all night," Sinatra said. "You wouldn't let a dog suffer like that." I was never heard from again in that movie. From the time I was born screaming in a bombed-out railroad station in Shanghai through the days I was known on the lot as America's most loyal Chinese American, because the Japs I came up with on the screen were fouler than even the white man imagined, I always get killed. I'm known in the industry as "The Chinese who dies." So I ask the question: Why me?

■ The answer is Charlie Chan of the movies. Our Father Which art in Hollywood, Charlie Chan be Thy Name. Amen. Everybody took to Charlie Chan, knew he was only passing but saw him as the real image of Chinamen anyway. That was in 1925. By 1936 the success of the Charlie Chan image filtered to the top, well-fixed in the minds of the finest people, including the first official Chinatown spokesman: Leong Gor Yun—a fake Chinatown author with a fake Chinese name, who wrote a fake book "Chinatown Inside Out."

America in its sinister wisdom invented a different movie form to irritate and mess on the minds of each of its minorities individually. For Indians it was the Western. The black movie was the courtroom drama where a black man would be accused of crime and then sit in a courtroom and listen to two white men discuss Abraham Lincoln and Karl Marx. The Chinese movie was the Charlie Chan movie and the road movie. Whites like Gary Cooper in *The General Died at Dawn*, Barbara Stanwyck in *The Bitter Tea of General Yen*, Alan Ladd in *China*, and James Stewart in *The Mountain Road* came to China out of Hollywood to get on a Chinese road over some mountains and discover that this road through China, bumping into love and hate, birth and death, is the road of life and runs into roadblocks, sideroads, and wham, a crossroads! But the beginning is Charlie Chan.

In the beginning there was Earl Derr Biggers, mild-mannered hack writer with a gift for cliches. In Hawaii, laying out on the lanai, sipping his Mai Tai and listening to the happy kanakas crooning harmoniously in the fields as they chopped the sugarcane, Derr Biggers was the picture of a contented Southern colonel sipping a julep on the verandah. He read about a Chinese detective before. And out of the void of this white man's mind, Charlie Chan was born.

In the tradition of 2100 feature films and stage productions with Chinese character leads, no Chinaman's ever played the role of Charlie Chan. Two Japanese in the early days when the Chan part was so small it was at the small print end of the credits, but no Chinaman. Not even when the old men of Fox and Monogram's 44 features had passed. Warner Oland and Sidney Toler were both dead and Roland Winters retired from playing out the last days of his career as someone's grandfather in James Garner and Jerry Lewis movies. All the classic Chans are gone and NBC and Universal Studios did prophesy Chan's second coming in color and sent NBC vice-president David Tebet out into the world saying he was looking for an "Oriental actor who spoke English in an accent understandable to U.S. audiences." Not even when they promised it out of the trade papers, gossip columns, and wire services did a Chinaman ever play Charlie Chan.

Keye Luke, the original Number One Son and still active in the postmidnight talk shows doing his Lionel Barrymore imitation, still looks in his forties and now and then shows up as a blind priest of Chinese mysticism who's overcome his handicap by reciting the drabber quotations of Kahlil Gibran on ABC's *Kung Fu.*

Keye spoke English in an accent good enough to be understood playing fools, converts to Catholicism and Oxford all with that same stiff, studied ineptitude of his Number One Son for over 40 years and was last seen renewing an old friendship with Gregory Peck that led directly to his being trampled to death by the Red Guard in *The Chairman.* Keye took a chance and auditioned for the part of his own father. He also had an idea of his own about playing Number One Son grown up. Keye Luke envisioned a television series featuring the adventures of Charlie Chan's Number One Son all grown up. A hip and modern Chinese American tough who might have been an all-American quarterback before a few years as a special agent of the F.B.I. "Charlie Chan worked for the police department," Keye notes. "This will be different. I will be a private detective." Keye Luke didn't get the part of Charlie Chan. And the Derr Biggers estate that owned Charlie Chan demanded the new Chan be just like the old ones. Keye's registered with Medicare now. Number One Son's in his sixties and still dreaming of going into private practice.

■ Victor Sen Yung, Number Two Son, was Chinatown San Francisco born and raised himself up through high school as a live-in houseboy for a white uptown family where he learned to speak English like he was born in Chicago, Illinois. He's the most talented Asian-American actor there ever was. He stole the show from Bette Davis in *The Letter,* and drove the censors at Paramount nuts with his ability to make anything he said to Loretta Young, in *China,* sound lecherous and aggressive. Scenes between him and Alan Ladd were cut from the finished film because Victor's hornrimmed glasses, skinny, smartass Chinese student was too much for Alan Ladd, who was on the road of life. Among the Yellow actors in Hollywood, Victor Sen Yung is remembered for being moody, pushy, totally out of his mind. He's thought of as being jinxed. I got the impression people were avoiding him. The lines yellow actors are given to speak have been pretty much the same for fifty years. But with Victor Sen Yung's ability to talk any kind of white American and European accent and give it a twirl and a question mark at the end of every phrase and pass it off as a Chinese accent, the lines took on some class.

Soon after Pearl Harbor, the United States Government in the form of the Office of War Information (OWI) notified Hollywood that Charlie Chan movies were now official anti-Jap propaganda. To signal the fact righteously to the Japs, Hollywood produced a grotesque parody of the Chan movies involving a Charlie Chan and his Number One Son who go from comic and lovable clowns to pitiful and loathsome reptiles, from comforting to sinister merely by going from Chinese to Japanese in *Across the Pacific,* John Huston's first big film after his smash *The Maltese Falcon.*

Sydney Greenstreet was a white man who's Jap at heart in Charlie Chan's white suit and white snapbrim . . . unsnapped. And Victor Sen Yung was the gunzel Joe Tatsuiko. He was to parody himself.

As Charlie Chan's Number Two Son he dressed in the latest fads — pleated pants and two-tone shoes. He took double, wham wham with his eyes back on white girls, and be bop baree bopped all kinds of American slang all ineptly, making Americans laugh. They admired the dumb son of Charlie Chan for wanting to be like them. With instinctive genius Victor Sen Yung produced a most distasteful and sinister Joe Tatsuiko merely by doing what Number Two Son did badly for comic relief, but doing it well, so well that, except for the eyes, the skin and hair, he was immaculately, perfectly American. Whites couldn't stand it. The sincere fumbling Number Two Son who was so shy he was rarely seen talking to anyone other than his father or the black chauffeur was now cocky, backslapping Joe Tatsuiko, looking Humphrey Bogart in the eye and saying, "Boy, it's good to find someone on this boat who speaks my language!" He was the first one Bogart shot and killed in the climactic scenes.

When NBC was sniffing the watering holes of the world for an Oriental actor to play an Oriental role, Victor Sen Yung was showing up as Hop Sing, the Cartwright boys' cook on TV's *Bonanza.* Benson Fong, Charlie Chan's Number Three Son, used to be so young, with such a sincere, trusting, handsome face that he got viciously shot up by the Japs in almost every movie he was in outside of the Charlie Chan movies. Today Benson Fong runs a string of sweet'n'sour suey joints and boasts of buying a new Cadillac every two years. He still gets killed in most of his movies and was last seen going to his maker in ABC's *Kung Fu.*

Benson Fong, Victor Sen Yung, and Keye Luke were all in Ross Hunter's 1961 production of *Flower Drum Song.* The film's director, Henry Koster, told me that musicals were usually the costliest form of Hollywood movie to make, because of the high salaries commanded by stars who were both actors and song and dance people. But *Flower Drum Song* didn't cost very much to make, Koster said, because "You don't have to pay Oriental actors as much as you do regular actors."

NBC and Universal didn't cast a yellow lead in the role of Charlie Chan because they hadn't found an Oriental actor that was "dynamic," had "charisma" and "star quality" — in other words, "balls" — enough to play the part of Charlie Chan: . . . a decrepit, hunched over, mealy mouthed, sycophantic, clumsy, more-than-slightly-effeminate, limp-wristed, bucktoothed detective you could tell was Chinese because he never used first-person pronouns "I", "Me," or "We" in the presence of whites. And to compound the offense, NBC trotted out their only black vice-president, Stan Robertson, to say, "We don't think it's offensive," telling us what white men used to tell blacks a generation ago, "We wanted to cast an Oriental, and we looked here and in London and in Hong Kong. Unfortunately, we never found an Oriental actor who could carry the movie."

Stan Robertson was Birmingham's revenge. The Chan movies of the For-ties and Fifties were on-screen off-screen double-visioned parables of racist order with whites on top, blacks on the bottom, and two kinds of Chinese in between. "I'm sure that any intelligent and proud Chinese would more or less resent the whole idea of Chan," Roland Winters, the last Chan, said. "Not so much Chan, because he wasn't too bad, but his, you know, the silly kids that did stupid things."

The Chinese and the silly kids that did stupid things had a servant, Bir-mingham. Birmingham was black — lowest fool on the totem pole and played by Mantan Moreland, last seen doing the same vaudeville routine he brought to the Chan films, in a Midas muffler commercial. Now in 1972, a black man speaking for NBC told us that being told not one of us was dynamic enough to play sleepy old Charlie Chan wasn't offensive.

Whites all over America weren't surprised to see a Chinaman with a black servant and talking nasty into the face of people like Willy Best in *Charlie Chan at the Race Track*. A film that featured Charlie Chan saying, "Murder without blood, like Amos without Andy." But it didn't look right to me. Word got around Hollywood that I was a troublemaker. A picture of Stepin Fetchit basking by his pool in Beverly Hills had Chinese servants in Mandarin collars serving him drinks. I sensed a primitive message running to the blacks out of the Charlie Chan movies.

■ I went to a tape recording of my agent's voice, and talked to it — my agent, Bessie Loo, the agent handling most of us yellows. I discovered I was dealing with one of the powers behind Charlie Chan. She's the only agent ever per-mitted to work as a studio casting director while working as an agent. She dealt with herself, casting her clients. They were all yellows. She delivered the yellows to the studio. Bessie Loo is the source of every Asian, Oriental, gook, Jap, Chinaman, Nip, Chink, Slopehead, Chinese, and Japanese you remember. And that lingering impression of bland indifference all of them mechanics, cooks, houseboys, orphans, honorable sons, and Japanese sol-diers combined leave you with is the result of Bessie Loo's genius.

"Bessie," I said to the playback of her voice, "I can't do this Chan movie. Not another one. I'm too old to still be playing his son. And the other ones . . . they've been on my conscience, Bessie, ever since I read Richard Wright's *Black Boy*. And Bessie, he wrote up an account of a black man down South who lets white folks kick him in the ass for a quarter, Bessie. And he just laughs and picks up the quarter off the scummy old floor with his lips! and wags his ass! And Shorty says he's going to the North, and they ask Shorty, 'Shorty, what're you gonna do up North?' And Shorty said, 'I'll pass for Chinese.' Listen, Bessie, they don't like us, and we're not even down South! I'm scared. I got a wife and kid."

And Bessie Loo, this ancient woman, a seventy-odd-year-old woman whose skin was like cocoons all over her, recorded on Mother's Day, "Well, of course, I'm not as sensitive as some of the other people. To me, I think it's sort of a comedy thing, you know."

"But, Bessie, the joke's on me."

"And I have no qualms about it because, after all, Charlie Chan was a good man. He represents the Chinese in a good light."

"But what about me? What about us? Our people?" I asked.

"All that is ignorance," Bessie shouted.

"Bessie, I'm going to kill Charlie Chan. I'm in this organization, you see . . ." I said, but Bessie's voice went on over mine. She didn't stop talking.

"When I first moved Among American! I've always lived Among American, ah, people! And I've gone into a higher level home!"

"Most of the time we go bowling once a week, but we all swore this blood oath, you know, Bessie? We all swore to kill Charlie Chan."

"You know at first they didn't accept us," Bessie said, and she should know. In the seventy-odd years of her life she's been through most of our history here. She remembers horse and buggies, and being the first Chinese-American public school teacher in San Francisco teaching in Chinatown's Commodore Stockton grammar school. "They didn't accept us. Why? I wore trousers and they laughed at us. Thinking, 'Ooooh, a girl wearing trousers!' And look at them now. And uh, at first they all seem to, you know, 'My goodness, a Chinese coming to our neighborhood!' They didn't like it. Even then I have an inferiority complex. Always, 'Aww gee, there's a white and I'm Oriental. I'm yellow.'"

"I'll walk onto that set tomorrow, Bessie. Walk up grinning my honorable son grin up to Charlie Chan and say, 'Geewhiz, pop, have I got a surprise for you!' and kill him dead. Then I will be a hero of my people."

"Awhile back I told you we were supposed to be seen and not heard, and it wasn't until I got away from home before I begin to express myself. Luckily, I lived in a home. An American home and they were nice to me. And gradually I felt the transition."

"Quit the science fiction, Bessie, and listen. I gotta kill Charlie Chan."

"And cuz they're human beings and I am too. And if they loved me, if they respect me, I'm sure others would."

"Way we got it figured, it's him or us, Bessie. No fooling."

"Now they have all the respect for me. And a large crowd. I'm the president of this and that and they're all American people. I have gone through a lot of humiliation and yet I come up smelling like a rose. It's up to you, you younger generation now. *Put your best foot forward!* That's what I say. And I sincerely mean it."

"I'm tellin ya this, Bess, with Chan out of the way, the coast will be clear!" I said, and the next thing I knew instead of going to the Chan set in the morning I died in a movie where Spencer Tracy tells the pilots, everyone in his leather jacket, that the Jap planes can't bank left and that Jap pilots laugh out loud when they bomb hospitals but they go down gentle, writing Haiku in their heads, singing them aloud breaking everybody's radio silence with a poetry reading around the American task force. The notion of Japanese kamikaze pilots going down, screaming engines whistling rivets out of the sky, mouthing original seventeen syllable poems about cherry blooms and frog-dump for the radios of the American ships to intercept, struck me funny. I never trusted Spencer Tracy again.

■ It's no secret that Charlie Chan was official U.S. Government propaganda controlled by the Office of War Information during WW2. In the ten Chan films made in the war years, Charlie Chan and his sons weren't busy smashing Jap spy rings or even obviously involved in the war effort. He continued solving high-society murders. His effectiveness as an anti-Japanese tool depended not on his exploits but his being visibly and actively not Japanese with all his heart and soul. The lives of Chinese and Chinese-Americans on and off the screen were pushed by American pop culture as images of the ideal American minority. Our mere and very being encouraged Americans to hate Japanese. We wore buttons that read "I am a loyal Chinese-American."

Later, as one of history's little ironies would have it, Chinamen and Japs were one in Hollywood's mind, and Chinese- and Japanese-Americans were used against the blacks now the way Chinese-Americans had been used against Japanese-Americans. *U.S. News and World Report* threw us at the blacks with "Success Story of One Minority Group in U.S." "Still being taught," they wrote, "is the old idea that people should depend on their own efforts—not a welfare check—in order to reach America's 'promised land.'" There are those in Chinatown who say the date of that story, December 26, 1966, was the day the San Francisco papers started their run of Negro gunman kills Chinese grocer stories. And with amazingly similar language, *Newsweek,* on June 21, 1971, ran a two-page spread headlined, *The Japanese American Success Story: Outwhiting the Whites.* Tom Wolfe said in *Esquire* that a Chinaman who was "loud, violent, sexually aggressive," was imitating blacks because "loud, violent, sexually aggressive" was "stuff that really stunned most Chinese." David Hilliard of the Black Panthers told the people of Chinatown they were "the Uncle Toms of the non-white peoples."

One of the masterminds behind bringing the Chinese- and Japanese-Americans together against the blacks was Phil Karlson. Having directed two Charlie Chan movies, *The Shanghai Cobra* and *Dark Alibi,* Phil Karlson was an old hand at the subtle art of portraying yellows as defective, pitifully naive children.

In 1960 Karlson became overseer of Japanese-America's modern image by directing *Hell to Eternity*—a slick stock war movie about a quaint Japanese-American family in East L.A. taking in an orphan white boy who grows up to become Jeffrey Hunter. This was the first American film to feature the evacuation of the Japanese-Americans off the West Coast. It also included a scene inside a relocation camp that made the barracks look like a rustic honeymoon lodge, or a knotty pine old folks' home.

Hell to Eternity foreshadowed the day ABC-TV would make Romeo a Japanese-American boy, and Juliet a mungy-looking white girl, Patty Duke, who marry secretly, while their families are in church one Sunday morning, December seventh, nineteen forty-one, call it *If Tomorrow Comes* (it was originally titled *My Husband the Enemy*), and air it as the Movie of the Week on Pearl Harbor Day. And NBC's Robert Northshield told everyone a cheap sad story instead of telling the truth about the least understood and most touchily remembered period in Japanese-American history. These TV offerings rehabilitate the Japanese-American image by substituting one white racist stereotype for another white racist stereotype. As in previous times when white men transformed the hateful black stud into the lovable Aunt Jemima, so now the white racist that had seen mad dog Japs was now white racist love that saw helpless pregnant women and little babies.

In the white universe a white man gets thrown into a concentration camp and it's *Some Call It Courage, The Great Escape, Stalag 17, Hogan's Heroes,* and a skinny bombardier with a cowlick quoting from William Faulkner's Nobel acceptance speech, "I believe man will not only endure, he will prevail," several years before he won the Nobel Prize in 1949. But we go to camp and it's either all mad dogs tearing our bodies apart on the barbed wire trying to get out and sabotage American factories, or it's all helpless pregnant women, little babies, withered old men having a long cry. My dying words to Richard Widmark in Lewis Milestone's *Halls of Montezuma,* come back to me like a child's prayer. On page 95, Scene 147 of the script, it looks like poetry:

> (gently chiding)
> Sergeant, I am surprised at you. You say you have been a long time in my country, and yet you seem to have forgotten that for generations my people think not of living well, but of dying well. Have you not studied our philosophy or military science, our judo wrestling? Do you not remember that we always take the obvious — and reverse it?
> (he pauses; then vigorously)
> So we reverse the role of life. To us, it is death that is desirable. It is the source of our strength.

The dying Jap officer I played and Robert Northshield's 1972 model Japanese-Americans are of the same mythical people. Whites were so sure they were right that hearing a Japanese say he thinks in backwards didn't shock them. I never heard John Wayne, explaining American thought to the Japanese, say anything like, "Have you not studied our philosophy, our baseball, our cowpunchin? Do you not remember that we always take the obvious — and reverse it?"

Death did become a way of life among Japanese-Americans, but not in the camps. Artists like Mine Okubo and writers like Toshio Mori, intellectuals and journalists that had been scattered around the country unaware or out of touch with each other, were thrown together in the camps and produced a Japanese-American cultural movement. There was life in those camps, bad as they were. Death after the camps, when Japanese-America came out of the desert killing themselves to be accepted by whites. America had shown them what it thought of Japanese things, so they set out to outwhite the whites. Toshio Mori wrote Japanese-America's epitaph:

> . . . We will leave individually, one by one, to some other locality and to some unknown beyond. . . . Our world will be gone, and there will be no more little Tokyos. Yes, we shall see no more the lantern parades and the kimonos of the past. Our days of hightop boots, jeans, and the uniform mackinaws will be gone. The "Tojo" hats will become useless with wear and tear, and grotesque in new surroundings. We shall move on willingly into the melting world of our land, forever to lose our racial identity, however impossible, and assuredly certain to drop our differences when we shall pass away from the earth of our mutual interest.

And by the late '60s Japanese-Americans were so proud of calling themselves

"The Quiet Americans" that their semi-official history, by Bill Hosokawa, was titled *Nisei: The Quiet Americans.*

■ For the Charlie Chan of the '70s NBC and Universal Studios preserved a white racist tradition. Ross Martin, a white actor best known for playing grotesques on TV's *Wild Wild West,* became the fourth white man to play Charlie Chan in 40 years . . . the fifth, if you count the short-lived TV series that starred J. Carroll Naish as Chan.

None of the Sons got the job as pop, and far from being bitter, Victor Sen Yung blames the blacks for the present scarcity of jobs for yellow actors and objects to Asian-Americans protesting against the casting practice because he fears white backlash in the form of no jobs at all for any yellow actor. Benson Fong doesn't talk about politics or religion or race. And the original Number One Son, Keye Luke, reveals that he has become resigned to white supremacy as a fact of life when he says, "There is one consideration that overrides all others, and that's box office. After all, this is not Oriental theatre, it's a white man's theatre. You have to cater to that."

When I wasn't Charlie Chan's son I was the Chinese who always dies. I died with funny last words, like looking at Alan Ladd and calling him Brother Number Four on my dying breath. "Goodbye, . . . Brother Number Fourer-erer . . ." I said and went limp, and slipped off the raft into the river. This Spencer Tracy movie was the first movie in which I died off screen. I'd never been *found* dead in a movie before. I'd never died alone without a scene before. Always before I passed and went limp as a movie star was pinning a medal to my bloody shirt, or was shot in the head by the star. I always have a relationship with the star. Like my best friend, Steve McQueen in *The Sand Pebbles,* shooting off the top of my head with his Springfield rifle. Or sometimes I'd die shouting something paradoxical. "The river does not contend against the willow, yet the doorknob still turns," I'd say, and crash, I was dead. I've never been cut up by a boozer who wore a surgical mask made from one cup of a Chinese nurse's bra. He's sniffed the insides of the nurse's bras before boiling them, and the audience had laughed, as if the sniffing of a sock pulled off a Chinese tit had been sneaked in the movie. The audience laughed when he sniffed round and round the stitching down inside the cup of one large bra, moved to boil it, then did a double take with his nose and sniffed a long hissing sniff of something that made him groan. And he sighed and said, "This fits my face perfectly," bringing the audience out of the dark laughing. I'd never been treated like that in a movie before. I'd never been left alone in a movie, to die away from the Yanks. For me, William Bendix had pulled the pin on a hand grenade, laid his arms out back behind his head, and on the throw shouted, "This is for Donald Duck!"

My only consolation was that someday, all of them, Keye Luke, Victor Sen Yung, Benson Fong, Richard Loo, all of them will find themselves in a movie, dying without a scene and end up like me, seen fit only as a fanatically faithful Chinese-Catholic convert, cooking and dusting for Humphrey Bogart passing himself off as a priest, at an out-of-the-way Chinese village on the road of life. In a scene with a beautiful woman horny for Bogart, Bogart said I was like a woman to him. He said I took care of him "like a good wife." Whatever it was I'd done, Hollywood hadn't forgiven me or forgotten. I stood up in the middle of the movies out of the seating section and asked the stars why I had to die and why they had to make me smile when Bogart likened me to a woman in front of a beautiful woman. I try to talk them out of leaving me alone to die. I'll die, but why do I have to be alone? If I could only be out of the room when Bogart likens me to a woman, or if I didn't understand English in this movie. And the people in the audience wait for Spencer Tracy and the airmen to leave me behind, see it becoming inevitable and weep for me, and they wait for the woman to knock on Bogart's door and come in and laugh.

Suggestions for Discussion

1. The Chinese characters represented in each of the three war films described at the opening of this essay are all "sympathetic" portraits of the Chinese. What objections does Chin have to such characterizations?
2. In what ways does Chin compare the representation of Blacks in American culture with that of Asians? What image does Chin mean to evoke with his description of Earl Derr Biggers composing Charlie Chan stories? What does he mean by the statement, "Stan Robertson was Birmingham's revenge"?
3. What comment is Chin making through his representation of the imagined dialogue between himself and Bessie Loo? How would you characterize the tone of that dialogue?
4. What kinds of characterizations of Asian Americans would Chin like to see in American films?

Suggestion for Writing and Comparison

1. Write a brief essay in which you compare and contrast Chin's criticism of white Americans' perception of Asian Americans with Ferris Takahashi's criticism in "Nisei, Nisei!"

STORIES

Ferris Takahashi

Ferris Takahashi (who also uses the pseudonyms M. H. Constable and Mary Takahashi) was born in Boston. She lived for a period of time in Chicago where she worked as a free-lance writer and later moved to Boulder, Colorado, with her husband who is a doctor.

Ferris Takahashi writes both poems and short stories. Her work has appeared in several nationally circulated magazines, but she has been published most often in *Common Ground* and the West Coast Japanese American periodical *Pacific Citizen*. Two distinct problems of adjustment to America are explored in her stories and her poems. "Nisei, Nisei!" (p. 277) is a response to prejudice which sees physical racial characteristics — such as the shape of an eye — as constituting either beauty or ugliness. The following short story, "The Widower," presents a problem of adjustment not peculiar to any one ethnic group (as the various chapters of this text will indicate): the conflict between first and second generation, or here, between Issei and Nisei.

The Widower

"Partake of a little nourishment, Sato-san," they said to him, offering tea. Why did they not prepare some rice and serve him strength-building soup? Emi would have had soup for him. Emi would let no person, least of all her husband, rise hungry from table. And he was hungry, he was not sick. He had not eaten since the night before the funeral . . . Why did not Emi hurry in from the kitchen, her white skin flushed pink, her long, narrow eyes bright with pleasure and the mist from a dish of hot food beading her smooth hair? Why should Emi not be here when all these friends and neighbors filled their house with such a pulse of abundant life?

All day there had been such a crush of people in the rooms. He felt like a drunken man, sick-brained and giddy. All did the same things, the proper things. They came to him whispering or in silence. His hands ached with pattings and pressings and squeezings. Then, after a while, the women, crowded together, twittered softly and the close air of the stuffy rooms vibrated like a gong. The men remained subdued — when, at last, the funeral was over and the last "Amen" raggedly repeated, it was the men who led him away.

To see a coffin let down into the ground was a terrible thing. Thinking of this, he had asked that the two children be taken to a neighbor's house. Himself, as the men turned him away from the grave where floral pieces were quickly set across tumbled earth, he had struggled. It was very necessary to wait and watch for a while in case the quiet one below should rouse and want to move . . . there had been such cases. He could see Emi now, half-laughing, half-angry, trying to make these men who called themselves his friends let go of his arms . . .

In the old land, in Japan, it was customary to cremate, but he had rejected cremation. He could not tell any of them that he wanted her secret body kept as it had been, as only he had known it. So soft, cushioning, smooth-skinned . . .

As he sat among the people on an uncomfortable chair which was American, just as all the conditions of the funeral were properly Christian and American, he found himself crying. This he had promised himself he would not do. He did not feel like crying. But as he looked down at his hands, they were wet . . . he saw the heave of his own chest and belly.

An eager response went through the room. The people, up to now so careful of decorum, seemed to have been waiting for this. The paroxysm of lament crackled from body to body. Everyone was sobbing softly.

Then the children were brought to him, one on either side of a neighbor whose face he had suddenly forgotten. He could not remember whom she was nor why she was there. This was a bad thing, to bring the children at this time. They would remember this.

He put his arms around them. They stared at him, shaken, waiting to take their cue from him.

"These are my children," he said. "Ken and Lily. Now I am going to be father and mother to them. Mother is not really gone. She has only given me part of her work to do."

■ "Partake of a little nourishment, Sato-san," they said to him and Mrs. Shio offered him hot rice wine in the formal way. This *sake* was best quality, no doubt, but he had become middle-aged, it no longer warmed his blood. The Shio family seemed to wait for him to speak. He could not understand why they had brought him to their house to meet a *baishakunin*. Surely they remembered how often Emi had visited here with Mrs. Shio, borrowed back and forth, come in and out . . .

"Kano-san was greatly respected in Nagoya," Mr. Shio said proudly. "He has assisted many families even here in the new country. He sees the grand-children growing up and flourishing."

"Even some of this younger generation grow up to respect what they scoffed at in their unripeness," the marriage broker said. "In my village near Nagoya, the making of the whole community's future was in my hands. Did a marriage broker not consider the social good, what disaster! Believe me, it is no easy work."

He spoke mincingly and made an elaborate gesture with the wine cup in his broad peasant hand.

"We have told you something about Sato-san, our life-long friend," Mr. Shio began. " – How he came young from the homeland, having already chosen his life-partner. Together they made a little business, a nursery of green plants. Together we became brothers in Christ when we joined the Church. But God willed to take away this good life-partner from our friend too soon. His children, Ken and Lily, will soon go to the high school. He has worked as one does not think of a man working – cooking, washing the clothes. He had no time to meet the widow ladies whom we knew around the Church . . . Why! He even used to carry his little girl on his back when he had to go out at night and would lead his boy by the hand rather than leave them alone . . . my wife has done all she could and his children have been to us as our own. But one must think of the future."

"All his friends have done what they could," Mrs. Shio put in. "But there is no substitute for a woman in the home. Only when she is finally gone, does a man realize what he lacks."

Mr. Sato looked down at his cup. Emi and he had married in a Western way, a bold way, choosing each other without the direction of parents or marriage-brokers.

"Thank you most abundantly," he said at last. "You are kind to feel a concern for me, unimportant as I am. When my children were young, I tried to be father and mother to them. I did not wish them to forget their mother, who loved them so. I wanted them to grow up as *her* children, not the children of another woman . . . but I see my words are becoming confusing to you . . . So now my children, Ken and Lily, will soon go to the high school. My boy will go to college, where he can increase his ability to follow a profession. My children will then begin to care for me in turn. . . . How could I presume . . . (he decided to use smooth words to soothe their feelings) . . . how could I presume to offer some worthy woman a struggling existence? For all I earn shall go to take care of my children. Your kindness is, nonetheless, most appreciated."

■ Again it was that day of the year which the old custom called the Day of the Dead, and in accord with his practice he brought potted plants from the nursery to Emi's grave, set them, tended the plot and cultivated the borders on the surrounding plots which had become as familiar as his own. His corner of the cemetery was no longer used and not often visited. He had much work to do to keep the area as it should be, for the custodians were glad to have him do their work and left him quite alone.

He knew the years had made him grey and silent. There had been a long time of war, during which he and everyone he knew had been taken away and put in a kind of family prison for no reason and then, with as little reason, released and set adrift. And coming back, he found that he had the work of his youth to re-do: the shattered greenhouse to repair, the growing plants to renew, even the corner of the cemetery to restore from wilderness.

Ken was now a college graduate. How proud a thing it had been to see him, how clutching a surprise to hear on that very day of achievement that Ken planned to marry, even before he had found the architectural job of which he dreamed.

Now Ken worked for a construction company and the babies had come fast, one and two, and were soon little children who lived the life of adults: they visited and had parties with their playmates and were so busy that they could not often travel across the city to see their grandfather. And Ken's wife was a modern girl who could cause a husband much anxiety with talk of nerves and uncertain health.

When Mr. Sato was making himself supper on the kerosene stove in the room back of the greenhouse, he liked to talk aloud to Ken and Lily as though they were still little, telling them not to wriggle and jump about so much, not to be always asking for candy and "cokes" but to eat the good food so that they would be tall and strong . . . And they had grown tall, much taller than their parents and Lily had written from the East Coast city where she worked, that she would soon be married to a fine young man, with a good job, a church member, too.

To the wedding he would go, if they should send for him, yes, he lived on the hope of it, but Lily had not written that there was room for him in the new life ahead. Indeed, a short, grey dull father in the young, bright apartment of the newly-weds! Indeed, such a father would have to hide himself when their friends came for very shame.

He wandered about his narrow room, touching the things which were always placed where he could be close to them: photographs of Ken and Lily through the years, a bowl from the homeland, a scroll of calligraphy Emi had given him long ago, being unable to read but dreaming even then of children more able than their parents.

Long, so long ago, he had begun to rebuild Emi's presence by a clever device:

"Ai, my back aches so, *mamma-san*," he would say. "Rub it for me — " and then feel the quick, strong hands at the small of his back and the downy pressure of her breast against his shoulder. He told her all the news of Ken and read Lily's letters over and over and together they marveled at these children who walked now in the sun of success.

There came a certain night of the Day of the Dead when all these small satisfactions were strangely, suddenly brought to nothing, and the nearness of Emi herself ceased to be. How often he had been able to remember the sound of her feet pattering towards the bed! He heard no sound as he groped around in the dark, looking for matches so that he might light the stove and make tea. Suddenly he began to sob, clumsy sobs, old man's crying. Then, without matches, without jacket, still in his house slippers, he went unsteadily out on the street, down to the phone booth on the corner.

He would call the Shios. He did not see them very often, for they too had moved across town and lived with Shizuo, their married son. But they would remember, of course they would remember.

"Shio-san? Here Sato. Yes, Sato . . . How goes it with you, with your son, your wife? My wife thinks of her so often. — No, no, I am quite well. I am quite well. I am in good health. . . . We thought that in spite of the hour you would come over to visit us. . . . In bed? It is then so late? . . No, no, I am not sick. I can call my son, Ken, if I need anything. Thank you. I am sorry. Excuse me, please, for troubling you. . ."

Across the city, the alert of the phone rang in the apartment of Ken Sato.

"Ken, is this you? Yeah, this is Shiz Shio. Hate to bother you this time of night, but look, it's something about your dad. — Yeah, sure, I know it's 2:30 in the morning; our whole family is up with *this* call from your dad. He just called up and my parents sleep in the living room beside the phone.

"He wanted them to come over and see him, jus' like that, middle of the night, and my dad worries and says I've got to call you right away. He was goin' to call you but I did it for him, he don't speak English so good, y'know. — No, not sick, more like raving. Out of his mind, talking like your Mom was there with him.

"Y'know, Ken, he oughtn't be living alone like he does. It's an unkindness to the old man — Naw, Ken, I din' mean it that way, I know you do all you can — Sure, Ken, you know what Alice and I been through, the old folks underfoot every minute and telling her how to bring up her kids . . . Here's my mother right now yakking about how she tried her best to help with the marriage-broker, it's Sato-san's own fault, I dunno what she means. Old folks, they get mixed up. It's a burden. — Sure, Ken, I know what you go through with your wife's nerves. Here's *my* ole lady now, says to cut out the jawin' and le's all get some sleep. — I din' wanna wake you up but nothing else would satisfy my dad but I call you right away. Maybe you can run over tomorrow and see what's going on . . ."

■ "Have a little orange juice, Papa— " Ken said, holding out a tumbler of the bitter fluid.

Here in this "nursing-home," tea was only to be had at mealtime. Not even always then, for the others who came to table were *hakujin* and to them were served milk, coffee and on the Sundays, cocoa. Why could there not be tea for an old man who could not digest these other beverages? Why did Ken press the glass of bitter juice into his hand although he had already sipped and put it away? Why did the *hakujin* woman in the white dress look in through the door so impatiently? Ken had just been telling Mr. Sato of the expense of this place, expense which paid for good food and a clean, healthful room. But the room behind the greenhouse was healthful, fresh with the woodsy odor of potting plants and running water. There was a strange smell in this place.

But Father was not to worry about expense, Ken was repeating in his grammar-school Japanese, mixed with many English words. Expense is nothing when a man wishes to care for his father. This is a fine place. The *hakujin* people here are kind and well-mannered, both the guests and those who attend to them. True, there is a home for elderly Japanese men in the city but it is much too crowded. It would not do in any case. The men there are indigent. What would the people say if Ken Sato's father were in a pauper's home? — Better to rest here — and it is only for a short time — in this fine, costly nursing home till health and strength return and no voices are heard which others cannot hear . . . until the wife of Ken is a little less nervous after the expected new baby and a house can be found where all the Sato family will be together.

Ken's eyeglasses rode up on the wrinkles of his forehead and a little dampness appeared in the creases of his nose. This was a grown man facing him, Mr. Sato realized, a man showing already the marks of middle age as he pushed his shoulders forward eagerly and rubbed with his forefinger nervously, tensely across his dry upper lip.

"You *are* comfortable here, Papa, aren't you? You *do* see that it's the best thing till things get straightened out — only till then?"

"Yes," Mr. Sato said. He did not want to say the word at all but Ken's lips seemed to shape it for him unconsciously; Ken's forehead wrinkled as though it could not relax unless the word was said: "It is very well here. Oh yes, yes, yes."

Suggestions for Discussion

1. How old is the widower at the opening of the story? How much time has elapsed at the conclusion? What is the function of the repetition of the phrase "Partake of a little nourishment, Sato-san"? How does this phrase relate to Ken's offer in the last section, "Have a little orange juice, Papa"?

2. What is the nature of the relationship that the widower experienced with his wife? Is the author successful in arousing the reader's sympathy for the widower?

3. What is the function of the Shio family in the story? How do the characterizations of Mr. and Mrs. Shio compare to that of the widower? Which of them has become more "Americanized"?

4. What "war" is mentioned in the second paragraph of section three? What happened to the Japanese Americans during that war?

5. How is the widower's relationship with his children depicted? Are they present when he tells them not to ask for candy and "cokes," to eat good food? What is the significance of the paragraphs concerning Lily's marriage?

6. What is the nature of Shiz Shio's idiom? Does Ken use the same idiom? Is his difficulty in relating to his father linguistic or cultural?
7. Define *sake, baishakunin,* and *hakujin;* what does the *-san* suffix indicate? How does Ferris Takahashi create the impression that the older characters are speaking in Japanese, despite her use of English?

Suggestion for Writing and Comparison

1. Is the problem of the "generation-gap" peculiar to the Issei-Nisei group, or do all ethnic groups experience a similar problem? Discuss with reference to your own personal experiences.

Hisaye Yamamoto

Hisaye Yamamoto, born in Redondo Beach, California, in 1921, has been writing since the early 1940's. Her work has been published in Black and Japanese American periodicals as well as in the *Kenyon Review, Harper's, Partisan Review, Furioso,* and the annual Martha Foley collection of *The Best American Short Stories.*

Hisaye Yamamoto's stories most often deal with young Nisei characters growing up in small Southern California towns (as she herself did); but her themes are generally the universal ones of spiritual and emotional isolation. "The Legend of Miss Sasagawara," which is set in a Japanese Relocation Camp during World War II, is representative of her approach: the author is far less concerned with the social significance of the external environment than with the internal state of the characters.

The Legend of Miss Sasagawara

Even in that unlikely place of wind, sand, and heat, it was easy to imagine Miss Sasagawara a decorative ingredient of some ballet. Her daily costume, brief and fitting closely to her trifling waist, generously billowing below, and bringing together arrestingly rich colors like mustard yellow and forest green, appeared to have been cut from a coarse-textured homespun; her shining hair was so long it wound twice about her head to form a coronet; her face was delicate and pale, with a fine nose, pouting bright mouth, and glittering eyes; and her measured walk said, "Look, I'm *walking!*" as though walking were not a common but a rather special thing to be doing. I first saw her so one evening after mess, as she was coming out of the women's latrine, going towards her barracks, and after I thought she was out of hearing, I imitated the young men of the Block (No. 33), and gasped, "Wow! How much does *she* weigh?"

"Oh, haven't you heard?" said my friend Elsie Kubo, knowing very well I had not. "That's Miss Sasagawara."

It turned out Elsie knew all about Miss Sasagawara, who with her father was new to Block 33. Where had she accumulated all her items? Probably a morsel here and a morsel there, and, anyway, I forgot to ask her sources, because the picture she painted was so distracting: Miss Sasagawara's father was a Buddhist minister, and the two had gotten permission to come to this Japanese evacuation camp in Arizona from one farther north, after the death there of Mrs. Sasagawara. They had come here to join the Rev. Sasagawara's brother's family, who lived in a neighboring Block, but there had been some trouble between them, and just this week the immigrant pair had gotten leave to move over to Block 33. They were occupying one end of the Block's lone empty barracks, which had not been chopped up yet into the customary four apartments. The other end had been taken over by a young couple, also new-comers to the Block, who had moved in the same day.

"And do you know what, Kiku?" Elsie continued. "Oooh, that gal is really temperamental. I guess it's because she was a ballet dancer before she got stuck in camp, I hear people like that are temperamental. Anyway, the Sasakis, the new couple at the other end of the barracks, think she's crazy. The day they all moved in, the barracks was really dirty, all covered with dust from the dust storms and everything, so Mr. Sasaki was going to wash the whole barracks down with a hose, and he thought he'd be nice and do the Sasaga-waras' side first. You know, do them a favor. But do you know what? Mr. Sasaki got the hose attached to the faucet outside and started to go in the door, and he said all the Sasagawaras' suitcases and things were on top of the Army cots and Miss Sasagawara was trying to clean the place out with a pail of water and a broom. He said, 'Here, let me flush the place out with a hose for you; it'll be faster.' And she turned right around and screamed at him, 'What are you trying to do? Spy on me? Get out of here or I'll throw this water on you!' He said he was so surprised he couldn't move for a minute, and before he knew it, Miss Sasagawara just up and threw that water at him, pail and all. Oh, he said he got out of that place fast, but fast. Madwoman, he called her."

But Elsie had already met Miss Sasagawara, too, over at the apartment of the Murakamis, where Miss Sasagawara was borrowing Mrs. Murakami's Singer, and had found her quite amiable. "She said she was thirty-nine years old—imagine, thirty-nine, she looks so young, more like twenty-five; but she said she wasn't sorry she never got married, because she's had her fun. She said she got to go all over the country a couple of times, dancing in the ballet."

And after we emerged from the latrine, Elsie and I, slapping mosquitoes in the warm, gathering dusk, sat on the stoop of her apartment and talked awhile, jealously of the scintillating life Miss Sasagawara had led until now and nos-talgically of the few ballets we had seen in the world outside (how faraway Los Angeles seemed!), but we ended up as we always did, agreeing that our mission in life, pushing twenty as we were, was first to finish college some-where when and if the war ever ended and we were free again, and then to find good jobs and two nice, clean young men, preferably handsome, prefera-bly rich, who would cherish us forever and a day.

My introduction, less spectacular, to the Rev. Sasagawara came later, as I noticed him, a slight and fragile-looking old man, in the Block mess hall (where I worked as a waitress, and Elsie, too) or laundry room or going to and from the latrine. Sometimes he would be farther out, perhaps going to the post-office or canteen or to visit friends in another Block or on some business to the Administration buildings, but wherever he was headed, however doubt-less his destination, he always seemed to be wandering lostly. This may have been because he walked so slowly, with such negligible steps, or because he wore perpetually an air of bemusement, never talking directly to a person, as though, being what he was, he could not stop for an instant his meditation on the higher life.

I noticed, too, that Miss Sasagawara never came to the mess hall herself. Her father ate at the tables reserved for the occupants, mostly elderly, of the end barracks known as the bachelors' dormitory. After each meal, he came up to the counter and carried away a plate of food, protected with one of the pinkish apple wrappers we waitresses made as wrinkleless as possible and put out for napkins, and a mug of tea or coffee. Sometimes Miss Sasagawara could be seen rinsing out her empties at the one double-tub in the laundry that was reserved for private dishwashing.

If any one in the Block or in the entire camp of 15,000 or so people had talked at any length with Miss Sasagawara (everyone happening to speak of her called her that, although her first name, Mari, was simple enough and rather pretty) after her first and only visit to use Mrs. Murakami's sewing machine, I never heard of it. Nor did she ever willingly use the shower room, just off the latrine, when anyone else was there. Once, when I was up past midnight writing letters and went for my shower, I came upon her under the full needling force of a steamy spray, but she turned her back to me and did not answer my surprised hello. I hoped my body would be as smooth and spare and well-turned when I was thirty-nine. Another time, Elsie and I passed in front of the Sasagawara apartment, which was really only a cubicle because the once-empty barracks had soon been partitioned off into six units for families of two, and we saw her there on the wooden steps, sitting with her wide, wide skirt spread splendidly about her. She was intent on peeling a grapefruit, which her father had probably brought to her from the mess hall that morning, and Elsie called out, "Hello there!" Miss Sasagawara looked up and stared, without recognition. We were almost out of earshot when I heard her call, "Do I know you?" and I could have almost sworn that she sounded hopeful, if not downright wistful, but Elsie, already miffed at having expended friendliness so unprofitably, seemed not to have heard, and that was that.

Well, if Miss Sasagawara was not one to speak to, she was certainly one to speak of, and she came up quite often as topic for the endless conversations which helped along the monotonous days. My mother said she had met the late Mrs. Sasagawara once, many years before the war, and to hear her tell it, a sweeter, kindlier woman there never was. "I suppose," said my mother, "that I'll never meet anyone like her again; she was a lady in every sense of the word." Then she reminded me that I had seen the Rev. Sasagawara before. Didn't I remember him as one of the three bhikshus who had read the sutras at Grandfather's funeral?

I could not say that I did. I barely remembered Grandfather, my mother's father. The only thing that came back with clarity was my nausea at the wake and the funeral, the first and only ones I had ever had occasion to attend, because it had been reproduced several times since—each time, in fact, that I had crossed again the actual scent or a suspicion of burning incense. Dimly I recalled the inside of the Buddhist temple in Los Angeles, an immense, murky auditorium whose high and huge platform had held, centered in the background, a great golden shrine touched with black and white. Below this platform, Grandfather, veiled by gauze, had slept in a long, grey box which just fitted him. There had been flowers, oh, such flowers, everywhere. And right in front of Grandfather's box had been the incense stand, upon which squatted two small bowls, one with a cluster of straw-thin sticks sending up white tendrils of smoke, the other containing a heap of coarse, grey powder. Each mourner in turn had gone up to the stand, bowing once, his palms touching in prayer, before he reached it; had bent in prayer over the stand; had taken then a pinch of incense from the bowl of crumbs and, bowing over it reverently, cast it into the other, the active bowl; had bowed, the hands praying again; had retreated a few steps and bowed one last time, the hands still joined, before returning to his seat. (I knew the ceremony well for having been severely coached in it on the evening of the wake.) There had been tears and tears and here and there a sudden sob.

And all this while, three men in black robes had been on the platform, one standing in front of the shining altar, the others sitting on either side, and the entire trio incessantly chanting a strange, mellifluous language in unison. From time to time there had reverberated through the enormous room, above the singsong, above the weeping, above the fragrance, the sharp, startling whang of the gong.

So, one of those men had been Miss Sasagawara's father. . . . This information brought him closer to me, and I listened with interest later when it was told that he kept here in his apartment a small shrine, much more intricately constructed than that kept by the usual Buddhist household, before which, at regular hours of the day, he offered incense and chanted, tinkling (in lieu of the gong) a small bell. What did Miss Sasagawara do at these prayer periods, I wondered; did she participate, did she let it go in one ear and out the other, or did she abruptly go out on the steps, perhaps to eat a grapefruit?

■ Elsie and I tired one day of working in the mess hall. And this desire for greener fields came almost together with the Administration announcement that henceforth the wages of residents doing truly vital labor, such as in the hospital or on the garbage trucks that went from mess hall to mess hall, would be upped to nineteen dollars a month instead of the common sixteen.

"Oh, I've always wanted to be a nurse!" Elsie confided, as the Block manager sat down to his breakfast after reading out the day's bulletin in English and Japanese.

"What's stopped you?" I asked.

"Mom," Elsie said. "She thinks it's dirty work. And she's afraid I'll catch something. But I'll remind her of the extra three dollars."

"It's never appealed to me much, either," I confessed. "Why don't we go over to garbage? It's the same pay."

Elsie would not even consider it. "Very funny. Well, you don't have to be a nurse's aide, Kiku. The hospital's short all kinds of help. Dental assistants, receptionists. . . . Let's go apply after we finish this here."

So, willy-nilly, while Elsie plunged gleefully into the pleasure of wearing a trim blue-and-white striped seersucker, into the duties of taking temperatures and carrying bed-pans, and into the fringe of medical jargon (she spoke very casually now of catheters, enemas, primiparas, multiparas), I became a relief receptionist at the hospital's front desk, taking my hours as they were assigned. And it was on one of my midnight-to-morning shifts that I spoke to Miss Sasagawara for the first time.

The cooler in the corridor window was still whirring away (for that desert heat in Summer had a way of lingering intact through the night to merge with the warmth of the morning sun), but she entered bundled in an extraordinarily long black coat, her face made petulant, not unprettily, by lines of pain.

"I think I've got appendicitis," she said breathlessly, without preliminary.

"May I have your name and address?" I asked, unscrewing my pen.

Annoyance seemed to outbalance agony for a moment, but she answered soon enough, in a cold rush, "Mari Sasagawara. Thirty-three-seven C."

It was necessary also to learn her symptoms, and I wrote down that she had chills and a dull aching at the back of her head, as well as these excruciating flashes in her lower right abdomen.

"I'll have to go wake up the doctor. Here's a blanket, why don't you lie down over there on the bench until he comes?" I suggested.

She did not answer, so I tossed the Army blanket on the bench, and when I returned from the doctors' dormitory, after having tapped and tapped on the door of young Dr. Moritomo, who was on night duty, she was still standing where I had left her, immobile and holding onto the wooden railing shielding the desk.

"Dr. Moritomo's coming right away," I said. "Why don't you sit down at least?"

Miss Sasagawara said, "Yes," but did not move.

"Did you walk all the way?" I asked incredulously, for Block 33 was a good mile off, across the canal.

She nodded, as if that were not important, also as if to thank me kindly to mind my own business.

Dr. Moritomo (technically, the title was premature; evacuation had caught him with a few months to go on his degree), wearing a maroon bathrobe, shuffled in sleepily and asked her to come into the emergency room for an examination. A short while later, he guided her past my desk into the laboratory, saying he was going to take her blood count.

When they came out, she went over to the electric fountain for a drink of water, and Dr. Moritomo said reflectively, "Her count's all right. Not appendicitis. We should keep her for observation, but the general ward is pretty full, isn't it? Hm, well, I'll give her something to take. Will you tell one of the boys to take her home?"

This I did, but when I came back from arousing George, one of the ambulance boys, Miss Sasagawara was gone, and Dr. Moritomo was coming out of the laboratory where he had gone to push out the lights. "Here's George, but that girl must have walked home," I reported helplessly.

"She's in no condition to do that. George, better catch up with her and take her home," Dr. Moritomo ordered.

Shrugging, George strode down the hall; the doctor shuffled back to bed; and soon there was the shattering sound of one of the old Army ambulances backing out of the hospital drive.

George returned in no time at all to say that Miss Sasagawara had refused to get on the ambulance. "She wouldn't even listen to me. She just kept walking and I drove alongside and told her it was Dr. Moritomo's orders, but she wouldn't even listen to me."

"She wouldn't?"

"I hope Doc didn't expect me to drag her into the ambulance."

"Oh, well," I said. "I guess she'll get home all right. She walked all the way up here."

"Cripes, what a dame!" George complained, shaking his head as he started back to the ambulance room. "I never heard of such a thing. She wouldn't even listen to me."

■ Miss Sasagawara came back to the hospital about a month later. Elsie was the one who rushed up to the desk where I was on day duty to whisper, "Miss Sasagawara just tried to escape from the hospital!"

"Escape? What do you mean, escape?" I said.

"Well, she came in last night, and they didn't know what was wrong with her, so they kept her for observation. And this morning, just now, she ran out of the ward in just a hospital nightgown and the orderlies chased after her and caught her and brought her back. Oh, she was just fighting them. But once they got her back to bed, she calmed down right away, and Miss Morris asked her what was the big idea, you know, and do you know what she said? She said she didn't want any more of those doctors pawing her. *Pawing* her, imagine!"

After an instant's struggle with self-mockery, my curiosity led me down the entrance corridor after Elsie, into the longer, wider corridor admitting to the general ward. The whole hospital staff appeared to have gathered in the room to get a look at Miss Sasagawara, and the other patients, or those of them that could, were sitting up attentively in their high, white, and narrow beds. Miss Sasagawara had the corner bed to the left as we entered and, covered only by a brief hospital apron, she was sitting on the edge with her legs dangling over the side. With her head slightly bent, she was staring at a certain place on the floor, and I knew she must be aware of that concentrated gaze, of trembling old Dr. Kawamoto (he had retired several years before the war, but he had been drafted here), of Miss Morris, the head nurse, of Miss Bowman, the nurse in charge of the general ward during the day, of the other patients, of the nurse's aides, of the orderlies, and of everyone else who tripped in and out abashedly on some pretext or other in order to pass by her bed. I knew this by her smile, for as she continued to look at that same piece of the floor, she continued, unexpectedly, to seem wryly amused with the entire proceedings. I peered at her wonderingly through the triangular peep-hole created by someone's hand on hip, while Dr. Kawamoto, Miss Morris, and Miss Bowman tried to persuade her to lie down and relax. She was as smilingly immune to tactful suggestions as she was to tactless gawking.

There was no future to watching such a war of nerves as this, and besides, I was supposed to be at the front desk, so I hurried back in time to greet a frantic young mother and father, the latter carrying their small son who had had a hemorrhage this morning after a tonsillectomy yesterday in the out-patient clinic.

A couple of weeks later, on the late shift, I found George, the ambulance driver, in high spirits. This time he had been the one selected to drive a patient to Phoenix, where special cases were occasionally sent under escort, and he was looking forward to the moment when, for a few hours, the escort would permit him to go shopping around the city and perhaps take in a new movie. He showed me the list of things his friends had asked him to bring back for them, and we laughed together over the request of one plumpish nurse's aide for the biggest, richest chocolate cake he could find.

"You ought to have seen Mabel's eyes while she was describing the kind of cake she wanted," he said. "Man, she looked like she was eating it already!"

Just then one of the other drivers, Bobo Kunitomi, came up and nudged George, and they withdrew a few steps from my desk.

"Oh, I ain't particularly interested in that," I heard George saying.

There was some murmuring from Bobo, of which I caught the words, "Well, hell, you might as well, just as long as you're getting to go out there."

George shrugged, then nodded, and Bobo came over to the desk and asked for pencil and paper. "This is a good place. . . ." he said, handing George what he had written.

Was it my imagination, or did George emerge from his chat with Bobo a little ruddier than usual? "Well, I guess I better go get ready," he said, taking leave. "Oh, anything you want, Kiku? Just say the word."

"Thanks, not this time," I said. "Well, enjoy yourself."

"Don't worry," he said. "I will!"

He had started down the hall when I remembered to ask, "Who are you taking, anyway?"

George turned around. "Miss Sa-sa-ga-wa-ra," he said, accenting every syllable. "Remember that dame? The one who wouldn't let me take her home?"

"Yes," I said. "What's the matter with her?"

George, saying not a word, pointed at his head and made several circles in the air with his first finger.

"Really?" I asked.

Still mum, George nodded in emphasis and pity before he turned to go.

■ How long was she away? It must have been several months, and when, towards late Autumn, she returned at last from the sanitarium in Phoenix, everyone in Block 33 was amazed at the change. She said hello and how are you as often and easily as the next person, although many of those she greeted were surprised and suspicious, remembering the earlier rebuffs. There were some who never did get used to Miss Sasagawara as a friendly being.

One evening when I was going toward the latrine for my shower, my youngest sister, ten-year-old Michi, almost collided with me and said excitedly, "You going for your shower now, Kiku?"

"You want to fight about it?" I said, making fists.

"Don't go now, don't go now! Miss Sasagawara's in there," she whispered wickedly.

"Well," I demanded. "What's wrong with that, honey?"

"She's scary. Us kids were in there and she came in and we finished, so we got out, and she said, 'Don't be afraid of me. I won't hurt you.' Gee, we weren't even afraid of her, but when she said that, gee!"

"Oh, go on home and go to bed," I said.

Miss Sasagawara was indeed in the shower and she welcomed me with a smile. "Aren't you the girl who plays the violin?"

I giggled and explained. Elsie and I, after hearing Menuhin on the radio, had, in a fit of madness, sent to Sears and Roebuck for beginners' violins that cost five dollars each. We had received free instruction booklets, too, but, unable to make heads or tails from them, we contented ourselves with occasionally taking the violins out of their paper bags and sawing every whichway away.

Miss Sasagawara laughed aloud—a lovely sound. "Well, you're just about as good as I am. I sent for a Spanish guitar. I studied it about a year once, but that was so long ago I don't remember the first thing and I'm having to start all over again. We'd make a fine orchestra."

That was the only time we really exchanged words, and some weeks later, I understood she had organized a dancing class from among the younger girls in the Block. My sister Michi, becoming one of her pupils, got very attached to her and spoke of her frequently at home. So I knew that Miss Sasagawara and her father had decorated their apartment to look oh, so pretty, that Miss Sasagawara had a whole big suitcase full of dancing costumes, and that Miss Sasagawara had just lots and lots of books to read.

The fruits of Miss Sasagawara's patient labor were put on show at the Block Christmas party, the second such observance in camp. Again, it was a gay, if odd, celebration. The mess hall was hung with red and green crêpe-paper streamers and the greyish mistletoe that grew abundantly on the ancient mesquite surrounding the camp. There were even electric decorations on the token Christmas tree. The oldest occupant of the bachelors' dormitory gave a tremulous monologue in an exaggerated Hiroshima dialect, one of the young boys wore a bow-tie and whispered a popular song while the girls shrieked and pretended to be growing faint, my mother sang an old Japanese song, four of the girls wore similar blue dresses and harmonized on a sweet tune, a little girl in a grass skirt and superfluous brassiere did a hula, and the chief cook came out with an ample saucepan and, assisted by the waitresses, performed the familiar *dojo-sukui*, the comic dance about a man who is merely trying to scoop up a few loaches from an uncooperative lake. Then Miss Sasagawara shooed her eight little girls, including Michi, in front, and while they formed a stiff pattern and waited, self-conscious in the rustly crêpe-paper dresses they had made themselves, she set up a portable phonograph on the floor and vigorously turned the crank.

Something was past its prime, either the machine or the record or the needle, for what came out was a feeble rasp but distantly related to the Mozart minuet it was supposed to be. After a bit I recognized the melody; I had learned it as a child to the words,

> When dames wore hoops and powdered hair,
> And very strict was e-ti-quette,
> When men were brave and ladies fair,
> They danced the min-u-et. . . .

And the little girls, who might have curtsied and stepped gracefully about under Miss Sasagawara's eyes alone, were all elbows and knees as they felt the Block's one-hundred-and-fifty or more pairs of eyes on them. Although there was sustained applause after their number, what we were benevolently approving was the great effort, for the achievement had been undeniably small. Then Santa came with a pillow for a stomach, his hands each dragging a bulging burlap bag. Church people outside had kindly sent these gifts, Santa announced, and every recipient must write and thank the person whose name he would find on an enclosed slip. So saying, he called by name each Block child under twelve and ceremoniously presented each eleemosynary package, and a couple of the youngest children screamed in fright at this new experience of a red and white man with a booming voice.

At the last, Santa called, "Miss Mari Sasagawara!" and when she came forward in surprise, he explained to the gathering that she was being rewarded for her help with the Block's younger generation. Everyone clapped and Miss Sasagawara, smiling graciously, opened her package then and there. She held up her gift, a peach-colored bath towel, so that it could be fully seen, and everyone clapped again.

■ Suddenly, I put this desert scene behind me. The notice I had long awaited, of permission to relocate to Philadelphia to attend college, finally came, and there was a prodigious amount of packing to do, leave papers to sign, and goodbyes to say. And once the wearying, sooty train trip was over, I found myself in an intoxicating new world of daily classes, afternoon teas, and evening concerts, from which I dutifully emerged now and then to answer the letters from home. When the beautiful semester was over, I returned to Arizona, to that glowing heat, to the camp, to the family, for although the war was still on, it had been decided to close down the camps, and I had been asked to go back and spread the good word about higher education among the young people who might be dispersed in this way.

Elsie was still working in the hospital, although she had applied for entrance into the cadet nurse corps and was expecting acceptance any day, and the long conversations we held were mostly about the good old days, the good old days when we had worked in the mess hall together, the good old days when we had worked in the hospital together.

"What ever became of Miss Sasagawara?" I asked one day, seeing the Rev. Sasagawara go abstractly by. "Did she relocate somewhere?"

"I didn't write you about her, did I?" Elsie said meaningfully. "Yes, she's relocated all right. Haven't seen her around, have you?"

"Where did she go?"

Elsie answered offhandedly. "California."

"California?" I exclaimed. "We can't go back to California. What's she doing in California?"

So Elsie told me: Miss Sasagawara had been sent back there to a state institution, oh, not so very long after I had left for school. She had begun slipping back into her aloof ways almost immediately after Christmas, giving up the dancing class and not speaking to people. Then Elsie had heard a couple of very strange, yes, very strange things about her. One thing had been told by young Mrs. Sasaki, that next-door neighbor of the Sasagawaras.

Mrs. Sasaki said she had once come upon Miss Sasagawara sitting, as was her habit, on the porch. Mrs. Sasaki had been shocked to the core to see that the face of this thirty-nine-year-old woman (or was she forty now?) wore a beatific expression as she watched the activity going on in the doorway of her neighbors across the way, the Yoshinagas. This activity had been the joking and loud laughter of Joe and Frank, the young Yoshinaga boys, and three or four of their friends. Mrs. Sasaki would have let the matter go, were it not for the fact that Miss Sasagawara was so absorbed a spectator of this horseplay that her head was bent to one side and she actually had one finger in her mouth as she gazed, in the manner of a shy child confronted with a marvel. "What's the matter with you, watching the boys like that?" Mrs. Sasaki had cried. "You're old enough to be their mother!" Startled, Miss Sasagawara had jumped up and dashed back into her apartment. And when Mrs. Sasaki had gone into hers, adjoining the Sasagawaras', she had been terrified to hear Miss Sasagawara begin to bang on the wooden walls with something heavy like a hammer. The banging, which sounded as though Miss Sasagawara were using all her strength on each blow, had continued wildly for at least five minutes. Then all had been still.

The other thing had been told by Joe Yoshinaga, who lived across the way from Miss Sasagawara. Joe and his brother slept on two Army cots pushed together on one side of the room, while their parents had a similar arrangement on the other side. Joe had standing by his bed an apple crate for a shelf, and he was in the habit of reading his sports and western magazines in bed and throwing them on top of the crate before he went to sleep. But one morning he had noticed his magazines all neatly stacked inside the crate, when he was sure he had carelessly thrown some on top the night before, as usual. This happened several times, and he finally asked his family whether one of them had been putting his magazines away after he fell asleep. They had said no and laughed, telling him he must be getting absent-minded. But the mystery had been solved late one night, when Joe gradually awoke in his cot with the feeling that he was being watched. Warily, he had opened one eye slightly and had been thoroughly awakened and chilled, in the bargain, by what he saw. For what he saw was Miss Sasagawara sitting there on his apple crate, her long hair all undone and flowing about her. She was dressed in a white nightgown and her hands were clasped on her lap. And all she was doing was sitting there watching him, Joe Yoshinaga. He could not help it, he had sat up and screamed. His mother, a light sleeper, came running to see what had happened, just as Miss Sasagawara was running out the door, the door they had always left unlatched, or even wide open in Summer. In the morning, Mrs. Yoshinaga had gone straight to the Rev. Sasagawara and asked him to do something about his daughter. The Rev. Sasagawara, sympathizing with her indignation in his benign but vague manner, had said he would have a talk with Mari.

And, concluded Elsie, Miss Sasagawara had gone away not long after. I was impressed, although Elsie's sources were not what I would ordinarily pay much attention to, Mrs. Sasaki, that plump and giggling young woman who always felt called upon to explain that she was childless by choice, and Joe Yoshinaga, who had a knack of blowing up, in his drawling voice, any incident in which he personally played even a small part (I could imagine the field day he had had with this one). Elsie puzzled aloud over the cause of Miss Sasagawara's derangement, and I, who had so newly had some contact with the recorded explorations into the virgin territory of the human mind, sagely explained that Miss Sasagawara had no doubt looked upon Joe Yoshinaga as the image of either the lost lover or the lost son. But my words made me uneasy by their glibness, and I began to wonder seriously about Miss Sasagawara for the first time.

Then there was this last word from Miss Sasagawara herself, making her strange legend as complete as I, at any rate, would probably ever know it. This came some time after I had gone back to Philadelphia and the family had joined me there, when I was neck deep in research for my final paper. I happened one day to be looking through the last issue of a small poetry magazine that had suspended publication midway through the war. I felt a thrill of recognition at the name, Mari Sasagawara, signed to a long poem, introduced as ". . . the first published poem of a Japanese-American woman who is, at present, an evacuee from the West Coast making her home in a War Relocation center in Arizona."

It was a *tour de force*, erratically brilliant and, through the first readings, tantalizingly obscure. It appeared to be about a man whose lifelong aim had been to achieve Nirvana, that saintly state of moral purity and universal wisdom. This man had in his way certain handicaps, all stemming from his having acquired, when young and unaware, a family for which he must provide. The day came at last, however, when his wife died and other circumstances made it unnecessary for him to earn a competitive living. These circumstances were considered by those about him as sheer imprisonment, but he had felt free for the first time in his long life. It became possible for him to extinguish within himself all unworthy desire and consequently all evil, to concentrate on that serene, eight-fold path of highest understanding, highest mindedness, highest speech, highest action, highest livelihood, highest recollectedness, highest endeavor, and highest meditation.

This man was certainly noble, the poet wrote, this man was beyond censure. The world was doubtless enriched by his presence. But say that someone else, someone sensitive, someone admiring, someone who had not achieved this sublime condition and who did not wish to, were somehow called to companion such a man. Was it not likely that the saint, blissfully bent on cleansing from his already radiant soul the last imperceptible blemishes (for, being perfect, would he not humbly suspect his own flawlessness?) would be deaf and blind to the human passions rising, subsiding, and again rising, perhaps in anguished silence, within the selfsame room? The poet could not speak for others, of course; she could only speak for herself. But she would describe this man's devotion as a sort of madness, the monstrous sort which, pure of itself and so with immunity, might possibly bring troublous, scented scenes to recur in the other's sleep.

Suggestions for Discussion

1. Who is the narrator? Why did the author select a first-person narrator rather than a third-person narrator for this story? Does the narrator act as a foil in any way to Miss Sasagarawa?
2. How does the setting contribute to the mood of the story? Does the author make a social commentary through her depiction of the Relocation Camp? How would you characterize the narrator's tone? Is she bitter about her experiences? Is Miss Sasagawara bitter about her experiences?

3. How does Yamamoto build a sense of mystery around Miss Sasagawara? What do the scenes in the shower, eating the grapefruit, and at the hospital add to her characterization? Why is the story entitled "The *Legend* of Miss Sasagawara"?
4. What is "wrong" with Miss Sasagawara? Are the suspicions of Mrs. Sasaki and Joe Yoshinaga correct? How does the narrator's attitude towards the two reflect on their suspicions?
5. Who is the central character of Miss Sasagawara's poem? How does the poem help to explain the mystery of Miss Sasagawara? How has Yamamoto prepared the reader for the conclusion of the story?

Suggestion for Writing and Comparison

1. Compare Yamamoto's account of life in the Relocation Camp with any of the accounts in the following books: Monica Itoi Sone's *Nisei Daughter*, Karen Kehoe's *City in the Sun*, Allan Bosworth's *America's Concentration Camps*, Diasuke Kitagawa's *Issei and Nisei: The Internment Years*, or Mine Okubo's *Citizen 13660*.

Toshio Mori

Toshio Mori, a Nisei (American child of Japanese immigrant parents), was born in California. As a young man he published in periodicals of the 1930's and early 1940's such as *The Coast, Common Ground, Pacific Citizen, New Directions,* and *The Writer's Forum.*

His first book *Yokohama, California,* a collection of stories from which "The Eggs of the World" and "The Seventh Street Philosopher" are taken, was ready for publication in 1941, before war was declared with Japan. After the declaration of war, the release of the book was postponed, and Mori, along with all the Japanese who were living on the West Coast, was sent to a relocation camp.

Yokohama, California was finally published in 1949. William Saroyan, who wrote the preface to the book, observed that despite the fact that Mori's prose style occasionally left something to be desired, he was nevertheless "one of the most important new writers in the country at the moment." "The Eggs of the World" and "The Seventh Street Philosopher" are representative of Mori's fiction: they are set in a Japanese American community where life is pedestrian (as it is in most communities), and a philosopher speaks to deaf ears.

The Eggs of the World

Almost everyone in the community knew Sessue Matoi as the heavy drinker. There was seldom a time when one did not see him staggering full of drink. The trouble was that the people did not know when he was sober or drunk. He was very clever when sober. The people were afraid to touch him. They were afraid of this man, sober or drunk, for his tongue and brains. They dared not coax him too solicitously or make him look ridiculous as they would treat the usual tipsy gentleman. The people may have had only contempt for him but they were afraid and silent. And Sessue Matoi did little work. We always said he practically lived on sake and wit. And that was not far from truth.

I was at Mr. Hasegawa's when Sessue Matoi staggered in the house with several drinks under his belt. About the only logical reason I could think of for his visit that night was that Sessue Matoi must have known that Mr. Hasegawa carried many bottles of Japan-imported sake. There was no other business why he should pay a visit to Hasegawa's. I knew Mr. Hasegawa did not tolerate drinking bouts. He disliked riotous scenes and people.

At first I thought Mr. Hasegawa might have been afraid of this drinker, and Sessue Matoi had taken advantage of it. But this was not the case. Mr. Hasegawa was not afraid of Sessue Matoi. As I sat between the two that night I knew I was in the fun, and as likely as any minute something would explode.

"I came to see you on a very important matter, Hasegawa," Sessue Matoi said without batting an eye. "You are in a very dangerous position. You will lose your life."

"What are you talking about?" Mr. Hasegawa said.

"You are in an egg," Sessue Matoi said. "You have seen nothing but the inside of an egg and I feel sorry for you. I pity you."

"What are you talking about? Are you crazy?" Mr. Hasegawa said.

"I am not crazy. I see you very clearly in an egg," Sessue Matoi said. "That is very bad. Pretty soon you will be rotten."

Mr. Hasegawa was a serious fellow, not taking to laughter and gaiety. But he laughed out loud. This was ridiculous. Then he remembered Sessue Matoi was drunk.

"What about this young fellow?" Mr. Hasegawa said, pointing at me.

Sessue Matoi looked me over quizzically. He appeared to study me from all angles. Then he said, "His egg is forming. Pretty soon he must break the shell of his egg or little later will find himself too weak to do anything about it."

I said nothing. Mr. Hasegawa sat with a twinkle in his eyes.

"What about yourself, Sessue Matoi?" he said. "Do you live in an egg?"

"No," Sessue Matoi said. "An egg is when you are walled in, a prisoner within yourself. I am free, I have broken the egg long ago. You see me as I am. I am not hidden beneath a shell and I am not enclosed in one either. I am walking on this earth with my good feet, and also I am drinking and enjoying, but am sad on seeing so many eggs in the world, unbroken, untasted, and rotten."

"Are you insulting the whole world or are you just insulting me?" Mr. Hasegawa said.

"I am insulting no one. Look, look me in the eye, Hasegawa. See how sober I am," he said. "I am not insulting you. I love you. I love the whole world and sober or drunk it doesn't make a bit of difference. But when I say an egg's an egg I mean it. You can't very well break the eggs I see."

"Couldn't you break the eggs for us?" Mr. Hasegawa said. "You seem to see the eggs very well. Couldn't you go around and break the shells and make this world the hatching ground?"

"No, no!" Sessue Matoi said. "You have me wrong! I cannot break the eggs. You cannot break the eggs. You can break an egg though."

"I don't get you," said Mr. Hasegawa.

"An egg is broken from within," said Sessue Matoi. "The shell of an egg melts by itself through heat or warmth and it's natural, and independent."

"This is ridiculous," said Mr. Hasegawa. "An egg can be broken from outside. You know very well an egg may be broken by a rap from outside."

"You can rape and assault too," said Sessue Matoi.

"This is getting to be fantastic," Mr. Hasegawa said. "This is silly! Here we are getting all burned up over a little egg, arguing over nonsense."

"This is very important to me," Sessue Matoi said. "Probably the only thing I know about. I study egg culture twenty-four hours. I live for it."

"And for sake," Mr. Hasegawa said.

"And for sake," Sessue Matoi said.

"Shall we study about sake tonight? Shall we taste the sake and you tell me about the flavor?" Mr. Hasegawa said.

"Fine, fine, fine!" said Mr. Matoi.

Mr. Hasegawa went back in the kitchen and we heard him moving about. Pretty soon he came back with a steaming bottle of sake. "This is Hakushika," he said.

"Fine, fine," Sessue Matoi said. "All brands are the same to me, all flavors match my flavor. When I drink I am drinking my flavor."

Mr. Hasegawa poured him several cups which Sessue Matoi promptly gulped down. Sessue Matoi gulped down several more. "Ah, when I drink sake I think of the eggs in the world," he said. "All the unopened eggs in the world."

"Just what are you going to do with all these eggs lying about? Aren't you going to do something about it? Can't you put some of the eggs aside and heat them up or warm them and help break the shells from within?" Mr. Hasegawa said.

"No," Sessue Matoi said. "I am doing nothing of the sort. If I do all you think I should do, then I will have no time to sit and drink. And I must drink. I cannot go a day without drinking because when I drink I am really going outward, not exactly drinking but expressing myself outwardly, talking very much and saying little, sadly and pathetically."

"Tell me, Sessue Matoi," said Mr. Hasegawa. "Are you sad at this moment? Aren't you happy in your paganistic fashion, drinking and laughing through twenty-four hours?"

"Now, you are feeling sorry for me, Hasegawa," Sessue Matoi said. "You are getting sentimental. Don't think of me in that manner. Think of me as the mess I am. I am a mess. Then laugh very hard, keep laughing very hard. Say, oh what an egg he has opened up! Look at the shells, look at the drunk without a bottle."

"Why do you say these things?" Mr. Hasegawa said. "You are very bitter."

"I am not bitter, I am not mad at anyone," Sessue Matoi said. "But you are still talking through the eggshell."

"You are insulting me again," Mr. Hasegawa said. "Do not allow an egg to come between us."

"That is very absurd," Sessue Matoi said, rising from his chair. "You are very absurd, sir. An egg is the most important and the most disturbing thing in the world. Since you are an egg you do not know an egg. That is sad. I say, good night, gentlemen."

Sessue Matoi in all seriousness bowed formally and then tottered to the door.

"Wait, Sessue Matoi," said Mr. Hasegawa. "You didn't tell me what you thought of the flavor of my sake."

"I did tell you," Sessue Matoi said. "I told you the flavor right along."

"That's the first time I ever heard you talking about the flavor of sake tonight," said Mr. Hasegawa.

"You misunderstand me again," said Sessue Matoi. "When you wish to taste the flavor of sake which I drank then you must drink the flavor which I have been spouting all evening. Again, good night, gentlemen."

Again he bowed formally at the door and staggered out of the house.

I was expecting to see Mr. Hasegawa burst out laughing the minute Sessue Matoi stepped out of the house. He didn't. "I suppose he will be around in several days to taste your sake. This must happen every time he comes to see you," I said.

"No," Mr. Hasegawa said. "Strangely, this is the first time he ever walked out like that. I cannot understand him. I don't believe he will be back for a long time."

"Was he drunk or sober tonight?" I said.

"I really don't know," said Mr. Hasegawa. "He must be sober and drunk at the same time."

"Do you really think we will not see him for awhile?" I said.

"Yes, I am very sure of it. To think that an egg would come between us!"

The Seventh Street Philosopher

He is what our community calls the Seventh Street philosopher. This is because Motoji Tsunoda used to live on Seventh Street sixteen or seventeen years ago and loved even then to spout philosophy and talk to the people. Today he is living on an estate of an old lady who has hired him as a launderer for a dozen years or so. Every once so often he comes out of his washroom, out of obscurity, to mingle among his people and this is usually the beginning of something like a furore, something that upsets the community, the people, and Motoji Tsunoda alike.

There is nothing like it in our community, nothing so fruitless and irritable which lasts so long and persists in making a show; only Motoji Tsunoda is unique. Perhaps his being alone, a widower, working alone in his sad washroom in the old lady's basement and washing the stuff that drops from the chute and drying them on the line, has quite a bit to do with his behavior when he meets the people of our community. Anyway when Motoji Tsunoda comes to the town and enters into the company of the evening all his silent hours and silent vigils with deep thoughts and books come to the fore and there is no stopping of his flow of words and thoughts. Generally, the people are impolite when Motoji Tsunoda begins speaking, and the company of the evening either disperse quite early or entirely ignore his philosophical thoughts and begin conversations on business or weather or how their friends are getting along these days. And the strangeness of it all is that Motoji Tsunoda is a very quiet man, sitting quietly in the corner, listening to others talk until the opportunity comes. Then he will suddenly become alive and the subject and all the subjects in the world become his and the company of the evening his audience.

When Motoji Tsunoda comes to the house he usually stays till one in the morning or longer if everybody in the family are polite about it or are sympathetic with him. Sometimes there is no subject for him to talk of, having talked himself out, but this does not slow him up. Instead he will think for a moment and then begin on his favorite topic: What is there for the individual to do today? And listening to him, watching him gesture desperately to bring over a point, I am often carried away by this meek man who launders for an old lady on weekdays. Not by his deep thoughts or crazy thoughts but by what he is and what he is actually and desperately trying to put across to the people and the world.

"Tsunoda-san, what are you going to speak on tonight?" my mother says when our family and Motoji Tsunoda settle down in the living room.

"What do you want to hear?" Motoji Tsunoda answers. "Shall it be about Shakyamuni's boyhood or shall we continue where we left off last week and talk about Dewey?"

That is a start. With the beginning of words there is no stopping of Motoji Tsunoda, there is no misery in his voice nor in his stance at the time as he would certainly possess in the old washroom. His tone perks up, his body becomes straight, and in a way this slight meek man becomes magnificent, powerful, and even inspired. He is proud of his debates with the numerous Buddhist clergymen and when he is in a fine fettle he delves into the various debates he has had in the past for the sake of his friends. And no matter what is said or what has happened in the evening Motoji Tsunoda will finally end his oration or debate with something about the tradition and the blood flow of Shakyamuni, St. Shinran, Akegarasu, and Motoji Tsunoda. He is not joking when he says this. He is very serious. When anyone begins kidding about it, he will sadly gaze at the joker and shake his head.

About this time something happened in our town which Motoji Tsunoda to this day is very proud of. It was an event which has prolonged the life of Motoji Tsunoda, acting as a stimulant, that of broadcasting to the world in general the apology of being alive.

It began very simply, nothing of deliberation, nothing of vanity or pride, but simply the eventual event coming as the phenomenon of chance. There was the talk about this time of Akegarasu, the great philosopher of Japan, coming to our town to give a lecture. He, Akegarasu, was touring America, lecturing and studying and visiting Emerson's grave, so there was a good prospect of having this great philosopher come to our community and lecture. And before anyone was wise to his move Motoji Tsunoda voluntarily wrote to Akegarasu, asking him to lecture on the night of July 14 since that was the date he had hired the hall. And before Motoji Tsunoda had received an answer he went about the town, saying the great philosopher was coming, that he was coming to lecture at the hall.

He came to our house breathless with the news. Someone asked him if he had received a letter of acceptance and Akegarasu had consented to come.

"No, but he will come," Motoji Tsunoda said. "He will come and lecture. Be sure of that."

For days he went about preparing for the big reception, forgetting his laundering, forgetting his meekness, working as much as four men to get the Asahi Auditorium in shape. For days ahead he had all the chairs lined up, capable of seating five hundred people. Then the word came to him that the great philosopher was already on his way to Seattle to embark for Japan. This left Motoji Tsunoda very flat, leaving him to the mercy of the people who did not miss the opportunity to laugh and taunt him.

'What can you do?" they said and laughed. "What can you do but talk?"

Motoji Tsunoda came to the house, looking crestfallen and dull. We could not cheer him up that night; not once could we lift him from misery. But the next evening, unexpectedly, he came running in the house, his eyes shining, his whole being alive and powerful. "Do you know what?" he said to us. "I have an idea! A great idea."

So he sat down and told us that instead of wasting the beautiful hall, all decorated and cleaned and ready for five hundred people to come and sit down, he, Motoji Tsunoda, would give a lecture. He said he had already phoned the two Japanese papers to play up his lecture and let the world know he is lecturing on July 14. He said for us to be sure to come. He said he had phoned all his friends and acquaintances and reporters to be sure to come. He said he was going home now to plan his lecture, he said this was his happiest moment of his life and wondered why he did not think of giving a lecture at the Asahi Auditorium before. And as he strode off to his home and to lecture plans, for a moment I believed he had outgrown the life of a launderer, outgrown the meekness and derision, outgrown the patheticness of it and the loneliness. And seeing him stride off with unknown power and unknown energy I firmly believed Motoji Tsunoda was on his own, a philosopher by rights, as all men are in action and thought a philosopher by rights.

We did not see Motoji Tsunoda for several days. However in the afternoon of July 14 he came running up our steps. "Tonight is the big night, everybody," he said. "Be sure to be there tonight. I speak on a topic of great importance."

"What's the time?" I said.

"The lecture is at eight," he said. "Be sure to come, everybody."

The night of July 14 was like any other night, memorable, fascinating, miserable; bringing together, under a single darkness, one night of performance, of patience of the world, the bravery of a single inhabitant and the untold braveries of all the inhabitants of the earth, crying and uncrying for salvation and crying just the same; beautiful gestures and miserable gestures coming and going; and the thoughts unexpressed and the dreams pursued to be expressed.

We were first to be seated and we sat in the front. Every now and then I looked back to see if the people were coming in. At eight-ten there were six of us in the audience. Motoji Tsunoda came on the platform and sat down and when he saw us he nodded his head. He sat alone up there, he was to introduce himself.

We sat an hour or more to see if some delay had caused the people to be late. Once Motoji Tsunoda came down and walked to the entrance to see if the people were coming in. At nine-eighteen Motoji Tsunoda stood up and introduced himself. Counting the two babies there were eleven of us in the audience.

When he began to speak on his topic of the evening, "The Apology of Living," his voice did not quiver though Motoji Tsunoda was unused to public speaking and I think that was wonderful. I do not believe he was aware of his audience when he began to speak, whether it was a large audience or a small one. And I think that also was wonderful.

Motoji Tsunoda addressed the audience for three full hours without intermission. He hardly even took time out to drink a glass of water. He stood before us and, in his beautiful sad way, tried with every bit of finesse and deep thought to reveal to us the beautiful world he could see and marvel at, but which we could not see.

Then the lecture was over and Motoji Tsunoda sat down and wiped his face. It was wonderful, the spectacle; the individual standing up and expressing himself, the earth, the eternity, and the audience listening and snoring, and the beautiful auditorium standing ready to accommodate more people.

As for Motoji Tsunoda's speech that is another matter. In a way, however, I thought he did some beautiful philosophizing that night. No matter what his words might have meant, no matter what gestures and what provoking issues he might have spoken in the past, there was this man, standing up and talking to the world, and also talking to vindicate himself to the people, trying as hard as he could so he would not be misunderstood. And as he faced the eleven people in the audience including the two babies, he did not look foolish, he was not just a bag of wind. Instead I am sure he had a reason to stand up and have courage and bravery to offset the ridicule, the nonsense, and the misunderstanding.

And as he finished his lecture there was something worth while for everyone to hear and see, not just for the eleven persons in the auditorium but for the people of the earth: that of his voice, his gestures, his sadness, his patheticness, his bravery, which are of common lot and something the people, the inhabitants of the earth, could understand, sympathize and remember for awhile.

Suggestions for Discussion

1. What is the relationship of the narrator to the community in "The Eggs of the World"? What does the sentence "The people may have had only contempt for him, but they were afraid and silent" indicate about the people? What aspect of the narrator's character is revealed when he says "About the only logical reason I could think of for his visit that night was that Sessue Matoi must have known that Mr. Hasegawa carried many bottles of Japan-imported sake"?

2. How does Sessue Matoi distinguish between being "hidden beneath a shell" and being "enclosed in one"?

3. The narrator is confused as to whether Sessue Matoi was drunk or sober. How is the following statement by Matoi an explanation: "All brands are the same to me, all flavors match my flavor. When I drink I am drinking my flavor"?

4. In what way is "the absurd" which Matoi discusses the same as the existentialist's "absurd"? Is it true that if "you are an egg you do not know an egg"? Is the egg an appropriate symbol for the state Matoi describes?

5. What is the community's response to Motoji Tsunoda in "The Seventh Street Philosopher"? Is the narrator's response different from the community's? Is he interested in Tsunoda's philosophy or in Tsunoda himself?

6. The narrator introduces the story of Tsunoda's public lecture as something having happened "in our town which Motoji Tsunoda to this day is very proud of." We are told that only eleven people come to hear Tsunoda speak. What is it that he is "very proud of"?

7. Discuss the following statement in relation to the rest of the story:

> The night of July 14 was like any other night, memorable, fascinating, miserable; bringing together, under a single darkness, one night of performance, of patience of the world, the bravery of a single inhabitant and the untold braveries of all the inhabitants of the earth, crying and uncrying for salvation and crying just the same; beautiful gestures and miserable gestures coming and going; and the thoughts unexpressed and the dreams pursued to be expressed.

Suggestions for Writing and Comparison

1. With reference to the following quotations from "The Eggs of the World," discuss the community's view of Matoi as opposed to the reader's view: a) "And Sessue Matoi did little work. We always said he practically lived on sake and wit." b) "When you wish to taste the flavor of sake which I drank then you must drink the flavor which I have been spouting all evening."

2. Discuss the narrator's apparent joy, in "The Seventh Street Philosopher," in his vision of "the individual standing up and expressing himself, the earth, the eternity, and the audience listening and snoring, and the beautiful auditorium standing ready to accommodate more people."

Lin Yutang

Lin Yutang was born in Fukien Province, China, in 1895. As a child he was sent to Christian schools where he learned English and Western subjects. After receiving his B.A. in Shanghai, he came to the United States where he earned an M.A. at Harvard, and he later traveled to Germany where he took a Ph.D. at Leipzig.

He returned to China briefly as a professor of English philosophy, but was blacklisted from the University at Peking when he declared himself a radical. Soon becoming disillusioned with the revolution, Lin Yutang returned to the United States to live. His best-selling book *My Country and My People* (1935) is particularly concerned with his criticism of revolutionary China.

In 1948 Lin Yutang was the head of the arts and letters division of UNESCO. He is also known as a lecturer, essayist, novelist, translator, and philosopher; his book of philosophical essays, *The Importance of Living* (1937), remains his best known work. More recently, he has published a translation from the Masters of Chinese Art, *The Chinese Theory of Art* (1967).

Chinatown Family (1948), from which the following excerpt is taken, is a novel of first generation immigrants. However, Tom, the central character, was brought to America as a child and has American scientific attitudes as a result of his education here. Elsie, his girlfriend, who was educated in China, introduces him to Taoism and the thought of Laotse and Chuangtse. The excerpt—slightly modified by the editors for consistency—thus becomes a rare example in our literature of an Americanized character discovering and accepting—rather than rejecting—the culture of his ancestors.

from
Chinatown Family

He lay back with one arm across his forehead, letting his other hand rest on Elsie's back. High up a patch of white cloud was moving slowly across the sky, and it seemed to him as if the earth he was lying on were visibly turning in silent motion on a mysterious voyage.

After a while he said, "What do the clams do when they shut up and dig into the sand? It must be all dark. What do they do?"

Elsie laughed. She liked Tom for asking such impossible questions. "What do they do? They eat and sleep, like you and me."

"Yes, the salt sea water must taste delicious to them. And they reproduce. Who tells them to?"

"What's bothering you, Tom?"

"Who tells the clams to build shells out of the calcium in sea water and dig into the sand and eat and sleep and reproduce like men? Who cares? I ask these questions but there is no answer."

"What makes you think we are more important than the clams?" Elsie asked.

"Aren't we?"

"Not a bit."

Tom sat up. "You don't mean to say you have an answer for me?"

Now Tom brought up his favorite Problem of the Feathers to show how insoluble it was. "Look at the parrot's crest, the peacock's tail, the lark's eyebrow. Who painted them? Take a single feather out of the peacock's tail. It is black here, green there, and gold there, and then it turns black again. Now tell me who did it. Who cares?"

"The answer is that we don't know."

Tom relaxed. "I thought perhaps you had an answer."

"It *is* an answer. We don't know."

He drew his finger along the sand.

"Why won't you take that for an answer?" said Elsie.

"What?"

"To know that we don't know. Tom, why do you puzzle about things so? You'll wreck your brains and never know."

"That was what I thought." Tom looked disappointed. "We know that we don't know."

"Tom, if you know that you don't know, you know. If you don't know that you don't know, you really don't know. Isn't that something to begin with?"

Tom got up and walked about as he always did when he was impatient.

"Daisow, do you know why we live?" he asked Flora.

"No. God wants us to live, I suppose."

"Do you know, Eva?"

"Don't know."

"Do you know why we live, Yiko?"

"Tom, sit down and don't act crazy, asking silly questions like that. Who knows?"

"Yeah, who knows?" said Tom, and he lay down again.

"Didn't I tell you?" said Elsie with a little smile.

"All right, you win."

Elsie noticed that there were thin lines of bruises on her legs. She rubbed them cautiously.

"Did you cut yourself?" Tom asked.

"I thought I felt something sting me in the water."

"Oh, it must have been the jellyfish."

"Tom, if you stop wondering, things get simpler. Don't assume that you are more important than the peacock or the clam, and you won't be so surprised."

"Yeah, or the jellyfish from which you got that sting."

"Or the jellyfish. Tao is in the jellyfish as it is in you or me. You'll be happier if you know that."

"Oh, the Tao again. And one part of Tao stings another part of Tao. Tao must be unkind."

"That is exactly what Laotse said. Tao is impersonal. It does not care."

"I thought you said you didn't know."

"There are things we can know, and things we cannot know. We cannot know the Tao."

"That does not really answer my question. And it does not lessen the mystery."

"Why should you want to? It is more beautiful like that. Life is limited and knowledge is limitless, and it is dangerous to pit the limited against the limitless, as Chuangtse says."

"Who says that?"

"Chuangtse. He says Tao is in ourselves. It is a part of the clam, a part of the jellyfish. Chuangtse says, 'Tao is in the ants, it is in the bricks and tiles, it is even in the excrement.'"

"What kind of religion are you preaching?" Flora asked.

"No religion. It is just a way of understanding things, of understanding life and the universe. Tao is in life, in the universe, in everything."

"What is this Taoism?" Flora asked again.

"I don't know how to put it briefly. Let me see. It is a philosophy of polarization, reversion and cycles, of the unity of all things, the leveling of all differences, the relativity of all standards." Turning to Tom, she said, "You ought to read Chuangtse."

She opened her handbag and took out a comb and began to reset her hair.

"Did you say polarization?"

"Yes, polarization."

"Elsie," said Flora, "I don't see how you know so much."

"I really don't know so very much. It is like you. You were brought up a Catholic and naturally you know a great deal about the Catholic faith. I was brought up with Taoism."

"But you must have read a great number of books."

"No, I haven't. My father said one ought not to read many books. One should read a few, the really good ones, and know them well. Tom, do you want to comb your hair?"

She offered the comb, and Tom took it.

"Give me your hand cream," he said.

She gave it to him, and he began to rub it into his hair.

"What are you doing, Tom?"

"That is Tom. You don't know him," said Eva with a laugh. "He cleans his shoes with Barbasol, shaves with it, and combs his hair with it."

Elsie broke into spasms of laughter. "Tom, you really are funny."

"Isn't it all one basic cream? They use different names to extort money from the ladies," said Tom.

"I bet you don't clean your teeth with it."

"I have tried, but it doesn't taste good. But Barbasol is a cleansing cream. If it cleans the skin, why shouldn't it clean the teeth?"

■ Laotse was a dazzling light, so blinding that it took some time for Tom's mind to adjust itself to him. You either have read Laotse or you haven't; if you have read and understood him, you are a changed man. "When the highest type of men hear the Tao, they try hard to live in accordance with it;

when the mediocre men hear the Tao, they seem to be aware and yet unaware of it; when the lowest type hear the Tao, they break into loud laughter. If it were not laughed at, it would not be Tao." Actually no one ever reads the book of Laotse without laughing at first, and many end by laughing at their own laughter. So it was with Tom. Furthermore, Laotse helped him to understand Elsie better.

She knew the book well. The first time they sat for an hour over the small paper-bound volume. It was probably the most exciting hour Tom had ever spent with her.

"Tom," she said, pointing to a page of the book, "this is just like you. 'He who stands on tiptoe does not stand firm; he who strains his strides does not walk well.'"

":Don't I walk very well?"

"You do. But you don't always get there first."

"I'm afraid I don't follow. But you don't get there by sitting still, either."

"Yes, you do."

"Elsie, either you are fooling me, or I am very stupid. This is all paradox."

"No, it isn't. It's just good sense."

He looked into her eyes, turned upon him from the shaded corner. She seemed one who heard all, knew all, absorbed all, but spoke no more than was necessary. Again he felt tremendous power in her reserve; it was new and exciting, almost frightening.

"Elsie, you are so calm."

"What do you mean?"

"I mean your point of view. You look at things differently from Eva, from Flora, from all the girls I know. You are so—relaxed."

"Relaxed?" That was all she said, as she held up the book again. After a few minutes they came to three lines that held Tom's attention:

> Movement overcomes cold.
> But keeping still overcomes heat.
> Who is calm and quiet becomes the guide of the universe.

"There it is! That is what I mean!" exclaimed Tom.

"That is not paradox, is it?" asked Elsie sweetly. Suddenly she smiled. "I must tell you what my father always said."

"What did he say?"

"He said that Laotse was for women and Confucius was for men. 'Know the male, but keep to the female,' was his favorite line. I'll show it to you."

Elsie rustled the pages of the well-thumbed volume until she found the passage:

> The Spirit of the Valley never dies.
> It is called the Mystic Female.
> The Door of the Mystic Female
> Is the root of heaven and earth.

"There, you see! 'The Female overcomes the Male by quietude.'"

"Is that why women always seem to yield and always win?"

Elsie smiled again. "Father used to tell me that Laotse called Tao the mother and not the father of heaven and earth. You take the book home with you. You see it is not too difficult. I know you will like it."

As Tom went home with the small volume rolled up in his hand, he felt as if he had met a new friend. That night after everybody had left and the restaurant was closed he took out the small volume and read in bed. Some passages caught his immediate attention.

> When the world lives in accord with Tao
> Racing horses are turned back to haul refuse carts.
> When the world lives not in accord with Tao
> Cavalry abounds in the countryside.

Laotse kept on turning out paradoxes for him. It was almost the philosopher's habit of speech.

> Because he does not contend, therefore none can contend with
>   him.
> He does nothing, and through him everything is done.

> Even in victory, there is no beauty,
> And who calls it beautiful
> Is one who delights in slaughter.
> The slaying of multitudes should be mourned with sorrow.
> A victory should be celebrated with the Funeral Rite.
> Therefore when two equally matched armies meet
> It is the man of sorrow who wins.

> All the world says my teaching resembles great folly
> Because it is great; therefore it resembles folly.
> If it did not resemble folly
> It would have long ago become petty indeed.

> My teachings are very easy to understand and very easy to practice,
> But no one can understand them and no one can practice them.
> In my words there is a principle;
> In the affairs of men there is a system.
> Because they know not these,
> They also know me not.
> Since there are few that know me
> Therefore I am distinguished.

Late in the night as Tom clicked off the light, he softly cried, "Hurray!" for the Old Boy.

Suggestions for Discussion

1. Explain the following statements: "If you know that you don't know, you know. If you don't know that you don't know, you really don't know." Are they more appropriate for the opening or the closing of a discussion?

2. In what way are characteristics of Taoist philosophy, "the unity of all things, the relativity of all standards," particularly relevant to twentieth-century thought?
3. Which of Tom's traits are particularly American? Which are Chinese? How does Elsie function as Tom's foil?

Suggestions for Writing and Comparison

1. For a general introduction to Chinese philosophy, see *Three Ways of Thought in Ancient China* by Arthur Waley. Both Taoist classics, the *I Ching* (or *Book of Changes*) and the *Tao Te Ching* (or *Way of Tao*), are available in modern translations.
2. Read Dylan Thomas' poem "The Force That Through the Green Fuse Drives the Flower." Compare Thomas' "force" with Lin Yutang's "tao" and discuss the differences between these concepts and the concept of a personal deity.

Bienvenido Santos

Bienvenido Santos was born in the Philippines in 1911. He came to America as a lecturer before World War II and with the outbreak of the war was forced to remain. At its conclusion he went back to the Philippines where he became the president of Legazpi College. In 1957 he again returned to the United States and worked in the creative writing program of the State University of Iowa.

Santos' poetry and fiction have been published widely in periodicals, including *The Literary Review, Story,* and *Beloit Poetry Journal.* He has also published collections of poems such as *The Wounded Stag* (1956) and several books of fiction including *Brother, My Brother* (1960) and *Villa Magdalena* (1965). Santos has been the recipient of Guggenheim and Rockefeller fellowships and the Republic Cultural Heritage Award for fiction.

The following story, "The Day the Dancers Came," as well as many of the stories in Santos' collection *You Lovely People* (1955), is concerned with the Filipino experience in America and presents an atmosphere much like the one depicted in Carlos Bulosan's Filipino American autobiography *America Is in the Heart.* The mood of "The Day the Dancers Came," which is one of pathos and loneliness (characteristic of Santos' fiction), should be compared to that of Bernard Malamud's "The First Seven Years" in the Jewish American chapter of this text (p. 441).

The Day the Dancers Came

As soon as Fil woke up, he noticed a whiteness outside, quite unusual for a morning in November. That fall, Chicago was sandman's town, sleepy valley, drowsy gray, slumbrous mistiness from sun up till noon when the clouds drifted away in cauliflower clusters and suddenly it was evening. The lights shone on the avenues like soiled lamps centuries old and the skyscrapers became monsters with a thousand sore eyes. But now, there was a brightness in the air and Fil knew what it was and he shouted, "Snow! It's snowing!"

Tony, who slept in the adjoining room, was awakened.

"What's that?" he asked.

"It's snowing," Fil said, peering at the swirling flakes and smiling as if he had ordered this and was satisfied with the prompt delivery. "Oh, they'd love this, they'd love this," he repeated.

From the bedroom came the sound of shattered springs, a deaf, battered accordion of sagging coils.

"Who'd love what?" Tony's voice came after the battery.

When Fil did not answer, Tony asked again, his voice now raised in annoyance.

"The dancers, of course," Fil answered, facing the bedroom. "They're arriving today. Maybe they've already arrived. And they'll see this snow and walk in it. It will be their first snow, I'm sure. Now they have something to remember about Chicago."

"How do you know it didn't snow in New York while they were there?" Tony asked, his words coming through the squeak and creak of thoroughly punished springs.

"Snow in New York in early November?" Fil said. "Are you crazy?"

"Who's crazy?" Tony replied. "Ever since you heard of those dancers from the Philippines coming to Chicago, you've been acting nuts. Loco. As if they're coming here just for you."

Tony chuckled.

Hearing it, Fil blushed. Perhaps it was true that he had been acting too eager ever since he had learned that the dancers were coming to Chicago from New York, but he couldn't help feeling the way he did. Tony had said it—it felt that way, as if the dancers were coming to Chicago specially for him.

Filemon Acayan, Filipino, was fifty, a U.S. citizen. He was a corporal in the U.S. Army, training at San Luis Obispo, California, on the day he was discharged honorably, in 1945, and one of thousands like him for whom the war ended abruptly that day in August after Hiroshima and who never had the chance to fight for the homeland. Instead, a few months later, he got his citizenship papers. Thousands of them, smart and small in their uniform, stood at attention in drill formation, in the scalding sun, and pledged allegiance to the flag and the republic for which it stands, their voices like a prayer recited in unison during the Eucharist at the Luneta. Soon after, he got back to work. To a new citizen, work meant many places and many ways, factories, hospitals and hotels, tending a rose garden and a hundred-year-old veteran of a border war, waiter and cook, and several odd jobs that bore no names. Now he was a special policeman in the post office. He had had pictures taken of himself in uniform with the blouse a bit too loose and long, looking like a musician, a doorman, salvation army bugler, anything but special policeman.

He was a few years younger than Tony—Antonio Bataller, a retired Pullman porter—but he looked older in spite of the fact that Tony had been bedridden most of the time for the last two years, suffering from a kind of wasting disease that had intrigued doctors. All over Tony's body, a gradual peeling was taking place. At first he thought it was merely tinea flava, a skin disease common among adolescents in the Philippines. It had started around the neck and now affected his extremities. His face looked as if it was healing from severe burns. Nevertheless, it was a young face, much younger than Fil's, who had never looked young.

"I'm becoming a white man," Tony had said once, chuckling softly.

It was the same chuckle Fil seemed to have heard now, but this was derisive, insulting.

Fil said, "I know who's nuts. It's the sick guy with the sick thoughts. You don't care for nothing but your pain, your imaginary pain."

"You're the imagining fellow. I got the real thing," Tony shouted from the room. He believed he had something worse than the whiteness spreading on his skin. There was a pain in his insides, like dull scissors scraping his intestines. Cancer. Angrily, he added, "What for I got retired?"

"You're old, man, old, that's what, and sick, yes, but not cancer," Fil said, turning toward the snow-filled sky. He pressed his face against the glass window. There's about an inch now on the ground, he thought, maybe more.

Tony had come out of the room, looking as if he had not slept all night. "I know it is," he said, as if it were an honor and a privilege to die of cancer and Fil was trying to deprive him of it. "Never a pain like this. One day, I'm just gonna die."

"Naturally. Who says you won't?" Fil argued, thinking how wonderful it would be if he could join the company of dancers from the Philippines, show them around, walk with them in the snow, watch their eyes as they stared about them, answer their questions, tell them everything they wanted to know about the changing seasons in this strange land. They would pick up fistfuls of snow, crunch it in their fingers or shove it into their mouths, as he did himself the first time, long, long ago, remembering the grated ice the Chinese sold in the store near the town plaza where he played *tatching* with an elder brother who, later, drowned in a sudden squall. How his mother had grieved over that death, who had not cried too much when his father died, a broken man. Now they were all gone, after a storm and suddenly, or lingeringly, in a season of drought, all, all of them he had loved. He continued, "All of us will die. One day. A medium bomb marked Chicago and this whole dump is *tapús*, finish. Who'll escape then?"

"Maybe your dancers will," Tony answered, now watching the snow himself. "I don't know what makes you so crazy about them."

"Of course, they will," Fil retorted, his voice sounding like a big assurance that all the dancers would be safe in his care. "The bombs won't be falling on this night. And when the dancers are back in the Philippines . . ."

Suddenly, he paused, as if he was no longer sure of what he was going to say. "But maybe, even in the Philippines the bombs gonna fall, no?" he said, gazing sadly at the falling snow.

"What's that to you?" Tony replied. "You got no more folks ove'der, right? I know it's nothing to me. I'll be dead before that."

"Let's talk about something nice," Fil said, the sadness spreading on his face as he tried to smile. "Tell me, how will I talk, how am I gonna introduce myself?"

He would go ahead with his plans. He was going to introduce himself to the dancers and volunteer to take them sight-seeing. His car was clean and ready for his guests. He had soaped the ashtrays, dusted off the floor boards and thrown away the old mats, replacing them with new plastic throw rugs. He had got himself soaking wet as he sprayed the car, humming as he worked. Bit by bit, stray songs from the islands came back to him. The dancers would sing and dance to these songs. He could sing broken phrases, unfinished bars. There were stretches of the forgotten between one phrase and another. Besides, popular songs he had since learned in America kept crowding out the songs of his country.

Fil shook his head as he waited for Tony to say something. "Gosh, I wish I had your looks, even with those white spots, then I could face everyone of them," he said, "but this mug . . ."

"That's the important thing, your mug. It's your calling card. It says,

Filipino. Countryman," Tony said.

"You're not fooling me, friend," Fil said. "This mug says, Ugly Filipino. It says, old-timer, *muchacho*. It says, Pinoy, *bejo*."

For Fil, time was the villain. In the beginning, the words he often heard were: too young, too young; but all of a sudden, too young became too old, too late. What had happened in between? A weariness, a mist covering all things. You don't have to look at your face in a mirror to know that you are old, suddenly old, grown useless for a lot of things and too late for all the lovely and splendid dreams you had wrapped up well against a day of need. The faces of all those you know had blended with other faces less familiar, strange.

When Fil worked as a menial in a hospital in Cook County, all day he touched filth and gore. He came home smelling of surgical soap and disinfectant. In the hospital, he took care of a row of bottles on a shelf, each bottle containing a stage of the human embryo in preservatives, from the lizard-like foetus of a few days, through the newly born infant, with the position unchanged, cold and cowering and afraid. Sometimes in his sleep, Fil dreamed of preserving the stages after infancy, but somewhere he drew a blank like the many years between too young and too old.

"It also says sucker," Tony was saying. "What for you want to invite them? Here? Aren't you ashamed of this hole?"

They had occupied the same apartment on West Sheridan Road for the past ten years and there had been no changes done or any repair made as if there was a tacit contest among all the apartments in the building as to which one was going to survive longest, untouched.

Tony had the bedroom to himself while Fil slept in the living room in a convertible bed. The carpet had lost its true color as if dust had settled on it permanently and had become imbedded in it, textured into a kind of loom where broken lines now stood for the design of what was once perhaps a pattern of beauty. Everything in the apartment was old, including the newspapers and magazines from the Philippines with dates as far back as ten years ago. The walls were eggshell bare except for a tiny crucifix which dropped on the floor every time the door swung against it with some force, but one of them always put it back.

The kitchen looked like an open closet with all sorts of deodorizers in open bottles and sprays. As soon as he woke up, Fil reached for the nearest one and began spraying the air as if a creature of decay had spawned stillbirths of stink during the night and these had to be removed.

On the kitchen wall was a shopping reminder with pegs and holes opposite spaces marked *salt, bread*, or whatever they needed. The pegs continually changed as various needs arose, except one opposite an article which Tony had added, pasting a piece of paper marked *Ligaya* on top of *starch*, which they never used. Ligaya is a girl's name, but it also means happiness. The peg remained stuck in the hole opposite *Ligaya*. For some time, both of them thought it clever and amusing.

In the kitchen, Fil felt he had something on his friend who could not cook as well as he.

"It's not a palace, I know," he said. "But who wants a palace when they can have the most delicious *adobo* here and the best boneless chicken with stuffing . . . yum . . . yum . . ."

Tony was angry, "Yum, yum, you're nuts," he said, "plain and simple loco. What for you want to spend and spend? You've been living on loose change practically all your life and now on treasury warrant so small, all full of holes and practically nothing, and still you want to spend for these dancing kids who don't know you and won't even send you a card afterwards."

"Never mind the cards," Fil answered. "Who wants cards? But don't you see, they'll be happy; and then, you know what? I'm going to keep their voices, their words and their singing and their laughter in my magic sound mirror."

The first time Fil heard his own voice played back in the tape recorder, he didn't believe it was his own, but as soon as he recognized it, the whole thing became to him pure magic. He bought a portable. Tony and he had fun making recordings to songs from the radio and listening to their own voices as they debated in English or in the dialect. It was evident, Fil showed more mastery. His style was florid, sentimental, poetic.

The machine was now several years old, but it still looked new. Fil had a stack of tape recordings, patiently labelled, songs and speeches. The songs were in English, but most of the speeches were in the dialect.

Without telling Tony, he had experimented on recording sounds, like the way a bed creaked, doors opening and closing, rain or sleet tapping on the glass window panes, footsteps through the corridor and on the threadbare rug. He played all the sounds back and tried to remember how it was on the day or night the sounds had been recorded. Did they bring back the moment? He was beginning to think that they did. He was learning to identify each of the sounds with a particular mood or fact. Sometimes, whimsically, he wished that there was a way of keeping a record of silence because it was to him the richest sound, like snow falling.

Now as he and Tony watched the snow blowing in the wind, he thought, what took care of that moment if memory didn't? Like time, memory was often a villain, a betrayer.

"As soon as they accept my invitation, I'll call you up," Fil said; adding hastily, "no, you don't have to do anything, but I'd want you to know so you'd be here to meet them."

"I'm going out myself," Tony said, "and I don't know what time I'm coming back." Then he added, "So you're not working today. Are you on leave?"

"For two days. While the dancers are here," Fil said.

"It still doesn't make sense to me," Tony said. "But, good luck, anyway."

"Aren't you going to see them tonight? That ticket I got you is a good seat, right in front," Fil said.

"I know. But I'm not sure I can come."

"What? You're not sure?" Fil could not believe it. The opportunity of a lifetime. Something must be wrong with Tony. He looked at him closely, saying nothing.

"I'd want to, but I'm sick, Fil. I tell you, I'm not feeling so good. My doctor will know today. He'll tell me," Tony said.

"What will he tell you?"

"How do I know?"

"I mean, what's he trying to find out?"

"If it's cancer," Tony said. Without saying another word, he went straight to his room.

Fil remembered those times, at night, when Tony kept him awake with his long-drawn out sighs of pain. When he called out to him, saying, "Tony! Tony, what's the matter?" the moaning ceased for a while. But afterwards, as if unable to hold the pain any longer, Tony screamed, deadening his cries with a pillow against his mouth. When Fil went to him then, Tony drove him away. Or he curled up in the bedsheets like a big infant suddenly hushed in its crying.

The next day, Tony looked all right. When Fil asked him about the night before, he replied, "I was dying," but it sounded more like disgust over a nameless annoyance. Fil had more misgivings over the whiteness spreading on Tony's skin. He had heard of leprosy. Every time he thought of that dreaded disease, he felt tears in his eyes. In all the years he had been in America, he had not had a friend until he met Tony whom he liked immediately and worshipped for all things the man had and which Fil knew he himself lacked.

"Fil, I can't find my boots, may I wear yours?" Tony's voice sounded strong and healthy.

"Sure, sure!" Fil answered. He didn't need boots. He loved to walk in the snow. Tony needed them.

They had been wearing each other's things. At first, they marked with their initials what each owned, but later, neither paid attention to the distinguishing marks. They wore each other's socks, shorts, handkerchiefs, ties, shoes, jackets, etc. Still they continued to exchange gifts on Christmas. Nobody sent them Christmas presents. Once in a rare while, they got Christmas cards, one from the florist near their apartment house, another from an insurance company. But they made merry on Christmas and drank a lot. Then it did not embarrass them to admit that they were fast friends, indeed. They shook hands on that; they shook hands on practically anything they said. Christmas Day was Armistice Day. They kept shaking hands and admiring each other's gifts. Drink affected them differently: Fil became boisterous and recited poems in the dialect and praised himself. Tony fell to giggling and cursing all the railroad companies of America. When they woke up the next morning, they glared at each other and, without a word, they cleaned up the mess, each obviously avoiding the other. Then one or the other left, but the next day, everything was normal again.

Now as he was getting ready to leave the apartment, Fil said, "Well, I'll be seeing you. Try to be home on time. I shall invite the dancers for luncheon or dinner, maybe tomorrow. But tonight, let's go to the theater together, ha?"

"I'll try," Tony answered.

There was no eagerness in his voice. He had returned to bed as if the morning, that early, had already wearied him.

As he was about to shut the door, Fil heard Tony saying, "Good luck." The voice was faint.

The air outside felt good. Fil lifted his face to the sky and closed his eyes as the snow and a wet wind drenched his face. He stood that way for some time, crying, more, more, more! to himself, drunk with snow and coolness. His car was parked a block away. As he walked toward it, he pushed one foot into the snow and studied the scar he made, a hideous shape among perfect footmarks. He felt strong as his lungs filled with the cold air, as if just now it did not matter too much that he was the way he looked and his English was the way it was. But perhaps, he could talk to the dancers in his dialect. Why not?

A heavy frosting of snow covered his ear, and as he wiped it off with his bare hands, he felt light and young, like a child at play, and once again, he raised his face to the sky and licked the flakes, cold and tasteless on his tongue.

■ When Fil arrived at the Hamilton, it seemed to him the Philippine dancers had taken over the hotel. They were all over the lobby, on the mezzanine, talking in groups animatedly, their teeth sparkling as they laughed, their eyes disappearing in mere slits of light. Some of the girls wore their black hair long. For a moment the sight seemed too much for him who had all but forgotten how beautiful Philippine girls were. He wanted to look away, but their loveliness held him. He must do something, close his eyes perhaps. As he did so, their laughter came to him like a breeze murmurous with sounds native to his land. It was happiness itself.

Later, he tried to relax, to appear inconspicuous. True, they were all very young, but there were a few elderly men and women who must be their chaperones or well-wishers like him. He smiled at everyone who happened to look toward him. Most of them smiled back, or rather seemed to smile, but it was quick, without recognition, and might not have been for him, but for someone else near or behind him..

His lips formed the words he was trying to phrase in his mind: *Ilocano ka? Bicol? Ano na, paisano? Comusta?* Or should he introduce himself? How? His lips trembled at the unfamiliar phrases, frightening him into deeper incoherence.

Suddenly he felt as if he had stumbled into company where he was not welcome. All the things he had been trying to hide now showed: the age in his face, his horny hands. He knew it the instant he wanted to shake hands with the first boy who had drawn close to him, smiling and friendly. Fil put his hands in his pocket. They were cold and damp.

Now he wished Tony were with him. Tony would know what to do. He would charm these young people with his smile and his learned words. Fil wanted to leave, but he seemed caught up in the tangle of moving bodies that merged and broke in a fluid strangle hold. Everybody was talking, mostly in English. Once in a while he heard exclamations in the dialect right out of the past, conjuring up playtime, long shadows of evening on the plaza, fiestas, *misa de gallo.*

There was music in their voices. This was home. This was homelessness. The paradox confused him, but that was how he felt, uncertain whether this feeling was not really regret over all the wasted years away from home. He loved them all — that was clearest in his mind, as he walked among the dancers, pretending he was not a stranger.

Time was passing and he had yet to talk to someone. Suppose he stood on a chair and addressed them in the manner of his flamboyant speeches, recorded in his magic sound mirror?

"Beloved countrymen, lovely children of the Pearl of the Orient Seas, listen to me. I'm Fil Acayan. I've come to volunteer my services. I'm yours to command. Your servant. Tell me where you want to go, what you want to see in Chicago. I know every foot of the lakeshore drive, all the gardens and the parks, the museums, the huge department stores, the planetarium. Let me be your guide. That's what I'm offering you, a free tour of Chicago, and finally, dinner at my apartment on West Sheridan Road—pork *adobo* and chicken *relleno*, name your dish. How about it, *paisanos?*"

No. That would be a foolish thing to do. They would laugh at him. He felt a dryness in his throat. He was sweating. As he wiped his face with a handkerchief, he bumped against a slim, short girl who quite gracefully stepped aside, and for a moment he thought he would swoon in the perfume that enveloped him. It was fragrance long forgotten, essence of *camia*, of *ilang-ilang*, and *dama de noche*.

Two boys with sleek, pomaded hair, were sitting near an empty chair. He sat down and said in the dialect, "May I invite you to my apartment?" The boys stood up, saying, "Excuse, please," and walked away. He mopped his brow, but instead of getting discouraged, as though he had moved another step beyond shamelessness, he grew bolder. Approaching another group, he repeated his invitation, and a girl with a mole on her upper lip, said, "Thank you, but we have no time." As he turned toward another group, he felt their eyes on his back. Once, a boy came toward him, but as soon as he began to speak, the boy said, "Pardon, please," and moved away.

They were always moving away. As if by common consent, they had decided to avoid him, ignore his presence. Perhaps it was not their fault. They must have been instructed to do so. Or was it his looks that kept them away? The thought was a sharpness inside him.

After a while, as he wandered about the mezzanine, among the dancers, but alone, he noticed that some were going down the stairs and others were crowding noisily into the two elevators, through the revolving door, out into the street. He followed the crowd going down the stairs. Beyond the glass doors, he saw them getting into a bus parked beside the subway entrance on Dearborn.

The snow had stopped falling; it was melting fast in the sun and turning into slush.

As he moved about aimlessly, he felt someone touch him on the sleeve. It was one of the dancers, a mere boy, tall and slim, who was saying, "Excuse, please." Fil realized he was in the way between another boy with a camera and a group posing in front of the hotel.

"Sorry," Fil said, jumping away.

The crowd burst out laughing. Then everything became a blur in his eyes, a moving picture out of focus, but gradually, the figures cleared, there was mud on the pavement on which the dancers stood posing, and the sun threw shadows at their feet.

Let them have fun, he said to himself, they're young and away from home. I have no business messing up their schedule, forcing myself on them.

He watched the dancers, till the last of them was on the bus. Their voices came to him, above the traffic sounds. They waved their hands and smiled toward him as the bus started. Fil raised his hand to wave back, but stopped suddenly, aborting the gesture. He turned to look behind him at whoever the dancers were waving their hands. There was no one there except his own reflection in the glass door, a double exposure of himself and a giant plant with its thorny branches around him like arms in a loving embrace.

■ Even before he opened the door to their apartment, Fil knew that Tony had not yet arrived. There were no boots outside on the landing. Somehow he felt relieved, for until then he did not know how he was going to explain his failure.

From the hotel, he had driven around, cruised by the lakeshore drive, beyond the city limits hoping he would see the dancers somewhere, in a park perhaps, taking pictures of the mist over the lake and the last gold on the trees now wet with melted snow, or on some picnic grounds, near a bubbling fountain, still taking pictures of themselves against a background of Chicago's gray and dirty skyscrapers. He slowed down every time he saw a crowd, but the dancers were nowhere along the way he took. Perhaps they had gone to the theater to rehearse. He turned back before reaching Evanston, wondering where the dancers could be then.

He felt weak but not hungry. Just the same, he ate, warming up some leftover food. The rice was cold, but the soup was hot and tasty. While he ate, he listened for footfalls.

Afterwards, he lay down on the sofa and a weariness came over him, but he tried hard not to sleep. As he stared at the ceiling, he felt like floating away in sleep, but he kept his eyes open, willing hard to remain awake.

He had stared at that ceiling so many years, he had memorized every part of it: a corner with stain and dirt, dried up after a long dampness, with lines curved like boundaries between countries where peace was permanent and no borders ever changed, and lines within like rivers touching the sea, estuaries and dots to mark a city, a cape or a peninsula; and cobwebs that grew in a thickening maze, color of rust and soot and age. Always as he gazed at *his* ceiling, he wondered whether the boundaries had changed in the night, what city had vanished after what compromises, whose was the loss, whose the cunning, that a spot called city was gone and other spots had come up, as yet nameless, until he had chosen for each an identity. It was a fascinating game which he could play all by himself and forget time passing.

He lay there wide-eyed till the cities and rivers and the boundaries were nothing now but dirt. He wanted to be awake when Tony arrived. But soon his eyes closed against a weary will, too tired and weak to fight back sleep — and then there were voices. Tony was in the room, eager, to tell his own bit of news.

"I've discovered a new way of keeping afloat," he was saying.

"Who wants to keep afloat?" Fil asked.

"Just in case. In a shipwreck, for example," Tony said.

"Never mind shipwreck. I must tell you about the dancers," Fil said.

"But this is important," Tony insisted. "With this method, you can keep floating indefinitely."

"What for indefinitely?" Fil asked.

"Say in a ship . . . I mean, in an emergency, you're stranded without help in the middle of the Pacific or the Atlantic, you must keep floating till help comes . . . if help comes," Tony explained.

"Better yet," Fil said, "find a way to reach shore before the sharks smell you. You discover that."

"I will," Tony said, without eagerness, as though certain that there was no such way, that, after all, his discovery was worthless.

"Now you listen to me," Fil said, sitting up abruptly. As he talked, in the dialect, Tony listened with increasing apathy.

"There they were," Fil began, his voice taking on the orator's pitch, "some of whom that could have been my children if I had not left home — or yours, Tony. They gazed around them with wonder, smiling at me, answering my questions, but grudgingly, edging away as if to be near me were wrong, a violation in their rule book. But it could be that every time I opened my mouth, I gave myself away. I talked to them in the dialect, Ilocano, Tagalog, Bicol, but no one listened. They avoided me. They had been briefed too well: Do not talk to strangers. Ignore their invitations. Be extra careful in the big cities like New York and Chicago, beware of the old-timers, the Pinoys. Most of them are bums. Keep away from them. Be on the safe side — stick together, entertain only those who have been introduced to you properly.

"I'm sure they had such instructions, safety measures, they must have called them. What then could I do, scream out my good intentions, prove my harmlessness and my love for them by beating my breast? Oh, but I loved them. You see, I was like them once. I, too, was nimble with my feet, graceful with my hands; and I had the tongue of a poet. Ask the village girls and the envious boys from the city — but first you have to find them. After these many years, it shall not be easy. You'll have to search every suffering face in the village gloom for a hint of youth and beauty or go where the graveyards are and the tombs under the lime trees. One such face . . . oh, God, what am I saying?

"All I wanted was to talk to them, guide them around Chicago, spend money on them so that they would have something special to remember about us here when they return to our country. They would tell their folks: We met a kind, old man, who took us to his apartment. It was not much of a place. It was old — like him. When we sat on the sofa in the living room, the bottom sank heavily, the broken springs touching the floor. But what a cook that man was! And how kind! We never thought that rice and *adobo* could be that delicious. And the chicken *relleno!* When someone asked what the stuffing was — we had never tasted anything like it — he smiled, saying, 'From heaven's supermarket,' touching his head and pressing his heart like a clown, as if heaven were there. He had this tape recorder, which he called magic sound mirror, and he had all of us record our voices. Say anything in the dialect, sing, if you please, our *kundiman*, please, he said, his eyes pleading, too. Oh, we had fun listening to the playback. When you're gone, the old man said, I shall listen to your voices with my eyes closed and you will be here again and I'll not be alone, not any more after this. We wanted to cry, but he looked very funny, so we laughed and he laughed with us.

"But, Tony, they would not come. They thanked me, but they said they had no time. Others said nothing. They looked through me. I didn't exist. Or worse, I was unclean. They were ashamed of me. How could I be Filipino?"

The memory, suddenly recalled, was a rock on his breast. He gasped for breath.

"Now, let me teach you how to keep afloat," Tony said, but it was not Tony's voice.

Fil was alone and crying for air. His eyes opened slowly till he began to breathe easily. The sky outside was gray. He looked at his watch—a quarter past five. The show would begin at eight. There was still time. Perhaps Tony would be home soon.

The apartment was warming up. The radiators sounded full of scampering rats. He had a recording of that in his sound mirror.

Fil smiled. He had an idea. He would take the sound mirror to the theater, go to his seat close to the stage, and make tape recordings of the singing and the dances.

Now he was wide awake and somehow pleased with himself. The more he thought of the idea of recording the dancers' performance, the better he felt. If Tony showed up now . . . He sat up, listening. The radiators were quiet. There were no footfalls, no sound of a key turning.

■ Late that night, back from the theater, Fil knew at once that Tony was back. The boots were outside the door. He, too, must be tired and should not be disturbed.

Fil had waited for him till the last possible moment and he had to drive fast. He didn't want too many people staring at him as he lugged the sound mirror to his seat out in front. He had hoped Tony would be there. Shortly before the lights went out, Fil placed the tape recorder on the seat reserved for Tony, next to his. He leaned back and watched, as the show began, manipulating the microphone, controls and tape quite deftly, keeping his eyes on the dancers. He would remember. After this, all he had to do was dub his memory of this night on the sounds recorded on the tape, and the dancers would be there again, frail and graceful and young.

An electric bulb high against a brick wall in the alley across the south window of the living room lighted his way to the sofa on which he placed the sound mirror, careful not to make any noise. He turned on the floor lamp, thinking as he removed his jacket that perhaps Tony was awake and waiting for him. They would listen together to a playback of the dances and the songs Tony had missed. Then he would tell Tony what happened that day, repeating part of the dream.

As he tiptoed toward Tony's bedroom, he heard the regular breathing of a man sound asleep. In the half-darkness, Tony's head showed darkly, deep in a pillow, on its side, his knees bent, almost touching the clasped hands under his chin, an oversized foetus in the last bottle. Quietly, Fil shut the door between them and walked to the sofa. Opening the case of the recorder, he looked around for a socket, and, finding one, plugged in the sound mirror, adjusted the tape, and turned the volume low. At first nothing but static and odd sounds came through, but soon after there was the patter of feet to the rhythms of a familiar melody.

All the beautiful boys and girls were in the room now, dancing and singing. A boy and a girl sat on the floor holding two bamboo poles on each end, flat on the floor, clapping them together, then apart, and pounding them on the boards, while dancers swayed and balanced their lithe forms, dipping their bare brown legs in and out the clapping bamboos, the pace gradually increasing into a fury of wood on wood, in a counterpoint of panic among the dancers in a harmonious flurry of toes and ankles escaping certain pain—crushed bones and bruised flesh, and humiliation. Other dances followed, accompanied by songs and live with the sounds of life and death in the old country: Igorots in G-strings, walking down a mountainside, peasants climbing up a hill on a rainy day; neighbors moving a house, their sturdy legs showing under a portable roof; lovers in Lent hiding their love among wild hedges, far from the stewing chapel; a distant gong sounding off a summons either to a feast or a wake. And finally, a prolonged ovation, thunderous, wave upon wave.

"Turn that thing off!" Tony's voice was distinct and sharp above the echoes of the shuddering gongs and the applause settling into silence.

Fil switched off the machine; in the sudden stillness, the voices turned into faces, familiar and near like gestures and touch, that stayed on even as the memory withdrew, bowing out, as it were, in a graceful exit, saying, thank you, thank you, before a ghostly audience that clapped hands in silence and stomped their feet in a sucking emptiness. He wanted to join the finale, such as it was, pretend that the curtain call included him, and attempt a shamefaced imitation of a graceful adieu, but he was stiff and old, incapable of grace; but he said, thank you, thank you, his voice sincere and contrite, grateful for the other voices and the sound of singing and the memory.

"Oh, my God . . ." the man in the other room cried, followed by a moan of such anguish that Fil fell on his knees, covering the sound mirror with his hands to muffle the sounds that had started again, it seemed to him, even after he had turned it off.

Then, quickly, he remembered.

"Tony, what did the doctor say? What did he say?" he shouted and listened breathless, no longer able to tell at the moment who had truly waited all day for the final sentence.

There was no answer. Meanwhile, under his hands, there was a flutter of wings, a shudder of gongs. What was Tony saying? Fil wanted to hear, he must know. His arms went around the dead machine as his head fell, resting on a loosened tape.

It was near morning then and sleep overpowered him like a wave that drew his body into a darkness where he floated on and on in a shoreless sea.

Suggestions for Discussion

1. Why is Fil able to accept the probable bombing of Chicago but not of the Philippines? What kind of significance have the dancers taken on for Fil?

2. What kind of comment on the lives of Tony and Fil is the statement "The peg remained stuck in the hole opposite *Ligaya"?* How aware are they of their situation?
3. A number of images are at work in the story. For example, how do the bottled embryos relate to Tony "curled up in the bedsheets like a big infant suddenly hushed in its crying" (p. 266)? When the dancers leave, Fil sees a reflection "of himself and a giant plant with its thorny branches around him in a loving embrace" (p. 269). Explain. Is there a central metaphor unifying these different images?
4. What is the meaning of " . . . no longer able to tell at the moment who had truly waited all day for the final sentence" (p. 272)? What is the significance of the story's conclusion?

Suggestion for Writing and Comparison

1. Compare the quality of the lives of the characters and the mood created in both Bernard Malamud's "The First Seven Years" (p. 441) and Santos' "The Day the Dancers Came."

Carlos Bulosan

Carlos Bulosan was born in the Philippine village of Mangus-
mana when it was still a wilderness. Although he began working at the age of five, he managed to obtain a small amount of
schooling and to become literate in both his native language
and in English. He left the Philippines in 1931 as a young man
of seventeen.

Bulosan came to California where several of his older
brothers worked as itinerant farmers, and he too found employment as a fruitpicker. He later traveled throughout the United
States by freight train, returning on several occasions to California where he was to become a labor leader.

Throughout his life he suffered from tuberculosis. During a
two-year stay in the Los Angeles County Hospital Bulosan began
to read seriously and to write. In a brief period of time, he produced several volumes of verse including *Letter From America*
(1942) and *The Voice of Bataan* (1943), a collection of short stories, *The Laughter of My Father* (1944), and an autobiography,
America Is in the Heart (1946). Bulosan died of tuberculosis in
1956. His letters were published posthumously in 1960 under
the title *Sound of Falling Light: Letters in Exile*.

The following poem, "History of a Moment," was written just
before the outbreak of World War II. It reflects the mood of tension, the hope and the fear regarding the outcome of that war,
particularly in the Pacific.

History of a Moment

Now listen. The steady fall of fine rain enriches
The land. Sunset is a red flower in the western sky.
Night breaks the moment and darkness moves eastward
Over America, and earthward, sprawling upon the continent.
5 It is the fluid tension of waiting in valleys and cities;
It is the last passionate longing in every heart
That beats remembering the final plunge to earth.

Listen to me then. Listen to me in the night
That ruins our illusion of violent discoveries.
10 Listen to my last words under the galaxies of eyes
And tongues that lash at every promise I make
For you. And now you prepare for my last will
And testament, for I leave you this heritage
Of vast patterns of land that is America. . . .

15 Remember how I walked under the bombers that time,
Bearing a new world of longing in my eager hands;
How I approached you through the battleships,
Saying: Here is a tiny green fruit from my country.
Remember how I sat back in the small sick-bed,
20 After the submarines and destroyers, saying:
Here is a historic seed growing in your country.

I am the tension of waiting in valleys and cities,
The longing in every heart that beats to see
America break through the darkness moving eastward.
25 I warn you and prepare for the final lash
Of armies and navies and the enduring love;
Living at a time when the night must lie,
I make no promise except this historic truth.

Suggestions for Discussion

1. How is the opening description of landscape — a fine rain, sunset, night — made to function in the human realm of tension, longing, and remembering?

2. How are the bombers and the battleships of the third stanza related to the small sick-bed? Why is the "fruit from my country" tiny and green? How does this imagery reflect the relationship of the U.S. to the Philippines at the beginning of the second World War?

3. Who is the narrator? Why does he identify himself in the final stanza? Were his warning and promise fulfilled?

Suggestion for Writing and Comparison

1. Compare "History of a Moment," written immediately preceding the Second World War, with Langston Hughes' "Let America Be America Again" (p. 108), which was written during the Depression. How does each poet—during ominous and, for some, hopeless times—reflect a hope for America's future?

Ferris Takahashi

(See p. 229 for Takahashi's story "The Widower" and a biographical sketch of the author.)

Nisei, Nisei!

I have no face —
This is a face,
(Nisei, Nisei!)
My face of astigmatic eyes,
5 Other eyes.

A composite of sneer and word,
The cherry blossom and the sword,
Where I hang as on gallows wood;
(Nisei, Nisei!)

10 Set in the island centuries
Of the mixed stock Yamato breeds.
(And this is censored:
No one reads
Of our dissimilarities,
15 Nisei, Nisei!)

Is this so yellow?
Brown and plain
White are the skins of old Japan.

I have no face.

20 My sallow cheek
Is greenish in the subway light,
My parents' mild and patient eyes
Mocked in these narrow apertures;
Look, glasses make this low-built nose
25 The shadow of a caricature.
(Nisei, Nisei!)

Give me the eyes that form my face!
All outside eyes, all looking down,
The eyes of every day that frown,
30 The starry world, the street, the job, the eating place —
All eyes I envy for their anonymity.
(Nisei, Nisei!)

This is mirage.
These are my twenty years of youth —
35 To look the thing I hate and what I am:
(Nisei, Nisei!)

Where is the heart to scour this enemy mask
Nailed on my flesh and artifact of my veins?
Where is the judge of the infernal poll
40 Where they vote round eyes honest and mine knave?

This is a dream.
These eyes, this face
(Nisei, Nisei!)
Clutched on my twitching plasm like a monstrous growth,
45 A twinning cyst of hair, of pulp, of teeth. . . .

Tell me this is no face,
This face of mine —
It is a face of Angloid eyes who hate.

Suggestions for Discussion

1. Who is the speaker in the poem? Why is "Nisei, Nisei!" put in parentheses? Explain the lines "(And this is censored:/No one reads/Of our dissimilarities,/Nisei, Nisei!)."
2. In what way do "astigmatic eyes" and "yellow skin" compose "no face . . . this enemy mask"?
3. What is meant by the final two lines, "This face of mine —/It is a face of Angloid eyes who hate"? Who sees through "Angloid eyes"?
4. What is the historical significance of the publication date of this poem in 1946?

Suggestion for Writing and Comparison

1. How do Ralph Ellison and Ferris Takahashi use invisibility and anonymity to explore the problems of identity? (See particularly the Prologue to Ellison's novel *Invisible Man*.)

Chiang Yee

Chiang Yee was born in Kiukiang, China, in 1903, a son of the painter Chiang Ho-an. Chiang Yee attended the National South-Eastern University in Nanking, where he received a Bachelor of Science degree in 1925. He was a lecturer in chemistry for one year, and then became governor and director of four districts.

In 1935 he went to England where he was appointed Lecturer in Chinese at London University. He also received recognition as an artist through a series of one-man shows of his paintings and drawings. Several years later he migrated to America.

Chiang Yee has written a number of critical works as well as novels, children's stories, and poems. He began the *Silent Traveller* series, which contains travel narrative, social observation, poetry, and paintings, in 1937 with *The Silent Traveller in Lakeland*. This was followed by a number of volumes with similar format including *The Silent Traveller in New York* (1950), *The Silent Traveller in Boston* (1959), and *The Silent Traveller in San Francisco* (1964).

"Arrival at Boston," from Chiang Yee's 1959 volume, captures the spirit of the *Silent Traveller* series, indicating the peripatetic narrator's lifelong quest after knowledge of all the "human world." The movement in the poem, suggested by the words "drifted" and "at leisure," is noticeably different from that in the next poem in this section by Kuangchi C. Chang (p. 281). Chiang Yee's arrival in the United States is as an urbane world traveller; Kuangchi Chang's arrival is as a political refugee.

Arrival at Boston

Originally I lived in Mount Lu,
A dumbman well-acquainted with travels.
Riding the storm and braving the waves
    I reached the Western land,
5 Having seen all the winds and rains of the
    human world.

After twenty years stay in Oxford, England,
I now drifted towards the Star-flag.
With no definite purpose
I stop at Boston temporarily,
10 Tracing at leisure the origin of the Yankees.

Suggestions for Discussion

1. This poem, printed originally both in Chinese characters and in English, is taken from Chiang Yee's book of travel essays *The Silent Traveller in Boston*. How does the book's title clarify Chiang's reference to himself in the second line of the poem as "a dumbman"?
2. What do "all the winds and rains of the / human world" signify? Why does the poet imply he has seen them *before* reaching the West?
3. What attitude is revealed in the phrases "at leisure" and "With no definite purpose"? What will this traveller find that would be missed by another who wants "to do Boston in a week"? Is Chiang's "purposelessness" exaggerated? If so, to what end?

Suggestion for Writing and Comparison

1. Discuss the differences between Chiang Yee's arrival in Boston and the "coolies'" arrival in California. Do economic and educational background affect the newcomer's welcome?

Kuangchi C. Chang

Kuangchi C. Chang was born in Shanghai, China. He received a classical education in Chinese literature and art before coming to America. He first travelled to this country in order to study architecture at Columbia University, and he returned to China after graduation. But in 1949 he came again to the United States where he remains as a refugee from Communism.

Kuangchi C. Chang has been a professor of Oriental Art at the University of Oklahoma and an architect for a New York City firm. His poetry and translations have appeared in various American periodicals such as *The American Scholar* and *Hudson Review*.

The following poem, "Garden of My Childhood," deals explicitly with the experience of the refugee, and it is his history, rather than that of the United States, which is scrutinized (compare Chiang Yee's "Arrival at Boston," p. 279). The walk to the garden of the narrator's childhood was paved "with pebbles of memory"; in his new garden in America "the unpebbled walk awaits tomorrow's footprints." Present-day America is once again a refuge for the "homeless, tempest-tost" of Emma Lazarus' poem (see the Introduction to Chapter 5, p. 411).

Garden of My Childhood

"Run, run, run,"
Whispered the vine,
"A horde is on the march no Great Wall can halt."
But in the garden of my childhood
5 The old maple was painting a sunset
And the crickets were singing a carol;
No, I had no wish to run.

"Run, run, run,"
Gasped the wind,
10 "The horde has entered the Wall."
Down the scorched plain rode the juggernaut
And crossed the Yangtse as if it were a ditch;
The proverbial rats had abandoned the ship
But I had no intention of abandoning
15 The garden of my childhood.

"Run, run, run,"
Roared the sea,
"Run before the bridge is drawn."
In the engulfed calm after the storm
20 The relentless tom-tom of the rice-sprout song

Finally ripped my armor,
And so I ran.

I ran past the old maple by the terraced hall
And the singing crickets under the latticed wall,
25 And I kept on running down the walk
Paved with pebbles of memory big and small
Without turning to look until I was out of the gate
Through which there be no return at all.

Now, eons later and worlds away,
30 The running is all done
For I am at my destination: Another garden,
Where the unpebbled walk awaits tomorrow's footprints,
Where my old maple will come with the sunset's glow
And my crickets will sing under the wakeful pillow.

Suggestions for Discussion

1. What is the effect of beginning the first three stanzas with the same three words? Which line in each of the first three stanzas emphasizes the movement in the poem?
2. What force has a "rice-sprout song" to rip "armor"? What various kinds of meaning have the armor and the rice-sprout song in relation to nature and to politics?
3. How does the movement of the poem change in the last two stanzas? Is the central metaphor of the poem, the garden, an effective counterpart to the movement? How is the garden at once past and future?

Suggestion for Writing and Comparison

1. Read the Sung Dynasty lyrics of Li Yu, Su Shih, or Li Ch'ing-chao. Compare mood and imagery in any one of their poems with that in Chang's "Garden of My Childhood."

Lloyd Tsugawa

Lloyd Tsugawa, born in Hawaii in 1946, attended schools in Hilo before coming to California with his family. He received his high school education in Los Angeles and then attended UCLA.

Lloyd Tsugawa is especially interested in the work of Thomas Merton and Herman Hesse. The interaction between Eastern and Western ways of thought—treated in Tsugawa's "Poem" —is the major theme of Hesse's novel *Siddhartha*.

Tsugawa's deft, sure touch in the use of imagery is evident both in the following poem and in "To Ripen," p. 304. His poems have appeared, as yet, only in literary magazines.

Poem

maybe if you didn't have
your belly full of gravity
your head cages
you could come play with me

5 I have never seen Kamakura
where footfalls complain not
but fall deep into moss
spoiled by full rain and shaded sun

maybe by the next ride out
10 the Buddy will wink coca-cola
and we'll never get to say
solemn things on his behalf

Suggestions for Discussion

1. Who is the speaker in the first stanza? Whom is he addressing? Where are they both located? Explain the lines "your belly full of gravity/your head cages."
2. What is the significance of "Kamakura" to Buddhism? What is meant by "footfalls complain not"? In what sense is the moss "spoiled" by rain and sun?
3. Why is the image "the Buddy will wink coca-cola" startling? How is this image a comment on the twentieth century?

Suggestion for Writing and Comparison

1. Compare the attitudes toward twentieth-century America expressed in Tsugawa's poem with those in Ferris Takahashi's story "The Widower" (p. 229). In each instance how is "Westernization" depicted in relation to Eastern culture?

Lawson Fusao Inada

Lawson Inada, a third-generation Japanese American, was born in Fresno, California, and raised in the predominantly Black area of West Fresno. In 1971 he published his first collection of poetry, *Before the War: Poems As They Happened.* His work has been frequently anthologized and he has also published in literary reviews, such as *Evergreen Review, Chicago Review,* and *Kayak.* Inada is a professor at Southern Oregon College in Ashland, Oregon.

Inada's poetry, described by Denise Levertov as "taut, sinewy, and full of energy," is often concerned with the Japanese American experience and his own place in that experience. In the following poem he takes his personal history as the basis of a political message to Asian brother and Asian sister.

Asian Brother, Asian Sister

For Yoshiko Saito

I

Not yet dawn,
but the neighbors have been here,
bringing condolences, assurances
that my pupils will be seen to:

5 though I am new to their village
they include me, are grateful
for what I do.

The teacups are rinsed.
The bedding is stacked.
10 While my wife wraps our basket
the children kneel on the tatami,
fingering the beads of the rosary like an abacus.
In their way, they are hushed,
and seem to sense the solemnity.

15 "Sa. Iki-ma-sho."

A cold wind greets us.
There will be snow soon
in this prefecture.

Burnt wood, sweet fields.
20 Not yet dawn.
In one of these houses,
my grandmother is rising to go to school

II

By sixteen,

she was in this country —

25 making a living, children
on the way.

I don't know what it cost
in passage, in the San Joaquin.

I'm beginning
30 to understand the conditions.

III

To get back to the source,
through doors

of dialects and restrictions . . .

Brazil to the south, this blue
35 shore on the horizon . . .

To get back to the source,
the need to leave

and bring it with you:

in 1912, they opened
40 the Fresno Fish Store.

IV

Ika, the squid,
to slither down your throat.

Saba, the mackerel,
to roast.

45 Maguro, the tuna —
slice it thin and raw.

Kani, the crab.
Aobi, the abalone.

All these
50 shipped in slick and shiney.

All these
to keep our seasons.

All these.

V

Grandmother never learned the language —
55 just a few
choice phrases to take care of business.
Grandfather ordered the fish.

But when the nice white man
bent down to her level and said
60 "How long you been here, Mama?"
she told him
"Come today fresh."

VI

Before the war, after
the old scrape of stench and scale,
65 she'd come to see what her new grandson could do.

Nine o'clock, but you've got to wake him,
so I can flip him in his crib.

Bring him down to the store tomorrow
so I can get him some manju,
70 let him chew on an ebi.

Part his hair in the middle,
slick it down,
so I can wheel him around to the people.

Listen, big baby — Mexican tunes
75 moving around the jukeboxes.
Listen, big fat round-headed baby in white shoes.

What chu mean
he's got small eyes?
What chu mean?
80 That's how he
supposed to be.
What chu mean?
Big fat baby in a hood.

In depths of bed,
85 to roll to where the shore was, undulating
coves and folds . . .

Drunks dancing wounded
under a wounded streetlight . . .

Then the Danish Creamery
90 screaming about its business
and we couldn't sleep.

Sing me. Sing me. Sing me
please about the pigeons
cooing home to the temple to roost.

95 Sing me. Please.

For our sweet tooth,
she kept a store

of canned fruit buried in the dirt
beside her barracks in Arkansas.

100 Water flopping over the furo's edges
as we entered, feet
sliding on slats,
a soft iceberg in the heat and steam . . .

So you've got a son in New Guinea,
105 another at some fort.
What do you do?
What have you *been* doing? —

try to keep busy and eat.

And as the children leave
110 to dicker with the enemy,
try to keep busy and eat.

Float around him,
bump and nudge him,
and try to keep busy and eat.

115 Shuffle off to the store
ten feet behind him
and try to keep busy and eat.

And when the sons take over,
try to keep busy and eat.

120 Go in and scream about the business.
Grandchildren stumbling
over their own skin in the suburbs,
hubcaps and money
cluttering the driveways . . .

125 One day they found her
flipping in a driveway like a fish.

If your hip is broken,
you can't ever go home —
roaming through Wakayama
130 for what the War didn't own.

If your hip is broken,
you can't ever go to Oregon.
You've got to wheel to your drawer
for your Issei medallion —

135 that steamer riding on a starry-striped sea.

If your hip is broken,
you've got to give that medallion
with a moan —

as though you could know.

VII

140 My grandmother is in the beauty
of release.
As the heart subsides,
as the blood runs its course,
she is gowned and attended,
145 chanting incantations to Buddha.

I am touched by the beauty,
by the peace
that is the end of her life —

fluttering eyelids,
150 the murmuring barely audible.

It is goodbye.

It is beautiful.

I do not need to cry.

As the sheet flows over in its purity,
155 I note the smoothness
of skin, the grey-blue hair
echoed faintly over the lips.

Then the sheet becomes a paper bag,
and she slips out of that sack
160 off the kitchen table

and lands on her back
on the linoleum,

naked, moaning, the impact
having stunned her into fright.

165 And she grabs both legs of mine
and bends the knees
and brings me down upon her

blue mouth without teeth,
food beginning to swell
170 in her belly

where I am

crying, and not yet born.

VIII

This house. This house.
The paths become trenches to the telephone, the bathroom . . .
175 This house. The scent of Orient

and seven existences.
This house. The bedrooms
tacked-on then sealed-off
as each moved to the colonies.

180 This house. Fifty years in this house.
Lie in front of the heater and dream,
flames eating the snowflake
mica that shudder with color
like fish-scales — blue, red — dream . . .

185 Lie in front of this heater
and knead the pus
where fish-fins stuck,
your dreams a fish
wilting over this heater . . .

190 This house. Creamery and cleavers
going at each other down the wintery street.

Bitches in alleys,
bottles in dreams . . .

Who knew the black whore in the alley
195 of this house —
dead a week, wrapped in leaves . . .

Tread lightly in this house.
Appliances try the edge of trenches.
Grandchildren balance on the shelves —
200 tassled
offspring of another culture . . .

This house. The basement
crammed with ballast —
dolls, kimonoes, swords . . .

205 This house. That survived the War
and got stoned.
This house. Exhausted fumes

gnawing the garden on the shore.

In the mist of that shore,
210 the chrysanthemum
droops and nods.

This house.

It drops into the freeway
and I drown.

IX

215 Then the doors burst open

and the people come flooding in —

from all over the San Joaquin
come to form the procession.

There is a trench to the temple.

220 When you are in that trench,
there is no room
for much movement:

all that you move from
comes in on you;
225 all that you do
is judged upon.

Trapped in the trench,
I am smothered in my people,
chanting in procession to the temple.

230 And when we emerge in the temple
I am five feet two,
flat-faced, bent-legged, epicanthic
as I will ever be . . .

Do my eyes lie?

235 My people see I am beautiful.

Yes. I am rocked in the lap of Buddha.
Yes. Incense owns my clothes.
Yes. I am wrapped in beads.

Yes. My people.
240 Grandmother, take me in your arms.

What you say, I will do.

X

The procession continues . . .
My grandfather migrates
to my mother's house, in the suburbs.
245 Even the chrysanthemum
finds new root, in the suburbs.

I have the medallion
forever sailing on my breast —
a family and the seven gods of luck
250 in the hold.

Brothers, Sisters,
understand this:

you are in passage —
wherever you go

255 you are slanted
down to the bone.

Do your eyes lie?

Brothers, Sisters,
understand this:

260 you are beautiful.

And your beautiful grandmother
is dancing in your eyes,

cooing and cooing you
home to roost.

Suggestions for Discussion

1. Who is the speaker in Part I of "Asian Brother, Asian Sister"? How does Part I relate to the rest of the poem? Explain the lines "In one of these houses/my grandmother is rising to go to school."

2. To what source does the speaker in Part III hope to return? How is the rest of the poem an attempt "to get back to the source"?

3. In what context does the speaker use the lines "Sing me/please about the pigeons/cooing home to the temple to roost" (Part VI)? How does the meaning of the lines change when he evokes them in the final part of the poem, "cooing and cooing you/home to roost"?

4. Explain the lines "Grandchildren stumbling/over their own skin in the suburbs,/hubcaps and money/cluttering the driveways . . ." in Part VI. How do the lives of the grandchildren contrast to that of the grandmother?

5. Discuss the meaning of the nightmare visions in Parts VII and VIII of the poem. What are the "trenches" in Part VIII? What do the "trenches" come to mean in Part IX? Explain the speaker's statement "When you are in that trench,/there is no room/for much movement."

6. Are the conflicts that the speaker describes throughout the poem resolved in the final part? Explain his statement "Wherever you go/you are slanted/down to the bone."

Suggestion for Writing and Comparison

1. Compare and contrast "Asian Brother, Asian Sister" with Pam Koo's "In the Hardware Store" (p. 300) and Harold Bond's "Letter to an Aunt" (p. 618). In each case, describe the relationship between the speaker and other family members.

Diana Chang

Diana Chang was born in New York, but at the age of eight months she went with her parents to China. The family lived for several years in Peiping, Nanking, and Shanghai. At the end of the Second World War they returned to the United States where Diana Chang graduated from Barnard College in 1949.

She was awarded a John Hay Whitney Foundation fellowship in order to complete her first novel, *The Frontiers of Love* (1956), which has been favorably compared to the popular *Love Is a Many Splendored Thing*. *The Frontiers of Love* was followed by *A Woman of Thirty* (1959) and *A Passion for Life* (1961).

Diana Chang's poems have been published in a number of American periodicals, including *Poetry* magazine. "On Seeing My Great-Aunt in a Funeral Parlor" and "Four Views in Praise of Reality" appeared in *The American Scholar* in 1955 and 1959.

In both the following poem and "Four Views in Praise of Reality," Diana Chang explores attitudes toward the inner world. Her aunt's legacy is that "She leaves us listening/Her speech is young somewhere." That inner life—transcending death—comes in conflict with physical objects in "Four Views." The existing objects seem to haunt the poet and make "His mind . . . desolate/In a metaphysical scene." "Four Views" should be compared to the poems of José Garcia Villa (p. 305–6), which deal in a similar way with the nature of reality, art, and philosophy.

On Seeing My Great-Aunt in a Funeral Parlor

She died away from home
Moved to floral rooms
Hotels of death are near

My aunt lies quiet here
5 The smiling winter bride
Her wedding bed the earth

My aunt receives the spade
Her stony flesh is frail
Her bones light as at birth

10 The trees are human veins
The sunset cries anew
Her blood was used in love

The old are girlish now
Going to their grooms
15 They marry mysteries

She travels past the light
She leaves us listening
Her speech is young somewhere

We are the sleeping guests
20 Talking in our night
On her happy dawn

The heart does leap in love
Though the growing spirit hurts
The pain of joy is life.

Four Views in Praise of Reality

1

All things beautiful begin
In imagination's small society:
The points of harmony are old houses
Quiet beyond the sound of the sea.

5 The painter makes bright squares
Of gold, his canvas is as dear
As sunshine in Schenectady.

New England's blue geography
Is closer to imagery
10 Than the circling of infinity.

2

Music is prismatic among these heights,
Where steep and dark the conversations run—
Nowhere in Manhattan does Euclid cease.

Music sings drily into toneless equations,
15 Its notes like cold stars constricted by time,
They repeat the fiction of a human position.

But hosannas to truth are mute and fair,
Their dumb warm circuits dominate
A low, miraculous firmament of air.

20 The innocence of a rose
Is what the poet wants,
A certain lack of philosophy
But definite roseness,

So that life will not look at him
25 Through the eyes of a green wall,
A fireplace, a clock, objects
That have each a place to begin,

Green, white, gold, their centers
Sing, while all night long
30 His mind is desolate
In a metaphysical scene.

4

The city does not seem to know
Its real estate in space and sky
May outlast your integrity,

35 Though in the windows of your eyes
The instinct for the absolute
Wanders in gradual suicide.

The city is wise and visible,
Certain of an actual view,
40 But you engage its reality.

Suggestions for Discussion

1. What are the origins of "hotel" and "hospital"? Discuss the meaning of the phrase "hotels of death" in "On Seeing My Great-Aunt."

2. What have funerals and wedding ceremonies in common? In what way is the aunt a "smiling winter bride"? How is the wedding image expanded later in the poem?

3. How is the paradoxical nature of death as a beginning rather than as an ending conveyed through the imagery? What is meant by "She travels past the light"?

4. What have "old houses," "the sound of the sea," and "sunshine" to do with "New England's blue geography" in "Four Views"? Why is the geography blue?

5. What does the poet mean by "The innocence of a rose" and "Green, white, gold, their centers/Sing"? How are the colors in opposition to the poet's mind? Why is her mind "desolate"?

6. What does the word "engage" mean in the context of the final line "But you engage its reality"? How is this engaging of reality opposed to "the circling of infinity" mentioned in the first section of the poem? How does "Four Views" "praise" reality?

Suggestions for Writing and Comparison

1. Compare Diana Chang's attitude toward death with that of James Agee in his couplet "And all our grief and every joy/To time's deep end will time destroy." In "On Seeing My Great-Aunt,"³ is time seen as an agent of destruction?
2. What is the difference between poetry and philosophy? Discuss Diana Chang's views in "Four Views" and those of Wallace Stevens as found in his poems "Sunday Morning" or "Peter Quince at the Clavier." Is poetry "essential" or "existential"?

Toyo Suyemoto

Toyo Suyemoto, a West Coast Japanese American, is a poet who employs both Oriental and Occidental traditions in her work. "Retrospect" and "A Gift of Quince" were both composed in the early 1940's when she was an inmate of the Japanese Relocation Center in Topaz, Utah. These poems were published in *The American Scholar* of December, 1945. The emotional intensity of Toyo Suyemoto's poetry and her mastery of the rhymed quatrain suggest her debt to Emily Dickinson.

Retrospect

No other shall have heard,
   When these suns set,
The gentle guarded word
   You may forget.

5 No other shall have known
   How spring decays
Where hostile winds have blown,
   And that doubt stays.

But I remember yet
10   Once heart was stirred
To song—until I let
   The sounds grow blurred.

And time—still fleet—delays
   While pulse and bone
15 Take count before the days
   Lock me in stone.

Gift of Quince

You placed a spring of scarlet quince
   In my curved hand, and then I knew
This was your answer to all that
   I asked of you:

5 The flame had never been put out,
   But that the eyes had been deceived
Until it burned again, until
   The heart believed.

Suggestions for Discussion

1. In "Retrospect," who is being addressed in the lines "The gentle guarded word/You may forget"? How is it suggested that the speaker will *not* forget?
2. What is the meaning of "hostile winds" in the poem "Retrospect"? What are their results? What words are used to contrast the momentary passage of the winds with their lasting effects?
3. In "Retrospect," how does the poet emphasize the contrast between "pulse and bone" and "stone"? What is meant by the phrase "before the days/Lock me in stone"?
4. In what way is "Gift of Quince" a companion poem to "Retrospect"? What part does the element of time play in the relationship of the poems?
5. What similarities unite the images of "the flame" and the "sprig of scarlet quince"? How are they set in opposition to the "stone" of "Retrospect"? In what way is "until/The heart believed" an answer to "until I let/The sounds grow blurred"?

Suggestion for Writing and Comparison

1. Compare the uses of "stone" as an image in Muriel Rukeyser's sonnet from *Letter to the Front* (p. 510), in Toyo Suyemoto's two poems, and in Diana Chang's "On Seeing My Great-Aunt in a Funeral Parlor" (p. 293). What aspect of death does each of these women poets use "stone" to represent?

Pam Koo

Pam Koo was born in San Diego, California, in 1954 and raised in predominantly white neighborhoods. In her own words, she "was a model student and constant teacher's pet. Learned to cash in on the stereotype. Smiled lots and looked bright: instant A's." She has been published in several little magazines and in *Crystal Clear and Cloudy*, an anthology of modern poetry.

Pam Koo's poetry generally tries to make brief, sharp statements about personal experiences. With great economy and deftness of imagery she is able to suggest to the reader far more than is made explicit in the poem.

Pauline

All night at the airport
after missing the last plane,
you slouched behind sunglasses,
staring ahead.

5 Remembering:
     Mom screaming in Chinese
     and sister, crazy, sad,
     flying through a window.
     Cement three stories down.

10 Now at home you cry at night.
Downstairs the phone rings
but you shut your eyes
and hear only the wind —
The wolf, you say,
15 and in the darkness below
the window, arms folded,
you rock alone
all night.

10/9 Afternoon

Coming into fall.
Chrysanthemum takes over
the trellis
where chinese stringbeans
5 were;
no vegetables grew this year.
Already too much rain
and grandmother

preens the leaves
10 of the orange tree,
hunting grasshoppers.

"I twist off their heads,"
she tells me.
She comes in, hair blown
15 and slippers muddy —
we know the oranges
must survive.
"They eat the young leaves —
damn them!"
20 I tell her
washing
her hands will prevent
grasshopper malaria.
Watching a smile
25 from her eyes,
finding her mouth —
a laugh gurgles.

"Oh yeah?"

In the Hardware Store

In the hardware store
I asked,
"Gramma, want to plant a garden this year?"
She said,
5 "Tend vines, fight white flies?
Watch everything dry in the sun?"

Eyeing each other, smiling,
I rattled a seed packet,
and she marched
10 to the clerk,
two envelopes — melons and tomatoes —
in each hand.

Suggestions for Discussion

1. Discuss the progression of "Pauline." How do the images and
the tone in each stanza relate to those in the other two stanzas
and produce a unified whole?

2. What details in the first stanza of "10/9 Afternoon" suggest the grandmother's involvement with growing things? What is the difference between the knowledge of the speaker and the knowledge of the grandmother? Who is the more convincing?
3. How does the hardware store setting in the last poem affect the rest of the poem? How does the speaker take both the reader and the grandmother out of the hardware store? What is the effect of the speaker's gesture?

Suggestion for Writing and Comparison

1. Write a short essay in which you discuss the characterization of the grandmother in "10/9 Afternoon" and "In the Hardware Store." How does Koo create character through language, tone, and action in these brief poems? Expand Koo's depiction. What else might we guess about the grandmother from the details that we are given in this poem?

Shisei Tsuneishi

Shisei Tsuneishi was born in 1888 in a farm village of the Prefecture of Kochi, Japan. He came to America at the age of nineteen, attended high school in Monrovia, California, and later became a student at the University of Southern California.

Tsuneishi began writing haiku in 1921 for the *Japanese American Daily News* in San Francisco. The following year he founded the Tachibana-Haiku Society, which is still flourishing in California and publishes a quarterly magazine devoted to haiku. Tsuneishi, who is now living in Los Angeles, is also an associate of the *Hototogisu,* Japan's leading haiku magazine.

The following poems, written originally in Japanese, were translated into English by the author. Tsuneishi has retained through his translations most of the technical requirements for the Japanese haiku such as the three lines of five, seven, and five syllables each. However, as English has more prepositions, articles, and conjunctions, occasionally there are lines with an extra syllable.

These poems are fine examples of the qualities which have made the haiku popular. Terse, sharp, and direct, the poems at once present an image and suggest something more. This "something more," which lies in the realm of feeling and thought, rather than being made explicit, is left to the reader's imagination.

Five Haiku

I

(*at Evergreen Cemetery*)

Dandelion flowers;
how many good friends of mine
sleep here, I wonder!

II

On awaking from
midday nap, I found myself
back in America.

III

(*at Wupatki National Monument, Arizona*)

Indians met their doom
at this very spot, I heard . . .
Wild flowers in bloom.

IV

Look, a green spider
upon the pink hollyhock,
chewing a bee alive!

V

Though old, I still harbor
unrealized dreams within me,
as the new year returns.

Suggestions for Discussion

1. What technique is employed throughout these poems to suggest
   the situation? How explicit are place and time made in each
   case? Is the situation usually central to the thought?
2. Although these haiku concern different subjects, the thought pattern in each often follows the same progression. For example,
   compare the functions of the first lines, second lines, and final
   lines in the first and third haiku. Explain how, although the obvious progressions—flowers to people, people to flowers—are
   opposite, the underlying thought patterns are similar.
3. Examine the second haiku. What is the situation that is made explicit in the poem? What is the probable story which the reader
   intuits? Do any of the other haiku suggest, in a similar way,
   longer stories?
4. It is the business of poetry to make us see and feel what we
   ordinarily ignore. Which of the haiku do you find most successful in this respect?

Suggestion for Writing and Comparison

1. Compare Carl Sandburg's poem "Grass" with Shisei Tsuneishi's first and third haiku. Discuss each poet's attitude toward
   nature as seen in the relations of grass, dandelions, and wild
   flowers to mankind and history.

Lloyd Tsugawa

(See p. 283 for Tsugawa's "Poem" and a biographical sketch of the author.)

To Ripen

I have set
as one might have fruit
green loving on a sill
to ripen
5 . . . to cause the sun to move
quickly and quietly to my window . . .

Suggestions for Discussion

1. In the classical period of Japanese poetry, preceding the seventeenth-century, most poets used the *tanka* form. It contains thirty-seven syllables, arranged five-seven-five-seven-seven. The *hokku* or *haiku* evolved from the *tanka* by the elimination of the last two lines. Hitomara, considered Japan's greatest poet, often used the *tanka* form. How close is the syllabic pattern of "To Ripen" to that of the traditional tanka? Does the poem seem in any way an expanded haiku?
2. Does "loving" resemble "fruit . . . on a sill"? Is the image in the last two lines, ". . . to cause the sun to move/quickly and quietly to my window," effective?

Suggestion for Writing and Comparison

1. Read several of Hitomara's tanka or the anthology *Sounds from the Unknown* (1963), edited by Lucille M. Nixon and Tomoe Tana, which contains tanka written by Japanese Americans. Write two or three "expanded haiku" using Lloyd Tsugawa's "To Ripen" as an example of a modern American variant of the form.

José Garcia Villa

José Garcia Villa was born in Manila, Philippines. He came to the United States in 1930 and has resided here ever since. Garcia Villa attended both the University of New Mexico and Columbia University. While still a student he began publishing short stories. He met with such success that in 1932 Edward O'Brien, for many years the editor of the annual *Best American Short Stories,* dedicated the collection of that year to him. O'Brien referred to Garcia Villa as being "among the half-dozen short story writers in America who count."

In 1933 Garcia Villa published *Footnote to Youth*, a collection of stories written in poetic prose. Since that time he has turned his attention to poetry. Garcia Villa's first volume of collected poems, *Have Come, Am Here* (1942), was hailed with great enthusiasm by critics such as Marianne Moore and Mark Van Doren. This book received the poetry award of the American Academy of Arts and Letters. It was followed in 1946 by *Selected Poems*, for which Edith Sitwell wrote a laudatory preface, and later by several other volumes of verse including *Selected Poems and New* (1958).

José Garcia Villa, who is also a painter and a mystic, has often been compared, in his childlike, visionary quality, to the English mystic-artist-poet William Blake.

Inviting a Tiger

Inviting a tiger for a weekend.
The gesture is not heroics but discipline.
The memoirs will be splendid.

Proceed to dazzlement, Augustine.
5 Banish little birds, graduate to tiger.
Proceed to dazzlement, Augustine.

Any tiger of whatever colour
The same as jewels any stone
Flames always essential morn.

10 The guest is luminous, peer of Blake.
The host is gallant, eye of Death.
If you will do this you will break

The little religions for my sake.
Invite a tiger for a weekend,
15 Proceed to dazzlement, Augustine.

Be Beautiful, Noble, Like the Antique Ant

Be beautiful, noble, like the antique ant,
Who bore the storms as he bore the sun,
Wearing neither gown nor helmet,
Though he was archbishop and soldier:
5 Wore only his own flesh.

Salute characters with gracious dignity:
Though what these are is left to
Your own terms. Exact: the universe is
Not so small but these will be found
10 Somewhere. Exact: they will be found.

Speak with great moderation: but think
With great fierceness, burning passion:
Though what the ant thought
No annals reveal, nor his descendants
15 Break the seal.

Trace the tracelessness of the ant,
Every ant has reached this perfection.
As he comes, so he goes,
Flowing as water flows,
20 Essential but secret like a rose.

Suggestions for Discussion

1. In "Inviting a Tiger," how does the medieval philosopher and theologian Augustine deal with "little birds"? To what end does Villa say "Proceed to dazzlement, Augustine"?
2. How would inviting a tiger for a weekend "break the little religions"? What is suggested by the phrase "eye of Death"?
3. What is the tone of "Inviting a Tiger"? What ideas are we asked to entertain? Finally, how are we meant to interpret "Invite a tiger for a weekend,/Proceed to dazzlement"?
4. In Garcia Villa's second poem, why do ants seem to be "uniformed"? Why is wearing only one's own flesh noble or beautiful or worthy of imitation?
5. How are the ant and human contrasted in the third stanza of Garcia Villa's second poem? How is this contrast explored further in the final stanza? Why are human lives said to be "existential," rather than "essential" like the rose or ant?

Suggestions for Writing and Comparison

1. Compare William Blake's "The Tiger" with José Garcia Villa's "Inviting a Tiger." How does each poet suit his diction and syntax to the subject?
2. Read the chapter in Jean-Paul Sartre's novel *Nausea* in which he discusses the tree-ness of the tree. How is this idea similar to the one expressed at the end of Garcia Villa's poem "Be Beautiful, Noble, Like the Antique Ant" in the lines "Every ant has reached this perfection . . . / Essential but secret . . ."?

Chapter 4
Hispanic American Writers

Oscar Zeta Acosta
Leonard Adamé
Alurista
Emilio Díaz Valcárel
Victor Hernandez Cruz

Luis Lloréns Torres
Felipe Luciano
Manuel J. Martinez
Americo Paredes
Prudencio de Pereda

Josef Rodriguez
Omar Salinas
Piri Thomas
Luis Valdez

Introduction

Until recent years, Hispanic American writers—Puerto Ricans, Chicanos, and Hispanos (Spaniards)—seldom chose to write in English, perhaps because Spanish is still the dominant language in many Hispanic American communities, and most Hispanic Americans are bilingual. But the late 1960's marked the beginning of a renaissance in Hispanic American writing. Young Chicanos, Puerto Ricans, and Hispanos have begun to produce belletristic literature written often in English, sometimes in Spanish, sometimes in a combination of the two languages, and sometimes in a *pachuco* dialect. Such conscious experimentation with language is often accompanied by themes of social awareness. It is no coincidence that many of the most important young Hispanic American writers of today are also political activists and leaders in the La Raza movement.

A few Hispanic Americans writing in English have been published in the United States throughout this century, and some have entered the mainstream of American writers. George Santayana, who came to America from Spain at the age of nine and was educated at Boston Latin School and Harvard University, is perhaps the best example. Santayana, who is especially known for his novel *The Last Puritan*, wrote all of his major works, including philosophical discourse and poetry, in English. Luís Muñoz Marin, a Puerto Rican (who later was elected governor of Puerto Rico), also became a mainstream writer in the 1920's. Muñoz Marin was part of a literary circle which included Horace Gregory, Sara Teasdale, and Vachel Lindsay. His poems and articles were often published in magazines such as *The Nation, The American Mercury,* and *Poetry.* Maria Christina Mena, who was born in Mexico in 1893 and migrated to the United States as a young girl, is another example. She published her first story in *Century Magazine* at the age of twenty. In 1928 she was included in the O'Brien annual collection of best American short stories, and critics stated that she had written the most comprehensive series of stories of Mexican life ever published in English.

But much of the material that was produced by Hispanic Americans during the early decades of the twentieth century was anonymous, and most of it was written in Spanish. The large American publishing houses had little interest in publishing works in the language of a minority group, and thus few of those writers have come down to us in literary history. Some of their works have been preserved through small, independent presses—such as the work of Santiago de la Hoz, a Chicano poet from Laredo, Texas, whose *Sinfonía de combate* appeared in 1904; but a vast amount has been lost or has yet to be transcribed. (For an example of transcription see Americo Paredes' "With His Pistol in His Hand," p. 328.)

The Spanish American writer Prudencio de Pereda published short stories and novels successfully from the 1930's all through the 40's and 50's; and Jaime de Angulo, another Spanish American, published *Indian Tales* in 1953. In the 1940's and 50's two Chicano writers of note came on the literary scene and received attention from mainstream publishers—Mario Suarez, whose sketches in English of *barrio* life appeared in several nationally circulated periodicals, and Jose Villarreal, whose novel *Pocho* was published by Doubleday. But it was not until the 1960's (and in the wake of the Black movement) that Hispanic American writing began to grow into a conscious literary movement, with ties based on language, culture, skin color, and economic problems.

■ In the long history of Spanish discovery, conquest, and influence in the Americas, the island of Puerto Rico was one of the first to be touched. It was visited by Columbus in 1493. Later used as a trading post by Spanish explorers, its native Arawak Indians were soon decimated and Africans imported to replace them as "forced labor." In Mexico an advanced Aztec civilization under Montezuma was conquered by Hernando Cortés during the years 1519–1521; but the Indians of Mexico, who were more numerous than those of the Caribbean, survived colonization. Within twenty years of the conquest of Mexico, the southern section of what was to be the United States, from South Carolina to California, had been explored by Spaniards. Fray Marcos and an African, Esteban, who was called the "Black Mexican," sought the mythical "Seven Cities of Cibolá"; they found Zuñi pueblos instead. The Grand Canyon was visited by a lieutenant of Coronado in 1540. Hernando de Soto landed in Florida and marched across country until he reached the Mississippi in 1541. The founding of St. Augustine, Florida, in 1565 preceded the building of forts and missions as far north as the Carolinas. And it was in the sixteenth century, eleven years before the Mayflower landed, that Santa Fe, New Mexico, was founded. Thus Spanish colonization in the Southeastern and Southwestern United States preceded that of the English in the Northeast or New England.

After the decline of Spain as a major power and the declaration of American independence from England, there was little significant Spanish immigration to this country for many years. One of the largest periods of immigration occurred much later in the 1850's, when nearly ten thousand Spaniards entered the United States. In other decades of the nineteenth century the number was considerably lower, particularly as compared with the influx from Germany, Italy, Russia, or Great Britain. Spanish immigration increased around the turn of the century but dropped severely in the 1920's with the passage of restrictive immigration laws. And during the period of the Spanish Civil War emigration from America exceeded immigration because many men returned to Spain in order to fight. Subsequent immigration has been minor.

In 1848, the United States gained a number of citizens through the treaty of Guadalupe Hidalgo, by which people living in the new territories of Texas, New Mexico, Arizona, and California were given the choice of leaving for Mexico or remaining as "new" American citizens. A mass movement occurred in the 1920's when immigration laws kept out many European and Asian laborers, thereby creating a need for workers which was to be filled by Mexican immigrants and nationals. More recently, the Immigration and Naturalization Service statistics indicate that in the 1950's over 350,000 Mexicans immigrated to the United States; and in 1963, 56,000 new Mexican Americans comprised the largest United States immigrant group.

Puerto Ricans have been migrating to the mainland for well over a hundred years. As early as 1910 there were Puerto Ricans in thirty-nine of the forty-six states. In 1917 Puerto Ricans were declared United States citizens by birth; therefore, neither passport nor visa was required for entry into the continental United States. However, it has only been since the conclusion of World War II that the number of Puerto Rican migrants has increased to make a significant social and economic difference to both Puerto Rico and the mainland.

The ties that Puerto Ricans and Chicanos have been able to retain with Puerto Rico and Mexico are often closer than the European American's ties with Europe, partly because of proximity. Frequent two-way travel is not uncommon and helps maintain cultural affiliations through many more generations than is possible for those with European background, who seldom or never visit their parents' or grandparents' homeland. Another obvious reason for the maintenance of the culture, and one that we have seen operating for several of the other minority groups considered in this book, is race prejudice and hostility on the part of the majority culture. The healthy, normal reaction of minorities has been to band together both for emotional sustenance and to preserve their culture from attack. The literature that has come out of the recent Hispanic American renaissance often illustrates this reaction and is more consistently "ethnic" (i.e., concerned with cultural and/or sociopolitical themes) than that of the various White Ethnic groups we consider in this text.

■ What most white Americans knew about Hispanic Americans until recently was often suggested to them by white American writers. Too few Hispanic Americans were speaking for themselves, but the literature about the Hispanic American was plentiful. (See, for example, Cecil Robinson's critical study on literature about Mexican Americans by Anglo writers, appropriately named *With the Ears of Strangers*). Such literary depictions ran the gamut from stereotyping of the "lazy Mexican" to treating him as a superior, spiritual being.

Early New England travelers to the Southwest were among the first Anglos to record their impressions. The literature of the Santa Fe Trail is extensive: it includes *Prose Poems and Sketches* (1834), by Albert Pike, in which the land and people of New Mexico are described; the classic of the genre, Josiah Gregg's *Commerce of the Prairies* (1851), which contains a comprehensive account of life among the Mexicans and Americans along the Santa Fe Trail; and one of the best known sea narratives, Richard Henry Dana's *Two Years Before the Mast* (1840), with its stereotyped picture of the California Mexican. (Dana says, for example, "nothing but the character of the people prevents Monterey from becoming a great town.")

Popular writers of the early 1900's such as Bret Harte and O. Henry reveal the racial attitudes prevalent at the time. O. Henry, for instance, mustered a most condescending tone to stereotype an old man as "a lineal Aztec, somewhat less than a thousand years old, who herded a hundred goats and lived in a continuous drunken dream from drinking *mescal*." This kind of writing is obviously the product of one who hears with the ears of a stranger.

Willa Cather, writing during a period when O. Henry was still very popular, chose to depict the Mexican American community as a refuge for the heroine of her novel *The Song of the Lark*. Thea Kronborg's family had little appreciation of esthetic values, and she found in Johnny Tellamantez, singer and guitarist, a sympathetic and sensitive friend. In a later novel, *Death Comes for the Archbishop*, one of Cather's characters notices what he believes to be a wholly admirable and even Christ-like quality in the Mexicans, "whose minds are not upon gain and worldly advancement."

John Steinbeck's Mexican American characters in *Tortilla Flat*, whom he calls *paesanos*, are dispossessed people who manage to live innocent, happy lives in spite of their lack of money or land. In Steinbeck's short story "Flight" the main character is Pepé, a nineteen-year-old "black" Mexican, unused to city ways. Pepé is destroyed in his eagerness to become a man, but Steinbeck emphasizes his nobility and tragic realization of his own humanity. Both Cather and Steinbeck, then, find values in the Mexican American community that are at odds with the generally pragmatic Anglo outlook.

Puerto Ricans have also been depicted by various Anglo writers. Arthur Laurent's play *West Side Story*, which was later made into a motion picture and a novel, attempts an honest but somewhat romanticized fictional presentation of Puerto Ricans and their various encounters with American systems. The Puerto Ricans of New York have also been the subject of numerous sociological studies: most notable are *The Puerto Rican Journey: New York's Newest Immigrants*, by C. Wright Mills, Clarence Senior, and Rose Golden; *The Newcomers: Negroes and Puerto Ricans in a Changing Metropolis*, by Oscar Handlin; and Oscar Lewis' famous work, *La Vida*. However, the most revealing work about the Puerto Ricans in New York is Piri Thomas' autobiographical novel *Down These Mean Streets* (see p. 364).

As a general rule, we can get the most accurate perception of an experience from a talented writer who has either lived that experience or observed it firsthand. And while most of us would agree that men have sometimes drawn good literary portraits of women and some white writers have written interesting works about members of minority groups, feminist criticism and ethnic criticism have now shown us that even the best depictions were frequently flawed by authors' false assumptions and generalizations regarding what are the internal truths about "the other."

■ The literary renaissance of La Raza was affirmed in 1969 with the "Spiritual Manifesto of Aztlan" which came out of the Chicano Denver Conference, and with the formation of similar Puerto Rican groups in New York such as the Young Lords Party. The "Spiritual Manifesto" recognized Hispanic American unity with the statement "We are a bronze people with a bronze culture. Before all the world, before all of North America, before all our brothers in the bronze continent, we are a nation, we are a union of free pueblos, we are Aztlan." It was this affirmation of a "bronze culture" that led to a new literary proliferation, which in turn is now strengthening that bronze culture.

Much of this literature has come out of the *barrio*—a term which means, literally, neighborhood. But the *barrio* is more than a locale: it is a cultural and spiritual zone with its own traditions and legends and heroes, its own art and graffiti and even calligraphy, and its own literary genres (such as the *corrido*—a ballad, usually meant to be sung, which appeared in the Southwest during the early decades of the twentieth century. The *corrido* was generally anonymous. Its lines are usually octosyllabic, with four lines to a stanza in an *abcb* rhyme scheme.). This literature has been further encouraged by the spread in the last few years of the older concept of *flor y canto* (literally, flower and song), a metaphorical conception of the humanistic, creative spirit of the individual which insists that people may transcend reality through art and literature.

The explosion of artistic creation where so recently there was only an occasional spurt is dramatically suggested by the many new periodicals devoted to Hispanic American writing (e.g., Puerto Rican periodicals in New York: *Guajana, La Nueve Sangre, P'alante, Unidad Latina;* Chicano periodicals: *El Grito, Con Safos, La Raza, Regeneracion, Bronzé*). It is further suggested by the publication of Hispanic Americans' novels and poetry by major publishers (e.g., Grove Press's publication of Spanish American author Floyd Salas' *Tatoo the Wicked Cross,* Doubleday's publication of Chicano author Richard Vasquez' *Chicano,* Random House's publication of two books of poetry by Puerto Rican author Victor Hernandez Cruz, *Snaps* and *Mainland*). The international recognition given to Luis Valdez' Teatro Campesino suggests that the Anglo public is now anxious to hear Hispanic American writers speak for themselves.

But perhaps the healthiest aspect of this literary renaissance is that Hispanic American writers have learned to speak to each other. This has resulted in a great prolification of Hispanic American publishing houses, including Quinto Sol Publications (publishers of *El Grito* magazine, as well as the Chicano anthology *El Espejo,* Rudolfo Anaya's novel *Bless Me, Ultima,* and Sergio Elizondo's collection of poetry *Perros y Antiperros*) and Barrio Publications (publishers of Abelardo Delgado's *Los Cuatro* and *Chicano: Twenty-Five Pieces of a Chicano Mind*).

Having learned to speak to each other, many more Hispanic Americans are writing belletristic literature, since they have a greater assurance of a sympathetic reading public with many shared experiences. What is apparent in the literature of some of the younger writers in this text, such as Alurista, is that there is little concern with the reaction of the white reader, since the author writes primarily for other Chicanos who share with him a *barrio* language, a culture, and a sociopolitical experience. But what is also apparent is that the white reader has much to learn from reading literature that was not first overheard with the ears of strangers and then translated through the author's own preconceptions and misconceptions, but rather was delivered directly by those who are speaking for themselves.

Manuel J. Martinez

Manuel J. Martinez, a Chicano of the Southwest, is a muralist, easel painter, and critic. Martinez' work is well known in the *barrios* of the Southwest. He has covered entire houses with his murals and he also has been an artist-spokesman for Cesar Chavez' United Farm Workers. Martinez believes that the Chicano artist must be communal, and that the new Chicano art is, like the modern art of Mexico, essentially a statement of social protest.

The Art of the Chicano Movement and the Movement of Chicano Art

To understand the present cultural values of our people, it is necessary to understand the history of Mexico, to which we are still closely related. Mexican history and artistic expressions bring life and cultural nationalism within emotional grasp.

Unlike many of the styles of contemporary art, many concepts and forms of Chicano art come from its own traditions. This is not to say that Chicano art is an imitation of Indian, Spanish, or Modern Mexican art, in technique or otherwise. The most *ancient* art of our history is purely Indian and is still considered the natural and most vital source of inspiration. Then following the conquest of Mexico came Colonial art which is based fundamentally on Spanish-European principles of the sixteenth and seventeenth centuries. And then came the Modern Mexican art movement dominated by artists who were Mestizo (the offspring of Indian and Spanish blood) and whose work has both Indian and European influences.

Chicano art is a newborn baby with Ancient Indian art as a mother, Spanish Colonial art as a father, and Modern Mexican art as a midwife. Or we can see it as a branch extending out into the southwest United States from the great Bronze Tree of Mexican art. Taking the roots of that tree for granted as being Indian and Spanish, we can move up to the trunk of the tree which is known as Modern Mexican art.

It would be wrong if we first looked up definitions of art in textbooks and then used them to determine the past principles from the modern artistic movement of Mexico. We should start from historical facts, not from abstract definitions.

What are some of the historical and artistic facts of the Modern art movement in Mexico? Or, from the Mexican point of view, what are some of the significant features in the development of this movement? Despite all the conflict, confusion, and bloodshed of the Mexican Revolution, it created a new spirit. A revolutionary spirit that inspired new leadership and began to be felt and expressed by the writers, the musicians, the poets, and the painters. Each felt that it was his duty and privilege to share his talents in the social cause of bringing about a new Mexico. Art for art's sake began to die. The new art would no longer serve as a privilege of the rich or a mere decoration. Since Mexico was largely illiterate, painting had to become the medium of visual education, monumental in size, and become public property.

Some of the more advanced artists and pioneers of this new aesthetic concept formed a group in 1922 known as the "Syndicate of painters, sculptors, and intellectual workers." Among those who allied themselves with this group and who brought forth the first original expression of Modern art on this continent were: Ramon Alva de la Canal, Jean Charlot, Fernando Leal, Xavier Guerrero, Carlos Medina, Roberto Montenegro, Jose Clemente Orozco, Fermin Revueltas, Diego Rivera, David Alfaro Sigueiros, and Maximo Pacheco.

The open-mindedness and foresight of Jose Vasconcelos, minister of education, must be given credit for opening the doors to the usefulness of monumental painting on the walls of public buildings. Under his program, Vasconcelos patronized the artists and they were given but one instruction: to paint Mexican subjects. It was the first collective attempt at mural painting in Modern art.

Then followed the fruits of the "Mexican Renaissance": the rebirth of creative enthusiasm and a time for the people to again recognize human values and their expressions in a creative form.

The Mexican painters have shown in their work the long and exciting history of the Mexican people. Great murals were done by men who sought truth and justice for their people and all of humanity. Mexican Modern art was essentially an art of the Revolution. Nowhere else in the world can the people of a country see so much of their own story told pictorially on the big walls of their public buildings.

Like the modern art of Mexico, the new Chicano art is essentially an art of social protest. Generally speaking, however, there are two types of Chicano art. The first is an art that makes up the cultural front of the Chicano movement that is sweeping the Southwest, an art that reflects the greatness and sacrifices of our past, an art that clarifies and intensifies the present desires of a people who will no longer be taken for granted as second-class citizens and whose time has come to stand up and fight for what is rightfully theirs as human beings.

The art of the Chicano movement serves as a shield to preserve and protect our cultural values from the mechanical shark of this society, that has been chewing and spitting out our beautiful language, music, literature, and art for over a hundred years. The artists use their own media in their own way to strengthen the unity of our people and they help to educate us about ourselves since the educational system has failed to do so.

The other type of Chicano art is created by artists who find it difficult to allow themselves to be used by any cause, by any institution, or by any government. They realize that the artist has spent centuries to free himself from the domination of a social hierarchy, the church, or government control. They love the past but refuse to be trapped by it. Their primary interest is to convey a point of view or an idea, whereas the Chicano artist of the movement generally uses any method to achieve his goal.

The Chicano artist who refuses to plunge into the movement, yet wishes to deal with social concerns in this society, cannot escape the realities in his life, in the lives of people around him, and in the times in which he lives. These things will inevitably begin to show in his work. Art works that are characterized as works of social protest are really just the product of the artist having to deal with the realities he sees. How does he respond to these realities? He writes a poem, a play, a song; he paints a picture, a mural; or models clay or wax.

The Chicano artist will work with his own "raw materials" of his social concerns in his own way. Most importantly, the artist is devoted to his art, and he loves color, form, composition, structure, and rhythm.

There are times when the Chicano artist, like other people, attempts to escape his humanness but cannot. His commitment is to himself and to humanity. He loves art and he loves his people. It is this love for humanity that he can reveal to others and in doing so help fulfill their humanness. This does not mean that he is not going to reveal the countless evils of our life but rather to show you that we must get back our humanness if we are to live in this world peacefully.

Suggestions for Discussion

1. According to Martinez, what is the parentage of Chicano art? How does it differ from its parents?
2. What are the two types of Chicano art that Martinez discusses? How does he distinguish between them? Which type does he seem to prefer? Need the two types be mutually exclusive?

Suggestion for Writing and Comparison

1. Which of the Chicano selections in this section fall into Martinez' first category of Chicano art? Which fall into the secondary category? Write an essay in which you discuss the selections that you feel to be most effective. Which category do they fall into?

STORIES

Prudencio de Pereda

Prudencio de Pereda was born in Brooklyn, New York, in 1912, the son of Spanish immigrants. As a child he spent some time visiting Spain, but he received most of his education in the United States. De Pereda was awarded his B. A. by the City College of New York and did graduate work at the University of Illinois. He later took a Master's degree in Library Science from the Pratt Institute Library School.

Prudencio de Pereda began his writing career with short stories for which he received almost immediate recognition. These early works were included in the *O. Henry Memorial Award Stories* for 1937 and O'Brien's *Best American Short Stories* for 1938 and 1940. His first novel, *All the Girls We Love,* was published in 1948. This was followed by several other novels, including *Fiesta: A Novel of Modern Spain* (1953) and *Windmills in Brooklyn* (1960).

The following story, "Conquistador," is set in de Pereda's own Brooklyn. Its first-person narrator looks back on his childhood when he first learned how terrible it is for the individual to compromise his dignity and his sense of self. The title, "Conquistador," is both ironic and straightforward in relation to the meaning of the story.

Conquistador

I thought, when I was young, that you worked according to your nationality. We were Spanish, and my father, grandfather, and uncles were all in the cigar business. There was a definite rule about this, I believed—a *law*. I thought so particularly during those times when I listened to my father and the other men of our family talk business, and heard them complain bitterly about the cigar business and about what a dishonorable trade it was, and how they were cursed the moment they took it up.

This used to surprise me—especially in regard to my father, because on the rare visits to his store it had seemed like a wonderful place. It had a broad, rich-looking, nickel-plated counter, neatly stacked with bright-colored boxes of cigars, and with shining hookahs and lighters along its top. The floor was white tile, and the inside wall of the store was a great mirror. The customers I'd seen had been well-dressed men with booming voices, rich gold chains around their full stomachs, and canes and gloves in their hands. There had been an air of wealth and strength in that store as I remembered it.

Still, my father was one of the most vehement in his denunciations of the cigar business. "Let them raise the blood to my face in shame," he once said, in his correct, intense Spanish, "if I permit any of my sons to go into this business. Yes. Let them do that!" I admired my father for his feelings, but felt that he was just talking, that my three brothers and I were all fated for the cigar business, just as my father and uncles had been. Indeed, even at this time, my older brother, who was only ten but figured himself a wise American, had already begun to do some special errands for my father. He would not only deliver boxes of cigars to the hotels in the neighborhood of my father's store in the Borough Hall section of Brooklyn, but would even take the elevated and go over the river and into the city to make deliveries.

When I begged him to tell me about this, he acted very casual and unafraid, and when, out of my genuine concern for him, I asked, "Aren't you going to be an aviator any more?" he said, "Sure! What's the matter with you? What d'you think I'm saving my money for?" I pitied him all the more, and worried myself inside for him. He was doomed—just as my father and uncles had been doomed. He would never be an aviator; nor would I ever be a bullfighter —and poor Justo would never have his big shoeshine parlor, or have his twin, Bifanio, as a sweeper. Bifanio hadn't made up his mind, yet, as to what he wanted to be, but the twins always did things together.

My older brother would never take me with him when he went on his errands. I was too young—though I was only two years younger than he. After we came home from school, he would put on his Sunday suit and new shoes and go down to my father's store on the trolley. I often wept as I pleaded with him to take me—just once, just this once! I didn't want to get into the cigar business, and was afraid of the city, but I would have risked anything to be allowed to ride on an elevated train.

My brother never relented, and my first experience in the cigar business came through an accident and without his help. It was something bigger than he'd ever done, and I should have felt boastful; instead, it filled me with terror and shame, and, at once, I understood the feelings of my father and the other men of our family.

■ How it happened was natural enough. Mother was making another try to have a girl, "a little sister," as she explained formally to us, and we three younger boys were farmed out. My older brother, Joe, stayed at home because he could do errands, make phone calls, and generally help around the house, and besides, as he explained to me, he was old enough to understand things. I didn't feel too bad, because I was going to Grandmother's and not to an aunt's, as the twins had. Going to Grandmother's had some responsibility, for there were always errands to be done and I would often have to act as translator. My grandmother spoke only about ten words of English, and my grandfather just a few more.

On the third day of my stay there—it was the Fourth of July—Grandfather had announced early that he wouldn't "go out" today. "Going out" meant going to work. My grandfather was in the most stigmatized form of the cigar business—he was a *teveriano* or "junk dealer," one of those itinerant salesmen who were scorned by the rest of the trade because they dealt completely in lies: in false labels, false representation, and false merchandise—very cheap cigars for which they secured exorbitant prices—and so brought still more disgrace to the Spaniards who had enough as it was by merely being in the legitimate cigar business.

I had heard all this at home—listening eagerly because the *teveriano* was certainly the most interesting of all the cigar men—but I'd never been able to connect the fabulous stories of *teverianos* with my mild, sad grandfather. For one thing, he was always very poor.

Grandmother didn't turn to look at him as she answered: "Do you observe American holidays, now?" She had a great dislike for everything American. She had been a great lady in Spain.

"One has to dance to the song they play," Grandfather said, shrugging his shoulders.

"And one has to pay the rent they ask!" Grandmother said this very sharply. I knew I should have left the room then, but I felt too sorry for my grandfather. He was growing very red. "We're at the fourth, now," Grandmother said. "That's five days late."

"I know that."

"Well?" Grandmother said, turning.

"I know that. I'm in accord with you. But not in front of the boy, please! Not in front of the boy, woman!"

"The boy knows it!"

"But not from me!" Grandfather stood up suddenly and came over to me. His hands were trembling. He took my arm and led me into the front parlor. He stood me by the window and sat down in the big chair. "Watch the celebrations!" he said. "Watch the celebrations!" I stared fixedly out the open window, knowing there weren't going to be any celebrations around here, but not wanting to tell my grandfather.

■ We stayed there only a short time, because the bell rang in a few moments—I couldn't see who it was—and quick, happy steps came up the stairs and we heard Agapito's voice greeting my grandmother. He called her "Dona," the most respectful title in Spanish, but he was laughing and warm as he talked.

Just as Grandfather was not, Agapito was the perfect example of the *teveri-ano*. He was still a very young man and had only been in America a short time, but he was easily the most famous—as well as the most criticized—of the salesmen. He was dressed that day as I imagined a *teveriano* would dress: a fine white linen suit, brown patent-leather shoes with button tops, a bright polka-dot bow tie, and a Panama straw with a multicolored band. When he came smiling into the front room, I thought he looked like the perfect man of the world, and he seemed to fill the room with brightness. He was very respectful to my grandfather, as he'd been to Grandmother, and when he suggested that they go out for a little bit, he said it in a quiet, serious voice. "We'll take the boy with us, yes?" he said, patting my shoulder and smiling at me. Agapito had neat white teeth and a small black mustache. He had a dark Spanish skin, and I thought he was very handsome. I'd always liked him, in spite of the stories I'd heard about him.

Grandfather answered Agapito's suggestion to go out by quietly shrugging his shoulders, but when Agapito suggested that they take me, his face took on the dark, stubborn look again.

"Yes, take the boy!" my grandmother called from the kitchen. "He hasn't been out. He may see some things. Holiday things." My grandfather shrugged his shoulders again.

■ We took a trolley—an open summer trolley—and we stayed on till the end of the line, and I saw that we'd come to the dock section. We could see the colored stacks of the big liners tied up at the piers. The big street was empty and quiet and that made the wonderful ships seem more intimate in the sun. Agapito kept pointing out things to me, but Grandfather walked along very quietly. He was dressed in his best black suit, with a black derby hat, and his face looked very worried. His black, drooping mustache made his face look very sad.

When we'd gone a few blocks, we turned into a side street and went into a small cigar store. I saw that this was Miguelin's. I knew Miguelin from seeing him at home and at the Spanish dances. He was a little, gray old man, and his store was dusty and old. He wrapped up seven new boxes of cigars for us, not wrapping them in brown paper but just with a heavy string so that you could see it was cigars and all the beautiful labels showed. Agapito gave him fourteen dollars. I counted them—and figured out that meant two dollars per box. Grandfather wanted to pay, but Agapito stopped him and made him put his wallet away. Agapito seemed to have charge of everything—he'd paid our fares on the trolley, too—and he would bend over and talk to Grandfather in a low voice while he patted him on the shoulder. I felt happy about this. I wanted my grandfather to lose his worry.

When we left Miguelin's, we turned to the big street again, and walked back the way we'd come. We walked very slowly, and Agapito kept talking to Grandfather and looking into each saloon that we passed. The saloons were the only places that were open today and there weren't many men in any of them. We were coming to a big one on the opposite corner, when Agapito said to my grandfather: "This one! This one seems good." The saloon had a big, bright shiny front and had a big hotel upstairs. I read the name "Monaghan" on the big sign over the swinging doors. As we crossed, Agapito took my hand firmly, and as we went in, I saw that the saloon was big and shiny and clean. It reminded me of my father's store. There was a big counter on one side with a great mirror on the wall and another counter on the other side with trays of food filling it all along. The tile floor was very clean and had no sawdust on it, and there was a big back room with tables that had white table-cloths.

Agapito stood inside the doorway, smiling and looking around as if he liked the place. Then, he led us over to the big counter with the mirror. We found a place easily because there were only a few men standing there, and Agapito placed the cigar boxes on the counter and nodded and smiled to the man behind the counter. He pointed to my grandfather and then to himself and said "Whiskey!" very plainly. He pronounced it "vhiskey." He patted me on the head, and smiled at the man again, and said, "Ginger ale!" He pronounced this well, except that he said "al" instead of "ale."

There was another man behind the counter, standing farther back. He had his jacket off and his sleeves rolled up, but he didn't have an apron on. He was a big man with a red face and he was smoking a big cigar. He had a gold chain across his vest and two big rings on his right hand, and he looked like one of my father's rich customers. When I stared at him, he winked at me and laughed. He'd been watching Agapito and my grandfather who were leaning on the big counter with their feet on the brass rail. Agapito had been talking in Spanish and laughing as he and my grandfather drank their whiskey.

The big man walked up to them slowly and patted the cigar boxes. Agapito turned his head up suddenly, in surprise, and then smiled at the big man and bowed to him.

"Havanas?" the big man said. He had a strong deep voice.

Agapito nodded quickly. "Yes! I am from Havana. I am from Havana."

"I mean the cigars," the big man said, laughing. He had brown teeth, but a nice face.

"Oh! Also, also!" Agapito said. He laughed and kept nodding his head. "From Havana, also. For my friend! I bring them." He pointed outside. "The ship! You understand? From Havana to Spain. I bring them to friend here. I stop off." He spoke in short spurts, but he pronounced very clearly. He stopped smiling and became very serious as he pulled one of the boxes out of the bundle, opened it with his little gold knife and picked out two cigars carefully. He handed them over to the big man and nodded vigorously when the big man seemed to hesitate.

"For Fourth of July!" Agapito said. He smiled again. "Happy Fourth of July!" He nodded and pressed the cigars into the man's hand.

The big man smelled the cigars and nodded to him. "Good flavor," he said. He turned and said something to the man in the apron and this man took the bottle and poured more whiskey into Agapito's and my grandfather's glasses. Agapito raised his glass to him, and then my grandfather did.

The big man kept smelling the cigars and then he patted the boxes again. "What would they cost? — How much?" he said, when Agapito looked puzzled. Agapito spread his hands. "For a friend," he said. "You understand. No. . . ." He made the motion with his hands again.

"Customs?" the big man said.

"Customs!" Agapito nodded quickly and smiled. He rubbed his hands. "No customs! Customs."

"Well, how much? How much, anyway?" The big man patted the boxes.

Agapito held a finger up, and turned to my grandfather. "This one seems to have money," he said in Spanish. "This one can pay."

"Take care, hombre," my grandfather said.

"No, don't disquiet yourself, Don Jose. I know what I'm doing." Agapito patted Grandfather's arm, turned to the big man and smiled. "My friend, here. He remember. He remember everything." He ran his finger up and down the boxes. "All the boxes. Seven! Sixty dollars. Cost for my friend."

■ Sixty dollars! This was a shock to me—if a man buys seven boxes of cigars for fourteen dollars, two dollars per box, and sells them for—sixty dollars! I understood why the big man made such a face and then laughed. I hadn't minded all the lies that Agapito had told because I knew that *teverianos* worked like that, but when he asked this high, high figure, I got shocked and embarrassed—and then, very frightened for us. The glass felt heavy in my hand, and I held my head down because I knew that I was blushing.

I'd heard that *teverianos* asked robber prices, but I never thought that Agapito would take the chance today, when he had my grandfather and me with him. He was going to get us into trouble. He was making us take a chance—because he wanted to. And we were all going to get into trouble.

The big man said something to Agapito and Agapito said, "Well—you know, sir. Havanas!"

I didn't hear the big man answer but then Agapito said very brightly, "You interested? You interested in cigars?" I hated his accent, now. His lying.

"I was looking for ten boxes. I could use ten boxes," the big man said slowly.

Agapito was talking in Spanish, then. He must have been talking to my grandfather. "You stay here," he said, still speaking respectfully. "I will run to Miguelin's and get three more boxes. I will run fast. You stay here. This is a good thing."

"Yes, hombre, it is," I heard my grandfather say. "Let him take these seven boxes and let us be through here. Let it stay a good thing."

"There is no danger," Agapito said quickly.

"If there is, entrust it to me," my grandfather said sternly and I looked up suddenly to see that his face had taken on the stubborn look again. "I wasn't thinking of that. I was thinking that we have a good thing. Let us take it, and be gone."

"I don't work like that," Agapito said. "You know that, Don Jose," he said more softly.

"Then, as you wish."

"You will stay?"

"As you wish!"

I watched, in rage but fascinated, as Agapito turned back to smile at the big man who was leaning on the counter with his old cigar in his mouth. Agapito brought his hands together. "We fix it," he said, and nodded. "Three more boxes, I will bring from the boat. For ten boxes"—he ran his fingers up and down the seven on the counter and held up three fingers—"ten boxes—for eighty dollars—for you!" He pointed at the big man.

The big man stared at Agapito for a moment, and then nodded and said, "Okay. Eighty dollars." What a fool this one is, too, I thought. His face looked stupid to me, now.

"You give me fifty dollars, now," Agapito said. He smiled. "I give money to guard—small money. You understand? My friend wait here, I come back. With three more."

Did Grandfather understand that? Did Grandfather know what Agapito was saying? I stared at his face, but couldn't see anything. I was weak with fright and fear, but I didn't dare say a word. The big man had taken out his wallet without hesitation and given Agapito five new bills—tens they must have been. Agapito smiled and nodded as he put them in his wallet quickly. He patted Grandfather on the arm, saying, "Don't worry yourself. I'll be back immediately," and then patted me on the head—I couldn't duck fast enough—and went out into the street.

■ I stared at the floor. I wouldn't look at my grandfather. I'd finished the ginger ale, but I wouldn't go over to put the glass on the counter. I heard the big man say something to Grandfather that Grandfather didn't answer. "No speak English, eh?" the big man said, and laughed. He took up the bundle of cigars and moved down to the end of the counter—where I could see him by just lifting my eyes a little—and he began to open every box.

I had to look at my grandfather, then. Did he see what danger we were in? He was staring at the mirror. His hands were steady, but he was sweating. I glared at him, at first, but then wanted to cry. I went up and put the glass by his side and he looked down at me and then turned to stare up at the big man as he was opening each box. Then, he turned back, finished his drink in one slug and turned to me. His back was to the big man and he put his hand on my shoulder. I could smell the whiskey on his breath as he bent down. "Get thee out of here," he said. "Act as if thou art going out calmly." My grandfather always used the familiar "thee" with us, and his voice was calm and easy now but I could see that he was sweating badly. His hand felt very tight on my shoulder. "Get thyself to the trolley station. Stand by the trees there and wait for me. No matter how long, I will come. Do nothing but wait for me. I will escape this in some way. I will get out, and get to thee. I will escape this and get to thee. In whatever way, I will.

"Without crying, thee!" he said. "Without crying!" I hadn't started to cry yet, but my lip had begun to tremble. I bit my lip and started to shake my head even before he'd finished. "And think well of me," he was saying. "Think well of me. I did not want this situation for thee. Thou wilt not? Thou wilt not do it?"

"No. I stay. I stay here with you." His face had the stubborn look again and he pushed my shoulder but held his grip tightly on it. He glared at me, but I kept shaking my head. "Stay, then!" he said. "Stay!" He dropped his hand from my shoulder but reached to take my hand and then turned to lean on the bar again, holding my hand. A moment later, when he poured more whiskey into his glass, he did it with his left hand, but poured it very neatly. He lifted the glass in his left hand, and began to sip the whiskey slowly.

■ Grandfather had been a waiter in Spain. He was very proud of that. He'd been a waiter at the best hotel in Tangier just before he'd come to the United States, and a prince, a duke, and two princesses had been among his patrons. My mother was born in Tangier, and, though she couldn't remember anything of her part in the life there, she told us many stories about it. The three years spent in Tangier had been the happiest time in the life of her family.

My grandmother's brother had come to the United States some years before and made an immediate success as a *teveriano*. He wrote glowing letters to my grandmother, telling her of the wonderful opportunities in the trade and urging her to make Jose, my grandfather, see reason and come to America. Does he want to be a waiter all his life? the brother would ask. He'd felt very bad when she'd married a waiter. He was her only brother and they were very close.

Grandfather was content. He didn't want to leave. The letters got more boastful, and then pleading. Finally, my granduncle sent enough money to pay first-class passage for all three and the pressure was too much for my grandfather. He consented, and he came to the United States with his family —to a tenement district in Hoboken, New Jersey. They moved to Brooklyn shortly after, when my aunt was born, but to a tenement district again, and they had never lived better than that. Grandfather—as Mother would say, in ending these stories—was just not a good salesman.

I was thinking these things as I gripped Grandfather's hand and stared up at him, and the anger that I'd felt before turned to pity. I love you, I thought. Once, I pulled his arm and said, "We could go to the bathroom—first me, then you—sneak out that way." He glared down at me with a stubborn look. "No. In no such manner. When we go, we go through the front door. We are men." He turned to stare at the mirror, but then turned quickly back to me. "Dost thou have to go to the toilet? Truly?"

I shook my head.

"Good!" he said, and turned to the mirror.

I thought we stood like that for a long time—it seemed like a long, long time to me—but Agapito said later that he'd only been gone sixteen minutes, that he'd counted them. Agapito's face was sweating when he came back, and his Panama was pushed back on his head, but he was smiling and looked very happy, and his clothes were still very neat. "I run! I run!" he said to the big man. "To ship. To ship and back!" He'd put the new boxes on the counter and was opening each one with his penknife and holding the open box up to the big man. The boxes looked very new and I thought that one of the labels looked wet. Surely, the big man would see, now. He would see the truth, now, I thought. And it would serve Agapito right. He'd be in it, now. Grandfather and I could run. We'd get away. Agapito was the one they'd hold.

The big man smelled every box and even touched the wet wrapper, but he nodded seriously and then stupidly took out his wallet and gave Agapito three more ten dollar bills. The man with the apron had filled Agapito's glass again and Agapito held out one of the bills to him, but he shook his head. Then, Agapito put the bills in his wallet and picked out a one-dollar bill that he folded and handed to the man in the apron. "For you," he said. "For you." He smiled and nodded. Then, he held up the whiskey, smiled and nodded again, and drank it in one gulp.

I had been tugging at Grandfather's hand, wanting to start, wanting us to go, but Grandfather held his tight grip and waited until Agapito had shaken hands with both men, and then he himself nodded to them, and we all turned towards the door.

We walked very slowly as we went outside and crossed the street. Grandfather wanted to walk fast, but Agapito was holding his arm and walking very slowly. "Don't worry yourself," he said, after a moment. "We'll turn down the first street. For now, we walk slowly — very slowly, and with dignity."

We turned down the first street, walked down that block, and then turned in the direction of the trolleys. As soon as we'd made this last turn, Agapito stopped and took out his wallet. He handed Grandfather three ten-dollar bills. Grandfather pushed them back. "Hombre!" he said, "don't embarrass me."

"Please!" Agapito said. "This is your share."

"It's too much."

"It's half. We were equally involved." Agapito pressed the bills into Grandfather's hand. "Equally!" he said, letting go.

Grandfather put the bills in his little black purse. "I'm very appreciative. Very!" he said.

"For nothing!" Agapito said. "For nothing!" As we walked, now, he was smiling and happy again. He took off his hat and rubbed his face with a big silk handkerchief. "One has to see these things, Don Jose. One has to see them. To believe them, one has to see them. Havanas!" he shook his head and laughed. "And you musn't feel that we cheat them!" he said, when Grandfather didn't answer. "This one buys them as Havanas. He gives them out as Havanas — probably at some festival — and those who take them, take them as Havanas, and smoke them. No matter how bad the cigars, for them they are Havanas. Yes, Don Jose. We sell Havanas — they buy Havanas!"

On the trolley, after he'd paid our fares, Agapito slipped a half dollar into the conductor's pocket. "For Fourth of July!" he said. The conductor blushed, and nodded. Later, Agapito stood up and took off his hat. "Life for the United States of America!" he called out. "Happy Fourth of July to everybody!" The two people who were sitting up at the front end of the trolley smiled and shook their heads. They thought he was drunk.

■ Agapito left, soon after we got home. Then, Grandmother went out. "I'll get some ham," she said. "We'll eat well, tonight." Grandfather and I were in the front room, and she'd come to the door. "The delicatessen has good ham."

Grandfather nodded. "We're most fortunate," he said, without looking up. "Most fortunate."

Grandmother turned back and stared at him with a cold face. She was dressed in her black skirt and black silk waist, and she looked like the pictures of the Queen Mother in the Spanish magazines we had, except that Grandmother was much more beautiful. "Yes," she said, in a calm voice. "Most fortunate. You, in particular! You needn't go out for some days, now. Perhaps grow a beard, here."

Grandfather got very red, but didn't look up. He shrugged his shoulders as Grandmother turned and went out. After a moment, he reached over to me and pulled me to the side of the chair. He kept his arm around me and patted my head. "Thou!" he said. He looked straight at me. "Thou must forget what thou heardst today, what thou sawst. All of it! Forget especially what thy grandmother said. She is a fine woman. Nothing of today was like her. It is I who am weak. The fault is mine. Thou wilt understand this some day. Thou wilt, yes. What thou must remember is this"—he pressed my shoulder—"that thou must be strong. Remember that! Let no woman—whether she be thy mother who is my own flesh, or the woman thou wilt marry—let none of them press thee or influence thee in choosing thy profession. Thou, thou alone, must move through the world to make thy money, thou alone must suffer—so thou must choose. And hold to that!

"Thou art the bullfighter, no?"

"Or one who guides an elevated train," I said. "One of those."

"Good. Thou might change, but whatever thou shouldst choose—hold to it. Grip it well."

I nodded.

"Dost thou know what she referred to in that of the beard?" he said, in a softer voice.

"No, Grandfather," I lied.

"Well, it was this: I had a fine beard when I was a waiter in Tangier. It was a full, well-cut beard and I was a fine figure with it. One afternoon, the major-domo—he who was chief of all our waiters—the major-domo, Don Felix, came to me and said, 'Jose, you must shave that beard. Too many patrons are coming in and talking to you and treating you as the major-domo. I regret this, but you must shave it, because there is only one major-domo here, and it is me. No one else can look like a major-domo. No one else will.'

"I went home to thy grandmother and told her this, and she said, 'Yes. The man has reason. You must shave your beard.' I had thought that she would have objections, that she would show anger. I had thought that she loved the beard as I did—it was a fine beard. But she did not—or, if she did, she would not let it stand before Don Felix's objection.

"So, I cut it off!" my grandfather said. He brushed his hand under his chin. "That was a mistake. I should have held to my first thought. I should have defended myself. I should have left my place and sought another job in Tangier—or Gibraltar or La Linea where there are fine hotels. *I* was doing the waiting, and *I* should have thought of *myself*." He stopped and stared at me. "Thou seest?" he said. "Stop thou at the first mistake. Stop there."

I nodded, and he pressed my shoulder again and then reached over and lifted me on to his lap. He cradled my head on his shoulder and rocked slowly back and forth. "We must gladden ourselves," he said, "before she comes. We must gladden ourselves and be smiling. This is difficult for her, too. Difficult. We must gladden ourselves, now. Yes! We must gladden ourselves for her."

I was nodding my head to say, Yes, when my forehead felt something wet, and I looked up and saw that the tears were falling down his cheeks.

Suggestions for Discussion

1. How does the title relate to the story? Who were the original *conquistadors?* Is the narrator's assertion at the beginning of the story that his grandmother "had been a great lady in Spain" correct?
2. What does the author accomplish by revealing the story through the eyes of a child? How does the narrator learn to understand "the feelings of my father and the other men of our family"? Why does the experience he shares with his grandfather fill him with "terror and shame"?
3. Why is Agapito's attire described in detail? Does Agapito function as a foil? What is the significance of the grandfather's attire?
4. What is the significance of Agapito's actions when they first enter the bar? Why does he order the whiskey "very plainly"? Why does he pretend to think that the man was inquiring as to his nationality?
5. At what point does the narrator's attitude towards Agapito change? Why? Does his attitude change again later in the story with Agapito's continued generosity?
6. Why are we told about the narrator's family background in the middle of the bar scene? Is this a flaw in the structure of the story?
7. What does growing a beard represent to the grandfather? What is the significance of his advice to the narrator about women? How does this advice relate to the meaning of the story? Is the depiction of women in this story sexist?

Suggestion for Writing and Comparison

1. Discuss the social, moral, and economic values in the story with particular reference to each character.

Americo Paredes

The following legend was written by Americo Parades, a Chicano, after tape recording many versions of it told by people still living along the Mexico-Texas border. "El Corrido de Gregorio Cortez," the border ballad or *corrido*, was the subject of Paredes' doctoral dissertation and his book *With His Pistol in His Hand* (1958). In his research Paredes found that a real Gregorio Cortez did exist and that the legend was based largely on truth. The real Cortez was born in 1875 on the Mexican side of the Border on a ranch between Matamoros and Reynosa. When he was twelve the family crossed the Border and moved to the Austin area of Texas. His brother's name was Romaldo rather than Román, and the incidents of the legend took place in Karnes County, pronounced in Spanish similarly to "El Carmen" of the legend.

Americo Paredes has dedicated *With His Pistol in His Hand* "to the memory of my father, who made a raid or two with Catarino Garza; and to all those old men who sat around on summer nights, in the days when there was a chaparral, smoking their cornhusk cigarettes and talking in low, gentle voices about violent things; while I listened."

The Legend of Gregorio Cortez

They still sing of him—in the *cantinas* and the country stores, in the ranches when men gather at night to talk in the cool dark, sitting in a circle, smoking and listening to the old songs and the tales of other days. Then the *guitarreros* sing of the border raids and the skirmishes, of the men who lived by the phrase, "I will break before I bend."

They sing with deadly-serious faces, throwing out the words of the song like a challenge, tearing savagely with their stiff, callused fingers at the strings of the guitars.

And that is how, in the dark quiet of the ranches, in the lighted noise of the saloons, they sing of Gregorio Cortez.

After the song is sung there is a lull. Then the old men, who have lived long and seen almost everything, tell their stories. And when they tell about Gregorio Cortez, the telling goes like this:

How Gregorio Cortez came to be in the county of El Carmen

That was good singing, and a good song; give the man a drink. Not like these pachucos nowadays, mumbling damn-foolishness into a microphone; it is not done that way. Men should sing with their heads thrown back, with their mouths wide open and their eyes shut. Fill your lungs, so they can hear you at the pasture's farther end. And when you sing, sing songs like *El Corrido de Gregorio Cortez*. There's a song that makes the hackles rise. You can almost see him there—Gregorio Cortez, with his pistol in his hand.

He was a man, a Border man. What did he look like? Well, that is hard to tell. Some say he was short and some say he was tall; some say he was Indian brown and some say he was blond like a newborn cockroach. But I'd say he was not too dark and not too fair, not too thin and not too fat, not too short and not too tall; and he looked just a little bit like me. But does it matter so much what he looked like? He was a man, very much of a man; and he was a Border man. Some say he was born in Matamoros; some say Reynosa; some say Hidalgo county on the other side. And I guess others will say other things. But Matamoros, or Reynosa, or Hidalgo, it's all the same Border; and short or tall, dark or fair, it's the man that counts. And that's what he was, a man.

Not a gunman, no, not a bravo. He never came out of a cantina wanting to drink up the sea at one gulp. Not that kind of man, if you can call that kind a man. No, that wasn't Gregorio Cortez at all. He was a peaceful man, a hard-working man like you and me.

He could shoot. Forty-four and thirty-thirty, they were the same to him. He could put five bullets into a piece of board and not make but one hole, and quicker than you could draw a good deep breath. Yes, he could shoot. But he could also work.

He was a vaquero, and a better one there has not ever been from Laredo to the mouth. He could talk to horses, and they would understand. They would follow him around, like dogs, and no man knew a good horse better than Gregorio Cortez. As for cattle, he could set up school for your best caporal. And if an animal was lost, and nobody could pick up a trail, they would send for Gregorio Cortez. He could always find a trail. There was no better tracker in all the Border country, nor a man who could hide his tracks better if he wanted to. That was Gregorio Cortez, the best vaquero and range man that there ever was.

But that is not all. You farmers, do you think that Gregorio Cortez did not know your business too? You could have told him nothing about cotton or beans or corn. He knew it all. He could look into the sky of a morning and smell it, sniff it the way a dog sniffs, and tell you what kind of weather there was going to be. And he would take a piece of dirt in his hands and rub it back and forth between his fingers—to see if the land had reached its point—and you would say he was looking into it. And perhaps he was, for Gregorio Cortez was the seventh son of a seventh son.

You piddling modern farmers, vain of yourselves when you make a bale! You should have seen the crops raised by Gregorio Cortez. And when harvesting came, he was in there with the rest. Was it shucking corn? All you could see was the shucks fly and the pile grow, until you didn't know there was a man behind the pile. But he was even better at cotton-picking time. He would bend down and never raise his head till he came out the other end, and he would be halfway through another row before the next man was through with his. And don't think the row he went through wasn't clean. No flags, no streamers, nothing left behind, nothing but clean, empty burrs where he had passed. It was the same when clearing land. There were men who went ahead of him, cutting fast along their strip in the early morning, but by noontime the man ahead was always Gregorio Cortez, working at his own pace, talking little and not singing very much, and never acting up.

For Gregorio Cortez was not of your noisy, hell-raising type. That was not his way. He always spoke low, and he was always polite, whoever he was speaking to. And when he spoke to men older than himself he took off his hat and held it over his heart. A man who never raised his voice to parent or elder brother, and never disobeyed. That was Gregorio Cortez, and that was the way men were in this country along the river. That was the way they were before these modern times came, and God went away.

He should have stayed on the Border; he should not have gone up above, into the North. But it was going to be that way, and that was the way it was. Each man has a certain lot in life, and no other thing but that will be his share. People were always coming down from places in the North, from Dallas and San Antonio and Corpus and Foro West. And they would say, "Gregorio Cortez, why don't you go north? There is much money to be made. Stop eating beans and tortillas and that rubbery jerked beef. One of these days you're going to put out one of your eyes, pull and pull with your teeth on that stuff and it suddenly lets go. It's a wonder all you Border people are not one-eyed. Come up above with us, where you can eat white bread and ham."

But Gregorio Cortez would only smile, because he was a peaceful man and did not take offense. He did not like white bread and ham; it makes people flatulent and dull. And he liked it where he was. So he always said, "I like this country. I will stay here."

But Gregorio Cortez had a brother, a younger brother named Román. Now Román was just like the young men of today, loud-mouthed and discontented. He was never happy where he was, and to make it worse he loved a joke more than any other thing. He would think nothing of playing a joke on a person twice his age. He had no respect for anyone, and that is why he ended like he did. But that is yet to tell.

Román talked to Gregorio and begged him that they should move away from the river and go up above, where there was much money to be made. And he talked and begged so, that finally Gregorio Cortez said he would go with his brother Román, and they saddled their horses and rode north.

Well, they did not grow rich, though things went well with them because they were good workers. Sometimes they picked cotton; sometimes they were vaqueros, and sometimes they cleared land for the Germans. Finally they came to a place called El Carmen, and there they settled down and farmed. And that was how Gregorio Cortez came to be in the county of El Carmen, where the tragedy took place.

Román's horse trade and what came of it

Román owned two horses, two beautiful sorrels that were just alike, the same color, the same markings, and the same size. You could not have told them apart, except that one of them was lame. There was an American who owned a little sorrel mare. This man was dying to get Román's sorrel—the good one—and every time they met he would offer to swap the mare for the horse. But Román did not think much of the mare. He did not like it when the American kept trying to make him trade.

"I wonder what this Gringo thinks," Román said to himself. "He takes me for a fool. But I'm going to make him such a trade that he will remember me forever."

And Román laughed a big-mouthed laugh. He thought it would be a fine joke, besides being a good trade. There were mornings when the American went to town in his buggy along a narrow road. So Román saddled the lame sorrel, led him a little way along the road, and stopped under a big mesquite that bordered on the fence. He fixed it so the spavined side was against the mesquite. Román waited a little while, and soon he heard the buggy coming along the road. Then he got in the saddle and began picking mesquites off the tree and eating them. When the American came around the bend, there was Román on his sorrel horse. The American stopped his buggy beside Román and looked at the horse with much admiration. It was a fine animal, exactly like the other one, but the American could not see the spavined leg.

"Changed your mind?" the American said.

Román stopped chewing on a mesquite and said, "Changed my mind about what?"

"About trading that horse for my mare."

"You're dead set on trading your mare for this horse of mine?" Román said.

"You know I am," the American said. "Are you ready to come round?"

"I'm in a trading mood," said Román. "With just a little arguing you might convince me to trade this horse for that worthless mare of yours. But I don't know; you might go back on the deal later on."

"I never go back on my word," the American said. "What do you think I am, a Mexican?"

"We'll see, we'll see," said Román. "How much are you willing to give in hand?"

"Enough to give you the first square meal you've had in your life," the American said.

Román just laughed, and it was all he could do to keep from guffawing. He knew who was getting the best of things.

So they made the deal, with Román still sitting on his spavined horse under the tree, chewing on mesquites.

"Where's the mare?" Román said.

"She's in my yard," said the American, "hung to a tree. You go get her and leave the horse there for me because I'm in a hurry to get to town."

That was how Román had figured it, so he said, "All right, I'll do it, but when I finish with these mesquites."

"Be sure you do, then," the American said.

"Sure, sure," said Román. "No hurry about it, is there?"

"All right," the American said, "take your time." And he drove off leaving Román still sitting on his horse under the mesquite, and as he drove off the American said, "Now isn't that just like a Mexican. He takes his time."

Román waited until the American was gone, and then he stopped eating mesquites. He got off and led the horse down the road to the American's yard and left him there in place of the little sorrel mare. On the way home Román almost fell off his saddle a couple of times, just laughing and laughing to think of the sort of face the American would pull when he came home that night.

The next morning, when Gregorio Cortez got up he said to his brother Román, "Something is going to happen today."

"Why do you say that?" asked Román.

"I don't know," said Gregorio Cortez. "I just know that something is going to happen today. I feel it. Last night my wife began to sigh for no reason at all. She kept sighing and sighing half the night, and she didn't know why. Her heart was telling her something, and I know some unlucky thing will happen to us today."

But Román just laughed, and Gregorio went inside the house to shave. Román followed him into the house and stood at the door while Gregorio shaved. It was a door made in two sections; the upper part was open and Román was leaning on the lower part, like a man leaning out of a window or over a fence. Román began to tell Gregorio about the horse trade he had made the day before, and he laughed pretty loud about it, because he thought it was a good joke. Gregorio Cortez just shaved, and he didn't say anything.

When what should pull in at the gate but a buggy, and the American got down, and the Major Sheriff of the county of El Carmen got down too. They came into the yard and up to where Román was leaning over the door, looking out.

The American had a very serious face. "I came for the mare you stole yesterday morning," he said.

Román laughed a big-mouthed laugh. "What did I tell you, Gregorio?" he said. "This Gringo Sanavabiche has backed down on me."

Now there are three saints that the Americans are especially fond of —Santa Anna, San Jacinto, and Sanavabiche—and of the three it is Sanavabiche that they pray to most. Just listen to an American any time. You may not understand anything else he says, but you are sure to hear him say, "Sanavabiche! Sanavabiche! Sanavabiche!" Every hour of the day. But they'll get very angry if you say it too, perhaps because it is a saint that belongs to them alone.

And so it was with the Major Sheriff of the county of El Carmen. Just as the words "Gringo Sanavabiche" came out of Román's mouth, the sheriff whipped out his pistol and shot Román. He shot Román as he stood there with his head thrown back, laughing at his joke. The sheriff shot him in the face, right in the open mouth, and Román fell away from the door, at the Major Sheriff's feet.

And then Gregorio Cortez stood at the door, where his brother had stood, with his pistol in his hand. Now he and the Major Sheriff met, each one pistol in hand, as men should meet when they fight for what is right. For it is a pretty thing to see, when two men stand up for their right, with their pistols in their hands, front to front and without fear. And so it was, for the Major Sheriff also was a man.

Yes, the Major Sheriff was a man; he was a gamecock that had won in many pits, but in Gregorio Cortez he met a cockerel that pecked his comb. The Major Sheriff shot first, and he missed; and Gregorio Cortez shot next, and he didn't miss. Three times did they shoot, three times did the Major

Sheriff miss, and three times did Gregorio Cortez shoot the sheriff of El Carmen. The Major Sheriff fell dead at the feet of Gregorio Cortez, and it was in this way that Gregorio Cortez killed the first sheriff of many that he was to kill.

When the Major Sheriff fell, Gregorio Cortez looked up, and the other American said, "Don't kill me; I am unarmed."

"I will not kill you," said Gregorio Cortez. "But you'd better go away."

So the American went away. He ran into the brush and kept on running until he came to town and told all the other sheriffs that the Major Sheriff was dead.

Meanwhile, Gregorio Cortez knew that he too must go away. He was not afraid of the law; he knew the law, and he knew that he had the right. But if he stayed, the Rangers would come, and the Rangers have no regard for law. You know what kind of men they are. When the Governor of the State wants a new Ranger, he asks his sheriffs, "Bring all the criminals to me." And from the murderers he chooses the Ranger, because no one can be a Ranger who has not killed a man. So Gregorio Cortez knew that the best thing for him was to go away, and his first thought was of the Border, where he had been born. But first he must take care of his brother, so he put Román in the buggy and drove into town, where his mother lived.

Now there was a lot of excitement in town. All the Americans were saddling up and loading rifles and pistols, because they were going out to kill Cortez. When all of a sudden, what should come rolling into town but the buggy, driven by Gregorio Cortez. They met him on the edge of town, armed to the teeth, on horseback and afoot, and he on the buggy, holding the reins lightly in his hands. Román was in the back, shot in the mouth. He could neither speak nor move, but just lay there like one who is dead.

They asked him, "Who are you?"

And he said to them, "I am Gregorio Cortez."

They all looked at him and were afraid of him, because they were only twenty or twenty-five, and they knew that they were not enough. So they stepped aside and let him pass and stood talking among themselves what would be the best thing to do. But Gregorio Cortez just drove ahead, slowly, without seeming to care about the men he left behind. He came to his mother's house, and there he took down his brother and carried him in the house. He stayed there until dawn, and during the night groups of armed men would go by the house and say, "He's in there. He's in there." But none of them ever went in.

At dawn Gregorio Cortez came out of his mother's house. There were armed men outside, but they made no move against him. They just watched as he went down the street, his hands resting on his belt. He went along as if he was taking a walk, and they stood there watching until he reached the brush and he jumped into it and disappeared. And then they started shooting at him with rifles, now that he was out of pistol range.

"I must get me a rifle," said Gregorio Cortez, "a rifle and a horse."

They gathered in a big bunch and started after him in the brush. But they could not catch Gregorio Cortez. No man was ever as good as him in hiding his own tracks, and he soon had them going around in circles, while he doubled back and headed for home to get himself a rifle and a horse.

How Gregorio Cortez rode the little sorrel mare all of five hundred miles

He went in and got his thirty-thirty, and then he looked around for the best horse he had. It is a long way from El Carmen to the Border, all of five hundred miles. The first thing he saw in the corral was the little sorrel mare. Gregorio Cortez took a good look at her, and he knew she was no ordinary mare.

"You're worth a dozen horses," said Gregorio Cortez, and he saddled the little mare.

But by then the whole wasp's nest was beginning to buzz. The President of the United States offered a thousand dollars for him, and many men went out to get Gregorio Cortez. The Major Sheriffs of the counties and all their sheriffs were out. There were Rangers from the counties, armed to the teeth, and the King Ranch Rangers from the Capital, the meanest of them all, all armed and looking for Cortez. Every road was blocked and every bridge guarded. There were trackers out with those dogs they call hounds, that can follow a track better than the best tracker. They had railroad cars loaded with guns and ammunition and with men, moving up and down trying to head him off. The women and children stayed in the houses, behind locked doors, such was the fear they all had of Gregorio Cortez. Every town from the Capital to the Border was watching out for him. The brush and the fields were full of men, trying to pick up his trail. And Gregorio Cortez rode out for the Border, through brush and fields and barbed wire fences, on his little sorrel mare.

He rode and rode until he came to a great broad plain, and he started to ride across. But just as he did, one of the sheriffs saw him. The sheriff saw him, but he hid behind a bush, because he was afraid to take him on alone. So he called the other sheriffs together and all the Rangers he could find, and they went off after Gregorio Cortez just as he came out upon the plain.

Gregorio Cortez looked back and saw them coming. There were three hundred of them.

"We'll run them a little race," said Gregorio Cortez.

Away went the mare, as if she had been shot from a gun, and behind her came the sheriffs and the Rangers, all shooting and riding hard. And so they rode across the plain, until one by one their horses foundered and fell to the ground and died. But still the little mare ran on, as fresh as a lettuce leaf, and pretty soon she was running all alone.

"They'll never catch me like that," said Gregorio Cortez, "not even with those dogs called hounds."

Another big bunch of sheriffs rode up, and they chased him to the edge of the plain, and into the brush went Cortez, with the trackers after him, but they did not chase him long. One moment there was a trail to follow, and next moment there was none. And the dogs called hounds sat down and howled, and the men scratched their heads and went about in circles looking for the trail. And Gregorio Cortez went on, leaving no trail, so that people thought he was riding through the air.

There were armed men everywhere, and he could not stop to eat or drink, because wherever he tried to stop armed men were there before him. So he had to ride on and on. Now they saw him, now they lost him, and so the chase went on. Many more horses foundered, but the mare still ran, and

Gregorio Cortez rode on and on, pursued by hundreds and fighting hundreds every place he went.

"So many mounted Rangers," said Gregorio Cortez, "to catch just one Mexican."

It was from the big bunches that he ran. Now and again he would run into little ones of ten or a dozen men, and they were so scared of him that they would let him pass. Then, when he was out of range they would shoot at him, and he would shoot back at them once or twice, so they could go back and say, "We met up with Gregorio Cortez, and we traded shots with him." But from the big ones he had to run. And it was the little sorrel mare that took him safe away, over the open spaces and into the brush, and once in the brush, they might as well have been following a star.

So it went for a day, and when night fell Cortez arrived at a place named Los Fresnos and called at a Mexican house. When the man of the house came out, Cortez told him, "I am Gregorio Cortez."

That was all he had to say. He was given to eat and drink, and the man of the house offered Gregorio Cortez his own horse and his rifle and his saddle. But Cortez would not take them. He thanked the man, but he would not give up his little sorrel mare. Cortez was sitting there, drinking a cup of coffee, when the Major Sheriff of Los Fresnos came up with his three hundred men. All the other people ran out of the house and hid, and no one was left in the house, only Gregorio Cortez, with his pistol in his hand.

Then the Major Sheriff called out, in a weepy voice, as the corrido says. He sounded as if he wanted to cry, but it was all done to deceive Gregorio Cortez.

"Cortez," the Major Sheriff said, "hand over your weapons. I did not come to kill you. I am your friend."

"If you come as my friend," said Gregorio Cortez, "why did you bring three hundred men? Why have you made me a corral?"

The Major Sheriff knew that he had been caught in a lie, and the fighting began. He killed the Major Sheriff and the second sheriff under him, and he killed many sheriffs more. Some of the sheriffs got weak in the knees, and many ran away.

"Don't go away," said Gregorio Cortez. "I am the man you are looking for. I am Gregorio Cortez."

They were more than three hundred, but he jumped their corral, and he rode away again, and those three hundred did not chase him any more.

He rode on and on, until he came to a river called the San Antonio. It is not much of a river, but the banks are steep and high, and he could not find a ford. So he rode to a ranch house nearby, where they were holding a baile because the youngest child of the house had been baptized that day, and he asked the man of the house about a ford.

"There are only two fords," the man said. "One is seven miles upstream and the other is seven miles down."

"I will take another look at the river," said Gregorio Cortez. He left the baile and rode slowly to the river. It was steep, and far below he could see the water flowing; he could barely see it because it was so dark. He stood there thinking, trying to figure out a way, when he heard the music at the baile stop.

He knew the Rangers were at the baile now. So he leaned over in his saddle and whispered in the mare's ear. He talked to her, and she understood. She came to the edge of the bank, with soft little steps, because she was afraid. But Gregorio Cortez kept talking to her and talking to her, and finally she jumped. She jumped far out and into the dark water below, she and Gregorio Cortez.

The other bank was not so high, but it was just as steep. Gregorio Cortez took out his reata, and he lassoed a stump high on the bank. He climbed up the rope and got a stick, and with the stick he worked on the bank as fast as he could, for he could hear the racket of the dogs. The ground was soft, and he knocked off part of the top, until he made something like a slope. Then he pulled and talked until the mare struggled up the bank to where he was. After that they rested up a bit and waited for the Rangers. Up they came with their dogs, to the spot where the mare had jumped. When they came up to the river's edge, Cortez fired a shot in the air and yelled at them, "I am Gregorio Cortez!"

Then he rode away, leaving them standing there on the other side, because none of them was brave enough to do what Cortez had done.

He rode on and on, and sometimes they chased him and sometimes he stood and fought. And every time he fought he would kill them a Ranger or two. They chased him across the Arroyo del Cíbolo and into the oak grove, and there they made him a corral. Then they sent the dogs away and sat down to wait, for they wanted to catch him asleep. Gregorio Cortez thought for a little while what he should do. Then he made his mare lie down on the ground, so she would not be hurt. After that Gregorio Cortez began talking to himself and answering himself in different voices, as if he had many men. This made the Rangers say to one another, "There is a whole army of men with Gregorio Cortez." So they broke up their corral and went away, because they did not think there were enough of them to fight Gregorio Cortez and all the men he had. And Gregorio Cortez rode away, laughing to himself.

He kept riding on and on, by day and by night, and if he slept the mare stood guard and she would wake him up when she heard a noise. He had no food or cigarettes, and his ammunition was running low. He was going along a narrow trail with a high barbed wire fence on one side and a nopal thicket on the other, and right before he hit a turn he heard horses ahead. The first man that came around the turn ran into Gregorio Cortez, with his pistol in his hand. There was a whole line of others behind the first, all armed with rifles, but they had to put the rifles away. Then Gregorio Cortez knocked over a tall nopal plant with his stirrup and made just enough room for his mare to back into while the Rangers filed by. He stopped the last one and took away his tobacco, matches, and ammunition. And then he rode away.

He rode on to La Grulla, and he was very thirsty, because he had not had water in a long time, and the mare was thirsty too. Near La Grulla there was a dam where the vaqueros watered their stock. But when Gregorio Cortez got there, he saw twenty armed men resting under the trees that grew close to the water. Gregorio Cortez stopped and thought what he could do. Then he went back into the brush and began rounding up cattle, for this was cattle country and steers were everywhere. Pretty soon he had two hundred head, and he drove them to water and while the cattle drank he and the mare drank too. After he had finished, some of the Rangers that were resting under the trees came over and helped him get the herd together again, and Gregorio Cortez rode off with the herd, laughing to himself.

He rode on and on, and by now he knew that the Rio Grande was near. He rode till he came to Cotulla, and there he was chased again. The little mare was tired, and now she began to limp. She had cut her leg and it was swelling up. Gregorio Cortez rode her into a thicket, and the Rangers made him a corral. But once in the brush, Gregorio Cortez led the mare to a coma tree and tied her there. He unsaddled her and hung the saddle to the tree, and he patted her and talked to her for a long while. Then he slipped out of the thicket, and the Rangers didn't see him because they were waiting for him to ride out. They waited for three days and finally they crept in and found only the mare and the saddle.

How El Teco sold Gregorio Cortez for a morral full of silver dollars

Gregorio Cortez was gone. While all the armed men were guarding the thicket where the mare was tied, he walked into Cotulla itself. He walked into town and mixed with the Mexicans there. He sat on the station platform and listened to other men while they talked of all the things that Gregorio Cortez had done. Then he went to a store and bought himself new clothes and walked out of the town. He went to the river and took a bath and then swam across, because the bridge was guarded. That sort of man was Gregorio Cortez. They don't make them like him any more.

He had only three cartridges left, one for one pistol and two for the other, and he had left his rifle with the mare. But he was very near the Rio Grande, and he expected to cross it soon. Still he needed ammunition, so he walked into El Sauz and tried to buy some, but they did not sell cartridges in that town. Then he thought of trying some of the houses, and chose one in which there was a pretty girl at the door because he knew it would be easier if he talked to a girl. There was not a woman that did not like Gregorio Cortez.

The girl was alone, and she invited him into the house. When he asked for ammunition, she told him she had none.

"My father has taken it all," she said. "He is out looking for a man named Gregorio Cortez."

Gregorio Cortez was embarrassed because he could see that the girl knew who he was. But she did not let on and neither did he. He stayed at the house for a while, and when he left she told him how to get to the Rio Grande by the quickest way.

Now all the people along the river knew that Gregorio Cortez was on the Border, and that he would soon cross, but no one told the sheriffs what they knew. And Gregorio Cortez walked on, in his new clothes, with his pistols in a morral, looking like an ordinary man, but the people he met knew that he was Gregorio Cortez. And he began to talk to people along the way.

Soon he met a man who told him, "You'll be on the other side of the river tonight, Gregorio Cortez."

"I think I will," he said.

"You'll be all right then," said the man.

"I guess so," said Gregorio Cortez.

"But your brother won't," the man said. "He died in the jail last night."

"He was badly wounded," said Gregorio Cortez. "It was his lot to die, but I have avenged his death."

"They beat him before he died," the man said. "The Rangers came to the jail and beat him to make him talk."

This was the first news that Gregorio Cortez had heard, and it made him thoughtful.

He walked on, and he met another man who said, "Your mother is in the jail, Gregorio Cortez."

"Why?" said Gregorio Cortez. "Why should the sheriffs do that to her?"

"Because she is your mother," the man said. "That's why. Your wife is there too, and so are your little sons."

Gregorio Cortez thought this over, and he walked on. Pretty soon he met another man who said, "Gregorio Cortez, your own people are suffering, and all because of you."

"Why should my own people suffer?" said Cortez. "What have I done to them?"

"You have killed many sheriffs, Gregorio Cortez," said the man. "The Rangers cannot catch you, so they take it out on other people like you. Every man that's given you a glass of water has been beaten and thrown in jail. Every man who has fed you has been hanged from a tree branch, up and down, up and down, to make him tell where you went, and some have died rather than tell. Lots of people have been shot and beaten because they were your people. But you will be safe, Gregorio Cortez; you will cross the river tonight."

"I did not know these things," said Gregorio Cortez.

And he decided to turn back, and to give himself up to the Governor of the State so that his own people would not suffer because of him.

He turned and walked back until he came to a place called Goliad, where he met eleven Mexicans, and among them there was one that called himself his friend. This man was a vaquero named El Teco, but Judas should have been his name. Gregorio Cortez was thirsty, and he came up to the eleven Mexicans to ask for water, and when El Teco saw Gregorio Cortez he thought how good it would be if he could get the thousand-dollar reward. So he walked up to Cortez and shook his hand and told the others, "Get some water for my friend Gregorio Cortez."

Then El Teco asked Gregorio Cortez to let him see the pistols he had, and that he would get him some ammunition. Gregorio Cortez smiled, because he knew. But he handed over the guns to El Teco, and El Teco looked at them and put them in his own morral. Then El Teco called the sheriffs to come and get Gregorio Cortez.

When Gregorio Cortez saw what El Teco had done, he smiled again and said to him, "Teco, a man can only be what God made him. May you enjoy your reward."

But El Teco did not enjoy the reward, though the sheriffs gave him the money, one thousand dollars in silver, more than a morral could hold. He did not enjoy it because he could not spend it anywhere. If he went to buy a taco at the market place, the taco vender would tell him that tacos were worth two thousand dollars gold that day. People cursed him in the streets and wished that he would be killed or die. So El Teco became very much afraid. He buried the money and never spent it, and he never knew peace until he died.

How Gregorio Cortez went to prison, but not for killing the sheriffs

When the sheriffs came to arrest Gregorio Cortez, he spoke to them and said, "I am not your prisoner yet. I will be the prisoner only of the Governor of the State. I was going to the Capital to give myself up, and that is where I'll go."

The sheriffs saw that he was in the right, so they went with him all the way to the Capital, and Cortez surrendered himself to the Governor of the State.

Then they put Cortez in jail, and all the Americans were glad, because they no longer were afraid. They got together, and they tried to lynch him. Three times they tried, but they could not lynch Gregorio Cortez.

And pretty soon all the people began to see that Gregorio Cortez was in the right, and they did not want to lynch him any more. They brought him gifts to the jail, and one day one of the judges came and shook the hand of Gregorio Cortez and said to him, "I would have done the same."

But Gregorio Cortez had many enemies, for he had killed many men, and they wanted to see him hanged. So they brought him to trial for killing the Major Sheriff of the county of El Carmen. The lawyer that was against him got up and told the judges that Cortez should die, because he had killed a man. Then Gregorio Cortez got up, and he spoke to them.

"Self-defense is allowed to any man," said Gregorio Cortez. "It is in your own law, and by your own law do I defend myself. I killed the sheriff, and I am not sorry, for he killed my brother. He spilled my brother's blood, which was also my blood. And he tried to kill me too. I killed the Major Sheriff defending my right."

And Gregorio Cortez talked for a long time to the judges, telling them about their own law. When he finished even the lawyer who was against him at the start was now for him. And all the judges came down from their benches and shook hands with Gregorio Cortez.

The judges said, "We cannot kill this man."

They took Gregorio Cortez all over the State, from town to town, and in each town he was tried before the court for the killing of a man. But in every court it was the same. Gregorio Cortez spoke to the judges, and he told them about the law, and he proved that he had the right. And each time the judges said, "This man was defending his right. Tell the sheriffs to set him free."

And so it was that Gregorio Cortez was not found guilty of any wrong because of the sheriffs he had killed. And he killed many of them, there is no room for doubt. No man has killed more sheriffs than did Gregorio Cortez, and he always fought alone. For that is the way the real men fight, always on their own. There are young men around here today, who think that they are brave. Dangerous men they call themselves, and it takes five or six of them to jump a fellow and slash him in the arm. Or they hide in the brush and fill him full of buckshot as he goes by. They are not men. But that was not the way with Gregorio Cortez, for he was a real man.

Now the enemies of Gregorio Cortez got together and said to each other, "What are we going to do? This man is going free after killing so many of our friends. Shall we kill him ourselves? But we would have to catch him asleep, or shoot him in the back, because if we meet him face to face there will be few of us left."

Then one of them thought of the little sorrel mare, and there they had a plan to get Gregorio Cortez. They brought him back to court, and the lawyer who was against him asked, "Gregorio Cortez, do you recognize this mare?"

"I do," said Gregorio Cortez. "And a better little mare there never was."

Then the lawyer asked him, "Have you ridden this mare?"

And Gregorio Cortez answered, "She carried me all the way from El Carmen to the Border, a distance of five hundred miles."

Then the lawyer asked him, "Is this mare yours?"

And Gregorio Cortez saw that they had him, but there was nothing he could do, because he was an honest man and he felt that he must tell the truth. He said no, the mare did not belong to him.

Then the judges asked Gregorio Cortez, "Is this true, Gregorio Cortez? Did you take this mare that did not belong to you?"

And Gregorio Cortez had to say that the thing was true.

So they sentenced Gregorio Cortez, but not for killing the sheriffs, as some fools will tell you even now, when they ought to know better. No, not for killing the sheriffs but for stealing the little sorrel mare. The judge sentenced him to ninety-nine years and a day. And the enemies of Gregorio Cortez were happy then, because they thought Cortez would be in prison for the rest of his life.

How President Lincoln's daughter freed Gregorio Cortez, and how he was poisoned and died

But Gregorio Cortez did not stay in prison long. Inside of a year he was free, and this is the way it came about. Every year at Christmastime, a pretty girl can come to the Governor of the State and ask him to give her a prisoner as a Christmas present. And the Governor then has to set the prisoner free and give him to the girl. So it happened to Cortez. One day President Lincoln's daughter visited the prison, and she saw Gregorio Cortez. As soon as she saw him she went up and spoke to him.

"I am in love with you, Gregorio Cortez," President Lincoln's daughter said, "and if you promise to marry me I will go to the Governor next Christmas and tell him to give you to me."

Gregorio Cortez looked at President Lincoln's daughter, and he saw how beautiful she was. It made him thoughtful, and he did not know what to say.

"I have many rich farms," President Lincoln's daughter said. "They are all my own. Marry me and we will farm together."

Gregorio Cortez thought about that. He could see himself already like a German, sitting on the gallery, full of ham and beer, and belching and breaking wind while a half-dozen little blond cockroaches played in the yard. And he was tempted. But then he said to himself, "I can't marry a Gringo girl. We would not make a matching pair."

So he decided that President Lincoln's daughter was not the woman for him, and he told her, "I thank you very much, but I cannot marry you at all."

But President Lincoln's daughter would not take his no. She went to the Governor and said, "I would like to have a prisoner for Christmas."

And the Governor looked at her and saw she was a pretty girl, so he said, "Your wish is granted. What prisoner do you want?"

And President Lincoln's daughter said, "I want Gregorio Cortez."

The Governor thought for a little while and then he said, "That's a man you cannot have. He's the best prisoner I got."

But President Lincoln's daughter shook her head and said, "Don't forget that you gave your word."

"So I did," the Governor said, "and I cannot go back on it."

And that was how Gregorio Cortez got out of prison, where he had been sentenced to ninety-nine years and a day, not for killing the sheriffs, as some fools will tell you, but for stealing the little sorrel mare. Gregorio Cortez kept his word, and he did not marry President Lincoln's daughter, and when at last she lost her hopes she went away to the north.

Still, the enemies of Gregorio Cortez did not give up. When they heard that he was getting out of prison they were scared and angry, and they started thinking of ways to get revenge. They got a lot of money together and gave it to a man who worked in the prison, and this man gave Cortez a slow poison just before Gregorio Cortez got out of jail.

And that was how he came to die, within a year from the day he got out of jail. As soon as he came out and his friends saw him, they said to each other, "This man is sick. This man will not last the year."

And so it was. He did not last the year. He died of the slow poison they gave him just before he was let out, because his enemies did not want to see him free.

And that was how Gregorio Cortez came to die. He's buried in Laredo some place, or maybe it's Brownsville, or Matamoros, or somewhere up above. To tell the truth, I don't know. I don't know the place where he is buried any more than the place where he was born. But he was born and lived and died, that I do know. And a lot of Rangers could also tell you that.

So does the corrido; it tells about Gregorio Cortez and who he was. They started singing the corrido soon after he went to jail, and there was a time when it was forbidden in all the United States, by order of the President himself. Men sometimes got killed or lost their jobs because they sang *El Corrido de Gregorio Cortez*. But everybody sang it just the same, because it spoke about things that were true.

Now it is all right to sing *El Corrido de Gregorio Cortez,* but not everybody knows it any more. And they don't sing it as it used to be sung. These new singers change all the old songs a lot. But even so, people still remember Gregorio Cortez. And when a good singer sings the song—good and loud and clear—you can feel your neck-feathers rise, and you can see him standing there, with his pistol in his hand.

Suggestions for Discussion

1. Why are the physical descriptions of Gregorio Cortez so indefinite? How is it important to the legend that Cortez be characterized as a peaceful man (not a bravo), a vaquero and a farmer, as well as a good shot?
2. What is the function of Román Cortez in the story? Does he serve as anything more than a foil to his brother Gregorio?
3. What roles do Román and the unnamed American play for each other in their first encounter? What expectations does each one fulfill for the other?
4. How is the "Major Sheriff" characterized? How is he contrasted with the Texas Rangers? What is the Mexican American community's assessment of the Ranger motto, "Shoot first, and ask questions later"?
5. What legendary abilities of Gregorio Cortez come to light in the chase? What part does the little sorrel mare play both in the action and in the revelation of character?
6. It is true that Gregorio Cortez was found guilty of horse theft and sentenced to prison for that crime rather than murder. Is the irony of this situation used effectively in the legend? Is Gregorio Cortez's death one befitting a hero? Do the power and vindictiveness of his "many enemies" seem plausible?

Suggestions for Writing and Comparison

1. Discuss Gregorio Cortez as a folk hero. What qualities does he share with Daniel Boone, John Henry, Jesse James, or Robin Hood? Does the phrase "with his pistol in his hand," which Paredes took for the title of his book, emphasize the most important aspect of Cortez's character?
2. Read Robert Graves' novel *Sergeant Lamb's America* (an account of the American Revolution from the point of view of a British infantryman) or any history of the Mexican War written by a Mexican. What insight is gained from reading "the other point of view"? In what way does the legend of Gregorio Cortez give "another picture" of the Texas-Mexico border?

Oscar Zeta Acosta

Oscar Acosta is a Chicano activist, writer, journalist, lawyer, and former candidate for sheriff in Southern California.

He is the author of *Autobiography of a Brown Buffalo* (1972), which traces a Chicano's sociopolitical awakening, and *The Revolt of the Cockroach People* (1973), a novel set in the Chicano ghetto of East Los Angeles during the late 1960's. *The Revolt of the Cockroach People* deals especially with the Chicano's conflict with the Catholic Church, the law, and bourgeoise hypocrisy. Both novels are thinly disguised autobiography.

"Perla Is a Pig," unlike the two social protest novels mentioned above, concentrates on a rural Chicano community, where the people are beset with superstition and mistrust. The theme is a universal one, suggesting the loneliness of those who are different, and pointing out that even in a "homogeneous" community there is seldom true homogeneity, and those who do not fit the pattern run the risk of being ostracized.

Perla Is a Pig

He was an old man who peddled corn in the Mexican *barrio* and he had gone five days now without a sale because the rumor had spread that he urinated in his cornfield.

On the evening of this fifth day he slowly pushed his orange cart to the pig's pen to dispose of the freshly cut corn. Those which had become yellow, he fed to the black sow.

"It is the same, Perla," the old man whispered in his native Spanish. "Our misfortune is your joy. Or so it seems." The fat, black pig grunted as it crushed the tender corn ears. "So eat and grow fatter. We'll have you when you're ready."

He chuckled and playfully threw one of the ears at the pig. Then he rolled the cart behind the one-room adobe shack and went to the water pump. He could see no one from there, for in the spring he had planted the tiny kernels of corn in circular furrows surrounding the shack, the pig's pen, and his outhouse. Now it was summer and the green stalks were higher than a man's head.

He removed his eye-patch that hid a purple socket, which he rubbed as though he were scrubbing an elbow, to clean the phlegmy, white particles that caked there during the day. He washed only his face. He did not trouble to roll up his sleeves and so his cuffs were always brown and wrinkled, as were his other garments. He dried his face with his shirt tails, then with his hands still wet, he flattened his few, thin strands of yellow hair.

He went into the outhouse to complete his toiletry. He laughed to himself of the new rumor as he urinated.

He took some corn and picked green squash growing alongside the plum tree next to the shack to prepare the meal for the guest he was expecting within the hour.

The corn had not yet cooked when the old man heard his guest's whistle. "I'm in here, Nico. Come on in," he responded.

Nico, the business invitee, was about half the old man's size. He wore a Levi jacket, Levi pants, and Llama boots. His brilliant black hair was immaculate. He wore a long mustachio, as did the Mexican cowboys in Texas from whom he had learned all there was to know of manhood. This same little man had also learned from his mother that no gentleman should be out in the streets without a pencil, a pad of paper, a comb, and, at the very least, fifty cents on his person.

He entered and said, "Ah, here you are, eh? I thought you might be out pissing." He giggled the shrill laugh of a dirty boy.

"Excuse my bad manners, but I'm at the stove now," the old man explained. "Sit down, Nico. Take all that weight off your feet."

Nicolas hung his nose over the boiling pots. "No meat, Huero?" he asked the old man whom they called *el Huero*, because of his light skin, green eye, and yellow hair.

"Sorry, but she's not ready yet."

"Ah, what luck. When my mother told me you said it was urgent, I thought, or at least I had hoped that you were ready to stick the knife in its throat."

"In her neck," the old man corrected.

"In its neck, in its throat, what does it matter? So long as we can get to it. I saw it when I came in. He's going to be beautiful, he'll bring in a lot."

"She is beautiful, Nico . . . Why don't you sit down?"

"Can I help?"

"No, just rest yourself."

"I thought you might want me to help set the table. I don't mind, Huero. Shall I get the wine glasses?"

"No, we won't need them. I thought we might drink some goats' milk. It's nice and fresh," the old man said, smiling.

"Goats' milk? Yes, it's nice. My mother serves it every night. Says it's supposed to be good for your liver."

"I know, you've told me. That's why I thought you might like it."

The little cowboy waited a moment. "I wouldn't mind trying some of your wine though, Huero," he suggested.

"Wine? But, Nico, what would your mother say? She'd smell it, you know."

"That is of no consequence, Huero! . . . besides, I can stop at Lodi's and get some sweets on the way home."

The old man turned and faced Nicolas. "Well, if you want. But don't tell the old lady. She's mad at me as it is. Like all the others, she wouldn't buy my corn today because of this new rumor. It's up to you."

"Jesus, hombre! I'm fifty-five! You think I worry about her?"

"Well, I don't know, Nico. She's what? Seventy-five?"

"I don't know. I suppose."

"I don't mind, Nico. You're the one living with her."

"So what? Come on, *viejo,* don't play games with me . . . I have to stop at Lodi's anyway. She wants some of that Mexican chocolate."

The two men ate the meal and drank the wine. They did not speak of the business for which the cowboy had come. When they finished, they sat outside and watched the orange, purple sun silently disappear somewhere behind the brown foothills surrounding their valley of San Joaquin. They sat on huge logs smoking slowly. The mosquitoes from the cornfield picked at the little cowboy. He constantly swung at them and cursed them. Huero, the older man, made no such motions. Even if one were to rest on his eyeless socket, he did not bother it.

"Well, Nico, we'd better start on the business," the old man said suddenly, throwing the cigarette at the water pump.

"Business! What business?" Nicolas asked with surprise.

"Don't come at me with foolishness, Nico. You know it well."

"If you have some, well go ahead, but I don't know what you have in mind," the little cowboy said innocently.

"Then why are you here?" Huero said impatiently. "Are you here only to eat and drink?"

"My mother only said you wanted me for dinner as a guest."

"Guest? Ah, what a guest! . . . You know, Nico, sometimes you are like a pimp."

"A pimp? A pimp! Huero, you slander me."

"Quiet yourself, I say it without malice. What I mean is, you try to hide your business, your true business, I mean."

"Business? That I am a pimp? You know, Huero, sometimes I seriously believe you're losing it. Maybe what they said was true . . . maybe you did lose your eye from syphilis."

"Don't start, Nico."

"Well, I don't know, Huero. How should I know? How does anyone know anything?"

"Let it alone, *viejo!*" the old man of one eye warned.

But the little cowboy would not let it alone. "God only knows, *viejo,* but I should know. I who am your friend. Your counselor. Your business agent. Of a truth, if anyone should know, if anyone should know how you lost your eye, it should be me. But you are stubborn, you don't know who your true friends are."

"Look, Nico, we haven't time for that. This new rumor is serious. I've not sold one *helote* all week."

"But it might be important to this case," Nicolas reasoned. "Perhaps the original rumor has not died down. Perhaps it is a recurrence of the same thing."

"It is not the same thing, you jackass! I tell you this is new gossip, a new rumor. Forget the others. I tell you I've not sold all week. You know corn must be sold within a day or two lest it rot."

"Huero, you are using too many vile names. I cannot concentrate when you are rude to me."

"He's gone and started another one on me, Nico. I know it is he. And you know the children need their corn."

"Who?"

"Ay, but look at what a mosquito you are! Who? Who else but the fat Spaniard, you runt!"

"Lodi? Lodi Ulloa?"

"And he's using the same tricks. He has no morals, that *español!* To use one's children to spread evil gossip shows poor education. To gain a business advantage one should not have to lie. He is poorly educated, that one is."

"Huero, if you have something to tell me, why do you hide it? I know nothing of any rumor. I know only of the ones I helped you with in the past."

"But why do you play the part of the cat with this mouse? If indeed you do not know, then why did you ask me if I was pissing in the cornfield when you first entered?"

"Well, that is a natural thing, Huero. Surely you know that."

"You think I don't know what you're doing? You think I am such a fool?" The old man brought out another cigarette. He lit it carefully, deliberately. He inhaled evenly and waited for the words to come to him; for now the bargaining had begun. His words came firmly: "So you know nothing of this new rumor, is that it, Nico? You have no knowledge of the pissing in the cornfield, of the condition of my sales. You are here only as a guest."

The counselor cowboy arose and stepped on the stub of his cigarette with the heel of his boot. "*Viejo,* I'm merely here sitting, smoking, and listening to the talk of a man who it seems to me has a problem, and who is talking like a mad one . . . A man, I should remind you, who claims to be a *Mejicano,* though he has blond hair and one green eye."

"*Ay, dios,* save me from this imbecile! I tell you we have work to do, we have plans to make, arrangements and terms of the agreement to decide . . . And if my color is different from the others, of what concern is that now?"

Nicolas scratched his ear. "How should I know? I remember some years back there was talk you were a gringo."

The old man did not speak now. He saw Nicolas pull at his ear with his thumb and forefinger. He watched him as he stared at the ground and occasionally at the sky which was now black and dotted with pinpoints of white and orange.

Nicolas paced the ground before the old man. Now and then he would stop and look directly into the old man's face. Now that the counselor cowboy was at work, the old man did not interfere. "Shall I tell you the details?" Nicolas finally asked.

"You know you have charge in the matter."

"With the thing about your being a gringo . . . sst! Nothing. A word here, a suggestion in the right ear . . . nothing! A child could have thought that one . . . That was the first rumor, no?"

"As I recall. And this is harder?"

"A gringo! Eh, it was so simple I've forgotten how I did it."

"You made me paint the Mexican flag on the cart."

"Ah, *si.* A flag . . . sst! A child could have done that one." The cowboy pulled up his slight shoulders. "But you shouldn't have taken it off. Who knows, if you had left it on, and it wasn't that bad looking, maybe you wouldn't be facing this now."

"It looked like a child's drawing," the old man said simply.

"What's that to you. It served its purpose. They thought you were a gringo, because of your color. They would not let you drink in peace at the cantina . . ."

"And so you had me paint a flag on my peddler's cart to prove I am a *Mejicano.*"

"Yes, if that's what it took, why not? They no longer bother you at the cantina with their questions, do they? I don't know, Huero, you bring these things on yourself."

"That's of no consequence now, Nico. Let's get on with it."

"No? But that's your problem. You concern yourself only with your own ways, with the things of today. You are like a mule, each day you must learn what you were taught the day before. You do not see the continuity of things."

"Don't start again, Nico," the old man pleaded.

"No, you are stubborn! You surround yourself too much with yourself thinking that by so doing you are hiding from others. But you are only calling attention to yourself."

"How's that?"

Nicolas stopped his pacing. Looking down at the corn peddler like a judge from his bench, he said, "Like this corn. Look at it!" He pointed to the circular furrows.

"What's that matter?"

"Well, look. *Jesus y Maria*, what a man you are! Who ever heard of a round field?"

"It helps the land. It rotates the soil, Nico."

"What a help! Don't you come at me with this foolishness. I know why you did this. And as you can see, everyone else knows."

"What? How's that?"

"To help the land! What nonsense. Who ever saw a round field of corn? It is clear to me, Huero. You did it to hide them. Do you think we are such fools? Even to the children it is clear."

"Hide? But what have I to hide?"

"Well, what else but the pig. And perhaps your plums. There is nothing else. Unless it was to hide your laziness. So that you could piss outside your house without being detected."

"I hide nothing, you *idiota!*" Huero exclaimed.

"But look at yourself. I try to help you. I give you counsel. You do well with my instructions at the beginning, but then as soon as you are doing well then you refuse to abide by my directions. Either you forget or you are a fool. When will you learn?" The cowboy shook his head and sucked at his teeth.

"I should have left that flag painted on my cart? What for? They took that, a child's drawing, as evidence of my *raza?* Anyway, I choose not to go to the cantina anymore."

"Yes, and now you come to me for help again."

"Yes, but I know that I will not always need the counsel of a spider. God will forgive me this weakness . . . but as I have said, this is a different matter."

"That is where you are a fool or a child. Can you not see it? Are you really such a *pendejo?*"

The old man pondered. "You really think this is the same thing?"

"It is for the same reasons," Nicolas said, tossing an obvious rule of law to the wind.

Huero tugged at the cigarette and nodded at the sky. He inhaled the warm breeze and fixed his gaze on Venus. "And the syphilis? That came after the gringo thing. Was that also part of it?"

Now the little cowboy from Texas was in his glory. "Exactly. Look . . . First it was the gringo. They would not give you the drinks, right? So you painted a flag. It was a simple idea, true, but it was good, and it worked . . . Then you removed it. And then what happened? Then they started the rumor of the syphilis; that you lost your eye because of syphilis."

"Well, it wasn't clear. It was sin, I think."

"Sin, syphilis, they are one and the same."

"Well, I don't know," nodded the old man.

The teacher continued without interest in the obvious past. "Look, dumb one. Pay attention. Sin, syphilis, what does it matter what they think. The reason behind the acceptance of a rumor hardly matters. What matters is that you cure them."

"I went to church as you suggested."

"Yes, you went to the mass . . . One time."

"I couldn't do it, Nico. I went the one time to show them where my religious thoughts were. I didn't mind that one time to prove to them, but to continue . . . Besides, the padre was a gringo, an Italian, they say."

"Sometimes I think you do have syphilis, Huero. It has spoiled your brain like a squash that has rotted from the frost. . . . Can't you see it was not for religion that I sent you there? It was to dispel the suggestion of sin."

"You believe that, Nicolas?"

"No, of course not. I am merely a counselor giving argument."

"I can't see it," the old man said, scratching his socket.

"Sure, look, it is very simple. If you had continued to go, if you had gone but a month and waited for the padre to hear of your sins. If you would have had the padre bless you in front of all the people . . . sst! You think Lodi would have dared start another rumor after that? Not even an *español* would be so stupid!"

The old man laughed fully. He slapped the ground and nodded slowly, saying, "*Ay, que cabron,* what a bastard you are! You have such crazy notions."

"It is not a thing to laugh at. You refused to carry out my instruction, you refused to go get blessed and so now what? Now you have to wear that patch over your eye, that is what. But that is not all, and this is what you still do not see . . . This thing of the pissing is the same thing."

"I guess I'm too old."

"Then listen . . . You've worn that patch for three years now. And the people have forgotten about the syphilis. But the patch was your idea, it was certainly not one of mine. I am like a surgeon. I cut away the roots. With that patch you merely delayed this new one. You merely hid the sin. Now Lodi has seen fit to start another one because you have been selling too well in the past few years . . . so there you have it. Listen to my counsel and you will be cured once and for all."

The crickets lessened their clicking and the frogs took up their place. Mosquitoes hummed and buzzed while the fireflies occasionally bit the night air. Now there was a suggestion of a moon, as the Mexican cowboy issued his judgment. The counselor paced before the old man. He smoked and sighed now and again. "I have it! I have found it!" Nicolas burst suddenly. "Ho, ho, there we have it, *viejo!*" he shouted to the old man.

"Has the wine gone to your head, Nico?" asked the old man, thinking that perhaps Nicolas was drunk.

"Si, Nico! Nicolas Bordona! Old Nico has done it again. Go and get us some wine, old man," the cowboy ordered.

"Sit down and tell me. Calm yourself before your heart falls to your feet," said the old man.

"No, give me some wine first!" Nicolas paraded before the peddler, like a proud bantam rooster after the battle. "Bah! who has need of wine when his head is full like mine?"

"Have you a good plan, a big one?" asked the old man.

"Good? You say *good? Ay, ay, ay!* Don't use such small words."

"Well, tell me. What clown do I play this time, doctor?"

"Sst! Clown? I'm not a beginner anymore, old man. My ideas have grown with me. I remember before I used to need the quiet of my home, a certain solitude, before they came to me . . . Clown? No more."

"Well hurry and say it, Nico," the old man was impatient with the cowboy's crowing.

"Yes, I'm growing big in my old age. You should see what ideas I have. Before, the thing of the flag, of the church, they were nothing. Sst! *Nada,* not a thing. A child, an idiot could have worked those up. But this one? I'm telling you, Huero, right from up there."

"You're telling me nothing, Nico."

"Nothing, I tell you," he continued without paying heed to the old man. "In those earlier years it was nothing . . ."

"For the love of God, Nico, say it and be done with it!"

With that the counselor returned to earth from his exaltation and began to unfold his plan before the peddler of corn who had gone five days without a sale because of the rumor in the Mexican *barrio* that said he urinated in his round cornfield. "Here you have it," began the cowboy. "This plan must dispel, once and for all, all the bad feelings of these people, these Mexicans of superstition. This plan must wipe out from their minds the idea that you are different, or that you are unclean. These are the things that tell the people that you are not one of us, and it is for these reasons that they accept the rumors about you. It is a universal occurrence that people will believe what they want to believe according to their feelings of the person in question; and these people, perhaps because they are but poor Mexicans, these people will believe any malicious gossip about you until you can show them . . ."

The old man interrupted, "Nico, please. I have no need for speeches."

"Oh? Then you do not want the basis, the reasoning behind the plan, is that it?"

"Just tell me what I must do, *por favor.*"

"I see. Here I will show you . . . You see, the people, including the children, they believe you have planted your round rows of corn to hide something. To hide what? you may ask. Well, that I do not know, but again you stand apart, again you show your difference and thus again you give them cause for suspicion. Maybe they think you have something special, your pig, your plums, who knows? But I do know that it is because of that that they find it so easy to accept the accusation of this pissing."

"Nico! Jesus, hombre, speak! Say something!"

"Yes, yes. You are without learning. You have no love of philosophy in you."

"It is not philosophy I seek from you, worm. Nor these devious words of yours. I only want to know what I must do to sell my corn. Now will you counsel me or shall I seek out another?"

The counselor sighed deeply and shook his head more in pity than in disgust at the old man of such little knowledge, and then he said, "You will give your plums to the children."

"Give my plums?"

"Yes. To get them, and this is why I like this plan, to get them to spread, as it were, a rumor come from you. In a word, to get them on your side."

The old man turned his one eye up toward the little cowboy. *Surely the wine has gone to this one's head,* the old man thought. *For I ask him to sell my corn and he tells me to give away my plums.*

The gnarled, black-trunked tree blossomed violet each spring and when the sun assaulted the hot fields in July the boys from the *barrio* crept through the tall, green, yellow stalks and stole away the old man's plums. He knew of their entrance, he saw them run through the field, their pockets laden with the purple fruit. He heard them giggle their fear away, but he never once in all those years prevented their taking, without asking, the gorgeous, tender fruit, sweet to the dry mouths of brown-baked Mexican boys.

"Give them my plums, eh? To get them on my side?"

"Yes, that is the first part. I will go and tell them that you have decided to give away your plums. Then, and this is where the plan intrigues me. Then I will go and see Lodi and compliment him on his good meat."

"His meat?"

"Yes, his meat. I will tell him he has the best meat in the entire valley . . . And then, and then, ho, ho, ho . . . and then I will tell him that others have said the same thing."

The old man scratched at his eyeless socket. "That he has good meat, the best in the valley."

"Yes, and then . . . but this is good! Then I will, ever so slowly, suggest to him that if I were he I'd raise the price. *It is worth it, Lodi,* I shall say. *Not only is it the best, but it saves us a trip to Riverbank; and above all, we do not have to deal with the gringos.* I can do such a thing, you know, Huero. You know I have a way with words. *Si, Lodi, were it not for you we would have to buy from those fucking gringos.* And then, Huero, as you shall see, and then he will in fact raise the price of his meat. And it would not surprise me if he raises all his prices, for I will blow up his head 'til it is like a pumpkin, you'll see."

The old man nodded in amazement. He could barely speak. "I see, he'll raise the price of his meat, that's it?"

"Sure. And then all you have to do is sell yours for about ten cents cheaper."

The old man shook his face and scratched at his head. He spoke quietly, "Nico, I am not selling meat; I'm trying to sell my corn."

"Well, sell meat, dumb one."

"But it is you who are the dumb one. I have no meat to sell."

"And the pig?"

"Perla? She is not ready yet."

"Ready? Why not? The animal looks good and ready to me."

Huero looked toward the pig's pen. "Then I am not ready, frog!"

"We must truly come from different countries, Huero. I cannot understand how it is your head works. Here I've arrived at a solution, what appears to me to be the ultimate solution to your problem. A plan that will not only help you sell your pig and your corn but most important it will endear you to these people. For as even you can see, when the women learn from their sons that you are a generous man given to kindness, they will think well of you. When you tell the children that you planted the round field to keep away the dust from the roads to protect your beautiful animal so that she would be clean, how can they not think well of you? . . . And then when these same women learn that the *español,* that fat one who is not a *Mejicano,* when they hear that he has raised all his prices . . . Can't you see it? There you are, a kind man selling clean pork at bargain prices on Sunday afternoon in front of the church . . . Jesus, hombre, it is a beauty!"

"What? What's this of the church? And this thing about the dust not getting on Perla, what is that? So again you would have me play the clown and tell more lies. Again you would have me fight one lie with another one."

"So what? What is that to you? Look, you fool, you'll sell cheaper, true, but you'll sell it all in one day, or in two at the most while the story circulates. It'll mean less work and then next week you can go back to your corn. By then that story will be dead . . . It is simple. You kill the pig tomorrow. You give the boys the plums and tell them the story. Sunday you take the pig to the church at twelve noon. I'll leave as they're saying the last prayers and when the women start coming out I'll tell them you're selling Perla for much less than what Lodi sells for. You watch, you'll sell all the pig before the sun has set."

The old man sat quietly. He looked to the moon. He nodded his head slowly as the blood rose to his head. He clenched his fists and shouted at the little Texan, "Jesus Christ! I must be as dumb as my pig. Why do I ask you to counsel me? Why must I always turn to the spiders and the mosquitoes for assistance? . . . All I want to do is sell my corn and be left in peace. If I don't sell it, the worms will have it. It is too late to have it dried for cornmeal; I've given it too much water for that. And even if the worms don't get to it the sun will take up the sweetness . . . And you will have me slaughter Perla when she is not ready . . . God, but I am surely a fool!"

The old man was explaining these things for himself, because he knew now that he had already committed himself to the plan by simply having asked the little man to counsel him. But he wanted, for a later time, to have this seeming rebellion as a comfort. He knew this would be his only outburst. Now he was but a soldier offering his distaste for war, knowing all along he would concede to his general.

He arose and went into his shack. He soon returned with two glasses full of wine. They drank slowly while the old man finished the examination of his conscience.

When he spoke again his voice was soft and without emotion. "I'll fix the pig and be at the church at noon. Take some corn on your way out. It is still fresh, I cut it only yesterday."

Nicolas had seen the old man like this before, so he did not speak further on the matter. He took only an armful of the green *helotes*. His fee was all the corn he desired throughout the season.

II

The old man had begun the fires under two large tin tubs filled with water. He honed at a long knife with a stone he had found at the river, while his pig snorted and grunted unaware and oblivious.

The line of boys came noisily through the dense field of green, yellow, brown stalks of seven, eight, nine feet. They walked in single file, all barefooted and in shortsleeved shirts or in none at all. They wore patched pants or swimming trunks. All were brown like earth, all had black eyes and brown hair too long or too short. Fifteen Mexican boys coming for their plums. They ceased their hornet's nest buzzing as they carefully approached the old man.

One came forward. "Well, here we are . . ." He hesitated. "Uh, Huero?"

The old man continued to sharpen the knife. *"¿Si muchachos?¿Que es?"*

The brown boy looked at his own mud-caked feet. "Well, Nico, Nicolas Bordona, he said . . . He said we could have the, some plums."

"Oh, *si, muchachos*." The old man hesitated, for he was unaccustomed to dealing with the children. "Take them. There they are."

"They have asked me to speak for them," the boy said.

"No we didn't!" One of the boys standing in file broke away. "You said we should let you talk, but I want to say it for myself."

"Well, speak," the old man said.

"Señor, Huero. We, I want to thank you for the plums . . . And I am sorry I told those lies about you. But I had to. My father says it is for my own good. He made me."

"You're one of the Ulloa boys?"

"Si, señor. But I didn't believe the story."

"It's all right. One has to obey his father. It is that way."

"I know. My mother said so too. But aren't you mad at me?"

"No, son. I am not angry with you. If a father tells his son to lie, then he must lie. Sometimes one must lie of necessity."

The boys murmured. "See?" one reminded the others.

"I said it too," the shortest one called in.

"Huero," another said, "Huero, I'm sorry I called you a . . . *el ciego*. I was just kidding."

"Eh, what does it matter? I wish I were blind. For all the good my one eye does me, I might as well be blind."

"You can see, can't you?"

"Some things. But if I were totally blind then the government would pay me. They give you money if you cannot see anything."

"Huero?" Another one called in. "Huero, I stole a piece of sugar cane once when you weren't looking."

"Ah, what's a piece of sugar cane?"

"Me, too, 'ero," the shortest one squealed. "Oh, no, it was a tomato, I think."

The others laughed at him and the old man smiled.

"One time you gave me too much change," another said, "and I kept it. I'm sorry."

Each one in his turn confessed his sin before the old man. He laughed or smiled and tried to offer consolation. But he was running out of absolutions. Although he had been amongst these children for seven years this was the first time they had come to him. The plan, the counselor's scheme, kept twisting within him. He looked at his sow and he saw the water giving up the steam. He ran his finger along the knife's edge. He used his eyeless socket to advantage. When he did not want others to see him he turned that void toward the speaker. When people told stories, or made attempts at laughing matter he wished not to hear, he would turn away from them. No one truly expected a man with one eye to have all his wits, or to be completely competent in his perception and therefore no one called this rudeness to his attention.

So now as the boys looked upon him without their accustomed rudeness, the scheme raced through him. He turned away from them because he did not like to look upon people when they could measure his emotion. He looked at his plum tree and at his pig. He exhaled deeply, resignedly, and decisively. "Look, *muchachos*, did not Nico tell you you could have the plums? Have I not said, take them? Well, take them, they are yours . . . Not just now, but whenever you want them. This year and the next. They are yours. It will be your tree."

"Always?" one asked.

"Yes. It is yours . . . but there is just one condition. You must do me just one favor in exchange . . . You must not tell anyone about this . . . You must keep this a secret between us. Not even the girls. Because, well . . . the more people know, the fewer plums it will be for you." He smiled and saw it was not so difficult to speak to them. He saw clearly that they were but little boys with dirty bare feet and that all he wanted was to peddle his corn.

"Huero, you say *always*? With your permission, may I ask, Are you going away?"

"Don't you like the plums, Huero?" another asked. "Do they make you sick? My mother says if you eat too many you'll get sick."

"No, I'm not going away. Not now, at least."

"But you are going away? You say not now?"

"Well, everyone goes away someday, you know."

The short one chirped in. "You mean to die? My dog died. My father said he was going away. I know he just died." This shortest one, a little bit of a boy, he was not the age of the others. He had merely come with his older brother to the feast.

"Boys, why don't you just take the plums?"

"Are you very sick?"

"No, not very sick," the old man answered.

"My dog had a sickness. His eye was all red, and white, too. It was ugly. He had blood in it. Is that what you have, 'ero?" the little one asked.

The other boys turned to him and with their eyes and their faces they tried to warn him, to silence him. Their embarrassment compelled them to turn away from the old man with one eye.

"Well, in a way it is my eye, *hijo*."

"Oh, I am sorry, 'ero. I'm very sorry you have the leprosy."

"Shut up, Paquito," his brother yelled.

"Why? I am sorry. And I know about it. The sisters told me about leprosy in catechism. It's like what Teto, my dog, that's what he had. He had it too. Isn't that what you have, 'ero?"

The old man chuckled. "I don't know, Paquito. Maybe I'll die of that like your dog. His name was Teto, eh?"

"*Si*. I called him that for my uncle Hector. And the sister said he just went away too. But I know he just died of the leprosy."

"I see. Well, look, boys, you've thanked me for the plums. I say you are welcome. Now take them, they are yours. They are ripe now."

The boys did not wait. They leaped to the tree and pulled at the branches. The purple tender balls came off with a touch. They ate as they picked more to stuff in their pockets. They yelled and pushed and buzzed and filled their mouths with the fruit. It was not a big tree. Shortly it was clean of the fruit. With their mouths purple and their pockets wet, they left down the same path through which they had entered.

The old man stirred the flames more. "*Bueno*, Perla, it is your time. I would have waited . . . but you have eaten well, have you not?"

What a pearl! he thought to himself as he drove the knife into her neck. He drained her blood, he sliced her skin, he burnt and scraped the bristles. He pulled the intestines. He preserved the brain and the eyes. He cut cleanly the meat from the fat.

Huero worked late into the night under a lamp beside the now thinned plum tree.

III

It was Sunday morning in the *barrio*. The old, wrinkled, burnt-skinned Mexican women, covered with black shawls, gathered at the entrance to the wooden building. The church steeple was crowned with a bleeding Christ and housed a hornets' nest.

The children in stiff bright clothes held back their laughter. They carried black or red or white missals. The men in tight, white starched collars and pin-striped black or brown suits smoked quickly before the mass began.

"Have you heard about the old man?" a woman asked several others.

The others came closer. "*Si, que lastima*, what a pity."

"El Huero, you mean?"

"My boy told me. It is sad."

"I wonder if we shouldn't send the men to inquire."

"I don't know, we might be intruding. I don't want to be a *metichi*."

"Yes, but, Rosa, when it is a thing like this . . ."

"But with him? It is different. He does not join us."

"Well, it is a shame. But I could not buy his corn after what was said. My man would have thrown it to the trash."

"I know. It is the same with me. Mine would have cracked a plate over my head . . . Still, he does have a heart. Like my boy said—he's a little sick this morning, I guess he ate too many . . ."

"Isn't that a coincidence? Manuelito is sick, too. You say yours ate too many? What's that?"

"The plums. You know, Paquito said the old man gave them some plums."

"Your boys are sick? You say Huero gave them . . ."

"*Si*, Paquito said all the boys went there . . ."

"All the boys. Elisa, what are you saying? Don't you know, didn't your boy tell you? My boy, Oscar, he told me that Huero had some bad illness. He's sick too. He's got stomach trouble."

"Wait a minute. Paquito . . . but he's just a baby, he said the old man had what his dog died of. He said the old man told him he was dying of leprosy. But surely, that is just a baby talking."

"Leprosy!"

"Now wait, just wait. My boy, Oscar, he never lies, he is a good honest boy; now he said, and he is no baby . . ."

"Well what is it, Rosa?"

"He did say the old man was sick, of a disease . . . You say leprosy? But he said it might just be a rumor . . ."

"*Jesus y Maria!* If they all went there, as you say . . . and he has leprosy . . . and now they are sick . . . *Dios mio!*"

Several of them crossed themselves. Two of them, without another word, turned and ran home. The others talked faster and louder and gathered momentum in their gesticulations. They called the men into their discussions.

The men laughed at them and called them *chirinoleras*. The men told their women to leave the old man alone. The men in their tight clothes returned to finish their cigarettes, for the priest had arrived.

The women continued in their anxiety. They quoted scripture to one another. One suggested it was not communicable. Another said it was the mark of Cain. They carried their grief into the church and prayed with the priest for all the sick.

But it was all too late. For the rumor had spread during the mass. During the collection, the rumor went round from one to the other, from pew to pew, that the old man had leprosy. The evidence was overwhelming, beyond a reasonable doubt. The Huero had leprosy as was proven by the illness of all the children who had eaten too many plums.

While the congregation recited their *Hail Marys*, the little cowboy slipped out to meet the old man who had rolled his cart near the entrance to the church.

"What's this about your illness?" The counselor wore a black suit and a green tie four inches wide.

"My illness? I am well."

"I don't get it all. I got here a little late. Mother wanted some fresh milk before I left. Look, here they come!" He spun around and hurried to the door to meet the women. But they would not stop to talk as was their custom. They only touched the priest's hand. They hurried away holding tightly to their children. They wanted to find a doctor. Some wanted to go to the older women, the very old and wiser women who counseled them in times of distress, the *viejitas* who found wild mint and red spinach among the peach trees for the illnesses of the children.

The women had no time for the politeness of the counselor who bid them seek out the old man's pork at bargain prices. Nicolas went from one to another pleading with them to look at the meat. They paid him no heed.

One of the women walked up to the old man standing by his cart, and the old man said, "*Ah, buenos dias, señoras.* I have nice fresh meat, thirty cents to the pound. The skins are crisp and the blood is red."

"Huero, I don't come here to buy. I must know, this is a serious thing. Did my son, Paquito, did he go to your house yesterday?"

The old man arranged the meat in the cart of two unnecessarily large wheels, one painted black and the other white. The cart itself was painted orange. "Paquito? Well, what did he tell you?"

"That doesn't matter, Huero. He is just a boy. But I must know for certain. Did he?"

"Don't ask me. I know nothing of your son."

Nicolas came to his defense. "Ladies, perhaps what you should do is buy some of these *chicharrones* for your children. You know how they like them."

"You stay out of this, Nicolas Bordona. This is very serious. We have to know. Huero, we know you are sick and we know some of the boys went to your house yesterday. We have to know which ones."

"I am sick? What is this of my being sick?" he asked the excited women who eyed the pork meat with the eye of the bargain hunter.

"*Si, viejo*, we know of it. It is out and we've got to know which boys were exposed. Now tell us!"

"*Señor* Huero, please, this is a serious thing. Even though the *padrecito* just told me it is not catching, still we should know. I'm sorry if she is rude, but we are all concerned," a younger one apologized.

"I'm not being rude, Carmen. But leprosy is a bad thing, don't you know?"

"Leprosy?" the old man asked. "I have leprosy?"

They all fixed their gaze upon him. "Well, do you deny it?"

The old man touched his eye patch. "Where did you hear that one?"

"From the . . . the boys told us. I think it was Rosa's boy, Paquito, and Elisa's boy, Oscar, he said you told them."

The old man smiled and remembered. He looked at the meat in the cart and he remembered the confessions he had heard the previous day. He saw again the boys scampering through the plum tree and he chuckled when he thought of Paquito's dog, Teto. With a twinkle in his eye he said, "I don't know, ladies. How would I know what I have. I have not talked to a doctor since I was but a child. How should I know for certain if I have leprosy . . . for that matter who can say he does not have it."

The women stared at him and looked with nervous eyes at one another. They tightened their shawls about them and some clutched at the missal or rosary they held in their hands.

"Well, we know, at least the father told Carmen that it is not catching . . . But you are right, who knows."

"Maybe it's just a coincidence that they're all sick," Carmen said.

"Or a warning," Rosa said as she hurried away.

Nicolas said, "But ladies, how about this beautiful meat?"

"The meat? . . . No, I think I'll wait."

"But it's fresh, and it is much less than at Lodi's," he wailed.

"No, Nico . . . I don't think my man would want me to buy just now. Maybe we'd better wait until tomorrow, after we see a doctor or talk to the *viejitas*, they should know."

Nicolas tried the last remaining worshippers. But their decision was the same. They would wait until the following day. If their sons were only sick from too many plums . . . perhaps they would reconsider.

So now I am a leper, the old man chuckled to himself as he covered the meat in the cart with a white cloth.

"How do you do it, Huero? Of all my clients how is it that you bring me the most hardships?"

"It is over with, Nico."

"But you can bring me some problems, can't you? You cannot keep my counsel. You must always play the part of the clown."

"Leave it be, Nico. It is done."

"No, wait, *viejo*. This was a business matter. You were to take my advice for a price."

"You can have your corn, hyena. You can have all that enormous belly of yours will hold. But away with you and your advice!"

"I don't know, Huero. First a gringo, then syphilis, then the pissing . . . Now leprosy . . . But why did you not deny it? Why did you let them know that is what it is. Are you such a *pendejo?*"

"What are you saying, frog face?"

"Ah, well, never you mind, old man. I'll come up with another plan. You see. We'll sell your pig yet."

"Pig? But it is you who are the *pendejo*. This is not a pig. This is but pork meat, can't you see that? . . . Perla is a pig!"

For the first time the counselor took notice of the old man's seriousness. The little cowboy's eyes fluttered and he bit at his mustachio. "Huero, you are disappointed because the plan did not work. But then you should not have said anything about this leprosy. You should have denied it. You should not have let them know you have it, or whatever it is . . . So that is what it is. I thought, for years I had known you'd lost that eye from something strange and mysterious."

Huero pushed his cart away. The counselor followed after him and tried to stop him. The old man pushed his hand away angrily. He mumbled curses at the cowboy. Nico placed himself in front of the cart.

"Jesus, hombre, but you are loco. *Cabron*, but you are weak in the head," Nico shouted.

"Loco? Yes, Nico, that I am. I am weak in the head. But as it goes, *He who has no head had better have good feet*. So get away from me before I run over you!"

Nicolas stepped away from the cart. "Jesus, but now you are like a wild one caged too long without water."

The old man advanced toward the little cowboy from Texas. "Nico, you know they say if a leper rubs his sore on sweet skin it will harden and fall off like cold wax. Want me to try it on you?"

Nicolas jumped back. "God, but now you've really gone off."

Huero laughed fully. His whole body trembled with delight as he watched the frightened little man scampering away with short steps like a busy field mouse.

The old man returned to his hut surrounded by circular furrows of tall corn stalks. He had planted it that way because he had read in a magazine that it did the soil good.

The Mexican peddler of corn hummed an old song as he dug a grave behind the plum tree. The grave was large enough for the coffin, which was the cart, stuffed with the meat of the pig that had once been his Perla.

He knew then, that he too, like Paquito's dog, would have to leave the Mexican *barrio* of Riverbank.

Suggestions for Discussion

1. What is the author's attitude toward Nico? What does he want us to understand about the character through descriptions such as, "He wore a long mustachio, as did the Mexican cowboys in Texas from whom he had also learned all there was to know of manhood," and the nature of the counsel he gives the old man?
2. How had the old man received Nico's counsel in the past? Why does he continue to seek his advice? Why does he accept the advice to kill Perla?
3. Why was the community so ready to believe the rumors about the old man? What is the author's view of the community? Why does the old man behave in suspect ways, such as planting his corn in circular furrows?
4. In Part III of the story Nico promises, "We'll sell your pig yet." What does the old man respond and what is the meaning of the response? Explain the title.
5. The story concludes, "He knew then, that he too, like Paquito's dog, would have to leave the Mexican *barrio* of Riverbank." Explain.

Suggestion for Writing and Comparison

1. In a brief essay, discuss an incident in which you have felt yourself to be an outsider. What were your reactions?

Emilio Díaz Valcárcel

Emilio Díaz Valcárcel, a Puerto Rican, was born in Trujillo Alto in 1929. He spent some time in New York where his work was recognized by a grant from the Guggenheim Foundation. He is presently considered one of Puerto Rico's most talented young writers. Díaz Valcárcel has published numerous short stories in both English and Spanish periodicals.

The following story, "Damián Sánchez, G.I.," was written in Spanish and translated into English by Lee Robinson. It was published in *San Juan Review*, a periodical in English devoted to Puerto Rican culture and literature. The story concerns the experiences of alienation and loneliness of an American soldier, a Puerto Rican, in an integrated but unfriendly army during the Korean War.

Damián Sánchez, G.I.

Fifteen minutes after taking off his shirt, private Damián Sánchez had turned darker and drenched with perspiration.

"What a country! When a man isn't shivering from the cold, he's choking from the heat."

The pick gleamed momentarily over his head and came down, stirring u tiny lumps of dry dirt.

The lieutenant walked up and down to inspect his men's work. A lieutenan is always a lieutenant, no matter if he's at the front or if, as now, he trains his men in a "rest area." His reddish face sweated profusely and his shirt was soaked under his armpits.

Damián Sánchez watched him and spoke in Spanish, so that the officer and the group of blond men digging at his side could not understand.

"When a man isn't shivering from cold, he is choking from heat."

The lieutenant wrinkled his brow and walked away. The soldiers watched Damián sullenly over their shoulders.

Trucks shook raspily along the nearby dirt road, leaving dense clouds of dust behind. The big dry leaves on the bushes were weighed down by a thick crust of dirt.

At night it would usually get cold. Then Damián used to take a little box he kept under his cot and, by the shaky light of a candle, he would read and re-read his precious letters. Sometimes the other men—those now working at his side—wondered if he was sane. For in the shadows the dark face of the Puerto Rican could be just dimly seen wrinkled in a wide smile, his teeth gleaming in the flickering candlelight. That was the time when he would have been with Diana, over there, at a movie or under a tree, squeezing her and firing up her blood. Once the Americans had heard him call out that name—Diana—and they woke up startled for it was three in the morning and the one who had called out was the damned *Porto Rican* and you had to be on the lookout.

Damián rested the handle of the pick against his thigh and pulled out his canteen. The hot heavy water oozed down his throat; feeling nauseous, he spat in anger. He wiped his forehead with his thumb, bent his head forward, and let the trickle of sweat drop on the removed ground.

"A hundred miles from the Chinese and we dig! I'd like to . . . !"

He felt the stares of the others humming over his temples, and laughed impudently without looking at any of them.

"I'd like to . . . !" he repeated in a louder voice.

■ Had Kim Wan been there, everything would be different. Poor Kim Wan had served in the 65th Infantry Regiment for two years and had learned Spanish and would joke with the men about wanting to go to *Puertorro* to take the women away from the Puerto Ricans. Everybody in the 65th would laugh at his jokes because a Korean is a human being just like the others and, besides, they had taken a liking to him. Once, on White Horse Hill, Kim Wan had cleaned up a couple of *mongoles*, thus saving the lives of many guys from Borinquen. So good was he, that once he got Damián a cousin of his at a reduced rate. They had gone together along high hard trails that crossed the rice paddies, the native in front, Damián slipping and stumbling on the early November frost.

"Tchon, buena yangar*baw*, two dollar," Kim Wan told him.

And they had sneaked into the first little shack of clay and straw. Going in, Damián felt the pleasant warmth that came from under the heavy wooden floor. Some very nice young women smiled at him so broadly that their dark little eyes became even more slanted. The rest was easy: the small doll room, the mat on the floor, the body sculptured in fine porcelain, the fever of a lusty man who had been sleeping for six months among soldiers and stinks and curses.

Damián leaned forward and began to take out the earth with his trench shovel. The sun lit a blaze on his naked back. The light tortured his senses, sucked the weak plants dry, dug at the scorched earth of the bomb-torn hills, boiled over the rocks and the ruined military weapons. The few trees existent crawled pitifully and terribly silent toward the sky, their branches like bones and their leaves completely still, like metal. Bees and flies buzzed insanely for the lack of a breeze. Suffocating under the foliage, a kec-cori would pierce the air from time to time with his desolate cry.

Some thirty yards away, Damián saw one of the men turn ashen, crumple slowly and fall on his face. He wanted to run over to him, for even if he was an American he was in need of help, but the hard face of the lieutenant stopped him.

He then gathered new strength and swung the pick furiously at the ground. The earth was softer now and the hole reached his knees already.

■ Of course, in the 65th he had to work even harder. There every corporal was bucking for a sergeant's stripes and every sergeant wanted to become an officer's right arm by taking advantage of the men of lowest rank, offering them as "volunteers" for any hard or dangerous task. After sunset, however, he used to gather with his countrymen to tell them of his plans, and he spoke for quite some time about his girl Diana, who was as ardent as any *geisha*, and told them that when he went back to *Puertorro* he would buy a little Ford and no woman would then be safe on the highway. He talked a lot and listened a lot to guys from Utuado and Morovis and Mayagüez and Trujillo and San Juan. But the new colonel with the pock-marked nose did not like the color of the Puerto Ricans at all, nor the mustaches of the Puerto Ricans, and least of all the language of the Puerto Ricans. After a while, to make things worse, orders came from above, from very far away from the front, and the regiment was disbanded and the Puerto Ricans distributed—like individual packages—among different combat units. Damián, since then, became.mute. Or almost mute. For they transferred good Kim Wan along with him, on the request of the Korean boy himself, and they had both ended in the same infantry company. Here everyone was blond and none of them spoke Spanish. At night, scaring the shadows away, the Oriental and the Puerto Rican would mix Asiatic, English and Spanish terms and talk in a low tone.

"You say Puerto Rico, *tagzán yangarbó?*"

"Many, many."

"*Semo semo Kórea?*"

"No. *Más, más . . . Tagzán,* more, see? And like the ones you see in the movies."

"*¿Las has visto?*"

"*¿Qué?*"

"The *yangarbó* in movies."

"*Yo ir a Puerto Rico*, okaee?"

Their new tent-mates growled at them. Damián always heard them mutter the same thing: "God-damn bastard, shut up." He already understood the curses and he bit his lips, not knowing how to reply. Kim Wan knew some English but preferred to speak Spanish even if he had to suffer the tantrums of the Americans.

Damián Sánchez leaned forward again to dig with his trench shovel. He felt exhausted; the hard work under the beating sun, the frustration of his natural wish to express himself not by sign language, created a deadening confusion in him. If only Kim Wan were with him! Damián reproached himself in silence for what had happened that night. But hadn't he been perfectly right in acting as he did?

With a grimy handkerchief he wiped his forehead, his neck and his armpits. Right in front of him, objects expanded and contracted and spun around.

■ Damián had drunk at least eight cans of beer on that Saturday night. Kim Wan was sitting at his side on the cot and his own hiccups made him shake from time to time; his slanted eyes watched unseeingly the group of men who, horselaughing and shouting drunkenly, were playing dice. Some of them pushed each other, falling all over the cots, or lay drunk on the floor, or fought over a drink of whiskey. Damián was quiet because it was Saturday night and he could not forget. Diana might be dancing at that very minute, not even remembering him. He bent over and pulled a little box from under his cot. When he straightened up, Kim Wan saw the tin can in his hand and asked, "Chop chop?"

"Sí. Pasteles . . . *pasteles criollos*, number one. Mamá sends, *mamasan,* see?"

The other nodded jerkily.

"Good?" he asked.

"Tchosoomnidá."

The Korean came closer and looked at the can. Damián took an opener out of his pocket and began to tear away the top. Kim Wan could hardly wait to taste the *pasteles*.

The other men had stopped playing games and they now watched the two friends in silence. They stood in a group at the end of the tent with an air of resignation, as if forced to tolerate some nonsense.

"Look at 'em," said one of them at last. "They look like a damn couple of lovers."

Kim Wan knew that a joke was going around and he smiled uneasily. Damián thought he understood. He sensed the eyes nailed on him, and his movements became as heavy as those of a child before an exacting teacher. The Korean, in order to break the silence, asked, *"Buena?"*

Damián tightened his jaw and did not say anything. He took out his mess kit and emptied half of the *pasteles* in it, which he then handed to Kim Wan. The other soldiers came closer, staggering, and looked on with tight lips. One of them moved forward, exclaiming, "Jesus! What the hell is this?"

They laughed raucously even though they didn't seem to want to do so. Damián fixed each one with cold attention, as if he were figuring out the best way to mow them down. He stared at the tin and began to eat without appetite, but firmly. One of them came close to Kim Wan, who did not dare to eat, and, practically putting his finger in the kit, asked, "Tell me, porky, what the hell is this?"

■ Kim Wan was shaking. He thought he'd make a joke in order to soften up the intruders, and said in halting English, "Don't know . . . It . . . it looks like shit . . ."

Damián saw his home and his island and Diana and his people outraged, nothing else. He jumped on the Korean, hitting his face cruelly with the tin can, sobbing crazily. He straightened up and kicked all around and bit arms and in turn was beaten all over. Before he passed out, he managed to shout frenziedly, *"Gringos maricones,* you are the shit!"

It seemed that the sun would never go down; it dehydrated the soldiers to the bone. An airplane passed over noisily—its shadow ran swiftly over the men and climbed the nearby brown hill. An odor of resin filled the valley, pinching nostrils anxious for air.

Damián sat on the edge of the foxhole, which now came up to his belt, and took off one of his boots. A stone had cut his heel.

"I shouldn't have hit him. The poor kid is in the hospital and only God knows whether he'll lose his eye. And me with a court martial probably . . ."

A whistle blew, making him raise his eyes. While he put his boot on, he thought of Diana and his parents and his island. Then he got up, put on his shirt, picked up his tools, thought again about Diana, and moved wearily toward the group of men who had already begun to fall into formation.

Suggestions for Discussion

1. How do the physical details fit the mood of the story? What is the significance of the digging of the hole?
2. How does the author show the main character's ambivalence toward Americans?
3. Why does Diana take on such importance? What significance is attached by Damián's fellow G. I.'s to the 3:00 A.M. scene? Does it disturb Damián?
4. Why does his friendship with Kim Wan serve to further isolate Damián? What makes Kim Wan preferable to the "blond men"?
5. What conflicts become evident in the *pasteles* scene? Why must they be resolved in the way they are? What aspect of Kim Wan's character becomes intolerable?

Suggestions for Writing and Comparison

1. Compare the contrast the loneliness of the main characters in "The Day the Dancers Came" by Bienvenido Santos (p. 261) and "Damián Sánchez, G. I." by Díaz Valcárcel. What relation have homesickness and physical isolation to a sense of alienation?
2. Read John Killens' *And Then We Heard the Thunder* for a picture of segregation and integration in the Armed Forces. How does Valcárcel's attitude differ from that of Killens?

Piri Thomas

Piri Thomas, born in 1928 in New York City's Spanish Harlem, was the oldest of seven children in a Puerto Rican family. Thomas grew up in the streets of Harlem's Puerto Rican *barrio*. It was not until he went to prison, at twenty-two, that he seriously began to read and became interested in writing. When Thomas was released from prison in 1956 he worked in a rehabilitation center for drug addicts. He later went to Puerto Rico to organize a similar rehabilitation center and there attended the University of Puerto Rico.

Piri Thomas wrote the narration for the film *Petey and Johnny*, which was concerned with Spanish Harlem. The film was awarded first prize in the documentary category at the 1964 Festival Dei Popoli in Florence, Italy. His novel *Savior, Savior, Hold My Hand,* was published in 1973.

The following excerpt is taken from an earlier autobiographical novel, *Down These Mean Streets* (1967). "Alien Turf" explores the problem of growing up by the code of the ghetto streets and the tenements. Thomas is concerned with showing how one triumphs and achieves manhood in a hostile environment.

Alien Turf

Sometimes you don't fit in. Like if you're a Puerto Rican on an Italian block. After my new baby brother, Ricardo, died of some kind of germs, Poppa moved us from 111th Street to Italian turf on 114th Street between Second and Third Avenue. I guess Poppa wanted to get Momma away from the hard memories of the old pad.

I sure missed 111th Street, where everybody acted, walked, and talked like me. But on 114th Street everything went all right for a while. There were a few dirty looks from the spaghetti-an'-sauce cats, but no big sweat. Till that one day I was on my way home from school and almost had reached my stoop when someone called: "Hey, you dirty fuckin' spic."

The words hit my ears and almost made me curse Poppa at the same time. I turned around real slow and found my face pushing in the finger of an Italian kid about my age. He had five or six of his friends with him.

"Hey, you," he said. "What nationality are ya?"

I looked at him and wondered which nationality to pick. And one of his friends said, "Ah, Rocky, he's black enuff to be a nigger. Ain't that what you is, kid?"

My voice was almost shy in its anger. "I'm Puerto Rican," I said. "I was born here." I wanted to shout it, but it came out like a whisper.

"Right here inna street?" Rocky sneered. "Ya mean right here inna middle of da street?"

They all laughed.

I hated them. I shook my head slowly from side to side. "Uh-uh," I said softly. "I was born inna hospital—inna bed."

"Umm, *paisan*—born inna bed," Rocky said.

I didn't like Rocky Italiano's voice. "Inna hospital," I whispered, and all the time my eyes were trying to cut down the long distance from this trouble to my stoop. But it was no good; I was hemmed in by Rocky's friends. I couldn't help thinking about kids getting wasted for moving into a block belonging to other people.

"What hospital, *paisan*?" Bad Rocky pushed.

"Harlem Hospital," I answered, wishing like all hell that it was 5 o'clock instead of just 3 o'clock, 'cause Poppa came home at 5. I looked around for some friendly faces belonging to grown-up people, but the elders were all busy yakking away in Italian. I couldn't help thinking how much like Spanish it sounded. Shit, that should make us something like relatives.

"Harlem Hospital?" said a voice. "I knew he was a nigger."

"Yeah," said another voice from an expert on color. "That's the hospital where all them black bastards get born at."

I dug three Italian elders looking at us from across the street, and I felt saved. But that went out the window when they just smiled and went on talking. I couldn't decide whether they had smiled because this new whatever-he-was was gonna get his ass kicked or because they were pleased that their kids were welcoming a new kid to their country. An older man nodded his head at Rocky, who smiled back. I wondered if that was a signal for my funeral to begin.

"Ain't that right, kid?" Rocky pressed. "Ain't that where all black people get born?"

I dug some of Rocky's boys grinding and pushing and punching closed fists against open hands. I figured they were looking to shake me up, so I straightened up my humble voice and made like proud. "There's all kinds of people born there. Colored people, Puerto Ricans like me, an'—even spaghetti-benders like you."

"That's a dirty fuckin' lie"—*bash*, I felt Rocky's fist smack into my mouth—"you dirty fuckin' spic."

I got dizzy and then more dizzy when fists started to fly from everywhere and only toward me. I swung back, *splat, bish*—my fist hit some face and I wished I hadn't, 'cause then I started getting kicked.

I heard people yelling in Italian and English and I wondered if maybe it was 'cause I hadn't fought fair in having hit that one guy. But it wasn't. The voices were trying to help me.

"Whas'sa matta, you no-good kids, leeva da kid alone," a man said. I looked through a swelling eye and dug some Italians pushing their kids off me with slaps. One even kicked a kid in the ass. I could have loved them if I didn't hate them so fuckin' much.

"You all right, kiddo?" asked the man.

"Where you live, boy?" said another one.

"Is the *bambino* hurt?" asked a woman.

I didn't look at any of them. I felt dizzy. I didn't want to open my mouth to talk, 'cause I was fighting to keep from puking up. I just hoped my face was cool-looking. I walked away from that group of strangers. I reached my stoop and started to climb the steps.

"Hey, spic," came a shout from across the street. I started to turn to the voice and changed my mind. "Spic" wasn't my name. I knew that voice, though. It was Rocky's. "We'll see ya again, spic," he said.

I wanted to do something tough, like spitting in their direction. But you gotta have spit in your mouth in order to spit, and my mouth was hurt dry. I just stood there with my back to them.

"Hey, your old man just better be the janitor in that fuckin' building."

Another voice added, "Hey, you got any pretty sisters? We might let ya stay onna block."

Another voice mocked, "Aw, fer Chrissake, where ya ever hear of one of them black broads being pretty?"

I heard the laughter. I turned around and looked at them. Rocky made some kind of dirty sign by putting his left hand in the crook of his right arm while twisting his closed fist in the air.

Another voice said, "Fuck it, we'll just cover the bitch's face with the flag an' fuck er for old glory."

All I could think of was how I'd like to kill each of them two or three times. I found some spit in my mouth and splattered it in their direction and went inside.

Momma was cooking, and the smell of rice and beans was beating the smell of Parmesan cheese from the other apartments. I let myself into our new pad. I tried to walk fast past Momma so I could wash up, but she saw me.

"My God, Piri, what happened?" she cried.

"Just a little fight in school, Momma. You know how it is, Momma, I'm new in school an' . . . ." I made myself laugh. Then I made myself say, "But Moms, I whipped the living —— outta two guys, an' one was bigger'n me."

"*Bendito*, Piri, I raise this family in Christian way. Not to fight. Christ says to turn the other cheek."

"Sure, Momma." I smiled and went and showered, feeling sore at Poppa for bringing us into spaghetti country. I felt my face with easy fingers and thought about all the running back and forth from school that was in store for me.

I sat down to dinner and listened to Momma talk about Christian living without really hearing her. All I could think of was that I hadda go out in that street again. I made up my mind to go out right after I finished eating. I had to, shook up or not; cats like me had to show heart.

"Be back, Moms," I said after dinner, "I'm going out on the stoop." I got halfway to the stoop and turned and went back to our apartment. I knocked.

"Who is it?" Momma asked.

"Me, Momma."

She opened the door. "*Qué pasa?*" she asked.

"Nothing, Momma, I just forgot something," I said. I went into the bedroom and fiddled around and finally copped a funny book and walked out the door again. But this time I made sure the switch on the lock was open, just in case I had to get back real quick. I walked out on that stoop as cool as could be, feeling braver with the lock open.

There was no sign of Rocky and his killers. After awhile I saw Poppa coming down the street. He walked like beat tired. Poppa hated his pick-and-shovel job with the WPA. He couldn't even hear the name WPA without getting a fever. *Funny*, I thought, *Poppa's the same like me, a stone Puerto Rican, and nobody in this block even pays him a mind. Maybe older people get along better'n us kids.*

Poppa was climbing the stoop. "Hi, Poppa," I said.

"How's it going, son? Hey, you sure look a little lumped up. What happened?"

I looked at Poppa and started to talk it outta me all at once and stopped, 'cause I heard my voice start to sound scared, and that was no good.

"Slow down, son," Poppa said. "Take it easy." He sat down on the stoop and made a motion for me to do the same. He listened and I talked. I gained confidence. I went from a tone of being shook up by the Italians to a tone of being a better fighter than Joe Louis and Pedro Montanez lumped together, with Kid Chocolate thrown in for extra.

"So that's what happened," I concluded. "And it looks like only the beginning. Man, I ain't scared, Poppa, but like there's nothin' but Italianos on this block and there's no me's like me except me an' our family."

Poppa looked tight. He shook his head from side to side and mumbled something about another Puerto Rican family that lived a coupla doors down from us.

I thought, *What good would that do me, unless they prayed over my dead body in Spanish?* But I said, "Man! That's great. Before ya know it, there'll be a whole bunch of us moving in, huh?"

Poppa grunted something and got up. "Staying out here, son?"

"Yeah, Poppa, for a little while longer."

From that day on I grew eyes all over my head. Anytime I hit that street for anything, I looked straight ahead, behind me and from side to side all at the same time. Sometimes I ran into Rocky and his boys — that cat was never without his boys — but they never made a move to snag me. They just grinned at me like a bunch of hungry alley cats that could get to their mouse anytime they wanted. That's what they made me feel like — a mouse. Not like a smart house mouse but like a white house pet that ain't got no business in the middle of cat country but don't know better 'cause he grew up thinking he was a cat — which wasn't far from wrong 'cause he'd end up as part of the inside of some cat.

Rocky and his fellas got to playing a way-out game with me called "One-finger-across-the-neck-inna-slicing-motion," followed by such gentle words as "It won't be long, spico." I just looked at them blank and made it to wherever I was going.

I kept wishing those cats went to the same school I went to, a school that was on the border between their country and mine, and I had *amigos* there — and there I could count on them. But I couldn't ask two or three *amigos* to break into Rocky's block and help me mess up his boys. I knew 'cause I had asked them already. They had turned me down fast, and I couldn't blame them. It would have been murder, and I guess they figured one murder would be better than four.

I got through the days trying to play it cool and walk on by Rocky and his boys like they weren't there. One day I passed them and nothing was said. I started to let out my breath. I felt great; I hadn't been seen. Then someone yelled in a high, girlish voice, "Yoo-hoo . . . Hey, *paisan* . . . we see yoo . . ." And right behind that voice came a can of evaporated milk — whoosh, clatter. I walked cool for ten steps then started running like mad.

This crap kept up for a month. They tried to shake me up. Every time they threw something at me, it was just to see me jump. I decided that the next fucking time they threw something at me I was gonna play bad-o and not run. That next time came about a week later. Momma sent me off the stoop to the Italian market on 115th Street and First Avenue, deep in Italian country. Man, that was stompin' territory. But I went, walking in the style which I had copped from the colored cats I had seen, a swinging and stepping down hard at every step. Those cats were so down and cool that just walking made a way-out sound.

Ten minutes later I was on my way back with Momma's stuff. I got to the corner of First Avenue and 114th Street and crushed myself right into Rocky and his fellas.

"Well-l, fellas," Rocky said. "Lookee who's here."

I didn't like the sounds coming out of Rocky's fat mouth. And I didn't like the sameness of the shitty grins spreading all over the boys' faces. But I thought, *No more! No more! I ain't gonna run no more.* Even so, I looked around, like for some kind of Jesus miracle to happen. I was always looking for miracles to happen.

"Say, *paisan*," one guy said, "you even buying from us *paisans*, eh? Man, you must wantta be Italian."

Before I could bite that dopey tongue of mine, I said, "I wouldn't be a guinea on a motherfucking bet."

"Wha-at?" said Rocky, really surprised. I didn't blame him; I was surprised myself. His finger began digging a hole in his ear, like he hadn't heard me right. "Wha-at? Say that again?"

I could feel a thin hot wetness cutting itself down my leg. I had been so ashamed of being so damned scared that I had peed on myself. And then I wasn't scared any more; I felt a fuck-it-all attitude. I looked real bad at Rocky and said, "Ya heard me. I wouldn't be a guinea on a bet."

"Ya little sonavabitch, we'll kick the shit outta ya," said one guy, Tony, who had made a habit of asking me if I had any sen-your-ritas for sisters.

"Kick the shit outta me yourself if you got any heart, you motherfuckin' fucker," I screamed at him. I felt kind of happy, the kind of feeling that you get only when you got heart.

Big-mouth Tony just swung out, and I swung back and heard all of Momma's stuff plopping all over the street. My fist hit Tony smack dead in the mouth. He was so mad he threw a fist at me from about three feet away. I faked and jabbed and did fancy dance steps. Big-mouth put a stop to all that with a punch in my mouth. I heard the home cheers of "Yea, yea, bust that spic wide open!" Then I bloodied Tony's nose. He blinked and sniffed without putting his hands to his nose, and I remembered Poppa telling me, "Son, if you're ever fighting somebody an' you punch him in the nose, and he just blinks an' sniffs without holding his nose, you can do one of two things: fight like hell or run like hell—'cause that cat's a fighter."

Big-mouth came at me and we grabbed each other and pushed and pulled and shoved. *Poppa,* I thought, *I ain't gonna cop out. I'm a fighter, too.* I pulled away from Tony and blew my fist into his belly. He puffed and butted my nose with his head. I sniffed back. *Poppa, I didn't put my hands to my nose.* I hit Tony again in that same weak spot. He bent over in the middle and went down to his knees.

Big-mouth got up as fast as he could, and I was thinking how much heart he had. But I ran toward him like my life depended on it; I wanted to cool him. Too late, I saw his hand grab a fistful of ground asphalt which had been piled nearby to fix a pothole in the street. I tried to duck; I should have closed my eyes instead. The shitty-gritty stuff hit my face, and I felt the scrappy pain make itself a part of my eyes. I screamed and grabbed for two eyes with one hand, while with the other I beat some kind of helpless tune on air that just couldn't be hurt. I heard Rocky's voice shouting, "Ya scum bag, ya didn't have to fight the spic dirty; you could've fucked him up fair and square!" I couldn't see. I heard a fist hit a face, then Big-mouth's voice: "Whatta ya hittin' me for?" and then Rocky's voice: "*Putana!* I ought ta knock all your fuckin' teeth out."

I felt hands grabbing at me between my screams. I punched out. *I'm gonna get killed,* I thought. Then I heard many voices: "Hold it, kid." "We ain't gonna hurt ya." "Je-*sus*, don't rub your eyes." "Ooooohhhh, shit, his eyes is fulla that shit."

You're fuckin' right, I thought, *and it hurts like* coño.

I heard a woman's voice now: "Take him to a hospital." And an old man asked: "How did it happen?"

"Momma, Momma," I cried.

"Comon, kid," Rocky said, taking my hand. "Lemme take ya home." I fought for the right to rub my eyes. "Grab his other hand, Vincent," Rocky said. I tried to rub my eyes with my eyelids. I could feel hurt tears cutting down my cheeks. "Come on, kid, we ain't gonna hurt ya," Rocky tried to assure me. "Swear to our mudders. We just wanna take ya home."

I made myself believe him, and trying not to make pain noises, I let myself be led home. I wondered if I was gonna be blind like Mr. Silva, who went around from door to door selling dish towels and brooms, his son leading him around.

"You okay, kid?" Rocky asked.

"Yeah," what was left of me said.

"A-huh," mumbled Big-mouth.

"He got much heart for a nigger," somebody else said.

A *spic*, I thought.

"For anybody," Rocky said. "Here we are, kid," he added. "Watch your step."

I was like carried up the steps. "What's your apartment number?" Rocky asked.

"One-B—inna back—ground floor," I said, and I was led there. Somebody knocked on Momma's door. Then I heard running feet and Rocky's voice yelling back, "Don't rat, huh, kid?" And I was alone.

I heard the door open and Momma say, "*Bueno*, Piri, come in." I didn't move. I couldn't. There was a long pause; I could hear Momma's fright. "My God," she said finally. "What's happened?" Then she took a closer look. "Ai-eeee," she screamed. "*Dios mío!*"

"I was playing with some kids, Momma," I said, "an' I got some dirt in my eyes." I tried to make my voice come out without the pain, like a man.

"*Dios eterno* — your eyes!"

"What's the matter? What's the matter?" Poppa called from the bedroom.

"*Está ciego!*" Momma screamed. "He is blind!"

I heard Poppa knocking things over as he came running. Sis began to cry. Blind, hurting tears were jumping out of my eyes. "Whattya mean, he's blind?" Poppa said as he stormed into the kitchen. "What happened?" Poppa's voice was both scared and mad.

"Playing, Poppa."

"Whatta ya mean, 'playing'?" Poppa's English sounded different when he got warm.

"Just playing, Poppa."

"Playing? Playing got all that dirt in your eyes? I bet my ass. Them damn Ee-ta-liano kids ganged up on you again." Poppa squeezed my head between the fingers of one hand. "That settles it — we're moving outta this damn section, outta this damn block, outta this damn shit."

Shit, I thought, *Poppa's sure cursin' up a storm.* I could hear him slapping the side of his leg, like he always did when he got real mad.

"Son," he said, "you're gonna point them out to me."

"Point who out, Poppa? I was playin' an' — "

"Stop talkin' to him and take him to the hospital!" Momma screamed

"*Pobrecito*, poor Piri," cooed my little sister.

"You sure, son?" Poppa asked. "You was only playing?"

"Shit, Poppa, I said I was."

Smack — Poppa was so scared and mad, he let it out in a slap to the side of my face.

"*Bestia!* Ani-*mul!*" Momma cried. "He's blind, and you hit him!"

"I'm sorry, son, I'm sorry," Poppa said in a voice like almost-crying. I heard him running back into the bedroom, yelling, "Where's my pants?"

Momma grabbed away fingers that were trying to wipe away the hurt in my eyes. "*Caramba*, no rub, no rub," she said, kissing me. She told Sis to get a rag and wet it with cold water.

Poppa came running back into the kitchen. "Let's go, son, let's go. Jesus! I didn't mean to smack ya, I really didn't," he said, his big hand rubbing and grabbing my hair gently.

"Here's the rag, Momma," said Sis.

"What's that for?" asked Poppa.

"To put on his eyes," Momma said.

I heard the smack of a wet rag, *blapt*, against the kitchen wall. "We can't put nothing on his eyes. It might make them worse. Come on, son," Poppa said nervously, lifting me up in his big arms. I felt like a little baby, like I didn't hurt so bad. I wanted to stay there, but I said, "Let me down, Poppa, I ain't no kid."

"Shut up," Poppa said softly. "I know you ain't, but it's faster this way."

"Which hospeetal are you taking him to?" Momma asked.

"Nearest one," Poppa answered as we went out the door. He carried me through the hall and out into the street, where the bright sunlight made a red hurting color through the crap in my eyes. I heard voices on the stoop and on the sidewalk: "Is that the boy?"

"A-huh. He's probably blinded."

"We'll get a cab, son," Poppa said. His voice loved me. I heard Rocky yelling from across the street, "We're pulling for ya, kid. Remember what we . . ." The rest was lost to Poppa's long legs running down to the corner of Third Avenue. He hailed a taxi and we zoomed off toward Harlem Hospital. I felt the cab make all kinds of sudden stops and turns.

"How do you feel, *hijo?*" Poppa asked.

"It burns like hell."

"You'll be okay," he said, and as an afterthought added, "Don't curse, son."

I heard cars honking and the Third Avenue el roaring above us. I knew we were in Puerto Rican turf, 'cause I could hear our language.

"Son."

"Yeah, Poppa."

"Don't rub your eyes, fer Christ sake." He held my skinny wrists in his one hand, and everything got quiet between us.

The cab got to Harlem Hospital. I heard change being handled and the door opening and Poppa thanking the cabbie for getting here fast. "Hope the kid'll be okay," the driver said.

I will be, I thought. *I ain't gonna be like Mr. Silva.*

Poppa took me in his arms again and started running. "Where's emergency, mister?" he asked someone.

"To your left and straight away," said a voice.

"Thanks a lot," Poppa said, and we were running again. "Emergency?" Poppa said when we stopped.

"Yes, sir," said a girl's voice. "What's the matter?"

"My boy's got his eyes full of ground-up tar an'—"

"What's the matter?" said a man's voice.

"Youngster with ground tar in his eyes, doctor."

"We'll take him, mister. You just put him down here and go with the nurse. She'll take down the information. Uh, you the father?"

"That's right, doctor."

"Okay, just put him down here.".

"Poppa, don't leave me," I cried.

"Sh, son, I ain't leaving you. I'm just going to fill out some papers, an' I'll be right back."

I nodded my head up and down and was wheeled away. When the rolling stretcher stopped, somebody stuck a needle in me and I got sleepy and started thinking about Rocky and his boys, and Poppa's slap, and how great Poppa was, and how my eyes didn't hurt no more . . .

I woke up in a room blind with darkness. The only lights were the ones inside my head. I put my fingers to my eyes and felt bandages. "Let them be, sonny," said a woman's voice.

I wanted to ask the voice if they had taken my eyes out, but I didn't. I was afraid the voice would say yes.

"Let them be, sonny," the nurse said, pulling my hand away from the bandages. "You're all right. The doctor put the bandages on to keep the light out. They'll be off real soon. Don't you worry none, sonny."

I wished she would stop calling me sonny. "Where's Poppa?" I asked coollike.

"He's outside, sonny. Would you like me to send him in?"

I nodded, "Yeah." I heard walking-away shoes, a door opening, a whisper, and shoes walking back toward me. "How do you feel, *hijo?*" Poppa asked.

"It hurts like shit, Poppa."

"It's just for awhile, son, and then off come the bandages. Everything's gonna be all right."

I thought, *Poppa didn't tell me to stop cursing.*

"And son, I thought I told you to stop cursing," he added.

I smiled. Poppa hadn't forgotten. Suddenly I realized that all I had on was a hospital gown. "Poppa, where's my clothes?" I asked.

"I got them. I'm taking them home an'—"

"Whatta ya mean, Poppa?" I said, like scared. "You ain't leavin' me here? I'll be damned if I stay." I was already sitting up and feeling my way outta bed. Poppa grabbed me and pushed me back. His voice wasn't mad or scared any more. It was happy and soft, like Momma's.

"Hey," he said, "get your ass back in bed or they'll have to put a bandage there too."

"Poppa," I pleaded. "I don't care, wallop me as much as you want, just take me home."

"Hey, I thought you said you wasn't no kid. Hell, you ain't scared of being alone?"

Inside my head there was a running of *Yeah, yeah, yeah,* but I answered "Naw, Poppa, it's just that Momma's gonna worry and she'll get sick an' everything, and—"

"Won't work, son," Poppa broke in with a laugh.

I kept quiet.

"It's only for a couple days. We'll come and see you an' everybody'll bring you things."

I got interested but played it smooth. "What kinda things, Poppa?"

Poppa shrugged his shoulders and spread his big arms apart and answered me like he was surprised that I should ask. "Uh . . . fruits and . . . candy and ice cream. And Momma will probably bring you chicken soup."

I shook my head sadly. "Poppa, you know I don't like chicken soup."

"So we won't bring chicken soup. We'll bring what you like. Goddammit, whatta ya like?"

"I'd like the first things you talked about, Poppa," I said softly. "But instead of soup I'd like"—I held my breath back, then shot it out—"some roller skates!"

Poppa let out a whistle. Roller skates were about $1.50, and that was rice and beans for more than a few days. Then he said, "All right, son, soon as you get home, you got 'em."

But he had agreed too quickly. I shook my head from side to side. Shit, I was gonna push all the way for the roller skates. It wasn't every day you'd get hurt bad enough to ask for something so little like a pair of roller skates. I wanted them right away.

"Fer Christ sakes," Poppa protested, "you can't use 'em in here. Why, some kid will probably steal 'em on you." But Poppa's voice died out slowly in a "you win" tone as I just kept shaking my head from side to side. "Bring 'em tomorrow," he finally mumbled, "but that's it."

"Thanks, Poppa."

"Don't ask for no more."

My eyes were starting to hurt like mad again. The fun was starting to go outta the game between Poppa and me. I made a face.

"Does it hurt, son?"

"Naw, Poppa. I can take it." I thought how I was like a cat in a movie about Indians, taking it like a champ, tied to a stake and getting like burned toast.

Poppa sounded relieved. "Yeah, it's only at first it hurts." His hand touched my foot. "Well, I'll be going now . . ." Poppa rubbed my foot gently and then slapped me the same gentle way on the side of my leg. "Be good, son," he said and walked away. I heard the door open and the nurse telling him about how they were gonna move me to the ward 'cause I was out of danger. "Son," Poppa called back, "you're *un hombre*."

I felt proud as hell.

"Poppa."

"Yeah, son?"

"You won't forget to bring the roller skates, huh?"

Poppa laughed. "Yeah, son."

I heard the door close.

Suggestions for Discussion

1. What is the significance of the title of this selection? What influence does the environment have on the characters? What does the narrator suggest by his use of terms such as "spaghetti country"?

2. What is the cause of the conflict between the narrator and Rocky's gang? Is Rocky consistent in his attitude towards the narrator? Why does Rocky hit "Big-Mouth"?

3. What is the narrator's relationship to his mother and to his father? What are the parents' attitudes towards fighting? What is the narrator's attitude towards fighting?

4. How would you characterize the language of this selection? Why does the narrator repeatedly use "four-letter words"? What is his father's attitude towards his language?

5. How old is the narrator at the time the action is taking place? Is his request for roller skates consistent with his characterization? Why does he demand that the skates be given to him immediately?

6. What does the father mean when he says "You're *un hombre*"? How does the narrator become "*un hombre*"? Why does he feel "proud as hell" because of his father's statement? How does his pride suggest *machismo?*

Suggestions for Writing and Comparison

1. Compare Piri Thomas' view of a ghetto with that of Claude Brown in his autobiographical novel *Manchild in the Promised Land* (1965). What attitudes towards ghetto life do the two authors share? Are there any similarities in their language and tone?
2. Read Oscar Lewis' study of Puerto Ricans in Puerto Rico and New York, *La Vida.* Which of Lewis' generalizations about the Puerto Rican are illustrated in this story? Would Thomas object to any of Lewis' generalizations?

POEMS
History and the American Dream

Omar Salinas

Omar Salinas was born in Robstown, Texas, in 1937. As a child he went with his family to Mexico where his mother died of tuberculosis at the age of twenty-seven. Salinas returned to the United States shortly thereafter and was brought up by his aunt and uncle. When he was nine he moved with them to Bakersfield, California, where he was only an average student in school because of difficulty with English, his second language.

After high school graduation Salinas attended several California colleges where he studied poetry, working his way through school as a dishwasher, construction worker, shoe salesman, and newspaper reporter. His collection of poems, *Crazy Gypsy,* was published in 1969. Salinas is also the co-editor, with Lillian Faderman, of *From the Barrio: A Chicano Anthology* (1973).

In "Aztec Angel," as well as in "This Day of Quixotic Expectation" (p. 395), Salinas combines surrealistic images with realistic observations. The narrator of "Aztec Angel" is aware of himself both as an "Aztec Angel" and as an outcast in a society where he feels himself, as a Chicano, more closely related to the "pachuco" than to the forces of orthodoxy and convention. The problem that Salinas suggests in "Aztec Angel" is also explored in other poems in this section in which the Hispanic American sees himself an outsider who is called variously "jíbaro," "spic," and "savage."

from
AZTEC ANGEL

I

I am an Aztec angel
   criminal
      of a scholarly
         society
5   I do favors
      for whimsical
         magicians
   where I pawn
     my heart
10   for truth
   and find
      my way
  through obscure
       streets
15   of soft spoken
         hara-kiris

II

I am an Aztec angel
  forlorn passenger
    on a train
20 of chicken farmers
    and happy children

III

I am the Aztec angel
  fraternal partner
    of an orthodox
25   society
  where pachuco children
    hurl stones
  through poetry rooms
and end up in a cop car
30   their bones itching
     and their hearts
    busted from malnutrition

IV

I am the Aztec angel
  who frequents bars
35 spends evenings
    with literary circles
  and socializes
    with spiks
  niggers and wops
40   and collapses on his way
    to funerals

V
Drunk
lonely
bespectacled
45   the sky
opens my veins
like rain
clouds go berserk
around me
50   my Mexican ancestors
chew my fingernails
I am an Aztec angel
offspring
of a tubercular woman
55   who was beautiful

Suggestions for Discussion

1. Who is the speaker in this poem? Does the *persona* remain the same throughout?
2. Compare the children of Section III with those in Section II. What does the statement "their hearts/busted from malnutrition" mean both literally and figuratively?
3. How are Sections IV and V related? In the context of this poem are "spiks/niggers and wops" friends or enemies? Are the words used in the "ordinary" sense, as pejorative terms? What is meant by the statement "my Mexican ancestors/chew my fingernails"?
4. How effective is the combination of visible "facts"—for example, "pachuco children/hurl stones"—with surrealistic happenings—for example, "clouds go berserk"? Can the personal or "inside" statement provide a valid comment upon twentieth-century life in the "outside" world?

Suggestion for Writing and Comparison

1. Discuss the use of surrealistic imagery. Is it suitable to the themes in "Aztec Angel"?

Felipe Luciano

Felipe Luciano, a Puerto Rican from New York, was born in 1947. He has published in several New York Puerto Rican periodicals such as *P'alante*. Luciano has also produced the film *Right On!* His work is represented in Matilla and Silén's anthology, *The Puerto Rican Poets*.

In "Message to a Dope Fiend" Luciano attacks the "counterrevolutionary" Chicanos and Puerto Ricans who, instead of fighting social oppression, internalize all their hatred and destroy themselves by "shooting up."

In "The Library" (p. 397), Luciano more gently attacks the counterrevolutionary in himself, because he loves books so much that he "almost forgot/Revolution was a thing of the streets."

Message to a Dope Fiend . . .

Spics going to the cooker
never realizing they've
been cooked
Mind shook, money took
5 And nothing to show for it
but raw scars, railroad tracks
on swollen arms
And abscesses of the mind

Go ahead spic
10 Stick it in your trigger finger
You ain't got nothing to lose
but your freedom
And yo' mama—who wails futilely at
the toilet door
15 wants to tear down the whole plumbing structure
but can't
'cause you still inside
shooting up, when you already been shot

You ain't got nothing to lose but your freedom
20 Shoot the poison, the smack of your oppressor
Shoot Papi, on 8th Ave. pulling a mule
cart
of cheap dresses
to be sold en la Marqueta
Shoot Mami, sweating like her brown ancestors
25 long ago, killed by Columbus and the Church,
to make that 60.00 in the tombs called factories
Machines rape your mother everyday and

spit her out
a whore —
Don't throw dagger stares at men
30 who cruelly crunch your
sisters buttocks between
slimy fingers
You ain't doing nothing
to change it spic
35 You ain't got nothing to lose
but your freedom

Shoot up our island
of Borinquen
populated by writhing snakes
40 who we nicely call gringos
Green Go
Green Go
Green Berets en el Yunque
Green Marines on Calle del Sol
45 Green bills passing from hand
to calloused palms,
and you shoot the poison 'cause you don't
want to stare at your own ugly reflection —
But it's there spic, hanging off the stoops,
50 dripping over on firescapes, in the eyes
of your hermanito, who wants to be
like you — when he grows up

Better get hip — Quit lying &
   jiving
& flying like you own something
55 'cause you don't own nothing but your chains
And when the revolution comes
very, very soon — you shoot, and I'll shoot
You shoot & I'll shoot, you shoot & I'll shoot —
And unless you shoot straight,
60 I'm gonna get you
Before you get yourself!

Suggestions for Discussion

1. What is the message that the narrator gives to the "dope fiend"?
   What is the narrator's attitude towards the addict? What would
   he prefer that the addict do?
2. What are the various meanings of "shoot" and "shot" in the
   poem? Explain the repeated line, "You shoot and I'll shoot."

Suggestion for Writing and Comparison

1. Compare Luciano's attitude toward the counterrevolutionary in this poem with that in his poem "The Library" (p. 397). What activity, according to Luciano, should the young Puerto Rican ideally engage in?

Victor Hernandez Cruz

Victor Hernandez Cruz was born in Aguas Buenas, Puerto Rico, and raised in New York. He has been publishing his poetry in major periodicals since high school, beginning with *Evergreen Review*'s publication of "Papo Got His Gun" in 1967. He has also published two volumes of poems with Random House, *Snaps* (1969) and *Mainland* (1973).

Allen Ginsberg has described Victor Hernandez Cruz' poetry as "Poesy news from space anxiety police age inner city, spontaneous urban American language as Williams wished, high school street consciousness transparent, original soul looking out intelligent Bronx windows."

Energy

is
red beans
ray barretto
banging away
5 steam out the
radio
the five-stair
steps
is mofongo
10 chuchifrito stand
outside down
the avenue
that long hill
of a block
15 before the train
is pacheco
playing with
bleeding
blue lips

The Man Who Came to the Last Floor

There was a Puerto Rican man who
came to New York
He came with a whole shopping bag
full of seeds strange to the big
5 city

He came and it was morning
and though many people thought the
sun was out this man wondered:
"Where is it"
10 "Y el sol donde esta" he asked
himself
He went to one of the neighborhoods
and searched for an apartment
He found one in the large somewhere
15 of New York
with a window overlooking a busy avenue
It was the kind of somewhere that is
usually elevatorless
Somewhere near wall/less
20 stairless
But this man enjoyed the wide space
of the room with the window that
overlooked the avenue
There was plenty of space
25 looking out of the window
There is a direct path to heaven
he thought
A wideness in front of the living
room
30 It was the sixth floor so he lived
on top of everybody in the building
The last floor of the mountain
He took to staring out of his sixth
floor window
35 He was a familiar sight every day
From his window he saw legs that
walked all day
Short and skinny fat legs
Legs that belonged to many people
40 Legs that walk embraced with nylon socks
Legs that ride bareback
Legs that were swifter than others
Legs that were always hiding
Legs that always had to turn around
45 and look at the horizon
Legs that were just legs against
the grey of the cement
People with no legs
He saw everything hanging out
50 from his room
Big city anywhere and his smile
was as wide as the space in front of him

One day his dreams were invaded by spirits

People just saw him change
55 Change the way rice changes when it is
sitting on top of fire
All kinds of things started to happen
at the top of the mountain
Apartamento number 32
60 All kinds of smells started to come out
of apartamento number 32
All kinds of visitors started to come
to apartamento number 32
Wild looking ladies showed up
65 with large earrings and bracelets
that jingled throughout the hallways
The neighborhood became rich in legend
One could write an encyclopedia if one
collected the rumors
70 But nothing bothered this man who was
on top of everybody's heads
He woke one day and put the shopping bag
full of seeds that he brought from the island
near the window
75 He said "para que aproveche el fresco"
So that it can enjoy the fresh air
He left it there for a day
Taking air
Fresh air
80 Grey air
Wet air
The avenue air
The blue legs air
The teen-agers who walked below
85 Their air
With their black hats with the red
bandana around them full of cocaine
That air
The heroin in the young girls that
90 moved slowly toward their local
high school
All the air from the outside
The shopping bag stood by the window
inhaling
95 Police air
Bus air
Car wind
Gringo air
Big mountain city air anywhere
100 That day this man from Puerto Rico
had his three radios on at the same time
Music coming from anywhere

Each station was different
Music from anywhere everywhere

105 The following day the famous
outline of the man's head once again showed
up on the sixth floor window
This day he fell into song
and his head was in motion
110 No one recalls exactly at what point
in the song he started flinging the
seeds of tropical fruits down to
the earth
Down to the avenue of somewhere big
115 city
But no one knew what he was doing
So all the folks just smiled
"El hombre esta bien loco, algo le
cogio la cabeza"
120 The man is really crazy
something has taken his head
He began to throw out the last of the
Mango seeds
A policeman was walking down the avenue
125 and all of a sudden took off his hat
A mango seed landed nicely into his
curly hair
It somehow sailed into the man's
scalp
130 Deep into the grease of his curls
No one saw it
And the policeman didn't feel it
He put his hat on and walked away
The man from Puerto Rico
135 was singing another pretty song
His eyes were closed and his head waved.

Two weeks later the policeman felt
a bump coming out of his head
"Holy shit" he woke up telling his wife
140 one day
"this bump is getting so big I can't
put my hat on my head"
He took a day off and went to see his
doctor about his growing bump
145 The doctor looked at it and said
it'll go away
The bump didn't go away
It went toward the sky
getting bigger each day
150 It began to take hold of his whole head

Every time he tried to comb his hair
all his hair would fall to the comb
One morning when the sun was really hot
his wife noticed a green leaf sticking
155 out from the tip of his bump
Another month passed and more and more
leaves started to show on this man's head
The highest leaf was now two feet above
his forehead
160 Surely he was going crazy he thought
He could not go to work with a mango
tree growing out of his head
It soon got to be five feet tall
and beautifully green
165 He had to sleep in the living room
His bedroom could no longer contain him
Weeks later a young mango showed up
hanging from a newly formed branch
"Now look at this" he told his wife
170 He had to drink a lot of water or he'd
get severe headaches
The more water he drank the bigger
the mango tree flourished over his head
The people of the somewhere city heard
175 about it in the evening news and there was
a line of thousands ringed around his
home
They all wanted to see the man who
had an exotic mango tree growing from
180 his skull
And there was nothing that could be done.

Everyone was surprised when they
saw the man who lived at the top of
the mountain come down with his shopping
185 bag and all his luggage
He told a few of his friends that
he was going back to Puerto Rico
When they asked him why he was going back
He told them that he didn't remember
190 ever leaving
He said that his wife and children
were there waiting for him
The other day he noticed that he was
not on his island he said
195 almost singing
He danced toward the famous corner
and waved down a taxi
"El Aire port" he said

He was going to the clouds
200 To the island
At the airport he picked up a newspaper
and was reading an article about a mango
tree
At least that's what he could make out of
205 the English
Que cosa he said   Wao
Why write about a Mango tree
There're so many of them
and they are everywhere
210 They taste goooooood
Como eh.

Suggestions for Discussion

1. What kind of energy is Cruz describing in the first poem? What are the uses of such energy?
2. In "The Man Who Came to the Last Floor," what is Cruz suggesting in the lines "and though many people thought the/sun was out this man wondered:/Where is it"? What significance is there in the Puerto Rican being "on top of everybody in the building/The last floor of the mountain"?
3. Can the poem be read as an allegory? If so, what is being suggested by the story of the mango tree growing out of the head of the policeman? What does the Puerto Rican's return to his island mean?

Suggestion for Writing and Comparison

1. What use has Cruz made of the Johnny Appleseed story? What elements of the traditional American tall tale has he borrowed? What has he borrowed from Richard Wright's short story "The Man Who Lived Underground"?

Luis Lloréns Torres

Luis Lloréns Torres, a Puerto Rican, was for many years a successful practicing lawyer. He decided one day, in much the same manner as Sherwood Anderson, that he preferred to write poetry, even at the risk of poverty. He became one of Puerto Rico's leading poets.

As the following poem indicates, Luis Lloréns Torres was particularly interested in the problems of the *jíbaro* and his position in the changing culture of the 1930's. *Jíbaro* is a Puerto Rican term comparable to the Mexican *campesino*; it means "countryman" and is subject to various interpretations, such as the *jíbaro* is kind and sturdy, or the *jíbaro* cares only for cockfights, dice, song, and rum.

Jíbaro

A *jíbaro* came to San Juan
And a bunch of Yankee-lovers
Came upon him in the park
Hoping to win him over.
5 They told him about Uncle Sam,
About Wilson and E. Roote,
About liberty, and the vote,
About the dollar, and about habeas corpus,
And the *jíbaro* answered: Mmmmm.

Suggestions for Discussion

1. When was Wilson President of the United States? Who is E. Roote? What was the relation of Puerto Rico to the United States at the time this poem was written?
2. What is suggested by the *jíbaro's* answer, "Mmmmm"? Is it said in ignorance, hope, despair, fear, or wisdom?

Suggestion for Writing and Comparison

1. Is Torres' poem of the 1930's relevant to the 1970's? Why?

Alurista

Alurista, a Chicano poet from California, is among the most prolific and popular of the young Hispanic American writers. He has published *Floricanto En Aztlan* (1971), *El Ombligo de Aztlan* (1971), and *Nationchild/Plumaroja* (1972). He has also been included in most Chicano anthologies and periodicals.

Alurista is representative of a new school of Chicano poets who write in a combination of English and *barrio* Spanish, the language of the Chicano. His poetry is often concerned with the loss of Chicano heritage in an oppressive Anglo society and the necessity of regaining that heritage. Both "We've Played Cowboys" and "Must Be the Season of the Witch" suggest variations on these themes.

We've Played Cowboys

We've played cowboys
    not knowing
nuestros charros
    and their countenance
5 con trajes de gala
    silver embroidery
on black wool
    Zapata rode in white
campesino white
10   and Villa in brown
y nuestros charros
    parade of sculptured gods
on horses
    — of flowing manes
15 proud
    erect
they galloped
and we've played cowboys
    — as opposed to indians
20 when ancestors of mis charros abuelos
indios fueron
    de la meseta central
and of the humid jungles of Yucatán
    nuestros MAYAS
25 if we must play
    cowboys
— con bigotes
      y ojos negros
    negro pelo
30 de firmeza y decisión
of our caballeros tigres.

let them be
let them have the cheekbones

Must Be the Season of the Witch

Must be the season of the witch
    la bruja
    la llorona
she lost her children
5   and she cries
en las barrancas of industry
    her children
devoured by computers
    and the gears
10 Must be the season of the witch
    I hear huesos crack
in pain
    y lloros
la bruja pangs
15   sus hijos han olvidado
la magia de Durango
    y la de Moctezuma
    —el Huiclamina
Must be the season of the witch
20 La bruja llora
sus hijos sufren; sin ella

Suggestions for Discussion

1. What were "we" (Chicanos) ignorant of when "we've played cowboys"? Who were Zapata and Villa? Why is it ironic that "we've played cowboys/—as opposed to indians"?
2. Explain the narrator's final statement that if we must play cowboys, "let them be/let them have the cheekbones."
3. What is being echoed in the title "Must Be the Season of the Witch"? How does that echo relate to the theme of the poem?
4. How has Alurista modernized the legend of *la llorna?* Why is she crying? What aspect of "History and the American Dream" is revealed in this poem?

Suggestion for Writing and Comparison

1. Read several versions of the *la llorna* legend (see, for example, *Chicano Literature: Text and Context* by Shular, et al. for a half-dozen versions). How is Alurista's version of the *la llorna* tale different from the others?

The Old Truths

Leonard Adamé

Leonard Adamé was born in the California San Joaquin Valley in 1947. He has toured the United States as a rock musician and still works with rock bands. Adamé is presently a poetry instructor in the La Raza program at California State University, Fresno. His poems have been published in *American Poetry Review, Transpacific Review,* and a number of anthologies, including Salinas and Faderman's *From the Barrio.*

Adamé is much less concerned with making social statements in his poetry than he is with capturing the universals of feeling through the point of view of one individual who happens to be a member of a minority group.

". . . in Chihuahua, Villa was shooting traitors"

my father
hugs him and smiles,
touches his forehead;
i bring chairs . . .
5   they talk
of that christmas eve: 1916
the family arriving
without food
in el paso,
10   the smaller ninos tired, cold —
how he left
for two hours
and came back to the box-car
with food, blankets
15   and dry firewood . . .
" . . . in Chihuahua, Villa was shooting traitors,
taking men, cattle . . . "

both now quiet
with remembering . . .

20   looking at him
i remember my grandmother.
his face, eyes,
his smell, all like hers
just before death

25   now,

we've come to visit,
to talk:
    i ask
if he feels well
30   he tells me
        to touch his stump,
        ("it doesn't hurt much")
if he eats enough
    ("they don't give me
35   what i want:
        a little soup,
        an egg,
        a few vegetables . . . ")
if he's comfortable
40   ("give me another blanket,
        the cooler is colder at night")

(grandfather, i still smell the corn
we picked,
i still feel
45 your whiskers, your hands lifting me,
the wind in my face
when you tossed me up . . .
    yet,
    in my 25 years
50   our talks
    would not fill a day . . .)

he asks of my sister's wedding
of my child
of where i've been;
55 i give answers my grandmother heard,
answers we know beforehand
    and grow tired of . . .

in december's air

11:30,
a boy, a little girl,
the dog quiet on their laps,
waiting for Nick the attendant
5 near Beacon Gas and Grocery's door-step

gathered
like kids in old photographs;
her nostrils frost-cracked,
their breath like steam
10 in december's air

i look
and want to be sorry

for the holes
in their T-shirts and shoes.
15 kneeling i ask
their names,
where they live,
why they sit here;
i say nothing
20 of the cold
soaking through their clothes
like water

trinidad, guadalupe,
charley their dog,
25 waiting
to buy candy
with the fifty cents
from grandma . . .
they point to
30 their house:
three vacant lots away;
the one with the light, they say,
can you see it?

Suggestions for Discussion

1. How is the grandfather in ". . . In Chihuahua" depicted in reminiscences and memory? How does that depiction relate to the
   present view of him? What is the function of the lines ". . . in
   Chihuahua Villa was shooting traitors,/taking men, cattle . . ."?
2. How well are the speaker and the grandfather able to communicate now? How well could they communicate in the past? Explain the lines "i give answers my grandmother heard,/answers
   we know beforehand . . ."
3. What is the effect of the simile "gathered/like kids in old photographs" in "in december's air"? What do we learn about the
   speaker and his view of the scene in the lines "i look/and want
   to be sorry/for the holes/in their T-shirts and shoes"?
4. How do the children view their own situation? What are we
   asked to understand through the statement about their home,
   "the one with the light . . ./can you see it?"

Suggestion for Writing and Comparison

1. Compare Adamé's depiction of a relationship with a grandparent
   with Lawson Inada's depiction in "Asian Brother, Asian Sister."
   What ties do both see between an older generation and a younger
   one? How does Inada's view of those ties differ from Adamé's?

Josef Rodriguez

Josef Rodriguez, a Chicano, was born in 1943 in Fowler, California. He attended California State University, Fresno, and the Pasadena Playhouse, where he directed his original drama, *Invocation at the Golden Gate Bridge.*

Josef Rodriguez has published in various little magazines and has written for the Edna Means Dramatic Bureau. He is presently working with a Southern California theatre group, the Los Angeles Inner City Repertory Company.

"Smoke" and "Prayer" are companion poems: the subject of the first is the narrator's brother and the subject of the second is the narrator's mother; both poems are variations on the theme of belief. In each the narrator's own stance is outside traditional belief: "Smoke" suggests that he is seeking his gods, and "Prayer," through its ironic tone, suggests that he has closed himself off from his mother's faith and receptivity—which is presented through images of receptacles, the well and the cup.

Smoke

My brother, a closed sphere,
Round against noises, and shadows, and me—
Nothing open but his nostrils,
Nothing moving but his heart—
5 Is so silent in his sleep—I speak in mine.
But I am quiet in my waking, while he speaks much.
And I would swallow smoke all the evenings of my hours,
And commune with my clay Gods
That rest in rows against my walls
10 Like dolls, and give a prayer to each.
Black lines of hair, scabs from wounds, my nails,
I offer a part of myself to each so each
Might eat.
I am a pagan, strong in rituals,
15 And while my brother, a circle of silence, sleeps with his,
I burn incense,
To my offended Gods. . . .

Prayer

My mother is a well of prayers,
She draws them in a rosary of pleas.
Her hands fall, angled in an ivory cup,
And rise, that God might bend to drink
5 Brushing the rim of fingers with cool lips.
Her face, that flickers as she gazes up
Above the candelabra of her knees,
Burns, in the petit point of lace and years.
"You. Answer me, I'll not believe
10 My fingers are, carved in this cup, a sieve."

Suggestions for Discussion

1. What kind of "Gods" are mentioned in "Smoke"? Can the phrase "I burn incense/To my offended Gods" be read in more than one way?
2. In "Smoke," who is the narrator's brother and how is he a "circle of silence"? What function does the brother serve in the poem? What does the title of the poem mean?
3. Within the context of the imagery of the well in "Prayer," what function do the rosary beads perform? How do the hands working the beads relate to the image?
4. What is unusual about the concept of prayer suggested in the lines "that God might bend to drink/Brushing the rim of fingers with cool lips"?
5. What is the effect of "sieve" as the last word in "Prayer"? Why is it necessary for the mother's fingers to be "carved in this cup"?

Suggestions for Writing and Comparison

1. Discuss the use of symbolism in "Smoke" with particular emphasis upon sleep, rituals, and smoke.
2. Discuss the controlling image in "Prayer." Notice, for example, the use of words such as *cup, well, sieve, draws,* and *rim.*

Omar Salinas

(See p. 376 for Salinas' "Aztec Angel" and a biographical sketch of the author.)

This Day of Quixotic Expectation

This day of quixotic
    expectation
       and lady like caution
       of clever mermaids
5   in my basement

       I am in an excitable
       nightingale parlor
       where troubled angels
          play cards
10   the sky is making noises
       my gypsy girl friend
          is drunk
       I am terribly angry

the world is aloof anyway
15   filled with belly buttons
       and murders

    last night's sex game
    was in keeping
       with my dogmatic
20   religion
my frog soup diet
    is causing nightmares
       my eye doctor is insane
       rides a camel
25   to work

   the bride looks lovely anyway
    in her church bell mansion

    tongues hang in the wind
       and I've got to shout
30   to be heard

  Isn't it silly
    talking to an adding machine
       at three o'clock
          in the morning

35   go back to boardwalk
                      friend
                you've just passed
                    the buck

             and I've just seen Hamlet
40   walk around the block
                 I've got to say hello
          ask him if Ophelia was pregnant
                  after all

Suggestions for Discussion

1. Explain the allusions to the game of "Monopoly," to the Bible, and to *Hamlet*. (For example, why is it that the narrator's *eye* doctor rides a camel to work?) Does the poet use these references to create the impression of order or chaos or bafflement? Are they effective in conjuring up a world known to the reader?
2. What is meant by the bride's "church bell mansion"? Why must the poet shout to be heard? Is his "dogmatic religion" different from the bride's church?
3. Is the conclusion of the poem in any sense a resolution? How has the "quixotic expectation" of the first stanza been fulfilled? Does the form of the poem — stanzaic pattern, movement from left to right, lack of punctuation — emphasize the tone of the conclusion?

Suggestions for Writing and Comparison

1. Compare the picture of twentieth-century decadence in Salinas' poem with that in T.S. Eliot's "Sweeney Among the Nightingales."
2. Compare Rodriguez's "Prayer" (p. 394) and Salinas' "This Day of Quixotic Expectation" with reference to religious allusions and imagery.

Felipe Luciano

(See p. 378 for Luciano's poem "Message to a Dope Fiend" and a biographical sketch of the author.)

The Library

Been seduced once or twice
The N.Y. Public Library raped me
viciously
Assaulted my nose with book smells
5 'Til I almost forgot
Revolution was a thing of the streets.
Men with herringbones and blue shirts
and thick-rimmed glasses have signs on them
That point to Flatbush
10 and the rabbi insisted that scholars and crematoriums
were Compatible.
Young whites, poring over books
Memorizing but never learning
and I wonder how they'll justify genocide.
15 "I was in the library, honest to God,
    I didn't even know."
Don't matter. The library tempts me
Sometimes worse than a woman
With wide baby-holding hips and thick
20 calves
Sometimes I wanna sleep on it, in it, through it
    and
Wake up and say, "Good morning books."
I've kissed books before, held them
25 close to my brown skin
Learned why my mother got moody at the end of every
    month
But they never taught me how to fight
Or how to run from cops sperm bullets
30 "Zig zag, Butchy, zig zag, don't run straight fool."
Taught me to know, but not to believe
Moms believe in God
I believe in revolution
We both believe in something
35 Devoutly.
So,
I guess I'll always be tempted
And sometimes raped.
"Got to go home now books. It's ten o'clock
40 and you're closing up.
God, I wish I could fuck you. G'nite."

Suggestion for Discussion

1. What is the prevailing image that Luciano uses to describe his attitude towards books? What suggestions are there of the narrator's ambivalence toward his attachment to books? Why is he ambivalent?

Suggestion for Writing and Comparison

1. Compare "The Library" with Victor Hernandez Cruz' "today is a day of great joy." How does each author view the role of the written word with regard to social or political revolution?

Victor Hernandez Cruz

(See p. 381 for Cruz' poems "Energy" and "The Man Who Came to the Last Floor" and for a biographical sketch of the author.)

today is a day of great joy

when they stop poems
in the mail   & clap
their hands & dance to
them
5 when women become pregnant
by the side of poems
the strongest sounds   making
the river go along

it is a great day

10 as poems fall down to
movie crowds   in restaurants
in bars

when poems start to
knock down walls   to
15 choke politicians
when poems scream &
begin to break the air

that is the time of
true poets   that is
20 the time of greatness

a true poet   aiming
poems   & watching things
fall to the ground

it is a great day.

Suggestion for Discussion

1. What does the speaker believe the function of poetry should be? How close does poetry now come to fulfilling that function?

Suggestion for Writing and Comparison

1. Write an essay in which you discuss what the function of poetry and the poet should or could be. For example, should the poet aim to change society and/or the individual? Is a true poet one who is "aiming/poems and watching things/fall to the ground"? Are there other functions for poetry?

Luis Valdez

Luis Valdez is a Chicano playwright from California's San Joaquin Valley. He is the founder of El Teatro Campesino, which, since its inception in 1965, has received worldwide attention as one of the best examples of guerrilla theater. El Teatro Campesino was founded by Valdez to educate the Chicano farmworkers about their racial and political problems. Valdez generally employs in his *actos* a form of social satire which has its roots in Chicano vaudeville theater. "Las Dos Caras del Patroncito" is one of the early *actos* of El Teatro Campesino, written in the midst of the Delano grape strike, and representative of Valdez's concerns and techniques.

Las Dos Caras del Patroncito

Characters: Esquirol
           Patroncito
           Armed guard

First Performance: The Grape Strike, Delano, California, on the picket line.

In September, 1965, six thousand farmworkers went on strike in the grape fields of Delano. During the first months of the ensuing Huelga, the growers tried to intimidate the struggling workers to return to the vineyards. They mounted shotguns in their pickups, prominently displayed in the rear windows of the cab; they hired armed guards; they roared by in their huge caruchas, etc. It seemed that they were trying to destroy the spirit of the strikers with mere materialistic evidence of their power. Too poor to afford La Causa, many of the huelgistas left Delano to work in other areas; most of them stayed behind to picket through the winter; and a few returned to the fields to scab, pruning vines. The growers started trucking in more esquiroles from Texas and Mexico.

In response to this situation—especially the phoney "scary" front of the rancheros, we created Dos Caras. *It grew out of an improvisation in the old pink house behind the Huelga office in Delano. It was intended to show the "two faces of the boss."*

(A FARMWORKER *enters, carrying a pair of pruning shears.)*

FARMWORKER. *(To audience.)* Buenos días! This is the ranch of my patroncito, and I come here to prune grape vines. My patrón bring me all the way from Mexico here to California—the land of sun and money! More sun than money. But I better get to jalar now because my patroncito he don't like to see me talking to strangers. *(There is a roar backstage.)* Ay, here he comes in his big car! I better get to work. *(He prunes.)*

(The PATRONCITO *enters, wearing a yellow pig face mask. He is driving an imaginary limousine, making the roaring sound of the motor.)*

PATRONCITO. Good morning, boy!
FARMWORKER. Buenos días, patroncito. *(His hat in his hands.)*
PATRONCITO. You working hard, boy?
FARMWORKER. Oh, sí, patrón! Muy hard! *(He starts working furiously.)*
PATRONCITO. Oh, you can work harder than that, boy. *(He works harder.)*
     Harder! *(He works harder.)* Harder! *(He works still harder.)* HARDER!
FARMWORKER. Ay, that's too hard, patrón!

(The PATRONCITO *looks downstage then upstage along the imaginary row of vines, with the* FARMWORKER's *head alongside his, following his movement.)*

PATRONCITO. How come you cutting all the wires instead of the vines, boy?
     (The FARMWORKER *shrugs helplessly, frightened and defenseless.)* Look, lemme show you something. Cut this vine here. *(Points to a vine.)* Now

this one. (FARMWORKER *cuts.*) Now this one. (FARMWORKER *cuts.*) Now this one. *(The* FARMWORKER *almost cuts the* PATRONCITO's *extended finger.)* HEH!

FARMWORKER. *(Jumps back.)* Ay!

PATRONCITO. Ain't you scared of me, boy? (FARMWORKER *nods.*) Huh, boy? (FARMWORKER *nods and makes a grunt signifying yes.*) What, boy? You don't have to be scared of me! I love my Mexicans. You're one of the new ones, huh? Come in from . . .

FARMWORKER. México, señor.

PATRONCITO. Did you like the truck ride, boy? (FARMWORKER *shakes head indicating no.*) What?!

FARMWORKER. I loved it, señor!

PATRONCITO. Of course you did. All my Mexicans love to ride in trucks! Just the sight of them barreling down the freeway makes my heart feel good; hands on their sombreros, hair flying in the wind, bouncing along happy as babies. Yes sirree, I sure love my Mexicans, boy!

FARMWORKER. *(Puts his arm around* PATRONCITO.*)* Oh, patrón.

PATRONCITO. *(Pushing him away.)* I love 'em about ten feet away from me, boy. Why, there ain't another grower in this whole damn valley that treats you like I do. Some growers got Filipinos, others got Arabs, me I prefer Mexicans. That's why I come down here to visit you, here in the field. I'm an important man, boy! Bank of America, University of California, Safeway stores—I got a hand in all of 'em. But look, I don't even have my shoes shined.

FARMWORKER. Oh, patrón, I'll shine your shoes! *(He gets down to shine* PATRONCITO's *shoes.)*

PATRONCITO. Nevermind, get back to work. Up, boy, up I say! *(The* FARMWORKER *keeps trying to shine his shoes.)* Come on, stop it. STOP IT!

(CHARLIE *"La Jura" or "Rent-a-Fuzz" enters like an ape. He immediately lunges for the* FARMWORKER.*)*

PATRONCITO. Charlie! Charlie, no! It's okay, boy. This is one of MY Mexicans! He was only trying to shine my shoes.

CHARLIE. You sure?

PATRONCITO. Of course! Now you go back to the road and watch for union organizers.

CHARLIE. Okay.

(CHARLIE *exits like an ape. The* FARMWORKER *is off to one side, trembling with fear.)*

PATRONCITO. *(To* FARMWORKER.*)* Scared you, huh boy? Well lemme tell you, you don't have to be afraid of him, AS LONG AS YOU'RE WITH ME, comprende? I got him around to keep an eye on them huelguistas. You ever heard of them, son? Ever heard of Huelga? Or Cesar Ch'vez?

FARMWORKER. Oh sí, patrón!

PATRONCITO. What?

FARMWORKER. Oh no, señor! Es comunista! Y la huelga es puro pedo. Bola de colorados, arrastrados, huevones! No trabajan porque no quieren!

PATRONCITO. That's right, son. Sic'em Sic'em, boy!

FARMWORKER. *(Really getting into it.)* Comunistas! Desgraciados! Mendigos huevones!

PATRONCITO. Good boy! (FARMWORKER *falls to his knees, hands in front of his chest like a docile dog; his tongue hangs out.* PATRONCITO *pats him on the head.)* Good boy.

(The PATRONCITO *steps to one side and leans over:* FARMWORKER *kisses his ass.* PATRONCITO *snaps up triumphantly.)*

PATRONCITO. Atta' baby! You're OK, Pancho.

FARMWORKER. *(Smiling.)* Pedro.

PATRONCITO. Of course you are. Hell, you got it good here!

FARMWORKER. Me?

PATRONCITO. Damn right! You sure as hell ain't got my problems, I'll tell you that. Taxes, insurance, supporting all them bums on welfare. You don't have to worry about none of that. Like housing: don't I let you live in my labor camp—nice, rent-free cabins, air-conditioned?

FARMWORKER. Sí señor, ayer se cayó la puerta.

PATRONCITO. What was that? ENGLISH.

FARMWORKER. Yesterday, the door fell off, señor. And there's rats también. Y los escusados, the restrooms—ay, señor, fuchi! *(Holds fingers to his nose.)*

PATRONCITO. AWRIGHT! (FARMWORKER *shuts up.)* So you gotta rough it a little—I do that every time I go hunting in the mountains. Why, it's almost like camping out, boy. A free vacation!

FARMWORKER. Vacation?

PATRONCITO. Free!

FARMWORKER. Qué bueno. Thank you, patrón!

PATRONCITO. Don't mention it. So what do you pay for housing, boy?

FARMWORKER. NOthing! *(Pronounced "naw-thing.")*

PATRONCITO. Nothing, right! Now what about transportation? Don't I let you ride free in my trucks? To and from the fields?

FARMWORKER. Sí, señor.

PATRONCITO. What do you pay for transportation, boy?

FARMWORKER. NOthing!

PATRONCITO. (*With* FARMWORKER.) Nothing! What about food? What do you eat, boy?

FARMWORKER. Tortillas y frijoles con chile.

PATRONCITO. Beans and tortillas. What's beans and tortillas cost, boy?

FARMWORKER. *(Together with* PATRÓN.) Nothing!

PATRONCITO. Okay! So what you got to complain about?

FARMWORKER. Nothing?

PATRONCITO. Exactly. You got it good! Now look at me: they say I'm greedy, that I'm rich. Well, let me tell you, boy, I got problems. No free housing for me, Pancho. I gotta pay for what I got. You see that car? How much you think a Lincoln Continental like that costs? Cash! $12,000! Ever write out a check for $12,000, boy?

FARMWORKER. No, señor.

PATRONCITO. Well, lemme tell you, it hurts. It hurts right here! *(Slaps his wallet in his hind pocket.)* And what for? I don't NEED a car like that. I could throw it away!

FARMWORKER. *(Quickly.)* I'll take it, patrón.

PATRONCITO. GIT YOUR GREASY HANDS OFFA IT! *(Pause.)* Now, let's take a look at my housing. No free air-conditioned mountain cabin for me. No sir! You see that LBJ Ranch Style house up there, boy? How much you think a house like that costs? Together with the hill, which I built? $350,000!

FARMWORKER. *(Whistles.)* That's a lot of frijoles, patrón.

PATRONCITO. You're tellin' me! *(Stops, looks toward house.)* Oh yeah, and look at that, boy! You see her coming out of the house, onto the patio by the pool? The blonde with the mink bikini?

FARMWORKER. What bikini?

PATRONCITO. Well, it's small but it's there. I oughta know—it cost me $5,000! And every weekend she wants to take trips—trips to L.A., San Francisco, Chicago, New York. That woman hurts. It all costs money! You don't have problems like that, muchacho—that's why you're so lucky. Me, all I got is the woman, the house, the hill, the land. *(Starts to get emotional.)* Those commie bastards say I don't know what hard work is, that I exploit my workers. But look at all them vines, boy! *(Waves an arm toward the audience.)* Who the hell do they think planted all them vines with his own bare hands? Working from sun-up to sunset! Shoving vine shoots into the ground! With blood pouring out of his fingernails. Working in the heat, the frost, the fog, the sleet! (FARMWORKER *has been jumping up and down trying to answer him.*)

FARMWORKER. You, patrón, you!

PATRONCITO. *(Matter of factly.)* Naw, my grandfather, he worked his ass off out here. BUT I inherited, and it's all mine!

FARMWORKER. You sure work hard, boss.

PATRONCITO. Juan . . . ?

FARMWORKER. Pedro.

PATRONCITO. I'm going to let you in on a little secret. Sometimes I sit up there in my office and think to myself: I wish I was a Mexican.

FARMWORKER. You?

PATRONCITO. Just one of my own boys. Riding in the trucks, hair flying in the wind, feeling all that freedom, coming out here to the fields, working under the green vines, smoking a cigarette, my hands in the cool soft earth, underneath the blue skies, with white clouds drifting by, looking at the mountains, listening to the birdies sing.

FARMWORKER. *(Entranced.)* I got it good.

PATRONCITO. What you want a union for, boy?

FARMWORKER. I don't want no union, patrón.

PATRONCITO. What you want more money for?

FARMWORKER. I don't want—I want more money!

PATRONCITO. Shut up! You want my problems, is that it? After all I explained to you? Listen to me, son, if I had the power, if I had the POWER . . . wait a minute, I got the power! *(Turns toward* FARMWORKER, *frightening him.)* Boy!

FARMWORKER. I din't do it, patrón.

PATRONCITO. How would you like to be a Rancher for a day?

FARMWORKER. Who me? Oh no, señor. I can't do that.

PATRONCITO. Shut up. Gimme that. *(Takes his hat, shears, sign.)*

FARMWORKER. No, patrón, por favor, señor! Patroncito!

PATRONCITO. *(Takes off his own sign & puts it on* FARMWORKER.*)* Here!

FARMWORKER. Patrón . . . cito. *(He looks down at "patroncito" sign.)*

PATRONCITO. Alright, now take the cigar. (FARMWORKER *takes cigar.*) And the whip. (FARMWORKER *takes whip.*) Now look tough, boy. Act like you're the boss.

FARMWORKER. Sí, señor. *(He cracks the whip & almost hits his foot.)*

PATRONCITO. Come on, boy! Head up, chin out! Look tough, look mean. (FARMWORKER *looks tough & mean.*) Act like you can walk into the governor's office and tell him off!

FARMWORKER. *(With unexpected force & power.)* Now, look here, Ronnie! (FARMWORKER *scares himself.*)

PATRONCITO. That's good. But it's still not good enough. Let'see. Here take my coat.

FARMWORKER. Oh no, patrón, I can't.

PATRONCITO. Take it!

FARMWORKER. No, señor.

PATRONCITO. Come on!

FARMWORKER. Chale.

(PATRONCITO *backs away from* FARMWORKER. *He takes his coat and holds it out like a bullfighter's cape, assuming the bullfighting position.)*

PATRONCITO. Uh-huh, toro.

FARMWORKER. Ay! *(He turns toward the coat and snags it with an extended arm like a horn.)*

PATRONCITO. Ole! Okay, now let's have a look at you. (FARMWORKER *puts on coat.*) Naw, you're still missing something! You need something!

FARMWORKER. Maybe a new pair of pants?

PATRONCITO. *(A sudden flash.)* Wait a minute! *(He touches his pig mask.)*

FARMWORKER. Oh, no! Patrón, not that! *(He hides his face.)*

(PATRONCITO *removes his mask with a big grunt.* FARMWORKER *looks up cautiously, sees the* PATRÓN's *real face & cracks up laughing.)*

FARMWORKER. Patrón, you look like me!

PATRONCITO. You mean . . . I . . . look like a Mexican?

FARMWORKER. Sí, señor!

(FARMWORKER *turns to put on the mask, and* PATRONCITO *starts picking up* FARMWORKER's *hat, sign, etc., and putting them on.)*

PATRONCITO. I'm going to be one of my own boys.

(FARMWORKER, *who has his back to the audience, jerks suddenly as he puts on "patroncito" mask. He stands tall and turns slowly, now looking very much like a patrón.*)

PATRONCITO. *(Suddenly fearful, but playing along.)* Oh, that's good! That's . . . great.

FARMWORKER. *(Booming, brusque, patrón-like.)* Shut up and get to work, boy!

PATRONCITO. Heh, now that's more like it!

FARMWORKER. I said get to work! *(He kicks* PATRONCITO.*)*

PATRONCITO. Heh, why did you do that for?

FARMWORKER. Because I felt like it, boy! You hear me, boy? I like your name, boy! I think I'll call you boy boy!

PATRONCITO. You sure learn fast, boy.

FARMWORKER. I said SHUT UP!

PATRONCITO. What an actor. *(To audience.)* He's good, isn't he?

FARMWORKER. Come 'ere boy.

PATRONCITO. *(His idea of a Mexican.)* Sí, señor, I theeenk.

FARMWORKER. I don't pay you to think, son. I pay you to work. Now look here — see that car? It's mine.

PATRONCITO. My Lincoln Conti- Oh, you're acting. Sure.

FARMWORKER. And that LBJ Ranch Style house, with the hill? That's mine too.

PATRONCITO. The house too?

FARMWORKER. All mine.

PATRONCITO. *(More & more uneasy.)* What a joker.

FARMWORKER. Oh, wait a minute. Respect, boy! *(He pulls off* PATRONCITO'*s farmworker hat.)* Do you see her? Coming out of *my* house, onto *my* patio by *my* pool? The blonde in the bikini? Well, she's mine too!

PATRONCITO. But that's my wife!

FARMWORKER. Tough luck, son. You see this land, all these vines? They're mine.

PATRONCITO. Just a damn minute here. The land, the car, the house, hill, and the cherry on top too? You're crazy! Where am I going to live?

FARMWORKER. I got a nice, air-conditioned cabin down in the labor camp. Free housing, free transportation —

PATRONCITO. You're nuts! I can't live in those shacks! They got rats, cockroaches. And those trucks are unsafe. You want me to get killed?

FARMWORKER. Then buy a car.

PATRONCITO. With what? How much you paying me here anyway?

FARMWORKER. Eighty-five cents an hour.

PATRONCITO. I was paying you a buck twenty-five!

FARMWORKER. I got problems, boy! Go on welfare!

PATRONCITO. Oh no, this is too much. You've gone too far, boy. I think you better gimme back my things. *(He takes off farmworker sign & hat, throws down shears, and tells the audience)* You know that damn Cesar Chavez is right? You can't do this work for less than two dollars an hour. No, boy, I think we've played enough. Give me back —

FARMWORKER. GIT YOUR HANDS OFFA ME, SPIC!

PATRONCITO. Now stop it, boy!

FARMWORKER. Get away from me, greaseball! (PATRONCITO *tries to grab mask.)* Charlie! Charlie!

(CHARLIE *the Rent-a-Fuzz comes bouncing in.* PATRONCITO *tries to talk to him.*)

PATRONCITO. Now listen, Charlie, I—
CHARLIE. *(Pushing him aside.)* Out of my way, Mex! *(He goes over to* FARM-WORKER.*)* Yeah, boss?
PATRONCITO. This union commie bastard is giving me trouble. He's trying to steal my car, my land, my ranch, and he even tried to rape my wife!
CHARLIE. *(Turning around, an infuriated ape.)* You touched a white woman, boy?
PATRONCITO. Charlie, you idiot, it's me! Your boss!
CHARLIE. Shut up!
PATRONCITO. Charlie! It's me!
CHARLIE. I'm gonna whup you good, boy! *(He grabs him.)*
PATRONCITO. (CHARLIE *starts dragging him out.*) Charlie! Stop it! Somebody help me! Help! Where's those damn union organizers? Where's Cesar Chavez? Help! Huelga! HUELGAAAAAA!

(CHARLIE *drags out the* PATRONCITO. *The* FARMWORKER *takes off the pig mask and turns toward the audience.*)

FARMWORKER. Bueno, so much for the patrón. I got his house, his land, his car—only I'm not going to keep 'em. He can have them. But I'm taking the cigar. Ay los watcho. *(Exit.)*

Fin

Suggestions for Discussion

1. To what extent are the characters in the play "believable"? Valdez is obviously not concerned with verisimilitude. Why? What is more important than realism in this play?
2. How is the farmworker's naiveté suggested early in the play? Is he ever totally naive?
3. What does the patroncito learn through the turnabout? What does the farmworker learn? Does the audience also learn or does Valdez take for granted a prior knowledge on the part of the audience?

Suggestion for Writing and Comparison

1. Compare the social satire of "Las Dos Caras del Patroncito" with Ossie Davis' social satire in "Purlie Victorious." Which techniques and devices do the two authors have in common? Which play is more successful?

Chapter 5
Jewish American Writers

Introduction

The Jewish American writer emerged as a major literary figure after World War II with the recognition of such poets and novelists as Karl Shapiro, Muriel Rukeyser, Saul Bellow, Norman Mailer, Philip Roth, and Bernard Malamud. However, Jewish Americans, who today number over 3 percent of our total population, began migrating to this country long before the American Revolution. The first migrants came in the mid-seventeenth century from the Iberian peninsula; the second group came in the mid-nineteenth century from Germany; the third group arrived from Eastern Europe in the late-nineteenth century; and the last migrants came as post-World War II refugees from all of Europe.

The history of the first Jewish migrants to America dates back as far as 1492, the same year that Columbus is said to have discovered America. In that year, the Jews of Spain were expelled from their country *en masse* for religious reasons. Shortly thereafter, the Jews of Portugal were also expelled from their country. Together these Sephardic Jews traveled to the New World where they settled in Brazil. But when the Portugese regained possession of Brazil in 1654, the Jews were again driven from their homes. Many of these Jews returned to the Old World, although a small group traveled to North America and settled in what was then New Amsterdam. Their number was soon augmented by new Jewish emigrants from Spain, Portugal, and various Latin American colonies. From this Sephardic immigrant group there emerged in later generations several distinguished American figures. Perhaps the most notable of these was Emma Lazarus, poet and literary correspondent of Ralph Waldo Emerson. Emma Lazarus first became conscious as a writer of her Jewishness when she learned of the horrors of the Russian pogroms. She was inspired by the plight of the Russian Jews to write not only of their problems, but also of the problems of the oppressed everywhere. Her poem "The New Colossus" (1883) was taken for the inscription at the base of the Statue of Liberty. Its concluding lines refer not merely to Jewish migrants but to all of the various immigrant groups:

Give me your tired, your poor,
Your huddled masses yearning to breathe free,
The wretched refuse of your teeming shore,
Send these, the homeless, tempest-tost, to me,
I lift my lamp beside the golden door!

At the time of the American Revolution there were barely three thousand Jews in the United States. Seventy-five years later there were approximately fifty thousand, most of them having come to America from Germany in the mass migration of the 1840's. This second wave of emigration reflected the chaos of Europe after the reign of Napoleon. These migrants came to America with many non-Jewish Germans who were also fleeing from hunger and oppression. Unlike the Sephardic Jews, however, the German Jews did not settle only on the Atlantic seaboard; they became pioneers in all parts of the growing country, settling in German American colonies rather than Jewish America ghettos. Edna Ferber, a descendant of these immigrants and the author of numerous popular books such as *Showboat* (1926) and *Giant* (1952), has recorded the experiences of German Jews who settled in the Middle West in *Fanny Herself* (1917), a somewhat autobiographical novel. Another American author, Gertrude Stein, an influential figure in twentieth-century literature, was also the descendant of German Jewish immigrants, the group which settled in the Northeast.

Gertrude Stein's grandparents, who prospered rather quickly in the United States, were representative of German Jews who had come to America in the middle of the nineteenth century. Indeed, by the time of the next mass migration—1880-1920, when the Eastern European emigrants arrived—the German Jews had been so "Americanized" that there was a general antipathy between them and the newer arrivals. The Eastern European emigrants came to America penniless with only the knowledge of a *shtetl* existence in Russia or Poland or Roumania. In this respect they were quite unlike their German co-religionists who had received a liberal education of a much more secular character in Western Europe. The German Jews, therefore, could more easily establish a national life outside of Jewish traditions. The Eastern European Jews, like the protagonist in Abraham Cahan's *The Rise of David Levinsky* (1917), were often Talmudic scholars with few secular skills, and they were forced to take the only jobs they could find in America, those of pushcart peddler and sweatshop tailor. Most of these immigrants settled on the lower East Side of New York and established a ghetto which flourished for several decades.

This ghetto produced many poets and writers of fiction, among them Eliakim Zunser, Morris Rosenfeld, and S. Libin, who wrote in Yiddish and had a great following among their fellow immigrants. Their work was often published in the ghetto papers such as *Arbeiter-Zeitung, Zukunft,* and *Vorwarts.* Even in the 1960's, a number of Jewish Americans continue to write in Yiddish and are published primarily in the few remaining Yiddish papers such as the *Vorwarts.* Contemporary Yiddish writers of this type are represented in this book by Aaron Kurtz and Isaac B. Singer. Kurtz's poem "Behold the Sea" (p. 503) comments on mid-century problems in an exploration of the similarities between anti-Jewish and anti-black prejudice; Singer's "The Little

Shoemakers" (p. 424) contrasts the old Eastern European ghetto life with mid-century American life.

The lives of the Eastern European Jews who came to America during the great migration (1880-1920) were recorded in a number of novels written in English by immigrants, such as Mary Antin's *The Promised Land* (1912), Rose Cohen's *Out of the Shadow* (1918), and Anzia Yezierska's *Salome of the Tenements* (1923). The most important of the early immigrant novelists was Abraham Cahan, whose short stories in the style of the Russian realists (written variously in Yiddish and English) were frequently published in peridicals of both languages. But it was Cahan's novels in English, particularly *Yekl: A Tale of the New York Ghetto* (1896) and *The Rise of David Levinsky* (1917), which gave him so substantial a literary reputation that he was proclaimed by William Dean Howells as "the novelist of 'new' New York."

The Rise of David Levinsky is one of the few immigrant novels of interest to readers other than literary historians. Perhaps the reason it has endured far longer than other immigrant novels of the period is that it reflects a quality beyond the narrow experiences of any one ethnic group, as does the best American literature. Critics such as Isaac Rosenfeld have pointed out that *The Rise of David Levinsky* is an American novel in the very center of the Jewish genre. Cahan was concerned not only with the story of the Jewish immigrant who makes a fortune in the new land, but also with an exploration of American myths, particularly the myth of American capitalism that "the millionaire finds nothing but emptiness at the top of the heap," and the myths implicit in phrases such as "rags to riches," "he worked himself up," and "poor little rich boy."

In the 1920's, several writers emerged in America who came from the older German Jewish stock, among them Paul Rosenfeld and Waldo Frank; and in the 1930's the conditions of the American ghettos and the Depression produced a number of Jewish novels of some note (primarily by writers of Eastern European backgrounds), including Henry Roth's *Call It Sleep* (1934), Michael Gold's *Jews Without Money* (1930), Clifford Odet's *Awake and Sing* (1935), and Meyer Levin's *The Old Bunch* (1937). But much of the work by Jewish writers during the 1920's and 1930's has been forgotten because it was concerned with conditions pertinent only to a single time and place.

Ralph Ellison (see p. 96) has observed that what the Jewish writer had to learn before he could find a lasting place in American literature was the "Americaness of his experiences." The Jewish writer, like any good ethnic writer, "had to see himself as American and project his Jewish experience as an experience unfolding within this pluralistic society." When this was done, Ellison suggests, it was possible to project this variant of the American experience as a metaphor for the whole. It is significant that one of the most important Jewish American novels, Saul Bellow's *The Adventures of Augie March* (1953), opens with the statement "I am an American, Chicago born." It is with a similar implication that another contemporary novelist, Herbert Gold, asserts: "The American Jewish community is most important to me as a writer because it is a mirror in which the rest of America can be seen."

Finally, World War II and the horrors of European anti-Semitism affected the American population by the admission of thousands of Jews to the United States through the Displaced Persons Act of 1948. The war also had a twofold effect on the Jewish American writer. On the one hand, he rediscovered his identity as a Jew, even if he had long ago left the ghetto and the religion. Muriel Rukeyser expresses this insight eloquently in her poem "Letter to the Front":

> To be a Jew in the twentieth century
> Is to be offered a gift. If you refuse,
> Wishing to be invisible, you choose
> Death of the spirit, the stone insanity.
> Accepting, take full life. Full agonies . . .

On the other hand, and paradoxically, because the horror and tragedy of Hitler's policy put a virtual end to anti-Semitism in the United States, the Jewish American writer was free to deal with more inclusive, more universal themes. Where he does deal with anti-Semitism, as Saul Bellow does in *The Victim* (1947) and Bruce Jay Friedman does in *Stern* (1962), that theme is usually incidental or subordinate. Karl Shapiro points out in this context that it has only been since World War II "that an American writer could write Jewishly and still be thought of as American."

Delmore Schwartz and Karl Shapiro, who have both found a permanent place in American poetry, also demonstrate this two-fold effect in their work. In 1939, as Hitler marched through Europe, Schwartz published his first book, which G. M. O'Donnell, the critic for *Poetry* magazine, said was "one of those rare first books that oblige an immediate recognition of its greatness." Schwartz's work, from the very beginning, suggested his concern with both Jewish themes as well as American or more universal ones. For example, his early verse play *Shenandoah* (1941), set in the Bronx, deals with the naming rites of a Jewish child. A longer poem, *Genesis, Book I* (1943), depicts an American boy of Russian Jewish background growing up in NewYork. And several of the poems in *Summer Knowledge,* a collection of verse composed between 1938 and 1958, explore the earliest heritage of the Jewish writer, the Old Testament—a heritage which often inspires the work of many other Jewish American writers such as Howard Nemerov and Karl Shapiro.

Karl Shapiro's first work to attract attention appeared in a New Directions collection, *Five Young Poets* (1941). The poet and critic Louise Bogan correctly predicted of these early poems by Shapiro that "his work will become a sort of touchstone for his generation." In 1958 Shapiro collected his poems dealing with Jewish subjects into a single volume entitled *Poems of a Jew.* But despite the subject matter, these poems are unparochial; Shapiro himself states his purpose in the introduction: "These poems . . . are for people who derive some strength of meaning from the writings of poets and who seek in the poet's mind some clue to their own thoughts." (See pp. 506–9 for two poems by Shapiro.)

The contemporary Jewish writer has attempted to explain, to interpret Jewishness—not especially the Jewishness concerned with religion or custom or social setting, but rather the Jewishness of spirit which involves a particular sensibility, an intensity, and a humor which is often ironic or, as it was called in the 1960's, a "black humor": a spirit not exclusively parochial. Most of the characters in the works of writers such as Bernard Malamud, Saul Bellow, and Philip Roth are Jewish, and yet they are not necessarily so. Malamud, for example, generally uses Jewish characters to explore the themes of suffering and prevailing. But in Malamud's novel *The Natural* (1952) the central character is an Anglo-Saxon baseball player who, having no connection with Jews or Jewishness, similarly suffers and prevails. Malamud believes that a writer's purpose is not limited to a regionalism but it is rather "to keep civilization from destroying itself." And while his main characters are most often Jewish because the circumstances of his environment have made him know that group best, his themes are never "merely Jewish." For example, the central character of *The Fixer* (1966) is a Russian Jew who is persecuted by the anti-Semitic Black Hundreds group in Kiev; but the theme of this novel is universal in that it concerns an innocent human being who is the victim of injustice. Significantly, Malamud had originally intended to make the central character a Black and to set the scene in America. The story took its final form only because Malamud discovered that he could more skillfully depict a Jewish character, but the thematic statement remained the same. (See p. 441 for Malamud's story "The First Seven Years.")

Saul Bellow, like Malamud, often employs characters who are reminiscent of those in the Yiddish tales of writers such as Sholom Aleichem and Isaac Bashevis Singer: the *schlemiel* or *schlamezl* character, whose hopes and plans, despite his struggles and good intentions, usually come to no good. Both Malamud and Bellow also make use of the character of the Jewish intellectual. However, neither Malamud nor Bellow is limited to these characterizations. In novels such as *The Adventures of Augie March* (1953) and *Henderson the Rain King* (1959), for example, Bellow is concerned with a characteristically American hero: the lusty adventurer who seeks his identity through outward pursuits, as opposed to the peculiarly Jewish hero whose environment is the ghetto and who typically seeks his identity through more intellectual experiences.

Philip Roth, a younger Jewish American writer, depicts characters that are quite unlike those of Bellow and Malamud. In particular contrast to Malamud, whose Jewish characters are very often impoverished, middle-aged urban dwellers, Roth's characters are, for the most part, middle-class, young, very Americanized, and even suburbanized. Yet like the other writers, his characters' ethnic affiliations are not as important as his themes, which are at least national. "Goodbye, Columbus" is representative: his central characters are a Jewish boy and girl—he is poor and she is rich, he is romantic and she is a product of her materialistic environment. The conflict is an American one. (See p. 460 for Roth's story "Eli, the Fanatic.")

Jewish American writers, unlike those of most other groups in this text, have become an acknowledged part of the mainstream of American literature. Perhaps this is because the melting-pot theory has worked better for American Jews than it has for members of visible minority groups, i.e., "the third world"; or perhaps it is because, as Ralph Ellison has suggested, the Jewish writer has been permitted to see himself as American and, at a propitious time, has succeeded in projecting his Jewish experience as a larger experience unfolding within this pluralistic society.

AN ESSAY

Leslie Fiedler

Leslie Fiedler, born in 1917, is one of America's foremost critics. He is the author of *Love and Death in the American Novel*
(1959, 1966) and *No! In Thunder: Essays on Myth and Literature* (1960), as well as fiction such as *Nude Croquet* (1969) and
The Last Jew in America (1966). Fiedler has been a professor at
Princeton, Columbia, and the University of Vermont.

The following essay on Saul Bellow, written shortly after the
publication of Bellow's *Adventures of Augie March,* extends
beyond the subject of Bellow and his work to an examination
of the role and the accomplishments of the Jewish writer in
America.

Saul Bellow

With the publication of *Seize the Day,* Saul Bellow has become not merely a writer with whom it is possible to come to terms, but one with whom it is *necessary* to come to terms — perhaps of all our novelists the one we need most to understand, if we are to understand what the novel is doing at the present moment. Bellow has endured the almost ritual indignities of the beginning fictionist: his first novel a little over-admired and read by scarcely anyone; his second novel once more critically acclaimed, though without quite the thrill of discovery, and still almost ignored by the larger public; his third novel, thick, popular, reprinted in the paperbacks and somewhat resented by the first discoverers, who hate seeing what was exclusively theirs pass into the public domain; and now a fourth book: a collection of stories, most of which have appeared earlier, a play, and a new novella.

Suddenly, the novelist whom we have not ceased calling a "young writer" (it is a habit hard to break and the final indignity) is established and forty, a part of our lives and something for the really young to define themselves against. But it has become clear that he will continue to write, that he is not merely the author of a novel or two, but a *novelist;* and this in itself is a triumph, a rarity in recent American literary history and especially among the writers with whom we associate Bellow. We think of the whole line of Jewish-American novelists, so like him in origin and aspiration, of Daniel Fuchs and Henry Roth and Nathanael West, those poets and annalists of the thirties who did not survive their age, succumbing to death or Hollywood or a sheer exhaustion of spirit and subject. Or we think of Bellow's own contemporaries, the *Partisan Review* group, urban Jews growing up under the threat of failure and terror, the depression and Spain and the hopelessly foreseen coming of war. We remember, perhaps, Isaac Rosenfeld or H. J. Kaplan or Oscar Tarcov or Delmore Schwartz or even Lionel Trilling, who had also to be twice-born, committed first to Stalinism and then to disenchantment, but who were capable of using imaginatively only the disenchantment. And remembering these, we recall beginnings not quite fulfilled, achievements which somehow betrayed initial promises. Certain short stories remain in our minds (flanked by all those essays, those explanations and rejoinders and demonstrations of wit): Kaplan's "The Mohammedans," Rosenfeld's "The Pyramids," Schwartz's "In Dreams Begin Responsibilities," Trilling's "The Other Margaret"; but where except in *The Dangling Man* and *The Victim* and *Augie March* do the themes and motifs of the group find full novelistic expression?

We must begin to see Bellow, then, as the inheritor of a long tradition of false starts and abject retreats and gray inconclusions. There is a sense in which he fulfills the often frustrated attempt to possess the American imagination and to enter the American cultural scene of a line of Jewish fictionists which goes back beyond the postwar generation through Ben Hecht and Ludwig Lewisohn to Abe Cahan. A hundred, a thousand one-shot novelists, ephemeral successes, and baffled eccentrics stand behind him, defining a subject: the need of the Jew in America to make clear his relationship to that country in terms of belonging or protest — and a language: a speech enriched by the dialectic and joyful intellectual play of Jewish conversation.

Bellow's own story is, then, like the archetypal Jewish dream a success story; since, like the standard characters in the tales of my grandfather (socialist though he was!), the novelist, too, has "worked himself up in America." Bellow's success must not be understood, however, as exclusively his own; for he emerges at the moment when the Jews for the first time move into the center of American culture, and he must be seen in the larger context. The background is familiar enough: the gradual breaking up of the Anglo-Saxon domination of our imagination: the relentless urbanization which makes rural myths and images no longer central to our experience; the exhaustion as vital themes of the Midwest and of the movement from the provinces to New York or Chicago or Paris; the turning again from West to East, from our own heartland back to Europe; and the discovery in the Jews of a people essentially urban, essentially Europe-oriented, a ready-made image for what the American longs to or fears he is being forced to become.

On all levels in the years since World War II, the Jewish-American writer feels imposed on him the role of being The American, of registering his experience for his compatriots and for the world as The American Experience. Not only his flirtation with Communism and his disengagement, but his very sense of exclusion, his most intimate awareness of loneliness and flight are demanded of him as public symbols. The Southerner and the Jew, the homosexual out of the miasma of Mississippi and the ex-radical out of the iron landscape of Chicago and New York — these seem the exclusive alternatives, contrasting yet somehow twinned symbols of America at mid-century. *Partisan Review* becomes for Europe and *Life* magazine the mouthpiece of intellectual America, not despite but because of its tiny readership and its specially determined contributors; and in Saul Bellow a writer emerges capable of transforming its obsessions into myths.

He must not, however, be seen only in this context. His appearance as the first Jewish-American novelist to stand at the center of American literature is flanked by a host of matching successes on other levels of culture and subculture. What Saul Bellow is for highbrow literature, Salinger is for upper middlebrow, Irwin Shaw for middle middlebrow, and Herman Wouk for lower middlebrow. Even on the lowbrow levels, where there has been no such truce with antisemitism as prosperity has brought to the middle classes, two young Jews in contriving Superman have invented for the comicbooks a new version of the Hero, the first purely urban incarnation of the most ancient of mythic figures. The acceptance of Bellow as the leading novelist of his generation must be paired off with the appearance of Marjorie Morningstar on the front cover of *Time*. On all levels, the Jew is in the process of being mythicized into the representative American.

There is a temptation in all this to a kind of assimilation with the most insipid values of bourgeois life in the United States. It is to Bellow's credit that he has at once accepted the full challenge implicit in the identification of Jew with America, and yet has not succumbed to the temptation; that he has been willing to accept the burden of success without which he might have been cut off from the central subject of his time; and that he has accomplished this without essential compromise. In *Augie March,* which is the heart of his work (though technically not as successful as *The Victim* or *Seize the Day*), he has risked the final absurdity: the footloose Jewish boy, harried by urban machiavellians, the picaresque *schlimazl* out of Fuchs or Nathanael West, becomes Huck Finn; or, if you will, Huck is transformed into the footloose Jewish boy. It is hard to know which way of saying it gives a fuller sense of the absurdity and importance of the transaction. The point is, I think, that the identification saves both halves of the combination from sentimental falsification: Huck Finn, who has threatened for a long time to dissolve into the snub-nosed little rascal, barefoot and overalled; and the Jewish *schlimazl,* who becomes only too easily the liberals' insufferable victim, say, Noah Acker-man in Irwin Shaw's *The Young Lions.*

The themes of Saul Bellow are not, after all, very different from those of the middlebrow Jewish novelists in step with whom he has "worked himself up"; but in treatment they become transformed. Like Wouk or Shaw, he, too, has written a War Novel: a book about the uncertainty of intellectual and Jew face to face with a commitment to regimentation and violence. But unlike Wouk and Shaw, Bellow has not merely taken the World War I novel of pro-test and adulterated it with popular front pieties. His intellectual is not shown up like Wouk's Keefer; his Jew does not prove himself as brave and brutal as his antisemitic buddies like Shaw's Ackerman or Wouk's Greenspan, whose presumable triumphs are in fact abject surrenders. The longing to relinquish the stereotyped protest of the twenties, no longer quite believed in, is present in Bellow's *Dangling Man,* but present as a *subject:* a temptation to be con-fronted, not a value to be celebrated.

Dangling Man is not an entirely successful book; it is a little mannered, a lit-tle incoherent, obviously a first novel. But it is fresh beyond all expectation, unlike any American war book before or since; for Bellow has realized that for his generation the war itself is an anticlimax (too foreknown from a score of older novels to be really lived), that their real experience is the waiting, the dangling, the indecision before the draft. His book therefore ends, as it should, with its protagonist about to leave for camp and writing in his journal: "Hurray for regular hours! And for the supervision of the spirit! Long live regimentation!" In the purest of ironies, the slogans of accommodation are neither accepted nor rejected, but suspended.

Similarly, in *The Victim* Bellow takes up what is, perhaps, the theme *par excellence* of the liberaloid novel of the forties: antisemitism. In proletarian novels, though many were written by Jews, this was a subject only peripher-ally treated; for the Jew in the Communist movement, Judaism was the ene-my, Zionism and the Jewish religion the proper butt of satire and dissent. But Hitler had made a difference, releasing a flood of pious protests against dis-crimination; from Arthur Miller's *Focus* to John Hersey's *The Wall,* via *Gen-tlemen's Agreement, The Professor's Umbrella,* etc., Jew and Gentile alike took up the subject over and over. In a time when the Worker had been re-placed by the Little Man as a focus for undiscriminating sympathy, the Little Jew took his place beside the Little Negro, the Little Chinese, the Little Para-plegic as a favorite victim. Even what passed for War Novels were often merely anti-antisemitic fictions in disguise, the war itself being treated only as an occasion for testing a Noble Young Jew under the pressure of ignorant hostility.

In the typical middlebrow novel, it was seldom a real Jew who was ex-posed to persecution; rather some innocent gentile who by putting on glasses mysteriously came to look Jewish or some high-minded reporter only pretending to be a Jew. In part what is involved is the commercial necessity for finding a gimmick to redeem an otherwise overworked subject; but in part what is at stake is surely a confusion in the liberal, middlebrow mind about what a Jew is anyhow: a sneaking suspicion that Jew-baiting is real but Jews are imaginary, just as, to the same mind, witch-hunting is real but witches only fictions.

In Bellow's book about antisemitism, *The Victim,* once more the confusion becomes the subject. It is Asa Leventhal, not the author, who is uncertain of what it means to be a Jew, because he does not know yet what it is to be a man; and neither he nor his author will be content with the simple equation: the victim equals the Jew, the Jew the victim. In *The Victim,* Jew and antisemite are each other's prey as they are each other's beloved. At the moment when the Jew in general, when the author himself as well as his protagonist, have moved into situations of security, however tenuous, inflicting injury in their scramble to win that security, Bellow alone among our novelists has had the imagination and the sheer nerve to portray the Jew, the Little Jew, as victimizer as well as victim. Allbee may be mad, a pathological antisemite and a bum, but his charge that Leventhal's success was achieved somehow at his expense is not utter nonsense. It is the necessary antidote to the self-pity of the Jew, one part of a total ambiguous picture. In the slow, gray, low-keyed exposition of *The Victim,* Leventhal's violence and his patience, his desire to exculpate himself and his sense of guilt, his haunting by the antisemite he haunts, become for us truths, part of our awareness of our place as Jews in the American scene.

As *The Victim* is Bellow's most specifically Jewish book, *Augie March* (in this, as in all other respects, a reaction from the former) is his most generally American. Its milieu is Jewish American, its speech patterns somehow molded by Yiddish, but its theme is the native theme of *Huckleberry Finn*: the rejection of power and commitment and success, the pursuit of a primal innocence. It is a strangely non-Jewish book in being concerned not with a man's rise but with his evasion of rising; and yet even in that respect it reminds us of *David Levinsky,* of the criticism of David implicit in the text and entrusted to the Socialist characters. It is as if David had been granted a son, a grandson, to try again — to seek a more genuine Americanism of noncommittal. Certainly, Bellow's character is granted a symbolic series of sexual successes to balance off the sexual failures of Cahan's protagonist. But the socialism of Cahan does not move his descendant; it has become in the meanwhile Soviet Communism, an alternative image of material success, and has failed; so that there is left to Augie only the denial of the values of capitalism without a corresponding allegiance, a desire to flee success from scene to scene, from girl to girl, from father to father — in favor of what? The most bitter of Happy Endings as well as the most negative, the truly American Happy Ending: no reunion with the family, no ultimately happy marriage, no return to the native place — only a limitless disponibility guarded like a treasure. It is, of course, the ending of *Huckleberry Finn,* an ending which must be played out as comedy to be tolerable at all; but unlike Twain, Bellow, though he has found the proper tone for his episodes, cannot recapture it for his close. *Augie,* which begins with such rightness, such conviction, does not know how to end; shriller and shriller, wilder and wilder, it finally whirls apart in a frenzy of fake euphoria and exclamatory prose.

Seize the Day is a pendant and resolution to *Augie March*. Also a study of success and failure, this time it treats them in contemporary terms rather than classic ones, reworking directly a standard middlebrow theme. Call it "The Death of a Salesman" and think of Arthur Miller. It is the price of failure in a world dedicated to success that Bellow is dealing with now; or more precisely, the self-consciousness of failure in a world where it is not only shameful but rare; or most exactly of all, the bitterness of success and failure become pawns in the deadly game between father and son. Bellow is not very successful when he attempts to deal with the sentimental and erotic relations that are the staples of the great European novels; his women tend to be nympholeptic projections, fantasies based on girls one never had; and his husbands and wives seem convincing only at the moment of parting. But he comes into his own when he turns to the emotional transactions of males inside the family: brother and brother, son and father—or father-hating son and machiavellian surrogate father. It is the muted rage of such relationships that is the emotional stuff of his best work; and in *Seize the Day,* it is the dialogues of Tommy and his old man, Tommy and the sharper Tamkin that move us, prepare us for Tommy's bleakest encounter: with himself and the prescience of his own death.

But how, we are left asking, has Bellow made tragedy of a theme that remains in the hands of Arthur Miller sentimentality and "good theater"? It is just this magical transformation of the most travestied of middlebrow themes which is Bellow's greatest triumph. That transformation is in part the work of style, a function of language. Bellow is in no sense an experimental writer; the scraps of avant-garde technique which survive in *The Dangling Man* are purged away in *The Victim;* yet he has managed to resist the impulse to lifeless lucidity which elsewhere has taken over in a literature reacting to the linguistic experiments of the twenties. There is always the sense of a living voice in his prose, for his books are all dramatic; and though this sometimes means a deliberate muting of rhetoric for the sake of characterization, it just as often provides occasions for a release of full virtuosity. Muted or released, his language is never dull or merely expedient, but always moves under tension, toward or away from a kind of rich, crazy poetry, a juxtaposition of high and low style, elegance and slang, unlike anything else in English except *Moby Dick,* though at the same time not unrelated in range and variety to spoken Yiddish.

Since Bellow's style is based on a certain conversational ideal at once intellectual and informal, dialogue is for him necessarily a distillation of his strongest effects. Sometimes one feels his characters' speeches as the main events of the books in which they occur; certainly they have the impact of words exchanged among Jews, that is to say, the impact of actions, not merely overheard but *felt,* like kisses or blows. Implicit in the direction of his style is a desire to encompass a world larger, richer, more disorderly and untrammeled than that of any other writer of his generation; it is this which impels him toward the picaresque, the sprawling, episodic manner of *Augie March.* But there is a counter impulse in him toward the tight, rigidly organized, underplayed style of *The Victim:* and at his best, I think, as in *Seize the*

Day, an ability to balance the two tendencies against each other: hysteria and catalepsy, the centrifugal and the centripetal in a sort of perilous rest.

But the triumphs of Bellow are not mere triumphs of style; sometimes indeed they must survive the collapse of that style into mannerism, mechanical self-parody. Beyond an ear, Bellow possesses a fortunate negative talent: a constitutional inability to dissolve his characters into their representative types, to compromise their individuality for the sake of a point. It is not merely that his protagonists refuse to blur into the generalized Little People, the Victims of sentimental liberalism; but that they are themselves portrayed as being conscious of their struggle against such debasement. That struggle is, indeed, the essence of their self-consciousness, their self-definition. Their invariable loneliness is felt by them and by us not only as a function of urban life and the atomization of culture, but as something *willed:* the condition and result of their search to know what they are.

More, perhaps, than any other recent novelist, Bellow is aware that the collapse of the proletarian novel, which marks the starting place of his own art, has meant more than the disappearance of a convention in the history of fiction. With the disappearance of the proletarian novel as a form there has taken place the gradual dissolution of the last widely shared definition of man: man as the product of society. If man seems at the moment extraordinarily lonely, it is not only because he finds it hard to communicate with his fellows, but because he has lost touch with any overarching definition of himself.

This Bellow realizes; as he realizes that it is precisely in such loneliness, once man learns not to endure but to *become* that loneliness, that man can rediscover his identity and his fellowship with others. We recognize the Bellow character because he is openly what we are in secret, because he is us without our customary defenses. Such a protagonist lives nowhere except in the City; he camps temporarily in boardinghouses or lonely hotels, sits by himself at the corner table of some seedy restaurant or climbs backbreaking stairways in search of another whose existence no one will admit. He is the man whose wife is off visiting her mother or has just left him; the man who returns to find his house in disorder or inhabited by a squalid derelict; the man who flees his room to follow the funeral of someone he never knew.

He is essential man, man stripped of success and belongingness, even of failure; he is man disowned by his father, unrecognized by his son, man without woman, man face to face with himself, which means for Bellow face to face not with a fact but a question: "What am I?" To which the only answer is: "He who asks!" But such a man is at once the Jew in perpetual exile and Huck Finn in whom are blended with perfect irony the twin American beliefs that the answer to all questions is always over the next horizon and that there is no answer now or ever.

Suggestions for Discussion

1. Fiedler suggests Bellow is "the inheritor of a long tradition" and that his story is "like the archetypal Jewish dream, a success story." Discuss Fiedler's reasons for making these statements.

2. This essay was first published in 1957. How many of the writers discussed have remained important through the 1970's?

3. What seems to be Fiedler's attitude toward the treatment of anti-Semitism in the novels of the forties?

4. What does Fiedler regard as Saul Bellow's "greatest triumph"? How has Bellow distinguished himself in character portrayal?

Suggestions for Writing and Comparison

1. After reading the selection from *Augie March* in this chapter, discuss the points on which you agree or disagree with Fiedler.

2. Review the authors in this chapter who are younger than Saul Bellow. Do they seem to be continuing in the tradition to which Fiedler believes Bellow belongs? Does there seem to be a movement away from the themes that preoccupy Bellow?

STORIES

Isaac Bashevis Singer

Isaac Bashevis Singer, born in Poland in 1904, has lived in the United States since 1935. For many years he has been on the staff of the *Jewish Daily Forward*, the leading Yiddish American newspaper. Singer has written most of his work in Yiddish, and all of his major books—which include the novels *The Family Moskat* (1950) and *The Magician of Lublin* (1960), the short-story collections *The Spinoza of Market Street* (1961) and *Gimpel the Fool* (1965), and the memoir *In My Father's Court* (1966)—have been translated into English. His work has been recognized by various grants and awards, and in 1965 he was elected to the National Institute of Arts and Letters. Kenneth Rexroth has called Singer "one of the most remarkable American authors who has ever lived."

"The Little Shoemakers," which is set in both a ghetto of Eastern Europe and a suburb of America, takes as its protagonist a typical Singer character, the simple, pious Jew who relates to the world in terms of his *shtetl* experience and his religious habits. Singer's depictions of the European ghetto and those who peopled it before the advent of Hitler have been compared to Sholom Aleichem's and mark Singer as a writer in the older Yiddish tradition.

The Little Shoemakers

I
The Shoemakers and Their Family Tree

The family of the little shoemakers was famous not only in Frampol but in the outlying district—in Yonev, Kreshev, Bilgoray, and even in Zamoshoh. Abba Shuster, the founder of the line, appeared in Frampol some time after Chmielnitzki's pogroms. He bought himself a plot of ground on the stubby hill behind the butcher stalls, and there he built a house that remained standing until just the other day. Not that it was in such fine condition—the stone foundation settled, the small windows warped, and the shingled roof turned a moldy green and was hung with swallows' nests. The door, moreover, sank into the ground; the banisters became bowlegged; and instead of stepping up onto the threshold, one was obliged to step down. All the same, it did survive the innumerable fires that devastated Frampol in the early days. But the rafters were so rotten that mushrooms grew on them, and when wood dust was needed to staunch the blood of a circumcision, one had only to break off a piece of the outer wall and rub it between one's fingers. The roof, pitched so steeply that the chimneysweep was unable to climb onto it to look after the chimney, was always catching fire from the sparks. It was only by the grace of God that the house was not overtaken by disaster.

The name of Abba Shuster is recorded, on parchment, in the annals of the Frampol Jewish community. It was his custom to make six pairs of shoes every year for distribution among widows and orphans; in recognition of his philanthropy the synagogue called him to the reading of the Torah under the honorific title, *Murenu*, meaning "our teacher."

His stone in the old cemetery had vanished, but the shoemakers knew a sign for the grave—nearby grew a hazelnut tree. According to the old wives, the tree sprang from Reb Abba's beard.

Reb Abba had five sons; they settled, all but one, in the neighboring towns; only Getzel remained in Frampol. He continued his father's charitable practice of making shoes for the poor, and he too was active in the gravediggers' brotherhood.

The annals go on to say that Getzel had a son, Godel, and that to Godel was born Treitel, and to Treitel, Gimpel. The shoemaker's art was handed down from one generation to the next. A principle was fast established in the family, requiring the eldest son to remain at home and succeed his father at the workbench.

The shoemakers resembled one another. They were all short, sandy-haired, and sound, honest workmen. The people of Frampol believed that Reb Abba, the head of the line, had learned shoemaking from a master of the craft in Brod, who divulged to him the secret of strengthening leather and making it durable. In the cellar of their house the little shoemakers kept a vat for soaking hides. God knows what strange chemicals they added to the tanning fluid. They did not disclose the formula to outsiders, and it was handed on from father to son.

As it is not our business to deal with all the generations of the little shoemakers, we will confine ourselves to the last three. Reb Lippe remained without heir till his old age, and it was taken for a certainty that the line would end with him. But when he was in his late sixties his wife died and he married an overripe virgin, a milkmaid, who bore him six children. The eldest son, Feivel, was quite well to do. He was prominent in community affairs, attended all the important meetings, and for years served as sexton of the tailors' synagogue. It was the custom in this synagogue to select a new sexton every Simchath Torah. The man so selected was honored by having a pumpkin placed on his head; the pumpkin was set with lighted candles, and the lucky fellow was led about from house to house and refreshed at each stop with wine and strudel or honeycakes. However, Reb Feivel happened to die on Simchath Torah, the day of rejoicing over the Law, while dutifully making these rounds; he fell flat in the market place, and there was no reviving him. Because Feivel had been a notable philanthropist, the rabbi who conducted his services declared that the candles he had borne on his head would light his way to Paradise. The will found in his strongbox requested that when he was carried to the cemetery, a hammer, an awl, and a last should be laid on the black cloth over his coffin, in sign of the fact that he was a man of peaceful industry who never cheated his customers. His will was done.

Feivel's eldest son was called Abba, after the founder. Like the rest of his stock, he was short and thickset, with a broad yellow beard, and a high fore-head lined with wrinkles, such as only rabbis and shoemakers have. His eyes were also yellow, and the over-all impression he created was that of a sulky hen. Nevertheless he was a clever workman, charitable like his forebears, and unequaled in Frampol as a man of his word. He would never make a promise unless he was sure he could fulfill it; when he was not sure he said: who knows, God willing, or maybe. Furthermore he was a man of some learning. Every day he read a chapter of the Torah in Yiddish translation and occupied his free time with chapbooks. Abba never missed a single sermon of the trav-eling preachers who came to town, and he was especially fond of the Biblical passages which were read in the synagogue during the winter months. When his wife, Pesha, read to him, of a Sabbath, from the Yiddish translation of the stories in the Book of Genesis, he would imagine that he was Noah, and that his sons were Shem, Ham, and Japheth. Or else he would see himself in the image of Abraham, Isaac, or Jacob. He often thought that if the Almighty were to call on him to sacrifice his eldest son, Gimpel, he would rise early in the morning and carry out his commands without delay. Certainly he would have left Poland and the house of his birth and gone wandering over the earth where God sent him. He knew the story of Joseph and his brothers by heart, but he never tired of reading it over again. He envied the ancients because the King of the Universe revealed Himself to them and performed miracles for their sake, but consoled himself by thinking that from him, Abba, to the Patriarchs, there stretched an unbroken chain of generations—as if he too were part of the Bible. He sprang from Jacob's loins; he and his sons were of the seed whose number had become like the sand and the stars. He was living in exile because the Jews of the Holy Land had sinned, but he awaited the Redemption, and he would be ready when the time came.

Abba was by far the best shoemaker in Frampol. His boots were always a perfect fit, never too tight or too roomy. People who suffered from chilblains, corns, or varicose veins were especially pleased with his work, claiming that his shoes relieved them. He despised the new styles, the gimcrack boots and slippers with fancy heels and poorly stitched soles that fell apart with the first rain. His customers were respectable burghers of Frampol or peasants from the surrounding villages, and they deserved the best. He took their measurements with a knotted string, as in the old days. Most of the Frampol women wore wigs, but his wife, Pesha, covered her head with a bonnet as well. She bore him seven sons, and he named them after his forefathers — Gimpel, Getzel, Treitel, Godel, Feivel, Lippe, and Chananiah. They were all short and sandy-haired like their father. Abba predicted that he would turn them into shoemakers, and as a man of his word he let them look on at the workbench while they were still quite young, and at times taught them the old maxim — good work is never wasted.

He spent sixteen hours a day at the bench, a sack spread on his knees, gouging holes with the awl, sewing with a wire needle, tinting and polishing the leather or scraping it with a piece of glass; and while he worked he hummed snatches from the canticles of the Days of Awe. Usually the cat huddled nearby and watched the proceedings as though she were looking after him. Her mother and grandmother had caught mice, in their time, for the little shoemakers. Abba could look down the hill through the window and see the whole town and a considerable distance beyond, as far as the road to Bilgoray and the pine woods. He observed the groups of matrons who gathered every morning at the butcher stalls and the young men and idlers who went in and out of the courtyard of the synagogue; the girls going to the pump to draw water for tea, and the women hurrying at dusk to the ritual bath.

Evenings, when the sun was setting, the house would be pervaded by a dusky glow. Rays of light danced in the corners, flicked across the ceiling, and set Abba's beard gleaming with the color of spun gold. Pesha, Abba's wife, would be cooking *kasha* and soup in the kitchen, the children would be playing, neighboring women and girls would go in and out of the house. Abba would rise from his work, wash his hands, put on his long coat, and go off to the tailors' synagogue for evening prayers. He knew that the wide world was full of strange cities and distant lands, that Frampol was actually no bigger than a dot in a small prayer book; but it seemed to him that his little town was the navel of the universe and that his own house stood at the very center. He often thought that when the Messiah came to lead the Jews to the Land of Israel, he, Abba, would stay behind in Frampol, in his own house, on his own hill. Only on the Sabbath and on Holy Days would he step into a cloud and let himself be flown to Jerusalem.

II
Abba and His Seven Sons

Since Gimpel was the eldest, and therefore destined to succeed his father, he came foremost in Abba's concern. He sent him to the best Hebrew teachers and even hired a tutor who taught him the elements of Yiddish, Polish, Russian, and arithmetic. Abba himself led the boy down into the cellar and showed him the formula for adding chemicals and various kinds of bark to the tanning fluid. He revealed to him that in most cases the right foot is larger than the left, and that the source of all trouble in the fitting of shoes is usually to be found in the big toes. Then he taught Gimpel the principles for cutting soles and inner soles, snub-toed and pointed shoes, high heels and low; and for fitting customers with flat feet, bunions, hammer toes, and calluses.

On Fridays, when there was always a rush of work to get out, the older boys would leave *cheder* at ten in the morning and help their father in the shop. Pesha baked *chalah* and prepared their lunch. She would grasp the first loaf and carry it, hot from the oven, blowing on it all the while and tossing it from hand to hand, to show it to Abba, holding it up, front and back, till he nodded approval. Then she would return with a ladle and let him sample the fish soup, or ask him to taste a crumb of freshly baked cake. Pesha valued his judgment. When she went to buy cloth for herself or the children she brought home swatches for him to choose. Even before going to the butcher she asked his opinion—what should she get, breast or roast, flank or ribs? She consulted him not out of fear or because she had no mind of her own, but simply be-cause she had learned that he always knew what he was talking about. Even when she was sure he was wrong, he would turn out to be right, after all. He never browbeat her, but merely cast a glance to let her know when she was being a fool. This was also the way he handled the children. A strap hung on the wall, but he seldom made use of it; he had his way by kindness. Even strangers respected him. The merchants sold him hides at a fair price and presented no objections when he asked for credit. His own customers trusted him and paid his prices without a murmur. He was always called sixth to the reading of the Torah in the tailors' synagogue—a considerable honor—and when he pledged or was assessed for money, it was never necessary to re-mind him. He paid up, without fail, right after the Sabbath. The town soon learned of his virtues, and though he was nothing but a plain shoemaker and, if the truth be told, something of an ignoramus, they treated him as they would a distinguished man.

When Gimpel turned thirteen, Abba girded the boy's loins in sackcloth and put him to work at the bench. After Gimpel, Getzel, Treitel, Godel, and Feivel became apprentices. Though they were his own sons and he supported them out of his earnings, he nevertheless paid them a wage. The two young-est boys, Lippe and Chananiah, were still attending the elementary *cheder*, but they too lent a hand at hammering pegs. Abba and Pesha were proud of them. In the morning the six workers trooped into the kitchen for breakfast, washed their six pairs of hands with the appropriate benediction, and their six mouths chewed the roasted groats and corn bread.

Abba loved to place his two youngest boys one on each knee, and sing an old Frampol song to them:

> *"A mother had*
> *Ten little boys,*
> *Oh, Lord, ten little boys!*
>
> *The first one was Avremele,*
> *The second one was Berele,*
> *The third one was called Gimpele,*
> *The fourth one was called Dovid'l,*
> *The fifth one was called Hershele . . ."*

And all the boys came in on the chorus:

"Oh, Lord, Hershele!"

Now that he had apprentices, Abba turned out more work, and his income grew. Living was cheap in Frampol, and since the peasants often made him a present of a measure of corn or a roll of butter, a sack of potatoes or a pot of honey, a hen or a goose, he was able to save some money on food. As their prosperity increased, Pesha began to talk of rebuilding the house. The rooms were too narrow, the ceiling was too low. The floor shook underfoot. Plaster was peeling off the walls, and all sorts of maggots and worms crawled through the woodwork. They lived in constant fear that the ceiling would fall on their heads. Even though they kept a cat, the place was infested with mice. Pesha insisted that they tear down this ruin and build a larger house.

Abba did not immediately say no. He told his wife he would think it over. But after doing so, he expressed the opinion that he would rather keep things as they were. First of all, he was afraid to tear down the house, because this might bring bad luck. Second, he feared the evil eye — people were grudging and envious enough. Third, he found it hard to part with the home in which his parents and grandparents, and the whole family, stretching back for generations, had lived and died. He knew every corner of the house, each crack and wrinkle. When one layer of paint peeled off the wall, another, of a different color, was exposed; and behind this layer, still another. The walls were like an album in which the fortunes of the family had been recorded. The attic was stuffed with heirlooms — tables and chairs, cobbler's benches and lasts, whetstones and knives, old clothes, pots, pans, bedding, salting boards, cradles. Sacks full of torn prayer books lay spilled on the floor.

Abba loved to climb up to the attic on a hot summer's day. Spiders spun great webs, and the sunlight filtering in through cracks, fell upon the threads in rainbows. Everything lay under a thick coat of dust. When he listened attentively he would hear a whispering, a murmuring and soft scratching, as of some unseen creature engaged in endless activity, conversing in an unearthly tongue. He was sure that the souls of his forefathers kept watch over the house. In much the same way he loved the ground on which it stood. The weeds were as high as a man's head. There was a dense growth of hairy and brambly vegetation all about the place — the very leaves and twigs would catch hold of one's clothing as though with teeth and claws. Flies and midges swarmed in the air and the ground crawled with worms and snakes of all descriptions. Ants had raised their hills in this thicket; field mice had dug their holes. A pear tree grew in the midst of this wilderness; every year, at the time of the Feast of the Tabernacle, it yielded small fruit with the taste and hardness of wood. Birds and bees flew over this jungle, great big golden-bellied flies. Toadstools sprang up after each rain. The ground was unkept, but an unseen hand guarded its fertility.

When Abba stood here looking up at the summer sky, losing himself in contemplation of the clouds, shaped like sailboats, flocks of sheep, brooms, and elephant herds, he felt the presence of God, His providence and His mercy. He could virtually see the Almighty seated on His throne of glory, the earth serving Him as a footstool. Satan was vanquished; the angels sang hymns. The Book of Memory in which were recorded all the deeds of men lay open. From time to time, at sunset, it even seemed to Abba that he saw the river of fire in the nether world. Flames leaped up from the burning coals; a wave of fire rose, flooding the shores. When he listened closely he was sure he heard the muffled cries of sinners and the derisive laughter of the evil host.

No, this was good enough for Abba Shuster. There was nothing to change. Let everything stand as it had stood for ages, until he lived out his allotted time and was buried in the cemetery among his ancestors, who had shod the sacred community and whose good name was preserved not only in Frampol but in the surrounding district.

III
Gimpel Emigrates to America

Therefore the proverb says: Man proposes, God disposes.

One day while Abba was working on a boot, his eldest son, Gimpel, came into the shop. His freckled face was heated, his sandy hair disheveled under the skullcap. Instead of taking his place at the bench, he stopped at his father's side, regarded him hesitantly, and at last said, "Father, I must tell you something."

"Well, I'm not stopping you," replied Abba.

"Father," he cried, "I'm going to America."

Abba dropped his work. This was the last thing he expected to hear, and up went his eyebrows.

"What happened? Did you rob someone? Did you get into a fight?"

"No, Father."

"Then why are you running away?"

"There's no future for me in Frampol."

"Why not? You know a trade. God willing, you'll marry some day. You have everything to look forward to."

"I'm sick of small towns; I'm sick of the people. This is nothing but a stinking swamp."

"When they get around to draining it," said Abba, "there won't be any more swamp."

"No, Father, that's not what I mean."

"Then what do you mean?" cried Abba angrily. "Speak up!"

The boy spoke up, but Abba couldn't understand a word of it. He laid into synagogue and state with such venom, Abba could only imagine that the poor soul was possessed: the Hebrew teachers beat the children; the women empty their slop pails right outside the door; the shopkeepers loiter in the streets; there are no toilets anywhere, and the public relieves itself as it pleases, behind the bathhouse or out in the open, encouraging epidemics and plagues. He made fun of Ezreal the Healer and of Mecheles the Marriage Broker, nor did he spare the rabbinical court and the bath attendant, the washerwoman and the overseer of the poorhouse, the professions and the benevolent societies.

At first Abba was afraid that the boy had lost his mind, but the longer he continued his harangue, the clearer it became that he had strayed from the path of righteousness. Jacob Reifman, the atheist, used to hold forth in Shebreshin, not far from Frampol. A pupil of his, a detractor of Israel, was in the habit of visiting an aunt in Frampol and had gathered quite a following among the good-for-nothings. It had never occurred to Abba that his Gimpel might fall in with this gang.

"What do you say, Father?" asked Gimpel.

Abba thought it over. He knew that there was no use arguing with Gimpel, and he remembered the proverb: A rotten apple spoils the barrel. "Well," he replied, "what can I do? If you want to go, go. I won't stop you."

And he resumed his work.

But Pesha did not give in so easily. She begged Gimpel not to go so far away; she wept and implored him not to bring shame on the family. She even ran to the cemetery, to the graves of her forefathers, to seek the intercession of the dead. But she was finally convinced that Abba was right: it was no use arguing. Gimpel's face had turned hard as leather, and a mean light showed in his yellow eyes. He had become a stranger in his own home. He spent that night out with friends, and returned in the morning to pack his prayer shawl and phylacteries, a few shirts, a blanket, and some hard-boiled eggs—and he was all set to go. He had saved enough money for passage. When his mother saw that it was settled, she urged him to take at least a jar of preserves, a bottle of cherry juice, bedding, pillows. But Gimpel refused. He was going to steal over the border into Germany, and he stood a better chance if he traveled light. In short, he kissed his mother, said good-by to his brothers and friends, and off he went. Abba, not wanting to part with his son in anger, took him in the wagon to the station at Reivetz. The train arrived in the middle of the night with a hissing and whistling, a racket and din. Abba took the headlights of the locomotive for the eyes of a hideous devil, and shied away from the funnels with their columns of sparks and smoke and their clouds of steam. The blinding lights only intensified the darkness. Gimpel ran around with his baggage like a madman, and his father ran after him. At the last moment the boy kissed his father's hand, and Abba called after him, into the darkness, "Good luck! Don't forsake your religion!"

The train pulled out, leaving a smell of smoke in Abba's nostrils and a ringing in his ears. The earth trembled under his feet. As though the boy had been dragged off by demons! When he returned home and Pesha fell on him, weeping, he said to her, "The Lord gave and the Lord has taken away. . . ."

■ Months passed without word from Gimpel. Abba knew that this was the way with young men when they leave home—they forget their dearest ones. As the proverb says: Out of sight, out of mind. He doubted that he would ever hear from him, but one day a letter came from America. Abba recognized his son's handwriting. Gimpel wrote that he crossed the border safely, that he saw many strange cities and spent four weeks on board ship, living on potatoes and herring because he did not want to touch improper food. The ocean was very deep and the waves as high as the sky. He saw flying fish but no mermaids or mermen, and he did not hear them singing. New York is a big city, the houses reach into the clouds. The trains go over the roofs. The gentiles speak English. No one walks with his eyes on the ground, everybody holds his head high. He met a lot of his countrymen in New York; they all wear short coats. He too. The trade he learned at home has come in very handy. He is *all right*; he is earning a living. He will write again, a long letter.

He kisses his father and mother and his brothers, and sends regards to his friends.

A friendly letter after all.

In his second letter Gimpel announced that he had fallen in love with a girl and bought her a diamond ring. Her name is Bessie; she comes from Rumania; and she works *at dresses.* Abba put on his spectacles with the brass frames and spent a long time puzzling this out. Where did the boy learn so many English words? The third letter stated that he was married and that *a reverend* had performed the service. He inclosed a snapshot of himself and wife.

Abba could not believe it. His son was wearing a gentleman's coat and a high hat. The bride was dressed like a countess in a white dress, with train and veil; she held a bouquet of flowers in her hand. Pesha took one look at the snapshot and began to cry. Gimpel's brothers gaped. Neighbors came running, and friends from all over town; they could have sworn that Gimpel had been spirited away by magic to a land of gold, where he had taken a princess to wife—just as in the storybooks the pack merchants brought to town.

To make a long story short, Gimpel induced Getzel to come to America, and Getzel brought over Treitel; Godel followed Treitel, and Feivel, Godel; and then all five brothers brought the young Lippe and Chananiah across. Pesha lived only for the mail. She fastened a charity box to the doorpost, and whenever a letter came she dropped a coin through the slot. Abba worked all alone. He no longer needed apprentices because he now had few expenses and could afford to earn less; in fact, he could have given up work altogether, as his sons sent him money from abroad. Nevertheless he rose at his usual early hour and remained at the bench until late in the evening. His hammer sounded away, joined by the cricket on the hearth, the mouse in its hole, the shingles crackling on the roof. But his mind reeled. For generations the little shoemakers had lived in Frampol. Suddenly the birds had flown the coop. Was this a punishment, a judgment, on him? Did it make sense?

Abba bored a hole, stuck in a peg, and murmured, "So—you, Abba, know what you're doing and God does not? Shame on you, fool! His will be done. Amen!"

IV
The Sack of Frampol

Almost forty years went by. Pesha had long since died of cholera, during the Austrian occupation. And Abba's sons had grown rich in America. They wrote every week, begging him to come and join them, but he remained in Frampol, in the same old house on the stubby hill. His own grave lay ready, next to Pesha's, among the little shoemakers; the stone had already been raised; only the date was missing. Abba put up a bench by the side of her grave, and on the eve of Rosh Hashonoh or during fasts, he went there to pray and read Lamentations. He loved it in the cemetery. The sky was so much clearer and loftier than in town, and a great, meaningful silence rose from the consecrated ground and the old gravestone overgrown with moss. He loved to sit and look at the tall white birches, which trembled even when no breeze blew, and at the crows balancing in the branches, like black fruit.

Before she died Pesha made him promise that he would not remarry and that he would come regularly to her grave with news of the children. He kept his promise. He would stretch out alongside the mound and whisper into her ear, as if she were still alive, "Gimpel has another grandchild. Getzel's youngest daughter is engaged, thank God. . . ."

The house on the hill was nearly in ruins. The beams had rotted away, and the roof had to be supported by stone posts. Two of the three windows were boarded over because it was no longer possible to fit glass to the frames. The floor was all but gone, and the bare ground lay exposed to the feet. The pear tree in the garden had withered; the trunk and branches were covered with scales. The garden itself was now overgrown with poisonous berries and grapes, and there was a profusion of the burrs that children throw about on Tishe b'Av. People swore they saw strange fires burning there at night, and claimed that the attic was full of bats which fly into girls' hair. Be that as it may, an owl certainly did hoot somewhere near the house. The neighbors repeatedly warned Abba to move out of this ruin before it was too late—the least wind might knock it over. They pleaded with him to give up working —his sons were showering him with money. But Abba stubbornly rose at dawn and continued at the shoemaker's bench. Although yellow hair does not readily change color, Abba's beard had turned completely white, and the white, staining, had turned yellow again. His brows had sprouted like brushes and hid his eyes, and his high forehead was like a piece of yellow parchment. But he had not lost his touch. He could still turn out a stout shoe with a broad heel, even if it did take a little longer. He bored holes with the awl, stitched with the needle, hammered his pegs, and in a hoarse voice sang the old shoemaker's song:

> "*A mother bought a billy goat,*
> *The* shochet *killed the billy goat,*
> *Oh, Lord, the billy goat!*
>
> *Avremele took its ears,*
> *Berele took its lung,*
> *Gimpele took the gullet,*
> *And Dovid'l took the tongue,*
> *Hershele took the neck. . . ."*

As there was no one to join him, he now sang the chorus alone:

> "*Oh, Lord, the billy goat!*"

His friends urged him to hire a servant, but he would not take a strange woman into the house. Occasionally one of the neighbor women came in to sweep and dust, but even this was too much for him. He got used to being alone. He learned to cook for himself and would prepare soup on the tripod, and on Fridays even put up the pudding for the Sabbath. Best of all, he liked to sit alone at the bench and follow the course of his thoughts, which had become more and more tangled with the years. Day and night he carried on conversations with himself. One voice asked questions, the other answered. Clever words came to his mind, sharp, timely expressions full of the wisdom of age, as though his grandfathers had come to life again and were conducting their endless disputations inside his head on matters pertaining to this world and the next. All his thoughts ran on one theme: What is life and what is death, what is time that goes on without stopping, and how far away is America? His eyes would close; the hammer would fall out of his hand; but he would still hear the cobbler's characteristic rapping—a soft tap, a louder one, and a third, louder still—as if a ghost sat at his side, mending unseen shoes. When one of the neighbors asked him why he did not go to join his sons, he would point to the heap on the bench and say, "*Nu,* and the shoes? Who will mend them?"

Years passed, and he had no idea how or where they vanished. Traveling preachers passed through Frampol with disturbing news of the outside world. In the tailors' synagogue, which Abba still attended, the young men spoke of war and anti-Semitic decrees, of Jews flocking to Palestine. Peasants who had been Abba's customers for years suddenly deserted him and took their trade to Polish shoemakers. And one day the old man heard that a new world war was imminent. Hitler—may his name vanish!—had raised his legions of barbarians and was threatening to grab up Poland. This scourge of Israel had expelled the Jews from Germany, as in the days of Spain. The old man thought of the Messiah and became terribly excited. Who knows? Perhaps this was the battle of Gog and Magog? Maybe the Messiah really was coming and the dead would rise again! He saw the graves opening and the little shoemakers stepping forth—Abba, Getzel, Treitel, Gimpel, his grandfather, his own father. He called them all into his house and set out brandy and cakes. His wife, Pesha, was ashamed to find the house in such condition, but "Never mind," he assured her, "we'll get someone to sweep up. As long as we're all together!" Suddenly a cloud appears, envelops the town of Frampol —synagogue, House of Study, ritual bath, all the Jewish homes, his own among them—and carries the whole settlement off to the Holy Land. Imagine his amazement when he encounters his sons from America. They fall at his feet, crying, "Forgive us, Father!"

When Abba pictured this event his hammer quickened in tempo. He saw the little shoemakers dress for the Sabbath in silks and satins, in flowing robes with broad sashes, and go forth rejoicing in Jerusalem. They pray in the Temple of Solomon, drink the wine of Paradise, and eat of the mighty steer and Leviathan. The ancient Jochanan the Shoemaker, renowned for his piety and wisdom, greets the family and engages them in a discussion of the Torah and shoemaking. Sabbath over, the whole clan returns to Frampol, which has become part of the Land of Israel, and re-enters the old home. Even though the house is as small as ever, it has miraculously grown roomy enough, like the hide of a deer, as it is written in the Book. They all work at one bench, Abbas, Gimpels, Getzels, Godels, the Treitels and the Lippes, sewing golden sandals for the daughters of Zion and lordly boots for the sons. The Messiah himself calls on the little shoemakers and has them take his measure for a pair of silken slippers.

One morning, while Abba was wandering among his thoughts, he heard a tremendous crash. The old man shook in his bones: the blast of the Messiah's trumpet! He dropped the boot he had been working on and ran out in ecstasy. But it was not Elijah the Prophet proclaiming the Messiah. Nazi planes were bombing Frampol. Panic spread through the town. A bomb fell near the synagogue, so loud that Abba felt his brain shudder in his skull. Hell opened before him. There was a blaze of lightning, followed by a blast that illuminated all of Frampol. A black cloud rose over the courtyard of the synagogue. Flocks of birds flapped about in the sky. The forest was burning. Looking down from his hill, Abba saw the orchards under great columns of smoke. The apple trees were blossoming and burning. Several men who stood near him threw themselves down on the ground and shouted to him to do the same. He did not hear them; they were moving their lips in dumbshow. Shaking with fright, his knees knocking together, he re-entered the house and packed a sack with his prayer shawl and phylacteries, a shirt, his shoemaker's tools, and the paper money he had put away in the straw mattress. Then he took up a stick, kissed the *mezzuzah*, and walked out the door. It was a miracle that he was not killed; the house caught fire the moment he left. The roof swung out like a lid, uncovering the attic with its treasures. The walls collapsed. Abba turned about and saw the shelf of sacred books go up in flames. The blackened pages turned in the air, glowing with fiery letters like the Torah given to the Jews on Mount Sinai.

V
Across the Ocean

From that day on, Abba's life was transformed beyond recognition – it was like a story he had read in the Bible, a fantastic tale heard from the lips of a visiting preacher. He had abandoned the house of his forefathers and the place of his birth and, staff in hand, gone wandering into the world like the Patriarch Abraham. The havoc in Frampol and the surrounding villages brought Sodom and Gomorrah to mind, burning like a fiery furnace. He spent his nights in the cemetery together with the other Jews, lying with his head on a gravestone – he too, as Jacob did at Beth-El, on the way from Beer Sheba to Haran.

On Rosh Hashonoh the Frampol Jews held services in the forest, with Abba leading the most solemn prayer of the Eighteen Benedictions because he was the only one with a prayer shawl. He stood under a pine tree, which served as an altar, and in a hoarse voice intoned the litany of the Days of Awe. A cuckoo and a woodpecker accompanied him, and all the birds roundabout twittered, whistled, and screeched. Late summer gossamers wafted through the air and trailed onto Abba's beard. From time to time a lowing sounded through the forest, like a blast on the ram's horn. As the Day of Atonement drew near, the Jews of Frampol rose at midnight to say the prayer for forgiveness, reciting it in fragments, whatever they could remember. The horses in the surrounding pastures whinnied and neighed, frogs croaked in the cool night. Distant gunfire sounded intermittently; the clouds shone red. Meteors fell; flashes of lightning played across the sky. Half-starved little children, exhausted from crying, took sick and died in their mothers' arms. There were many burials in the open fields. A woman gave birth.

Abba felt he had become his own great-great-grandfather, who had fled Chmielnitzki's pogroms, and whose name is recorded in the annals of Frampol. He was ready to offer himself in Sanctification of the Name. He dreamed of priests and Inquisitions, and when the wind blew among the branches he heard martyred Jews crying out, "Hear, O Israel, the Lord our God, the Lord is One!"

Fortunately Abba was able to help a good many Jews with his money and shoemaker's tools. With the money they hired wagons and fled south, toward Rumania; but often they had to walk long distances, and their shoes gave out. Abba would stop under a tree and take up his tools. With God's help, they surmounted danger and crossed the Rumanian frontier at night. The next morning, the day before Yom Kippur, an old widow took Abba into her house. A telegram was sent to Abba's sons in America, informing them that their father was safe.

You may be sure that Abba's sons moved heaven and earth to rescue the old man. When they learned of his whereabouts they ran to Washington and with great difficulty obtained a visa for him; then they wired a sum of money to the consul in Bucharest, begging him to help their father. The consul sent a courier to Abba, and he was put on the train to Bucharest. There he was held a week, then transferred to an Italian seaport, where he was shorn and deloused and had his clothes steamed. He was put on board the last ship for the United States.

It was a long and severe journey. The train from Rumania to Italy dragged on, uphill and down, for thirty-six hours. He was given food, but for fear of touching anything ritually unclean he ate nothing at all. His phylacteries and prayer shawl got lost, and with them he lost all track of time and could no longer distinguish between Sabbath and weekdays. Apparently he was the only Jewish passenger on board. There was a man on the ship who spoke German, but Abba could not understand him.

It was a stormy crossing. Abba spent almost the whole time lying down, and frequently vomited gall, though he took nothing but dry crusts and water. He would doze off and wake to the sound of the engines throbbing day and night, to the long, threatening signal blasts, which reeked of fire and brimstone. The door of his cabin was constantly slamming to and fro, as though an imp were swinging on it. The glassware in the cupboard trembled and danced; the walls shook; the deck rocked like a cradle.

During the day Abba kept watch at the porthole over his bunk. The ship would leap up as if mounting the sky, and the torn sky would fall as though the world were returning to original chaos. Then the ship would plunge back into the ocean, and once again the firmament would be divided from the waters, as in the Book of Genesis. The waves were a sulphurous yellow and black. Now they would saw-tooth out to the horizon like a mountain range, reminding Abba of the Psalmist's words: "The mountains skipped like rams, the little hills like lambs." Then they would come heaving back, as in the miraculous Parting of the Waters. Abba had little learning, but Biblical references ran through his mind, and he saw himself as the prophet Jonah, who fled before God. He too lay in the belly of a whale and, like Jonah, prayed to God for deliverance. Then it would seem to him that this was not ocean but limitless desert, crawling with serpents, monsters, and dragons, as it is written in Deuteronomy. He hardly slept a wink at night. When he got up to relieve himself, he would feel faint and lose his balance. With great difficulty he would regain his feet and, his knees buckling under, go wandering, lost, down the narrow, winding corridor, groaning and calling for help until a sailor led him back to the cabin. Whenever this happened he was sure that he was dying. He would not even receive decent Jewish burial, but be dumped in the ocean. And he made his confession, beating his knotty fist on his chest and exclaiming, "Forgive me, Father!"

Just as he was unable to remember when he began his voyage, so he was unaware when it came to an end. The ship had already been made fast to the dock in New York harbor, but Abba hadn't the vaguest notion of this. He saw huge buildings and towers, but mistook them for the pyramids of Egypt. A tall man in a white hat came into the cabin and shouted something at him, but he remained motionless. At last they helped him dress and led him out on deck, where his sons and daughters-in-law and grandchildren were waiting. Abba was bewildered; a crowd of Polish landowners, counts and countesses, gentile boys and girls, leaped at him, hugged him, and kissed him, crying out in a strange language, which was both Yiddish and not Yiddish. They half led, half carried him away, and placed him in a car. Other cars arrived, packed with Abba's kinfolk, and they set out, speeding like shot arrows over bridges, rivers, and roofs. Buildings rose up and receded, as if by magic, some of the buildings touching the sky. Whole cities lay spread out before him; Abba thought of Pithom and Rameses. The car sped so fast, it seemed to him the people in the streets were moving backward. The air was full of thunder and lightning; a banging and trumpeting, it was a wedding and a conflagration at once. The nations had gone wild, a heathen festival . . .

His sons were crowding around him. He saw them as in a fog and did not know them. Short men with white hair. They shouted, as if he were deaf.

"I'm Gimpel!"

"Getzel!"

"Feivel!"

The old man closed his eyes and made no answer. Their voices ran together; everything was turning pell-mell, topsy-turvy. Suddenly he thought of Jacob arriving in Egypt, where he was met by Pharaoh's chariots. He felt, he had lived through the same experience in a previous incarnation. His beard began to tremble; a hoarse sob rose from his chest. A forgotten passage from the Bible stuck in his gullet.

Blindly he embraced one of his sons and sobbed out, "Is this you? Alive?"

He had meant to say: "Now let me die, since I have seen thy face, because thou art yet alive."

VI
The American Heritage

Abba's sons lived on the outskirts of a town in New Jersey. Their seven homes, surrounded by gardens, stood on the shore of a lake. Every day they drove to the shoe factory, owned by Gimpel, but on the day of Abba's arrival they took a holiday and prepared a feast in his honor. It was to be held in Gimpel's house, in full compliance with the dietary laws. Gimpel's wife, Bessie, whose father had been a Hebrew teacher in the old country, remembered all the rituals and observed them carefully, going so far as to cover her head with a kerchief. Her sisters-in-law did the same, and Abba's sons put on the skullcaps they had once worn during Holy Days. The grandchildren and great-grandchildren, who did not know a word of Yiddish, actually learned a few phrases. They had heard the legends of Frampol and the little shoemakers and the first Abba of the family line. Even the gentiles in the neighborhood were fairly well acquainted with this history. In the ads Gimpel published in the papers, he had proudly disclosed that his family belonged to the shoe-making aristocracy:

> Our experience dates back three hundred years to the Polish city of Brod, where our ancestor, Abba, learned the craft from a local master. The community of Frampol, in which our family worked at its trade for fifteen generations, bestowed on him the title of Master in recognition of his charitable services. This sense of public responsibility has always gone hand in hand with our devotion to the highest principles of the craft and our strict policy of honest dealing with our customers.

The day Abba arrived, the papers in Elizabeth carried a notice to the effect that the seven brothers of the famous shoe company were welcoming their father from Poland. Gimpel received a mass of congratulatory telegrams from rival manufacturers, relatives, and friends.

It was an extraordinary feast. Three tables were spread in Gimpel's dining-room; one for the old man, his sons, and daughters-in-law, another for the grandchildren, and the third for the great-grandchildren. Although it was broad daylight, the tables were set with candles — red, blue, yellow, green — and their flames were reflected from the dishes and silverware, the crystal glasses and the wine cups, the decanters reminiscent of the Passover Seder. There was an abundance of flowers in every available corner. To be sure, the daughters-in-law would have preferred to see Abba properly dressed for the occasion, but Gimpel put his foot down, and Abba was allowed to spend his first day in the familiar long coat, Frampol style. Even so, Gimpel hired a photographer to take pictures of the banquet — for publication in the newspa-pers — and invited a rabbi and a cantor to the feast to honor the old man with traditional song.

Abba sat in an armchair at the head of the table. Gimpel and Getzel brought in a bowl and poured water over his hands for the benediction before eating. The food was served on silver trays, carried by colored women. All sorts of fruit juices and salads were set before the old man, sweet brandies, cognac, caviar. But Pharaoh, Joseph, Potiphar's wife, the Land of Goshen, the chief baker, and the chief butler spun round and round in his head. His hands trembled so that he was unable to feed himself, and Gimpel had to help him. No matter how often his sons spoke to him, he still could not tell them apart. Whenever the phone rang he jumped — the Nazis were bombing Fram-pol. The entire house was whirling round and round like a carousel; the ta-bles were standing on the ceiling and everyone sat upside down. His face was sickly pale in the light of the candles and the electric bulbs. He fell asleep soon after the soup course, while the chicken was being served. Quickly they led him to the bedroom, undressed him, and called a doctor.

He spent several weeks in bed, in and out of consciousness, fitfully dozing as in a fever. He even lacked the strength to say his prayers. There was a nurse at his bedside day and night. Eventually he recovered enough to take a few steps outdoors, in front of the house, but his senses remained disordered. He would walk into clothes closets, lock himself into the bathroom and forget how to come out; the doorbell and the radio frightened him; and he suffered constant anxiety because of the cars that raced past the house. One day Gimpel brought him to a synagogue ten miles away, but even here he was bewildered. The sexton was clean-shaven; the candelabra held electric lights; there was no courtyard, no faucet for washing one's hands, no stove to stand around. The cantor, instead of singing like a cantor should, babbled and croaked. The congregation wore tiny little prayer shawls, like scarves around their necks. Abba was sure he had been hauled into church to be converted. . . .

When spring came and he was no better, the daughters-in-law began to hint that it wouldn't be such a bad idea to put him in a home. But something unforeseen took place. One day, as he happened to open a closet, he noticed a sack lying on the floor which seemed somehow familiar. He looked again and recognized his shoemaker's equipment from Frampol: last, hammer and nails, his knife and pliers, the file and the awl, even a broken-down shoe. Abba felt a tremor of excitement; he could hardly believe his eyes. He sat down on a footstool and began to poke about with fingers grown clumsy and stale. When Bessie came in and found him playing with a dirty old shoe, she burst out laughing.

"What are you doing, Father? Be careful, you'll cut yourself, God forbid!"

That day Abba did not lie in bed dozing. He worked busily till evening and even ate his usual piece of chicken with greater appetite. He smiled at the grandchildren when they came in to see what he was doing. The next morning, when Gimpel told his brothers how their father had returned to his old habits, they laughed and thought nothing more of it — but the activity soon proved to be the old man's salvation. He kept at it day after day without tiring, hunting up old shoes in the clothes closets and begging his sons to supply him with leather and tools. When they gave in, he mended every last pair of shoes in the house — man, woman, and child's. After the Passover holidays the brothers got together and decided to build a little hut in the yard. They furnished it with a cobbler's bench, a stock of leather soles and hides, nails, dyes, brushes — everything even remotely useful in the craft.

Abba took on new life. His daughters-in-law cried, he looked fifteen years younger. As in the Frampol days, he now rose at dawn, said his prayers, and got right to work. Once again he used a knotted string as a measuring tape. The first pair of shoes, which he made for Bessie, became the talk of the neighborhood. She had always complained of her feet, but this pair, she insisted, were the most comfortable shoes she had ever worn. The other girls soon followed her example and also had themselves fitted. Then came the grandchildren. Even some of the gentile neighbors came to Abba when they heard that in sheer joy of the work he was turning out custom-made shoes. He had to communicate with them, for the most part, in gestures, but they got along very well. As for the younger grandchildren and the great-grandchildren, they had long been in the habit of standing at the door to watch him work. Now he was earning money, and he plied them with candies and toys. He even whittled a stylus and began to instruct them in the elements of Hebrew and piety.

One Sunday, Gimpel came into the workshop and, no more than half in earnest, rolled up his sleeves and joined Abba at the bench. The other brothers were not to be outdone, and on the following Sunday eight work stools were set up in the hut. Abba's sons spread sackcloth aprons on their knees and went to work, cutting soles and shaping heels, boring holes and hammering pegs, as in the good old days. The women stood outside, laughing, but they took pride in their men, and the children were fascinated. The sun streamed in through the windows, and motes of dust danced in the light. In the high spring sky, lofting over the grass and the water, floated clouds in the form of brooms, sailboats, flocks of sheep, herds of elephants. Birds sang; flies buzzed; butterflies fluttered about.

Abba raised his dense eyebrows, and his sad eyes looked around at his heirs, the seven shoemakers: Gimpel, Getzel, Treitel, Godel, Feivel, Lippe, and Chananiah. Their hair was white, though yellow streaks remained. No, praise God, they had not become idolaters in Egypt. They had not forgotten their heritage, nor had they lost themselves among the unworthy. The old man rattled and bumbled deep in his chest, and suddenly began to sing in a stifled, hoarse voice:

> *"A mother had*
> *Ten little boys,*
> *Oh, Lord, ten little boys!*
>
> *The sixth one was called Velvele,*
> *The seventh one was Zeinvele,*
> *The eighth one was called Chenele,*
> *The ninth one was called Tevele,*
> *The tenth one was called Judele . . ."*

And Abba's sons came in on the chorus:

> *"Oh, Lord, Judele!"*

— Translated by Isaac Rosenfeld

Suggestions for Discussion

1. Why does Singer begin the story with a history of the family's settlement in Frampol? Do the first and second sections of the story add in any way to our understanding of what happens to Abba in the last sections?
2. What is Abba's attitude toward his profession? How does this relate to his attitude toward his religion?
3. Section III begins with the proverb "Man proposes, God disposes." How is this proverb illustrated in the action?
4. What is Abba's response to Gimpel's declaration that he is going to America? Why? Is Abba finally able to understand the reason that his son wants to leave Frampol?

5. What is the probable date of the son's migration to America (see Section IV)? What is the historical significance of that period in American immigration? (See also Allon Schoener's *Portal to America: The Lower East Side: 1870–1925.*)
6. Explain the meaning of the following passages:

> Abba was bewildered; a crowd of Polish landowners, counts and countesses, gentile boys and girls, leaped at him, hugged him, and kissed him, crying out in a strange language, which was both Yiddish and not Yiddish.

> Gimpel's wife, Bessie, whose father had been a Hebrew teacher in the old country, remembered all the rituals and observed them carefully, going so far as to cover her head with a kerchief. Her sisters-in-law did the same, and Abba's sons put on the skullcaps they had once worn during Holy Days.

7. In what ways, besides the superficial ones of age and wealth, have Abba's sons changed? In what ways have they remained the same? What seems to be of permanent value to them?

Suggestions for Writing and Comparison

1. How would you describe the tone and mood of "The Little Shoemakers"? Is the story ever *merely* funny or sad? What does it have in common with the stories of Sholom Aleichem? Does it contain any elements of the fairy tale?
2. See William Pillin's poem "Miserere," p. 501. Do any of the personalities that Pillin mentions in reference to the inhabitants of the European ghettos characterize the people of "The Little Shoemakers"?

Bernard Malamud

Bernard Malamud was born in 1914 in Brooklyn, New York, where he has spent much of his life. His father was a storekeeper who resembled, in many ways, the central character of one of Malamud's most important novels, *The Assistant* (1957).

Malamud received his B.A. from the College of the City of New York in 1936, and his M.A. from Columbia University in 1942. He is the author of the short-story collections *The Magic Barrel* (1958) and *Idiots First* (1963), as well as several novels, including *A New Life* (1961), *The Fixer* (1966), and *The Tenants* (1971). He has been the recipient of numerous literary awards, such as the Rosenthal Award of the National Institute of Arts and Letters, the Daroff Memorial Award, and the National Book Award.

The Magic Barrel, from which "The First Seven Years" was taken, shows Malamud's characteristically profound concern for human existence and the sacredness of human life. His characters, as represented by Sobel in "The First Seven Years," are frequently maimed by life or society, and yet they are able to retain an inner beauty, a goodness and integrity that is visible to the more perceptive.

The First Seven Years

Feld, the shoemaker, was annoyed that his helper, Sobel, was so insensitive to his reverie that he wouldn't for a minute cease his fanatic pounding at the other bench. He gave him a look, but Sobel's bald head was bent over the last as he worked and he didn't notice. The shoemaker shrugged and continued to peer through the partly frosted window at the near-sighted haze of falling February snow. Neither the shifting white blur outside, nor the sudden deep remembrance of the snowy Polish village where he had wasted his youth could turn his thoughts from Max the college boy, (a constant visitor in the mind since early that morning when Feld saw him trudging through the snow-drifts on his way to school) whom he so much respected because of the sacrifices he had made throughout the years — in winter or direst heat — to further his education. An old wish returned to haunt the shoemaker: that he had had a son instead of a daughter, but this blew away in the snow for Feld, if anything, was a practical man. Yet he could not help but contrast the diligence of the boy, who was a peddler's son, with Miriam's unconcern for an education. True, she was always with a book in her hand, yet when the opportunity arose for a college education, she had said no she would rather find a job. He had begged her to go, pointing out how many fathers could not afford to send their children to college, but she said she wanted to be independent. As for education, what was it, she asked, but books, which Sobel, who diligently read the classics, would as usual advise her on. Her answer greatly grieved her father.

A figure emerged from the snow and the door opened. At the counter the man withdrew from a wet paper bag a pair of battered shoes for repair. Who he was the shoemaker for a moment had no idea, then his heart trembled as he realized, before he had thoroughly discerned the face, that Max himself was standing there, embarrassedly explaining what he wanted done to his old shoes. Though Feld listened eagerly, he couldn't hear a word, for the opportunity that had burst upon him was deafening.

He couldn't exactly recall when the thought had occurred to him, because it was clear he had more than once considered suggesting to the boy that he go out with Miriam. But he had not dared speak, for if Max said no, how would he face him again? Or suppose Miriam, who harped so often on independence, blew up in anger and shouted at him for his meddling? Still, the chance was too good to let by: all it meant was an introduction. They might long ago have become friends had they happened to meet somewhere, therefore was it not his duty—an obligation—to bring them together, nothing more, a harmless connivance to replace an accidental encounter in the subway, let's say, or a mutual friend's introduction in the street? Just let him once see and talk to her and he would for sure be interested. As for Miriam, what possible harm for a working girl in an office, who met only loud-mouthed salesmen and illiterate shipping clerks, to make the acquaintance of a fine scholarly boy? Maybe he would awaken in her a desire to go to college; if not—the shoemaker's mind at last came to grips with the truth—let her marry an educated man and live a better life.

When Max finished describing what he wanted done to his shoes, Feld marked them, both with enormous holes in the soles which he pretended not to notice, with large white-chalk x's, and the rubber heels, thinned to the nails, he marked with o's, though it troubled him he might have mixed up the letters. Max inquired the price, and the shoemaker cleared his throat and asked the boy, above Sobel's insistent hammering, would he please step through the side door there into the hall. Though surprised, Max did as the shoemaker requested, and Feld went in after him. For a minute they were both silent, because Sobel had stopped banging, and it seemed they understood neither was to say anything until the noise began again. When it did, loudly, the shoemaker quickly told Max why he had asked to talk to him.

"Ever since you went to high school," he said, in the dimly-lit hallway, "I watched you in the morning go to the subway to school, and I said always to myself, this is a fine boy that he wants so much an education."

"Thanks," Max said, nervously alert. He was tall and grotesquely thin, with sharply cut features, particularly a beak-like nose. He was wearing a loose, long slushy overcoat that hung down to his ankles, looking like a rug draped over his bony shoulders, and a soggy, old brown hat, as battered as the shoes he had brought in.

"I am a business man," the shoemaker abruptly said to conceal his embarrassment, "so I will explain you right away why I talk to you. I have a girl, my daughter Miriam—she is nineteen—a very nice girl and also so pretty that everybody looks on her when she passes by in the street. She is smart, always with a book, and I thought to myself that a boy like you, an educated boy—I thought maybe you will be interested sometime to meet a girl like this." He laughed a bit when he had finished and was tempted to say more but had the good sense not to.

Max stared down like a hawk. For an uncomfortable second he was silent, then he asked, "Did you say nineteen?"

"Yes."

"Would it be all right to inquire if you have a picture of her?"

"Just a minute." The shoemaker went into the store and hastily returned with a snapshot that Max held up to the light.

"She's all right," he said.

Feld waited.

"And is she sensible—not the flighty kind?"

"She is very sensible."

After another short pause, Max said it was okay with him if he met her.

"Here is my telephone," said the shoemaker, hurriedly handing him a slip of paper. "Call her up. She comes home from work six o'clock."

Max folded the paper and tucked it away into his worn leather wallet.

"About the shoes," he said. "How much did you say they will cost me?"

"Don't worry about the price."

"I just like to have an idea."

"A dollar—dollar fifty. A dollar fifty," the shoemaker said.

At once he felt bad, for he usually charged two twenty-five for this kind of job. Either he should have asked the regular price or done the work for nothing.

Later, as he entered the store, he was startled by a violent clanging and looked up to see Sobel pounding with all his might upon the naked last. It broke, the iron striking the floor and jumping with a thump against the wall, but before the enraged shoemaker could cry out, the assistant had torn his hat and coat from the hook and rushed out into the snow.

■ So Feld, who had looked forward to anticipating how it would go with his daughter and Max, instead had a great worry on his mind. Without his temperamental helper he was a lost man, especially since it was years now that he had carried the store alone. The shoemaker had for an age suffered from a heart condition that threatened collapse if he dared exert himself. Five years ago, after an attack, it had appeared as though he would have either to sacrifice his business upon the auction block and live on a pittance thereafter, or put himself at the mercy of some unscrupulous employee who would in the end probably ruin him. But just at the moment of his darkest despair, this Polish refugee, Sobel, appeared one night from the street and begged for work. He was a stocky man, poorly dressed, with a bald head that had once been blond, a severely plain face and soft blue eyes prone to tears over the sad books he read, a young man but old—no one would have guessed thirty. Though he confessed he knew nothing of shoemaking, he said he was apt and would work for a very little if Feld taught him the trade. Thinking that with, after all, a landsman, he would have less to fear than from a complete stranger, Feld took him on and within six weeks the refugee rebuilt as good a shoe as he, and not long thereafter expertly ran the business for the thoroughly relieved shoemaker.

Feld could trust him with anything and did, frequently going home after an hour or two at the store, leaving all the money in the till, knowing Sobel would guard every cent of it. The amazing thing was that he demanded so little. His wants were few; in money he wasn't interested—in nothing but books, it seemed—which he one by one lent to Miriam, together with his profuse, queer written comments, manufactured during his lonely rooming house evenings, thick pads of commentary which the shoemaker peered at and twitched his shoulders over as his daughter, from her fourteenth year, read page by sanctified page, as if the word of God were inscribed on them. To protect Sobel, Feld himself had to see that he received more than he asked for. Yet his conscience bothered him for not insisting that the assistant accept a better wage than he was getting, though Feld had honestly told him he could earn a handsome salary if he worked elsewhere, or maybe opened a place of his own. But the assistant answered, somewhat ungraciously, that he was not interested in going elsewhere, and though Feld frequently asked himself what keeps him here? why does he stay? he finally answered it that the man, no doubt because of his terrible experiences as a refugee, was afraid of the world.

After the incident with the broken last, angered by Sobel's behavior, the shoemaker decided to let him stew for a week in the rooming house, although his own strength was taxed dangerously and the business suffered. However, after several sharp nagging warnings from both his wife and daughter, he went finally in search of Sobel, as he had once before, quite recently, when over some fancied slight—Feld had merely asked him not to give Miriam so many books to read because her eyes were strained and red—the assistant had left the place in a huff, an incident which, as usual, came to nothing for he had returned after the shoemaker had talked to him, and taken his seat at the bench. But this time, after Feld had plodded through the snow to Sobel's house—he had thought of sending Miriam but the idea became repugnant to him—the burly landlady at the door informed him in a nasal voice that Sobel was not at home, and though Feld knew this was a nasty lie, for where had the refugee to go? still for some reason he was not completely sure of—it may have been the cold and his fatigue—he decided not to insist on seeing him. Instead he went home and hired a new helper.

Having settled the matter, though not entirely to his satisfaction, for he had much more to do than before, and so, for example, could no longer lie late in bed mornings because he had to get up to open the store for the new assistant, a speechless, dark man with an irritating rasp as he worked, whom he would not trust with the key as he had Sobel. Furthermore, this one, though able to do a fair repair job, knew nothing of grades of leather or prices, so Feld had to make his own purchases; and every night at closing time it was necessary to count the money in the till and lock up. However, he was not dissatisfied, for he lived much in his thoughts of Max and Miriam. The college boy had called her, and they had arranged a meeting for this coming Friday night. The shoemaker would personally have preferred Saturday, which he felt would make it a date of the first magnitude, but he learned Friday was Miriam's choice, so he said nothing. The day of the week did not matter. What mattered was the aftermath. Would they like each other and want to be friends? He sighed at all the time that would have to go by before he knew for sure. Often he was tempted to talk to Miriam about the boy, to ask whether she thought she would like his type—he had told her only that he considered Max a nice boy and had suggested he call her—but the one time he tried she snapped at him—justly—how should she know?

At last Friday came. Feld was not feeling particularly well so he stayed in bed, and Mrs. Feld thought it better to remain in the bedroom with him when Max called. Miriam received the boy, and her parents could hear their voices, his throaty one, as they talked. Just before leaving, Miriam brought Max to the bedroom door and he stood there a minute, a tall, slightly hunched figure wearing a thick, droopy suit, and apparently at ease as he greeted the shoe-maker and his wife, which was surely a good sign. And Miriam, although she had worked all day, looked fresh and pretty. She was a large-framed girl with a well-shaped body, and she had a fine open face and soft hair. They made, Feld thought, a first-class couple.

Miriam returned after 11:30. Her mother was already asleep, but the shoe-maker got out of bed and after locating his bathrobe went into the kitchen, where Miriam, to his surprise, sat at the table, reading.

"So where did you go?" Feld asked pleasantly.

"For a walk," she said, not looking up.

"I advised him," Feld said, clearing his throat, "he shouldn't spend so much money."

"I didn't care."

The shoemaker boiled up some water for tea and sat down at the table with a cupful and a thick slice of lemon.

"So how," he sighed after a sip, "did you enjoy?"

"It was all right."

He was silent. She must have sensed his disappointment, for she added, "You can't really tell much the first time."

"You will see him again?"

Turning a page, she said that Max had asked for another date.

"For when?"

"Saturday."

"So what did you say?"

"What did I say?" she asked, delaying for a moment—"I said yes."

Afterwards she inquired about Sobel, and Feld, without exactly knowing why, said the assistant had got another job. Miriam said nothing more and began to read. The shoemaker's conscience did not trouble him; he was satisfied with the Saturday date.

During the week, by placing here and there a deft question, he managed to get from Miriam some information about Max. It surprised him to learn that the boy was not studying to be either a doctor or lawyer but was taking a business course leading to a degree in accountancy. Feld was a little disappointed because he thought of accountants as bookkeepers and would have preferred "a higher profession." However, it was not long before he had investigated the subject and discovered that Certified Public Accountants were highly respected people, so he was thoroughly content as Saturday approached. But because Saturday was a busy day, he was much in the store and therefore did not see Max when he came to call for Miriam. From his wife he learned there had been nothing especially revealing about their meeting. Max had rung the bell and Miriam had got her coat and left with him — nothing more. Feld did not probe, for his wife was not particularly observant. Instead, he waited up for Miriam with a newspaper on his lap, which he scarcely looked at so lost was he in thinking of the future. He awoke to find her in the room with him, tiredly removing her hat. Greeting her, he was suddenly inexplicably afraid to ask anything about the evening. But since she volunteered nothing he was at last forced to inquire how she had enjoyed herself. Miriam began something non-committal but apparently changed her mind, for she said after a minute, "I was bored."

When Feld had sufficiently recovered from his anguished disappointment to ask why, she answered without hesitation, "Because he's nothing more than a materialist."

"What means this word?"

"He has no soul. He's only interested in things."

He considered her statement for a long time but then asked, "Will you see him again?"

"He didn't ask."

"Suppose he will ask you?"

"I won't see him."

He did not argue; however, as the days went by he hoped increasingly she would change her mind. He wished the boy would telephone, because he was sure there was more to him than Miriam, with her inexperienced eye, could discern. But Max didn't call. As a matter of fact he took a different route to school, no longer passing the shoemaker's store, and Feld was deeply hurt.

Then one afternoon Max came in and asked for his shoes. The shoemaker took them down from the shelf where he had placed them, apart from the other pairs. He had done the work himself and the soles and heels were well built and firm. The shoes had been highly polished and somehow looked better than new. Max's Adam's apple went up once when he saw them, and his eyes had little lights in them.

"How much?" he asked, without directly looking at the shoemaker.

"Like I told you before," Feld answered sadly. "One dollar fifty cents."

Max handed him two crumpled bills and received in return a newly-minted silver half dollar.

He left. Miriam had not been mentioned. That night the shoemaker discovered that his new assistant had been all the while stealing from him, and he suffered a heart attack.

■ Though the attack was very mild, he lay in bed for three weeks. Miriam spoke of going for Sobel, but sick as he was Feld rose in wrath against the idea. Yet in his heart he knew there was no other way, and the first weary day back in the shop thoroughly convinced him, so that night after supper he dragged himself to Sobel's rooming house.

He toiled up the stairs, though he knew it was bad for him, and at the top knocked at the door. Sobel opened it and the shoemaker entered. The room was a small, poor one, with a single window facing the street. It contained a narrow cot, a low table and several stacks of books piled haphazardly around on the floor along the wall, which made him think how queer Sobel was, to be uneducated and read so much. He had once asked him, Sobel, why you read so much? and the assistant could not answer him. Did you ever study in a college someplace? he had asked, but Sobel shook his head. He read, he said, to know. But to know what, the shoemaker demanded, and to know, why? Sobel never explained, which proved he read much because he was queer.

Feld sat down to recover his breath. The assistant was resting on his bed with his heavy back to the wall. His shirt and trousers were clean, and his stubby fingers, away from the shoemaker's bench, were strangely pallid. His face was thin and pale, as if he had been shut in this room since the day he had bolted from the store.

"So when you will come back to work?" Feld asked him.

To his surprise, Sobel burst out, "Never."

Jumping up, he strode over to the window that looked out upon the miserable street. "Why should I come back?" he cried.

"I will raise your wages."

"Who cares for your wages!"

The shoemaker, knowing he didn't care, was at a loss what else to say.

"What do you want from me, Sobel?"

"Nothing."

"I always treated you like you was my son."

Sobel vehemently denied it. "So why you look for strange boys in the street they should go out with Miriam? Why you don't think of me?"

The shoemaker's hands and feet turned freezing cold. His voice became so hoarse he couldn't speak. At last he cleared his throat and croaked, "So what has my daughter got to do with a shoemaker thirty-five years old who works for me?"

"Why do you think I worked so long for you?" Sobel cried out. "For the stingy wages I sacrificed five years of my life so you could have to eat and drink and where to sleep?"

"Then for what?" shouted the shoemaker.

"For Miriam," he blurted— "for her."

The shoemaker, after a time, managed to say, "I pay wages in cash, Sobel," and lapsed into silence. Though he was seething with excitement, his mind was coldly clear, and he had to admit to himself he had sensed all along that Sobel felt this way. He had never so much as thought it consciously, but he had felt it and was afraid.

"Miriam knows?" he muttered hoarsely.

"She knows."

"You told her?"

"No."

"Then how does she know?"

"How does she know?" Sobel said, "because she knows. She knows who I am and what is in my heart."

Feld had a sudden insight. In some devious way, with his books and commentary, Sobel had given Miriam to understand that he loved her. The shoemaker felt a terrible anger at him for his deceit.

"Sobel, you are crazy," he said bitterly. "She will never marry a man so old and ugly like you."

Sobel turned black with rage. He cursed the shoemaker, but then, though he trembled to hold it in, his eyes filled with tears and he broke into deep sobs. With his back to Feld, he stood at the window, fists clenched, and his shoulders shook with his choked sobbing.

Watching him, the shoemaker's anger diminished. His teeth were on edge with pity for the man, and his eyes grew moist. How strange and sad that a refugee, a grown man, bald and old with his miseries, who had by the skin of his teeth escaped Hitler's incinerators, should fall in love, when he had got to America, with a girl less than half his age. Day after day, for five years he had sat at his bench, cutting and hammering away, waiting for the girl to become a woman, unable to ease his heart with speech, knowing no protest but desperation.

"Ugly I didn't mean," he said half aloud.

Then he realized that what he had called ugly was not Sobel but Miriam's life if she married him. He felt for his daughter a strange and gripping sorrow, as if she were already Sobel's bride, the wife, after all, of a shoemaker, and had in her life no more than her mother had had. And all his dreams for her — why he had slaved and destroyed his heart with anxiety and labor — all these dreams of a better life were dead.

The room was quiet. Sobel was standing by the window reading, and it was curious that when he read he looked young.

"She is only nineteen," Feld said brokenly. "This is too young yet to get married. Don't ask her for two years more, till she is twenty-one, then you can talk to her."

Sobel didn't answer. Feld rose and left. He went slowly down the stairs but once outside, though it was an icy night and the crisp falling snow whitened the street, he walked with a stronger stride.

But the next morning, when the shoemaker arrived, heavy-hearted, to open the store, he saw he needn't have come, for his assistant was already seated at the last, pounding leather for his love.

Suggestions for Discussion

1. What qualities in Max attract the shoemaker? What is the signif-icance of the questions Max asks about Miriam? Is Max a sym-pathetic character?
2. What framework does the author provide for the introduction of Sobel's history? Why does Feld think Sobel stays with him? Does it seem an adequate answer for a man of Sobel's charac-ter?
3. At what point does the reader realize that Sobel is interested in Miriam? What insight is gained by seeing "the courtship" of Max and Miriam from her father's point of view? What does Feld understand by Miriam's statement "He has no soul"? Characterize the style in which the "end of the courtship" is described. What effect does this narration have on the reader?
4. Explain what Sobel meant when he said he read "to know." Why doesn't Feld understand this? Would Max have understood?

5. To what Biblical story does the title refer? How does the title relate to the last sentence in the story?
6. Define "tragedy," "melodrama," "sentimentality," and "pathos." Which, if any, of these terms characterizes "The First Seven Years"? Why is the story moving?

Suggestions for Writing and Comparison

1. Compare the characterization in Ralph Ellison's "Did You Ever Dream Lucky?" (p. 96) to that in Malamud's "The First Seven Years." In what respects are the two sets of characters "ethnic"? In what ways are they universal? Do Ellison and Malamud share any techniques of characterization?
2. What is an "education"? Is Max or Sobel the "educated man"? Read John Henry Newman's *The Idea of a University* and compare his attitudes concerning the purpose of a university with the statement "He read, he said, to know" from Malamud's story.

Saul Bellow

Saul Bellow was born in Lachine, Quebec, in 1915. Two years before his birth his father had migrated to Canada from St. Petersburg, Russia. Because of Bellow's family background and his geographical environment he had to learn Yiddish, English, Hebrew, and French as a child. He lived in an impoverished section of Montreal until the family moved to Chicago in 1924.

In 1937 Bellow received a B.S. degree with a major in anthropology and sociology from Northwestern University. A short period in graduate school convinced him that he did not want to be a social scientist. After he completed his military service he produced his first novel, *Dangling Man* (1944), which was concerned with a young man from Chicago waiting to do his turn in the military. This was followed by *The Victim* (1947), a provocative study of the complexities of anti-Semitism and moral guilt; *The Adventures of Augie March* (1953), a twentieth-century picaresque novel, whose hero, while not autobiographical, reflects both Bellow's Jewish background and his roots in North America; and several other novels, including *Henderson the Rain King* (1959), the story of an American millionaire who goes to Africa to find a cure for his soul sickness, and *Mr. Sammler's Planet* (1970), a study of alienation and reaction to the militant movements of the 1960's.

In 1954, Bellow won the National Book Award for *The Adventures of Augie March.* For *Herzog* (1964), he received a second National Book Award, as well as the Prix International de Litterature. He has taught at Bard College and at the University of Chicago, the University of Minnesota, and Princeton.

The following selection is an excerpt from *The Adventures of Augie March.* The stream-of-consciousness technique of *Herzog* is here foreshadowed in the handling of Augie. The peculiarities of the language—alternately crude and intellectual, aphoristic and prolix—lead us into Augie's personal vision of his world. Augie's Grandma Lausch is typical of Bellow's characters in her individualism, or as Philip Roth has suggested, it is not so much that Bellow has created a character as that we are convinced by his writing that "Grandma Lausch IS."

(See Leslie Fiedler's essay "Saul Bellow" on p. 416.)

The Adventures of Augie March

I am an American, Chicago born—Chicago, that somber city—and go at things as I have taught myself, free-style, and will make the record in my own way: first to knock, first admitted; sometimes an innocent knock, sometimes a not so innocent. But a man's character is his fate, says Heraclitus, and in the end there isn't any way to disguise the nature of the knocks by acoustical work on the door or gloving the knuckles.

Everybody knows there is no fineness or accuracy of suppression; if you hold down one thing you hold down the adjoining.

My own parents were not much to me, though I cared for my mother. She was simple-minded, and what I learned from her was not what she taught, but on the order of object lessons. She didn't have much to teach, poor woman. My brothers and I loved her. I speak for them both; for the elder it is safe enough; for the younger one, Georgie, I have to answer—he was born an idiot—but I'm in no need to guess, for he had a song he sang as he ran dragfooted with his stiff idiot's trot, up and down along the curl-wired fence in the backyard:

> Georgie Mahchy, Augie, Simey
> Winnie Mahchy, evwy, evwy love Mama.

He was right about everyone save Winnie, Grandma Lausch's poodle, a pursy old overfed dog. Mama was Winnie's servant, as she was Grandma Lausch's. Loud-breathing and wind-breaking, she lay near the old lady's stool on a cushion embroidered with a Berber aiming a rifle at a lion. She was personally Grandma's, belonged to her suite; the rest of us were the governed, and especially Mama. Mama passed the dog's dish to Grandma, and Winnie received her food at the old lady's feet from the old lady's hands. These hands and feet were small; she wore a shriveled sort of lisle on her legs and her slippers were gray—ah, the gray of that felt, the gray despotic to souls—with pink ribbons. Mama, however, had large feet, and around the house she wore men's shoes, usually without strings, and a dusting or mobcap like somebody's fanciful cotton effigy of the form of the brain. She was meek and long, round-eyed like Georgie—gentle green round eyes and a gentle freshness of color in her long face. Her hands were work-reddened, she had very few of her teeth left—to heed the knocks as they come—and she and Simon wore the same ravelly coat-sweaters. Besides having round eyes, Mama had circular glasses that I went with her to the free dispensary on Harrison Street to get. Coached by Grandma Lausch, I went to do the lying. Now I know it wasn't so necessary to lie, but then everyone thought so, and Grandma Lausch especially, who was one of those Machiavellis of small street and neighborhood that my young years were full of. So Grandma, who had it all ready before we left the house and must have put in hours plotting it out in thought and phrase, lying small in her chilly small room under the featherbed, gave it to me at breakfast. The idea was that Mama wasn't keen enough to do it right. That maybe one didn't need to be keen didn't occur to us; it was a contest. The dispensary would want to know why the Charities didn't pay for the glasses. So you must say nothing about the Charities, but that sometimes money from my father came and sometimes it didn't, and that Mama took boarders. This was, in a delicate and choosy way, by ignoring and omitting certain large facts, true. It was true enough for *them,* and at the age of nine I could appreciate this perfectly. Better than my brother Simon, who was too blunt for this kind of maneuver and, anyway, from books, had gotten hold of some English schoolboy notions of honor. *Tom Brown's Schooldays* for many years had an influence we were not in a position to afford.

Simon was a blond boy with big cheekbones and wide gray eyes and had the arms of a cricketer—I go by the illustrations; we never played anything but softball. Opposed to his British style was his patriotic anger at George III. The mayor was at that time ordering the schoolboard to get history books that dealt more harshly with the king, and Simon was very hot at Cornwallis. I admired this patriotic flash, his terrific personal wrath at the general, and his satisfaction over his surrender at Yorktown, which would often come over him at lunch while we ate our bologna sandwiches. Grandma had a piece of boiled chicken at noon, and sometimes there was the gizzard for bristleheaded little Georgie, who loved it and blew at the ridgy thing more to cherish than to cool it. But this martial true-blood pride of Simon's disqualified him for the crafty task to be done at the dispensary; he was too disdainful to lie and might denounce everybody instead. I could be counted on to do the job, because I enjoyed it. I loved a piece of strategy. I had enthusiasms too; I had Simon's, though there was never much meat in Cornwallis for me, and I had Grandma Lausch's as well. As for the truth of these statements I was instructed to make—well, it was a fact that we had a boarder. Grandma Lausch was our boarder, not a relation at all. She was supported by two sons, one from Cincinnati and one from Racine, Wisconsin. The daughters-in-law did not want her, and she, the widow of a powerful Odessa businessman—a divinity over us, bald, whiskery, with a fat nose, greatly armored in a cutaway, a double-breasted vest, powerfully buttoned (his blue photo, enlarged and retouched by Mr. Lulov, hung in the parlor, doubled back between the portico columns of the full-length mirror, the dome of the stove beginning where his trunk ended)—she preferred to live with us, because for so many years she was used to direct a house, to command, to govern, to manage, scheme, devise, and intrigue in all her languages. She boasted French and German besides Russian, Polish, and Yiddish; and who but Mr. Lulov, the retouch artist from Division Street, could have tested her claim to French? And he was a serene bogus too, that triple-backboned gallant tea-drinker. Except that he had been a hackie in Paris, once, and if he told the truth about that might have known French among other things, like playing tunes on his teeth with a pencil or singing and keeping time with a handful of coins that he rattled by jigging his thumb along the table, and how to play chess.

Grandma Lausch played like Timur, whether chess or klabyasch, with palatal catty harshness and sharp gold in her eyes. Klabyasch she played with Mr. Kreindl, a neighbor of ours who had taught her the game. A powerful stub-handed man with a large belly, he swatted the table with those hard hands of his, flinging down his cards and shouting *"Shtoch! Yasch! Menél! Klabyasch!"* Grandma looked sardonically at him. She often said, after he left, "If you've got a Hungarian friend you don't need an enemy." But there was nothing of the enemy about Mr. Kreindl. He merely, sometimes, sounded menacing because of his drill-sergeant's bark. He was an old-time Austro-Hungarian conscript, and there was something soldierly about him: a neck that had strained with pushing artillery wheels, a campaigner's red in the face, a powerful bite in his jaw and gold-crowned teeth, green cockeyes and soft short hair, altogether Napoleonic. His feet slanted out on the ideal of Frederick the Great, but he was about a foot under the required height for guardsmen. He had a masterly look of independence. He and his wife—a woman quiet and modest to the neighbors and violently quarrelsome at home—and his son, a dental student, lived in what was called the English basement at the front of the house. The son, Kotzie, worked evenings in the corner drugstore and went to school in the neighborhood of County Hospital, and it was he who told Grandma about the free dispensary. Or rather, the old woman sent for him to find out what one could get from those state and county places. She was always sending for people, the butcher, the grocer, the fruit peddler, and received them in the kitchen to explain that the Marches had to have discounts. Mama usually had to stand by. The old woman would tell them, "You see how it is—do I have to say more? There's no man in the house and children to bring up." This was her most frequent argument. When Lubin, the caseworker, came around and sat in the kitchen, familiar, bald-headed, in his gold glasses, his weight comfortable, his mouth patient, she shot it at him: "How do you expect children to be brought up?" While he listened, trying to remain comfortable but gradually becoming like a man determined not to let a grasshopper escape from his hand. "Well, my dear, Mrs. March could raise your rent," he said. She must often have answered—for there were times when she sent us all out to be alone with him—"Do you know what things would be like without me? You ought to be grateful for the way I hold them together." I'm sure she even said, "And when I die, Mr. Lubin, you'll see what you've got on your hands." I'm one hundred per cent sure of it. To us nothing was ever said that might weaken her rule by suggesting it would ever end. Besides, it would have shocked us to hear it, and she, in her miraculous knowledge of us, able to be extremely close to our thoughts—she was one sovereign who knew exactly the proportions of love, respect, and fear of power in her subjects—understood how we would have been shocked. But to Lubin, for reasons of policy and also because she had to express feelings she certainly had, she must have said it. He had a harassed patience with her of "deliver me from such clients," though he tried to appear master of the situation. He held his derby between his thighs (his suits, always too scanty in the pants, exposed white socks and bulldog shoes, crinkled, black, and bulging with toes), and he looked into the hat as though debating whether it was wise to release his grasshopper on the lining for a while.

"I pay as much as I can afford," she would say.

She took her cigarette case out from under her shawl, she cut a Murad in half with her sewing scissors and picked up the holder. This was still at a time when women did not smoke. Save the intelligentsia—the term she applied to herself. With the holder in her dark little gums between which all her guile, malice, and command issued, she had her best inspirations of strategy. She was as wrinkled as an old paper bag, an autocrat, hard-shelled and jesuitical, a pouncy old hawk of a Bolshevik, her small ribboned gray feet immobile on the shoekit and stool Simon had made in the manual-training class, dingy old wool Winnie whose bad smell filled the flat on the cushion beside her. If wit and discontent don't necessarily go together, it wasn't from the old woman that I learned it. She was impossible to satisfy. Kreindl, for example, on whom we could depend, Kreindl who carried up the coal when Mama was sick and who instructed Kotzie to make up our prescriptions for nothing, she called "that trashy Hungarian," or "Hungarian pig." She called Kotzie "the baked apple"; she called Mrs. Kreindl "the secret goose," Lubin "the shoe-maker's son," the dentist "the butcher," the butcher "the timid swindler." She detested the dentist, who had several times unsuccessfully tried to fit her with false teeth. She accused him of burning her gums when taking the impressions. But then she tried to pull his hands away from her mouth. I saw that happen: the stolid, square-framed Dr. Wernick, whose compact forearms could have held off a bear, painfully careful with her, determined, concerned at her choked screams, and enduring her scratches. To see her struggle like that was no easy thing for me, and Dr. Wernick was sorry to see me there too, I know, but either Simon or I had to squire her wherever she went. Here particularly she needed a witness to Wernick's cruelty and clumsiness as well as a shoulder to lean on when she went weakly home. Already at ten I was only a little shorter than she and big enough to hold her small weight.

"You saw how he put his paws over my face so I couldn't breathe?" she said. "God made him to be a butcher. Why did he become a dentist? His hands are too heavy. The touch is everything to a dentist. If his hands aren't right he shouldn't be let practice. But his wife worked hard to send him through school and make a dentist of him. And I must go to him and be burned because of it."

The rest of us had to go to the dispensary—which was like the dream of a multitude of dentists' chairs, hundreds of them in a space as enormous as an armory, and green bowls with designs of glass grapes, drills lifted zigzag as insects' legs, and gas flames on the porcelain swivel trays—a thundery gloom in Harrison Street of limestone county buildings and cumbersome red street-cars with metal grillwork on their windows and monarchical iron whiskers of cowcatchers front and rear. They lumbered and clanged, and their brake tanks panted in the slushy brown of a winter afternoon or the bare stone brown of a summer's, salted with ash, smoke, and prairie dust, with long stops at the clinics to let off clumpers, cripples, hunchbacks, brace-legs, crutch-wielders, tooth and eye sufferers, and all the rest.

So before going with my mother for the glasses I was always instructed by the old woman and had to sit and listen with profound care. My mother too had to be present, for there must be no slip-up. She must be coached to say nothing. "Remember, Rebecca," Grandma would re-repeat, "let him answer everything." To which Mama was too obedient even to say yes, but only sat and kept her long hands folded on the bottle-fly iridescence of the dress the old woman had picked for her to wear. Very healthy and smooth, her color; none of us inherited this high a color from her, or the form of her nose with nostrils turned back and showing a little of the partition. "You keep out of it. If they ask you something, you look at Augie like this." And she illustrated how Mama was to turn to me, terribly exact, if she had only been able to drop her habitual grandeur. "Don't tell anything. Only answer questions," she said to me. My mother was anxious that I should be worthy and faithful. Simon and I were her miracles or accidents; Georgie was her own true work in which she returned to her fate after blessed and undeserved success. "Augie, listen to Grandma. Hear what she says," was all she ever dared when the old woman unfolded her plan.

"When they ask you, 'Where is your father?' you say, 'I don't know where, miss.' No matter how old she is, you shouldn't forget to say 'miss.' If she wants to know where he was the last time you heard from him, you must tell her that the last time he sent a money order was about two years ago from Buffalo, New York. Never say a word about the Charity. The Charity you should never mention, you hear that? Never. When she asks you how much the rent is, tell her eighteen dollars. When she asks where the money comes from, say you have boarders. How many? Two boarders. Now, say to me, how much rent?"

"Eighteen dollars."

"And how many boarders?"

"Two."

"And how much do they pay?"

"How much should I say?"

"Eight dollars each a week."

"Eight dollars."

"So you can't go to a private doctor, if you get sixty-four dollars a month. The eyedrops alone cost me five when I went, and he scalded my eyes. And these specs"—she tapped the case—"cost ten dollars the frames and fifteen the glasses."

Never but at such times, by necessity, was my father mentioned. I claimed to remember him; Simon denied that I did, and Simon was right. I liked to imagine it.

"He wore a uniform," I said. "Sure I remember. He was a soldier."

"Like hell he was. You don't know anything about it."

"Maybe a sailor."

"Like hell. He drove a truck for Hall Brothers laundry on Marshfield, that's what he did. *I* said he used to wear a uniform. Monkey sees, monkey does; monkey hears, monkey says." Monkey was the basis of much thought with us. On the sideboard, on the Turkestan runner, with their eyes, ears, and mouth covered, we had see-no-evil, speak-no-evil, hear-no-evil, a lower trinity of the house. The advantage of lesser gods is that you can take their names any way you like. "Silence in the courthouse, monkey wants to speak; speak, monkey, speak." "The monkey and the bamboo were playing in the grass . . ." Still the monkeys could be potent, and awesome besides, and deep social critics when the old woman, like a great lama—for she is Eastern to me, in the end—would point to the squatting brown three, whose mouths and nostrils were drawn in sharp blood-red, and with profound wit, her unkindness finally touching greatness, say, "Nobody asks you to love the whole world, only to be honest, *ehrlich*. Don't have a loud mouth. The more you love people the more they'll mix you up. A child loves, a person respects. Respect is better than love. And that's respect, the middle monkey." It never occurred to us that she sinned mischievously herself against that convulsed speak-no-evil who hugged his lips with his hands; but no criticism of her came near our minds at any time, much less when the resonance of a great principle filled the whole kitchen.

She used to read us lessons off poor Georgie's head. He would kiss the dog. This bickering handmaiden of the old lady, at one time. Now a dozy, long-sighing crank and proper object of respect for her years of right-minded but not exactly lovable busyness. But Georgie loved her—and Grandma, whom he would kiss on the sleeve, on the knee, taking knee or arm in both hands and putting his underlip forward, chaste, lummoxy, caressing, gentle and diligent when he bent his narrow back, blouse bagging all over it, whitish hair pointy and close as a burr or sunflower when the seeds have been picked out of it. The old lady let him embrace her and spoke to him in the following way: "Hey, you, boy, clever *junge,* you like the old Grandma, my minister, my *cavalyer?* That's-a-boy. You know who's good to you, who gives you gizzards and necks? Who? Who makes noodles for you? Yes. Noodles are slippery, hard to pick up with a fork and hard to pick up with the fingers. You see how the little bird pulls the worm? The little worm wants to stay in the ground. The little worm doesn't want to come out. Enough, you're making my dress wet." And she'd sharply push his forehead off with her old prim hand, having fired off for Simon and me, mindful always of her duty to wise us up, one more animadversion on the trustful, loving, and simple surrounded by the cunning-hearted and tough, a fighting nature of birds and worms, and a desperate mankind without feelings. Illustrated by Georgie. But the principal illustration was not Georgie but Mama, in her love-originated servitude, simple-minded, abandoned with three children. This was what old lady Lausch was driving at, now, in the later wisdom of her life, that she had a second family to lead.

And what must Mama have thought when in any necessary connection my father was brought into the conversation? She sat docile. I conceive that she thought of some detail about him—a dish he liked, perhaps meat and potatoes, perhaps cabbage or cranberry sauce; perhaps that he disliked a starched collar, or a soft collar; that he brought home the *Evening American* or the *Journal.* She thought this because her thoughts were always simple; but she felt abandonment, and greater pains than conscious mental ones put a dark streak to her simplicity. I don't know how she made out before, when we were alone after the desertion, but Grandma came and put a regulating hand on the family life. Mama surrendered powers to her that maybe she had never known she had and took her punishment in drudgery; occupied a place, I suppose, among women conquered by a superior force of love, like those women whom Zeus got the better of in animal form and who next had to take cover from his furious wife. Not that I can see my big, gentle, dilapidated, scrubbing, and lugging mother as a fugitive of immense beauty from such classy wrath, or our father as a marble-legged Olympian. She had sewed buttonholes in a coat factory in a Wells Street loft and he was a laundry driver —there wasn't even so much as a picture of him left when he blew. But she does have a place among such women by the deeper right of continual payment. And as for vengeance from a woman, Grandma Lausch was there to administer the penalties under the standards of legitimacy, representing the main body of married womankind.

Still the old lady had a heart. I don't mean to say she didn't. She was tyrannical and a snob about her Odessa luster and her servants and governesses, but though she had been a success herself she knew what it was to fall through susceptibiltiy. I began to realize this when I afterward read some of the novels she used to send me to the library for. She taught me the Russian alphabet so that I could make out the titles. Once a year she read *Anna Karenina* and *Eugene Onegin*. Occasionally I got into hot water by bringing a book she didn't want. "How many times do I have to tell you if it doesn't say *roman* I don't want it? You didn't look inside. Are your fingers too weak to open the book? Then they should be too weak to play ball or pick your nose. For that you've got strength! *Bozhe moy!* God in Heaven! You haven't got the brains of a cat, to walk two miles and bring me a book about religion because it says Tolstoi on the cover."

The old *grande dame,* I don't want to be misrepresenting her. She was suspicious of what could have been, given one wrong stitch of heredity, a family vice by which we could have been exploited. She didn't want to read Tolstoi on religion. She didn't trust him as a family man because the countess had had such trouble with him. But although she never went to the synagogue, ate bread on Passover, sent Mama to the pork butcher where meat was cheaper, loved canned lobster and other forbidden food, she was not an atheist and free-thinker. Mr. Anticol, the old junky she called (search me why) "Rameses" —after the city named with Pithom in the Scriptures maybe; no telling what her inspirations were—was that. A real rebel to God. Icy and canny, she would listen to what he had to say and wouldn't declare herself. He was ruddy, and gloomy; his leathery serge cap made him flat-headed, and his alley calls for rags, old iron—"recks aline," he sung it—made him gravel-voiced and gruff. He had tough hair and brows and despising brown eyes; he was a studious, shaggy, meaty old man. Grandma bought a set of the *Encyclopedia Americana*—edition of 1892, I think—from him and saw to it that Simon and I read it; and he too, whenever he met us, asked, "How's the set?" believing, I reckon, that it taught irreverence to religion. What had made him an atheist was a massacre of Jews in his town. From the cellar where he was hidden he saw a laborer pissing on the body of his wife's younger brother, just killed. "So don't talk to me about God," he said. But it was he that talked about God, all the time. And while Mrs. Anticol stayed pious, it was his idea of grand apostasy to drive to the reform synagogue on the high holidays and park his pink-eye nag among the luxurious, whirl-wired touring cars of the rich Jews who bared their heads inside as if they were attending a theater, a kind of abjectness in them that gave him grim entertainment to the end of his life. He caught a cold in the rain and died of pneumonia.

Grandma, all the same, burned a candle on the anniversary of Mr. Lausch's death, threw a lump of dough on the coals when she was baking, as a kind of offering, had incantations over baby teeth and stunts against the evil eye. It was kitchen religion and had nothing to do with the giant God of the Creation who turned back the waters and exploded Gomorrah, but it was on the side of religion at that. And while we're on that side I'll mention the Poles—we were just a handful of Jews among them in the neighborhood—and the swollen, bleeding hearts on every kitchen wall, the pictures of saints, baskets of death flowers tied at the door, communions, Easters, and Christmases. And sometimes we were chased, stoned, bitten, and beat up for Christ-killers, all of us, even Georgie, articled, whether we liked it or not, to this mysterious trade. But I never had any special grief from it, or brooded, being by and large too larky and boisterous to take it to heart, and looked at it as needing no more special explanation than the stone-and-bat wars of the street gangs or the swarming on a fall evening of parish punks to rip up fences, screech and bawl at girls, and beat up strangers. It wasn't in my nature to fatigue myself with worry over being born to this occult work, even though some of my friends and playmates would turn up in the middle of these mobs to trap you between houses from both ends of a passageway. Simon had less truck with them. School absorbed him more, and he had his sentiments anyway, a mixed extract from Natty Bumppo, Quentin Durward, Tom Brown, Clark at Kaskaskia, the messenger who brought the good news from Ratisbon, and so on, that kept him more to himself. I was just a slow understudy to this, just as he never got me to put in hours on his Sandow muscle builder and the gimmick for developing the sinews of the wrist. I was an easy touch for friendships, and most of the time they were cut short by older loyalties. I was pals longest with Stashu Kopecs, whose mother was a midwife graduated from the Aesculapian School of Midwifery on Milwaukee Avenue. Well to do, the Kopecses had an electric player piano and linoleums in all the rooms, but Stashu was a thief, and to run with him I stole too: coal off the cars, clothes from the lines, rubber balls from the dime store, and pennies off the newsstands. Mostly for the satisfaction of dexterity, though Stashu invented the game of stripping in the cellar and putting on girls' things swiped from the clotheslines. Then he too showed up in a gang that caught me one cold afternoon of very little snow while I was sitting on a crate frozen into the mud, eating Nabisco wafers, my throat full of the sweet dust. Foremost, there was a thug of a kid, about thirteen but undersized, hard and grieved-looking. He came up to accuse me, and big Moonya Staplanski, just out of the St. Charles Reformatory and headed next for the one at Pontiac, backed him up.

"You little Jew bastard, you hit my brother," Moonya said.

"I never did. I never even saw him before."

"You took away a nickel from him. How did you buy them biscuits else, you?"

"I got them at home."

Then I caught sight of Stashu, hayheaded and jeering, pleased to sickness with his deceit and his new-revealed brotherhood with the others, and I said, "Hey, you lousy bed-wetter, Stashu, you know Moon ain't even got a brother."

Here the kid hit me and the gang jumped me, Stashu with the rest, tearing the buckles from my sheepskin coat and bloodying my nose.

"Who is to blame?" said Grandma Lausch when I came home. "You know who? You are, Augie, because that's all the brains you have to go with that piss-in-bed *accoucherka's* son. Does Simon hang around with them? Not Simon. He has too much sense." I thanked God she didn't know about the stealing. And in a way, because that was her schooling temperament, I suspect she was pleased that I should see where it led to give your affections too easily. But Mama, the prime example of this weakness, was horrified. Against the old lady's authority she didn't dare to introduce her feelings during the hearing, but when she took me into the kitchen to put a compress on me she nearsightedly pored over my scratches, whispering and sighing to me, while Georgie tottered around behind her, long and white, and Winnie lapped water under the sink.

Suggestions for Discussion

1. In what way is the opening paragraph a statement about the narrator, the style of writing, and the form of the novel? What is meant by the phrase "go at things as I have taught myself, free-style"?

2. Consider Bellow's prose style: for example, how is the action advanced in the midst of so many insertions, digressions, and interruptions? What is gained by this approach? In spite of the seeming chaos of the story, is it well-constructed?

3. Augie refers to Grandma Lausch as "the old lady," "grande dame," and an "Eastern lama." Is each term justified by her actions or physical characteristics or possessions?

4. Analyze the long paragraph on p. 457 beginning "The old *grande dame* . . ." What elements of the essay and the short story does it contain? What "rules of paragraph development" as taught in composition classes does it violate? How is it effective?

5. Augie identifies himself in the opening paragraph by saying "I am an American, Chicago born." Later he says "I'll mention the Poles—we were just a handful of Jews among them in the neighborhood." According to Bellow's story, what makes a non-religious American a Jew?

Suggestions for Writing and Comparison

1. Define *picaresque* and *Bildungsroman*. Illustrate, by giving examples from this excerpt, how *Augie March* partakes of the qualities of both forms.

2. Compare Bellow's Augie March with J. D. Salinger's Holden Caulfield in *Catcher in the Rye*. Which of the characters is more mature, more honest, more daring?

Philip Roth

Philip Roth was born in Newark, New Jersey, in 1933. He graduated Phi Beta Kappa from Bucknell University in 1954, and he
received a Master's degree from the University of Chicago in
1955. While still in his early twenties, his stories were published
in *Chicago Review, Commentary, Esquire, Harper's, The New
Yorker,* and *The Paris Review. Goodbye, Columbus,* which won
Roth the National Book Award, was published when he was
twenty-six. This work was followed by several novels, including
Letting Go (1962), *When She Was Good* (1967), *Portnoy's
Complaint* (1968), and *The Breast* (1972).

Roth has been on the faculty of the University of Chicago,
Iowa State, and Princeton. His importance as an American writer
has been widely recognized by critics.

"Eli, the Fanatic" appeared in the *Goodbye, Columbus*
collection of short stories. Unlike Malamud's stories, which
generally focus on poor urban Jews, "Eli, the Fanatic," as well
as most of the stories in *Goodbye, Columbus,* is concerned
with the middle-class suburban Jew. But Roth's ethnic concern
in "Eli, the Fanatic" — the problem of assimilation and identification — is subordinate to his universal concern — the problem
of being a *Mensch,* a human being.

Eli, The Fanatic

Leo Tzuref stepped out from back of a white column to welcome Eli Peck.
Eli jumped back, surprised; then they shook hands and Tzuref gestured him
into the sagging old mansion. At the door Eli turned, and down the slope of
lawn, past the jungle of hedges, beyond the dark, untrampled horse path, he
saw the street lights blink on in Woodenton. The stores along Coach House
Road tossed up a burst of yellow — it came to Eli as a secret signal from his
townsmen: "Tell this Tzuref where we stand, Eli. This is a modern community,
Eli, we have our families, we pay taxes . . ." Eli, burdened by the message,
gave Tzuref a dumb, weary stare.

"You must work a full day," Tzuref said, steering the attorney and his
briefcase into the chilly hall.

Eli's heels made a racket on the cracked marble floor, and he spoke above
it. "It's the commuting that's killing," he said, and entered the dim room
Tzuref waved open for him. "Three hours a day . . . I came right from the
train." He dwindled down into a harp-backed chair. He expected it would be
deeper than it was and consequently jarred himself on the sharp bones of his
seat. It woke him, this shiver of the behind, to his business. Tzuref, a bald

shaggy-browed man who looked as if he'd once been very fat, sat back of an empty desk, halfway hidden, as though he were settled on the floor. Everything around him was empty. There were no books in the bookshelves, no rugs on the floor, no draperies in the big casement windows. As Eli began to speak Tzuref got up and swung a window back on one noisy hinge. "May and it's like August," he said, and with his back to Eli, he revealed the black circle on the back of his head. The crown of his head was missing! He returned through the dimness — the lamps had no bulbs — and Eli realized all he'd seen was a skullcap. Tzuref struck a match and lit a candle, just as the half-dying shouts of children at play rolled in through the open window. It was as though Tzuref had opened it so Eli could hear them.

"Aah, now," he said. "I received your letter."

Eli poised, waiting for Tzuref to swish open a drawer and remove the letter from his file. Instead the old man leaned forward onto his stomach, worked his hand into his pants pocket, and withdrew what appeared to be a week-old handkerchief. He uncrumpled it; he unfolded it; he ironed it on the desk with the side of his hand. "So," he said.

Eli pointed to the grimy sheet which he'd gone over word-by-word with his partners, Lewis and McDonnell. "I expected an answer," Eli said. "It's a week."

"It was so important, Mr. Peck, I knew you would come."

Some children ran under the open window and their mysterious babble — not mysterious to Tzuref, who smiled — entered the room like a third person. Their noise caught up against Eli's flesh and he was unable to restrain a shudder. He wished he had gone home, showered and eaten dinner, before calling on Tzuref. He was not feeling as professional as usual — the place was too dim, it was too late. But down in Woodenton they would be waiting, his clients and neighbors. He spoke for the Jews of Woodenton, not just himself and his wife.

"You understood?" Eli said.

"It's not hard."

"It's a matter of zoning . . ." and when Tzuref did not answer, but only drummed his fingers on his lips, Eli said, "We didn't make the laws . . ."

"You respect them."

"They protect us . . . the community."

"The law is the law," Tzuref said.

"Exactly!" Eli had the urge to rise and walk about the room.

"And then of course" — Tzuref made a pair of scales in the air with his hands — "the law is not the law. When is the law that is the law not the law?" He jiggled the scales. "And vice versa."

"Simply," Eli said sharply. "You can't have a boarding school in a residential area." He would not allow Tzuref to cloud the issue with issues. "We thought it better to tell you before any action is undertaken."

"But a house in a residential area?"

"Yes. That's what residential means." The DP's English was perhaps not as good as it seemed at first. Tzuref spoke slowly, but till then Eli had mistaken it for craft — or even wisdom. "Residence means home," he added.

"So this is my residence."

"But the children?"

"It is their residence."

"*Seventeen* children?"

"Eighteen," Tzuref said.

"But you *teach* them here."

"The Talmud. That's illegal?"

"That makes it school."

Tzuref hung the scales again, tipping slowly the balance.

"Look, Mr. Tzuref, in America we call such a place a boarding school."

"Where they teach the Talmud?"

"Where they teach period. You are the headmaster, they are the students."

Tzuref placed his scales on the desk. "Mr. Peck," he said, "I don't believe it . . ." but he did not seem to be referring to anything Eli had said.

"Mr. Tzuref, that is the law. I came to ask what you intend to do."

"What I *must* do?"

"I hope they are the same."

"They are." Tzuref brought his stomach into the desk. "We stay." He smiled. "We are tired. The headmaster is tired. The students are tired."

Eli rose and lifted his briefcase. It felt so heavy packed with the grievances, vengeances, and schemes of his clients. There were days when he carried it like a feather—in Tzuref's office it weighed a ton.

"Goodbye, Mr. Tzuref."

"Sholom," Tzuref said.

Eli opened the door to the office and walked carefully down the dark tomb of a corridor to the door. He stepped out on the porch and, leaning against a pillar, looked down across the lawn to the children at play. Their voices whooped and rose and dropped as they chased each other round the old house. The dusk made the children's game look like a tribal dance. Eli straightened up, started off the porch, and suddenly the dance was ended. A long piercing scream trailed after. It was the first time in his life anyone had run at the sight of him. Keeping his eyes on the lights of Woodenton, he headed down the path.

And then, seated on a bench beneath a tree, Eli saw him. At first it seemed only a deep hollow of blackness—then the figure emerged. Eli recognized him from the description. There he was, wearing the hat, that hat which was the very cause of Eli's mission, the source of Woodenton's upset. The town's lights flashed their message once again: "Get the one with the hat. What a nerve, what a nerve . . ."

Eli started towards the man. Perhaps he was less stubborn than Tzuref, more reasonable. After all, it was the law. But when he was close enough to call out, he didn't. He was stopped by the sight of the black coat that fell down below the man's knees, and the hands which held each other in his lap. By the round-topped, wide-brimmed Talmudic hat, pushed onto the back of his head. And by the beard, which hid his neck and was so soft and thin it fluttered away and back again with each heavy breath he took. He was asleep, his side-locks curled loose on his cheeks. His face was no older than Eli's.

Eli hurried towards the lights.

The note on the kitchen table unsettled him. Scribblings on bits of paper had made history this past week. This one, however, was unsigned. "Sweetie," it said, "I went to sleep. I had a sort of Oedipal experience with the baby today. Call Ted Heller."

She had left him a cold soggy dinner in the refrigerator. He hated cold soggy dinners, but would take one gladly in place of Miriam's presence. He was ruffled, and she never helped that, not with her infernal analytic powers. He loved her when life was proceeding smoothly—and that was when she loved him. But sometimes Eli found being a lawyer surrounded him like quicksand—he couldn't get his breath. Too often he wished he were pleading for the other side; though if he were on the other side, then he'd wish he were on the side he was. The trouble was that sometimes the law didn't seem to be the answer, *law* didn't seem to have anything to do with what was aggravating everybody. And that, of course, made him feel foolish and unnecessary . . . Though that was not the situation here—the townsmen had a case. But not *exactly*, and if Miriam were awake to see Eli's upset, she would set about explaining his distress to him, understanding him, forgiving him, so as to get things back to Normal, for Normal was where they loved one another. The difficulty with Miriam's efforts was they only upset him more; not only did they explain little to him about himself or his predicament, but they convinced him of *her* weakness. Neither Eli nor Miriam, it turned out, was terribly strong. Twice before he'd faced this fact, and on both occasions had found solace in what his neighbors forgivingly referred to as "a nervous breakdown."

Eli ate his dinner with his briefcase beside him. Halfway through, he gave in to himself, removed Tzuref's notes, and put them on the table, beside Miriam's. From time to time he flipped through the notes, which had been carried into town by the one in the black hat. The first note, the incendiary:

To whom it may concern:

Please give this gentleman the following: Boys shoes with rubber heels and soles.

> 5 prs size 6c
> 3 prs size 5c
> 3 prs size 5b
> 2 prs size 4a
> 3 prs size 4c
> 1 pr size 7b
> 1 pr size 7c

Total 18 prs. boys shoes. This gentleman has a check already signed. Please fill in correct amount.

> L. TZUREF
> Director, Yeshivah of
> Woodenton, N. Y.
> (5/8/48)

"Eli, a regular greenhorn," Ted Heller had said. "He didn't say a word. Just handed me the note and stood there, like in the Bronx the old guys who used to come around selling Hebrew trinkets."

"A Yeshivah!" Artie Berg had said. "Eli, in Woodenton, a Yeshivah! If I want to live in Brownsville, Eli, I'll live in Brownsville."

"Eli," Harry Shaw speaking now, "the old Puddington place. Old man Puddington'll roll over in his grave. Eli, when I left the city, Eli, I didn't plan the city should come to me."

Note number two:

Dear Grocer:

Please give this gentleman ten pounds of sugar. Charge it to our account, Yeshivah of Woodenton, NY—which we will now open with you and expect a bill each month. The gentleman will be in to see you once or twice a week.

L. TZUREF, Director
(5/10/48)

P. S. Do you carry kosher meat?

"He walked right by my window, the greenie," Ted had said, "and he nodded, Eli. He's my *friend* now."

"Eli," Artie Berg had said, "he handed the damn thing to a *clerk* at Stop N' Shop—and in that hat yet!"

"Eli," Harry Shaw again, "it's not funny. Someday, Eli, it's going to be a hundred little kids with little *yamalkahs* chanting their Hebrew lessons on Coach House Road, and then it's not going to strike you funny."

"Eli, what goes on up there—my kids hear strange sounds."

"Eli, this is a modern community."

"Eli, we pay taxes."

"Eli."

"Eli!"

"*Eli!*"

At first it was only another townsman crying in his ear; but when he turned he saw Miriam, standing in the doorway, behind her belly.

"Eli, sweetheart, how was it?"

"He said no."

"Did you see the other one?" she asked.

"Sleeping, under a tree."

"Did you let him know how people feel?"

"He was sleeping."

"Why didn't you wake him up? Eli, this isn't an everyday thing."

"He was tired!"

"Don't shout, please," Miriam said.

" 'Don't shout. I'm pregnant. The baby is heavy.' " Eli found he was getting angry at nothing she'd said yet; it was what she was going to say.

"He's a very heavy baby the doctor says," Miriam told him.

"Then sit *down* and make my dinner." Now he found himself angry about her not being present at the dinner which he'd just been relieved that she wasn't present at. It was as though he had a raw nerve for a tail, that he kept stepping on. At last Miriam herself stepped on it.

"Eli, you're upset. I understand."

"You *don't* understand."

She left the room. From the stairs she called, "I do, sweetheart."

It was a trap! He would grow angry knowing she would be "understanding." She would in turn grow more understanding seeing his anger. He would in turn grow angrier . . . The phone rang.

"Hello," Eli said.

"Eli, Ted. So?"

"So nothing."

"Who is Tzuref? He's an American guy?"

"No. A DP. German."

"And the kids?"

"DP's too. He teaches them."

"What? What subjects?" Ted asked.

"I don't know."

"And the guy with the hat, you saw the guy with the hat?"

"Yes. He was sleeping."

"Eli, he sleeps with the *hat?*"

"He sleeps with the hat."

"Goddam fanatics," Ted said. "This is the twentieth century, Eli. Now it's the guy with the hat. Pretty soon all the little Yeshivah boys'll be spilling down into town."

"Next thing they'll be after our daughters."

"Michele and Debbie wouldn't look at them."

"Then," Eli mumbled, "you've got nothing to worry about, Teddie," and he hung up.

In a moment the phone rang. "Eli? We got cut off. We've got nothing to worry about? You worked it out?"

"I have to see him again tomorrow. We can work something out."

"That's fine; Eli. I'll call Artie and Harry."

Eli hung up.

"I thought you said *nothing* worked out." It was Miriam.

"I did."

"Then why did you tell Ted *something* worked out?"

"It did."

"Eli, maybe you should get a little more therapy."

"That's enough of that, Miriam."

"You can't function as a lawyer by being neurotic. That's no answer."

"You're ingenious, Miriam."

She turned, frowning, and took her heavy baby to bed.

The phone rang.

"Eli, Artie. Ted called. You worked it out? No trouble?"

"Yes."

"When are they going?"

"Leave it to me, will you, Artie? I'm tired. I'm going to sleep."

■ In bed Eli kissed his wife's belly and laid his head upon it to think. He laid it lightly, for she was that day entering the second week of her ninth month. Still, when she slept, it was a good place to rest, to rise and fall with her breathing and figure things out. "If that guy would take off that crazy hat. I know it, what eats them. If he'd take off that crazy hat everything would be all right."

"What?" Miriam said.

"I'm talking to the baby."

Miriam pushed herself up in bed. "Eli, please, baby, shouldn't you maybe stop in to see Dr. Eckman, just for a little conversation?"

"I'm fine."

"Oh, sweetie!" she said, and put her head back on the pillow.

"You know what your mother brought to this marriage — a sling chair and a goddam New School enthusiasm for Sigmund Freud."

Miriam feigned sleep, he could tell by the breathing.

"I'm telling the kid the truth, aren't I, Miriam? A sling chair, three months to go on a *New Yorker* subscription, and *An Introduction to Psychoanalysis*. Isn't that right?"

"Eli, must you be aggressive?"

"That's all you worry about, is your insides. You stand in front of the mirror all day and look at yourself being pregnant."

"Pregnant mothers have a relationship with the fetus that fathers can't understand."

"Relationship my ass. What is my liver doing now? What is my small intestine doing now? Is my island of Langerhans on the blink?"

"Don't be jealous of a little fetus, Eli."

"I'm jealous of your island of Langerhans!"

"Eli, I can't argue with you when I know it's not me you're really angry with. Don't you see, sweetie, you're angry with yourself."

"You and Eckman."

"Maybe he could help, Eli."

"Maybe he could help you. You're practically lovers as it is."

"You're being hostile again," Miriam said.

"What do you care — it's only *me* I'm being hostile towards."

"Eli, we're going to have a beautiful baby, and I'm going to have a perfectly simple delivery, and you're going to make a fine father, and there's absolutely no reason to be obsessed with whatever is on your mind. All we have to worry about — " she smiled at him " — is a name."

Eli got out of bed and slid into his slippers. "We'll name the kid Eckman if it's a boy and Eckman if it's a girl."

"Eckman Peck sounds terrible."

"He'll have to live with it," Eli said, and he went down to his study where the latch on his briefcase glinted in the moonlight that came through the window.

He removed the Tzuref notes and read through them all again. It unnerved him to think of all the flashy reasons his wife could come up with for his reading and rereading the notes. "Eli, why are you so *preoccupied* with Tzuref?" "Eli, stop getting *involved*. Why do you think you're getting *involved*, Eli?" Sooner or later, everybody's wife finds their weak spot. His goddam luck he had to be neurotic! Why couldn't he have been born with a short leg.

He removed the cover from his typewriter, hating Miriam for the edge she had. All the time he wrote the letter, he could hear what she would be saying about his not being *able* to let the matter drop. Well, her trouble was that she wasn't *able* to face the matter. But he could hear her answer already: clearly, he was guilty of "a reaction formation." Still, all the fancy phrases didn't fool

Eli: all she wanted really was for Eli to send Tzuref and family on their way, so that the community's temper would quiet, and the calm circumstances of their domestic happiness return. All she wanted were order and love in her private world. Was she so wrong? Let the world bat its brains out—in Woodenton there should be peace. He wrote the letter anyway:

Dear Mr. Tzuref:

Our meeting this evening seems to me inconclusive. I don't think there's any reason for us not to be able to come up with some sort of compromise that will satisfy the Jewish community of Woodenton and the Yeshivah and yourself. It seems to me that what most disturbs my neighbors are the visits to town by the gentleman in the black hat, suit, etc. Woodenton is a progressive suburban community whose members, both Jewish and Gentile, are anxious that their families live in comfort and beauty and serenity. This is, after all, the twentieth century, and we do not think it too much to ask that the members of our community dress in a manner appropriate to the time and place.

Woodenton, as you may not know, has long been the home of well-to-do Protestants. It is only since the war that Jews have been able to buy property here, and for Jews and Gentiles to live beside each other in amity. For this adjustment to be made, both Jews and Gentiles alike have had to give up some of their more extreme practices in order not to threaten or offend the other. Certainly such amity is to be desired. Perhaps if such conditions had existed in prewar Europe, the persecution of the Jewish people, of which you and those 18 children have been victims, could not have been carried out with such success—in fact, might not have been carried out at all.

Therefore, Mr. Tzuref, will you accept the following conditions? If you can, we will see fit not to carry out legal action against the Yeshivah for failure to comply with township Zoning ordinances No. 18 and No. 23. The conditions are simply:

1. The religious, educational, and social activities of the Yeshivah of Woodenton will be confined to the Yeshivah grounds.

2. Yeshivah personnel are welcomed in the streets and stores of Woodenton provided they are attired in clothing usually associated with American life in the 20th century.

If these conditions are met, we see no reason why the Yeshivah of Woodenton cannot live peacefully and satisfactorily with the Jews of Woodenton —as the Jews of Woodenton have come to live with the Gentiles of Woodenton. I would appreciate an immediate reply.

Sincerely,
ELI PECK, Attorney

Two days later Eli received his immediate reply:

Mr. Peck:

The suit the gentleman wears is all he's got.

Sincerely,
LEO TZUREF, Headmaster

■ Once again, as Eli swung around the dark trees and onto the lawn, the children fled. He reached out with his briefcase as if to stop them, but they were gone so fast all he saw moving was a flock of skullcaps.

"Come, come . . ." a voice called from the porch. Tzuref appeared from behind a pillar. Did he *live* behind those pillars? Was he just watching the children at play? Either way, when Eli appeared, Tzuref was ready, with no forewarning.

"Hello," Eli said.

"Sholom."

"I didn't mean to frighten them."

"They're scared, so they run."

"I didn't do anything."

Tzuref shrugged. The little movement seemed to Eli strong as an accusation. What he didn't get at home, he got here.

Inside the house they took their seats. Though it was lighter than a few evenings before, a bulb or two would have helped. Eli had to hold his briefcase towards the window for the last gleamings. He removed Tzuref's letter from a manila folder. Tzuref removed Eli's letter from his pants pocket. Eli removed the carbon of his own letter from another manila folder. Tzuref removed Eli's first letter from his back pocket. Eli removed the carbon from his briefcase. Tzuref raised his palms. ". . . It's all I've got . . ."

Those upraised palms, the mocking tone—another accusation. It was a crime to keep carbons! Everybody had an edge on him—Eli could do no right.

"I offered a compromise, Mr. Tzuref. You refused."

"Refused, Mr. Peck? What is, is."

"The man could get a new suit."

"That's all he's got."

"So you told me," Eli said.

"So I told you, so you know."

"It's not an insurmountable obstacle, Mr. Tzuref. We have stores."

"For that too?"

"On Route 12, a Robert Hall—"

"To take away the one thing a man's got?"

"Not take away, *replace*."

"But I tell you he has nothing. *Nothing.* You have that word in English? *Nicht? Gornisht?*"

"Yes, Mr. Tzuref, we have the word."

"A mother and a father?" Tzuref said. "No. A wife? No. A baby? A little ten-month-old baby? No! A village full of friends? A synagogue where you knew the feel of every seat under your pants? Where with your eyes closed you could smell the cloth of the Torah?" Tzuref pushed out of his chair, stirring a breeze that swept Eli's letter to the floor. At the window he leaned out, and looked, beyond Woodenton. When he turned he was shaking a finger at Eli. "And a medical experiment they performed on him yet! That leaves nothing, Mr. Peck. Absolutely nothing!"

"I misunderstood."

"No news reached Woodenton?"

"About the suit, Mr. Tzuref. I thought he couldn't afford another."

"He can't."

They were right where they'd begun. "Mr. Tzuref!" Eli demanded. "*Here?*" He smacked his hand to his billfold.

"Exactly!" Tzuref said, smacking his own breast.

"Then we'll buy him one!" Eli crossed to the window and taking Tzuref by the shoulders, pronounced each word slowly. "We-will-pay-for-it. All right?"

"Pay? What, diamonds!"

Eli raised a hand to his inside pocket, then let it drop. Oh stupid! Tzuref, father to eighteen, had smacked not what lay under his coat, but deeper, under the ribs.

"Oh . . ." Eli said. He moved away along the wall. "The suit is all he's got then."

"You got my letter," Tzuref said.

Eli stayed back in the shadow, and Tzuref turned to his chair. He swished Eli's letter from the floor, and held it up. "You say too much . . . all this reasoning . . . all these conditions . . ."

"What can I do?"

"You have the word 'suffer' in English?"

"We have the word suffer. We have the word law too."

"Stop with the law! You have the word suffer. Then try it. It's a little thing."

"They won't," Eli said.

"But you, Mr. Peck, how about you?"

"I am them, they are me, Mr. Tzuref."

"Aach! You are us, we are you!"

Eli shook and shook his head. In the dark he suddenly felt that Tzuref might put him under a spell. "Mr. Tzuref, a little light?"

Tzuref lit what tallow was left in the holders. Eli was afraid to ask if they couldn't afford electricity. Maybe candles were all they had left.

"Mr. Peck, who made the law, may I ask you that?"

"The people."

"No."

"Yes."

"Before the people."

"No one. Before the people there was no law." Eli didn't care for the conversation, but with only candlelight, he was being lulled into it.

"Wrong," Tzuref said.

"We make the law, Mr. Tzuref. It is our community. These are my neighbors. I am their attorney. They pay me. Without law there is chaos."

"What you call law, I call shame. The heart, Mr. Peck, the heart is law! God!" he announced.

"Look, Mr. Tzuref, I didn't come here to talk metaphysics. People use the law, it's a flexible thing. They protect what they value, their property, their well-being, their happiness—"

"Happiness? They hide their shame. And you, Mr. Peck, you are shameless?"

"We do it," Eli said, wearily, "for our children. This is the twentieth century . . ."

"For the goyim maybe. For me the Fifty-eighth." He pointed at Eli. "That is too old for shame."

Eli felt squashed. Everybody in the world had evil reasons for his actions. Everybody! With reasons so cheap, who buys bulbs. "Enough wisdom, Mr. Tzuref. Please. I'm exhausted."

"Who isn't?" Tzuref said.

He picked Eli's papers from his desk and reached up with them. "What do you intend for us to do?"

"What you must," Eli said. "I made the offer."

"So he must give up his suit?"

"Tzuref, Tzuref, leave me be with that suit! I'm not the only lawyer in the world. I'll drop the case, and you'll get somebody who won't talk compromise. Then you'll have no home, no children, nothing. Only a lousy black suit! Sacrifice what you want. I know what I would do."

To that Tzuref made no answer, but only handed Eli his letters.

"It's not me, Mr. Tzuref, it's them."

"They are you."

"No," Eli intoned, "I am me. They are them. You are you."

"You talk about leaves and branches. I'm dealing with under the dirt."

"Mr. Tzuref, you're driving me crazy with Talmudic wisdom. This is that, that is the other thing. Give me a straight answer."

"Only for straight questions."

"Oh, God!"

Eli returned to his chair and plunged his belongings into his case. "Then, that's all," he said angrily.

Tzuref gave him the shrug.

"Remember, Tzuref, you called this down on yourself."

"*I* did?"

Eli refused to be his victim again. Double-talk proved nothing.

"Goodbye," he said.

But as he opened the door leading to the hall, he heard Tzuref.

"And your wife, how is she?"

"Fine, just fine." Eli kept going.

"And the baby is due when, any day?"

Eli turned. "That's right."

"Well," Tzuref said, rising. "Good luck."

"You know?"

Tzuref pointed out the window—then, with his hands, he drew upon himself a beard, a hat, a long, long coat. When his fingers formed the hem they touched the floor. "He shops two, three times a week, he gets to know them."

"He *talks* to them?"

"He sees them."

"And he can tell which is my wife?"

"They shop at the same stores. He says she is beautiful. She has a kind face. A woman capable of love . . . though who can be sure."

"*He* talks about *us,* to *you?*" demanded Eli.

"You talk about us, to her?"

"Goodbye, Mr. Tzuref."

Tzuref said, "Sholom. And good luck—I know what it is to have children. Sholom," Tzuref whispered, and with the whisper the candles went out. But the instant before, the flames leaped into Tzuref's eyes, and Eli saw it was not luck Tzuref wished him at all.

Outside the door, Eli waited. Down the lawn the children were holding hands and whirling around in a circle. At first he did not move. But he could not hide in the shadows all night. Slowly he began to slip along the front of the house. Under his hands he felt where bricks were out. He moved in the shadows until he reached the side. And then, clutching his briefcase to his chest, he broke across the darkest spots of the lawn. He aimed for a distant glade of woods, and when he reached it he did not stop, but ran through until he was so dizzied that the trees seemed to be running beside him, fleeing not towards Woodenton but away. His lungs were nearly ripping their seams as he burst into the yellow glow of the Gulf station at the edge of town.

■ "Eli, I had pains today. Where were you?"

"I went to Tzuref."

"Why didn't you call? I was worried."

He tossed his hat past the sofa and onto the floor. "Where are my winter suits?"

"In the hall closet. Eli, it's May."

"I need a strong suit." He left the room, Miriam behind him.

"Eli, talk to me. Sit down. Have dinner. Eli, what are you doing? You're going to get moth balls all over the carpet."

He peered out from the hall closet. Then he peered in again—there was a zipping noise, and suddenly he swept a greenish tweed suit before his wife's eyes.

"Eli, I love you in that suit. But not now. Have something to eat. I made dinner tonight—I'll warm it."

"You've got a box big enough for this suit?"

"I got a Bonwit's box, the other day. Eli, *why?*"

"Miriam, you see me doing something, let me do it."

"You haven't eaten."

"I'm *doing* something." He started up the stairs to the bedroom.

"Eli, would you please tell me what it is you want, and why?"

He turned and looked down at her. "Suppose this time you give me the reasons *before* I tell you what I'm doing. It'll probably work out the same anyway."

"Eli, I want to help."

"It doesn't concern you."

"But I want to help *you*," Miriam said.

"Just be quiet, then."

"But you're upset," she said, and she followed him up the stairs, heavily, breathing for two.

"Eli, what now?"

"A shirt." He yanked open all the drawers of their new teak dresser. He extracted a shirt.

"Eli, batiste? With a tweed suit?" she inquired.

He was at the closet now, on his knees. "Where are my cordovans?"

"Eli, why are you doing this so compulsively? You look like you *have* to do something."

"Oh, Miriam, you're supersubtle."

"Eli, stop this and talk to me. Stop it or I'll call Dr. Eckman."

Eli was kicking off the shoes he was wearing. "Where's the Bonwit box?"

"Eli, do you want me to have the baby right *here!*"

Eli walked over and sat down on the bed. He was draped not only with his own clothing, but also with the greenish tweed suit, the batiste shirt, and under each arm a shoe. He raised his arms and let the shoes drop onto the bed. Then he undid the necktie with one hand and his teeth and added that to the booty.

"Underwear," he said. "He'll need underwear."

"Who!"

He was slipping out of his socks.

Miriam kneeled down and helped him ease his left foot out of the sock. She sat with it on the floor. "Eli, just lie back. Please."

"Plaza 9-3103."

"What?"

"Eckman's number," he said. "It'll save you the trouble."

"Eli—"

"You've got that goddam tender 'You need help' look in your eyes, Miriam, don't tell me you don't."

"I don't."

"I'm not flipping," Eli said.

"I know, Eli."

"Last time I sat in the bottom of the closet and chewed on my bedroom slippers. That's what I did."

"I know."

"And I'm not doing that. This is not a nervous breakdown, Miriam, let's get that straight."

"Okay," Miriam said. She kissed the foot she held. Then, softly, she asked, "What *are* you doing?"

"Getting clothes for the guy in the hat. Don't tell me why, Miriam. Just let me do it."

"That's all?" she asked.

"That's all."

"You're not leaving?"

"No."

"Sometimes I think it gets too much for you, and you'll just leave."

"What gets too much?"

"I don't *know*, Eli. Something gets too much. Whenever everything's peaceful for a long time, and things are nice and pleasant, and we're expecting to be even happier. Like now. It's as if you don't think we *deserve* to be happy."

"Damn it, Miriam! I'm giving this guy a new suit, is that all right? From now on he comes into Woodenton like everybody else, is that all right with you?"

"And Tzuref moves?"

"I don't even know if he'll take the suit, Miriam! What do you have to bring up moving!"

"Eli, I didn't bring up moving. Everybody did. That's what everybody wants. Why make everybody un*happy*. It's even a law, Eli."

"Don't tell me what's the law."

"All right, sweetie. I'll get the box."

"*I'll* get the box. Where is it?"

"In the basement."

When he came up from the basement, he found all the clothes neatly folded and squared away on the sofa: shirt, tie, shoes, socks, underwear, belt, and an old gray flannel suit. His wife sat on the end of the sofa, looking like an anchored balloon.

"Where's the green suit?" he said.

"Eli, it's your loveliest suit. It's my favorite suit. Whenever I think of you, Eli, it's in that suit."

"Get it out."

"Eli, it's a Brooks Brothers suit. You say yourself how much you love it."

"Get it out."

"But the gray flannel's more practical. For shopping."

"Get it out."

"You go overboard, Eli. That's your trouble. You won't do anything in moderation. That's how people destroy themselves."

"I do *everything* in moderation. That's my trouble. The suit's in the closet again?"

She nodded, and began to fill up with tears. "Why does it have to be *your* suit? Who are you even to decide to give a suit? What about the others?" She was crying openly, and holding her belly. "Eli, I'm going to have a baby. Do we need all *this?*" and she swept the clothes off the sofa to the floor.

At the closet Eli removed the green suit. "It's a J. Press," he said, looking at the lining.

"I hope to hell he's happy with it!" Miriam said, sobbing.

■ A half hour later the box was packed. The cord he'd found in the kitchen cabinet couldn't keep the outfit from popping through. The trouble was there was too much: the gray suit *and* the green suit, an oxford shirt as well as the batiste. But let him have two suits! Let him have three, four, if only this damn silliness would stop! And a hat — of course! God, he'd almost forgotten the hat. He took the stairs two at a time and in Miriam's closet yanked a hatbox from the top shelf. Scattering hat and tissue paper to the floor, he returned downstairs, where he packed away the hat he'd worn that day. Then he looked at his wife, who lay outstretched on the floor before the fireplace. For the third time in as many minutes she was saying, "Eli, this is the real thing."

"Where?"

"Right under the baby's head, like somebody's squeezing oranges."

Now that he'd stopped to listen he was stupefied. He said, "But you have two more weeks . . ." Somehow he'd really been expecting it was to go on not just another two weeks, but another nine months. This led him to suspect, suddenly, that his wife was feigning pain so as to get his mind off delivering the suit. And just as suddenly he resented himself for having such a thought. God, what had he become! He'd been an unending bastard towards her since this Tzuref business had come up — just when her pregnancy must have been most burdensome. He'd allowed her no access to him, but still, he was sure, for good reasons: she might tempt him out of his confusion with her easy answers. He could be tempted all right, it was why he fought so hard. But now a sweep of love came over him at the thought of her contracting womb, and his child. And yet he would not indicate it to her. Under such splendid marital conditions, who knows but she might extract some promise from him about his concern with the school on the hill.

■ Having packed his second bag of the evening, Eli sped his wife to Woodenton Memorial. There she proceeded not to have her baby, but to lie hour after hour through the night having at first oranges, then bowling balls, then basketballs, squeezed back of her pelvis. Eli sat in the waiting room, under the shattering African glare of a dozen rows of fluorescent bulbs, composing a letter to Tzuref.

Dear Mr. Tzuref:
   The clothes in this box are for the gentleman in the hat. In a life of sacrifice what is one more? But in a life of no sacrifices even one is impossible. Do you see what I'm saying, Mr. Tzuref? I am not a Nazi who would drive eighteen children, who are probably frightened at the sight of a firefly, into homelessness. But if you want a home here, you must accept what we have to offer. The world is the world, Mr. Tzuref. As you would say, what is, is. All we say to this man is change your clothes. Enclosed are two suits and two shirts, and everything else he'll need, including a new hat. When he needs new clothes let me know.
   We await his appearance in Woodenton, as we await friendly relations with the Yeshivah of Woodenton.

He signed his name and slid the note under a bursting flap and into the box. Then he went to the phone at the end of the room and dialed Ted Heller's number.
   "Hello."
   "Shirley, it's Eli."
   "Eli, we've been calling all night. The lights are on in your place, but nobody answers. We thought it was burglars."
   "Miriam's having the baby."
   "At home?" Shirley said. "Oh, Eli, what a fun-idea!"
   "Shirley, let me speak to Ted."
   After the ear-shaking clatter of the phone whacking the floor, Eli heard footsteps, breathing, throat-clearing, then Ted. "A boy or a girl?"
   "Nothing yet."
   "You've given Shirley the bug, Eli. Now she's going to have *our* next one at home."
   "Good."
   "That's a terrific way to bring the family together, Eli."
   "Look, Ted, I've settled with Tzuref."
   "When are they going?"
   "They're not exactly going, Teddie. I settled it—you won't even know they're there."
   "A guy dressed like 1000 B. C. and I won't know it? What are you thinking about, pal?"

"He's changing his clothes."

"Yeah, to what? Another funeral suit?"

"Tzuref promised me, Ted. Next time he comes to town, he comes dressed like you and me."

"What! Somebody's kidding somebody, Eli."

Eli's voice shot up. "If he says he'll do it, he'll do it!"

"And, Eli," Ted asked, "he said it?"

"He said it." It cost him a sudden headache, this invention.

"And suppose he doesn't change, Eli. Just suppose. I mean that *might* happen, Eli. This might just be some kind of stall or something."

"No," Eli assured him.

The other end was quiet a moment. "Look, Eli," Ted said, finally, "he changes. Okay? All right? But they're still up there, aren't they? *That* doesn't change."

"The point is you won't know it."

Patiently Ted said, "Is this what we asked of you, Eli? When we put our faith and trust in you, is that what we were asking? We weren't concerned that this guy should become a Beau Brummell, Eli, believe me. We just don't think this is the community for them. And, Eli, we isn't me. The Jewish members of the community appointed me, Artie, and Harry to see what could be done. And we appointed you. And what's happened?"

Eli heard himself say, "What happened, happened."

"Eli, you're talking in crossword puzzles."

"My wife's having a baby," Eli explained, defensively.

"I realize that, Eli. But this is a matter of zoning, isn't it? Isn't that what we discovered? You don't abide by the ordinance, you go. I mean I can't raise mountain goats, say, in my backyard—"

"This isn't so simple, Ted. People are involved—"

"People? Eli, we've been through this and through this. We're not just dealing with people—these are religious fanatics is what they are. Dressing like that. What I'd really like to find out is what goes on up there. I'm getting more and more skeptical, Eli, and I'm not afraid to admit it. It smells like a lot of hocus-pocus abracadabra stuff to me. Guys like Harry, you know, they think and they think and they're afraid to admit what they're thinking. I'll tell you. Look, I don't even know about this Sunday school business. Sundays I drive my oldest kid all the way to Scarsdale to learn Bible stories . . . and you know what she comes up with? This Abraham in the Bible was going to kill his own *kid* for a sacrifice. She gets nightmares from it, for God's sake! You call that religion? Today a guy like that they'd lock him up. This is an age of science, Eli. I size people's feet with an X-ray machine, for God's sake. They've disproved all that stuff, Eli, and I refuse to sit by and watch it happening on my own front lawn."

"Nothing's happening on your front lawn, Teddie. You're exaggerating, nobody's sacrificing their kid."

"You're damn right, Eli—I'm not sacrificing mine. You'll see when you have your own what it's like. All the place is, is a hideaway for people who can't face life. It's a matter of *needs*. They have all these superstitions, and why do you think? Because they can't face the world, because they can't take their place in society. That's no environment to bring kids up in, Eli."

"Look, Ted, see it from another angle. We can convert them," Eli said, with half a heart.

"What, make a bunch of Catholics out of them? Look, Eli—pal, there's a good healthy relationship in this town because it's modern Jews and Protestants. That's the point, isn't it, Eli? Let's not kid each other. I'm not Harry. The way things are now are fine—like human beings. There's going to be no pogroms in Woodenton. Right? 'Cause there's no fanatics, no crazy people—" Eli winced, and closed his eyes a second—"just people who respect each other, and leave each other be. Common sense is the ruling thing, Eli. I'm for common sense. Moderation."

"Exactly, exactly, Ted. I agree, but common sense, maybe, says make this guy change his clothes. Then maybe—"

"Common sense says that? Common sense says to me they go and find a nice place somewhere else, Eli. New York is the biggest city in the world, it's only 30 miles away—why don't they go there?"

"Ted, give them a chance. Introduce them to common sense."

"Eli, you're dealing with *fanatics*. Do they display common sense? Talking a dead language, that makes sense? Making a big thing out of suffering, so you're going oy-oy-oy all your life, that's common sense? Look, Eli, we've been through all this. I don't know if you know—but there's talk that *Life* magazine is sending a guy out to the Yeshivah for a story. With pictures."

"Look, Teddie, you're letting your imagination get inflamed. I don't think *Life's* interested."

"But I'm interested, Eli. And we thought you were supposed to be."

"I am," Eli said, "I am. Let him just change the clothes, Ted. Let's see what happens."

"They live in the medieval ages, Eli—it's some superstition, some *rule*."

"Let's just *see*," Eli pleaded.

"Eli, every day—"

"One more day," Eli said. "If he doesn't change in one more day . . ."

"What?"

"Then I get an injunction first thing Monday. That's that."

"Look, Eli—it's not up to me. Let me call Harry—"

"You're the spokesman, Teddie. I'm all wrapped up here with Miriam having a baby. Just give me the day—them the day."

"All right, Eli. I want to be fair. But tomorrow, that's all. Tomorrow's the judgment day, Eli, I'm telling you."

"I hear trumpets," Eli said, and hung up. He was shaking inside—Teddie's voice seemed to have separated his bones at the joints. He was still in the phone booth when the nurse came to tell him that Mrs. Peck would positively not be delivered of a child until the morning. He was to go home and get some rest, he looked like *he* was having the baby. The nurse winked and left.

But Eli did not go home. He carried the Bonwit box out into the street with him and put it in the car. The night was soft and starry, and he began to drive the streets of Woodenton. Square cool windows, apricot-colored, were all one could see beyond the long lawns that fronted the homes of the townsmen. The stars polished the permanent baggage carriers atop the station wagons in the driveways. He drove slowly, up, down, around. Only his tires could be heard taking the gentle curves in the road.

What peace. What incredible peace. Have children ever been so safe in their beds? Parents—Eli wondered—so full in their stomachs? Water so warm in its boilers? Never. Never in Rome, never in Greece. Never even did walled cities have it so good! No wonder then they would keep things just as they were. Here, after all, were peace and safety—what civilization had been working toward for centuries. For all his jerkiness, that was all Ted Heller was asking for, peace and safety. It was what his parents had asked for in the Bronx, and his grandparents in Poland, and theirs in Russia or Austria, or wherever else they'd fled to or from. It was what Miriam was asking for. And now they had it—the world was at last a place for families, even Jewish families. After all these centuries, maybe there just had to be this communal toughness—or numbness—to protect such a blessing. Maybe that was the trouble with the Jews all along—too soft. Sure, to live takes guts . . . Eli was thinking as he drove on beyond the train station, and parked his car at the darkened Gulf station. He stepped out, carrying the box.

At the top of the hill one window trembled with light. What *was* Tzuref doing up there in that office? Killing babies—probably not. But studying a language no one understood? Practicing customs with origins long forgotten? Suffering sufferings already suffered once too often? Teddie was right—why keep it up! However, if a man chose to be stubborn, then he couldn't expect to survive. The world is give-and-take. What sense to sit and brood over a suit. Eli would give him one last chance.

He stopped at the top. No one was around. He walked slowly up the lawn, setting each foot into the grass, listening to the shh shhh shhhh his shoes made as they bent the wetness into the sod. He looked around. Here there was nothing. Nothing! An old decaying house—and a suit.

On the porch he slid behind a pillar. He felt someone was watching him. But only the stars gleamed down. And at his feet, off and away, Woodenton glowed up. He set his package on the step of the great front door. Inside the cover of the box he felt to see if his letter was still there. When he touched it, he pushed it deeper into the green suit; which his fingers still remembered from winter. He should have included some light bulbs. Then he slid back by the pillar again, and this time there was something on the lawn. It was the second sight he had of him. He was facing Woodenton and barely moving across the open space towards the trees. His right fist was beating his chest. And then Eli heard a sound rising with each knock on the chest. What a moan! It could raise hair, stop hearts, water eyes. And it did all three to Eli, plus more. Some feeling crept into him for whose deepness he could find no word. It was strange. He listened—it did not hurt to hear this moan. But he wondered if it hurt to make it. And so, with only stars to hear, he tried. And it did hurt. Not the bumble-bee of noise that turned at the back of his throat and winged out his nostrils. What hurt buzzed down. It stung and stung inside him, and in turn the moan sharpened. It became a scream, louder, a song, a crazy song that whined through the pillars and blew out to the grass, until the strange hatted creature on the lawn turned and threw his arms wide, and looked in the night like a scarecrow.

Eli ran, and when he reached the car the pain was only a bloody scratch across his neck where a branch had whipped back as he fled the greenie's arms.

■ The following day his son was born. But not till one in the afternoon, and by then a great deal had happened.

First, at nine-thirty the phone rang. Eli leaped from the sofa—where he'd dropped the night before—and picked it screaming from the cradle. He could practically smell the hospital as he shouted into the phone. "Hello, yes!"

"Eli, it's Ted. Eli, he *did* it. He just walked by the store. I was opening the door, Eli, and I turned around and I swear I thought it was you. But it was him. He still walks like he did, but the clothes, Eli, the clothes."

"Who?"

"The greenie. He has on man's regular clothes. And the suit, it's a beauty."

The suit barreled back into Eli's consciousness, pushing all else aside. "What color suit?"

"Green. He's just strolling in the green suit like it's a holiday. Eli . . . is it a Jewish holiday?"

"Where is he now?"

"He's walking straight up Coach House Road, in this damn tweed job. Eli, it worked. You were right."

"We'll see."

"What next?"

"We'll see."

He took off the underwear in which he'd slept and went into the kitchen where he turned the light under the coffee. When it began to perk he held his head over the pot so it would steam loose the knot back of his eyes. It still hadn't when the phone rang.

"Eli, Ted again. Eli, the guy's walking up and down every street in town. Really, he's on a tour or something. Artie called me, Herb called me. Now Shirley calls that he just walked by our house. Eli, go out on the porch you'll see."

Eli went to the window and peered out. He couldn't see past the bend in the road, and there was no one in sight.

"Eli?" He heard Ted from where he dangled over the telephone table. He dropped the phone into the hook, as a few last words floated up to him —"Eliyousawhim . . . ?" He threw on the pants and shirt he'd worn the night before and walked barefoot on to his front lawn. And sure enough, his apparition appeared around the bend: in a brown hat a little too far down on his head, a green suit too far back on the shoulders, an unbuttoned-down button-down shirt, a tie knotted so as to leave a two-inch tail, trousers that cascaded onto his shoes—he was shorter than that black hat had made him seem. And moving the clothes was that walk that was not a walk, a tiny-stepped shlumpy gait. He came round the bend, and for all his strangeness—it clung to his whiskers, signaled itself in his locomotion—he looked as if he belonged. Eccentric, maybe, but he belonged. He made no moan, nor did he invite Eli with wide-flung arms. But he did stop when he saw him. He stopped and put a hand to his hat. When he felt for its top, his hand went up too high. Then it found the level and fiddled with the brim. The fingers fiddled, fumbled, and when they'd finally made their greeting, they traveled down the fellow's face and in an instant seemed to have touched each one of his features. They dabbed the eyes, ran the length of the nose, swept over the hairy lip, until they found their home in the hair that hid a little of his collar. To Eli the fingers said, *I have a face, I have a face at least.* Then his hand came through the beard and when it stopped at his chest it was like a pointer—and the eyes asked a question as tides of water shifted over them. *The face is all right, I can keep it?* Such a look was in those eyes that Eli was still seeing them when he turned his head away. They were the hearts of his jonquils, that only last week had appeared—they were the leaves on his birch, the bulbs in his coach lamp, the droppings on his lawn: those eyes were the eyes in his head. They were his, he had made them. He turned and went into his house and when he peeked out the side of the window, between shade and molding, the green suit was gone.

The phone.

"Eli, Shirley."

"I saw him, Shirley," and he hung up.

He sat frozen for a long time. The sun moved around the windows. The coffee steam smelled up the house. The phone began to ring, stopped, began again. The mailman came, the cleaner, the bakery man, the gardener, the ice cream man, the League of Women Voters lady. A Negro woman spreading some strange gospel calling for the revision of the Food and Drug Act knocked at the front, rapped the windows, and finally scraped a half-dozen pamphlets under the back door. But Eli only sat, without underwear, in last night's suit. He answered no one.

Given his condition, it was strange that the trip and crash at the back door reached his inner ear. But in an instant he seemed to melt down into the crevices of the chair, then to splash up and out to where the clatter had been. At the door he waited. It was silent, but for a fluttering of damp little leaves on the trees. When he finally opened the door, there was no one there. He'd expected to see green, green, green, big as the doorway, topped by his hat, waiting for him with those eyes. But there was no one out there, except for the Bonwit's box which lay bulging at his feet. No string tied it and the top rode high on the bottom.

The coward! He couldn't do it! He couldn't!

The very glee of that idea pumped fuel to his legs. He tore out across his back lawn, past his new spray of forsythia, to catch a glimpse of the bearded one fleeing naked through yards, over hedges and fences, to the safety of his hermitage. In the distance a pile of pink and white stones—which Harriet Knudson had painted the previous day—tricked him. "Run," he shouted to the rocks, "run, you . . ." but he caught his error before anyone else did, and though he peered and craned there was no hint anywhere of a man about his own size, with white, white, terribly white skin (how white must be the skin of his body!) in cowardly retreat. He came slowly, curiously, back to the door. And while the trees shimmered in the light wind, he removed the top from the box. The shock at first was the shock of having daylight turned off all at once. Inside the box was an eclipse. But black soon sorted from black, and shortly there was the glassy black of lining, the coarse black of trousers, the dead black of fraying threads, and in the center the mountain of black: the hat. He picked the box from the doorstep and carried it inside. For the first time in his life he *smelled* the color of blackness: a little stale, a little sour, a little old, but nothing that could overwhelm you. Still, he held the package at arm's length and deposited it on the dining room table.

Twenty rooms on a hill and they store their old clothes with me! What am I supposed to do with them? Give them to charity? That's where they came from. He picked up the hat by the edges and looked inside. The crown was smooth as an egg, the brim practically threadbare. There is nothing else to do with a hat in one's hands but put it on, so Eli dropped the thing on his head. He opened the door to the hall closet and looked at himself in the full-length mirror. The hat gave him bags under the eyes. Or perhaps he had not slept well. He pushed the brim lower till a shadow touched his lips. Now the bags under his eyes had inflated to become his face. Before the mirror he unbuttoned his shirt, unzipped his trousers, and then, shedding his clothes, he studied what he was. What a silly disappointment to see yourself naked in a hat. Especially in that hat. He sighed, but could not rid himself of the great weakness that suddenly set on his muscles and joints, beneath the terrible weight of the stranger's strange hat.

He returned to the dining room table and emptied the box of its contents: jacket, trousers, and vest (*it* smelled deeper than blackness). And under it all, sticking between the shoes that looked chopped and bitten, came the first gleam of white. A little fringed serape, a gray piece of semiunderwear, was crumpled at the bottom, its thready border twisted into itself. Eli removed it and let it hang free. What is it? For warmth? To wear beneath underwear in the event of a chest cold? He held it to his nose but it did not smell from Vick's or mustard plaster. It was something special, some Jewish thing. Special food, special language, special prayers, why not special BVD's? So fearful was he that he would be tempted back into wearing his traditional clothes —reasoned Eli—that he had carried and buried in Woodenton everything, including the special underwear. For that was how Eli now understood the box of clothes. The greenie was saying, Here, I give up. I refuse even to be tempted. We surrender. And that was how Eli continued to understand it until he found he'd slipped the white fringy surrender flag over his hat and felt it clinging to his chest. And now, looking at himself in the mirror, he was momentarily uncertain as to who was tempting who into what. Why *did* the greenie leave his clothes? Was it even the greenie? Then who was it? And why? But, Eli, for Christ's sake, in an age of science things don't happen like that. Even the goddam pigs take drugs . . .

■ Regardless of who was the source of the temptation, what was its end, not to mention its beginning, Eli, some moments later, stood draped in black, with a little white underneath, before the full-length mirror. He had to pull down on the trousers so they would not show the hollow of his ankle. The greenie, didn't he wear socks? Or had he forgotten them? The mystery was solved when Eli mustered enough courage to investigate the trouser pockets. He had expected some damp awful thing to happen to his fingers should he slip them down and out of sight—but when at last he jammed bravely down he came up with a khaki army sock in each hand. As he slipped them over his toes, he invented a genesis: a G.I.'s present in 1945. Plus everything else lost between 1938 and 1945, he had also lost his socks. Not that he had lost the socks, but that he'd had to stoop to accepting these, made Eli almost cry. To calm himself he walked out the back door and stood looking at his lawn.

On the Knudson back lawn, Harriet Knudson was giving her stones a second coat of pink. She looked up just as Eli stepped out. Eli shot back in again and pressed himself against the back door. When he peeked between the curtain all he saw were paint bucket, brush, and rocks scattered on the Knudsons' pink-spattered grass. The phone rang. Who was it—Harriet Knudson? Eli, there's a Jew at your door. *That's me.* Nonsense, Eli, I saw him with my own eyes. *That's me, I saw you too, painting your rocks pink.* Eli, you're having a nervous breakdown again. Jimmy, Eli's having a nervous breakdown again. Eli, this is Jimmy, hear you're having a little breakdown, anything I can do, boy? Eli, this is Ted, Shirley says you need help. Eli, this is Artie, you need help. Eli, Harry, you need help you need help . . . The phone rattled its last and died.

"God helps them who help themselves," intoned Eli, and once again he stepped out the door. This time he walked to the center of his lawn and in full sight of the trees, the grass, the birds, and the sun, revealed that it was he, Eli, in the costume. But nature had nothing to say to him, and so stealthily he made his way to the hedge separating his property from the field beyond and he cut his way through, losing his hat twice in the underbrush. Then, clamping the hat to his head, he began to run, the threaded tassels jumping across his heart. He ran through the weeds and wild flowers, until on the old road that skirted the town he slowed up. He was walking when he approached the Gulf station from the back. He supported himself on a huge tireless truck rim, and among tubes, rusted engines, dozens of topless oil cans, he rested. With a kind of brainless cunning, he readied himself for the last mile of his journey.

"How are you, Pop?" It was the garage attendant, rubbing his greasy hands on his overalls, and hunting among the cans.

Eli's stomach lurched and he pulled the big black coat round his neck.

"Nice day," the attendant said and started around to the front.

"Sholom," Eli whispered and zoomed off towards the hill.

■ The sun was directly overhead when Eli reached the top. He had come by way of the woods, where it was cooler, but still he was perspiring beneath his new suit. The hat had no sweatband and the cloth clutched his head. The children were playing. The children were always playing, as if it was that alone that Tzuref had to teach them. In their shorts, they revealed such thin legs that beneath one could see the joints swiveling as they ran. Eli waited for them to disappear around a corner before he came into the open. But something would not let him wait—his green suit. It was on the porch, wrapped around the bearded fellow, who was painting the base of a pillar. His arm went up and down, up and down, and the pillar glowed like white fire. The very sight of him popped Eli out of the woods onto the lawn. He did not turn back, though his insides did. He walked up the lawn, but the children played on; tipping the black hat, he mumbled, "Shhh . . . shhhh," and they hardly seemed to notice.

At last he smelled paint.

He waited for the man to turn to him. He only painted. Eli felt suddenly that if he could pull the black hat down over his eyes, over his chest and belly and legs, if he could shut out all light, then a moment later he would be home in bed. But the hat wouldn't go past his forehead. He couldn't kid himself—he was there. No one he could think of had forced him to do this.

The greenie's arm flailed up and down on the pillar. Eli breathed loudly, cleared his throat, but the greenie wouldn't make life easier for him. At last, Eli had to say "Hello."

The arm swished up and down; it stopped—two fingers went out after a brush hair stuck to the pillar.

"Good day," Eli said.

The hair came away; the swishing resumed.

"Sholom," Eli whispered and the fellow turned.

The recognition took some time. He looked at what Eli wore. Up close, Eli looked at what he wore. And then Eli had the strange notion that he was two people. Or that he was one person wearing two suits. The greenie looked to be suffering from a similar confusion. They stared long at one another. Eli's heart shivered, and his brain was momentarily in such a mixed-up condition that his hands went out to button down the collar of his shirt that somebody else was wearing. What a mess! The greenie flung his arms over his face.

"What's the matter . . ." Eli said. The fellow had picked up his bucket and brush and was running away. Eli ran after him.

"I wasn't going to hit . . ." Eli called. "Stop . . ." Eli caught up and grabbed his sleeve. Once again, the greenie's hands flew up to his face. This time, in the violence, white paint spattered both of them.

"I only want to . . ." But in that outfit Eli didn't really know what he wanted. "To talk . . ." he said finally. "For you to look at me. Please, just *look* at me . . ."

The hands stayed put, as paint rolled off the brush onto the cuff of Eli's green suit.

"Please . . . please," Eli said, but he did not know what to do. "Say something, speak *English*," he pleaded.

The fellow pulled back against the wall, back, back, as though some arm would finally reach out and yank him to safety. He refused to uncover his face.

"Look," Eli said, pointing to himself. "It's your suit. I'll take care of it."

No answer—only a little shaking under the hands, which led Eli to speak as gently as he knew how.

"We'll . . . we'll moth-proof it. There's a button missing"—Eli pointed—"I'll have it fixed. I'll have a zipper put in . . . Please, please—just look at me . . ." He was talking to himself, and yet how could he stop? Nothing he said made any sense—that alone made his heart swell. Yet somehow babbling on, he might babble something that would make things easier between them. "Look . . ." He reached inside his shirt to pull the frills of underwear into the light. "I'm wearing the special underwear, even . . . Please," he said, "*please, please, please*" he sang, as if it were some sacred word. "Oh, *please* . . ."

Nothing twitched under the tweed suit—and if the eyes watered, or twinkled, or hated, he couldn't tell. It was driving him crazy. He had dressed like a fool, and for what? For this? He reached up and yanked the hands away.

"There!" he said—and in that first instant all he saw of the greenie's face were two white droplets stuck to each cheek.

"Tell me—" Eli clutched his hands down to his sides—"Tell me, what can I do for you, I'll do it . . ."

Stiffly, the greenie stood there, sporting his two white tears.

"Whatever I can do . . . Look, look, what I've done *already*." He grabbed his black hat and shook it in the man's face.

And in exchange, the greenie gave him an answer. He raised one hand to his chest, and then jammed it, finger first, towards the horizon. And with what a pained look! As though the air were full of razors! Eli followed the finger and saw beyond the knuckle, out past the nail, Woodenton.

"What do you want?" Eli said. "I'll bring it!"

Suddenly the greenie made a run for it. But then he stopped, wheeled, and jabbed that finger at the air again. It pointed the same way. Then he was gone.

And then, all alone, Eli had the revelation. He did not question his understanding, the substance or the source. But with a strange, dreamy elation, he started away.

■ On Coach House Road, they were double-parked. The Mayor's wife pushed a grocery cart full of dog food from Stop N' Shop to her station wagon. The President of the Lions Club, a napkin around his neck, was jamming pennies into the meter in front of the Bit-in-Teeth Restaurant. Ted Heller caught the sun as it glazed off the new Byzantine mosaic entrance to his shoe shop. In pinkened jeans, Mrs. Jimmy Knudson was leaving Halloway's Hardware, a paint bucket in each hand. Roger's Beauty Shoppe had its doors open—women's heads in silver bullets far as the eye could see. Over by the barbershop the pole spun, and Artie Berg's youngest sat on a red horse, having his hair cut; his mother flipped through *Look*, smiling: the greenie had changed his clothes.

And into this street, which seemed paved with chromium, came Eli Peck. It was not enough, he knew, to walk up one side of the street. That was not enough. Instead he walked ten paces up one side, then on an angle, crossed to the other side, where he walked ten more paces, and crossed back. Horns blew, traffic jerked, as Eli made his way up Coach House Road. He spun a moan high up in his nose as he walked. Outside no one could hear him, but he felt it vibrate the cartilage at the bridge of his nose.

Things slowed around him. The sun stopped rippling on spokes and hubcaps. It glowed steadily as everyone put on brakes to look at the man in black. They always paused and gaped, whenever he entered the town. Then in a minute, or two, or three, a light would change, a baby squawk, and the flow continue. Now, though lights changed, no one moved.

"He shaved his beard," Eric the barber said.

"Who?" asked Linda Berg.

"The . . . the guy in the suit. From the place there."

Linda looked out the window.

"It's Uncle Eli," little Kevin Berg said, spitting hair.

"Oh, God," Linda said, "Eli's having a nervous breakdown."

"A nervous breakdown!" Ted Heller said, but not immediately. Immediately he had said "Hoooly . . ."

Shortly, everybody in Coach House Road was aware that Eli Peck, the nervous young attorney with the pretty wife, was having a breakdown. Everybody except Eli Peck. He knew what he did was not insane, though he felt every inch of its strangeness. He felt those black clothes as if they were the skin of his skin—the give and pull as they got used to where he bulged and buckled. And he felt eyes, every eye on Coach House Road. He saw headlights screech to within an inch of him, and stop. He saw mouths: first the bottom jaw slides forward, then the tongue hits the teeth, the lips explode, a little thunder in the throat, and they've said it: Eli Peck Eli Peck Eli Peck Eli Peck. He began to walk slowly, shifting his weight down and forward with each syllable: E—li—Peck—E—li—Peck—E—li—Peck. Heavily he trod, and as his neighbors uttered each syllable of his name, he felt each syllable shaking all his bones. He knew who he was down to his marrow—they were telling him. Eli Peck. He wanted them to say it a thousand times, a million times, he would walk forever in that black suit, as adults whispered of his strangeness and children made "Shame . . . shame" with their fingers.

"It's going to be all right, pal . . ." Ted Heller was motioning to Eli from his doorway. "C'mon, pal, it's going to be all right . . ."

Eli saw him, past the brim of his hat. Ted did not move from his doorway, but leaned forward and spoke with his hand over his mouth. Behind him, three customers peered through the doorway. "Eli, it's Ted, remember Ted . . ."

Eli crossed the street and found he was heading directly towards Harriet Knudson. He lifted his neck so she could see his whole face.

He saw her forehead melt down to her lashes. "Good morning, Mr. Peck."

"Sholom," Eli said, and crossed the street where he saw the President of the Lions.

"Twice before . . ." he heard someone say, and then he crossed again, mounted the curb, and was before the bakery, where a delivery man charged past with a tray of powdered cakes twirling above him. "Pardon me, Father," he said, and scooted into his truck. But he could not move it. Eli Peck had stopped traffic.

He passed the Rivoli Theater, Beekman Cleaners, Harris' Westinghouse, the Unitarian Church, and soon he was passing only trees. At Ireland Road he turned right and started through Woodenton's winding streets. Baby carriages stopped whizzing and creaked—"Isn't that . . ." Gardeners held their clipping. Children stepped from the sidewalk and tried the curb. And Eli greeted no one, but raised his face to all. He wished passionately that he had white tears to show them . . . And not till he reached his own front lawn, saw his house, his shutters, his new jonquils, did he remember his wife. And the child that must have been born to him. And it was then and there he had the awful moment. He could go inside and put on his clothes and go to his wife in the hospital. It was not irrevocable, even the walk wasn't. In Woodenton memories are long but fury short. Apathy works like forgiveness. Besides, when you've flipped, you've flipped—it's Mother Nature.

What gave Eli the awful moment was that he turned away. He knew exactly what he could do but he chose not to. To go inside would be to go halfway. There was more . . . So he turned and walked towards the hospital and all the time he quaked an eighth of an inch beneath his skin to think that perhaps he'd chosen the crazy way. To think that he'd *chosen* to be crazy! But if you chose to be crazy, then you weren't crazy. It's when you didn't choose. No, he wasn't flipping. He had a child to see.

"Name?"

"Peck."

"Fourth floor." He was given a little blue card.

In the elevator everybody stared. Eli watched his black shoes rise four floors.

"Four."

He tipped his hat, but knew he couldn't take it off.

"Peck," he said. He showed the card.

"Congratulations," the nurse said, ". . . the grandfather?"

"The father. Which room?"

She led him to 412. "A joke on the Mrs.?" she said, but he slipped in the door without her.

"Miriam?"

"Yes?"

"Eli."

She rolled her white face towards her husband. "Oh, Eli . . . Oh, Eli."

He raised his arms. "What could I do?"

"You have a son. They called all morning."

"I came to see him."

"Like *that!*" she whispered harshly. "Eli, you can't go around like that."

"I have a son. I want to see him."

"Eli, why are you doing this to me!" Red seeped back into her lips. "*He's* not your fault," she explained. "Oh, Eli, sweetheart, why do you feel guilty about everything? Eli, change your clothes. I forgive you."

"Stop forgiving me. Stop understanding me."

"But I love you."

"That's something else."

"But, sweetie, you *don't* have to dress like that. You didn't do anything. You don't have to feel guilty because . . . because everything's all right. Eli, can't you see that?"

"Miriam, enough reasons. Where's my son?"

"Oh, please, Eli, don't flip now, I need you now. Is that why you're flipping—because I need you?"

"In your selfish way, Miriam, you're very generous. I want my son."

"Don't flip now. I'm afraid, now that he's out." She was beginning to whimper. "I don't know if I love him, now that he's out. When I look in the mirror, Eli, he won't be there . . . Eli, Eli, you look like you're going to your own funeral. Please, can't you leave well enough *alone?* Can't we just have a family?"

"No."

In the corridor he asked the nurse to lead him to his son. The nurse walked on one side of him, Ted Heller on the other.

"Eli, do you want some help? I thought you might want some help."

"No."

Ted whispered something to the nurse; then to Eli he whispered, "Should you be walking around like this?"

"Yes."

In his ear Ted said, "You'll . . . frighten the kid . . ."

"There," the nurse said. She pointed to a bassinet in the second row and looked, puzzled, to Ted. "Do I go in?" Eli said.

"No," the nurse said. "She'll roll him over." She rapped on the enclosure full of babies. "Peck," she mouthed to the nurse on the inside.

Ted tapped Eli's arm. "You're not thinking of doing something you'll be sorry for . . . are you, Eli? Eli—I mean you know you're still Eli, don't you?"

In the enclosure, Eli saw a bassinet had been wheeled before the square window.

"Oh, Christ. . . ." Ted said. "You don't have this Bible stuff on the brain—" And suddenly he said, "You wait, pal." He started down the corridor, his heels tapping rapidly.

Eli felt relieved—he leaned forward. In the basket was what he'd come to see. Well, now that he was here, what did he think he was going to say to it? I'm your father, Eli, the Flipper? I am wearing a black hat, suit, and fancy underwear, all borrowed from a friend? How could he admit to this reddened ball—*his* reddened ball—the worst of all: that Eckman would shortly convince him he wanted to take off the whole business. He couldn't admit it! He wouldn't do it!

Past his hat brim, from the corner of his eye, he saw Ted had stopped in a doorway at the end of the corridor. Two interns stood there smoking, listening to Ted. Eli ignored it.

No, even Eckman wouldn't make him take it off! No! He'd wear it, if he chose to. He'd make the kid wear it! Sure! Cut it down when the time came. A smelly hand-me-down, whether the kid liked it or not!

Only Teddie's heels clacked; the interns wore rubber soles—for they were there, beside him, unexpectedly. Their white suits smelled, but not like Eli's.

"Eli," Ted said, softly, "visiting time's up, pal."

"How are you feeling, Mr. Peck? First child upsets everyone. . . ."

He'd just pay no attention; nevertheless, he began to perspire, thickly, and his hat crown clutched his hair.

"Excuse me—Mr. Peck. . . ." It was a new rich bass voice. "Excuse me, rabbi, but you're wanted . . . in the temple." A hand took his elbow, firmly; then another hand, the other elbow. Where they grabbed, his tendons went taut.

"Okay, rabbi. Okay okay okay okay okay okay. . . ." He listened; it was a very soothing word, that okay. "Okay okay everything's going to be okay." His feet seemed to have left the ground some, as he glided away from the window, the bassinet, the babies. "Okay easy does it everything's all right all right—"

But he rose, suddenly, as though up out of a dream, and flailing his arms, screamed: "*I'm the father!*"

But the window disappeared. In a moment they tore off his jacket—it gave so easily, in one yank. Then a needle slid under his skin. The drug calmed his soul, but did not touch it down where the blackness had reached.

Suggestions for Discussion

1. Define *in medias res*. How does it apply to the opening of this story?
2. What is the significance of Eli's mistaking Tzuref's skullcap for a deformity of the head? What else does Eli misunderstand in talking with Tzuref later in the story?
3. In what context does Eli think and act? How does the context change during the course of the story?
4. What is the function of the three men of suburbia, Ted Heller, Artie Berg, and Harry Shaw? Do they comprise a chorus in any way? Is there any significance in their names or the name of the town, Woodenton?
5. In his second encounter with Tzuref, what does Eli come to understand by the statement "The suit is all he's got"? If Eli understands Tzuref, why does he give the man another suit? Why one, or rather two, of his own?
6. What do Eli's statement that "This is not a nervous break-down" and Ted Heller's warning that "Tomorrow's the judge-ment day, Eli" suggest about Eli's actions on the following day? How does his behavior differ from that during his previous "breakdowns"? How does the "nervous breakdown" function on both literal and symbolic levels? How dominant are the themes of guilt and retribution in this story? What is the basis of the guilt?
7. How do the women—Miriam, Shirley, and Harriet—resemble Harry, Artie, and Ted? What is the significance of Harriet's painting her rocks pink? Is it fitting that she is the one to say "Eli, there's a Jew at your door"?
8. Who is the first to recognize Eli in his "new suit"? Of what folk tale does the author seem to be reminding us? How does that story relate to the conflict of reality and appearance?
9. Why does Eli, dressed as he is, go to see his son? How is the hospital scene a comment on twentieth-century America? Is it an appropriate conclusion to the story?
10. What does the title of the story mean? According to *whom* is Eli a fanatic?

Suggestions for Writing and Comparison

1. Use "Eli, the Fanatic" as a point of departure for an essay en-titled "Clothes Make the Man."
2. Read the prologue to Ralph Ellison's *Invisible Man*. Compare Roth's and Ellison's relation of alienation and identification to "visibility."

Grace Paley

Grace Paley is a New Yorker, a "somewhat combative pacifist and cooperative anarchist." She is an extraordinary short story writer. Her first book, *The Little Disturbances of Man,* was published in 1959. Her most recent, *Enormous Changes at the Last Minute* (1974), is the one from which the following story was taken. Susan Sontag has said of Grace Paley, "She is that rare kind of writer, a natural, with a voice like no one else's: funny, sad, lean, modest, energetic, acute. Like the great modern Russian writers, she demonstrates a possible unity of the art of consciousness and the naturalness of conscience."

"The Long-Distance Runner" is the story of a woman who returns to her old neighborhood in order to learn "what in the world is coming next."

The Long-Distance Runner

One day, before or after forty-two, I became a long-distance runner. Though I was stout and in many ways inadequate to this desire, I wanted to go far and fast, not as fast as bicycles and trains, not as far as Taipei, Hingwen, places like that, islands of the slant-eyed cunt, as sailors in bus stations say when speaking of travel, but round and round the country from the seaside to the bridges, along the old neighborhood streets a couple of times, before old age and urban renewal ended them and me.

I tried the country first, Connecticut, which being wooded is always full of buds in spring. All creation is secret, isn't that true? So I trained in the wide-zoned suburban hills where I wasn't known. I ran all spring in and out of dogwood bloom, then laurel.

People sometimes stopped and asked me why I ran, a lady in silk shorts halfway down over her fat thighs. In training, I replied and rested only to answer if closely questioned. I wore a white sleeveless undershirt as well, with excellent support, not to attract the attention of old men and prudish children.

Then summer came, my legs seemed strong. I kissed the kids goodbye. They were quite old by then. It was near the time for parting anyway. I told Mrs. Raftery to look in now and then and give them some of that rotten Celtic supper she makes.

I told them they could take off any time they wanted to. Go lead your private life, I said. Only leave me out of it.

A word to the wise . . . said Richard.

You're depressed Faith, Mrs. Raftery said. Your boy friend Jack, the one you think's so hotsy-totsy, hasn't called and you're as gloomy as a tick on Sunday.

Cut the folkshit with me, Raftery, I muttered. Her eyes filled with tears because that's who she is: folkshit from bunion to topknot. That's how she got liked by me, loved, invented and endured.

When I walked out the door they were all reclining before the television set, Richard, Tonto and Mrs. Raftery, gazing at the news. Which proved with moving pictures that there *had* been a voyage to the moon and Africa and South America hid in a furious whorl of clouds.

I said, Goodbye. They said, Yeah, O.K., sure.

If that's how it is, forget it, I hollered and took the Independent subway to Brighton Beach.

At Brighton Beach I stopped at the Salty Breezes Locker Room to change my clothes. Twenty-five years ago my father invested $500 in its future. In fact he still clears about $3.50 a year, which goes directly (by law) to the Children of Judea to cover their deficit.

No one paid too much attention when I started to run, easy and light on my feet. I ran on the boardwalk first, past my mother's leafleting station — between a soft-ice-cream stand and a degenerated dune. There she had been assigned by her comrades to halt the tides of cruel American enterprise with simple socialist sense.

I wanted to stop and admire the long beach. I wanted to stop in order to think admiringly about New York. There aren't many rotting cities so tan and sandy and speckled with citizens at their salty edges. But I had already spent a lot of life lying down or standing and staring. I had decided to run.

■ After about a mile and a half I left the boardwalk and began to trot into the old neighborhood. I was running well. My breath was long and deep. I was thinking pridefully about my form.

Suddenly I was surrounded by about three hundred blacks.

Who you?

Who that?

Look at her! Just look! When you seen a fatter ass?

Poor thing. She ain't right. Leave her, you boys, you bad boys.

I used to live here, I said.

Oh yes, they said, in the white old days. That time too bad to last.

But we loved it here. We never went to Flatbush Avenue or Times Square. We loved our block.

Tough black titty.

I like your speech, I said. Metaphor and all.

Right on. We get that from talking.

Yes my people also had a way of speech. And don't forget the Irish. The gift of gab.

Who they? said a small boy.

Cops.

Nowadays, I suggested, there's more than Irish on the police force.

You right, said two ladies. More more, much much more. They's French Chinamen Russkies Congoleans. Oh missee, you too right.

I lived in that house, I said. That apartment house. All my life. Till I got married.

Now that *is* nice. Live in one place. My mother live that way in South Carolina. One place. Her daddy farmed. She said. They ate. No matter winter war bad times. Roosevelt. Something! Ain't that wonderful! And it weren't cold! Big trees!

That apartment. I looked up and pointed. There. The third floor.

They all looked up. So what! You blubrous devil! said a dark young man. He wore horn-rimmed glasses and had that intelligent look that City College boys used to have when I was eighteen and first looked at them.

He seemed to lead them in contempt and anger, even the littlest ones who moved toward me with dramatic stealth singing, Devil, Oh Devil. I don't think the little kids had bad feeling because they poked a finger into me, then laughed.

Still I thought it might be wise to keep my head. So I jumped right in with some facts. I said, How many flowers' names do you know? Wild flowers, I mean. My people only knew two. That's what they say now anyway. Rich or poor, they only had two flowers' names. Rose and violet.

Daisy, said one boy immediately.

Weed, said another. That *is* a flower, I thought. But everyone else got the joke.

Saxifrage, lupine, said a lady. Viper's bugloss, said a small Girl Scout in medium green with a dark green sash. She held up a *Handbook of Wild Flowers*.

How many you know, fat mama? a boy asked warmly. He wasn't against my being a mother or fat. I turned all my attention to him.

Oh sonny, I said, I'm way ahead of my people. I know in yellows alone: common cinquefoil, trout lily, yellow adder's-tongue, swamp buttercup and common buttercup, golden sorrel, yellow or hop clover, devil's-paintbrush, evening primrose, black-eyed Susan, golden aster, also the yellow pickerel-weed growing down by the water if not in the water, and dandelions of course. I've seen all these myself. Seen them.

You could see China from the boardwalk, a boy said. When it's nice.

I know more flowers than countries. Mostly young people these days have traveled in many countries.

Not me. I ain't been nowhere.

Not me either, said about seventeen boys.

I'm not allowed, said a little girl. There's drunken junkies.

But *I! I!* cried out a tall black youth, very handsome and well dressed. I am an African. My father came from the high stolen plains. *I* have been everywhere. I was in Moscow six months, learning machinery. I was in France, learning French. I was in Italy, observing the peculiar Renaissance and the people's sweetness. I was in England, where I studied the common law and the urban blight. I was at the Conference of Dark Youth in Cuba to understand our passion. I am now here. Here am I to become an engineer and return to my people, around the Cape of Good Hope in a Norwegian sailing vessel. In this way I will learn the fine old art of sailing in case the engines of the new society of my old inland country should fail.

We had an extraordinary amount of silence after that. Then one old lady in a black dress and high white lace collar said to another old lady dressed exactly the same way, Glad tidings when someone got brains in the head not fish juice. Amen, said a few.

Whyn't you go up to Mrs. Luddy living in your house, you lady, huh? The Girl Scout asked this.

Why she just groove to see you, said some sarcastic snickerer.

She got palpitations. Her man, he give it to her.

That ain't all, he a natural gift-giver.

I'll take you, said the Girl Scout. My name is Cynthia. I'm in Troop 355, Brooklyn.

I'm not dressed, I said, looking at my lumpy knees.

You shouldn't wear no undershirt like that without no runnin number or no team writ on it. It look like a undershirt.

Cynthia! Don't take her up there, said an important boy. Her head strange. Don't you take her. Hear?

Lawrence, she said softly, you tell me once more what to do I'll wrap you round that lamppost.

Git! she said, powerfully addressing *me*.

In this way I was led into the hallway of the whole house of my childhood.

■ The first door I saw was still marked in flaky gold, 1A.

That's where the janitor lived, I said. He was a Negro.

How come like that? Cynthia made an astonished face. How come the janitor was a black man?

Oh Cynthia, I said. Then I turned to the opposite door, first floor front, 1B. I remembered. Now, here, this was Mrs. Goreditsky, very very fat lady. All her children died at birth. Born, then one, two, three. Dead. Five children, then Mr. Goreditsky said, I'm bad luck on you Tessie and he went away. He sent $15 a week for seven years. Then no one heard.

I know her, poor thing, said Cynthia. The city come for her summer before last. The way they knew, it smelled. They wropped her up in a canvas. They couldn't get through the front door. It scraped off a piece of her. My uncle Ronald had to help them, but he got disgusted.

Only two years ago. She was still here! Wasn't she scared?

So we all, said Cynthia. White ain't everything.

Who lived up here, she asked, 2B? Right now, my best friend Nancy Rosalind lives here. She got two brothers, and her sister married and got a baby. She very light-skinned. Not her mother. We got all colors amongst us.

Your best friend? That's funny. Because it was *my* best friend. Right in that apartment. Joanna Rosen.

What become of her? Cynthia asked. She got a running shirt too?

Come on Cynthia, if you really want to know, I'll tell you. She married this man, Marvin Steirs.

Who's he?

I recollected his achievements. Well, he's the president of a big corporation, JoMar Plastics. This corporation owns a steel company, a radio station, a new Xerox-type machine that lets you do twenty-five different pages at once. This corporation has a foundation, The JoMar Fund for Research in Conservation. Capitalism is like that, I added, in order to be politically useful.

How come you know? You go over their house a lot?

No. I happened to read all about them on the financial page, just last week. It made me think: a different life. That's all.

Different spokes for different folks, said Cynthia.

I sat down on the cool marble steps and remembered Joanna's cousin Ziggie. He was older than we were. He wrote a poem which told us we were lovely flowers and our legs were petals, which nature would force open no matter how many times we said no.

Then I had several other interior thoughts that I couldn't share with a child, the kind that give your face a blank or melancholy look.

Now you're not interested, said Cynthia. Now you're not gonna say a thing. Who lived here, 2A? Who? Two men lives here now. Women coming and women going. My mother says, Danger sign: Stay away, my darling, stay away.

I don't remember, Cynthia. I really don't.

You got to. What'd you come for, anyways?

Then I tried. 2A. 2A. Was it the twins? I felt a strong obligation as though remembering was in charge of the *existence* of the past. This is not so.

Cynthia, I said, I don't want to go any further. I don't even want to remember.

Come on, she said, tugging at my shorts, don't you want to see Mrs. Luddy, the one lives in your old house? That be fun, no?

No. No, I don't want to see Mrs. Luddy.

Now you shouldn't pay no attention to those boys downstairs. She will like you. I mean, she is kind. She don't like most white people, but she might like you.

No Cynthia, it's not that, but I don't want to see my father and mother's house now.

I didn't know what to say. I said, Because my mother's dead. This was a lie, because my mother lives in her own room with my father in the Children of Judea. With her hand over her socialist heart, she reads the paper every morning after breakfast. Then she says sadly to my father, Every day the same. Dying . . . dying, dying from killing.

My mother's dead Cynthia. I can't go in there.

Oh . . . oh, the poor thing, she said, looking into my eyes. Oh, if my mother died, I don't know what I'd do. Even if I was old as you. I could kill myself. Tears filled her eyes and started down her cheeks. If my mother died, what would I do? She is my protector, she won't let the pushers get me. She hold me tight. She gonna hide me in the cedar box if my Uncle Rudford comes try to get me back. She *can't* die, my mother.

Cynthia – honey – she won't die. She's young. I put my arm out to comfort her. You could come live with me, I said. I got two boys, they're nearly grown up. I missed it, not having a girl.

What? What you mean now, live with you and boys. She pulled away and ran for the stairs. Stay way from me, honky lady. I know them white boys. They just gonna try and jostle my black womanhood. My mother told me about that, keep you white honky devil boys to your devil self, you just leave me be you old bitch you. Somebody help me, she started to scream, you hear. Somebody help. She gonna take me away.

She flattened herself to the wall, trembling. I was too frightened by her fear of me to say, honey, I wouldn't hurt you, it's me. I heard her helpers, the voices of large boys crying, We coming, we coming, hold your head up, we coming. I ran past her fear to the stairs and up them two at a time. I came to my old own door. I knocked like the landlord, loud and terrible.

Mama not home, a child's voice said. No, no, I said. It's me! a lady! Someone's chasing me, let me in. Mama not home, I ain't allowed to open up for nobody.

It's me! I cried out in terror. Mama! Mama! let me in!

The door opened. A slim woman whose age I couldn't invent looked at me. She said, Get in and shut that door tight. She took a hard pinching hold on my upper arm. Then she bolted the door herself. Them hustlers after you. They make me pink. Hide this white lady now, Donald. Stick her under your bed, you got a high bed.

Oh that's O.K. I'm fine now, I said. I felt safe and at home.

You in my house, she said. You do as I say. For two cents, I throw you out.

I squatted under a small kid's pissy mattress. Then I heard the knock. It was tentative and respectful. My mama don't allow me to open. Donald! someone called. Donald!

Oh no, he said. Can't do it. She gonna wear me out. You know her. She already tore up my ass this morning once. Ain't *gonna* open up.

■ I lived there for about three weeks with Mrs. Luddy and Donald and three little baby girls nearly the same age. I told her a joke about Irish twins. Ain't Irish, she said.

Nearly every morning the babies woke us at about 6:45. We gave them all a bottle and went back to sleep till 8:00. I made coffee and she changed diapers. Then it really stank for a while. At this time I usually said, Well listen, thanks really, but I've got to go I guess. I guess I'm going. She'd usually say, Well, guess again. *I* guess you ain't. Or if she was feeling disgusted she'd say, Go on now! Get! You wanna go, I guess by now I have snorted enough white lady stink to choke a horse. Go on!

I'd get to the door and then I'd hear voices. I'm ashamed to say I'd become fearful. Despite my wide geographical love of mankind, I would be attacked by local fears.

There was a sentimental truth that lay beside all that going and not going. It *was* my house where I'd lived long ago my family life. There was a tile on the bathroom floor that I myself had broken, dropping a hammer on the toe of my brother Charles as he stood dreamily shaving, his prick halfway up his undershorts. Astonishment and knowledge first seized me right there. The kitchen was the same. The table was the enameled table common to our class, easy to clean, with wooden undercorners for indigent and old cockroaches that couldn't make it to the kitchen sink. (However, it was not the same table, because I have inherited that one, chips and all.)

The living room was something like ours, only we had less plastic. There may have been less plastic in the world at that time. Also, my mother had set beautiful cushions everywhere, on beds and chairs. It was the way she expressed herself, artistically, to embroider at night or take strips of flowered cotton and sew them across ordinary white or blue muslin in the most delicate designs, the way women have always used materials that live and die in hunks and tatters to say: This is my place.

Mrs. Luddy said, Uh huh!

Of course, I said, men don't have that outlet. That's how come they run around so much.

Till they drunk enough to lay down, she said.

Yes, I said, on a large scale you can see it in the world. First they make something, then they murder it. Then they write a book about how interesting it is.

You got something there, she said. Sometimes she said, Girl you don't know *nothing*.

We often sat at the window looking out and down. Little tufts of breeze grew on that windowsill. The blazing afternoon was around the corner and up the block.

You say men, she said. Is that men? she asked. What you call — a Man?

Four flights below us, leaning on the stoop, were about a dozen people and around them devastation. Just a minute, I said. I had seen devastation on my way, running, gotten some of the pebbles of it in my running shoe and the dust of it in my eyes. I had thought with the indignant courtesy of a citizen, This is a disgrace to the City of New York which I love and am running through.

But now, from the commanding heights of home, I saw it clearly. The tenement in which Jack my old and present friend had come to gloomy manhood had been destroyed, first by fire, then by demolition (which is a swinging ball of steel that cracks bedrooms and kitchens). Because of this work, we could see several blocks wide and a block and a half long. Crazy Eddy's house still stood, famous 1510 gutted, with black window frames, no glass, open laths. The stubbornness of the supporting beams! Some persons or families still lived on the lowest floors. In the lots between, a couple of old sofas lay on their fat faces, their springs sticking up into the air. Just as in wartime a half-dozen ailanthus trees had already found their first quarter inch of earth and begun a living attack on the dead yards. At night, I knew animals roamed the place, squalling and howling, furious New York dogs and street cats and mighty rats. You would think you were in Bear Mountain Park, the terror of venturing forth.

Someone ought to clean that up, I said.

Mrs. Luddy said, Who you got in mind? Mrs. Kennedy? —

Donald made a stern face. He said, That just what I gonna do when I get big. Gonna get the Sanitary Man in and show it to him. You see that, you big guinea you, you clean it up right now! Then he stamped his feet and fierced his eyes.

Mrs. Luddy said, Come here, you little nigger. She kissed the top of his head and gave him a whack on the backside all at one time.

Well, said Donald, encouraged, look out there now you all! Go on I say, look! Though we had already seen, to please him we looked. On the stoop men and boys lounged, leaned, hopped about, stood on one leg, then another, took their socks off, and scratched their toes, talked, sat on their haunches, heads down, dozing.

Donald said, Look at them. They ain't got self-respect. They got Afros *on* their heads, but they don't know they black *in* their heads.

I thought he ought to learn to be more sympathetic. I said, There are reasons that people are that way.

Yes, ma'am, said Donald.

Anyway, how come you never go down and play with the other kids, how come you're up here so much?

My mama don't like me do that. Some of them is bad. Bad. I might become a dope addict. I got to stay clear.

You just a dope, that's a fact, said Mrs. Luddy.

He ought to be with kids his age more, I think.

He see them in school, miss. Don't trouble your head about it if you don't mind.

Actually, Mrs. Luddy didn't go down into the street either. Donald did all the shopping. She let the welfare investigator in, the meterman came into the kitchen to read the meter. I saw him from the back room, where I hid. She did pick up her check. She cashed it. She returned to wash the babies, change their diapers, wash clothes, iron, feed people, and then in free half hours she sat by that window. She was waiting.

I believed she was watching and waiting for a particular man. I wanted to discuss this with her, talk lovingly like sisters. But before I could freely say, Forget about that son of a bitch, he's a pig, I did have to offer a few solid facts about myself, my kids, about fathers, husbands, passers-by, evening companions, and the life of my father and mother in this room by this exact afternoon window.

I told her for instance, that in my worst times I had given myself one extremely simple physical pleasure. This was cream cheese for breakfast. In fact, I insisted on it, sometimes depriving the children of very important articles and foods.

Girl, you don't know nothing, she said.

Then for a little while she talked gently as one does to a person who is innocent and insane and incorruptible because of stupidity. She had had two such special pleasures for hard times she said. The first, men, but they turned rotten, white women had ruined the best, give them the idea their dicks made of solid gold. The second pleasure she had tried was wine. She said, I do like wine. You *has* to have something just for yourself by yourself. Then she said, But you can't raise a decent boy when you liquor-dazed every night.

White or black, I said, returning to men, they did think they were bringing a rare gift, whereas it was just sex, which is common like bread, though essential.

Oh, you can do without, she said. There's folks does without.

I told her Donald deserved the best. I loved him. If he had flaws, I hardly noticed them. It's one of my beliefs that children do not have flaws, even the worst do not.

Donald was brilliant—like my boys except that he had an easier disposition. For this reason I decided, almost the second moment of my residence in that household, to bring him up to reading level at once. I told him we would work with books and newspapers. He went immediately to his neighborhood library and brought some hard books to amuse me. *Black Folktales* by Julius Lester and *The Pushcart War,* which is about another neighborhood but relevant.

Donald always agreed with me when we talked about reading and writing. In fact, when I mentioned poetry, he told me he knew all about it, that David

Henderson, a known black poet, had visited his second-grade class. So Donald was, as it turned out, well ahead of my nosy tongue. He was usually very busy shopping. He also had to spend a lot of time making faces to force the little serious baby girls into laughter. But if the subject came up, he could take *the* poem right out of the air into which language and event had just gone.

An example: That morning, his mother had said, Whew, I just got too much piss and diapers and wash. I wanna just sit down by that window and rest myself. He wrote a poem:

> Just got too much pissy diapers
> and wash and wash
> just wanna sit down by that window
> and look out
>   ain't nothing there.

Donald, I said, you are plain brilliant. I'm never going to forget you. For God's sakes don't you forget me.

You fool with him too much, said Mrs. Luddy. He already don't even remember his grandma, you never gonna meet someone like her, a curse never come past her lips.

I do remember, Mama, I remember. She lying in bed right there. A man standing in the door. She say, Esdras, I put a curse on you head. You worsen tomorrow. How come she said like that?

Gomorrah, I believe Gomorrah, she said. She know the Bible inside out.

Did she live with you?

No. No, she visiting. She come up to see us all, her children, how we doing. She come up to see sights. Then she lay down and died. She was old.

I remained quiet because of the death of mothers. Mrs. Luddy looked at me thoughtfully, then she said:

My mama had stories to tell, she raised me on. *Her* mama was a little thing, no sense. Stand in the door of the cabin all day, sucking her thumb. It was slave times. One day a young field boy come storming along. He knock on the door of the first cabin hollering, Sister, come out, it's freedom. She come out. She say, Yeah? When? He say, Now! It's freedom now! Then he knock at the next door and say, Sister! It's freedom! Now! From one cabin he run to the next cabin, crying out, Sister, it's freedom now!

Oh I remember that story, said Donald. Freedom now! Freedom now! He jumped up and down.

You don't remember nothing boy. Go on, get Eloise, she want to get into the good times.

Eloise was two but undersized. We got her like that, said Donald. Mrs. Luddy let me buy her ice cream and green vegetables. She was waiting for kale and chard, but it was too early. The kale liked cold. You not about to be here November, she said. No, no. I turned away, lonesomeness touching me and sang our Eloise song:

> Eloise loves the bees
> the bees they buzz
> like Eloise does.

Then Eloise crawled all over the splintery floor, buzzing wildly.

Oh you crazy baby, said Donald, buzz buzz buzz.

Mrs. Luddy sat down by the window.

You all make a lot of noise, she said sadly. You just right on noisy.

The next morning Mrs. Luddy woke me up.

Time to go, she said.

What?

Home.

What? I said.

Well, don't you think your little spoiled boys crying for you? Where's Mama? They standing in the window. Time to go lady. This ain't Free Vacation Farm. Time we was by ourself a little.

Oh Ma, said Donald, she ain't a lot of trouble. Go on, get Eloise, she hollering. And button up your lip.

She didn't offer me coffee. She looked at me strictly all the time. I tried to look strictly back, but I failed because I loved the sight of her.

Donald was teary, but I didn't dare turn my face to him, until the parting minute at the door. Even then, I kissed the top of his head a little too forcefully and said, Well, I'll see you.

On the front stoop there were about half a dozen midmorning family people and kids arguing about who had dumped garbage out of which window. They were very disgusted with one another.

Two young men in handsome dashikis stood in counsel and agreement at the street corner. They divided a comment. How come white womens got rotten teeth? And look so old? A young woman waiting at the light said, Hush . . .

I walked past them and didn't begin my run till the road opened up somewhere along Ocean Parkway. I was a little stiff because my way of life had used only small movements, an occasional stretch to put a knife or teapot out of reach of the babies. I ran about ten, fifteen blocks. Then my second wind came, which is classical, famous among runners, it's the beginning of flying.

In the three weeks I'd been off the street, jogging had become popular. It seemed that I was only one person doing her thing, which happened like most American eccentric acts to be the most "in" thing I could have done. In fact, two young men ran alongside of me for nearly a mile. They ran silently beside me and turned off at Avenue H. A gentleman with a mustache, running poorly in the opposite direction, waved. He called out, Hi, senora.

Near home I ran through our park, where I had aired my children on weekends and late-summer afternoons. I stopped at the northeast playground, where I met a dozen young mothers intelligently handling their little ones. In order to prepare them, meaning no harm, I said, In fifteen years, you girls will be like me, wrong in everything.

■ At home it was Saturday morning. Jack had returned looking as grim as ever, but he'd brought cash and a vacuum cleaner. While the coffee perked, he showed Richard how to use it. They were playing tick tack toe on the dusty wall.

Richard said, Well! Look who's here! Hi!

Any news? I asked.

Letter from Daddy, he said. From the lake and water country in Chile. He says it's like Minnesota.

He's never been to Minnesota, I said. Where's Anthony?

Here I am, said Tonto, appearing. But I'm leaving.

Oh yes, I said. Of course. Every Saturday he hurries through breakfast or misses it. He goes to visit his friends in institutions. These are well-known places like Bellevue, Hillside, Rockland State, Central Islip, Manhattan. These visits take him all day and sometimes half the night.

I found some chocolate-chip cookies in the pantry. Take them, Tonto, I said. I remember nearly all his friends as little boys and girls always hopping, skipping, jumping and cookie-eating. He was annoyed. He said, No! Chocolate cookies is what the commissaries are full of. How about money?

Jack dropped the vacuum cleaner. He said, No! They have parents for that.

I said, Here, five dollars for cigarettes, one dollar each.

Cigarettes! said Jack. Goddamnit! Black lungs and death! Cancer! Emphysema! He stomped out of the kitchen, breathing. He took the bike from the back room and started for Central Park, which has been closed to cars but opened to bicycle riders. When he'd been gone about ten minutes, Anthony said, It's really open only on Sundays.

Why didn't you say so? Why can't you be decent to him? I asked. It's important to me.

Oh Faith, he said, patting me on the head because he'd grown so tall, all that air. It's good for his lungs. And his muscles! He'll be back soon.

You should ride too, I said. You don't want to get mushy in your legs. You should go swimming once a week.

I'm too busy, he said. I have to see my friends.

Then Richard, who had been vacuuming under his bed, came into the kitchen. You still here, Tonto?

Going going gone, said Anthony, don't bat your eye.

Now listen, Richard said, here's a note. It's for Judy, if you get as far as Rockland. Don't forget it. Don't open it. Don't read it. I know he'll read it.

Anthony smiled and slammed the door.

Did I lose weight? I asked. Yes, said Richard. You look O.K. You never look too bad. But where were you? I got sick of Raftery's boiled potatoes. Where were you, Faith?

Well! I said. Well! I stayed a few weeks in my old apartment, where Grandpa and Grandma and me and Hope and Charlie lived, when we were little. I took you there long ago. Not so far from the ocean where Grandma made us very healthy with sun and air.

What are you talking about? said Richard. Cut the baby talk.

Anthony came home earlier than expected that evening because some people were in shock therapy and someone else had run away. He listened to me for a while. Then he said, I don't know what she's talking about either.

Neither did Jack, despite the understanding often produced by love after absence. He said, Tell me again. He was in a good mood. He said, You can even tell it to me twice.

I repeated the story. They all said, What?

Because it isn't usually so simple. Have you known it to happen much nowadays? A woman inside the steamy energy of middle age runs and runs. She finds the houses and streets where her childhood happened. She lives in them. She learns as though she was still a child what in the world is coming next.

Suggestions for Discussion

1. Why does the narrator want to become a runner?
2. How is the narrator characterized in the first three pages of the story? Compare the first sketch with the later development. Does she become less a type and more a three-dimensional character?
3. As the narrator first arrives in the old neighborhood she says she was surrounded by "about three hundred blacks." A dialogue ensues in which old white times are compared with new black times. On the basis of the details, how different is the old from the new neighborhood?
4. What happens to the narrator's attempt at friendship with Cynthia? What is Cynthia's reaction?
5. Compare Mrs. Luddy's household and her relations to her children with that of the narrator.
6. Discuss the meaning of the final paragraph in the story. Do you agree?

Suggestion for Writing and Comparison

1. Compare the attitudes to the "old neighborhood" found in the Paley story with those in Gregory Corso's poem "Birthplace Revisited" (see p. 599).

William Pillin

William Pillin was born in the Ukraine and came to the United States as a young man. He is currently a resident of California. His first book of collected poems appeared in 1939. He has published several other books, including *Theory of Silence* (1949), *Passage After Midnight* (1951), and *Dance Without Shoes* (1956). *Dance Without Shoes* was a selection of the Book Club for Poetry and also won Pillin the Jeannette Sewell Davis Prize. "Miserere" is one of the poems from *Passage After Midnight*.

"Miserere" is a poem of mourning. Its subject is the six million Jews who were killed by the Nazis. In "Miserere," Pillin refuses to idealize all Hitler's victims, to mourn for them because they were all great beauties and poets and philosophers; he suggests rather that many of them may have been hunchbacked or conniving or usurious. But he cries for humanity which has been destroyed in them. Pillin's sensibility, his concern for the seemingly unlovely, should be compared to that of Bernard Malamud (p. 441).

Miserere

I will not endow you with a false glow
ghetto
or say that only poets and seers
died in your ashes.
5   Many mourn the scholars and dreamers,
the beautiful innocent talented victims.
I will spare my tears for the
loudmouthed unhappy conniving
jews
10 the usurious lenders,

tuberculous hunchbacked
scum of the ghettos (the sweeping of Europe).
For them I will weep,
                 for the whores
15 pale in the doorways, for the spiderous tradesmen
with their false measures
                   and for all the grey sparrows
hopping about the winters of Poland
                   the grief of whose eyes
20 went up in thin smoke like a final prayer.

For them I will weep, I want them returned,
the dwellers of dives, brothels and taverns.
I want them
back as they were, piteous, ignoble,
25 instead of these grey ashes
that like a winding sheet settles on shivering Europe.

Suggestions for Discussion

1. What is the connection between the "grey sparrows" of the second stanza and the "grey ashes" of the last? How does the title of the poem suggest "greyness"?
2. If the people the poet mentions were as "piteous" and "ignoble" as he says, why does he "want them back"?
3. The poet can serve as prophet and seer, realist, historian of joy and sorrow, as well as maker or creator. Which of these functions is Pillin fulfilling in writing this poem? Is there a "central duty" of a poet? Does Pillin fulfill this duty?

Suggestion for Writing and Comparison

1. Do we need to be reminded, as Pillin seems to say, of people other than "the beautiful innocent talented victims"? Why or why not?

Aaron Kurtz

Aaron Kurtz was born in Osve, Russia, in 1891. He came to America as a child, and for much of his life he lived in the New York ghetto. Kurtz produced several volumes of verse, including *Chaos* (1920), *The Golden City* (1935), and *Marc Chagall* (1947). During the 1940's he was particularly influential as a "proletarian" writer. He was also the editor of several magazines, among them the Yiddish *Heintike Lieder*. Kurtz died in 1964.

Aaron Kurtz was one of the many twentieth-century Jewish American poets who continue to write in Yiddish. (See especially the anthology *Onions and Cucumbers and Plums: Forty-Six Yiddish Poems*, translated and edited by Sarah Zweig Betsky, for other Yiddish poets.) The following excerpt from Kurtz's poem "Behold the Sea" explores the nature of brotherhood and bigotry. In these lines Kurtz explicitly identifies the Black's problem in the United States with the Jew's problem in Nazi Germany.

from
Behold the Sea

. . . They got you last night.
I saw you clubbed.
I recognized the nightsticks: they were thorny twigs

From the tree from where I saw
5 your brother lynched.
They felt the same as those they used
on my Father in Maidenek.

I saw a boot step on your throat last night:
it was the same boot that stepped on my young sister's throat.

10 I saw you shot last night.
I saw the gun: it was the gun they used
on my brother in Dachau . . .

I saw clear white, pure white
from White House to the Ku Klux Klan's white robes
15 and the white gardenias in the lapels of justice —
white guns booming in Mississippi courthouses.
white guns on campuses proclaiming
white law of love and brotherhood . . .

I saw Christ flog you on the chain gang.
20 I saw Christ put the torch to your brother on a heartbroken tree.
I saw Christ torture you on Times Square.
(That wasn't Christ at all, of course — it was Judas raving he was Christ, with
    thumb on trigger).
I saw your children chased from a white open hydrant on a hot day in Alex-
    andria. I wanted to cry,
but would not dare
25 after I heard your mothers crying from a million
smoke holes in the black belt.
I heard the wise old trees of Georgia cry the cry of your lynched sons.
I saw the scabrous,
filthy walls of Harlem cry the cry of your clean heart . . .

30 One day at dawn
I saw the toppled white tombstones of your great
rise and grow
taller than
the tallest lynch trees of your land.
35   I saw Paul
standing on the beach — singing
across the sea
I heard his mighty voice, tragic thunder of
man's heart, rearing through the waves. I thought it was
40 the roaring sea, singing
to our brother, singing to
our might.

— translated from the Yiddish by the author.

Suggestions for Discussion

1. What are Maidenek and Dachau? In what sense are the clubs
and boots and guns used there the same as those at an American
lynching? Are "brother," "sister," and "father" used figuratively
or literally in the first four stanzas? To what "families" do these
people belong?
2. Explain the symbolic use of trees in the poem. What relation do
they have to hope, despair, and death (see especially the last
stanza)?
3. The speaker says "I wanted to cry, but would not dare." Why
didn't he dare?
4. Who is "Paul" and who is "our brother" (see the final stanza)?
How does the "sea" mentioned in this stanza relate to the previously mentioned "trees"?

Suggestions for Writing and Comparison

1. Read *Negro and Jew: An Encounter in America,* edited by Shlomo Katz. What problems do Blacks and Jews have in common? How have these problems been acknowledged?
2. Read Gordon Allport's *The Nature of Prejudice.* Discuss briefly the bigoted personality as drawn by Kurtz. Is the poet's view in accord with the social scientist's findings?

Karl Shapiro

Karl Shapiro was born in 1913, in Baltimore, Maryland. In between studies at the University of Virginia and Johns Hopkins
University he worked as a clerk, a salesman, and a librarian. His
first full length book of poems, *Person, Place, and Thing* (1944),
received extremely favorable reviews. His second volume of
verse, *V-Letter and Other Poems* (1945), won the Pulitzer Prize.
Shapiro is also the author of a number of other works, including *Essay on Rime* (1945), *Bibliography of Modern Prosody*
(1948), and *Poems of a Jew* (1958).

Shapiro has been on the faculties of Johns Hopkins, Iowa
State, the University of California, and the University of Ne-
braska. He is a member of the American Academy of Arts and
Letters and has served as Consultant in Poetry to the Library of
Congress. He has also edited *Poetry: A Magazine of Verse* and
Prairie Schooner.

Shapiro's poems are very often concerned with personal
experiences. He has said himself that he generally writes about
"myself, my house, my street, and my city." In taking this personal approach in a poem such as "The 151st Psalm," the God
of flowers and green pastures has become "the table on which
I lean . . . the plate from which I eat." In the following poem,
"University," Shapiro explores the seemingly commonplace
aspects of prejudice rather than the monstrous lynchings and
persecutions which are, for example, the subject of Aaron
Kurtz's "Behold the Sea" (p. 503). It is not idealized democracy,
the American dream, which is found in Shapiro's poem, but
everyday experience in which deans of a university would "humor the snob and lure the lout."

University

To hurt the Negro and avoid the Jew
Is the curriculum. In mid-September
The entering boys, identified by hats,
Wander in a maze of mannered brick
5   Where boxwood and magnolia brood
And columns with imperious stance
Like rows of ante-bellum girls
    Eye them, outlanders.

In whited cells, on lawns equipped for peace,
10   Under the arch, and lofty banister,

Equals shake hands, unequals blankly pass;
The exemplary weather whispers, "Quiet, quiet"
   And visitors on tiptoe leave
   For the raw North, the unfinished West
15   As the young, detecting an advantage,
      Practice a face.

Where, on their separate hill, the colleges,
Like manor houses of an older law,
Gaze down embankments on a land in fee,
20 The Deans, dry spinsters over family plate,
   Ring out the English name like coin,
   Humor the snob and lure the lout.
   Within the precincts of this world
      Poise is a club.

25 But on the neighboring range, misty and high,
The past is absolute: some luckless race
Dull with inbreeding and conformity
Wears out its heart, and comes barefoot and bad
   For charity or jail. The scholar
30 Sanctions their obsolete disease;
   The gentleman revolts with shame
      At his ancestor.

And the true nobleman, once a democrat,
Sleeps on his private mountain. He was one
35 Whose thought was shapely and whose dream was broad;
This school he held his art and epitaph.
   But now it takes from him his name,
   Falls open like a dishonest look,
   And shows us, rotted and endowed,
40   Its senile pleasure.

The 151st Psalm

Are You looking for us? We are here.
Have You been gathering flowers, Elohim?
We are Your flowers, we have always been.
When will You leave us alone?
5 We are in America.
We have been here three hundred years.
And what new altar will You deck us with?

Whom are You following, Pillar of Fire?
What barn do You seek shelter in?
10 At whose gate do You whimper
In this great Palestine?
Whose wages do You take in this New World?
But Israel shall take what it shall take,
Making us ready for Your hungry Hand!

15 Immigrant God, You follow me;
You go with me, You are a distant tree;
You are the beast that lows in my heart's gates;
You are the dog that follows at my heel;
You are the table on which I lean;
20 You are the plate from which I eat.

Shepherd of the flocks of praise,
Youth of all youth, ancient of days,
Follow us.

Suggestions for Discussion

1. Judging by the description in "University" "of mannered brick/
   Where boxwood and magnolia brood," in what section of
   the United States is the University located? What President of
   this country, a democrat (small "d"), founded a university and
   wanted the fact inscribed on his tomb?
2. What kinds of behavior are contrasted in the second and third
   stanzas? How is "Poise is a club" doubly ironic? How is it implied that the gentleman "revolts . . ./At his ancestor"? Why is
   it "with shame"?
3. How is the "true nobleman" of the final stanza contrasted with
   "the gentleman" of the previous stanza? How has the passage of
   time distorted the shapely thought and broad dream? Does the
   "senile pleasure" of the last line relate to the "curriculum" mentioned in the first stanza?
4. How does the question "Are You looking for us?" relate to the
   title "The 151st Psalm"? In what other ways does the poet indicate an interim since the Biblical psalms were composed?
5. How would you characterize the God depicted in the second
   poem? What do the words "looking for," "seek," and "follow"
   suggest? Is God shown "hounding" his people as in Francis
   Thompson's "The Hound of Heaven"?
6. What Jewish religious rituals are suggested by the list in the
   third stanza? What is the purpose of the rituals for the speaker?
7. The last three lines bear the weight of the whole poem. Why
   does the poet telescope a seven-line stanza into three lines?
   What layers of meaning are contained in the phrase "the flocks
   of praise"? How is the paradoxical "Youth of all youth, ancient
   of days" a particularly appropriate way to address God?

Suggestions for Writing and Comparison

1. Is it the function of poetry to present ugliness? On what grounds can the anger of Shapiro's "University" or Pillin's "Miserere" (p. 501) be justified?
2. Read John Donne's sonnet "Batter My Heart Three-Personed God." Compare the attitude of the poet to God in the sonnet and in "The 151st Psalm." What do the poets ask of God?

Muriel Rukeyser

Muriel Rukeyser was born in New York City in 1913. She attended Vassar, Harvard, and Columbia. One of her earliest works was a biography of the American physicist Willard Gibbs (1942), which was acclaimed among the finest biographies of the year. She has published collections of poetry, including *Theory of Flight* (1935), *A Turning Wind* (1938), *Beast in View* (1944), *Orpheus* (1949), *Selected Poems* (1951), and *Waterlily Fire* (1962). Ms. Rukeyser is also the author of critical studies such as *The Life of Poetry* (1949). She has been a Guggenheim Fellow and has received awards from the American Academy of Arts and Letters and the National Institute of Arts and Letters.

Often Muriel Rukeyser's poems are about personal anguish, and the diction in them is that of myth and dream, as in "Beast in View" (p. 531). The following poem, "Letter to the Front," like another of her poems, "Akiba," is different, however, in that it deals with an historical situation of public concern. Yet the language of "Letter to the Front" is of personal argument, and the historical situation of World War II becomes merely a setting for individual decision.

from
Letter to the Front

To be a Jew in the twentieth century
Is to be offered a gift. If you refuse,
Wishing to be invisible, you choose
Death of the spirit, the stone insanity.
5 Accepting, take full life. Full agonies:
Your evening deep in labyrinthine blood
Of those who resist, fail, and resist; and God
Reduced to a hostage among hostages.

The gift is·torment. Not alone the still
10 Torture, isolation; or torture of the flesh.
That may come also. But the accepting wish,
The whole and fertile spirit as guarantee
For every human freedom, suffering to be free,
Daring to live for the impossible.

Suggestions for Discussion

1. Discuss the effectiveness of the sonnet form as used by Rukeyser. Is the rhyme scheme Petrarchan or Shakespearean? What is the controlling image or metaphor? How is it ironic?
2. Explain the following phrases: "the stone insanity," "Your evening deep in labyrinthine blood," and "fertile spirit as guarantee."
3. How does being "a Jew in the twentieth century" relate to "the accepting wish"? Are the poems by William Pillin (p. 501) and Aaron Kurtz (p. 503) poems of "acceptance"?

Suggestions for Writing and Comparison

1. Compare and contrast this poem with Countee Cullen's "Yet Do I Marvel" (p. 117). Comment on the use of the sonnet form and the attitudes toward ethnic identification in both poems.
2. Read Albert Camus' *The Myth of Sisyphus* and discuss the existential ideas of commitment or "engagement" and living in good faith in relation to Rukeyser's "accepting wish."

Denise Levertov

Denise Levertov, born in 1923 in England, is of Russian-Jewish
and Welsh background. She came to the United States in 1948.
Levertov has taught writing at a variety of colleges and universities, including C.C.N.Y., Berkeley, and M.I.T. In a recent book
of essays, *The Poet and the World,* she discusses her teaching,
the world of poetry, and the world of American education. Her
volumes of poetry include *Jacob's Ladder, Relearning the Alphabet,* and *To Stay Alive.*

In "Illustrious Ancestors" Levertov learns from her own
ancestors, the tailor and the rabbi, how to be a poet, to write
"poems direct as what the birds said."

Illustrious Ancestors

The Rav
of Northern White Russia declined,
in his youth, to learn the
language of birds, because
5 the extraneous did not interest him; nevertheless
when he grew old it was found
he understood them anyway, having
listened well, and as it is said, "prayed
    with the bench and the floor." He used
10 what was at hand—as did
Angel Jones of Mold, whose meditations
were sewn into coats and britches.
    Well, I would like to make,
thinking some line still taut between me and them,
15 poems direct as what the birds said,
hard as a floor, sound as a bench,
mysterious as the silence when the tailor
would pause with his needle in the air.

Suggestions for Discussion

1. Discuss what the poet is suggesting about poetry when she uses
   the following words to describe it: "taut," "direct," "mysterious," "hard as a floor," "sound as a bench."
2. What do the Rav and Angel Jones have in common? In what
   way are they illustrious?

Suggestion for Writing and Comparison

1. Read Eugen Herrigel's *Zen and the Art of Archery*. Compare the Zen concept of a master with Levertov's comment about the Rav who came to understand the language of birds without studying it. Could the Rav be considered a master in the Zen sense?

Hyam Plutzik

Hyam Plutzik, like so many Jewish writers, was born in Brooklyn, New York. However, unlike the others, he was raised in the country in Connecticut. He attended Trinity College and Yale University, and during the Depression he worked as a newspaperman.

Plutzik has been published frequently in magazines and anthologies. He is the author of *Aspects of Proteus* (1949), *Apples from Shinar* (1959), and *Horatio* (1961). His poetry has received several awards, including the National Institute of Arts and Letters Award and the Poetry Awards Prize.

The following poem, "On the Photograph of a Man I Never Saw," suggests two themes that are recurrent in the literature of American ethnic groups: both the second- and third-generation American's awareness of the differences between himself and his ancestors, and his consciousness of loss of a traditional culture. Plutzik's themes should be compared especially with those in Jacob Sloan's "I Was My Father" (p. 520) and Virginia Tatarian's "Photograph of Five Ancestors" (p. 613). Plutzik's style in "On the Photograph of a Man I Never Saw" resembles that in his poem "Argumentum ad Hominem" (p. 530): both contain several brief, sharp stanzas presented in a "falling" pattern which work to wed form and content.

On the Photograph of a Man I Never Saw

My grandfather's beard
Was blacker than God's
Just after the tablets
Were broken in half.

5   My grandfather's eyes
    Were sterner than Moses'
    Just after the worship
    Of the calf.

        O ghost! ghost!
10   You foresaw the days
        Of the fallen Law
        In the strange place.

        Where ten together
        Lament David,
15   Is the glance softened?
        Bowed the face?

Suggestions for Discussion

1. What qualities of temperament does the poet infer from physical characteristics such as a black beard? Why is the grandfather connected with Moses?
2. What do the breaking of the tablets and the worship of the calf signify? How are these Biblical incidents related to the present day?
3. What is the meaning of the change from anger to lament, from references about Moses to mention of David? Is the ghost truly appeased? What is suggested by the implication that there is barely a *minyan?* (Jewish law requires a *minyan,* i.e., at least ten men gathered together, before a religious ceremony may be held.)

Suggestions for Writing and Comparison

1. Compare the references to Moses in this poem with those to Abraham in Delmore Schwartz's poem on p. 526. Do the patriarchs make similar impressions on the two poets?
2. What kind of communication is possible between the grandson and his unseen grandfather? Aside from genetics, what has the grandson inherited?

Rhoda Schwartz

Rhoda Schwartz is a second-generation American of Russian-Jewish descent. She is an editor of *The American Poetry Review*. Her poetry has appeared in *The Nation* and in the anthology *About Women,* and she is also scheduled for publication in two forthcoming anthologies, *Jewish American Literature* and *Doing the Unknown.* Ms. Schwartz lives in Philadelphia, Pennsylvania.

In her poems Rhoda Schwartz celebrates her father, who went to Bialystok prison for demonstrating against the tsar, and her grandmother, whose house overlooks Odessa. Through them, their images, and their stories, she attempts to understand the word "pogrom," to decipher her heritage.

Dark Moon

There is a long field covered with the bodies of matchstick peasants.
Legs and arms askew,
they remind me of a game I knew as a child,
but these matchsticks cannot be moved or lifted.
5 The bodies stretch for miles.
Hair is clotted moss mixed with the short grasses.
I feel like a dark moon
passing over all of this.
Bullet holes are hidden by blue blouses, dirty
10 and wrinkled, they'll never be clean.
You never told me things were as bad as this.
How can I understand a word like *pogrom?*
When the dark moon is gone, the bodies
will have disappeared and I'll be in a different hemisphere
15 shining on lovers.

Why can't you eat? Why do you run to hide
your books when there's a knock on the door?
Where did they bury
your mother? Your father?

20 You are in a parade. I see the red blouse and white
pants you wear like a uniform. Stop
laughing for a minute and listen to your daughter.
I'm afraid.

Old Photographs

1.

We are returning together. The train is late at every
stop on the way, detained by the banging of switchmen and
flares. It's the dead of winter. Snow has made bones
out of the trees. The huts are covered by drifts so
5 white our eyes hurt in the morning. Our conversation is
disjointed. We won't be able to stand it when the
train gets in. Candles burn in the aisles. We are
lurching towards the next day and the next. You keep
telling me I should go back to Russia. The train is
10 a black holocaust going through the mountains. Tomorrow,
we will be there. It is never the same. Someday, tell
me how beautiful it was when we went back together.
Say my name.

2.

My Russian great-grandmother: I would not be surprised to see
15 a crow sitting on her shoulder. Black silk dress—pleats heavy
and twisted like the rills of the Caucasus, she stands erect in
her garden—the long, slender hands touching the knob of the
summer chair. Is she brown with age or is it the old sepia
photograph? She is frowning. She says, to no one in particular,
20 what can I do with the 15-year-old up-start, my grandson,
in Bialystok prison for six months because he hates the Tsar, loves
Chekhov and marched in a parade before the revolution?

My father's friends are throwing rolls to him over the prison
walls with messages. He laughs. I love him.

25 He told me his grandmother hit him with Russian birch twigs to
subdue him. When he tried to row across the Dneiper
in a boat smaller than a toy, they laughed.
Father, when you hid your books in the hayloft, and argued with
Gogol late at night, I was there in your sperm waiting to hear
30 your story.

The ship that brought you to America had no library. You cursed its
keel—the hunger—the gold slipped through your fingers when you
disembarked. The shore was lonely. I want you to know I would have
loved you if I could have loved you, still hidden in your sperm
35 with Gogol and Pushkin. What a foursome. I would have
lost to you on purpose. I wish I could tear
down every Russian birch tree that hurt you before I could say I was
    sorry.

3.

The walls were taller than the prison
at Bialystok. You were shorter than the guards. Did you ever spit
40 at them—kick the dirt and yell down with the Tsar, or did you eat
your black bread quietly, pee in a trench, dig holes
for posts and think about the time you would leave for America?

4.

I am dreaming of you sitting in a buggy with your uncle,
holding the reins of an old horse. The reins look like
45 dried tobacco leaves. I think of your wallet, the same
color and texture, whenever I reach into a drawer of silk
scarves and suddenly touch it. I am old
and wrinkled as the tobacco leaf. I swim into daydreams
about you.
50 You are smiling because you are young and your hair is black
and curly and Pushkin is waiting for you back in the hayloft.
You were a romantic; a sensualist even then. Sometimes,
I wake up crying because I've seen you in a pine box, eyes
closed against living. You told me to always
55 be full of love and gentle with men. I try to remember.

5.

When you came to America, why did you think
the St. Lawrence River was like the Dneiper and try to row
across it in a rowboat? You were too slight
to do it, but you did it
60 while the steamships blew their horns in anger.
You told me the fog was rolling in like puffs of black cotton
and you were scared.
They let you off with a warning—
You sold expensive things to millionaires
65 and became a capitalist.
I used to pretend your name was Marco Polo
when you opened the packing crates
and showed me Italian linens, Spanish shawls and Chinese
vases. We put them all in a row and talked about them.
70 I was your best audience. It was hard for either
one of us to spell Czechoslovakia.

Suggestions for Discussion

1. Why is the title "Dark Moon" appropriate for the first poem?
What is the effect of the phrase "bodies of matchstick peasants"?

2. Why does the narrator say, finally, "I'm afraid"? Is she afraid of the past, of "pogroms," of her parent's laughter, or of the dark moon?

3. In the introductory stanza of "Old Photographs," is the setting real or imagined? How do old photographs relate to a train journey?

4. What are the narrator, her father, Gogol, and Pushkin doing? To what does "I would have/lost to you on purpose" refer?

5. Discuss the details of color and texture used throughout "Old Photographs." Do they seem to make a portrait of a romantic, a sensualist, a revolutionary? Are these necessarily contradictions?

6. Reread the last two lines of the poem. What is their tone? Do they make an effective close or do they seem irrelevant?

Suggestion for Writing and Comparison

1. Read Hyman Plutzik's "On the Photograph of a Man I Never Saw" (p. 514) and Virginia Tartarian's "Photograph of Five Ancestors" (p. 613). Compare the use to which each of these poets, and Rhoda Schwartz, has put the "photograph" device.

Jacob Sloan

Jacob Sloan, born in Brooklyn, New York, in 1918, is a graduate of Brooklyn College and the Seminary College of Jewish
Studies of the Jewish Theological Seminary. He is responsible
for many of the translations in *Language of Faith,* a volume of
Jewish prayers, as well as the translations of *Passover Hagga-
dah* (1953) and Isaac Bashevis Singer's *Satan in Goray* (1955).
Sloan is also the editor of the *American Jewish Yearbook* and
the recipient of the Louis LaMed prize for translations. A
collection of his poems, *Generation of Journey,* appeared in
1945. His more recent poems have been published frequently
by periodicals such as *Commentary.*

"I Was My Father" represents in three stages the ambivalence and the conflict of a second-generation American: his
realization of his unalterable heritage and his determination to
succeed where his immediate predecessor has not ("to outfather father"); his realization of the father's spirit and generosity
which he could not hope to equal, even if he desired to; and
finally, his realization that he must bury the father and inherit
himself, for good or for bad.

I Was My Father

I was my father: a bald, full-lipped man
with absent eyes, hoarse throat and mouth of wit,
studied heresy at the cabin hearth,
and bought the *Times* the first day off the ship.
5 I was my father; fought the kids who mocked
his poor wild pinching of the spitball class,
missed him like a tooth when I awoke
into adolescence, swore, harassed,
to outfather father: wish, work, win
10 what he had never dared, or lost. O,
but I was not my father, shrugged away
from his: "I know Job is very strong.
But a man can longer live with Psalms."
I was not my father; could not hope to say
15 to my wife the famous solace: "Why
cry? Who knows whether he who found
it, did not need the lost purse more than I?"

*"What hast thou here, and whom hast thou here that thou hast
hewed thee out here a sepulchre . . . a sepulchre on high?" (Isa. 22:16).*

I am myself—not yet, but shall be

less than I become, more than I do,
20 equal to my friends, less than my love,
more than my work, less than my poetry.
Making and unmaking myself man,
rabbi and charlatan and the between,
and hide myself and give myself away,
25 and say less than I think, more than I mean.
I build a house which I may not inhabit,
and sow a vineyard which I may not reap,
and play with children who are not my own,
and read a language I may never speak —
30 and joke and err and plan to be forgiven.
I am all these I do; like Hamlet, have
offenses more than thoughts; but no sword,
except the word I cast into the river.

Suggestions for Discussion

1. How is the son the father—that is, what does he accept as his own (see the first stanza)? What abilities of the father has the son lost?
2. In what ways does the speaker mean he "swore . . . to outfather father"? How does the use of "sepulchre" in the quotation from *Isaiah* relate to the poem?
3. Discuss how Sloan's narrator uses parallel sentence structure and forms of riddle in identifying himself. Are the contructions appropriate to the problem?

Suggestion for Writing and Comparison

1. Compare the inheritance you have from an immigrant ancestor with the poet's inheritance from his father.

Allen Ginsberg

Allen Ginsberg was born in Paterson, New Jersey, in 1926. In the 1950's he earned a national reputation as one of the leading spokesmen of the Beat generation and the San Francisco Beat poets. Ginsberg has described his own compositions as being made of "language . . . intuitively chosen as in a trance and dream" and "rhythms from breath into the breast and belly."

Ginsberg's work has been published in the Beat journal *Beatitude* as well as in periodicals such as *Playboy, Evergreen Review, Esquire,* and *New Directions.* He has also written several books of poems published in the 1960's such as *Howl, Kaddish, Reality Sandwiches,* and *Empty Mirrors.*

"*Kaddish* for Naomi Ginsberg: 1894-1956" was written in 1959 and published in 1961. *Kaddish* is the Jewish prayer for the dead; in this poem it refers to Ginsberg's prayers for and remembrances of his mother, Naomi. The whole poem contains five parts: "proem, narrative, hymmnn, lament, litany and fugue"; the following selections are from the first two sections of *Kaddish.*

from
Kaddish

For Naomi Ginsberg 1894-1956

Strange now to think of you, gone without corsets & eyes, while I walk on the sunny pavement of Greenwich Village.

downtown Manhattan, clear winter noon, and I've been up all night, talking, talking, reading the Kaddish aloud, listening to Ray Charles blues shout blind on the phonograph

the rhythm the rhythm—and your memory in my head three years after—And read Adonais' last triumphant stanzas aloud—wept, realizing how we suffer—

And how Death is that remedy all singers dream of, sing, remember, prophesy as in the Hebrew Anthem, or the Buddhist Book of Answers—and my own imagination of a withered leaf—at dawn—

5 Dreaming back thru life, Your time—and mine accelerating toward Apocalypse,

the final moment—the flower burning in the Day—and what comes after,

looking back on the mind itself that saw an American city

a flash away, and the great dream of Me or China, or you and a phantom Russia, or a crumpled bed that never existed—

like a poem in the dark—escaped back to Oblivion—

10 No more to say, and nothing to weep for but the Beings in the Dream, trapped in its disappearance,

sighing, screaming with it, buying and selling pieces of phantom, worshipping each other,

worshipping the God included in it all—longing or inevitability?—while it lasts, a Vision—anything more?

It leaps about me, as I go out and walk the street, look back over my shoulder, Seventh Avenue, the battlements of window office buildings shouldering each other high, under a cloud, tall as the sky an instant —and the sky above—an old blue place.

or down the Avenue to the South, to—as I walk toward the Lower East Side—where you walked 50 years ago, little girl—from Russia, eating the first poisonous tomatoes of America—frightened on the dock—

15 then struggling in the crowds of Orchard Street toward what?—toward Newark—

toward candy store, first home-made sodas of the century, hand-churned ice cream in backroom on musty brownfloor boards—

Toward education marriage nervous breakdown, operation, teaching school, and learning to be mad, in a dream—what is this life?

Toward the Key in the window—and the great Key lays its head of light on top of Manhattan, and over the floor, and lays down on the sidewalk —in a single vast beam, moving, as I walk down First toward the Yiddish Theater—and the place of poverty

you knew, and I know, but without caring now—Strange to have moved thru Paterson, and the West, and Europe and here again,

20 with the cries of Spaniards now in the doorstoops doors and dark boys on the street, fire escapes old as you

—Tho you're not old now, that's left here with me—

Myself, anyhow, maybe as old as the universe—and I guess that dies with us—enough to cancel all that comes—

What came is gone forever every time—

. . . .

Back! You! Naomi! Skull on you! Gaunt immortality and revolution come —small broken woman—the ashen indoor eyes of hospitals, ward greyness on skin—

25   'Are you a spy?' I sat at the sour table, eyes filling with tears— 'Who are you? Did Louis send you?— The wires—'

in her hair, as she beat on her head—'I'm not a bad girl—don't murder me! —I hear the ceiling—I raised two children—'

Two years since I'd been there— I started to cry—She stared—nurse broke up the meeting a moment—I went into the bathroom to hide, against the toilet white walls

'The Horror' I weeping—to see her again—'The Horror'—as if she were dead thru funeral rot in—'The Horror!'

I came back she yelled more—they led her away—'You're not Allen—' I watched her face—but she passed by me, not looking—

30   Opened the door to the ward,—she went thru without a glance back, quiet suddenly—I stared out—she looked old—the verge of the grave—'All the Horror!'

Another year, I left NY—on West Coast in Berkeley cottage dreamed of her soul—that, thru life, in what form it stood in that body, ashen or manic, gone beyond joy—

near its death—with eyes—was my own love in its form, the Naomi, my mother on earth still—sent her long letter—& wrote hymns to the mad—Work of the merciful Lord of Poetry.

that causes the broken grass to be green, or the rock to break in grass—or the Sun to be constant to earth—Sun of all sunflowers and days on bright iron bridges—what shines on old hospitals—as on my yard—

Returning from San Francisco one night, Orlovsky, in my room—Whalen in his peaceful chair—a telegram from Gene, Naomi dead—

35   Outside I bent my head to the ground under the bushes near the garage —knew she was better—

at last—not left to look on Earth alone—2 years of solitude—no one, at age nearing 60—old woman of skulls—once long-tressed Naomi of Bible—

or Ruth who wept in America—Rebecca aged in Newark—David remembering his Harp, now lawyer at Yale

or Svul Avrum—Israel Abraham—myself—to sing in the wilderness toward God—O Elohim!—so to the end—2 days after her death I got her letter—

Strange Prophecies anew! She wrote—'The key is in the window, the key is in the sunlight at the window—I have the key—Get married Allen don't take drugs—the key is in the bars, in the sunlight in the window.

40
                                  Love,
                                    your mother'

which is Naomi—

Suggestions for Discussion

1. Is this excerpt an appropriate "Kaddish" in tone and spirit?
2. Discuss the significance of the following lines from the opening stanza: "Death is that remedy all singers dream of . . ." and "No more to say, and nothing to weep for but the Beings in the Dream, trapped in its disappearance."
3. The poet makes use of a walk around Manhattan to compare the past with the present. How are the changes he notices relevant to his mother and to her life?
4. What is meant by the phrase "the key in the window" in the first and third stanzas?

5. The poet says of himself "myself—to sing in the wilderness toward God—O Elohim!" How does this image of the poet coincide with what you know of Allen Ginsberg through the popular press—newspapers, *Time*, *Life*, *Esquire?*

Suggestions for Writing and Comparison

1. Discuss Ginsberg's combination of tradition with unconventional language and poetic form. Is his approach effective?
2. Compare the influence of the death of a father on his son in James Baldwin's story "Death of the Prophet" (in *Commentary*, March 1950) with the death of the mother in Ginsberg's poem. Note carefully the elements of religion and rebellion.

Delmore Schwartz

Delmore Schwartz was born in Brooklyn, New York, in 1913. He attended several universities, including the University of Wisconsin, New York University, and Harvard. He received his B. A. in philosophy in 1935.

Schwartz was granted his first significant publishing opportunity by New Directions Publishers, who included his work in the *New Directions in Prose and Poetry* annual of 1937. In 1939, New Directions published his first collection, *In Dreams Begin Responsibilities,* which contains a story, a long poem, lyrics, and a play. Schwartz also wrote a verse play, *Shenandoah,* as well as other collections of short stories and poetry, including *The World Is a Wedding* (1948) and *Summer Knowledge* (1959). In 1959 he received the Bollingen Prize in Poetry for *Summer Knowledge,* and in 1960, six years before his death, he received the Shelley Memorial Prize.

The two poems in this text by Delmore Schwartz give an indication of the range of his ability. "The Self Unsatisfied Runs Everywhere" is a sonnet of personal experience: the emptiness of Manhattan on a Sunday morning. The following poem, "Abraham," on the other hand, is one of his poems on Biblical subjects which were originally included in *Summer Knowledge*. "Abraham," like its companion poems "Sarah" and "Jacob," is a dramatic monologue. The patriarch appears here as "a mere boy" and as an erring, "endlessly anxious" man vacillating between the extremes of doubt and confidence. The characterization is somewhat irreverent and altogether human.

Abraham

> *(To J. M. Kaplan)*

I was a mere boy in a stone-cutter's shop
When, early one evening, my raised hand
Was halted and the soundless voice said:
"Depart from your father and your country
5 And the things to which you are accustomed.
Go now into a country unknown and strange
I will make of your children a great nation,

Your generations will haunt every generation of all the nations,
They will be like the stars at midnight, like the sand of the sea."
10 Then I looked up at the infinite sky,
Star-pointing and silent, and it was then, on that evening, that I
Became a man: that evening of my manhood's birthday.

I went then to Egypt, the greatest of nations.
There I encountered the Pharaoh who built the tombs,
15 Great public buildings, many theatres, and seashore villas:
And my wife's beauty was such that, fearing his power and lust,
I called her my sister, a girl neither for him nor for me.
And soon was fugitive, a nomad again.
Living alone with my sister, becoming very rich
20 In all but children, in herds, in possessions, the herds continually
Increased my possessions through prodigies of progeny.

From time to time, in the afternoon's revery
In the late sunlight or the cool of the evening
I called to mind the protracted vanity of that promise
25 Which had called me forth from my father's house unwillingly
Into the last strangeness of Egypt and the childless desert.
Then Sarah gave me her handmaid, a young girl
That I might at least at last have children by another
And later, when a great deal else had occurred,
30 I put away Hagar, with the utmost remorse
Because the child was the cause of so much rivalry and jealousy.
At last when all this had passed or when
The promise seemed the parts of dream,
When we were worn out and patient in all things
35 The stranger came, suave and elegant,
A messenger who renewed the promise, making Sarah
Burst out laughing hysterically!

But the boy was born and grew and I saw
What I had known, I knew what I had seen, for he
40 Possessed his mother's beauty and his father's humility,
And was not marked and marred by her sour irony and my endless anxiety.

Then the angel returned, asking that I surrender
My son as a lamb to show that humility
Still lived in me, and was not altered by age and prosperity.

45 I said nothing, shocked and passive. Then I said but to myself alone:
"This was to be expected. These promises
Are never unequivocal or unambiguous, in this
As in all things which are desired the most:
I have had great riches and great beauty.
50 I cannot expect the perfection of every wish
And if I deny the command, who knows what will happen?"

Delmore Schwartz 527

But his life was forgiven and given back to me:
His children and their children are an endless nation:
Dispersed on every coast. And I am not gratified
55 Nor astonished. It has never been otherwise:
Exiled, wandering, dumbfounded by riches,
Estranged among strangers, dismayed by the infinite sky,
An alien to myself until at last the caste of the last alienation,
The angel of death comes to make the alienated and indestructible one a part
    of his famous society.

The Self Unsatisfied Runs Everywhere

Sunday and sunlight ashen on the Square,
Hard wind, high blue, and clouded pennant sky,
Fifth Avenue empty in the autumn air,
As if a clear photograph of a dead day.
5 It was the Lord's day once, solemn and full
—Now I in an aftermath, desire spent,
Move with a will appeased and see a gull,
Then gulls drop from an arch—scythes of descent!—

Having, I think, no wish beyond the foam
10 Toppling to them at each fresh exercise,
Knowing success like fountains, perhaps more wise
Than one who hesitantly writes a poem
—But who, being human, wishes to be a gull,
Knows nothing much, though birds are beautiful.

Suggestions for Discussion

1. What is narrative poetry? How does it differ from lyric poetry?
   Is "Abraham" narrative or lyric?
2. How formal is the language in "Abraham"? Does it seem appropriate for a patriarch? Does Schwartz use a definite meter and
   rhyme scheme? Why? What is the difference between free verse
   and blank verse?
3. Compare Schwartz's account of Abraham's story with the account given in Genesis. What changes has Schwartz made?
   What do we know about the characters from this poem that is
   only barely suggested in the Biblical account?
4. What is the diaspora? How does Abraham make reference to it?
   Define "dumbfounded," "dismayed," and "alien" in the context
   of the last stanza.

5. How does the image of Fifth Avenue on Sunday contrast with "the Lord's day . . . solemn and full" in "The Self Unsatisfied Runs Everywhere"? How is the speaker's mood akin to that of Fifth Avenue?
6. Is the phrase "scythes of descent" an accurate description of the flight of gulls? How does the phrase relate to Sunday, the Lord's day?
7. What elements of both the Petrarchan and Shakespearean forms does "The Self Unsatisfied" have? How is the phrase "Knows nothing much" a peculiar and therefore ironic comment for the last line of a sonnet? (Compare, for example, the concluding couplets in Shakespeare's sonnets XIV and CXVI.)

Suggestions for Writing and Comparison

1. See Schwartz's volume of poetry *Summer Knowledge* for his treatment of other Biblical characters. Compare Schwartz's delineation of any character with that in the Bible. Show how he changes, modernizes, or merely makes explicit that which was implicit in the original.
2. Rembrandt painted a series of Biblical portraits. Compare his characterization of Abraham with that of Schwartz. For instance, does Rembrandt find Abraham's humility as important as Schwartz does?
3. Read Wallace Stevens' poem "Sunday Morning." Compare Stevens' observations of the flight of birds on Sunday with those of Schwartz in "The Self Unsatisfied."

Hyam Plutzik

(See p. 514 for Plutzik's poem "On the Photograph of a Man I
Never Saw" and a biographical sketch of the author.)

Argumentum ad Hominem

Who has seen the pageant
Of the falling leaf
Has won a grief
Prouder than joy:

5   Has seen them fall,
One and by one,
The folk of the sun
Kissing the earth,

      Will know, will know,
10   What stuff is king
Of everything,
And its regent who.

Suggestions for Discussion

1. Define "argumentum ad hominem." Why is it usually considered a specious argument? How does this title relate to the
   poem?
2. How is this particular "grief/Prouder than joy"? How are leaves
   "The folk of the sun"? How does this "Kissing the earth" by
   the leaves "win" us "a grief/Prouder than joy"?
3. Define "stuff," "king," and "regent." How can "stuff" reign?
   Over what does it reign? Who is the "regent"?
4. Notice the meter and rhyme scheme of the poem. Are such brief
   lines appropriate to the diction and ideas? What is suggested by
   the fact that the first and last words of the poem are identical?

Suggestion for Writing and Comparison

1. Read Gerard Manley Hopkins' "Spring and Fall: To Margaret."
   Compare Hopkins' and Plutzik's methods of relating falling
   leaves to grief.

Muriel Rukeyser

(See p. 510 for the excerpt from Rukeyser's *Letter to the Front* and a biographical sketch of the author.)

Beast in View

Configurations of time and singing
    Bring me to a dark harbor where
    The chase is drawn to a beginning.
    And all the myths are gathered there.

5 I know the trees as fountains and the stars'
    Far fires fountains and your love
    A vivid fountain, and the bars
    Broken about me let me move

Among the fountains. At last seeing
10   I came here by obscure preparing,
    In vigils and encounters being
    Both running hunter and fierce prey waring.

I hunted and became the followed,
    Through many lives fleeing the last me,
15   And changing fought down a far road
    Through time to myself as I will be.

Chaos prepared me, and I find the track,
    Through life and darkness seek my myth—
    Move toward it, hunting grow more like,
20   Draw near, and know it through our path.
    Know only that we run one path.

Suggestions for Discussion

1. Why does the poet say that "The chase is drawn to a beginning" instead of the expected "drawn to a close"? How is the poem about both endings and beginnings?
2. Why should it be necessary for the bars to be "broken" in order to "Let me move/Among the fountains"? What various kinds of "fountains" are mentioned in the poem?
3. How does "Both running hunter and fierce pray waring" relate to "fought . . ./Through time to myself as I will be"? What kind of "fighting" took place and to what end?

4. How do the run-on lines build momentum and push the rhythm through an intricate rhyme scheme? What is the danger of a rhyme scheme as demanding as the one in this poem? What is the effect of reversal of techniques—end-stopped lines with fewer rhymes—in the final stanza?
5. How are the images of chaos and the path in the final stanza prefigured in the title and the opening stanza? Is there a central metaphor in the poem?

Suggestion for Writing and Comparison

1. The title for Muriel Rukeyser's poem was taken from the following stanza by John Dryden:

All, all of a piece throughout;
Thy chase had a beast in view;
Thy wars brought nothing about;
Thy lovers were all untrue,
'Tis well an old age is out,
And time to begin a new.

How does "Beast in View" suggest the coming of a new age? Is the Rukeyser poem an historical or a personal statement?

Denise Levertov

(See p. 512 for Levertov's poem "Illustrious Ancestors" and a biographical sketch of the author.)

Somebody Trying

"That creep Tolstoy," she sobbed.
"He . . . He . . . couldn't even . . ."
Something about his brother dying.

The serfs' punishments
5 have not ceased to suppurate on their backs.
Woodlots. People. Someone crying

under the yellow
autumn birchgrove drove him
wild: A new set of resolves:

10 When gambling, that almost obsolete fever,
or three days with the gypsies
sparked him into pure ego, he could,

just the same, write home, "Sell them."
It's true. "Still," (someone who loved her said,
15 cold and firm while she dissolved,

hypocrite, in self disgust, *lectrice*)
"Still, he kept on. He wrote
all that he wrote; and seems to have understood

better than most of us:
20 to be human isn't easy. It's not
easy to be a serf or a master and learn

that art. It takes nerve. Bastard. Fink.
Yet the grief
trudging behind his funeral, he earned."

A Hunger

Black beans, white sunlight.
These have sufficed.

Approval of mothers, of brothers,
of strangers—a plunge of the hands
5 in sifted flour, over the wrists.
It gives pleasure.

And being needed. Being loved for that.
Being forgiven.

What mountains there are
10 to border solitude and provide
limits, blue or
dark as raisins.

But hunger: a hunger there is
refuses. Refuses the earth.

Suggestions for Discussion

1. In the sentence from "Somebody Trying" "It's not/easy to be a serf or a master and learn/that art," to what does "that art" refer? What "takes nerve"?
2. Discuss the ambivalent attitude to Tolstoy found in the poem. Is the difference between the life and work of an artist usually so obvious?
3. Compare the first and last couplets in "A Hunger." Are "beans" and "sunlight" symbolic of what Levertov means by "the earth"?
4. What is the effect of the use of "beans," "sifted flour," and "raisins" as imagery? How do these images relate to solitude and hunger?

Suggestion for Writing and Comparison

1. The refusal in the final couplet of "A Hunger" runs counter to the approval mentioned earlier. Can the poem be read in the light of the poet's being a woman writing during the reemergence of the women's movement? Write an essay in which you discuss the conflict between a hunger which refuses and the approval which gives pleasure.

Rhoda Schwartz

(See p. 516 for Schwartz's "Dark Moon" and "Old Photographs," and for a biographical sketch of the author.)

Grand-mama

Grand-mama lifts the crystal tea glass to her
lips and sips through the cube of sugar clenched
between her teeth. A gold tooth gleams
in the candlelight as she smiles at me.
5 The flickering light has made a couch for us and I listen
for her wisdom to fill the room. Tell me more,
I beg, as I smell the lemon perfume of
her dress. Her dog whimpers in sleep near the stove
and we are alone in the stone house that overlooks
10 Odessa. She whispers poems in my ear about
blossoms turning to steel. I do not understand
her sudden gloom or why she stirs her nearly
empty glass over and over again with the old silver
spoon. Around and around it swirls until
15 I am walking near a beach with her
and kicking debris with my naked feet, looking
for my father — waiting for him to be washed
up by the sea.

I look at the white
20 shawl knotted underneath her chin — her head is bobbing
in half-sleep.
The lines on her face deepen.
She expels a soft moan
and a tiny drop of spittle hangs on the corner of her lips.
25 She does not speak for a long time. There is a banging
far away in the hills somewhere where someone wants
to be home. A night squall of rain is coming in on
the steps of darkness and rattles the panes. The heavy
smell of her oldness is everywhere. I wipe my
30 hands on my dress and look at the ring she has given
me. It slides off my finger and rolls across
the room. It sparkles in the darkness
in waves of pain.
Don't leave me grand-mama.

Suggestions for Discussion

1. Tea, flickering candlelight, and lemon perfume contrast sharply with poems "about/blossoms turning to steel." Is Grand-mama as wise and comforting as she first seems?
2. The images in the second stanza suggest age and decay. What does the narrator seem to be afraid of? What does she mean by "Don't leave me grand-mama," if her grandmother is already dead?

Suggestion for Writing and Comparison

1. Read Leonard Adamé's poem "In Chihuahua . . ." and compare his portrait of his grandfather with Rhoda Schwartz's portrait of her grandmother. How close do the poets seem to feel to their grandparents?

Chapter 6
White Ethnic Writers

Introduction

I t is impossible to characterize White Ethnic writing in the space of an introductory essay because of the great diversity of both the literature and the groups to which the writers belong. We have selected for this section writers with Polish, Armenian, Italian, Irish, Basque, Greek, and Swedish backgrounds. While this selection has been to some extent arbitrary and in all cases limited to writers with literary merit as well as ethnic awareness, we have kept in mind particularly those groups that have had a recent resurgence of ethnic identification. Such resurgence has occurred amid members of ethnic groups who have risen above the socioeconomic status of their immigrant parents or grandparents, but who still remain in what is called the "working class." Generally, those that have attained a status above the working class have retained less of their ethnic identification. The renewed White Ethnic awareness suggests that the old melting-pot theory was somewhat simplistic (and — writers such as Michael Novak assert — harmful, in that it takes a negative view of diversity). Working-class White Ethnics contrast their own situation to that of the middle-class and upper-middle-class white Anglo-Saxon Protestants, whom they see as having created a mainstream America to which White Ethnics no more belong than do Blacks or Chicanos.

Well over 40 million immigrants have come to this country since the United States declared its independence from England. Many of the Americans who comprise our present population identify themselves simply as "American," with little awareness of the ethnic background of their ancestors. However, this country is still made up of a sizable number of first- and second-generation white Americans. Of the foreign-born and their children, about 4.5 million still identify their background as Italian, almost 3 million as Polish, more than 2 million as Russian, almost 2 million as Irish, and 1 million as Swedish.

In the seventeenth and eighteenth centuries the English comprised the greatest number of migrants to America; however, since their contribution to American letters has never been neglected, as any American literature textbook will indicate, they must be outside the scope of our concern. In the early nineteenth century, one of the predominant immigrant groups was the Irish.

This group gave birth to a number of writers who were distinctly Irish American, such as poets John Boyle O'Reilly and Richard Henry Wilde, journalist Peter Finley Dunne, and novelist James T. Farrell. But this group also gave birth to such wholly "American" writers as Edgar Allan Poe, William Dean Howells, and Henry James, who can no more be considered minority-group authors than the German Americans H. H. Mencken or Theodore Dreiser.

Between 1820 and 1930 more than 4.25 million Irish immigrants came to the United States. They left Ireland for a variety of reasons: famine, political persecution, religious persecution—but the majority of them shared the problem of poverty. Like many immigrant groups, the Irish arrived in New York and, having no money to go further, were forced to settle in nearby urban slums. The Irish were the first to encounter the prejudice and hostility which were later inflicted, in varying degrees, on almost every new immigrant group. This was undoubtedly because their situation was similar to that of many later American immigrants: they arrived in great numbers, they were unskilled laborers, and their appearance was considered strange or foreign by the "settled" Americans. Like the Blacks and the Jews, they became figures of comic ridicule on the American stage. The Irish suffered the antipathy of groups such as the American Protective Association and later the Ku Klux Klan, and many job advertisers stated specifically, "No Irish need apply." Some of the problems which faced this group and their immediate descendants are depicted in Betty Smith's popular sentimental novel *A Tree Grows in Brooklyn*, in James T. Farrell's noted *Studs Lonigan* trilogy of the 1930's (which is set in the Irish ghetto of Chicago), and in *A Touch of the Poet*, a play by the Irish American Pulitzer Prize and Nobel Prize winner Eugene O'Neill.

However, despite the troubles of the Irish in the United States and the hostility which they encountered, they themselves typically took on the attitudes of older Americans toward newer immigrants. Peter Finley Dunne's Irish bartender Mr. Dooley wryly observed in 1902:

> As a pilgrim father that missed the first boat, I must raise me claryon voice again' the invasion iv this fair land be th' paupers an' arnychists in Europe. Ye bet I must—because I'm here first.

For some years it appeared as though the problems of adjustment of the Irish American were over, as was dramatically illustrated in 1960 with the election to the Presidency of a Catholic, the grandson of an Irish immigrant. In a short story which James Farrell wrote for *Commentary* in 1954, he expressed his conviction that the Irish had already melted into American life: the hero of "Danny O'Neill Was Here" returns to the Chicago ghetto of his youth, now no longer the poor son of Irish parents but a successful writer. Danny represents the cultural and financial achievement of the Irish American as Farrell saw it: the slum of his youth is no longer an Irish ghetto; it is now inhabited by Blacks. In more recent times, however, with the rise of White Ethnic consciousness, there is some suggestion that Irish American social problems are still very real, and that Irish Americans have not melted together with other groups and forgotten their own group identity.

The largest immigrant groups to arrive in the latter part of the nineteenth century were the Italians and the Eastern Europeans. Between 1820 and

1930 more than 4.5 million Italians arrived in the United States, most of them having come during the peak period around the turn of the century. They too went through the usual "period of adjustment," lived in dirty, overcrowded areas, were plagued by poverty, discrimination, and all the concomitant discomforts. Like the Irish Americans, the Italian Americans produced a number of writers whose literature expressed particular awareness of their background. One of the earliest of them was Arturo Giovannetti, who came to the United States in 1900 and worked as a coal miner in Pennsylvania. As late as 1931 Giovannetti's collection of poems *Arrows in the Gale,* published in 1914, was hailed as "one of the most significant social documents ever produced in America."

Pietro di Donato, author of *Christ in Concrete,* a literary sensation of the 1930's, was also an Italian American laborer. The hero of di Donato's novel, patterned after his father, is an Italian immigrant who labors as a construction worker with the hope of someday earning enough money to take his family out of the tenement district. He dies just as his dreams are about to be realized (see p. 552). Similar themes and characters are employed by other Italian American writers (see, for example, O. Peragello's study *Italian American Authors and Their Contribution to American Literature*).

Many Italian American writers, such as Bernard De Voto and John Ciardi, have come into the mainstream of American literature, but their work occasionally expresses some awareness of an ethnic working-class background. Ciardi's early collection of verse, *Homeward to America* (1940), as well as later collections including *As If* (1955), contains a number of poems which suggest that he feels both a nostalgia for and a distance from his ethnic background (see p. 606 for an example of Ciardi's verse).

The ethnic literature of first- and second-generation Americans is very often concerned not only with particular problems of a minority group, but also with urban problems in general, since most of these groups—the Irish, the Italians, the Poles, and the Greeks are outstanding examples—were forced to settle in urban ghettos. There are, however, several exceptions. The Basques, for instance, settled almost exclusively in Nevada, where they worked as shepherds; indeed, they were originally allowed into the country over the quota restriction because their skills were needed by the Nevada sheepmen who found it difficult to recruit local labor. Similarly, the Scandinavians settled in rural areas of states such as Minnesota or South Dakota, where they became farmers.

Although such groups were not forced to contend with ethnic problems specifically connected to urban dwelling, there were other cultural difficulties which confronted them as forcefully as members of minority groups who settled in the big cities. For example, the problems of the estrangement between immigrant parents and American-born children are common to both rural and urban dwellers. The Basque American writer Robert Laxalt (see p. 589) suggests this situation in his novel *Sweet Promised Land* (1957), when he laments, "In a little while, even our sons would forget, and the old country people would be only a dimming memory, and names would mean nothing, and the melting would be done." The same sentiment is suggested in Ole Rölvaag's trilogy *Giants in the Earth, Peder Victorious,* and *Their Father's God,* which is concerned with the conflict and alienation between first- and second-generation Norwegian Americans.

The Scandinavians, who came to America for economic rather than political or religious reasons, were different from most immigrant groups in that the social atmosphere in their new land was not unlike what they had known in the old country. A more representative, though much smaller, immigrant group was composed of Armenians who came here as refugees from persecution and encountered a culture quite foreign to that which they had known. Before 1894 there were only 3000 Armenians living in America. The real tide of immigration occurred after the conquest of Armenia and the massacre which followed. The Armenians thus without a homeland, like the Jews before 1948, sought refuge in America. From 1894 to 1930 over 100,000 Armenians entered the United States, where they settled in both rural and urban areas. Although the Armenians do not comprise one of the larger immigrant groups, there are several Armenian American authors who often write on ethnic themes. The most famous of these is William Saroyan, born in the Armenian community of Fresno, California, the son of refugees. Saroyan's short stories are anthologized in most American literature textbooks and have been collected in volumes such as *The Daring Young Man on the Flying Trapeze*. They frequently deal with the problems of American minority-group life—problems common to Italians, Germans, Jews, and Native Americans, as well as Armenians. Saroyan is perhaps the only Armenian American author of international repute, but a number of others, such as Richard Hagopian, Emmanuel Varandyan, Harold Bond (pp. 601, 618), Virginia Tatarian (p. 613), and Mihran H. Azhderian, have provided in their poetry and prose glimpses into the life of a representative American ethnic group.

Statistics on immigration may provide us with facts, but writers themselves best reveal what it means to live with the facts. Although the American writer is often concerned with the problems of his particular ethnic group, he is also well aware of problems of the individual, and especially problems of the artist. The artist's difficulty can be twofold: not only may he feel himself alienated from the majority culture by virtue of his ethnic background, but he may also feel himself alienated from his own ethnic group by virtue of his artistic sensibilities. This dilemma is suggested in Harold Bond's poem "Letter to an Aunt" (p. 618). The sense of two-ness, of belonging both to an ethnic group and to the larger American society, is frequently explored in this chapter. Both sociologists and writers have forecast the end of two-ness—the day the melting will be done, for better or for worse—but this day is yet to come, as the following portraits of American society testify.

AN ESSAY

Michael Novak

Michael Novak teaches at the State University of New York and is the author of *The Rise of the Unmeltable Ethnics* (1972), as well as various articles published in *Harper's* and *Saturday Review*. Novak challenges the concept of America as a melting pot, noting that a sense of ethnic identity is retained for generations by the non-WASP: "The long voyage of immigration is not completed when in the new land a man enters his first boardinghouse, or takes his wife to an apartment of their own. Immigration lasts at least a hundred years." As a Catholic and a Slovak, he has noticed the absence of Catholics and Slovaks from the traditional American approach to history. Novak observes, "I was taught to be proud of being Slovak, but to recognize that others wouldn't know what it meant."

The publication of *The Rise of the Unmeltable Ethnics* in 1972 is an indication of a renewed ethnic awareness, usually among third-generation Americans.

White Ethnic

Growing up in America has been an assault upon my sense of worthiness. It has also been a kind of liberation and delight.

There must be countless women in America who have known for years that something is peculiarly unfair, yet who have found it only recently possible, because of Women's Liberation, to give tongue to their pain. In recent months, I have experienced a similar inner thaw, a gradual relaxation, a willingness to think about feelings heretofore shepherded out of sight.

I am born of PIGS—those Poles, Italians, Greeks, and Slavs, non-English-speaking immigrants, numbered so heavily among the workingmen of this nation. Not particularly liberal, nor radical, born into a history not white Anglo-Saxon and not Jewish—born outside what in America is considered the intellectual mainstream. And thus privy to neither power nor status nor intellectual voice.

Those Poles of Buffalo and Milwaukee—so notoriously taciturn, sullen, nearly speechless. Who has ever understood them? It is not that Poles do not feel emotion: what is their history if not dark passion, romanticism, betrayal, courage, blood? But where in America is there anywhere a language for voicing what a Christian Pole in this nation feels? He has no Polish culture left him, no Polish tongue. Yet Polish feelings do not go easily into the idiom of happy America, the America of the Anglo-Saxons and, yes, in the arts, the Jews. (The Jews have long been a culture of the word, accustomed to exile, skilled in scholarship and in reflection. The Christian Poles are largely of peasant origin, free men for hardly more than a hundred years.) Of what shall the man of Buffalo think, on his way to work in the mills, departing from his relatively dreary home and street? What roots does he have? What language of the heart is available to him?

The PIGS are not silent willingly. The silence burns like hidden coals in the chest.

All four of my grandparents, unknown to one another, arrived in America from the same country in Slovakia. My grandfather had a small farm in Pennsylvania; his wife died in a wagon accident. Meanwhile, a girl of fifteen arrived on Ellis Island, dizzy, a little ill from witnessing births and deaths and illnesses aboard the crowded ship, with a sign around her neck lettered "PASSAIC." There an aunt told her of the man who had lost his wife in Pennsylvania. She went. They were married. Inheriting his three children, each year for five years she had one of her own; she was among the lucky, only one died. When she was twenty-two, mother of seven, her husband died. And she resumed the work she had begun in Slovakia at the town home of a man known to us now only as "the Professor": she housecleaned and she laundered.

I heard this story only weeks ago. Strange that I had not asked insistently before. Odd that I should have such shallow knowledge of my roots. Amazing to me that I do not know what my family suffered, endured, learned, hoped these past six or seven generations. It is as if there were no project on which we all have been involved. As if history, in some way, began with my father and with me.

Let me hasten to add that the estrangement I have come to feel derives not only from a lack of family history. All my life, I have been made to feel a slight uneasiness when I must say my name. Under challenge in grammar school concerning my nationality, I had been instructed by my father to announce proudly: "American." When my family moved from the Slovak ghetto of Johnstown to the WASP suburb on the hill, my mother impressed upon us how well we must be dressed, and show good manners, and behave—people think of us as "different" and we mustn't give them any cause. "Whatever you do, marry a Slovak girl," was other advice to a similar end: "They cook. They clean. They take good care of you. For your own good."

When it was revealed to me that most movie stars and many other professionals had abandoned European names in order to feed American fantasies, I felt only a little sadness. One of my uncles, for business reasons and rather late in life, changed his name too, to a simple German variant. Not long, either, after World War II.

Nowhere in my schooling do I recall an attempt to put me in touch with my own history. The strategy was clearly to make an American of me. English literature, American literature; and even the history books, as I recall them, were peopled mainly by Anglo-Saxons from Boston (where most historians seemed to live). Not even my native Pennsylvania, let alone my Slovak forebears, counted for very many paragraphs. I don't remember feeling envy or regret: a feeling, perhaps, of unimportance, of remoteness, of not having heft enough to count.

The fact that I was born a Catholic also complicated life. What is a Catholic but what everybody else is in reaction against? Protestants reformed "the Whore of Babylon," others were "enlightened" from it, and Jews had reason to help Catholicism and the social structures it was rooted in to fall apart. My history books and the whole of education hummed in upon that point (during crucial years I attended a public, not a parochial, school): to be modern is decidedly not to be medieval; to be reasonable is not to be dogmatic; to be free is clearly not to live under ecclesiastical authority; to be scientific is not to attend ancient rituals, cherish irrational symbols, indulge in mythic practices. It is hard to grow up Catholic in America without becoming defensive, perhaps a little paranoid, feeling forced to divide the world between "us" and "them."

We had a special language all our own, our own pronunciation for words we shared in common with others (Augustine, contemplative), sights and sounds and smells in which few others participated (incense at Benediction of the Most Blessed Sacrament, Forty Hours, wakes, and altar bells at the silent consecration of the Host); and we had our own politics and slant on world affairs. Since earliest childhood, I have known about a "power elite" that runs America: the boys from the Ivy League in the State Department, as opposed to the Catholic boys from Hoover's FBI who, as Daniel Moynihan once put it, keep watch on them. And on a whole host of issues, my people have been, though largely Democratic, conservative: on censorship, on Communism, on abortion, on religious schools . . . Harvard and Yale long meant "them" to us.

The language of Spiro Agnew, the language of George Wallace, excepting its idiom, awakens childhood memories in me of men arguing in the barbershop, of my uncle drinking so much beer he threatened to lay his dick upon the porch rail and wash the whole damn street with steaming piss—while cursing the niggers in the mill, below, and the Yankees in the mill, above: millstones he felt pressing him. Other relatives were duly shocked, but everybody loved Uncle George: he said what he thought.

We did not feel this country belonged to us. We felt fierce pride in it, more loyalty than anyone could know. But we felt blocked at every turn. There were not many intellectuals among us, not even very many professional men. Laborers mostly. Small businessmen, agents for corporations perhaps. Content with a little, yes, modest in expectation. But somehow feeling cheated. For a thousand years the Slovaks survived Hungarian hegemony, and our strategy here remained the same: endurance and steady work. Slowly, one day, we would overcome.

A special word is required about a complicated symbol: sex. To this day my mother finds it hard to spell the word intact, preferring to write "s--." Not that much was made of sex in our environment. And that's the point: silence. Demonstrative affection, emotive dances, exuberance Anglo-Saxons seldom seem to share; but on the realities of sex, discretion. Reverence, perhaps; seriousness, surely. On intimacies, it is as though our tongues had been stolen. As though in peasant life for a thousand years the context had been otherwise. Passion, yes; romance, yes; family and children, certainly; but sex, rather a minor part of life.

Imagine, then, the conflict in the generation of my brothers, sister, and myself. (The book critic for the *New York Times* reviews on the same day two new novels of fantasy: one a pornographic fantasy to end all such fantasies [he writes], the other about a mad family representing in some comic way the redemption wrought by Jesus Christ. In language and verve, the books are rated even. In theme, the reviewer notes his embarrassment in reporting a religious fantasy, but no embarrassment at all about the preposterous pornography.) Suddenly, what for a thousand years was minor becomes an all-absorbing investigation. It is, perhaps, one drama when the ruling classes (I mean subscribers to *The New Yorker,* I suppose) move progressively, generation by generation since Sigmund Freud, toward consciousness-raising sessions in Clit. Lib., but wholly another when we stumble suddenly upon mores staggering any expectation our grandparents ever cherished.

■ Yet more significant in the ethnic experience in America is the intellectual world one meets: the definition of values, ideas, and purposes emanating from universities, books, magazines, radio, and television. One hears one's own voice echoed back neither by spokesmen of "Middle America" (so complacent, smug, nativist, and Protestant), nor by "the intellectuals." Almost unavoidably, perhaps, education in America leads the student who entrusts his soul to it in a direction that, lacking a better word, we might call liberal: respect for individual conscience, a sense of social responsibility, trust in the free exchange of ideas and procedures of dissent, a certain confidence in the ability of men to "reason together" and to adjudicate their differences, a frank recognition of the vitality of the unconscious, a willingness to protect workers and the poor against the vast economic power of industrial corporations, and the like.

On the other hand, the liberal imagination has appeared to be astonishingly universalist, and relentlessly missionary. Perhaps the metaphor "enlightenment" offers a key. One is initiated into light. Liberal education tends to separate children from their parents, from their roots, from their history, in the cause of a universal and superior religion. One is taught, regarding the unenlightened (even if they be one's Uncles George and Peter, one's parents, one's brothers perhaps), what can only be called a modern equivalent of *odium theologicum.* Richard Hofstadter described anti-intellectualism in America, more accurately in nativist America than in ethnic America, but I have yet to encounter a comparable treatment of anti-unenlightenment among our educated classes.

In particular, I have regretted and keenly felt the absence of that sympathy for PIGS that simple human feeling might have prodded intelligence to muster: that same sympathy that the educated find so easy to conjure up for black culture, Chicano culture, Indian culture, and other cultures of the poor. In such cases, one finds, the universalist pretensions of liberal culture are suspended: some groups, at least, are entitled to be both different and respected. Why do the educated classes find it so difficult to want to understand the man who drives a beer truck, or the fellow with a helmet working on a site across the street with plumbers and electricians, while their sensitivities race easily to Mississippi or even Bedford-Stuyvesant?

There are deep secrets here, no doubt, unvoiced fantasies and scarcely admitted historical resentments. Few persons, in describing "Middle Americans," "the Silent Majority," or Scammon and Wattenberg's "typical American voter," distinguish clearly enough between the nativist American and the ethnic American. The first is likely to be Protestant, the second Catholic. Both may be, in various ways, conservative, loyalist, and unenlightened. Each has his own agonies, fears, betrayed expectations. Neither is ready, quite, to become an ally of the other. Neither has the same history behind him here. Neither has the same hopes. Neither is living out the same psychic voyage. Neither shares the same symbols or has the same sense of reality. The rhetoric and metaphors differ.

There is overlap, of course. But country music is not a polka, a successful politician in a Chicago ward needs a very different "common touch" from the one used by the county clerk in Normal; the urban experience of immigration lacks that mellifluous, optimistic, biblical vision of the good America that springs naturally to the lips of politicians from the Bible Belt. The nativist tends to believe with Richard Nixon that he "knows America and the American heart is good." The ethnic tends to believe that every American who preceded him has an angle, and that he, by God, will one day find one too. (Often, ethnics complain that by working hard, obeying the law, trusting their political leaders, and relying upon the American Dream they now have only their own naïveté to blame for rising no higher than they have.)

It goes without saying that the intellectuals do not love Middle America, and that for all the good warm discovery of America that preoccupied them during the 1950's, no strong tide of respect accumulated in their hearts for the Yahoos, Babbitts, Agnews, and Nixons of the land. Willie Morris, in *North Toward Home,* writes poignantly of the chill, parochial outreach of the liberal sensibility, its failure to engage the humanity of the modest, ordinary little man west of the Hudson. The intellectual's map of the United States is succinct: "Two coasts connected by United Airlines."

Unfortunately, it seems, the ethnics erred in attempting to Americanize themselves, before clearing the project with the educated classes. They learned to wave the flag and to send their sons to war. (The Poles in World War I were 4 percent of the population but took 12 percent of the casualties.) They learned to support their President—an easy task, after all, for those accustomed abroad to obeying authority. And where would they have been if Franklin Roosevelt had not sided with them against established interests? They knew a little about Communism, the radicals among them in one way, and by far the larger number of conservatives in another. Not a few exchange letters to this day with cousins and uncles who did not leave for America when they might have, whose lot is demonstrably harder and less than free.

Finally, the ethnics do not like, or trust, or even understand the intellectuals. It is not easy to feel uncomplicated affection for those who call you "pig," "fascist," "racist." One had not yet grown accustomed not to hearing "Hunkie," "Polack," "Spic," "Mick," "Dago," and the rest. At no little sacrifice, one had apologized for foods that smelled too strong for Anglo-Saxon noses, moderated the wide swings of Slavic and Italian emotion, learned decorum, given oneself to education American style, tried to learn tolerance and assimilation. Each generation criticized the earlier for its authoritarian and European and old-fashioned ways. "Up-to-date" was a moral lever. And now when the process nears completion, when a generation appears that speaks without accent and goes to college, still you are considered pigs, fascists, and racists.

Racists? Our ancestors owned no slaves. Most of us ceased being serfs only in the last 200 years—the Russians in 1861. What have we got against blacks or blacks against us? Competition, yes, for jobs and homes and communities; competition, even, for political power. Italians, Lithuanians, Slovaks, Poles are not, in principle, against "community control," or even against ghettos of our own. Whereas the Anglo-Saxon model appears to be a system of atomic individuals and high mobility, our model has tended to stress communities of our own, attachment to family and relatives, stability, and roots. We tend to have a fierce sense of attachment to our homes, having been homeowners less than three generations: a home is almost fulfillment enough for one man's life. We have most ambivalent feelings about suburban assimilation and mobility. The melting pot is a kind of homogenized soup, and its mores only partly appeal to us: to some, yes, and to others, no.

It must be said that we think we are better people than the blacks. Smarter, tougher, harder working, stronger in our families. But maybe many of us are not so sure. Maybe we are uneasy. Emotions here are delicate. One can understand the immensely more difficult circumstances under which the blacks have suffered, and one is not unaware of peculiar forms of fear, envy, and suspicion across color lines. How much of all this we learned in America, by being made conscious of our olive skin, brawny backs, accents, names, and cultural quirks, is not plain to us. Racism is not our invention; we did not bring it with us; we found it here. And should we pay the price for America's guilt? Must all the gains of the blacks, long overdue, be chiefly at our expense? Have we, once again, no defenders but ourselves?

Michael Novak   547

■ Television announcers and college professors seem so often to us to be speaking in a code. When they say "white racism," it does not seem to be their own traditions they are impugning. Perhaps it is paranoia, but it seems that the affect accompanying such words is directed at steelworkers, auto workers, truck drivers, and police—at us. When they say "humanism" or "progress," it seems to us like moral pressure to abandon our own traditions, our faith, our associations, in order to reap higher rewards in the culture of the national corporations—that culture of quantity, homogeneity, replaceability, and mobility. They want to grind off all the angles, hold us to the lathes, shape us to be objective, meritocratic, orderly, and fully American.

In recent years, of course, a new cleavage has sprung open among the intellectuals. Some seem to speak for technocracy—for that alliance of science, industry, and humanism whose heaven is "progress." Others seem to be taking the view once ascribed to ecclesiastical conservatives and traditionalists: that commitment to enlightenment is narrow, ideological, and hostile to the best interests of mankind. In the past, the great alliance for progress sprang from the conviction that "knowledge is power." Both humanists and scientists could agree on that, and labored in their separate ways to make the institutions of knowledge dominant in society: break the shackles of the Church, extend suffrage to the middle classes and finally to all, win untrammeled liberty for the marketplace of ideas. Today it is no longer plain that the power brought by knowledge is humanistic. Thus the parting of the ways.

Science has ever carried with it the stories and symbols of a major religion. It is ruthlessly universalist. If its participants are not "saved," they are nonetheless "enlightened," which isn't bad. And every single action of the practicing scientist, no matter how humble, could once be understood as a contribution to the welfare of the human race; each smallest gesture was invested with meaning, given a place in a scheme, and weighted with redemptive power. Moreover, the scientist was in possession of "the truth," indeed of the very meaning of and validating procedures for the word. His role was therefore sacred.

Imagine, then, a young strapping Slovak entering an introductory course in the Sociology of Religion at the nearby state university or community college. Is he sent back to his Slovak roots, led to recover paths of experience latent in all his instincts and reflexes, given an image of the life of his grandfather that suddenly, in recognition, brings tears to his eyes? Is he brought to a deeper appreciation of his Lutheran or Catholic heritage and its resonances with other bodies of religious experience? On the contrary, he is secretly taught disdain for what his grandfather *thought* he was doing when he acted or felt or imagined through religious forms. In the boy's psyche, a new religion is implanted: power over others, enlightenment, an atomic (rather than a communitarian) sensibility, a contempt for mystery, ritual, transcendence, soul, absurdity, and tragedy; and deep confidence in the possibilities of building a better world through scientific understanding. He is led to feel ashamed for the statistical portrait of Slovak immigrants which shows them to be conservative, authoritarian, not given to dissent, etc. His teachers instruct him with the purest of intentions, in a way that is value free.

To be sure, certain radical writers in America have begun to bewail "the laying on of culture" and to unmask the cultural religion implicit in the American way of science. Yet radicals, one learns, often have an agenda of their own. What fascinates *them* among working-class ethnics are the traces, now almost lost, of *radical* activities among the working class two or three generations ago. Scratch the resentful boredom of a classroom of working-class youths, we are told, and you will find hidden in their past some formerly imprisoned organizer for the CIO, some Sacco/Vanzetti, some bold pamphleteer for the IWW. All this is true. But supposing that a study of the ethnic past reveals that most ethnics have been, are, and wish to remain, culturally conservative? Suppose, for example, they wish to deepen their religious roots and defend their ethnic enclaves? Must a radical culture be "laid on" them?

America has never confronted squarely the problem of preserving diversity. I can remember hearing in my youth bitter arguments that parochial schools were "divisive." Now the public schools are attacked for their commitment to homogenization. Well, how *does* a nation of no one culture, no one language, no one race, no one history, no one ethnic stock continue to exist as one, while encouraging diversity? How can the rights of all, and particularly of the weak, be defended if power is decentralized and left to local interests? The weak have ever found strength in this country through local chapters of national organizations. But what happens when the national organizations themselves—the schools, the unions, the federal government—become vehicles of a new, universalistic, thoroughly rationalized, technological culture?

Still, it is not that larger question that concerns me here. I am content today to voice the difficulties in the way of saying what I wish to say, when I wish to say it. The tradition of liberalism is a tradition I have had to acquire, despite an innate skepticism about many of its structural metaphors (free marketplace, individual autonomy, reason naked and undisguised, enlightenment). Radicalism, with its bold and simple optimism about human potential and its anarchic tendencies, has been, despite its appeal to me as a vehicle for criticizing liberalism, freighted with emotions, sentiments, and convictions about men that I cannot bring myself to share.

In my guts, I do not feel that institutions are "repressive" in any meaning of the word that leaves it meaningful; the "state of nature" seems to me, emotionally, far less liberating, far more undifferentiated and confining. I have not dwelt for so long in the profession of the intellectual life that I find it easy to be critical and harsh. In almost everything I see or hear or read, I am struck first, rather undiscriminatingly, by all the things I like in it. Only with second effort can I bring myself to discern the flaws. My emotions and values seem to run in affirmative patterns.

My interest is not, in fact, in defining myself over against the American people and the American way of life. I do not expect as much of it as all that. What I should like to do is come to a better and more profound knowledge of who I am, whence my community came, and whither my son and daughter, and their children's children, might wish to head in the future: I want to have a history.

More and more, I think in family terms, less ambitiously, on a less than national scale. The differences implicit in being Slovak, and Catholic, and lower-middle class seem more and more important to me. Perhaps it is too much to try to speak to all peoples in this very various nation of ours. Yet it does not seem evident that by becoming more concrete, accepting one's finite and limited identity, one necessarily becomes parochial. Quite the opposite. It seems more likely that by each of us becoming more profoundly what we are, we shall find greater unity, in those depths in which unity irradiates diversity, than by attempting through the artifices of the American "melting pot" and the cultural religion of science to become what we are not.

There is, I take it, a form of liberalism not wedded to universal Reason, whose ambition is not to homogenize all peoples on this planet, and whose base lies rather in the imagination and in the diversity of human stories: a liberalism I should be happy to have others help me to find.

Suggestions for Discussion

1. How does Novak explain the paradox which he states in the first paragraph: that growing up in America has been an assault upon his sense of worthiness as well as a kind of liberation and delight? According to Novak, what is the strategy involved in making "an American" of the child of the immigrant? What is his view of that strategy?

2. What split does Novak see between American intellectuals and white ethnics? Does he seem to be objective in discussing this split or do his sympathies seem to lie more with one side than the other?

3. How does Novak distinguish between the nativist and the ethnic? He asserts, "I want to have a history." Is he suggesting that other groups, such as nativists, have a history which has been denied the White Ethnic? Explain.

Suggestion for Writing and Comparison

1. Read Gino Baroni's essay "The Ethnic Bag" (*Washingtonian*, July 1970). Compare Baroni's view of what White Ethnics should strive for in the future with that of Novak. Discuss the position that is closer to your own.

<u>STORIES</u>

Pietro di Donato

Pietro di Donato was born in 1911 in West Hoboken, New Jersey, the son of Italian immigrants. His father, a bricklayer, was killed when the building on which he was working collapsed. His mother died a few years later, and di Donato, still a child himself, was forced to quit school in the eighth grade in order to support the large family. He took up his father's position as a bricklayer in the daytime and continued his education at night through evening school and a program of reading which included especially the Russian novelists.

Di Donato's first story, "Christ in Concrete," was published in *Esquire* in 1937. The following year he took the story as the first chapter of a book by the same name. *Christ in Concrete* became an immediate literary sensation.

Di Donato has since been published in various periodicals including *American Mercury* and Martha Foley's *Best American Short Stories.* He is the author of several other books, including *The Woman* (1958) and *Three Circles of Light* (1960).

Like Upton Sinclair's earlier novel *The Jungle*, di Donato's work criticizes the intolerable conditions of immigrant labor in the early decades of the twentieth century and is also concerned with the immigrant's role in the making of America. The protagonist of "Christ in Concrete," Geremio, is a tragic figure who tries to wrest a piece of the American dream for himself and his family, but is sacrificed through monstrous, calculating economics.

Christic in Concrete

March whistled stinging snow against the brick walls and up the gaunt girders. Geremio, the foreman, swung his arms about, and gaffed the men on.

Old Nick, the 'Lean,' stood up from over a dust-flying brick pile, and tapped the side of his nose.

'Master Geremio, the devil himself could not break his tail any harder than we here.'

Burly Vincenzo of the walrus moustache, and known as the 'Snoutnose,' let fall the chute door of the concrete hopper and sang over in the Lean's direction: 'Mari-Annina's belly and the burning night will make of me once more a milk-mouthed stripling lad . . .'

The Lean loaded his wheelbarrow and spat furiously. 'Sons of two-legged dogs . . . despised of even the devil himself! Work! Sure! For America beautiful will eat you and spit your bones into the earth's hole! Work!' And with that his wiry frame pitched the barrow violently over the rough floor.

Snoutnose waved his head to and fro and with mock pathos wailed, 'Sing on, oh guitar of mine . . .'

Short, cherry-faced Joe Chiappa, the scaffoldman, paused with hatchet in hand and tenpenny spike sticking out from small dice-like teeth to tell the Lean as he went by, in a voice that all could hear, 'Ah, father of countless chicks, the old age is a carrion!'

Geremio chuckled and called to him: 'Hey, little Joe, who are you to talk? You and big-titted Cola can't even hatch an egg, whereas the Lean has just to turn the doorknob of his bedroom and old Philomena becomes a balloon!'

Coarse throats tickled and mouths opened wide in laughter.

Mike, the 'Barrel-mouth,' pretended he was talking to himself and yelled out in his best English . . . he was always speaking English while the rest carried on in their native Italian: 'I don't know myself, but somebodys whose gotta bigga buncha keeds and he alla times talka from somebodys elsa!'

Geremio knew it was meant for him and he laughed. 'On the tomb of Saint Pimplelegs, this little boy my wife is giving me next week shall be the last! Eight hungry Christians to feed is enough for any man.'

Joe Chiappa nodded to the rest. 'Sure, Master Geremio had a telephone call from the next bambino. Yes, it told him it had a little bell there instead of a rosebush . . . It even told him its name!'

'Laugh, laugh all of you,' returned Geremio, 'but I tell you that all my kids must be boys so that they some day will be big American builders. And then I'll help them to put the gold away in the basements for safe keeping!'

A great din of riveting shattered the talk among the fast-moving men. Geremio added a handful of 'Honest' tobacco to his corncob, puffed strongly, and cupped his hands around the bowl for a bit of warmth. The chill day caused him to shiver, and he thought to himself, 'Yes, the day is cold, cold . . . but who am I to complain when the good Christ himself was crucified?

'Pushing the job is all right (when has it been otherwise in my life?) but this job frightens me. I feel the building wants to tell me something; just as one Christian to another. I don't like this. Mr. Murdin tells me, "Push it up!"

That's all he knows. I keep telling him that the underpinning should be doubled and the old material removed from the floors, but he keeps the inspector drunk and . . . "Hey, Ashes-ass! Get away from under that pilaster! Don't pull the old work. Push it away from you or you'll have a nice present for Easter if the wall falls on you!" . . . Well, with the help of God I'll see this job through. It's not my first, nor the . . . "Hey, Patsy number two! Put more cement in that concrete; we're putting up a building, not an Easter cake!" '

Patsy hurled his shovel to the floor and gesticulated madly. 'The padrone Murdin-sa tells me, "Too much, too much! Lil' bit is plenty!" And you tell me I'm stingy! The rotten building can fall after I leave!'

Six floors below, the contractor called: 'Hey Geremio! Is your gang of dagos dead?'

Geremio cautioned to the men: 'On your toes, boys. If he writes out slips, someone won't have big eels on the Easter table.'

The Lean cursed that 'the padrone could take the job and shove it . . .!'

Curly-headed Sandino, the roguish, pigeon-toed scaffoldman, spat a clod of tobacco-juice and hummed to his own music.

'Yes, certainly yes to your face, master padrone . . . and behind, this to you and all your kind!'

The day, like all days, came to an end. Calloused and bruised bodies sighed, and numb legs shuffled towards shabby railroad flats. . . .

'Ah, *bella casa mio*. Where my little freshets of blood, and my good woman await me. Home where my broken back will not ache so. Home where midst the monkey chatter of my piccolinos I will float off to blessed slumber with my feet on the chair and the head on the wife's soft full breast.'

These great child-hearted ones leave each other without words or ceremony, and as they ride and walk home, a great pride swells the breast. . . .

'Blessings to Thee, oh Jesus. I have fought winds and cold. Hand to hand I have locked dumb stones in place and the great building rises. I have earned a bit of bread for me and mine.'

The mad day's brutal conflict is forgiven, and strained limbs prostrate themselves so that swollen veins can send the yearning blood coursing and pulsating deliciously as though the body mountained leaping streams.

The job alone remained behind . . . and yet, they too, having left the bigger part of their lives with it. The cold ghastly beast, the Job, stood stark, the eerie March wind wrapping it in sharp shadows of falling dusk.

That night was a crowning point in the life of Geremio. He bought a house! Twenty years he had helped to mould the New World. And now he was to have a house of his own! What mattered that it was no more than a wooden shack? It was his own!

He had proudly signed his name and helped Annunziata to make her X on the wonderful contract that proved them owners. And she was happy to think that her next child, soon to come, would be born under their own rooftree. She heard the church chimes, and cried to the children: 'Children, to bed! It is near midnight. And remember, shut-mouth to the *paesanos!* Or they will send the evil eye to our new home even before we put foot.'

The children scampered off to the icy yellow bedroom where three slept in one bed and three in the other. Coltishly and friskily they kicked about under the covers; their black iron-cotton stockings not removed . . . what! and freeze the peanut-little toes?

Said Annunziata, 'The children are so happy, Geremio; let them be, for even I would a Tarantella dance.' And with that she turned blushing. He wanted to take her on her word. She patted his hands, kissed them, and whispered, 'Our children will dance for us . . . in the American style some day.'

Geremio cleared his throat and wanted to sing. 'Yes, with joy I could sing in a richer feeling than the great Caruso.' He babbled little old country couplets and circled the room until the tenant below tapped the ceiling.

Annunziata whispered: 'Geremio, to bed and rest. Tomorrow is a day for great things . . . and the day on which our Lord died for us.'

The children were now hard asleep. Heads under the cover, over . . . moist noses whistling, and little damp legs entwined.

In bed Geremio and Annunziata clung closely to each other. They mumbled figures and dates until fatigue stilled their thoughts. And with chubby Johnnie clutching fast his bottle and warmed between them . . . life breathed heavily, and dreams entertained in far, far worlds, the nation-builder's brood.

But Geremio and Annunziata remained for a while staring into darkness, silently.

'Geremio?'

'Yes?'

'This job you are now working. . . .'

'So?'

'You used always to tell about what happened on the jobs . . . who was jealous, and who praised. . . .'

'You should know by now that all work is the same. . . .'

'Geremio. The month you have been on this job, you have not spoken a word about the work . . . And I have felt that I am walking in a dream. Is the work dangerous? Why don't you answer . . .?'

Job loomed up damp, shivery grey. Its giant members waiting.

Builders quietly donned their coarse robes, and waited.

■ Geremio's whistle rolled back into his pocket and the symphony of struggle began.

Trowel rang through brick and slashed mortar rivets were machine-gunned fast with angry grind Patsy number one check Patsy number two check the Lean three check Vincenzo four steel bellowed back at hammer donkey engines coughed purple Ashes-ass Pietro fifteen chisel point intoned stone thin steel whirred and wailed through wood liquid stone flowed with dull rasp through iron veins and hoist screamed through space Carmine the Fat twenty-four and Giacomo Sangini check . . . The multitudinous voices of a civilization rose from the surroundings and welded with the efforts of the Job.

To the intent ear, Nation was voicing her growing paints, but, hands that create are attached to warm hearts and not to calculating minds. The Lean as he fought his burden on looked forward to only one goal, the end. The barrow he pushed, he did not love. The stones that brutalized his palms, he did not love. The great God Job, he did not love. He felt a searing bitterness and a fathomless consternation at the queer consciousness that inflicted the ever mounting weight of structure that he HAD TO! HAD TO! raise above his shoulders! When, when and where would the last stone be? Never . . . did he bear his toil with the rhythm of song! Never . . . did his gasping heart knead the heavy mortar with lilting melody! A voice within him spoke a wordless language.

The language of worn oppression and the despair of realizing that his life had been left on brick piles. And always, there had been hunger and her bastard, the fear of hunger.

Murdin bore down upon Geremio from behind and shouted:

'Goddamnit, Geremio, if you're givin' the men two hours off today with pay, why the hell are they draggin' their tails? And why don't you turn that skinny old Nick loose, and put a young wop in his place?'

'Now, listen-a to me, Mister Murdin——'

'Don't give me that! And bear in mind that there are plenty of good barefoot men in the streets who'll jump for a day's pay!'

'Padrone — padrone, the underpinning gotta be make safe and——'

'Lissenyawopbastard! If you don't like it, you know what you can do!'

And with that he swung swaggering away.

The men had heard, and those who hadn't knew instinctively.

The new home, the coming baby, and his whole background, kept the fire from Geremio's mouth and bowed his head. 'Annunziata speaks of scouring the ashcans for the children's bread in case I didn't want to work on a job where . . . But am I not a man, to feed my own with these hands? Ah, but day will end and no boss in the world can then rob me of the joy of my home!'

Murdin paused for a moment before descending the ladder.

Geremio caught his meaning and jumped to, nervously directing the rush of work . . . No longer Geremio, but a machine-like entity.

The men were transformed into single, silent beasts. Snoutnose steamed through ragged moustache whip-lashing sand into mixer Ashes-ass dragged under four by twelve beam Lean clawed wall knots jumping in jaws masonry crumbled dust billowed thundered choked. . . .

At noon, Geremio drank his wine from an old-fashioned magnesia bottle and munched a great pepper sandwich . . . no meat on Good Friday. Said one, 'Are some of us to be laid off? Easter is upon us and communion dresses are needed and . . .'

That, while Geremio was dreaming of the new house and the joys he could almost taste. Said he: 'Worry not. You should know Geremio.' It then all came out. He regaled them with his wonderful joy of the new house. He praised his wife and children one by one. They listened respectfully and returned him well wishes and blessings. He went on and on. . . . 'Paul made a radio — all by himself, mind you! One can hear Barney Google and many American songs! How proud he.'

The ascent to labour was made, and as they trod the ladder, heads turned and eyes communed with the mute flames of the brazier whose warmth they were leaving, not with willing heart, and in that fleeting moment, the breast wanted so, so much to speak of hungers that never reached the tongue.

About an hour later, Geremio called over to Pietro: 'Pietro, see if Mister Murdin is in the shanty and tell him I must see him! I will convince him that the work must not go on like this . . . just for the sake of a little more profit!'

Pietro came up soon. 'The padrone is not coming up. He was drinking from a large bottle of whisky and cursed in American words that if you did not carry out his orders——'

Geremio turned away disconcerted, stared dumbly at the structure and mechanically listed in his mind's eye the various violations of construction safety. An uneasy sensation hollowed him. The Lean brought down an old piece of wall and the structure palsied. Geremio's heart broke loose and out-thumped the floor's vibrations, a rapid wave of heat swept him and left a chill touch in its wake. He looked about to the men, a bit frightened. They seemed usual, life-size, and moved about with the methodical deftness that made the moment then appear no different than the task of toil had ever been.

Snoutnose's voice boomed into him. 'Master Geremio, the concrete is rea—dy!'

'Oh, yes, yes, Vincenz.' And he walked gingerly towards the chute, but, not without leaving behind some part of his strength, sending out his soul to wrestle with the limbs of Job, who threatened in stiff silence. He talked and joked with Snoutnose. Nothing said anything, nor seemed wrong. Yet a vague uneasiness was to him as certain as the foggy murk that floated about Job's stone and steel.

'Shall I let the concrete down now, Master Geremio?'

'Well, let me see—no, hold it a minute. Hey, Sandino! Tighten the chute cables!'

Snoutnose straightened, looked about, and instinctively rubbed the sore small of his spine. 'Ah,' sighed he, 'all the men feel as I—yes, I can tell. They are tired but happy that today is Good Friday and we quit at three o'clock . . .' And he swelled in human ecstasy at the anticipation of food, drink, and the hairy flesh-tingling warmth of wife, and then, extravagant rest. In truth, they all felt as Snoutnose, although perhaps with variations on the theme.

It was the Lean only who had lived, and felt otherwise. His soul, accompanied with time, had shredded itself in the physical war to keep the physical alive. Perhaps he no longer had a soul, and the corpse continued from momentum. May he not be the Slave, working on from the birth of Man—He of whom it was said, 'It was not for Him to reason?' And probably He who, never asking, taking, nor vaunting, created God and the creatable? Nevertheless, there existed in the Lean a sense of oppression suffered, so vast that the seas of time could never wash it away.

Geremio gazed about and was conscious of seeming to understand many things. He marvelled at the strange feeling which permitted him to sense the familiarity of life. And yet—all appeared unreal, a dream pungent and nostalgic. Life, dream, reality, unreality, spiralling ever about each other. 'Ha,' he chuckled, 'how and from where do these thoughts come?'

Snoutnose had his hand on the hopper latch and was awaiting the word from Geremio. 'Did you say something, Master Geremio?'

'Why, yes, Vincenz, I was thinking—funny! A—yes, what is the time—yes, that is what I was thinking.'

'My American can of tomatoes says ten minutes from two o'clock. It won't be long now, Master Geremio.'

Geremio smiled. 'No, about an hour . . . and then, home.'

'Oh, but first we stop at Mulberry Street, to buy their biggest eels, and the other finger-licking stuffs.'

Geremio was looking far off, and for a moment happiness came to his heart without words, a warm hand stealing over. Snoutnose's words sang to him pleasantly, and he nodded.

'And Master Geremio, we ought really to buy the seafruits with the shells — you know, for the much needed steam they put into the——'

He flushed despite himself and continued. 'It is true, I know it — especially the juicy clams . . . uhmm, my mouth waters like a pump.'

Geremio drew on his unlit pipe and smiled acquiescence. The men around him were moving to their tasks silently, feeling of their fatigue, but absorbed in contemplations the very same as Snoutnose's. The noise of labour seemed not to be noise, and as Geremio looked about, life settled over him a grey concert — grey forms, atmosphere, and grey notes . . . Yet his off-tone world felt so near, and familiar.

'Five minutes from two,' swished through Snoutnose's moustache.

Geremio automatically took out his watch, rewound, and set it. Sandino had done with the cables. The tone and movement of the scene seemed to Geremio strange, differently strange, and yet, a dream familiar from a time-less date. His hand went up in motion to Vincenzo. The molten stone gurgled low, and then with heightening rasp. His eyes followed the stone-cementy pudding, and to his ears there was no other sound than its flow. From over the roofs somewhere, the tinny voice of *Barney Google* whined its way, hooked into his consciousness and kept itself a revolving record beneath his skull-plate.

'Ah, yes, Barney Google, my son's wonderful radio machine . . . wonderful Paul.' His train of thought quickly took in his family, home and hopes. And with hope came fear. Something within asked, 'Is it not possible to breathe God's air without fear dominating with the pall of unemployment? And the terror of production for Boss, Boss and Job? To rebel is to lose all of the very little. To be obedient is to choke. Oh, dear Lord, guide my path.'

Just then, the floor lurched and swayed under his feet. The slipping of the underpinning below rumbled up through the undetermined floors.

Was he faint or dizzy? Was it part of the dreamy afternoon? He put his hands in front of him and stepped back, and looked up wildly. 'No! No!'

The men poised stricken. Their throats wanted to cry out and scream but didn't dare. For a moment they were a petrified and straining pageant. Then the bottom of their world gave way. The building shuddered violently, her supports burst with the crackling slap of wooden gunfire. The floor vomited upward. Geremio clutched at the air and shrieked agonizingly. 'Brothers, what have we done? Ahhhh-h, children of ours!' With the speed of light, balance went sickeningly awry and frozen men went flying explosively. Job tore down upon them madly. Walls, floors, beams became whirling, solid, splintering waves crashing with detonations that ground man and material in bonds of death.

The strongly shaped body that slept with Annunziata nights and was perfect in all the limitless physical quantities, thudded as a worthless sack amongst the giant debris that crushed fragile flesh and bone with centrifugal intensity.

Darkness blotted out his terror and the resistless form twisted, catapulted insanely in its directionless flight, and shot down neatly and deliberately between the empty wooden forms of a foundation wall pilaster in upright position, his blue swollen face pressed against the form and his arms outstretched, caught securely through the meat by the thin round bars of reinforcing steel.

The huge concrete hopper that was sustained by an independent structure of thick timber, wavered a breath or so, its heavy concrete rolling uneasily until a great sixteen-inch wall caught it squarely with all the terrific verdict of its dead weight and impelled it downward through joists, beams and masonry, until it stopped short, arrested by two girders, an arm's length above Geremio's head; the grey concrete gushing from the hopper mouth, and sealing up the mute figure.

Giacomo had been thrown clear of the building and dropped six floors to the street gutter, where he lay writhing.

The Lean had evinced no emotion. When the walls descended, he did not move. He lowered his head. One minute later he was hanging in mid-air, his chin on his chest, his eyes tearing loose from their sockets, a green foam bubbling from his mouth and his body spasming, suspended by the shreds left of his mashed arms pinned between a wall and a girder.

A two-by-four hooked little Joe Chiappa up under the back of his jumper and swung him around in a circle to meet a careening I-beam. In the flash that he lifted his frozen cherubic face, its shearing edge sliced through the top of his skull.

When Snoutnose cried beseechingly, 'Saint Michael!' blackness enveloped him. He came to in a world of horror. A steady stream, warm, thick, and sickening as hot wine bathed his face and clogged his nose, mouth, and eyes. The nauseous syrup that pumped over his face, clotted his moustache red and drained into his mouth. He gulped for air, and swallowed the rich liquid scarlet. As he breathed, the pain shocked him to oppressive semiconsciousness. The air was wormingly alive with cries, screams, moans and dust, and his crushed chest seared him with a thousand fires. He couldn't see, nor breathe enough to cry. His right hand moved to his face and wiped at the gelatinizing substance, but it kept coming on, and a heart-breaking moan wavered about him, not far. He wiped his eyes in subconscious despair. Where was he? What kind of dream was he having? Perhaps he wouldn't wake up in time for work, and then what? But how queer; his stomach beating him, his chest on fire, he sees nothing but dull red, only one hand moving about, and a moaning in his face!

The sound and clamour of the rescue squads called to him from far off.

Ah, yes, he's dreaming in bed, and far out in the streets, engines are going to a fire. Oh poor devils! Suppose his house were on fire? With the children scattered about in the rooms he could not remember! He must do his utmost to break out of this dream! He's swimming under water, not able to raise his head and get to the air. He must get back to consciousness to save his children!

He swam frantically with his one right hand, and then felt a face beneath its touch. A face! It's Angelina alongside of him! Thank God, he's awake! He tapped her face. It moved. It felt cold, bristly, and wet. 'It moves so. What is this?' His fingers slithered about grisly sharp bones and in a gluey, stringy, hollow mass, yielding as wet macaroni. Grey light brought sight, and hysteria punctured his heart. A girder lay across his chest, his right hand clutched a grotesque human mask, and suspended almost on top of him was the twitching, faceless body of Joe Chiappa. Vincenzo fainted with an inarticulate sigh. His fingers loosed and the bodyless-headless face dropped and fitted to the side of his face while the drippings above came slower and slower.

The rescue men cleaved grimly with pick and axe.

Geremio came to with a start . . . far from their efforts. His brain told him instantly what had happened and where he was. He shouted wildly. 'Save me! Save me! I'm being buried alive!'

He paused exhausted. His genitals convulsed. The cold steel rod upon which they were impaled froze his spine. He shouted louder and louder. 'Save me! I am hurt badly! I can be saved, I can—save me before it's too late!' But the cries went no farther than his own ears. The icy wet concrete reached his chin. His heart was appalled. 'In a few seconds I shall be entombed. If I can only breathe, they will reach me. Surely they will!' His face was quickly covered, its flesh yielding to the solid, sharp-cut stones. 'Air! Air!' screamed his lungs as he was completely sealed. Savagely, he bit into the wooden form pressing upon his mouth. An eighth of an inch of its surface splintered off. Oh, if he could only hold out long enough to bite even the smallest hole through to air! He must! There can be no other way! He is responsible for his family! He cannot leave them like this! He didn't want to die! This could not be the answer to life! He had bitten half way through when his teeth snapped off to the gums in the uneven conflict. The pressure of the concrete was such, and its effectiveness so thorough, that the wooden splinters, stumps of teeth, and blood never left the choking mouth.

Why couldn't he go any farther?

Air! Quick! He dug his lower jaw into the little hollowed space and gnashed in choking agonized fury. 'Why doesn't it go through? Mother of Christ, why doesn't it give? Can there be a notch, or two-by-four stud behind it? Sweet Jesu! No! No! Make it give. . . . Air! Air!'

He pushed the bone-bare jaw maniacally; it splintered, cracked, and a jagged fleshless edge cut through the form, opening a small hole to air. With a desperate burst the lung-prisoned air blew an opening through the shredded mouth and whistled back greedily a gasp of fresh air. He tried to breathe, but it was impossible. The heavy concrete was settling immutably, and its rich cement-laden grout ran into his pierced face. His lungs would not expand, and were crushing in tighter and tighter under the settling concrete.

'Mother mine—mother of Jesu-Annunziata—children of mine—dear, dear, for mercy, Jesu-Guiseppe e 'Maria,' his blue-foamed tongue called. It then distorted in a shuddering coil and mad blood vomited forth. Chills and fire played through him and his tortured tongue stuttered, 'Mercy, blessed Father—salvation, most kind Father—Saviour—Saviour of His children help me—adored Saviour—I kiss your feet eternally—you are my Lord—there is but one God—you are my God of infinite mercy—Hail Mary divine Virgin —our Father who art in heaven hallowed be thy—name—our Father—my Father,' and the agony excrucited with never-ending mount, 'our Father —Jesu, Jesu, soon Jesu, hurry dear Jesu Jesu! Je-sssu . . .!' His mangled voice trebled hideously, and hung in jerky whimperings.

The unfeeling concrete was drying fast, and shrinking into monolithic density. The pressure temporarily de-sensitized sensation; leaving him petrified, numb, and substanceless. Only the brain remained miraculously alive.

'Can this be death? It is all too strangely clear. I see nothing nor feel nothing, my body and senses are no more, my mind speaks as it never did before. Am I or am I not Geremio? But I am Geremio! Can I be in the other world? I never was in any other world except the one I knew of; that of toil, hardship, prayer . . . of my wife who awaits with child for me, of my children and the first home I was to own. Where do I begin in this world? Where do I leave off? Why? I recall only a baffled life of cruelty from every direction. And hope was always as painful as fear, the fear of displeasing, displeasing the people and ideas whom I could never understand; laws, policemen, priests, bosses, and a rag with colours waving on a stick. I never did anything to these things. But what have I done with my life? Yes, my life! No one else's! Mine—mine—MINE—Geremio! It is clear. I was born hungry, and have always been hungry for freedom—life! I married and ran away to America so as not to kill and be killed in Tripoli for things they call "God and Country." I've never known the freedom I wanted in my heart. There was always an arm upraised to hit at me. What have I done to them? I did not want to make them toil for me. I did not raise my arm to them. In my life I could never breathe, and now without air, my mind breathes clearly for me. Wait! There has been a terrible mistake! A cruel crime! The world is not right! Murderers! Thieves! You have hurt me and my kind, and have taken my life from me! I have long felt it—yes, yes, yes, they have cheated me with flags, signs and fear . . . I say you can't take my life! I want to live! My life! To tell the cheated to rise and fight! Vincenz! Chiappa! Nick! Men! Do you hear me? We must follow the desires within us for the world has been taken from us; we, who made the world! Life!'

Feeling returned to the destroyed form.

'Ahhh-h, I am not dead yet. I knew it—you have not done with me. Torture away! I cannot believe you, God and Country, no longer!' His body was fast breaking under the concrete's closing wrack. Blood vessels burst like mashed flower stems. He screamed. 'Show yourself now, Jesu! Now is the time! Save me! Why don't you come! Are you there! I cannot stand it—ohhh, why do you let it happen—it is bestial—where are you! Hurry, hurry, hurry! You do not come! You make me suffer, and what have I done! Come, come—come now—now save me, save me now! Now, now, now! If you are God, save me!'

The stricken blood surged through a weltering maze of useless pipes and exploded forth from his squelched eyes and formless nose, ears and mouth, seeking life in the indifferent stone.

'Aie—aie, aie—devils and Saints—beasts! Where are you—quick, quick, it is death and I am cheated—cheat—ed! Do you hear, you whoring bastards who own the world? Ohhh-ohhhh aie-aie—hahahaha!' His bones cracked mutely and his sanity went sailing distorted in the limbo of the subconscious.

With the throbbing tones of an organ in the hollow background, the fighting brain disintegrated and the memories of a baffled lifetime sought outlet.

He moaned the simple songs of barefoot childhood, scenes flashed desperately on and off in disassociated reflex, and words and parts of words came pitifully high and low from his inaudible lips, the hysterical mind sang cringingly and breathlessly, 'Jesu my Lord my God my all Jesu my Lord my God my all Jesu my Lord my God my all Jesu my Lord my God my all,' and on as the whirling tempo screamed now far, now near, and came in soul-sickening waves as the concrete slowly contracted and squeezed his skull out of shape.

Suggestions for Discussion

1. How is the double characterization of Geremio as foreman and father introduced? Why is it appropriate that his wife's name is Annunziata? Is his role at home consistent with his attitude on the job toward his men?
2. How does old Nick, the Lean, function in the story? What is his goal? How is he contrasted with Geremio? Why does Geremio keep him on the job?
3. What do Geremio's cries to the men mean: "Brothers, what have we done? Ahhh-h, children of ours!"? Were the men responsible? Who are their "children"?
4. What is the nature of the social protest in Geremio's review of his life? Why is the following sentence ironic: "I married and ran away to America so as not to kill and be killed in Tripoli for things they call 'God and Country'"? What part do both God and Country play in the whole story?
5. It has been said that slavery in the South was preferable to the horrifying working conditions in the North. Would any of the characters in this story have preferred slavery to their condition?
6. "Christ in Concrete" was written during the Depression and first published in 1937. In what way does the story reflect the social attitudes of the period?

Suggestions for Writing and Comparison

1. Discuss the nature of the symbolism used in di Donato's short story with particular emphasis on the title "Christ in Concrete" and on the words capitalized throughout the story.
2. Compare the heroic qualities of Geremio with those of Gregorio Cortez in Americo Paredes' "The Legend" (p. 328). Is Geremio or Cortez more saintly, more wronged, more romanticized?

Harry Mark Petrakis

Harry Mark Petrakis was born in St. Louis, Missouri, in 1923, the son of immigrant parents from Greece. He attended the University of Illinois from 1940 to 1941 and supported himself variously as a steelworker, real estate salesman, and speech writer while he wrote short stories. In 1957 Petrakis received an *Atlantic* First Award and a Benjamin Franklin Citation for his stories. A novel, *Lion at My Heart*, appeared in 1959. This was followed by *The Odyssey of Kostas Volakis*, which received the 1964 award from Friends of American Writers, and a collection of short stories, *Pericles on 31st Street*, which was one of the final nominees for the 1965 National Book Award. A later novel, *A Dream of Kings,* is concerned, as is most of his work, with Greeks living in America.

The following short story, "The Wooing of Ariadne," is taken from *Pericles on 31st Street.* Petrakis believes that the greatest influence on his writing is the philosophy, poetry, and fiction of the acclaimed Greek author Nikos Kazantzakis, who, like the parents of Petrakis, was born on the island of Crete. And indeed Marko Palamas, the hero of "The Wooing of Ariadne," bears a striking resemblance to Kazantzakis' character Zorba in his vibrancy and passion. What Marko lacks in *savoir faire* he more than makes up for in vitality and unselfconscious charm.

The Wooing of Ariadne

I knew from the beginning she must accept my love — put aside foolish female protestations. It is the distinction of the male to be the aggressor and the cloak of the female to lend grace to the pursuit. Aha! I am wise to these wiles.

I first saw Ariadne at a dance given by the Spartan brotherhood in the Legion Hall on Laramie Street. The usual assemblage of prune-faced and banana-bodied women smelling of virtuous anemia. They were an outrage to a man such as myself.

Then I saw her! A tall stately woman, perhaps in her early thirties. She had firm and slender arms bare to the shoulders and a graceful neck. Her hair was black and thick and piled in a great bun at the back of her head. That grand abundance of hair attracted me at once. This modern aberration women have of chopping their hair close to the scalp and leaving it in fantastic disarray I find revolting.

I went at once to my friend Vasili, the baker, and asked him who she was.

"Ariadne Langos," he said. "Her father is Janco Langos, the grocer."

"Is she engaged or married?"

"No," he said slyly. "They say she frightens off the young men. They say she is very spirited."

"Excellent," I said and marveled at my good fortune in finding her unpledged. "Introduce me at once."

"Marko," Vasili said with some apprehension. "Do not commit anything rash."

I pushed the little man forward. "Do not worry, little friend," I said. "I am a man suddenly possessed by a vision. I must meet her at once."

We walked together across the dance floor to where my beloved stood. The closer we came the more impressive was the majestic swell of her breasts and the fine great sweep of her thighs. She towered over the insignificant applecore women around her. Her eyes, dark and thoughtful, seemed to be restlessly searching the room.

Be patient, my dove! Marko is coming.

"Miss Ariadne," Vasili said. "This is Mr. Marko Palamas. He desires to have the honor of your acquaintance."

She looked at me for a long and piercing moment. I imagined her gauging my mighty strength by the width of my shoulders and the circumference of my arms. I felt the tips of my mustache bristle with pleasure. Finally she nodded with the barest minimum of courtesy. I was not discouraged.

"Miss Ariadne," I said, "may I have the pleasure of this dance?"

She stared at me again with her fiery eyes. I could imagine more timid men shriveling before her fierce gaze. My heart flamed at the passion her rigid exterior concealed.

"I think not," she said.

"Don't you dance?"

Vasili gasped beside me. An old prune-face standing nearby clucked her toothless gums.

"Yes, I dance," Ariadne said coolly. "I do not wish to dance with you."

"Why?" I asked courteously.

"I do not think you heard me," she said. "I do not wish to dance with you."

Oh, the sly and lovely darling. Her subterfuge so apparent. Trying to conceal her pleasure at my interest.

"Why?" I asked again.

"I am not sure," she said. "It could be your appearance, which bears considerable resemblance to a gorilla, or your manner, which would suggest closer alliance to a pig."

"Now that you have met my family," I said engagingly, "let us dance."

"Not now," she said, and her voice rose. "Not this dance or the one after. Not tonight or tomorrow night or next month or next year. Is that clear?"

Sweet, sweet Ariadne. Ancient and eternal game of retreat and pursuit. My pulse beat more quickly.

Vasili pulled at my sleeve. He was my friend, but without the courage of a goat. I shook him off and spoke to Ariadne.

"There is a joy like fire that consumes a man's heart when he first sets eyes on his beloved," I said. "This I felt when I first saw you." My voice trembled under a mighty passion. "I swear before God from this moment that I love you."

She stared shocked out of her deep dark eyes and, beside her, old prune-face staggered as if she had been kicked. Then my beloved did something which proved indisputably that her passion was as intense as mine.

She doubled up her fist and struck me in the eye. A stout blow for a woman that brought a haze to my vision, but I shook my head and moved a step closer.

"I would not care," I said, "if you struck out both my eyes. I would cherish the memory of your beauty forever."

By this time the music had stopped, and the dancers formed a circle of idiot faces about us. I paid them no attention and ignored Vasili, who kept whining and pulling at my sleeve.

"You are crazy!" she said. "You must be mad! Remove yourself from my presence or I will tear out both your eyes and your tongue besides!"

You see! Another woman would have cried, or been frightened into silence. But my Ariadne, worthy and venerable, hurled her spirit into my teeth.

"I would like to call on your father tomorrow," I said. From the assembled dancers who watched there rose a few vagrant whispers and some rude laughter. I stared at them carefully and they hushed at once. My temper and strength of arm were well known.

Ariadne did not speak again, but in a magnificent spirit stamped from the floor. The music began, and men and women began again to dance. I permitted Vasili to pull me to a corner.

"You are insane!" he said. He wrung his withered fingers in anguish. "You assaulted her like a Turk! Her relatives will cut out your heart!"

"My intentions were honorable," I said. "I saw her and loved her and told her so." At this point I struck my fist against my chest. Poor Vasili jumped.

"But you do not court a woman that way," he said.

"*You* don't, my anemic friend," I said. "Nor do the rest of these sheep. But I court a woman that way!"

He looked to heaven and helplessly shook his head. I waved good-by and started for my hat and coat.

"Where are you going?" he asked.

"To prepare for tomorrow," I said. "In the morning I will speak to her father."

I left the hall and in the street felt the night wind cold on my flushed cheeks. My blood was inflamed. The memory of her loveliness fed fuel to the fire. For the first time I understood with a terrible clarity the driven heroes of the past performing mighty deeds in love. Paris stealing Helen in passion, and Menelaus pursuing with a great fleet. In that moment if I knew the whole world would be plunged into conflict I would have followed Ariadne to Hades.

I went to my rooms above my tavern. I could not sleep. All night I tossed in restless frenzy. I touched my eye that she had struck with her spirited hand.

Ariadne! Ariadne! my soul cried out.

In the morning I bathed and dressed carefully. I confirmed the address of Langos, the grocer, and started to his store. It was a bright cold November morning, but I walked with spring in my step.

■ When I opened the door of the Langos grocery, a tiny bell rang shrilly. I stepped into the store piled with fruits and vegetables and smelling of cabbages and greens.

A stooped little old man with white bushy hair and owlish eyes came toward me. He looked as if his veins contained vegetable juice instead of blood, and if he were, in truth, the father of my beloved I marveled at how he could have produced such a paragon of women.

"Are you Mr. Langos?"

"I am," he said and he came closer. "I am."

"I met your daughter last night," I said. "Did she mention I was going to call?"

He shook his head somberly.

"My daughter mentioned you," he said. "In thirty years I have never seen her in such a state of agitation. She was possessed."

"The effect on me was the same," I said. "We met for the first time last night, and I fell passionately in love."

"Incredible," the old man said.

"You wish to know something about me," I said. "My name is Marko Palamas. I am a Spartan emigrated to this country eleven years ago. I am forty-one years old. I have been a wrestler and a sailor and fought with the resistance movement in Greece in the war. For this service I was decorated by the king. I own a small but profitable tavern on Dart Street. I attend church regularly. I love your daughter."

As I finished he stepped back and bumped a rack of fruit. An orange rolled off to the floor. I bent and retrieved it to hand it to him, and he cringed as if he thought I might bounce it off his old head.

"She is a bad-tempered girl," he said. "Stubborn, impatient and spoiled. She has been the cause of considerable concern to me. All the eligible young men have been driven away by her temper and disposition."

"Poor girl," I said. "Subjected to the courting of calves and goats."

The old man blinked his owlish eyes. The front door opened and a battleship of a woman sailed in.

"Three pounds of tomatoes, Mr. Langos," she said. "I am in a hurry. Please to give me good ones. Last week two spoiled before I had a chance to put them into Demetri's salad."

"I am very sorry," Mr. Langos said. He turned to me. "Excuse me, Mr. Poulmas."

"Palamas," I said. "Marko Palamas."

He nodded nervously. He went to wait on the battleship, and I spent a moment examining the store. Neat and small. I would not imagine he did more than hold his own. In the rear of the store there were stairs leading to what appeared to be an apartment above. My heart beat faster.

When he had bagged the tomatoes and given change, he returned to me and said, "She is also a terrible cook. She cannot fry an egg without burning it." His voice shook with woe. "She cannot make pilaf or lamb with squash." He paused. "You like pilaf and lamb with squash?"

"Certainly."

"You see?" he said in triumph. "She is useless in the kitchen. She is thirty years old, and I am resigned she will remain an old maid. In a way I am glad because I know she would drive some poor man to drink."

"Do not deride her to discourage me," I said. "You need have no fear that I will mistreat her or cause her unhappiness. When she is married to me she will cease being a problem to you." I paused. "It is true that I am not pretty by the foppish standards that prevail today. But I am a man. I wrestled Zahundos and pinned him two straight falls in Baltimore. A giant of a man. Afterward he conceded he had met his master. This from Zahundos was a mighty compliment."

"I am sure," the old man said without enthusiasm. "I am sure."

He looked toward the front door as if hoping for another customer.

"Is your daughter upstairs?"

He looked startled and tugged at his apron. "Yes," he said. "I don't know. Maybe she has gone out."

"May I speak to her? Would you kindly tell her I wish to speak with her."

"You are making a mistake," the old man said. "A terrible mistake."

"No mistake," I said firmly.

The old man shuffled toward the stairs. He climbed them slowly. At the top he paused and turned the knob of the door. He rattled it again.

"It is locked," he called down. "It has never been locked before. She has locked the door."

"Knock," I said. "Knock to let her know I am here."

"I think she knows," the old man said. "I think she knows."

He knocked gently.

"Knock harder," I suggested. "Perhaps she does not hear."

"I think she hears," the old man said. "I think she hears."

"Knock again," I said. "Shall I come up and knock for you?"

"No, no," the old man said quickly. He gave the door a sound kick. Then he groaned as if he might have hurt his foot.

"She does not answer," he said in a quavering voice. "I am very sorry she does not answer."

"The coy darling," I said and laughed. "If that is her game." I started for the front door of the store.

I went out and stood on the sidewalk before the store. Above the grocery were the front windows of their apartment. I cupped my hands about my mouth.

"Ariadne!" I shouted. "Ariadne!"

The old man came out the door running disjointedly. He looked frantically down the street.

"Are you mad?" he asked shrilly. "You will cause a riot. The police will come. You must be mad!"

"Ariadne!" I shouted. "Beloved!"

■ A window slammed open, and the face of Ariadne appeared above me. Her dark hair tumbled about her ears.

"Go away!" she shrieked. "Will you go away!"

"Ariadne," I said loudly. "I have come as I promised. I have spoken to your father. I wish to call on you."

"Go away!" she shrieked. "Madman! Imbecile! Go away!"

By this time a small group of people had assembled around the store and were watching curiously. The old man stood wringing his hands and uttering what sounded like small groans.

"Ariadne," I said. "I wish to call on you. Stop this nonsense and let me in."

She pushed farther out the window and showed me her teeth.

"Be careful, beloved," I said. "You might fall."

She drew her head in quickly, and I turned then to the assembled crowd.

"A misunderstanding," I said. "Please move on."

Suddenly old Mr. Langos shrieked. A moment later something broke on the sidewalk a foot from where I stood. A vase or a plate. I looked up, and Ariadne was preparing to hurl what appeared to be a water pitcher.

"Ariadne!" I shouted. "Stop that!"

The water pitcher landed closer than the vase, and fragments of glass struck my shoes. The crowd scattered, and the old man raised his hands and wailed to heaven.

Ariadne slammed down the window.

The crowd moved in again a little closer, and somewhere among them I heard laughter. I fixed them with a cold stare and waited for some one of them to say something offensive. I would have tossed him around like sardines, but they slowly dispersed and moved on. In another moment the old man and I were alone.

I followed him into the store. He walked an awkward dance of agitation. He shut the door and peered out through the glass.

"A disgrace," he wailed. "A disgrace. The whole street will know by nightfall. A disgrace."

"A girl of heroic spirit," I said. "Will you speak to her for me? Assure her of the sincerity of my feelings. Tell her I pledge eternal love and devotion."

The old man sat down on an orange crate and weakly made his cross.

"I had hoped to see her myself," I said. "But if you promise to speak to her, I will return this evening."

"That soon?" the old man said.

"If I stayed now," I said, "it would be sooner."

"This evening," the old man said and shook his head in resignation. "This evening."

I went to my tavern for a while and set up the glasses for the evening trade. I made arrangements for Pavlakis to tend bar in my place. Afterward I sat alone in my apartment and read a little of majestic Pindar to ease the agitation of my heart.

Once in the mountains of Greece when I fought with the guerrillas in the last year of the great war, I suffered a wound from which it seemed I would die. For days high fever raged in my body. My friends brought a priest at night secretly from one of the captive villages to read the last rites. I accepted the coming of death and was grateful for many things. For the gentleness and wisdom of my old grandfather, the loyalty of my companions in war, the years I sailed between the wild ports of the seven seas, and the strength that flowed to me from the Spartan earth. For one thing only did I weep when it seemed I would leave life, that I had never set ablaze the world with a burning song of passion for one woman. Women I had known, pockets of pleasure that I tumbled for quick joy, but I had been denied mighty love for one woman. For that I wept.

■ In Ariadne I swore before God I had found my woman. I knew by the storm-lashed hurricane that swept within my body. A woman whose majesty was in harmony with the earth, who would be faithful and beloved to me as Penelope had been to Ulysses.

That evening near seven I returned to the grocery. Deep twilight had fallen across the street, and the lights in the window of the store had been dimmed. The apples and oranges and pears had been covered with brown paper for the night.

I tried the door and found it locked. I knocked on the glass, and a moment later the old man came shuffling out of the shadows and let me in.

"Good evening, Mr. Langos."

He muttered some greeting in answer. "Ariadne is not here," he said. "She is at the church. Father Marlas wishes to speak with you."

"A fine young priest," I said. "Let us go at once."

I waited on the sidewalk while the old man locked the store. We started the short walk to the church.

"A clear and ringing night," I said. "Does it not make you feel the wonder and glory of being alive?"

The old man uttered what sounded like a groan, but a truck passed on the street at that moment and I could not be sure.

At the church we entered by a side door leading to the office of Father Marlas. I knocked on the door, and when he called to us to enter we walked in.

Young Father Marlas was sitting at his desk in his black cassock and with his black goatee trim and imposing beneath his clean-shaven cheeks. Beside the desk, in a dark blue dress sat Ariadne, looking somber and beautiful. A bald-headed, big-nosed old man with flint and fire in his eyes sat in a chair beside her.

"Good evening, Marko," Father Marlas said and smiled.

"Good evening, Father," I said.

"Mr. Langos and his daughter you have met," he said and he cleared his throat. "This is Uncle Paul Langos."

"Good evening, Uncle Paul," I said. He glared at me and did not answer. I smiled warmly at Ariadne in greeting, but she was watching the priest.

"Sit down," Father Marlas said.

I sat down across from Ariadne, and old Mr. Langos took a chair beside Uncle Paul. In this way we were arrayed in battle order as if we were opposing armies.

A long silence prevailed during which Father Marlas cleared his throat several times. I observed Ariadne closely. There were grace and poise even in the way her slim-fingered hands rested in her lap. She was a dark and lovely flower, and my pulse beat more quickly at her nearness.

"Marko," Father Marlas said finally. "Marko, I have known you well for the three years since I assumed duties in this parish. You are most regular in your devotions and very generous at the time of the Christmas and Easter offerings. Therefore, I find it hard to believe this complaint against you."

"My family are not liars!" Uncle Paul said, and he had a voice like hunks of dry hard cheese being grated.

"Of course not," Father Marlas said quickly. He smiled benevolently at Ariadne. "I only mean to say —"

"Tell him to stay away from my niece," Uncle Paul burst out.

"Excuse me, Uncle Paul," I said very politely. "Will you kindly keep out of what is not your business."

Uncle Paul looked shocked. "Not my business?" He looked from Ariadne to Father Marlas and then to his brother. "Not my business?"

"This matter concerns Ariadne and me," I said. "With outside interference it becomes more difficult."

"Not my business!" Uncle Paul said. He couldn't seem to get that through his head.

"Marko," Father Marlas said, and his composure was slightly shaken. "The family feels you are forcing your attention upon this girl. They are concerned."

"I understand, Father," I said. "It is natural for them to be concerned. I respect their concern. It is also natural for me to speak of love to a woman I have chosen for my wife."

"Not my business!" Uncle Paul said again, and shook his head violently.

"My daughter does not wish to become your wife," Mr. Langos said in a squeaky voice.

"That is for your daughter to say," I said courteously.

■ Ariadne made a sound in her throat, and we all looked at her. Her eyes were deep and cold, and she spoke slowly and carefully as if weighing each word on a scale in her father's grocery.

"I would not marry this madman if he were one of the Twelve Apostles," she said.

"See!" Mr. Langos said in triumph.

"Not my business!" Uncle Paul snarled.

"Marko," Father Marlas said. "Try to understand."

"We will call the police!" Uncle Paul raised his voice. "Put this hoodlum under a bond!"

"Please!" Father Marlas said. "Please!"

"Today he stood on the street outside the store," Mr. Langos said excitedly. "He made me a laughingstock."

"If I were a younger man," Uncle Paul growled, "I would settle this without the police. Zi-ip!" He drew a callused finger violently across his throat.

"Please," Father Marlas said.

"A disgrace!" Mr. Langos said.

"An outrage!" Uncle Paul said.

"He must leave Ariadne alone!" Mr. Langos said.

"We will call the police!" Uncle Paul said.

"Silence!" Father Marlas said loudly.

With everything suddenly quiet he turned to me. His tone softened.

"Marko," he said and he seemed to be pleading a little. "Marko, you must understand."

Suddenly a great bitterness assailed me, and anger at myself, and a terrible sadness that flowed like night through my body because I could not make them understand.

"Father," I said quietly, "I am not a fool. I am Marko Palamas and once I pinned the mighty Zahundos in Baltimore. But this battle, more important to me by far, I have lost. That which has not the grace of God is far better in silence."

I turned to leave and it would have ended there.

"Hoodlum!" Uncle Paul said. "It is time you were silent!"

I swear in that moment if he had been a younger man I would have flung him to the dome of the church. Instead I turned and spoke to them all in fire and fury.

"Listen," I said. "I feel no shame for the violence of my feelings. I am a man bred of the Spartan earth and my emotions are violent. Let those who squeak of life feel shame. Nor do I feel shame because I saw this flower and loved her. Or because I spoke at once of my love."

No one moved or made a sound.

"We live in a dark age," I said. "An age where men say one thing and mean another. A time of dwarfs afraid of life. The days are gone when mighty Pindar sang his radiant blossoms of song. When the noble passions of men set ablaze cities, and the heroic deeds of men rang like thunder to every corner of the earth."

I spoke my final words to Ariadne. "I saw you and loved you," I said gently. "I told you of my love. This is my way—the only way I know. If this way has proved offensive to you I apologize to you alone. But understand clearly that for none of this do I feel shame."

I turned then and started to the door. I felt my heart weeping as if waves were breaking within my body.

"Marko Palamas," Ariadne said. I turned slowly. I looked at her. For the first time the warmth I was sure dwelt in her body radiated within the circles of her face. For the first time she did not look at me with her eyes like glaciers.

"Marko Palamas," she said and there was a strange moving softness in the way she spoke my name. "You may call on me tomorrow."

Uncle Paul shot out of his chair. "She is mad too!" he shouted. "He has bewitched her!"

"A disgrace!" Mr. Langos said.

"Call the police!" Uncle Paul shouted. "I'll show him if it's my business!"

"My poor daughter!" Mr. Langos wailed.

"Turk!" Uncle Paul shouted. "Robber!"

"Please!" Father Marlas said. "Please!"

I ignored them all. In that winged and zestful moment I had eyes only for my beloved, for Ariadne, blossom of my heart and black-eyed flower of my soul!

Suggestions for Discussion

1. What impression does the reader form of the narrator from the opening paragraph? What effect upon mood and tone result from telling the story from the viewpoint of the main character?

2. Does the Ariadne of this story resemble the one in Greek myths? Which of the mythical lovers, Theseus or Dionysus, does the suitor Marko Palamas most resemble? Is there any significance in the fact that Palamas owns a tavern?

3. What kind of a man is Ariadne's father? What is his opinion of his unmarried daughter of thirty?
4. Does Petrakis want to suggest that it is characteristic of a tavern owner, wrestler, sailor, and resistance fighter to sit down "to read a little of majestic Pindar to ease the agitation of [his] heart"? Why should Palamas read Pindar rather than any other Greek poet at that moment?
5. In the scene at the priest's office, what causes the change in Palamas' attitude? How does this change reveal character?

Suggestions for Writing and Comparison

1. Discuss the function of humor in the story. Is it sophisticated, witty, or bitter comedy?
2. Read either *Zorba the Greek* or *Freedom or Death* by Nikos Kazantzakis and compare either of Kazantzakis' heroes with Harry Petrakis' Marko Palamas. Is Palamas a particularly Greek character?

Richard Bankowsky

Richard Bankowsky, born in New Jersey in 1928, is a second generation Polish American. He holds degrees from both Yale and Columbia University, and he has taught at the State University of Iowa and Sacramento State College.

Bankowsky's major work is a tetralogy—*The Glass Rose* (1958), *After Pentecost* (1961), *On a Dark Night* (1964), and *The Pale Criminals* (1967)—which is comprised primarily of characters living in Anderson, a Polish American community in New Jersey. In its variety of characters and classes and in its abundance of fictitious socio-geographic detail, Bankowsky's Anderson may be likened to William Faulkner's Yoknapatawpha County.

After Pentecost, from which the following selection is taken, moves backward and forward in time between events which occur in 1926 and 1946. The scene shifts from Germany to New Jersey to Poland. The excerpt which follows is a story within a story—an inset story—which takes place in 1946 in New Jersey. The main character of the inset, Josef Janosz, is both a foil to and a prefiguration of the major character in the novel, Novak. Josef's castle is symbolic of the life Novak has built for himself and his family in the new country. Novak's attempt at suicide—which opens this story—follows on the news of a woman's survival of the Second World War, as Janosz's contemplated suicide had followed on the death of his daughter. In both the inset and the entire novel Bankowsky reveals the interrelatedness and dependence of one human being on another.

from

After Pentecost

Today, all of a sudden, as tired as he was, he was thinking as clearly and sensibly as he had ever thought in his life; standing there at the railing looking down into the still water as though waiting for something to appear suddenly out from under the bridge, watching his leg rising over the rail, and just smiling to himself, thinking, "Yes, I must be only dreaming after all. Because there is no reason for it now . . . and nothing is different. And I have the children and Martha. And we will grow old together, and there will be peace. And that is all I need now. I am just so tired . . . I feel I could sleep forever," looking down into the dark water, the streetlights mirrored in the flat surface below the bridge, thinking, "I have been thinking about the river for so long now, that I am even dreaming of it. It must be; only a dream could be so unreasonable. Because what would be the reason to do it now when there is

no need for it at all since nothing at all is different, nothing has changed?
. . . All I need is a little sleep, which is exactly what I am doing now, dreaming it all away once and for all and forever. Why, today has probably not even come yet, and where I really am right now is still back in bed last night only dreaming it is today"; the water, looking solid enough to walk on, beginning to rise now, coming up to claim him lazily as in a dream . . .

■ When old Jozef Janosz's Zofia died, all the good women of Anderson who saw him sitting there beside the coffin—sitting there with his eyes open but not seeing and his lips going but not speaking and with the rosary beads wrapped around his hands—all of them agreed that it would have been kinder if he had died, for surely now there was nothing for him, nothing but to sit there in the great house and wait to die himself, in the great unpainted house which he had built with his own hands and which had been fifteen long years in the building.

In the old country, Janosz had been a carpenter, a very fine carpenter, and so it had not been possible, as it had been for the others who had been only farmers, for Janosz to go to work in a factory. And since here in Anderson there was never any work for a fine carpenter, and no one could expect Janosz to go to work for one of those pushing construction companies across the river in Prescott, where there would always be some stupid Irish or Italian foreman trying to tell him how he should drive a nail, telling him, Janosz, who had been the finest carpenter in the entire section of the old country, how to build a house; so rather than go to work in the factory, Janosz the carpenter became Janosz the junkman, for whom there was always plenty of work.

The good women of the town would see him early every morning sitting there in his wagon under the beach umbrella, the reins loose in his hands and his mouth going with tobacco, his already tired but steady horse clopping along toward the bridge to Prescott and the towns beyond, where Janosz would ring the old cowbells strung across the wagon bed and yell in his best English, "Reksy, papiry, junky." And at night, the wagon full of old automobile tires and all kinds of rags and papers and junk, they would see him slumped there under the umbrella, probably already asleep, the wagon rumbling back over the bridge into Anderson behind the still tired but steady horse, and the old cowbells quietly rattling complines under the lamps.

There was so much work for Janosz the junkman, in fact, that it was not very long before he had sent back to the old country for his family and his good wife, and it was then that he first began making the great boast in the taverns. He would say that when his family got to America he would make sure that none of his sons ever had to go to work in a factory, and that with them helping him in his junk business he would some day build his family a great house, a regular castle, and that this house would have twenty rooms and each of them would be twice as large as any two rooms in the usual house of the town, and that he would build it all himself, with the help of his sons of course, for surely no one could dispute that Janosz had been the finest carpenter in the entire section of the old country. He would only talk like this when he had had a little too much to drink of course, and then he would sing very loudly, and show them his money and laugh at them for having to break their backs in the factories to make somebody else rich, and brag like that about the great house with the twenty rooms. And so when his good wife and his family finally came to live with him together with the horse and the junk, all in the tin-and-tarpaper shack on the edge of town at the foot of the Anderson Hill, the good women of the town would yell at him from their windows as he rumbled by in his wagon. "Pan Janosz," they would yell, "when will you invite us of the town to see your fine new house?" and, "Tell us, Pan Janosz, how does your good wife keep such a fine big house clean, Janosz? Twenty rooms, Janosz." And the men would joke him at the taverns, and so he soon stopped going to them and kept to himself, and after a while the good women even stopped yelling at him from their windows.

His good wife would tell the women at the meat market that her husband was a good man but was stubborn as a cow, and his sons would tell the Sisters at the school that though their Tata could not come to Mass with his family on Sunday morning, because that was the only free time he had to sort the junk since the rest of the week was all work from before sunup till long after sundown, that he would always say the rosary with them every night before they went to bed. But what was the good of money if you had to sacrifice your immortal soul for it, the good women would tell his wife, and what was the good of money if you could not at least enjoy it a little, when you have to live in a tarpaper shack together with a horse and a pile of junk and you never went to the beer gardens or had any friends and your young boys never even went out to the picture houses in Prescott across the river. But they had all of them forgotten about the boast of the great house. And so on that morning in 1910 when Janosz rumbled down the side of the hill and through the town toward the bridge with the wagon full of sawed-off sections of the trunks of trees, the good women of the town, hanging out of their windows or coming from the grocery stores with the hard rolls and the pickles for their husbands' lunch pails before the whistles blew in the factories across the river, just looked, because for the first time in over a dozen years Janosz, instead of simply spitting tobacco juice into the street as he passed, actually rattled his old cowbells at them and tipped his battered old cap.

They soon learned that he had bought an acre of land atop the Anderson Hill, bought it the very week after his wife had told him she was pregnant again. And it was many months before he had even a small section of the land cleared, and all the good women were sure he would be dead long before the year ended, what with his working all day with his junk business and half the night up on the hill. But at the end of the year he was still very much alive, and when Zofia was born his wife told how happy he was that she was a girl because he already had three sons and that was enough, and how he told her that since this was the first of their children to be born in the new country, the great house he would build would be especially for her, and that very night he went out and started digging the cellar of his "castle for my Zofia."

Zofia was already seven years old when the Great War came and it was clear to all by that time that Janosz had not just been talking when he had boasted that his house would be a castle. It had taken him four years just to dig his cellar, and the good women understood how terrible it must have been every single day of that entire four years for his wife to get up in the morning and be drawn to the window to look out on that little hole in the side of that great hill and not be able to notice any change at all. For there was not much one spade could do to the side of a hill in a few hours of a night, and Janosz got very little help from his sons. Two of them had to go to work in the factory in order to support the family because Janosz now put away every penny he made in his junk business for his house, and the youngest one was still in school and was truly a lazy boy. And so Janosz had to work alone, even in the wintertime before the snow finally came, picking away in the frozen ground; and when the snow finally would come covering the hill and lying deep in the hole that was to be the cellar of Janosz's house, his good wife would tell how difficult it was to live with him, and that it was a crazy man who would fight with his sons like that and call them worthless and lazy when really they worked very hard in the factories to support him and his family, a crazy man who would curse at them and then stomp out of the shack and trudge up the side of the hill with the kerosene lamp and just stand there in the snow spitting tobacco juice into a hole in the ground.

And when the war came and his sons left the factory and said good-bye to their younger brother and kissed their little sister and their good mother and then trudged up the side of the hill in the snow to say good-bye to their father and went away to France and never came home again, his wife told the good women that she thanked God, yes thanked Him for taking her sons from her if that was the only way He could get her husband to give up his foolish dream. Because when the news came that first Alex had been lost and then Thaddeus, Janosz just stopped working on the hill and never even went up there for almost a year. But on the Sunday night after little Zofia's First Holy Communion there was a light up on the hill again, the light of a small kerosene lamp moving in the dark clearing atop the moon-bright hill. And then the building began. And on Sundays, which Janosz would spend almost entirely up on the hill after the junk had been sorted, he would have the company of his little Zofia, who would come home from Mass with her good mother and take off her white communion veil and white shoes and put on her overalls and sneakers and after helping her Tata finish sorting the junk would walk with him up the side of the hill to work on their house. For as Janosz would say, he could not ever hope to get it done if it was not for his little Zofia's big help, and that if his son would do even half as much work as she did, instead of spending his time at the dances in the Prescott Polish Home and in the car of that good-for-nothing Italian girl from Prescott, whose brothers would surely make him marry her, that it would be no time at all before the work would be finished and the house done.

But the brothers of the good-for-nothing Italian girl from Prescott did not make Janosz's son marry their sister; instead, he ran away with her one spring and then there was only Janosz and his good wife and his little Zofia and the horse and junk left in the tin-and-tarpaper shack at the foot of the Anderson Hill. And then it was not long until there were only two of them and the horse and junk, for that winter they carried the coffin out of the shack and buried it in the frozen cemetery. Old Janosz cried of course when he threw the carnation into the hole, and he cried even harder when he knelt down in the snow to wipe the tears out of little Zofia's eyes. But that night there was a light on the hill as usual, and the next morning the good women of the town began yelling out of their windows again as he rumbled out of town in the wagon. "Pan Janosz," they yelled, "how is it you found time to go to the funeral of your poor dead wife? Surely, Janosz, you cannot afford to miss a whole day away from your house," and, "Who will live in your big house now, Janosz, when your Zofia takes a husband? Your horse, Janosz?" But he just spat some tobacco juice into the street and rode on by and at night there were the cowbells rattling complines in the streets as usual and later the small light on the hill.

And when the good women sent the pastor of the Holy Rosary Church to talk to him because they were worried about Zofia's having to sleep all alone in that shed half the night there on the very edge of town, he told the pastor that surely he could take care of his own, that his Zofia was happy and they needed nothing from anybody. "Father, I send my Zofia to your school, and she has never missed Mass a single day since her Mama died. So please be so good as to leave us alone, Father. My Zofia is healthy and she is happy. All you need to do is look at her and you can see. Zofia, are you not happy?" And so the Pastor came back and told them that Pan Janosz had been very polite and that he was bringing up his daughter as a good Catholic and that surely it was his privilege to be left alone if he wished it. After that the good women of the town washed their hands of old Jozef Janosz and his little daughter Zofia, and every morning from their windows in the town they would see Janosz's house growing up out of the side of the hill, mysteriously almost, almost as though it were not really being built by a man at all.

It was, just as Janosz had promised, a truly great house. It had twenty-one rooms, and sitting up there atop the hill under the sun it looked like nothing less than a castle. The entire first floor was built of stone, and it was larger than any of the great houses of the rich in Prescott's Third Ward or in the other towns Janosz visited with his junk wagon, and it had many more balconies, and its spires were like that of a cathedral. Indeed, it was the spires which brought the men up the side of the hill that Sunday. It was spring and the trees were still without leaves. Janosz and his Zofia were working on the skeleton of the tallest spire, each of them on separate ladders reaching up from the point of the main roof. She was helping him hold the young pine tree which by custom was nailed to the highest point on the house when the frame was completed, and which when finally taken down was a sign to all that the building was finally finished and only the painting remained. Janosz was tied to the spire with ropes, and hammering, and every once in a while spitting into the wind, and so he did not even hear them when they hollered up at him. Zofia came down however and talked to them for a few minutes. They told her that they had got together at Mass and decided to come and help him with the spires, because surely this was no kind of work for a man who was no longer as young as he used to be and whose ladders were surely not the best—not to mention a thirteen-year-old girl who could get dizzy climbing so high and fall. But she simply thanked them, and said that her Tata would refuse, that it was good of them but she and her Tata needed no help and they would be done soon anyway, and then went back into the house and climbed back out of the attic window onto the main roof and back up the ladder to the spire, her pale blond hair blowing long in the wind.

And then the real spring came and the trees were no longer without leaves, and then the summer was there, and then it was gone, and by the time the first snow came the roofs were all finished, and just in time too. For it was true, Janosz was no longer as young as he used to be and now he slept slumped over the reins in his wagon every morning and did not even seem to see the women hanging out of their windows or going to the store for their husbands' lunches, for the horse knew the way as well as he—down Maple Avenue, to Main and then to Anderson Avenue and over the Market Street Bridge into Prescott. And though he still had plenty of strength, more than most men half his age, it was still plain to all that there was pain in his bones when he lifted a barrel of scrap iron into the wagon, and the good women said among themselves when they saw that the roofs were finally completed, that if there had been one more shingle to place or one more nail to drive up there in the wind, surely Janosz could not have done it, for it was certain that a man of his age had long passed the days of climbing ladders. But the roofs were finished and all the work was being done on the inside of the house, and by the time spring came round again the day finally arrived when the young pine tree could be removed from the spire as a sign that except for the painting, Janosz's castle was finished at last.

■ At that point in his story the old man paused and spat against the pot stove, the tobacco juice sizzling and skittering against the glowing iron. The old gaunt skeleton of a horse, still harnessed to the junk wagon, nosed about in the haymow, intermittently and quietly clattering the cowbells strung across the wagon bed full of old automobile tires and all kinds of rags and papers and junk, and the rain was loud on the tin-and-tarpaper roof. From the pallet beside the haymow, naked and warm under the horse blanket after the hot wine—the wet tin cups empty now, sizzling and skittering on the pot stove —Novak watched the old man in the kerosene glow of the lamp, wringing out his soaking-wet clothes over the catch-buckets scattered about under the roof, and hanging them in the rafters over the stove to dry; the old man shaking and bent over with too much age and drink, who in his junk-buying trips across the river in Prescott and the towns beyond was perhaps no longer strong enough to lift a barrel of scrap iron into the wagon bed all alone, but was nonetheless capable of dragging a full-grown and unconscious man out of the Prescott River and lifting him unaided into that same wagon bed; puttering about now and telling his story, for what reason or to make what point Novak did not even bother to consider, lying there half dozing in the old man's pallet after the warm wine, listening, the story told in the good adequate peasant Polish, the old man's healthy tobacco-stained teeth gleaming in the ancient skull, his voice rattling away again amid the rafters, saying, "It snowed that Sunday, or rather the night before. A beautiful warm moist snow that whitened the branches of the trees below the hill and the roofs of the town beyond—the first Easter snow in thirty years. And we stood there on the main roof, me and my Zofia, reaching the ladder up to the high spire and watching the good women of the town in their coats and shawls and galoshes coming down Maple Avenue past my shack and toward the hill, together with their husbands and children and dogs even, so that it looked like not only the entire neighborhood but the entire town was coming to celebrate the completion of our house. For even though from the roofs we could not see what it was they were carrying, I knew they were coming with the Easter roasts and the wine and the homemade breads I had not tasted since my good wife died.

And so I did not know what to think even after my Zofia told me how just before Mass that morning she had gone and told the Sister that today would be the day of the taking down of the young pine, and how after the Gospel, the pastor had put aside his written-down Easter sermon and talked instead all about how with the aid of grace and complete faith, men could still make miracles in this world, and how with much hard work and much faith, even the poorest of our people could some day hope to build a great castle in this country, even if the castle only existed in the cathedral of his immortal soul. And as my Zofia told me of it, the church bells in the steeple of the Holy Rosary Church rang out the consecration of the Host at the noon Mass across the bridge and the valley and up the side of the hill. And then my Zofia climbed up the ladder, her long hair blowing in the wind. And as I stood there on the main roof holding the ladder against the spire, I watched her remove the young pine and stand there on the rungs waving to the good women of the town and their husbands and their children and even their dogs who were coming across the fields from the shack and up the side of the hill. And I could see them waving back. And then the snow began to slide out from under me and I could hear the good women of the town scream against the side of the hill."

He did not even cry at the funeral, he said. And all the good women of the town said many kind things to him, but he did not hear; and after the casket was in the ground, he just walked with his eyes staring but not seeing and with his lips moving but not speaking and with the rosary beads wrapped around his hands. He walked straight out of the cemetery without even saying thank you to the good women who had been so kind. And as he walked back "home" down the slush-covered streets—the first April snow in thirty years—he agreed with the women that it would have been kinder if he too had died, for surely now there was nothing for him. "And I could not understand it. I could not understand any of it. Why would a good and merciful God allow such a thing? And I tried to explain it to myself. I told myself that perhaps I had been wrong from the very beginning, that surely it had always been as my wife had said, I was a stubborn and willful man and now God had punished me. But then it was not for me to try to explain the ways of God, I told myself finally, and I spat into the snow and just sat there on the stump looking up at my Zofia's castle and thought what a good joke it would be to turn the whole thing into a stable for my horse."

And as the old man spoke, Novak could almost see him sitting there as darkness fell, spitting and thinking how he had built himself a house to die in; his castle there amid the radiant clean snow, looming big as a cathedral under the moon; the lights of the town below one after the other slowly and steadily going out until finally the whole town was dark and asleep; then the sky turning red over the hill, the great flames rosing the snow and scorching the leafless trees, and the lights of the town below one after the other coming on again, and the shouting and the running about; the good women in their shawls and overcoats and galoshes hurrying down Maple Avenue together with their husbands and children and dogs even, so that it looked as if not only the entire neighborhood but the entire town was coming to warm their hands, all of them amazed to find only the horse and the wagon and the unsorted junk there in the shack at the foot of the hill, saying later among themselves as they stood there in the circle around Janosz's castle looking up at the great devouring flames, saying it looked as though they had not only lost Janosz's miracle, but old Jozef Janosz himself.

"But they were wrong," the old man said, "because the next morning my old wagon was there in the streets under their windows as always." And as he went on, Novak did not even need to listen to the rest of it, for he could see it all himself, could see the old man slumped there under the umbrella behind the already tired and now almost unmoving horse, the reins loose in his hands and his mouth going with the tobacco; just sitting there under the umbrella paying no attention at all to the nods of the good women of the town hanging out of their windows or going to the store for the hard rolls and the sour pickles for their husbands' lunch pails, probably not even hearing the good mornings, just sitting there and spitting the tobacco juice into the cool morning air, the wagon bed full of all kinds of charred and blackened timbers and sinks and faucets and bathtubs and pipes and doorknobs and chandeliers and probably even a spire or two above which the old cowbells rattled matins in the slush-covered Anderson streets.

■ How he had managed to stay awake as the old man told his sentimental story, Novak did not consider. But almost immediately the old man finished, his voice rattling amid the rafters, saying, "I have been telling myself all these years that it was simply a matter of cowardice; that any real man would have set himself afire along with the house. But now I see that it was not that, after all. Because, tell me, my foolish friend, where would you be now if Janosz had done twenty years ago what you had tried to do last night, eh? Janosz would not only have set himself on fire that night, but you too, eh, my son," Novak fell asleep.

Suggestions for Discussion

1. Describe the style of the brief opening section at the river? Does it contain any elements of the stream-of-consciousness technique?
2. How does the frame of the story — Novak's attempted suicide — relate to the story proper? Discuss the themes of life, death, and responsibility in both the frame of the story and the story proper.
3. How do the neighbors function in the story? Are they cruel or kind? In what way do their comments add to the characterization of Janosz?
4. What is the "American Dream" for Janosz? Would the house have been the ultimate realization of the Dream or is the house merely symbolic?
5. What is the difference between a tragic character and a pathetic character? Is Janosz tragic or pathetic? Why?
6. What is meant by the line in the conclusion "Janosz would not only have set himself on fire that night, but you too, eh, my son"? According to the conclusion, what is the reason Janosz did not commit suicide after his daughter's death?

Suggestions for Writing and Comparison

1. Compare and contrast Bankowsky's prose style with that of William Faulkner (see especially any of the Yoknapatawpha County novels such as *Sartoris, The Sound and the Fury,* or *The Hamlet*).
2. Discuss the concept of the American Dream as it appears in the excerpt from *After Pentecost* and Isaac Bashevis Singer's "The Little Shoemakers" (p. 424). Does either of the stories suggest fulfillment of the Dream?

James T. Farrell

James T. Farrell was born in 1904 in Chicago, Illinois, of Irish parentage. He received his elementary and high-school education at Catholic parochial schools and later attended De Paul University, the University of Chicago, and New York University.

In 1932 Farrell published *Young Lonigan,* the first book of the *Studs Lonigan* trilogy, which is concerned with the Irish ghetto of Chicago's South Side before and during the Depression. This was followed by *The Young Manhood of Studs Lonigan* (1934) and *Judgement Day* (1935). More recently, Farrell has published *Saturday Night and Other Stories* (1958) and *Lonely for the Future* (1967). Farrell is considered among the strongest of the American naturalist writers. His stories have been translated into twenty languages.

Farrell's characters are generally lower-middle-class second- or third-generation Americans of Irish descent. The *Studs Lonigan* trilogy, as well as a number of other stories by Farrell, including "The Oratory Contest," is set in the slum area of Chicago which was once one of the largest Irish ghettos in America. "The Oratory Contest" is concerned with the despairing self-image of one such ghetto dweller, and the distance that he perceives between himself and the son for whom he has great aspirations.

The Oratory Contest

Facing the bathroom mirror, Gerry O'Dell practiced for the contest, and he imagined the thunder of applause that would greet him at the conclusion of his oration. His mother called him, and he said that he was coming. He met his dad in the hallway, and Mr. O'Dell looked at his narrow-faced, small, sixteen-year-old son with a mingling of pride and humility.

"Well, Gerry, how do you feel? The old soupbone in your throat loosened up?" the father asked.

"Yes, Dad," Gerry nervously answered.

"Gerry, your mother and I are mighty proud of you, and we'll be giving you all the . . . the moral support we can tonight. Don't get worried because you're speaking in public, or because of the size of the crowd. Ah, anyway, Gerry, oratory is certainly a great gift for a boy to have," the father said, putting his hairy hands into his blue trouser pockets and rocking backward on his heels. "Gerry, if a man has the makings of a great orator in him, he need have no fears of getting ahead in life."

"George, don't be making the boy nervous. Gerald, supper is ready," the mother called.

"Martha, I was only explaining to him," the father apologetically explained.

"Father, you mustn't be saying any more now," she said in a nagging tone.

The father followed his son into the dining room, and he seemed to have been hurt as the family sat down for supper.

"Well, Sis, how did school go today?" the father asked, cutting into his lamb chop and looking at his pigtailed daughter while Gerry talked with his brother, Michael, about Sister Sylvester, the eighth-grade teacher at Saint Catherine's grammar school.

"I was spelled down," Ellen said.

"What word did you miss, Sis?"

"Interest, Daddy."

"Maybe you'll do better the next time."

"But, gee, Daddy, I tried so hard. I could have cried right then and there like a baby," she said.

"That's just too bad! Too bad that you couldn't show off before Georgie Schaeffer," Michael said, making a wry face at his sister.

"Is that so!"

Mrs. O'Dell told her younger children to stop arguing and eat their supper. It was no time to be disturbing Gerald. The family ate, and the father cast continued glances of approval and pride at his oldest son.

"Gerry, where did you learn the things you're talking about tonight? You must certainly have studied a lot to learn them," the father said.

"I read the Constitution, and the editorials on it that have been printed recently in *The Chicago Questioner*. And then, of course, there was my civics course, and Father Robert gave me lots of suggestions, and he spent an awful lot of time helping me rehearse my speech. He helped me get it written and to get my delivery set in my mind," Gerry said.

"Gerry, when I heard you give your oration at the semifinals, I was a mighty proud father, I was."

Gerry smiled self-consciously.

"After you finish high school, you'll have to go to college. I want you to get a fine education."

"But, Dad, how can I?" Gerry said, looking hopefully at his father.

"You ought to be able to get a job and study law in the evenings downtown at Saint Vincent's."

"That's what I'll have to do," Gerry said disconsolately.

"Of course, something might turn up," the father said.

"George, that is what you've been saying for twenty years," Mrs. O'Dell said sarcastically.

"Martha, you can't say that I ain't tried. I've provided for you and the children as well as I could, and I always brought my pay home to you untouched. I don't see where you have any right to complain when a man has always done his best."

"George, I'm not complaining. It's just that after all these years I'm tired out. Look how long we're married, and we don't even own our own home."

"We will yet. I mean it! I swear we will! A fellow at the barns was telling me yesterday that he can get a ticket on the English Sweepstakes. Now suppose I should win that! One hundred thousand dollars! Say, we'd be rolling in wealth. You know, Martha, you never can tell what will happen in life. Now last year, I remember reading in the papers where some foreigner, a cook in some New York hotel, won over a hundred thousand dollars on a sweepstakes ticket."

"And you're not that cook. You've been talking yourself blue in the face about winning in baseball pools almost as long as I can remember. And what have you won? What?"

"Didn't I win twenty-five dollars on a baseball pool last year?"

"Yes, and how much did you spend buying tickets during the year?"

"Gee, give a man a chance."

"Give you a chance! That's all I've ever given you."

"Have it your way then. But three years ago Tom Foley, who runs a car on Western Avenue, won five hundred, didn't he? If he can have luck like that, what's to stop me from having it?"

"You're not Tom Foley."

"Aw, Ma!" O'Dell whined, causing Gerry to glance at him quickly in disgust.

"I can't be listening to all your nonsense, George. I got to see that the boys get ready for tonight," she said when they had finished their tea and dessert.

"Gee, Ma, are you sure you can't come?" Gerry said as she arose from the table, a small, broad, fat-cheeked woman in her forties whose stomach was swollen out.

"Gerald, your mother isn't feeling up to snuff this evening. But I'll be thinking of you, speaking and saying a little prayer to the Lord that you'll win the prize. Your mother knows that her son is going to take the prize, and she'll be just as happy whether she hears you or not, just as long as you telephone me the minute you get out of the hall," the mother said.

"Ma, can I go?" the sister asked.

"You got to stay home with your mother," the father said while Gerry kissed Mrs. O'Dell goodbye and left.

■ Mrs. O'Dell sat knitting baby socks in the dining room, and the daughter was bent over her school books at the table. The father entered the cramped room and asked his wife for some money. She slowly arose and waddled to their bedroom. She drew a two-dollar bill from a large leather pocketbook and handed it to him.

"George, I get spells. I'm afraid," she said.

"Don't worry, Martha. Gerry is a chip off the old block, and he has the makings of a fine orator. Why, he already orates better than a lot of lawyers and politicians I've heard," he said.

"It's not that, George. I'm too old now and this one is going to be a harder ordeal than when I was younger and had the others. Oh, George, I'm afraid! I can't bear to think of leaving you and the children without their mother."

Worried, he gently patted her back, tenderly caressed her unkempt black hair.

"I feel as if I can't carry the load inside of me. And my back gets so sore. I had a dream last night, and it's a premonition. I fear I shan't be pulling through. Oh, George, hold me, kiss me like you used to a long time ago! I can't bear it, the thought of dying and leaving you with an infant baby."

She sobbed in his arms. Holding her, he felt as if paralyzed. He sensed in her the mystery of woman which enabled them to bring forth a man's child. He was filled with respect, awed into speechlessness. He kissed her, clasped her tightly, his feelings reverential. He thought of how they were going along now, and of how they were past knowing and feeling again what they had known and felt in those first burning days of their marriage. Now it was just having sympathy with each other, being used to one another, having their family, their duties, and the obligations which they had to meet together, the feeling of liking, more than loving, each other, and wanting to be proud of their kids. He kissed her again.

Michael called his dad from the doorway. The parents blushed with embarrassment. They turned their heads aside. The father gruffly told his son that he was coming. He kissed his wife a final goodbye.

■ It was a muggy, misty March evening. Walking to the streetcar line with his son, O'Dell turned memories of other times over and over in his mind. He remembered his courtship and the days when he was younger and had worked nights, and of how at this time, on this kind of a night, he would be driving his car along Ashland Avenue. He wished that it were still those days and that he were young instead of a motorman rapidly getting old as his family was beginning to grow up. It was strange now to think of himself in other days, to think of what he had been, to realize how he had not at all known what life had in store for himself and his young bride. And now they both knew. And just to think that there had been a time when this boy, Michael, beside him had not been born, and neither had Gerry. Gerry had once been in his mother's womb just as the latest newcomer was at this very moment. He remembered the coming of his three children, Martha's shrieks and agonies, his own apprehensions and worries, the helpless feeling that had come over him, the drowsy tiredness on Martha's face after each delivery. He was afraid for it to happen all over again, afraid that this new one was going to mean trouble. *Death!* He wished that it were over with. Yes, and he wished that he were a young motorman again, instead of being pretty close on toward the declining years of middle age. He shook his head wistfully thinking of how now, for years, day after day, he had driven streetcars. And he had been driving them before the boy at his side was born, and even before Gerry had been on the way. Gerry had turned out fine, but not just exactly what he had imagined Gerry would be. Ah, nothing in life turned out just as a man imagined that it would turn out. And this new one? When it would be Gerry's age, he and Martha, if the Lord spared them both, they would be old. He trembled at the thought of this new one, and it turned his mind to thoughts of the years, of death, the end of them both.

"Mickey, you always want to be good to your mother. Help her all you can while you've got her, because you'll never realize how much she means to you until she's gone," he said.

"Yes, Dad," the boy dutifully replied, the father's words merely giving him the feeling that the old man was just preaching a little in order to hear himself talk.

"You won't have her with you always, you know."

They boarded a streetcar and stood on the rear platform talking with the conductor, who was a friend of Mr. O'Dell's. O'Dell told his friend where they were going and why. The conductor told O'Dell that one of his girls was a smart one like that, too, and she had just won a prize button in school for writing. But anyway, that girl of his, she was a great kid, and a smart one, too. Then they had to get off at Sixty-third Street and change for an eastbound car.

■ O'Dell became increasingly timid as the car approached the school auditorium of Mary Our Mother. He tried to force a feeling of reassurance upon himself, thinking that he was just as good as any man, telling himself that he was a freeborn American who earned his living by honest work. He had just as much right as any man to come to this contest and hear his own boy whom he was educating out of his hard-earned money. He was an honest man, and work was honorable, and what if he was a motorman and some of the fathers of Gerry's classmates were higher up on the ladder than he? No, there was no need of his being ashamed. America was a democratic country. Still, he was shy. He knew that he would feel out of place. But he was proud of his son, and he knew that Gerry was going to win out over the sons of richer fathers, and . . . he felt that he just wouldn't be in place, and that maybe he shouldn't have come.

And he realized that Gerry, instead of waiting for him and Michael, had gone ahead. Gerry, he suddenly felt, was ashamed of him. He argued with himself that the boy had had to get there early, and that, anyway, he had been nervous about the contest and restless, like a colt before the start of a race. But still, no, he could not rid his mind of that thought.

He noticed other people on the sidewalk, walking in the same direction as he, and he heard them talking. Some of them sounded like parents, and he was sure that many of them must be the fathers and mothers of boys who went to Mary Our Mother. Did any of them, he wondered, have thoughts such as he? Well, before this evening was over they were all going to know about Gerald O'Dell.

And at home, there was Martha, her body big and swollen. He wished that she had come along. And she was at home, knitting away. He was responsible for her condition, and if he had curbed himself, well, they wouldn't be having this worry and this danger, and all the expense and sacrifice that it would involve, and she would be at his side, and they would both be so proud and happy, hearing Gerry win with his oration. How good it would be to have Martha at his side, both of them hearing the whole auditorium applaud her boy, her own flesh and blood. And she would not be granted this pleasure. He could just see her at home, knitting, silent, afraid. And she was going to be hurt, and this new child was going to be, maybe, so hard at her age, and oh, God forbid that she should die.

In front of the auditorium, he saw boys of varying ages, some only a year or so older than his Michael, other lads of seventeen and eighteen in long pants. He looked about to see if Gerry were among them, but he wasn't. He would like to tell them who he was, the father of Gerry O'Dell.

"Mike, here we are," he said in an attempt to be whimsical.

He handed two complimentary tickets to the lad collecting them at the door, and in a humble mood he followed the usher to seats in the center of the auditorium. He looked shyly about the lighted hall, seeing a confusion of strange faces, the people moving down the aisles to seats, and he was excited and expectant. He wanted it to begin. He glanced up toward the stage, with the stand and a row of chairs in front of the drawn red curtain. The boys, judges, and the honored guests, including a number of priests, some of whom might be Gerry's teachers, would all sit in those chairs. And again he felt out of place, humbly so. He felt that in the auditorium there must be the fathers of many of Gerry's classmates, men who had gone so much further in the world than he had, men who could afford to send their sons to good colleges.

He remembered the sight of the lads outside, and it caused him to think of how Gerry must have an entire life closed out to his father and mother, a life they could never get their little fingers on. He glanced sidewise at Michael, who was awkwardly twisting in his seat and looking about at faces with a boy's alive and curious eyes. And what did he see? What? Michael, too, and the girl, they had their lives that were closed to their father and mother, and as they grew older they would both drift further and further away.

"Like it, Mickey?" he asked, wanting to get close to his son, to be like a pal with him.

Michael smiled, muttered an absorbed uhuh.

"Some day you'll be going to the school here, too, and maybe, like Gerry, you'll be winning oratorical contests and prizes."

"I'd rather be on the football team."

"Maybe you can do both."

Michael smiled frankly, and the father suddenly found his mood dissipating under the smile. He did not feel himself to be such a stranger to Michael.

■ He was conscious of the movement of people, priests in the rear, the hall filling up, and he guessed that it was going to start. Suddenly the orchestra began a scratchy prelude, and O'Dell told himself that it must be fine music. Like those around him, he sat quiet, a little hushed. Glad, too, that it was starting. He waited, entertained but anxious, through the elocution contests, when first-year students recited pieces. The junior contest followed, and four boys delivered famous orations. O'Dell thought that the tall boy who delivered a speech of Senator Hoar's defending the retention of the Philippine Islands had been the best. All of them had been good, but his boy would be better. And that was what he was waiting for.

He heard more music, idly reflecting that the priests here at Mary Our Mother must be giving the boys a good education. Anxiety was working within him like a pump. Right after the music Gerry would speak. He gripped and clasped his hands. Michael stirred. He tapped him, whispering to be quiet and to act well-mannered. The music, carried through by violins, seemed like the distant sounds of a waterfall, and they lulled within him. Dreamily he visualized Gerry speaking, imagined the lad's future as a great lawyer, and he thought of how boys in oratorical contests such as this one would, in years to come, be delivering the famous speeches and orations of Senator Gerald O'Dell. Gerald O'Dell, his son, the boy whose education had cost him sacrifices.

And now Gerry, small and freckled, was on the platform. He seemed so calm, as if there was not a worry in his head. He stood there, straight, dignified, and, ah, but wouldn't he be a pride to his father in the years to come. He was speaking. O'Dell leaned forward, listening attentively as his son's deep and full voice carried down the auditorium.

So the first step is, what is the Constitution?

O'Dell was in a spell, completely under the sway of his son's words, and he nodded his head as Gerry's voice rose in the final introductory statement which suggested that the United States and the Constitution are inseparable, and that without one there could not be the other.

And to all of us who are true Americans, our Constitution is sacred, the creed of those rights which are guaranteed to every one of us as an enduring pledge of our liberties.

Gerry spoke without halt, retaining not only the absorbed attention of his father but also of nearly everyone in the auditorium. He continued, declaiming that the defense of the Constitution, and of the principles which it embodied, was a sacred duty to be held inviolable, and that he who did not, nor would not, uphold these principles did not deserve to be called an American. He added that he who holds public office and willingly betrays his trust cannot be called an American. But in his talk he was not primarily interested in such men, even though they wantonly betrayed their public trust. He was concerned with something more vital, the betrayal of the fundamental principles on which the Constitution was founded, that of States' rights, individual liberty. And men, men in public affairs, were, because of ignorance or perversity or even malice, seeking to destroy that principle by advocating the passage of a Federal Maternity Act and a law establishing a Federal Education Department. These men wanted to abolish child labor by an act of Congress, even though the Constitution did not grant this prerogative to Congress.

O'Dell smiled when the boy quoted the late Champ Clark.

If the groups seeking Federal assistance would put their burdens on the state legislatures where they belong, Congress would have time for the work which, under the Constitution, belongs to Congress.

Continuing, Gerry referred to this tendency toward centralization, seeking to prove that it was unjustified. And then, with cleanly contrived gestures and a rising voice, he concluded:

Should we allow our rights to be taken from us? No! Wherever this tendency to centralization shows its serpentine head, we shall fight it, because it is a menace to us, to everyone who is a liberty-loving American, and we must fight this menace. And defending our liberties, we shall take a slogan from some recent words of a Cabinet member, Herbert Hoover: "It is time to decentralize." Our forefathers, Washington, Jefferson, and Madison, fought to give us our rights. Shall we let them be stripped away from us? Never! We will defend our rights. We will raise our voices until we are heard and our voices resound. Yes, we will even shout: It is time to decentralize.

Gerry O'Dell bowed to the audience. He turned and walked to his place among the others on the stage, while the applause thundered. The father clapped himself weary, restraining strong impulses to shout and stamp his feet. Tears welled in his eyes. He smiled with a simple and childlike joy. Unable to check himself, he turned to the man on his left and said:

"That's my boy."

"Smart lad."

The remaining speeches in the senior oratorical contest seemed dull and uninteresting to him. His boy had it all over these other lads. And he felt himself justified in these impressions when the judges anounced their decision, and amid a second strong burst of clapping Gerald O'Dell was announced the winner of the gold medal in the Senior Oratorical Contest. O'Dell rushed out to a drugstore to telephone the news to Martha. Then he and Michael went back. The tag end of the crowd was filtering out. Boys were coming out in groups, standing, talking, dispersing with the crowd. He searched for Gerry. Gerry would certainly have waited. A boy came out. It was Gerry. No! He searched again. Gerry must be inside, being congratulated. He went in, but found the stage empty. Gerry must have gone. He told himself that Gerry had known that his father would wait to see him, congratulate him, buy him a treat, and that then they would go home together. And Gerry had not waited. He still looked anxiously about at the disappearing faces. Where was he? He asked a boy in a lingering group of students if any of them had seen Gerald O'Dell. They hadn't. He said that he was Gerald's father. They said Gerald had spoken well and deserved his victory. He stood with Michael. Only a few scattered groups remained in front of the hall. Feeling blank, he told himself, yes, Gerry had gone. He solemnly led Michael away, both of them silent. He asked himself why Gerry hadn't waited, and he knew the answer to his question.

Suggestions for Discussion

1. What socioeconomic details of the O'Dell family life does Farrell provide us? What is his purpose in depicting such details?
2. How does O'Dell regard himself and how is he regarded by his family? Why does Gerry leave the auditorium before his father has a chance to congratulate him? Is Farrell making any general statements about the inevitable conflict between the "educated" young and their parents?
3. Why does Farrell choose to quote at length from Gerry's speech? What does the speech tell us about Gerry's character and his self-identity?

Suggestions for Writing and Comparison

1. Compare the relationship between uneducated fathers and educated sons as they are depicted in this story and in the excerpt from Laxalt's *Sweet Promised Land*. How does the conflict between the generations differ in these two stories?
2. Read one of the novels from Farrell's *Studs Lonigan* trilogy. Does Farrell's view of the Irish American in that novel and in "The Oratory Contest" (both written in the 1930's) continue to describe Irish Americans, or has that group "melted" together with other White Ethnic groups and lost its distinctiveness?

Robert Laxalt

Robert Laxalt was born in 1923 in Alturas, California, the son of a Basque sheepherder. He attended the University of Santa Clara and the University of Nevada, from which he received his B.A. in 1947. Laxalt has been a UPI correspondent and a Library of Congress consultant on Basque history and culture. He is also the recipient of a Fulbright Research Fellowship.

Laxalt's work has been published in periodicals such as *Atlantic* and *Saturday Evening Post. Sweet Promised Land* (1957), an autobiographical novel, was followed by *A Man in the Wheatfield* (1964) and other writings about Basque Americans.

The following story, an excerpt from *Sweet Promised Land,* touches on many of the themes explored by various writers in this text, including the conflicts between generations and cultures (see "The Oratory Contest," p. 581, and the excerpt from *Go Tell It on the Mountain,* p. 90).

from
Sweet Promised Land

Nothing he could have worn would have made any difference. He was as out of place in this New York café as the tuxedoed waiter would have been in a dusty horse corral. In this dimly lighted gathering of well-groomed people with soft faces and hands, he was an oddity with a leathered and creased face and hands that looked more like darkened wood than flesh.

As we entered the café and followed the headwaiter to the table, people turned and watched. Some regarded him with curious expressions, and a few with a resentment for which they could probably not find words. There was one, a pretty and tailored lady just beginning to gray, whose eyes softened, as if she could remember an old country father with a graven face, who had been a workingman too.

And yet, in spite of this scrutiny, my father was not ill at ease. Instead, he was as interested in the people about him as they were in him. He sat there as quietly and detachedly as if he were in a darkened movie house, observing everything and everyone in the café. His expression was as rapt as a child's and he was having just as much fun.

The waiters seemed to intrigue him the most. His eyes followed them relentlessly as they moved about, taking in their stiff shirt fronts and black ties and short jackets, and, mostly, the stiff correctness of their manner.

It was inevitable that my father's first altercation would be with a waiter. The warning came when we ordered a drink before dinner, and my father asked for a little glass of claret. He held up his thumb and forefinger to designate that he wanted "a short one." The waiter looked twice, and then smiled in understanding.

We made it though the soup and the salad without incident. It began when the waiter came to take away our salad plates and put on others for the main course. He collected John's and mine, and then reached for my father's. But he could not lift it, because my father was holding it to the table with both hands.

"I'm sorry," said the waiter. "I thought you were finished."

"I am finished," said my father.

"Oh," said the waiter, and again reached for the salad plate. My father held on.

"May I take your plate, sir?" said the waiter.

"No," said my father mildly.

The waiter stood in confused silence for a moment. "But I have to put another plate there, sir."

My father shook his head. "It's all right," he said. "Don't go to any bother."

The waiter blinked and then smiled weakly. "Oh, it's no bother at all," he said, and again reached for the plate.

This time, my father put his hands over the plate to protect it. The waiter stopped short and straightened up. He looked at us in something akin to frenzy, and John gestured with his head. The waiter retreated to the back of the room and stood there watching us from a long distance. He was pale and he still had a plate in his hands.

"Pop," said John. "Why don't you give him your plate?"

My father shrugged. "It's clean enough," he said.

This time John blinked. "I don't understand what you mean."

"They shouldn't waste a plate," said my father. "This one's fine."

John regarded my father for a long moment. "It's really no bother," he said. "They've got a washer back there that does all the work."

"Well, they might run short," my father said.

"I'm telling you, Pop," said John. "There's no danger." He took a deep drag of his cigarette and leaned forward again. "Pop," he said. "You're going to get that waiter in trouble."

"What?" said my father concernedly.

"It's this way," said John. "They're supposed to put a new plate on for each course. That's the way the management wants it. If the waiter doesn't do it and one of the managers sees him, he gets fired on the spot."

"I never heard of such a thing," my father said.

"It's true," said John. "That waiter's probably worried plenty by now."

"Well, hell," said my father. "Tell him to take it then."

John signaled for the waiter and he came forward. When John nodded his head that it was all right, he reached out gingerly and took the salad plate. "I'm sorry, poor fellow," said my father. "I didn't know you was that close to losing your job."

"Oh, that's all right," said the waiter, comprehending nothing at this stage.

After that, he seemed to expect anything. When dinner was done, my father helped him clear the crumbs from the table by gathering his own into his cupped hand. The waiter merely held out his hand to receive them. When my father was through dropping them in, the waiter said, "Thank you."

And later, when he brought us the check, he stood by with inscrutable countenance as my father pulled his passport and wallet bundle out of his pocket, set it on the table, unwound the black inner-tube band, untied the string, and gave him the money. He also gave him a big tip, and said, "It was a fine dinner. I really enjoyed it. How about you boys?"

And the waiter said in a voice without strength, "Well, I'm very happy."

When we left, John and I turned to look. The waiter was still at the table. His head was bowed and he was resting with both hands braced on the back of a chair.

■ He may not have been able to understand the manners of a New York café, but he knew a prize fight. This he could understand, because it was old and pure and without guise. On this, he could pronounce judgments like: "He reminds me of Dempsey, this Marciano does. He isn't so clever or quick as Dempsey, but he's got that same killer blood in him. La Starza is courageous, but he's not the best man. He's whipped already."

As each man who loves a prize fight comes for his own reason, so had he his. It was the reason why they came out of the hills of early Nevada—prospectors and buckaroos and sheepherders on foot and horseback—all come to watch a fight. Because this was something they knew. Like the men in the ring, they too had stood alone and fought alone, with their only weapons the hands that God gave them, and the fight was everything they had ever done and seen and felt. In that square was spoken the only language they understood, undisguised by subtleties and exposed for all the world to see. They saw and recognized the blind and stupid courage of an animal, they saw the beautiful courage of men who were afraid and yet fought, and they saw caution and fatal hesitation and cowardice.

And when it was over, they went away satisfied with the decisive knowledge of victory or defeat. A man had won and a man had been beaten, and the thing was settled, and it was not like the helpless inconclusion of argument.

It was something that all the old country men who had come to a new land could understand. Because they too had had to stand alone and without home to turn to for help, because they had forsaken home, and this was their new country, and they were fighting for acceptance.

It was the reason why we brothers had had to have our baptism of blood in the prize ring. It was the reason why each of us in his own turn, without urging from my father and to the hurt of my mother, had had to find his way alone into that square of light from which there is no escape, to know the terror of being alone and fighting alone, to taste the wild triumph of winning alone, and the bitter and lonely pain of defeat.

It was the reason why the sons of old country people everywhere must fight a little harder and do something better with their lives. Because we were born of old country people in a new land, and, right or wrong, we had not felt equal to those around us, and had had to do a little more than they in everything we did.

And in that ring were two like us, born of old country people, who had won their battle already, to show the way, and that it could be done, to the thousands of sons of old country people who were there watching them.

All of us together were of a generation born of old country people who spoke English with an accent and prayed in another language, who drank red wine and cooked their food in the old country way, and peeled apples and pears after dinner.

We were among the last whose names would tell our blood and the kind of faces we had, to know another language in our homes, to suffer youthful shame because of that language and refuse to speak it, and a later shame because of what we had done, and hurt because we had caused a hurt so deep it could never find words.

And the irony of it was that our mothers and fathers were truer Americans than we, because they had forsaken home and family, and gone into the unknown of a new land with only courage and the hands that God gave them, and had given us in our turn the right to be born American.

And in a little while, even our sons would forget, and the old country people would be only a dimming memory, and names would mean nothing, and the melting would be done.

■ The cabdriver made the first comment on our way to the overseas airport. We had said good-by to John at the hotel, so that he could make an early train back to Washington, and now my father and I were Paris-bound.

The cabdriver was on a tirade about the Puerto Ricans. From the glibness of his talk, it was obvious that this was one of his pet peeves, and that he had covered this ground many times before.

"The damn town's full of 'em," he said. "You'll see when you get to that airport. The place is crawling with 'em." He shook his head and sighed with gubernatorial authority. "I don't know what we're going to do about 'em."

"Well, why are they so much trouble?" I asked, out of curiosity.

He was patient, and showed it. "They're just no damn good. You get next to 'em and you'll find out," he warned. "Pick your pocket in a minute," and he snapped his fingers. A little later, he said, "I'd hate to get caught in a dark alley with some of 'em. Cut your throat just like that!" and he made a kkk sound to illustrate his point.

My father and I both grinned. It was exactly what I had whispered to him about the cabdriver when we first got in.

But he was right about one thing. After we had finished our business at the Air France ticket window and settled down for a wait, we saw that there were indeed a good many Puerto Ricans around. They were coming and going in such a steady flow that I could not understand how so many planes could be landing and taking off. But after a while, we realized that most of them were families coming to greet someone or see them off.

What the cabdriver had said must have made an impression on me, because I noticed that the other people in the terminal seemed to give them a wide berth. And they were indeed dressed differently, with dazzling arrangements of pegged pants and long coats and bright ties. And many of them had knife scars on their faces.

My father had been watching them with no little curiosity. "They don't look so bad," he said.

"Well, I don't know, Pop," I said. "I'd still leave them alone."

I guess I should have remembered a time in Nevada when the Mexican shearing crews came to clip the wool for our sheep, as they did every year for all the outfits. Most times, they were made up of older men who had been on the crews for a long time. But that year there were two young ones with them, who we learned were about twenty years old. After the first few days of working together in the corrals, we came to know them. They were friendly, and at night they would often bring their guitars to the cabin and teach us songs in Spanish. After we came to like them, it came as a shock one night to learn that they both carried knives, that at home in southern California they wore pegged pants and got into knife fights, that they were of the "Pachucos" we had been hearing so much about.

But that had happened in the hills, and things and people are different in the city, or so I thought. I should have known what was to happen, because my father was that way.

No matter where he went, he would strike up a conversation with anybody who happened to be near him. When we first sat down, there was a prosperous-looking man of about my father's age sitting next to us. He had a bulky brief case and he was reading a newspaper.

When my father first spoke to him, he was genuinely surprised and even a little irritated. But after a few minutes, they were in a lively conversation. My father learned that he was going to England on business, that he did it all the time, and that he knew both Senator Pat McCarran, whom my father knew from the days when the family was in sheep and about whose fieriness in the hills he could tell a few anecdotes, and Senator George Malone, whom my father and my uncle had met on horseback in the deserts many times. And, among other things, my father learned how the export business was doing these days.

A little later, after the businessman had bid him a warm good-by and boarded his plane, my father got into a conversation, first in English and then Italian, with a barber, and he learned all about the barber business both in New York and in Italy, where the man had his start.

All I could do was wonder when the time would come when someone would insult my father for daring to speak to a stranger. The wait for our own plane dragged into hours because of some kind of engine trouble. I stood up from time to time and wandered about the terminal, and once I came back to where my father was sitting to ask him if he wanted another cup of coffee. He didn't, and so I took my leave with the warning, "You know, I don't think I'd fool around with those Puerto Ricans. There's no use taking chances."

My father said nothing, but I had a suspicion then my words were wasted. And I was right. No sooner was I settled in the coffeeshop then I saw through the glass partition that my father was in a conversation with not one, but four of them. If he had chosen them by hand, he could not have picked four more dangerous-looking companions. It must just have started, because from their expressions the Puerto Ricans were still regarding my father with distance. But as I watched, they warmed up to it, and soon they all seemed to be talking and waving their hands at the same time. I knew it had to be in Spanish, because my father could speak that tongue too.

By the time I finished my coffee, they were getting along famously. But when I joined my father, the Puerto Ricans grew a little wary, and things never really got back to where they were, even though all I did was listen.

One of the Puerto Ricans was saying something to my father in Spanish. I groped for the meaning, but could not understand. One of the others, seeing my puzzlement, translated it into English with a thick accent.

"He was saying there is no chance for a Puerto Rican in America."

"But why?" my father asked.

"Because there is nothing we can do here. There is no work, and what there is is no good for a man."

"Then why do you come?" my father asked.

The Puerto Rican lifted his hands. "There is no chance in Puerto Rico either. When we were young, they always said this was a rich land. Maybe it is, but someone else must have it, because we don't. We are tired of waiting to get rich."

"But your people stay here," my father said.

Another of the Puerto Ricans answered him. "Why not? There is nothing else to do. They have no place to go."

"Why don't they go with you?" my father said.

The Puerto Rican shook his head and spoke for a long time, but my translator was more brief. "Brazil is a long way from here and from Puerto Rico too. Some are going, but not many. They do not want to say good-by to their families and their friends, and they do not know what they will find there. They are afraid. And so they live here, millions of them, to be treated worse than a Negro many times. Because the Americans think we are all lazy, that we are criminals, and that we want to live like pigs. But we are human men too, and, even if we have our lazy ones and our criminals, the Americans have them too."

"I don't think they would treat you that way if there were not so many of you, and with nothing to do," my father said.

The first Puerto Rican nodded his head. "That is part of it, all right. But still, it is a hurt not to be thought of as a people with self-respect."

"How do you know it will be different in Brazil?" my father said.

The first Puerto Rican spoke passionately. "This much we know. Brazil is a new country, and the land is rich, rich enough to give a man a good living if he works for it. A Puerto Rican can homestead there. And when a man has land, then he has self-respect and he will be respected. That is the way we want to live, not like this in New York."

My father agreed, adding, "But you cannot blame this country. It has been good for me and many like me."

"I do not blame this country," the Puerto Rican said. "All I say is this. The time of opportunity for poor people from another country is almost gone here. Now, they must find another America."

The loud-speaker called the departure of a plane. This time, the Puerto Ricans listened intently until it was repeated. Then they picked up their handbags and prepared to go. But, before they left, they looked at us almost shyly, and one of them, the one who had been doing most of the talking, held out his hand to my father. He seemed almost afraid to do so. But my father grasped it firmly, and there was a flash of white teeth in a dark face, and the grateful warmth of black eyes smiling.

"*Con Dios*," my father said.

"And He with you, good friend," the Puerto Ricans said, and then were gone.

Suggestions for Discussion

1. Why has the narrator chosen to describe his father "as if he were in a darkened movie house"? Is this a particularly apt simile for the man's behavior?
2. Why does John invent the story of the waiter's being fired? What does this incident reveal about both the father and the sons?
3. Are the comparisons between the prize fight and the lives of "old country" men and their sons valid? What is meant by the statement "each of us in his own turn, without urging from my father and to the hurt of my mother, had had to find his way alone into that square of light from which there is no escape, to know the terror of being alone and fighting alone"?
4. What is the narrator referring to when he says "And in a little while, even our sons would forget, . . . and the melting would be done"? To what extent has this phenomenon taken place?

Suggestion for Writing and Comparison

1. Discuss the themes of America as a land of opportunity and as a melting pot. (For some help on this, see Carl Wittke's *We Who Built America: The Saga of the Immigrant* [1964 edition], John F. Kennedy's *A Nation of Immigrants,* or Michael Novak's *The Rise of the Unmeltable Ethnics.*)

Joe Papaleo

Joe Papaleo was born in New York in 1925, the son of Italian immigrants. He received his A.B. degree from Sarah Lawrence College and then studied at the University of Florence. Upon his return to the United States he became an instructor at Sarah Lawrence.

Papaleo, who has been writing poetry and fiction since his early years at college, has published continuously, although not prolifically, from his poems of the 1940's, which appeared in *Common Ground,* to a recent novel, *All the Comforts* (1967).

Like many of the selections in this text, "Italian to the Moon Over New York" views the conflicts between the immigrant and the American-born, or between the older generation of White Ethnics and the young. Papleo despairs that communication is not possible since the young seem to be blind to "unbought luxury."

Italian to the Moon Over New York

How many nights have you coldly gestured
while I missed the moments when the years flew,
and now I question your pendant face.
Gracious Moon, I have come
5 again in anguish
to admire you.
You watched the last night
upon the bay when I
might have sung to you.
10 You followed the ship
whose hopeful ones dreamed
of a golden trip
to a golden city.
Did you see me disappear
15 within a frame house
for my adopted years?
When did you see
the metamorphosis
of me? When children
20 mocked my halted speech?
If they could see reflected
in your light, how we
were young together
by olive trees, skies
25 that defy remembering,
could they be young
as one should be young?
But they hardly look
toward the sky,
30 and I must try
remembering again
what was too short
but happiness enough.
If they would only
35 turn their eyes to you,
with unbought luxury
we could admire you
whole evenings long
within a sky of song.

Suggestions for Discussion

    1. How are time and the moon used as a frame for the poem? What
    is suggested by "a golden trip/to a golden city"?

2. How do the "frame house" and the narrator's "halted speech" relate to his "metamorphosis"? What kind of a metamorphosis has he undergone?

3. What *persona* is the poet assuming (Papaleo was born in New York) when he says "we/were young together/by olive trees, skies/that defy remembering"? How might this *persona* relate to the "golden trip/to a golden city"?

Suggestion for Writing and Comparison

1. Comment on the last six lines of the poem as they relate to the American dream. Is this a poem about hope or fulfillment?

Gregory Corso

Gregory Corso was born in New York City of young Italian immigrant parents. When Corso was still a child his mother returned to Italy and he was raised alternately by his father and
by foster parents. Much of his childhood was spent in the Italian and the Irish ghettoes of New York. He attended school until the sixth grade.

At the age of seventeen, Corso was convicted of robbery and
sent to prison for three years. It was there that he first felt himself free to think, feel, and write. He immersed himself in the
works of Chatterton, Marlowe, and Shelley, and then began
writing his own poems. In 1950, Corso met the Beat poet Allen
Ginsberg, who first taught him about contemporary poetry.

At the height of the Beat movement, in 1956, Corso went to
San Francisco, the home of the Beats, and, with the publication
of *Gasoline* (1958) and *The Happy Birthday of Death* (1960),
became one of the foremost spokesmen for that group. More
recently, his play *The Little Black Door on the Left* has been
published in the "black" humor anthology *"pardon me, sir, but
is my eye hurting your elbow?"* (1968).

Corso's two poems included here, "Birthplace Revisited,"
which follows, and "Uccello" (p. 611), examine extraordinary
poses and surfaces. In returning to his birthplace the character
in the first poem assumes a gangster stance, "with raincoat"
and "hand on gat," taken seemingly from the movies of his
childhood. Thus the real garbage cans that "haven't stopped
smelling" of "Birthplace Revisited" are in direct contrast to the
Renaissance banners, caparizoned horses, and golden princes
who "will never die on that battlefield" of "Uccello." These two
poems were written by a son of Italian immigrants who recalls
both the smelly tenements of his childhood and the golden age
of Italy, the Renaissance.

Birthplace Revisited

I stand in the dark light in the dark street
and look up at my window, I was born there.
The lights are on; other people are moving about.
I am with raincoat; cigarette in mouth,
5 hat over eye, hand on gat.
I cross the street and enter the building.
The garbage cans haven't stopped smelling.
I walk up the first flight; Dirty Ears
aims a knife at me . . .
10 I pump him full of lost watches.

Suggestions for Discussion

1. Who is the speaker, the "I," in this poem? When does the speaker's pose become obvious?
2. Aside from the suggestion of Salvador Dali's limp watches in "lost watches," what surreal qualities or dream images dominate the poem?
3. What is the significance of time in the poem? For example, what is the relation of the "lost watches" to the title, "Birthplace Revisited"?

Suggestion for Writing and Comparison

1. Read James T. Farrell's story "Danny O'Neill Was Here" (*Commentary*, Vol. 18, 1954) for another attitude toward a birthplace revisited. Compare and contrast the two views.

Harold Bond

Harold Bond was born in Boston, Massachusetts, in 1939. His parents, both Armenians who fled the Turkish massacres, met one another in Marseilles, France, in 1932 and came to the United States in the same year.

Bond received an A.B. in English-Journalism from Northeastern University in 1962 and an M.F.A. in Creative Writing from the University of Iowa in 1967. He was editor of *Ararat* magazine from 1969 to 1970, and he has also held editorial positions in newspaper and book publishing. Presently living in Melrose, Massachusetts, Bond has taught workshops in poetry writing for both children and adults.

Bond's poetry has appeared in such publications as *The New Yorker, Harper's Magazine, Saturday Review,* and *The New Republic,* and in more than a dozen anthologies, including *The Young American Poets, Getting into Poetry,* and *New Voices in American Poetry*. His works have been translated in Armenia and the Middle East, and he has read his poetry at schools throughout the Northeast. Bond's books include *The Northern Wall* (1969), *3 x 3* (1969), *Dancing on Water* (1970), and *Fragments of an Earlier Life* (in press).

Both poems included here by Harold Bond, "The Chance," which follows, and "Letter to an Aunt" (p. 618), explore the consequences of one's personal history. "The Chance" presents an "American" school in which the Irish teacher tells the Armenian student how to arrange Indian feathers. The child-narrator of the poem associates being an Armenian with being called "dumb." In "Letter to an Aunt," however, the poet speaks of the old country massacres and then states: "This is blood. This is what I am."

The Chance

First grade. I am the skinny
one with the foreign accent. I am
so scared I think I will wee
in my pants. Miss Breen is teaching us
5 colors. We are cutting out
strips of paper in the fashion of
Indian feathers. We must

order them in descending hues on
a black headband. I cannot
10 understand Miss Breen. It is not done

the way it should be: blue with
yellow and black with white. Unless I
do something soon Miss Breen will
say I am a dumb Armenian. So

15 without looking I shuffle
my feathers in my hand. I paste them
over my headband. I spill
my pastepot, and I know I will wee
now because here comes Miss Breen,
20 only Miss Breen says, Good, Harold, good,
blue after purple and green

after blue. It happened, it happened
like a rainbow, like a swatch
of oil on water, eight feathers thieved
25 in perfect succession one
on the other. Miss Breen did not say
I am a dumb Armenian,
and I do not even have to wee.

Suggestions for Discussion

1. Why are the speaker's age and situation particularly relevant to
the meaning of the poem? How are diction and syntax employed? For example, why does the child say "We must/order
them in descending hues"?
2. What is there in the school situation that makes the child say "I
am/so scared I think I will wee/in my pants"? What is suggested
by the teacher's name?
3. Has the poet been successful in recreating the emotional anx-
ieties of childhood? Can the poem be read as a comment on the
process of Americanization as it takes place in schools? What
does the title mean?

Suggestion for Writing and Comparison

1. Which aspects of childhood are explored in John Ciardi's "Elegy" (p. 606) and in Bond's "The Chance"? Which poem seems
more the accurate portrayal of childhood feelings, which one
more the adult reworking of childhood recollections?

May Swenson

May Swenson, like Carl Sandburg, was the child of Swedish immigrants. Born in Logan, Utah, she graduated from Utah State University and then went to New York City where she has lived and worked for many years.

Ms. Swenson has been an editor for New Directions Publishing Company and has had her own poetry published in periodicals such as *Poetry, Saturday Review, Atlantic, Harper's,* and *The New Yorker.* She is the recipient of a Guggenheim Fellowship as well as grants from the National Institute of Arts and the Ford Foundation. Her volumes of poetry include *To Mix With Time* (1963), *Poems to Solve* (1966), and *Half Sun, Half Sleep* (1967).

As might be inferred from the title of her latest volume, *Half Sun, Half Sleep,* May Swenson's poems often portray the processes of awakening. Two poems, "The Magnolia" and "Daffodils" (p. 615), show flowers waiting in the shade and opening to light. The following poem, "Things in Common," shows a city employee awakening—with the help of "the mess down South"—to an awareness of the existence of the fifty-year old "elevator boy" in the building where she works.

Things in Common

We have a good relationship, the elevator boy and I.
I can always be cheerful with him.
We make jokes. We both belong to the TGIF Club.
No matter how artificial and stiff I've had to be in the office,
5 seems like I can be natural with *him.*
We have basic things in common—
the weather, baseball, hangovers,
the superiority of Friday over Monday.

It's true I make it a point to be pleasant to him. Why?
10 Honest, its because I really like him.
Individually, I mean.
There's something about him—relaxed and balanced
like a dancer or a cat—
as if he knows who he is and where he's at.
15 At least he knows how to act like that.
Wish I could say the same for myself.

I like his looks, his manner, his red shirt,
the smooth panther shape to his head and neck.

I like it that he knows I don't mean to flirt —
20 even though I really like him.
I feel he knows I know the score.
It's all in the gleam of his eyes,
the white of his teeth, when he slides back the door
and says, "TGIF, Ma'am, have a nice weekend."

25 He's strong muscled, good looking — could be 35 —
though with his cap off he's 50, I suppose.
So am I. Hope he thinks I look younger too.
I want him to like it that my eyes are blue —
I want him to really like me.
30 We look straight at each other when we say goodnight.
Is he thinking it's only an accident I'm white?
"TGIF," we say. "Have a nice weekend."

That's the way it's been so far.
We have a good relationship, just the two of us
35 and the little stool on which he never sits, in the car.
Fridays I work late. I'm the last one down.
Been, let's see, 11 years now. . .
These days I hug the newspaper to me so the headlines won't show.
Why he never has a paper I don't know.
40 Probably not supposed to read in the elevator.

Lately I've asked myself why don't I say:
"What do you think of the mess down South, Willie?
Or for that matter, right here in D.C.?"
Wish I dared ask him. Or that he'd find a way to put it to me.
45 I'd like to say bluntly, "Willie, will there be war?"
Neither of us has been able to say it so far.
Will I dare, someday? I doubt it . . . Not *me*, to *him*. . . .
"Thank God It's Friday," we say. "Have a nice weekend."

Suggestions for Discussion

> 1. What *persona* has the poet assumed as the speaker of this
> poem? What is the woman's probable job "in the office"? In the
> light of her other ways of speaking, how natural does the line
> "seems like I can be natural with *him*" sound?

2. Discuss the effect of the placement of these three lines one after the other:

> I want him to really like me.
> We look straight at each other when we say goodnight.
> Is he thinking it's only an accident I'm white?

What mental process do the above lines suggest?
3. How does the refrain " 'TGIF,' we say. 'Have a nice weekend' " relate to the title? What do the two people in the poem really have in common?

Suggestions for Writing and Comparison

1. Discuss the line "Will I dare, someday? I doubt it . . . Not *me*, to *him* . . ." as a comment upon the previous statement "We have a good relationship." What aspects of appearance and reality in the "good relationship" are explored in the poem?
2. Read James Baldwin's essay "Stranger in the Village" in his book *Notes of a Native Son*. Comment on the roles of "insider" and "outsider" as seen by the speakers in Swenson's poem and Baldwin's essay.

John Ciardi

John Ciardi was born in Boston, Massachusetts, in 1916, the son of Carminantonio and Concetta Ciardi, Italian immigrants. The father, who was a laborer, a tailor, and an insurance man, died when Ciardi was a child.

In 1938 Ciardi received his A.B. degree from Tufts College. The following year he received an M.A. degree from the University of Michigan. *Homeward to America,* his first book of poems, was published in 1940. This was followed by several critical studies, translations, and volumes of poetry, including a verse translation of Dante's *The Inferno* (1954), a study on reading poetry, *How Does a Poem Mean?* (1960), and a 1962 collection of poems, *In Fact.*

Ciardi is popularly known as a master of the short essay and the well-turned phrase, but he is also a poet, a critic of poetry, and, for many years, the poetry editor of *Saturday Review.* He is particularly interested in the work of Robert Frost, and much of Ciardi's poetry shows qualities in common with those of Frost. The following poem, "Elegy," for example, may be compared — in its effect of conversational speech and in its manner of usage of the run-on line — with Robert Frost's well-known "Birches."

"Elegy," a song of remembrance for the poet's father who died when the poet was three, laments the necessary "adjustments" that the Italian farmer, "born with a spade in his hand," was forced to make in order to survive in a new culture. In "Letter to Mother" Ciardi recognizes that all his parents' bravery and struggles must be repeated again by him, that one generation's victories cannot be "inherited" by the next generation.

Elegy

My father was born with a spade in his hand and traded it
for a needle's eye to sit his days cross-legged on tables
till he could sit no more, then sold insurance, reading
the ten-cent-a-week lives like logarithms from
5 the Tables of Metropolitan to their prepaid tombstones.

Years of the little dimes twinkling on kitchen tables
at Mrs. Fauci's at Mrs. Locatelli's at Mrs. Cataldo's
(*Arrividerla, signora. A la settimana prossima. Mi saluta,
la prego, il marito. Ciao, Anna. Bye-bye.*)
10 —known as a Debit. And with his ten-year button

he opened a long dream like a piggy bank, spilling the dimes
like mountain water into the moss of himself, and bought

ten piney lots in Wilmington. Sunday by Sunday
he took the train to his woods and walked under the trees
15 to leave his print on his own land, a patron of seasons.

I have done nothing as perfect as my father's Sundays
on his useless lots. Gardens he dreamed from briar tangle
and the swampy back slope of his ridge rose over him
more flowering than Brazil. Maples transformed to figs,
20 and briar to blood-blue grapes in his look around

when he sat on a stone with his wine-jug and cheese beside him,
his collar and coat on a branch, his shirt open,
his derby back on his head like a standing turtle. A big
man he was. When he sang *Celeste Aida* the woods
25 filled as if a breeze were swelling through them.

When he stopped, I thought I could hear the sound still moving.
—Well, I have lied, Not so much lied as dreamed it.
I was three when he died. It was someone else—my sister—
went with him under the trees. But if it was her
30 memory then, it became mine so long since

I will owe nothing on it, having dreamed it from all
the nights I was growing, the wet-pants man of the family.
I have done nothing as perfect as I have dreamed him
from old-wives tales and the running of my blood.
35 God knows what queer long darks I had no eyes for

followed his stairwell weeks to his Sunday breezeways.
But I will swear the world is not well made that rips
such gardens from the week. Or I should have walked
a saint's way to the cross and nail by nail
40 hymned out my blood to glory, for one good reason.

Letter to Mother

It was good. You found your America. It was worth all
The coming: the fading figures in the never-again doorway,
The rankness of steerage, the landing in fog.
Yes, and the tenement, the reek and the shouting in the streets
5 All that night and the terror. It was good, it was all good.
It is important only that you came.

And it is good to remember that this blood, in another body, your body,
        arrived.
There is dynastic example in a single generation of this blood, and the
        example good,
But, Mother, I can promise you nothing.

10 This traveling is across the sprung longitudes of the mind
And the blood's latitudes. I have made a sextant of heart
And nailed my bearings to sun, but from the look-out
There is no hailing yet of the hoped-for land.
Only the enormous, wheeling, imperative sea,
15 And the high example of this earlier coming—

But there will be no Americas discovered by analogy.

Suggestions for Discussion

1. What image of the father is created in the first and second stanzas of "Elegy"? How does this portrait contrast with the one in the next three stanzas?
2. What is the effect of the statement "Well, I have lied"? Why has the poet chosen this particular moment to interrupt himself?
3. In what meter is the poem "Elegy" written? Is the beat primarily iambic, trochaic, or anapestic? Is the rhythm conversational or formal, "American" or "British"? Is there any suggestion of accent or dialect other than in the lines written in Italian?
4. What did the mother in "Letter to Mother" find in America, literally and symbolically? Explain the lines "It is important only that you came" and "There is dynastic example in a single generation of this blood."
5. What is a "sextant"? What is the dominant imagery of stanza three? How does that imagery relate to the first stanza?
6. Explain the speaker's statement that "there will be no Americas discovered by analogy."

Suggestions for Writing and Comparison

1. What aspects of "Elegy" are "ethnic"? Are there specific or indirect references to religion or nationality? What aspects of the poem are universal?
2. In the excerpt from Laxalt's *Sweet Promised Land* (p. 589) the narrator says that "each of us in his own turn, without urging from my father and to the hurt of my mother, had had to find his way alone into that square of light from which there is no escape, to know the terror of being alone and fighting alone." Relate Laxalt's statement to Ciardi's "Letter to Mother."

Sharon Hucklenbroich

Sharon Hucklenbroich was born in St. Louis, Missouri, in 1939, a third-generation American of Polish background. She quit school at the age of sixteen and has been largely self-educated. She has worked as a waitress, carhop, dog groomer, answering-service manager, factory carpenter, motel maid, and carnival barker, and has lived in St. Louis, Los Angeles, Hollywood, Las Vegas, San Diego, San Francisco, San Jose, Sausalito, and Denver. She writes, she says, because "I'm greedy and don't want to lose anything. My poems place things beyond time's blur. They *keep*."

"Genealogy" is concerned with discovering one's roots and finding that as a woman, as a member of a younger generation, and as an American, those roots are all but cut.

Genealogy

There was of course
my father. My old man.
Out of some back-country Polish pride
wanting to be called "Dad." (A firm and friendly word. A man-to-man.)
5 Poor soul, he longed for sons, and bred four women,
and never liked to hear the word "Papa."
He stood behind the big black barberchair
supporting us all on 60¢ haircuts,
and looking like a 1940's movie hero,
10 holding in his left hand the comb for all the world,
and in his right the steel barber-shears,
cutting, cutting, cutting.

Suggestions for Discussion

1. What kind of a relationship does the speaker have with her father? Once we understand the nature of that relationship, what does the title come to mean?
2. Why would the father not like the word "Papa"? What does "a 1940's movie hero" look like?
3. Beyond the literal level, what does the last line suggest?

Suggestion for Writing and Comparison

1. Refer to Rhoda Schwartz's "Dark Moon" (p. 516), "Old Photographs" (p. 517), and "Grand-mama" (p. 535), and to Virginia Tatarian's "Photograph of Five Ancestors" (p. 613). Compare the speakers' attitudes toward their genealogy with that of the speaker in Hucklenbroich's poem.

Gregory Corso

(See p. 599 for Corso's poem "Birthplace Revisited" and a biographical sketch of the author.)

Uccello

They will never die on that battlefield
nor the shade of wolves recruit their hoard like brides of
wheat on all horizons   waiting there to consume battle's end
There will be no dead to tighten their loose bellies
5   no heap of starched horses to redsmash their bright eyes
or advance their eat of dead
They would rather hungersulk with mad tongues
than believe that on that field no man dies

They will never die who fight so embraced
10   breath to breath   eye knowing eye   impossible to die
or move   no light seeping through   no maced arm
nothing but horse outpanting horse   shield brilliant upon
shield   all made starry by the dot ray of a helmeted eye
ah   how difficult to fall between those knitted lances
15   And those banners! angry as to flush insignia across its
erasure of sky
You'd think he'd paint his armies by the coldest rivers
have rows of iron skulls flashing in the dark
You'd think it impossible for any man to die
20   each combatant's mouth is a castle of song
each iron fist a dreamy gong   flail resounding flail
like cries of gold
how I dream to join such battle!
a silver man on a black horse with red standard and striped
25   lance   never to die but to be endless
a golden prince of pictorial war

Suggestions for Discussion

1. In what way does the opening line of the poem characterize the
paintings of Uccello? Do his paintings contain "wolves" or
"skulls" or a "heap of starched horses"?

2. In a painting, how can a man's mouth be "a castle of song"?
3. What aspect of Renaissance painting fascinates the twentieth-century poet Corso? Is it Uccello himself or the man in Uccello's painting who is "a golden prince of pictorial war"?

Suggestion for Writing and Comparison

1. Examine Picasso's *Guernica,* which was painted in memory of the town of Guernica that was destroyed in the Spanish Civil War. Write a poem in which you attempt to capture the essence of the painting, suiting your verse form to the form of the painting.

Virginia Tatarian

Virginia Tatarian was born in 1940 in Providence, Rhode Island, of Armenian parents who came to the United States as refugees. As a child she moved with her family to an Armenian community in Fresno, California, the home of another Armenian American writer of international reputation, William Saroyan. Virginia Tatarian received her A.B. at Fresno State College and her M.A. at the State University of Iowa. She has been published in several literary magazines.

The poem which follows, "Photograph of Five Ancestors," revives, quickens the people in a faded photograph. Their embarrassment, "a sense of heat," remains, for they were "ordinary men" in the same sense as the people in William Pillin's "Miserere" (p. 501). Another poem, "On the Photograph of a Man I Never Saw" by Hyam Plutzik (p. 514), similarly explores a second-generation American's response to the photograph of a European ancestor whom he has never met.

Photograph of Five Ancestors

Age and the quick hands
of American children must
have moved upon these faces
to fade them so. Men are caught

5   in the usual camera stance
of starched and formal bones, yet
there remains a sense
of heat, unschooled as an instinct.

For one enduring moment,
10   they are grand as bishops or elks
but cannot forget that
this is a kind of pretence,

like children who play at
not being children, serious
15   in unfamiliar dress, at
home, on rainy afternoons.

Suggestions for Discussion

1. What is the tone of the poem? What is the effect of a phrase such as "grand as bishops or elks"?

2. How are the children contrasted to the photograph? In what way does the photograph resemble the children?
3. What is the effect of the final stanza? What aspect of human life is explored in it?

Suggestions for Writing and Comparison

1. Compare and contrast Tatarian's poem with Hyam Plutzik's "On the Photograph of a Man I Never Saw" (p. 514). How do the attitudes of the two poets toward the respective photographs differ? What is the significance of the people in the photographs to each poet?
2. Write an essay in which you describe a photograph, with particular reference to past and present or appearance and reality.

May Swenson

(See p. 603 for Swenson's poem "Things in Common" and a biographical sketch of the author.)

The Magnolia

In the shade
each tight cone

untwists to a goblet.
Under light

5 the rim widens,
splits like silk.
Seven spatulate

white flakes
float open, purple
10 dregs at the nape.

Daffodils

Yellow telephones
in a row in the garden
are ringing,
shrill with light.

5 Old fashioned spring
brings earliest models out
each April the same,
naive and classical.

Look into the yolk-
10 colored mouthpieces
alert with echoes.
Say hello to time.

Suggestions for Discussion

1. The difference between metaphor and simile lies in the difference between comparisons implied or made explicit. Which poetic device does Swenson use in "The Magnolia" and "Daffodils"? Why?

2. Why does the poet vary the stanza length in "The Magnolia"? Is it significant that phrases such as "the rim widens" and "float open" appear in the last two stanzas?
3. What is the effect of comparing an object of nature, a daffodil, with an object such as a telephone, which is so much a part of the machine age? Is the metaphor successful?

Suggestion for Writing and Comparison

1. Compare Swenson's use of imagery with that in the *haiku* or *tanka*. See, for example, the poems of Richard Wright (p. 153), and Shisei Tsuneishi (p. 302), or any of the poems in *Sounds from the Unknown* (1963), an anthology of Japanese American poetry edited by Lucille M. Nixon and Tomoe Tana.

Sharon Hucklenbroich

(See p. 609 for Hucklenbroich's "Genealogy" and a biographical sketch of the author.)

Awakening

I have been asleep, not restfully.
I have been a small brown bear. Hibernating.
Tricked into an untimed winter.
Fat and furred, I lay me down with you. Now,
5   the mirror of your eyes reflects
your lean and mangy season. I am hungry.
Hungry. You have left no scrap of meat, no
stiffening honeycomb to suck; not even
a few pale slugs hidden beneath these
10 worn stones. I need a mouthful of water
to green my days. There is no brook here. (I
seem to remember one, but that
was long ago, and want can be deceptive.)
I turn and shake myself, and blink at
15 the unaccustomed sunlight
poured through the opening of this cave.
In a moment, I shall totter stiffly through the
rainbow door. I shall not even visit you
in sleep.

Suggestions for Discussion

1. What is the controlling metaphor of the poem? Trace its use throughout the poem. How successfully does that metaphor help convey the meaning of the poem?
2. What is the probable situation of the poem? Translate the metaphorical action of the poem into that situation.

Suggestion for Writing and Comparison

1. Write a poem in which you use a controlling metaphor describing an individual in terms of an animal. Show how that individual acts within a particular mood or a relationship. The metaphor should fit the emotional state of the character.

Harold Bond

(See p. 601 for Bond's poem "The Chance" and a biographical sketch of the author.)

Letter to an Aunt

I am writing by candle from the Cape.
An August storm has blown the power down.
The house is in darkness;
trees are screaming at my window.
5 I hope to finish before the candles stop.
You have seen my poems
and find them generally black.
I am forced to show you I can laugh.
Yesterday at Zack's there was a drummer
10 who played with reversed sticks.
He told me he tries to make sounds,
mostly makes noise.
We laughed. This I think funny, you will not.
And is, in any case, peripheral to the purpose.
15 Anyone can laugh.

What I am to write you of is belief.
Today I spent the afternoon
on a seacliff under a lighthouse.
Every stalk in sight was broken by the wind.
20 I almost cried. This you think funny, I do not.
This is belief. This I cannot explain.
I am also to write you of blood.
My mother told me once I am alive now
only because she was at a missionary's
25 when her village was bombed in the war.
This is blood. This is what I am.
I have never gone hungry
or lacked a place to sleep.
If I write black, know that, like the storm
30 outside, like the lack of light
inside, it has no image, form, color,
is only belief and blood and what it is.